FIFTH EDITION

CONTEMPORARY BEHAVIOR THERAPY

MICHAEL D. SPIEGLER

Providence College

DAVID C. GUEVREMONT

Woonsocket Education Department

WADSWORTH
CENGAGE Learning™

Australia • Brazil • Japan • Korea • Mexico • Singapore • Spain • United Kingdom • United States

WADSWORTH
CENGAGE Learning

Contemporary Behavior Therapy, Fifth Edition
Michael D. Spiegler and David C. Guevremont

Senior Publisher: Linda Schreiber

Executive Editor: Jon-David Hague

Assistant Editor: Paige Leeds

Editorial Assistant: Kelly Miller

Marketing Manager: Elisabeth Rhoden

Marketing Assistant: Molly Felz

Marketing Communications Manager: Talia Wise

Content Project Management: Pre-Press PMG

Creative Director: Rob Hugel

Art Director: Vernon Boes

Production Technology Analyst: Adam Grafa

Print Buyer: Linda Hsu

Rights Acquisitions Account Manager, Text: Roberta Broyer

Rights Acquisitions Account Manager, Image: Don Schlotman

Production Service: Pre-Press PMG

Copy Editor: Pre-Press PMG

Cover Designer: Andy Norris

Cover Image: Rick McEwan

Compositor: Pre-Press PMG

For product information and technology assistance contact us at **Cengage Learning Customer & Sales Support, 1-800-354-9706.**

For permission to use material from this text or product submit all requests online at **www.cengage.com/permissions**
Further permissions questions can be e-mailed to
permissionrequest@cengage.com

Library of Congress Control Number: 2009925797
ISBN-13: 978-0-495-50906-6
ISBN-10: 0-495-50906-X

Wadsworth
10 Davis Drive
Belmont, CA 94002-3098
USA

Cengage Learning is a leading provider of customized learning solutions with office locations around the globe, including Singapore, the United Kingdom, Australia, Mexico, Brazil, and Japan. Locate your local office at **www.cengage.com/global**.

Cengage Learning products are represented in Canada by Nelson Education, Ltd.

To learn more about Wadsworth, visit **www.cengage.com/wadsworth**

Purchase any of our products at your local college store or at our preferred online store **www.cengagebrain.com**

Printed in the United States of America
2 3 4 5 15 14 13 12

FIFTH EDITION

CONTEMPORARY BEHAVIOR THERAPY

To George A. Raymond

A very unique person in my life whose knowledge about all things great and small, psychological and nonpsychological; penchant for precision and detail; love of the nuances of the English language; generosity of spirit; and friendship have enriched my life for so many years. And I am unanimous in that.

ABOUT THE AUTHOR

Michael D. Spiegler (Ph.D., clinical psychology, Vanderbilt University) is professor of psychology at Providence College and was formerly director of the Community Training Center at the Palo Alto VA Hospital and assistant professor of psychology at the University of Texas at Austin. His contributions to behavior therapy include the development of the first skills training program for the treatment of chronic psychiatric disorders and his pioneering work in film modeling therapy. His other areas of research include observational learning, anxiety, the treatment of obesity, and active learning. Professor Spiegler is coauthor of *Personality: Strategies and Issues* and *The Community Training Center* and coeditor of *Contemporary Psychotherapies for a Diverse World*. He regularly presents workshops and courses on college textbook writing. His nonprofessional passions include his wife and family, flying his plane, mountains, listening to early music, and savoring wine.

PREFACE

Thank you for reading this preface. Few people read prefaces, so I want to reinforce your extraordinary behavior by answering one of the questions you may be curious about: How is this book different from other behavior therapy textbooks? *Contemporary Behavior Therapy* is simultaneously an introduction for beginning students and a comprehensive, scholarly review and resource for advanced students and professionals. To make this a "teaching book"—one from which students can easily learn—I have written in a casual, inviting style and have employed many pedagogical features, including the following:

- *Unifying principles and themes* that are initially presented in brief, introductory chapters and then illustrated throughout the book
- *A consistent behavioral perspective*, including the use of behavioral principles—such as prompting, shaping, reinforcement, modeling, and behavior rehearsal—to teach behavioral principles and procedures, and the use of behavioral rather than trait descriptions of clients' problems
- *Unique conceptual schemes* that organize the currently diverse field of behavior therapy
- *Numerous cases* that are integrated into the text and provide rich detail about the application of behavior therapy to a wide array of disorders
- *Participation Exercises* that provide students with hands-on experience with behavior therapy principles and procedures to promote active learning
- *Many illustrations* (including photographs and cartoons) that are functional rather than decorative
- *Integration of clinical, research, professional, and ethical facets* of the practice of behavior therapy

Contemporary Behavior Therapy has been written for readers in a variety of disciplines, and applications and examples are drawn from diverse fields. Readers need no previous background because all the basic concepts are presented in Chapters 3 and 4. Theoretical, methodological, and professional issues in behavior therapy are set off as In Theory boxes so that they can be omitted in courses in which their content is not germane.

What makes this book a scholarly review of behavior therapy is its comprehensiveness and critical evaluation. All of the major behavior therapy procedures are discussed, and the latest research findings are presented, synthesized, and critically evaluated. The literature review is documented with more than 2,200 references, a quarter of which were published since the last edition appeared in 2003.

What's new about the fifth edition of *Contemporary Behavior Therapy?* First of all, this edition was written solely by Michael Spiegler. When David Guevremont told me that he would not have time to collaborate on this revision due to other professional commitments, I felt a great loss. Not only was David's contribution to the book valuable, but we had a wonderful professional and personal collaboration. Writing a textbook is a major undertaking over a protracted period, and the enduring satisfaction comes in the process rather than the end product. I missed working with David this time around, but I am grateful for his legacy that still remains in this edition and for our continued friendship.

Since the publication of the previous edition of *Contemporary Behavior Therapy*, the field of behavior therapy has burgeoned, and the fifth edition has been expanded accordingly. The book now includes:

- An increased emphasis on the application of behavior therapy with culturally diverse clients
- Coverage of new therapies, including behavioral activation, functional analytic psychotherapy, and cognitive reprocessing therapy
- Expanded coverage of relapse prevention, treatment of addictive behaviors, integrated behavioral couple therapy, and treatment of posttraumatic stress disorder related to the 9/11 attacks and the Iraq war
- A new discussion of evaluating efficacy versus effectiveness and the role of meta-analytic studies
- A new chapter on third-generation behavior therapies, including major sections on Acceptance and Commitment Therapy, dialectical behavior therapy, and mindfulness-based cognitive therapy

As in previous editions, *Contemporary Behavior Therapy* is divided into three parts. The first part presents the fundamental principles of behavior therapy, which are repeatedly illustrated and drawn on in subsequent chapters. The second part covers all the major behavior therapy procedures used today. The third part first illustrates broader applications of behavior therapy principles and procedures to behavioral medicine and psychological disorders with primary physical characteristics; it then presents a final evaluation of and commentary on the present status and future of behavior therapy.

I have written the fifth edition of *Contemporary Behavior Therapy* as a teacher, researcher, and clinician. As a teacher, I have incorporated many pedagogical practices to facilitate learning, including stressing general principles, actively engaging students in learning about behavior therapy; and providing numerous examples and everyday illustrations to which students can relate. As a researcher, I appreciate the importance of empirically validating treatment procedures. Thus, not only have I presented the evidence for the efficacy and effectiveness of behavior therapy procedures by describing studies, but I also have critically evaluated them and discussed their limitations. As a clinician, I find the practice of behavior therapy to be challenging, stimulating, and reinforcing. I have striven to impart that in my writing in the hope of inspiring future behavior therapists.

ACKNOWLEDGMENTS

I am grateful to many people who facilitated the writing of this book.

My editor, Jon-David Hague, contributed his experience and intellect to making the book happen.

Abigail Greshik shepherded the book through its production. I am grateful for her knowledge, competence, care, and reliability, which enhanced the quality of the book you are holding. Moreover, Abby is a delightful person who was a pleasure to work with.

Kaitlin O'Donnell's careful reading of copyedited manuscript and proofs and her perceptive suggestions made for a clearer and cleaner presentation in many instances. Lauren Moses hunted down many of the hundreds of references I perused, Diane Wilkes-Smith was my Word wizard, and Lauren Jubinville worked out some of the kinks I experienced during the past year. Adam Miller played a major role in preparing the name index, and Zach Odachowski did some critical checking of proofs. Annmarie Mullen, the consummate secretary, provided assistance in so many ways. To be complete, Cynthia Finis was always there to keep me attending to details.

I am indebted to Amy Ustjanauskas for the invaluable assistance she provided in so many ways during the writing phase. Her attention to details, coupled with an awareness of the big picture; perceptive conceptual and editorial feedback and suggestions; efficiency; and dedication were exceptional and absolutely made the book better.

Thanks to my colleague-friends who gave me feedback, advice, and especially support: Chris Bloom, Tom Guilmette, Mary Harmon-Vukić, Mary O'Keeffe, George Raymond, and Jennifer Van Reet.

As always, my best friend Rick McEwan covered me, on and off belay.

For understanding, or at least accepting, the priority of "the book" for a protracted period, I thank my family. The joy and nachas I continually receive from my granddaughters, Amelia and Megan Fink, were a source of balance during frenetic periods. Writing this book, and all I do, is partially maintained by the modeling and reinforcement provided by the two people who picked me up from the hospital steps (or at least that's how they explained it to me): my loving parents, Lillian and Julie Spiegler. Finally, and most important, the gold medal for standing by her man goes to my wife and soul mate, Arlene. For her love and support, for understanding my need to spend so many hours in my study, and for "stending" me, I am grateful, always and forever.

Michael D. Spiegler

CONTENTS

CHAPTER **3 The Behavioral Model 31**

CHAPTER **4 The Process of Behavior Therapy 47**

CHAPTER **12** **Cognitive-Behavioral Therapy:** Cognitive Restructuring **303**

PART **3** **Applications to Somatic Problems and Contemporary Behavior Therapy in Perspective 419**

CHAPTER **15** **Applications of Behavior Therapy to Medical Disorders 421**

CASE STUDIES, PARTICIPATION EXERCISES, AND IN THEORY BOXES

CASE STUDIES

PARTICIPATION EXERCISES

IN THEORY BOXES

A NOTE TO READERS

As you journey through this book, you should be aware of several topographical features that will help you learn about behavior therapy and make your reading easier.

- Each chapter begins with an outline of its contents, and I suggest you look it over before starting to read.
- References are designated by superscript numbers that correspond to reference notes at the end of each chapter.
- All major behavior therapy terms are printed in **boldface type** at the point where they are first formally defined. These terms also are succinctly defined in a comprehensive Glossary of Behavior Therapy Terms at the back of the book.
- Should you be unfamiliar with some of the psychological disorders discussed, there also is a Glossary of Psychological Disorders and Problems at the back of the book.

Three features are set off from the main text.

- *Cases* are a continuous part of the text discussion, so you should read them as you come to them.
- *Participation Exercises* will give you hands-on experience with behavior therapy principles and procedures. Instructions for when to read and complete each Participation Exercise are provided in the text or in a footnote. Some of the Participation Exercises require work sheets and some have answers, both of which you will find in the Student Resource Manual on the Web at www.wadsworth.com/psychology/spiegler.

- *In Theory* boxes describe theoretical, methodological, and professional issues related to behavior therapy, and you should read them as soon as you come to a logical pause in the text.

Finally, important information and ideas are presented in tables and figures, so look at them carefully when they are referred to in the text. Finally, spending a moment with photos and cartoons will help you learn and remember the material.

In writing the fifth edition of *Contemporary Behavior Therapy*, I have incorporated suggestions from students who have read previous editions. I'd like to hear your comments and suggestions. Please write me at spiegler@ providence.edu; I will respond.

I hope you will enjoy reading and learning about behavior therapy.

PART ONE

Basic Principles

Imagine that you are about to enjoy a delicious three-course dinner. Consider each of the three parts of this book as one of the courses. In Part One, we serve the appetizers: the ideas that will prepare your palate for the rest of the dinner. You'll begin with an overview of the field of behavior therapy in Chapter 1, followed in Chapter 2 by a look at the historic events that shaped contemporary behavior therapy. Chapter 3 introduces the behavioral model, the principles that underlie behavior therapy. Chapter 4 explains how the behavioral model is applied to behavior therapy, describes the basic processes involved in implementing behavior therapy, and discusses how the success of behavior therapy is evaluated. Finally, Chapter 5 describes behavioral assessment, the methods behavior therapists use to gather information about clients' problems and measure clients' progress in therapy.

The first course is about to be served. Bon appétit.

Behavior Therapy

Introduction

Opening a textbook for the first time is like walking into a psychotherapist's office for the initial visit. Both students and clients arrive with general expectations about what is going to happen. Students assume the author will teach them, just as new clients in psychotherapy expect the therapist will help them with their problems.

Being taught and being helped are all too often passive processes. As teachers and behavior therapists, we believe that for education and psychotherapy to be most effective, students and clients must actively participate in the process. In behavior therapy, clients are involved in choosing and implementing therapy procedures. In education, students learn best when they actively learn, and we have written this book in ways that promote active learning.

One way you will actively learn about behavior therapy is through Participation Exercises that will give you hands-on experience with the ideas, concepts, and procedures used in behavior therapy. Some Participation Exercises take a very brief time to complete, and these should be done when you come to them in the chapter. Others require a bit more time; it is best to do them before continuing your reading, but you can do them later. Finally, some exercises are more extensive and must be done after you read the chapter. We will suggest when to do each Participation Exercise, either in the text or in a footnote. The first Participation Exercise is one you should complete before you continue reading. It will take just a couple of minutes.

PARTICIPATION EXERCISE 1-1

What Do You Know About Behavior Therapy?

You have no doubt heard about behavior therapy. How accurate is your picture of behavior therapy? This exercise can help answer that question. Read each of the following statements, and write down whether you think it is primarily true or primarily false.

1. Behavior therapy is the application of well-established laws of learning.
2. Behavior therapy directly changes symptoms of a disorder.
3. A trusting relationship between client and therapist is not necessary for behavior therapy to be effective.
4. Behavior therapy does not deal with problems of feelings, such as depression and anger.
5. Generally, little verbal interchange takes place between the therapist and client in behavior therapy.
6. The client's cooperation is not necessary for behavior therapy to be successful.
7. Most clients in behavior therapy are treated in fewer than five sessions.
8. Behavior therapy is not applicable to changing mental processes such as thoughts and beliefs.
9. Positive reinforcement works better with children than with adults.
10. Many behavior therapy procedures use painful or aversive treatments.

11. Behavior therapy primarily deals with relatively simple problems, such as phobias (for example, fear of snakes) or undesirable habits (for instance, smoking).
12. The behavior therapist determines the goals of therapy.
13. The behavior therapist primarily is responsible for the success of therapy.
14. Because behavior therapy treats the symptoms of a disorder and not its underlying cause, once the symptoms are removed, others will develop because the cause of the symptoms has not been treated.

You may have recognized that many of the statements are false. In fact, all of them are predominantly false. They are all myths or misconceptions about behavior therapy.

TERMINOLOGY AND SCOPE

Behavior therapy also is called *behavior modification* and *cognitive-behavioral therapy.* Behavior therapists occasionally distinguish among the terms, but the distinctions are not standard.[1] *Behavior modification* originally referred to procedures that change the consequences of behaviors (such as reinforcement) and the stimulus conditions that elicited behaviors (such as the physical setting). However, *behavior modification* sometimes is used as a generic term to refer to *any* procedure that modifies behaviors, including some rather radical procedures ranging from lobotomies to wilderness survival courses,[2] which are totally unrelated to behavior therapy. The term **cognitive-behavioral therapy** specifically refers to treatments that change cognitions (such as thoughts and beliefs) that are influencing psychological problems. *Behavior therapy* is the broadest and "purest" term, and we will use it to refer to the entire field of therapy you will be learning about.

Major Goal

The major goal of behavior therapy is to help clients with psychological problems, a goal it shares with other forms of psychotherapy. Examples of psychological problems include anxiety, depression, interpersonal difficulties, problems with sexual functioning, and bizarre behaviors (such as hearing voices). Psychological problems often are personally maladaptive and distressing to clients, may violate social norms, and may be disturbing to other people (for example, parents may be troubled by their child's aggressive acts). Such problems are often referred to as *mental illness, emotional disturbance, psychopathology,* and *abnormal behavior,* each of which has a particular connotation. In this book, we use more neutral terms: *psychological problem, psychological* or *psychiatric disorder, problem behavior,* and *problem.*

In addition to treating psychological disorders, the principles and procedures of behavior therapy have been harnessed for a variety of purposes, including to improve everyday functioning, such as work productivity and child rearing;[3] to deal with societal problems, such as safety hazards and recycling;[4] to enhance athletic performance;[5] to reduce perfectionism in graduate students;[6] and to prevent and treat the physical and psychological effects of medical disorders.[7]

WHAT IS BEHAVIOR THERAPY?

If the statements in Participation Exercise 1-1 reveal something of what behavior therapy is *not*, then just what is behavior therapy? Unfortunately, no single, agreed-upon definition exists.[8] Behavior therapy is both diverse and evolving, so it is difficult to define concisely.

Defining Themes of Behavior Therapy

Instead of a general definition, we propose four defining themes that are at the core of behavior therapy: scientific, active, present focus, and learning focus.[9] These themes are interrelated and overlap in their influence on the practice of behavior therapy.

Scientific

The essence of behavior therapy is a commitment to a scientific approach that involves *precision* and *empirical evaluation*.[10] All aspects of behavior therapy are defined precisely, including the behaviors targeted for change, treatment goals, and assessment and therapy procedures. Treatment protocols that spell out the details of particular therapy procedures have been developed for a number of behavior therapies.[11] Using such protocols enables therapists to employ the same procedures that have already proven efficacious. As another example of precision, clients' progress is monitored before, during, and after therapy using *quantitative* measurements of the behaviors to be changed.

Conclusions about the effectiveness of behavior therapies are based on the results of empirical research[12] rather than the subjective judgments of therapists or testimonials from satisfied clients.[13] This standard, which behavior therapists have always used, has been highlighted in recent years with the advent of managed care. Managed-care companies are only willing to pay for psychotherapy that has a track record of success with the client's identified psychiatric disorder, and many behavior therapies are on their list of preferred treatments because they are empirically supported.

Active

In behavior therapy, clients engage in specific actions to alleviate their problems. In other words, clients *do* something about their difficulties, rather than just talk about them. Behavior therapy is an *action therapy,* in contrast to a *verbal therapy* (such as psychoanalysis or client-centered therapy). In verbal psychotherapies, the dialogue between the client and therapist is the major mode through which therapy techniques are implemented. In action therapies, conversations between the client and therapist are predominantly for exchanging information. The therapy itself primarily consists of tasks the client does. In therapy sessions, examples would be role-playing problem situations, rehearsing coping skills, and imaging anxiety-evoking situations while actively countering the anxiety with muscle relaxation. Outside of therapy sessions, clients may monitor their problem behaviors during the course of their daily activities and practice applying coping skills, for example. Specific therapeutic tasks clients perform in their everyday environments, called **homework assignments,** are an integral part of behavior therapy.[14] The

What the Bleep do we Know?

logic for implementing treatment in the client's natural environments is simple: The client's problem is treated where it is occurring, which is in the client's everyday life. "Taking therapy home" makes it more likely that the changes that occur during therapy will transfer to the client's life and continue after therapy has ended.[15] For instance, in the treatment of antisocial behaviors, children and adolescents are taught problem-solving skills in therapy sessions. But the crucial part of the treatment occurs when the clients practice these skills at home or in school.[16] For instance, school interventions that are coordinated with treatment in therapy sessions has proved beneficial for such diverse problems as attention disorders,[17] adolescent depression,[18] disruptive behaviors,[19] bullying,[20] and obesity.[21]

The term **in vivo** (Latin for *in life*) is used to designate therapy procedures that are implemented in the client's natural environment. In vivo therapy can be implemented in one of three ways. First, the therapist may work directly with the client in the client's natural environment. This approach is costly in terms of therapists' time and is therefore used only occasionally. Second, the therapist can train people in the client's life, such as parents, spouses, and teachers, to assist in the treatment, such as by administering reinforcers.[22] Third, clients can serve as their own change agents by carrying out therapy procedures on their own with therapist instructions and monitoring.[23] Thus, those responsible for implementing treatment include not only behavior therapists but also other people who serve as *change agents,* including relatives, friends, teachers, and clients themselves.

Clients' serving as their own change agents illustrates the **self-control approach** commonly used in behavior therapy.[24] Self-control approaches have three important advantages. First, being responsible for the change is personally empowering.[25] Second, clients who are instrumental in changing their own behaviors are more likely to maintain the change. Third, clients who become skilled in dealing with their problems may be able to cope with future problems on their own,[26] which makes a self-control approach cost-effective in the long run.

Present Focus

The focus of behavior therapy is in the present. Behavior therapists assume that clients' problems, which occur in the present, are influenced by current conditions. Accordingly, behavioral assessment focuses on the client's current, rather than past, circumstances to find the factors responsible for the client's problems. Then, behavior therapy procedures are employed to change the current factors that are affecting the client's behaviors. This emphasis contrasts with other types of psychotherapy, such as psychoanalytic therapy, which assume that the major influences on clients' problems reside in the past.

Learning Focus

An emphasis on learning is a final theme that defines behavior therapy and distinguishes it from other types of psychotherapy. Learning is important in three different respects. First, the behavioral model holds that most problem behaviors develop, are maintained, and change primarily through learning. Behavior therapists do not believe that *all* behaviors are primarily a function of learning because some behaviors are strongly influenced by heredity and biology. Nonetheless, virtually all behaviors are affected by learning, even if they have biological components.

Second, behavior therapy provides clients with learning experiences in which new (adaptive) behaviors replace old (maladaptive) behaviors. Thus, there is a strong *educational* component in behavior therapy, and behavior therapists often serve as teachers.

Third, the development of some behavior therapies was originally based on basic learning principles, and theories of learning (such as classical and operant conditioning) often are used to explain why behavior therapy procedures work.

Common Characteristics of Behavior Therapy

In addition to the defining themes in behavior therapy just described, four common characteristics of behavior therapy help distinguish it from other forms of psychotherapy: individualized therapy, stepwise progression, treatment packages, and brevity.

Individualized Therapy

In behavior therapy, standard therapy and assessment procedures are tailored to each client's unique problem, the specific circumstances in which the problem occurs, and the client's personal characteristics.[27] For instance, reinforcement is used to get clients of all ages to engage in adaptive behaviors. However, the specific reinforcer is likely to vary with the client's age as well as a host of other demographic factors, including cultural identification. For example, cream cheese might be a reinforcer for a Jewish-American 3-year-old while kimchi—a spicy Korean cabbage dish—might be a reinforcer for a Korean-American of the same age.

Stepwise Progression

Behavior therapy often proceeds in a stepwise progression, moving from simple to complex, from easier to harder, or from less threatening to more threatening. For example, a girl who was socially withdrawn was taught—through modeling and reinforcement—to interact with peers in steps: initially playing by herself in the presence of peers, then playing with peers, and finally initiating play with peers. Similarly, a man who was afraid of heights gradually was exposed to higher elevations during treatment, beginning a few feet off the ground and ending on top of a 10-story building.

Treatment Packages

Two or more behavior therapy procedures often are combined in a **treatment package** to increase the effectiveness of the therapy. This practice is analogous to the treatment of many medical problems, such as combining medication, diet, and exercise for cardiovascular disease.

There are two caveats about treatment packages. First, although it might be expected that the combination of two or more effective treatments would be more beneficial to the client than just using one of the treatments, that is not always the case. Comparing the success of combined therapies with each of the component therapies alone may indicate that one or more of the components are as potent by themselves. For example, exposure therapy for obsessive-compulsive disorder and social phobia is as effective as combining exposure therapy with cognitive-behavioral therapies, whereas cognitive-behavioral treatment packages are more effective than specific treatments for other anxiety disorders.[28] Second, although treatment packages can be more effective than specific treatments, combining therapies may lengthen treatment.[29]

Treatment packages are the norm in behavior therapy today. This is important to keep in mind as you begin to read about specific behavior therapies in Chapter 6. To facilitate your learning about behavior therapies, they will be introduced individually. Then, as you become familiar with specific therapies, increasingly you will read about treatment packages made up of the specific therapies.

Brevity

Behavior therapy is relatively brief, generally involving fewer therapy sessions and often less overall time than many other types of therapy. This results, in part, from the use of homework assignments in particular and the self-control approach in general. The length of therapy varies considerably with the problem being treated. Usually, the more complex and severe the problem, the longer is the treatment duration. For example, one survey revealed that the average number of hours required to treat specific phobias with behavior therapy was 13.4, compared with 46.4 for obsessive-compulsive disorder.[30] Treatment duration also varies with the particular behavior therapy used.

THERAPIST–CLIENT RELATIONSHIP IN BEHAVIOR THERAPY

The relationship between the therapist and the client is important in all forms of psychotherapy,[31] and with some psychotherapies it is the most critical factor. In behavior therapy, the relationship is considered *a necessary but not a sufficient condition* for successful treatment.[32] Behavior therapists presume that their clients are helped primarily by the specific change techniques used rather than by their relationship with the therapist. However, clients in behavior therapy may attribute their improvement more to the therapist–client relationship than to the therapy procedures.[33] Nonetheless, from the behavior therapist's perspective, the therapist–client relationship is analogous to the role of anesthesia in surgery.

> Somebody goes . . . for surgery because there are certain procedures that need to be implemented. In order for these procedures to take place, the person must be under anesthesia; the anesthesia facilitates what is really important [that is, the surgical procedures]. However, if anything goes wrong with the anesthesia during

the surgery, then that becomes the priority. Similarly . . . a good . . . [therapist–client relationship] is necessary and often crucial. Without it you just can't proceed.[34]

The therapist–client relationship in behavior therapy facilitates the implementation of specific therapy procedures in a variety of ways, including increasing the client's positive expectations and hope for success; encouraging the client to complete homework assignments that involve risk taking; overcoming obstacles that arise in therapy, including clients' not complying with the treatment; and increasing the potency of the therapist's praise and approval.[35]

Collaboration between the therapist and client is a hallmark of behavior therapy.[36] Behavior therapists share their expertise so that clients become knowledgeable partners in their therapy. Decisions about therapy goals and treatment procedures are made jointly. For instance, behavior therapists provide information about treatment options, describing what each of the appropriate therapies entails and the effectiveness of each (based on research findings). Clients then can decide on the type of treatment that is best suited to their needs and personal preferences.

MANY VARIATIONS OF BEHAVIOR THERAPY

Behavior therapy is not a single technique. There are many different forms of behavior therapy—in other words, many behavior therapies. These therapies are unified by the defining themes and common characteristics you read about earlier. The following examples illustrate the variety of behavior therapy procedures that exist; the chapters in which they are introduced appear in parentheses.

Self-Instructional Training (Chapter 13): In a predominantly Latino-American junior high school, students were required to speak English in class. However, many of the first generation immigrant students often reverted to Spanish because they could express themselves better in their native tongue. They were taught to subvocally say, "Speak only English," to remind themselves each time they raised their hand to speak in class.

Modeling and Behavior Rehearsal (Chapter 11): A woman was intimidated by her boss and consequently was unable to speak to him about problems at work. She learned to express her desires appropriately to her boss by observing her therapist demonstrate effective ways to tell superiors politely yet forcefully about dissatisfactions and personal preferences [modeling]. The woman then practiced these behaviors—initially with her therapist and later with other people who were less threatening than her boss—before she attempted to speak with her boss [behavior reversal].

Response Cost (Chapter 7): A 7-year-old boy, who was big for his age, frequently bullied smaller children. To decrease the boy's bullying, the boy's teacher instituted a rule specifying that he would miss recess or gym, his favorite school activities, each time he was caught fighting.

Positive Reinforcement (Chapter 6): A sixth-grade boy was doing poorly in school because he was spending an average of only 20 minutes a day on his homework. The therapist suggested that his parents have him earn privileges by spending appropriate time on his homework. The boy was allowed to play with friends, have an evening snack, and talk on the phone only after he spent the designated time on homework.

Stress Inoculation Training (Chapter 13): A business executive drank excessively when he arrived home each evening after a frustrating day at the office. To help the man deal with his frustration, the therapist taught him appropriate coping skills, including muscle relaxation and self-instructions. In therapy, the client role-played being in various frustrating situations and practiced applying the coping skills. Then, he used the skills in his everyday life whenever he felt frustrated and had the urge to drink.

Extinction and Differential Reinforcement of Other Behaviors (Chapter 7): On several occasions, a young mother had beaten her 3-year-old son when he had a temper tantrum. The more the mother tried to get her son to stop crying, the angrier she got; eventually she hit the child. The mother was taught to ignore her son during a temper tantrum [extinction] and to reinforce him with attention when he began engaging in any other behaviors [differential reinforcement of other behaviors]. This treatment package was designed not only to reduce the frequency and duration of her son's temper tantrums but also to help the mother cope with her frustration and eliminate her abusing her child.

Systematic Desensitization (Chapter 9): A college student was doing poorly in school because she panicked during examinations. To overcome her test anxiety, the student first was taught muscle relaxation. While relaxed, she visualized increasingly more anxiety-evoking situations (beginning with hearing the announcement that an exam would be given in 2 weeks and ending with being unable to answer an exam question). The objective was to substitute relaxation for the anxiety associated with test situations.

Token Economy and Shaping (Chapters 8 and 6, respectively): A 36-year-old man who was hospitalized for the treatment of schizophrenia was extremely socially withdrawn. He was placed in a token economy program in which he earned tokens (poker chips) for engaging in increasing levels of social interaction. At first he earned tokens for minimally interacting with others (for instance, asking a nurse for something he wanted) and later for extended social interactions (for example, having a conversation with another patient while they worked on a project together) [shaping]. The man could exchange the tokens he earned for a variety of reinforcers (such as watching TV and playing pool).

Cognitive-Behavioral Couple Therapy (Chapter 13): A gay couple who had been together for 11 years sought help because of their difficulty resolving conflicts, which arose frequently, and because they believed that they no longer loved each other. For dealing with conflicts, they were taught problem-solving strategies that involved generating many potential solutions to disagreements and then evaluating them to select the optimal solution. For the couple's second complaint, the therapist instructed each partner to perform several behaviors each day that the other partner considered an indication of caring.

Cognitive Restructuring (Chapter 12): A college student avoided going to social functions (which he desperately wanted to do) because he was afraid that he was socially awkward. He learned to substitute positive, reassuring thoughts (for example, "I just need to be myself, and I will fit in") for his habitual negative, self-deprecating thoughts (for example, "I'm going to make a fool of myself") which lowered his social anxiety and allowed him to attend social functions.

Acceptance and Commitment Therapy (Chapter 14): A college student avoided going to social functions (which he desperately wanted to do) because he was afraid that he was socially awkward. He learned to accept and defuse (separate from) his habitual negative, self-deprecating thoughts (for example, "I'm going to make a fool of myself") by recognizing that they were just thoughts (in other words, "I am having the thought that I will make a fool of myself") which allowed him to attend social functions while still having his critical thoughts and feeling anxious.

Even from the small sample of behavior therapy procedures just presented, it is clear that many diverse behavior therapies are used to treat a wide array of problems. Also, the same problem can be treated with very different behavioral strategies, as was illustrated in the last two examples in which the college student suffering from social anxiety could be treated by either *cognitive restructuring* or *Acceptance and Commitment Therapy*. Why are there so many behavior therapies?

One advantage of having multiple treatments for the same problem is that therapies vary in their suitability for particular problems, clients, and circumstances. Clients' preferences make a difference in the success of therapy because clients are more willing to engage in and stick to a treatment they believe will work.[37] Also, different therapies may target different aspects of the same problem. For example, in treating anger in children, one study showed that problem-solving therapy and social skills training were both successful in reducing aggression, conduct problems, and the frequency of anger expression.[38] However, problem-solving therapy was more effective in reducing hostile intentions in anger-provoking situations and developing adaptive ways of thinking about conflict situations; in contrast, social skills training was more effective in developing anger control skills. Thus, depending on the nature of a client's specific problem, one therapy might be more suitable than another.

ETHICAL ISSUES IN BEHAVIOR THERAPY

The two major potential ethical issues in behavior therapy concern *depriving clients of their rights* and *harming clients*. Throughout this book, we will, from time to time, raise ethical questions in relevant contexts. As you read, be alert for instances where ethical issues could arise. In addition, consider the ways in which behavior therapy protects clients from ethical violations.

For example, you have already read about the active role clients play in deciding on their treatment goals and the specific therapy procedures used to achieve them. This practice not only increases the chances that the treatment will be successful because clients are actively involved in their therapy,[39] but it also gives clients freedom of choice, which protects clients' rights.

Ethical violations occasionally occur in behavior therapy, and there are a small number of well-documented incidents. Most involved clients who had little or no power, especially institutionalized individuals such as prison inmates.[40] To help prevent such incidents, behavior therapists have developed guidelines for the ethical practice of behavior therapy.[41] Table 1-1 presents examples of the questions that should be answered for each therapy case.

TABLE **1-1**
Examples of Ethical Questions That Should Be Answered for Each Therapy Case

A. Have the goals of treatment been adequately considered?
  1. To ensure that the goals are explicit, are they written?
  2. Has the client's understanding of the goals been ensured by having the client restate them orally or in writing?
  3. Have the therapist and client agreed on the goals of therapy?
  4. Will serving the client's immediate interests be contrary to the client's long-term interest?

B. Has the choice of treatment methods been adequately considered?
  1. Does the published literature show the procedure to be the best one available for that problem?
  2. Has the client been told of alternative procedures that might be preferred by the client on the basis of significant differences in discomfort, treatment time, cost, or degree of demonstrated effectiveness?

C. Is the client's participation voluntary?
  1. Have possible sources of coercion on the client's participation been considered?
  2. If treatment is legally mandated, has the available range of treatments and therapists been offered?

  3. Can the client withdraw from treatment without a penalty or financial loss that exceeds actual clinical costs?

D. Has the adequacy of treatment been evaluated?
  1. Have quantitative measures of the problem and its progress been obtained?
  2. Have the measures of the problem and its progress been made available to the client during treatment?

E. Has the confidentiality of the treatment relationship been protected?
  1. Has the client been told who has access to the records?
  2. Are records available only to authorized persons?

F. Is the therapist qualified to provide treatment?
  1. Has the therapist had training or experience in treating problems like the client's?
  2. If deficits exist in the therapist's qualifications, has the client been informed?
  3. If the therapist is not adequately qualified, is the client referred to other therapists or has supervision by a qualified therapist been provided? Is the client informed of the supervisory relation?

Source: Adapted from *Ethical issues for human services*, 1977, pp. v-vi.

Finally, in considering ethical issues related to behavior therapy, bear in mind that the ethical issues that can potentially arise in behavior therapy are relevant to all psychotherapies.

PURPOSE OF THIS BOOK

The purpose of this book is to introduce you to contemporary behavior therapy. We first will present its general principles and then illustrate how they are applied to treat clients' problems. Although this book is not intended to teach you to be a behavior therapist, you may be able to apply many of the principles and some of the procedures to deal with minor problems in your everyday life. However, if you develop a psychological problem that seriously affects your life and does not resolve itself quickly, you should consult with a professional. You can find guidelines for choosing a behavior therapist in the Appendix.

SUMMARY

1. The basic aim of behavior therapy is to help clients deal with psychological problems. Behavior therapy principles and procedures also are used to modify everyday problems.
2. There is no single, agreed-upon definition of behavior therapy. Behavior therapy can be characterized by four defining themes: scientific, active, present focus, and learning focus.
3. The scientific approach entails precisely defining treatment goals, assessment procedures, and therapy procedures; continuously monitoring clients' progress using quantitative measurements; and evaluating the effectiveness of procedures through controlled research.
4. Behavior therapy is active in that clients do more than just talk about their problems. Clients engage in specific therapeutic tasks in therapy sessions and in their everyday environments where their problems are occurring.
5. Behavior therapy focuses on the present. Current conditions are assumed to influence the clients' present problems, and behavior therapy procedures change these current conditions.
6. In behavior therapy, problem behaviors are assumed to be acquired and/or changeable through learning; therapy therefore focuses on learning. Also, theories of learning often are used to explain why behavior therapies work.
7. Four common characteristics further define behavior therapy. Behavior therapy is individualized for each client, proceeds in a stepwise progression, often involves the combination of two or more therapies in a treatment package, and tends to be relatively brief.
8. In behavior therapy, the therapist–client relationship is considered necessary but not sufficient for successful treatment because it is the specific change techniques used that are most relevant to treatment success. Collaboration between the therapist and client, such as in setting goals and choosing therapy procedures, is a hallmark of behavior therapy.

9. Behavior therapy consists of a wide variety of different treatment procedures.

10. As with all psychotherapies, ethical issues can arise in behavior therapy. The two major potential issues are depriving clients of their rights and harming clients. Behavior therapy practices provide for some internal protections against ethical violations.

REFERENCE NOTES

1. Martin & Pear, 2007; Wilson, 1978.
2. For example, Krakauer, 1995, p. 75.
3. Hawkins & Forsyth, 1997.
4. For example, Austin, Hackett, Gravina, & Lebbon, 2006; Farrell, Cox, & Geller, 2007; Iyer & Kashyap, 2007; Spiegler & Guevremont, 1998.
5. For example, Sheard & Golby, 2006; Smith, Smoll, & Cumming, 2007.
6. Kearns, Forbes, & Gardiner, 2007.
7. For example, García, Simón, Durán, Canceller, & Aneiros, 2006; Hoffman, Papas, Chatkoff, & Kerns, 2007.
8. Kazdin & Wilson, 1978.
9. Compare with Cottraux, 1993.
10. Wilson, 1997a.
11. For example, Carroll & Rounsaville, 2008.
12. Barlow, 2000; Chambless & Hollon, 1998; Kendall, 1998; Kendall & Chambless, 1998.
13. Date, 1996; Persons, 1994.
14. For example, Addis & Jacobson, 2000; Burns & Sprangler, 2000; Kazantzis, Deane, Ronan, & L'Abate, 2005.
15. For example, Edelman & Chambless, 1993; Risley, 1995.
16. Kazdin, 2003.
17. For example, Fabiano & Pelham, 2003; Waschbusch, Pelham, & Massetti, 2005.
18. Possel, Baldus, Horn, Groen, & Hautzinger, 2005.
19. For example, Hawken & Hess, 2006.
20. Hirschstein & Frey, 2006.
21. Spiegel & Foulk, 2006.
22. Petronko, Harris, & Kormann, 1994.
23. For example, Israel, Guile, Baker, & Silverman, 1994; Rokke, Tomhave, & Jocic, 1999, 2000; Silverman, Ginsburg, & Kurtines, 1995.
24. Rehm & Rokke, 1988.
25. For example, Israel, Guile, Baker, & Silverman, 1994.
26. For example, Otto & Gould, 1995; Otto & Pollack, 1994.
27. Association for Behavioral and Cognitive Therapies, 2008.
28. Deacon & Abramowitz, 2005.
29. For example, Turner, Beidel, Spaulding, & Brown, 1995.
30. Turner, Beidel, Spaulding, & Brown, 1995.
31. Gaston, Goldfried, Greenberg, Horvath, Raue, & Watson, 1995.
32. Fleece, 1995; Raue, Castonguay, & Goldfried, 1993; Raue & Goldfried, 1994.
33. Raue & Goldfried, 1994.
34. Gaston, Goldfried, Greenberg, Horvath, Raue, & Watson, 1995, p. 5, italics in original.
35. Gaston, Goldfried, Greenberg, Horvath, Raue, & Watson, 1995; Keijsers, Schaap, & Hoogduin, 2000; Kohlenberg & Tsai, 1995; Raue & Goldfried, 1994.
36. Association for Behavioral and Cognitive Therapies, 2008.
37. DeAngelis, 2008.
38. Sukhodolsky, Golub, Stone, & Orban, 2005.
39. Bandura, 1969.
40. For example, Cotter, 1967.
41. For example, Davison, 1976; Davison & Stuart, 1975; Stolz, 1977.

2

Antecedents of Contemporary Behavior Therapy

Behavior therapy has "a long past but a short history."[1] In rudimentary forms, behavior therapy is very old. Humans have been using behavioral principles to modify people's behaviors for thousands of years (such as parents' rewarding children for good behaviors). Although these everyday applications are generally haphazard, they can be effective. To treat serious problems, a systematic approach is necessary. The formal, systematic application of behavioral principles to treat psychological problems—that is, behavior therapy—is about 60 years old.

HISTORICAL PRECURSORS

A number of historical treatments for psychological disorders closely resemble contemporary behavior therapies. For example, Pliny the Elder, a 1st-century C.E. Roman scholar, treated drinking problems using the fundamental principle of aversion therapy. He created an aversion to alcohol by putting putrid spiders at the bottom of the problem drinker's glass.[2] An early account of a cognitive therapy strategy in treating depression is portrayed in a 10th-century Icelandic story.[3] In Egil's saga, a daughter helps her grieving father overcome his severe depression by getting him to engage in sequentially more active behaviors, which results in his feeling better.

At the close of the 18th century, Jean-Marc-Gaspard Itard attempted to socialize the "Wild Boy of Aveyron," a child who grew up without human contact.[4] To teach the boy language and other social behaviors, Itard employed procedures similar to contemporary behavior therapies used to treat children with autistic disorder, including modeling, prompting, shaping, and time out from positive reinforcement.[5]

In the early 19th century, Alexander Maconochie, a captain in the Royal Navy, was put in charge of a British penal colony located on Norfolk Island, Australia.[6] To rehabilitate the prisoners, Maconochie established a point system that allowed each prisoner to redeem himself by performing appropriate behaviors. In Maconochie's words, "When a man keeps the key of his own prison, he is soon persuaded to fit it into the lock." Despite the apparent success of this early token economy, Maconochie's superiors disapproved of his innovative methods and denigrated their effectiveness.[7]

An 1845 paper presented to the Royal Academy of Medicine in Paris reported on the treatment of a 30-year-old wine merchant for his obsessional thoughts by François Leuret, a physician. Leuret had the man recite song lyrics, behaviors that competed with his disturbing, repetitive thoughts.[8] And, in his book, *Chastity or Our Secret Sins*, Dio Lewis treated a man preoccupied with sexual thoughts by telling the man that sensual ideas are dangerous and that they would startle him when they came to mind. When this occurred, Lewis instructed the man to immediately engage in a competing response, such as thinking about something else or engaging in physical exercise.[9] These procedures are similar to some present-day cognitive-behavioral interventions.

These early harbingers of behavior therapy procedures have only historical significance because they have had no real influence on the development of contemporary behavior therapy.[10]

EARLY EXPERIMENTAL WORK

John B. Watson

The inspiration for contemporary behavior therapy came from experimental work on learning carried out at the beginning of the 20th century. Russian physiologist Ivan Pavlov is credited with the first systematic account of what has come to be called *classical* (or *Pavlovian*) *conditioning*.[11] In this form of learning, a neutral stimulus (one that elicits no particular response) is repeatedly paired with a stimulus that naturally elicits a particular response. The result is that eventually the neutral stimulus alone elicits the response. In Pavlov's well-known experiments with dogs, a neutral stimulus, such as a light or a tone, was paired with food, a stimulus that reflexively produces salivation. After repeated pairings of these two stimuli, the light or tone alone began to elicit salivation. This classical conditioning process is shown in Figure 2-1.

In addition to his important laboratory experiments with animals, Pavlov wrote about the application of learning procedures to treat psychological disorders.[12] Pavlov's critical contribution to behavior therapy, however, was the influence his work had on John B. Watson, an experimental psychologist at Johns Hopkins University. Watson is the founder of *behaviorism*, the school of psychology on which behavior therapy was largely based. Watson's behaviorism emphasized the importance of objectively studying behaviors by dealing only with directly observable stimuli and responses and rejected mentalistic concepts, such as consciousness, thought, and imagery.[13]

In 1924, Mary Cover Jones, one of Watson's students, successfully treated a 3-year-old boy named Peter, who had an intense fear of rabbits.[14] The therapy consisted of two basic procedures. First, Peter watched other children happily playing with a rabbit, which may have led Peter to realize that rabbits were not necessarily frightening. Then, Jones gradually exposed Peter to the rabbit. She placed a caged rabbit in the room while Peter was eating a

Mary Cover Jones

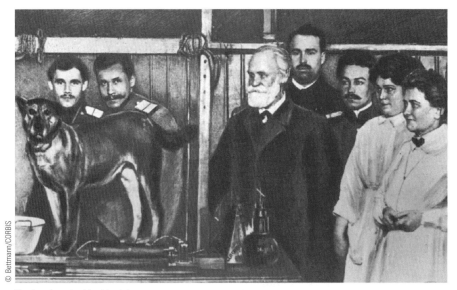

Pavlov (center) in his lab

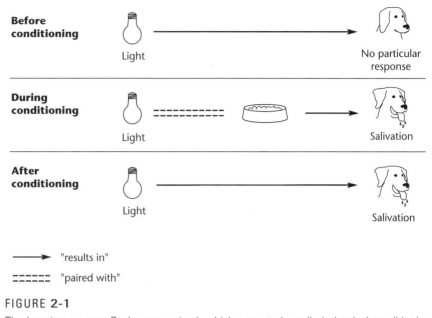

Before conditioning

Light → No particular response

During conditioning

Light ===== (bowl) → Salivation

After conditioning

Light → Salivation

——————▶ "results in"

====== "paired with"

FIGURE 2-1

The learning process Pavlov recognized, which came to be called *classical conditioning*

Edward Thorndike

favorite food. The cage was at a sufficient distance so that its presence did not interfere with Peter's eating and did not upset him. Over a number of days, Jones brought the rabbit closer to Peter, always keeping it at a distance that was comfortable for Peter. Jones eventually took the rabbit out of the cage and gradually brought it closer to Peter. Following this treatment, Peter was able to comfortably hold and play with the rabbit. Years later, Jones's two treatment procedures—modeling therapy and in vivo desensitization—were refined and now are widely used behavior therapies for the treatment of fears.

Hobart and Willie Mowrer also were influenced by Pavlov's classical conditioning principles. In 1935, they began a treatment program for nocturnal enuresis (bedwetting) at the New Haven Children's Center.[15] The treatment taught children to awaken when they felt tension in their bladder so that they could go to the toilet to urinate rather than wet the bed. To accomplish this, a special pad under the bedsheet activated a bell when a small amount of urine contacted it.[16] Thus, as soon as children began to urinate, they were awakened by the bell. After bladder tension and awakening were paired a number of times, a full bladder alone woke the child. Their bell-and-pad technique proved highly successful and is still used today.

At the same time that Pavlov was studying classical conditioning, psychologist Edward Thorndike at Columbia University was investigating the strengthening and weakening of behaviors by systematically changing their consequences (reinforcement and punishment, respectively).[17] This type of learning came to be called *operant* (or *instrumental*) *conditioning*.

Photographer: Special Collections & University Archives, University of Illinois at Chicago Library

Willie & Hobart Mowrer

In a different arena, Edmund Jacobson, a physiologist at the University of Chicago in the 1930s, was experimenting with skeletal muscle relaxation as a treatment for tension associated with a wide array of psychological and physical disorders, including generalized anxiety, phobias, depression, hypertension, colitis, tics, and stuttering.[18] Jacobson's *progressive relaxation* is the basis for the extensive use of muscle relaxation in behavior therapy.

GROWING DISCONTENT WITH PSYCHOANALYSIS

Despite the effectiveness of some early behavior therapy efforts,[19] contemporary behavior therapy did not begin in earnest until the 1950s.[20] The genesis of behavior therapy was influenced to a significant degree by the nature and status of psychoanalysis, the prevailing model of psychotherapy in the 1950s.

Psychoanalysis, originally developed by Sigmund Freud, focuses on exploring clients' early childhood experiences and attempting to uncover unconscious conflicts and desires, which are hypothesized to be the causal factors of psychological disorders. The objective is for clients to gain insight about the origin of their problems. Insight is believed to be the key to change; for this reason, psychoanalysis and similar therapies are called *insight therapies*.

Psychoanalysis was the only major approach to psychotherapy during the first half of the 20th century. However, after World War II, doubts about the usefulness of psychoanalysis as a general treatment method began to mount.

TABLE **2-1**

Differences Between Psychoanalysis and Behavior Therapy

	Psychoanalysis	Behavior Therapy
Locus of time	Past	Present
Mode of treatment	Verbal	Action-oriented
Treatment strategy	Indirectly explore client's past and unconscious as related to client's problem	Identify and directly change present maintaining conditions of client's problem
How techniques are applied	Same for all clients	Customized for each client
Length of treatment	Lengthy	Brief
Evidence for effectiveness	Uncontrolled, qualitative case studies	Controlled, quantitative experiments

Hans Eysenck

Because psychoanalysis is such a lengthy process—often requiring years—it could not meet the needs of the large number of veterans who required psychological treatment as a result of the war.

This growing discontent with traditional psychoanalytic psychotherapy received a major impetus from a 1952 retrospective study by British psychologist Hans Eysenck (pronounced EYE-zink).[21] Eysenck investigated the effectiveness of insight therapies by examining records from hospitals and insurance companies. He concluded that people treated by traditional insight psychotherapy were no more likely to improve than those who received no treatment at all. Subsequent reanalysis of Eysenck's data showed that his conclusion was exaggerated.[22] Nonetheless, Eysenck's original conclusion did serve as an impetus for psychotherapists to seriously question the benefits of traditional psychotherapy and to seek more effective alternatives. A major alternative was behavior therapy. Table 2-1 highlights the differences between psychoanalysis and behavior therapy.

FORMAL BEGINNINGS OF CONTEMPORARY BEHAVIOR THERAPY

Contemporary behavior therapy formally began in the 1950s simultaneously in the United States and Canada, South Africa, and Great Britain.

Developments in North America

B. F. Skinner

Beginning in the 1930s, psychologist B. F. Skinner at Harvard University began his extensive investigation of operant conditioning with pigeons and rats. Like Pavlov, Skinner speculated about the therapeutic uses of learning principles,[23] but he himself did not carry his ideas to fruition. It remained for his students and followers to apply operant principles to therapy.

In the early 1950s, Ogden Lindsley, then a graduate student working with Skinner, directed a series of studies to determine the feasibility of applying operant conditioning procedures to adults with severe psychiatric disorders.[24] His initial research demonstrated that patients in psychiatric hospitals

Courtesy of University of Kansas, University Archives

Ogden Lindsley

FIGURE 2-2

Sketch of the patient's stance that Haughton and Ayllon reinforced in their demonstration study

Source: Haughton & Ayllon, 1965, p. 96.

whose behaviors seemed aimless would consistently perform simple tasks when given meaningful reinforcers. Lindsley's initial investigations could not legitimately be considered therapy. However, they led to the development of sophisticated procedures, derived from operant conditioning principles, to treat complex human problems. Incidentally, Lindsley may have been the first to formally use the term *behavior therapy* to describe the systematic use of learning procedures to treat psychological disorders.[25]

In the late 1950s, Teodoro Ayllon (pronounced eye-YONE), at the Saskatchewan Hospital in Canada, performed now-classic demonstrations of the effectiveness of operant principles in modifying severely disturbed behaviors of psychiatric patients.[26] Ayllon's demonstrations were instrumental in overcoming the widespread resistance to the behavioral model. According to psychoanalysis, the model still prevailing at the time, psychological disorders are the result of deep-seated, unconscious conflicts. This implied that successful treatment had to delve into those conflicts.[27] As an indirect challenge to this psychoanalytic notion, Ayllon and his colleague Eric Haughton showed that a behavior that might be considered a symptom of a psychiatric disorder could be created simply by reinforcing it and then could be eliminated simply by withdrawing the reinforcement.[28] The behavior they chose was holding a broom in an upright position (see Figure 2-2). Their subject was a 54-year-old female patient with schizophrenia who had been hospitalized for 23 years and who spent most of her time lying in bed or sitting on a couch. A psychiatrist who was unaware of the origins of the patient's broom-holding made the following comments after observing the patient's behavior.

> Her constant and compulsive pacing holding a broom . . . could be seen as a ritualistic procedure, a magical action. When regression conquers the associative process, primitive and archaic forms of thinking control the behavior. Symbolism is a predominant mode of expression of deep-seated unfulfilled desires and instinctual impulses. . . .
>
> Her broom could then be:
>
> 1. a child that gives her love and she gives him in return her devotion;
> 2. a phallic symbol;
> 3. the sceptre of an omnipotent queen.[29]

This explanation is consistent with the psychoanalytic model that postulates complex and deep-rooted causes of behavior. However, Haughton and Ayllon demonstrated that alternative and much simpler and more straightforward explanations for psychiatric symptoms might exist, which was a revolutionary idea at the time.

In 1961, Ayllon collaborated with Nathan Azrin, another of Skinner's former students, to design the first comprehensive token economy at Anna State Hospital in Illinois.[30] A token economy provides clients with token reinforcers (such as poker chips or points) to motivate them to perform desired behaviors; the patient can exchange tokens for actual reinforcers (for instance, a snack or time watching TV). The Anna State Hospital token economy paved the way for the widespread application of this treatment method.

Early Resistance to Behavior Therapy

In setting up their token economy, Ayllon and Azrin, like most other early behavior therapists, encountered considerable resistance from the hospital staff. Most of the staff did not believe that the new behavioral treatment methods could be effective and were reluctant to support Ayllon and Azrin's program. As was typical of behavior therapy efforts at the time, the Anna State Hospital token economy was an experimental program funded by a research grant, which separated it from the mainstream hospital programs. Resisting the new treatment model, the staffs of other hospital programs were reluctant to refer patients to the token economy program, especially patients with whom they were having some success. Therefore, the patients who were referred to Ayllon and Azrin's experimental program were those who had not responded to traditional treatments and were considered incurable. Naturally, this "stacked the deck" against the new behavior therapy program. Ironically, these unfavorable conditions turned out to be a blessing in disguise. The token economy resulted in remarkable changes in the so-called incurable patients, which only strengthened the case for the effectiveness of behavior therapy procedures. This cycle of facing *skepticism* from traditional professionals, having to work under *adverse conditions*, and nonetheless *demonstrating effectiveness* was a common experience for early behavior therapists through at least the mid-1970s.

Developments in South Africa

Meanwhile, in South Africa, psychiatrist Joseph Wolpe had become disenchanted with psychoanalytic methods of treatment. In the 1950s, he developed several keystone behavior therapies, most notably systematic desensitization used to treat fear and anxiety. Systematic desensitization involves exposing clients to mental images of anxiety-evoking situations while engaging in a behavior that competes with anxiety, such as skeletal muscle relaxation (based on Jacobson's progressive relaxation). Wolpe explained his procedures in terms of classical conditioning and neurophysiological concepts.[31] His work was seminal, and he is sometimes referred to as the founder of behavior therapy.[32]

Prominent among the professionals whom Wolpe trained in South Africa were Arnold Lazarus and Stanley Rachman. Lazarus initially made important contributions by adapting systematic desensitization to groups of clients and to children.[33] Throughout his career, Lazarus has strongly advocated extending the boundaries of behavior therapy. He developed innovative therapy techniques on the basis of their effectiveness rather than their being derived from existing theories[34]—in contrast to Wolpe, whose work always was tightly bound to learning theory. Since 1966, Lazarus has practiced and taught behavior therapy in the United States. Rachman, who had collaborated with Lazarus in South Africa, emigrated to Great Britain in 1959 to work closely with Eysenck. Rachman introduced desensitization to British behavior therapists, and he became one of behavior therapy's foremost advocates and researchers in Great Britain.[35]

Arnold Lazarus

Stanley Rachman

Developments in Great Britain

Great Britain was the third major breeding ground for contemporary behavior therapy. The development of behavior therapy in Great Britain was spearheaded by Eysenck at the Institute of Psychiatry at the University of London. This work was facilitated by M. B. Shapiro,[36] who, as director of the Clinical-Teaching Section, advocated validating behavior therapies by systematically comparing individual clients' behaviors during periods of therapy and periods without therapy (as in reversal studies; see Chapter 4), as did Skinner and his associates.[37] This emphasis is but one commonality among the early behavior therapists in North America, South Africa, and Great Britain. As is often the case in the history of science, similar approaches develop simultaneously and independently. Nonetheless, behavior therapy in North America, South Africa, and Great Britain in the 1950s presented a strong and fairly unified alternative to traditional psychoanalytic therapy.

EARLY ETHICAL CONCERNS ABOUT BEHAVIOR THERAPY

In its formative years, there were some ethical concerns about behavior therapy that were, in large measure, artifacts of the time. One ethical concern was the possible danger that behavior therapy techniques would be used to control people. In part, this notion may have arisen from misunderstandings about some of the terminology that behavior therapists used, such as references to "*controlling* variables," "experimental *control*," and the "*manipulation* of contingencies." Coincidentally, behavior therapy emerged in a period of heightened vigilance about external control (such as by governments), about the invasion of personal privacy (as through electronic eavesdropping and computer storage of personal information), and about the abuse of civil liberties (for instance, of institutionalized patients and prisoners). "Reacting to the seemingly unchecked growth of these influences, many citizens . . . [came] to adopt positions that are highly critical of any and all behavior influence efforts."[38]

A number of early ethical criticisms of behavior therapy arose out of confusion as to what behavior therapy was and what it was not. These criticisms occurred most frequently when the term *behavior modification* was used (rather than *behavior therapy*). *Behavior modification* was mistakenly confused with *any* procedure that modifies behavior, including psychosurgery (such as lobotomies), electroconvulsive shock therapy (ECT), drugs, brainwashing, sensory deprivation, and even torture.[39] A survey of articles indexed under *behavior modification* in the *New York Times* over a 5-year period revealed that the term was incorrectly used approximately half the time.[40] In some cases, the treatment procedures referred to as *behavior modification* had absolutely no relationship to behavior therapy, such as the use of a drug that causes a brief period of paralysis of the muscles (including those of the respiratory system) as punishment for prisoners.[41]

The extent to which the name of a therapy procedure can influence people's perceptions of it is illustrated by a study titled "A Rose by Any Other Name . . . : Labeling Bias and Attitudes Toward Behavior Modification."[42] In this experiment, undergraduate and graduate students evaluated a video of a teacher using reinforcement procedures in a special education class. All the students saw the same video, but half were told that it illustrated "behavior modification" and half were told that it illustrated "humanistic education." Compared with students who viewed the procedures as "behavior modification," those who viewed them as "humanistic education" gave the teacher significantly more favorable ratings and considered the teaching method significantly more likely to promote academic learning and emotional growth. Apparently, a rose by any other name may not smell as sweet.

ACCEPTANCE AND GROWTH OF BEHAVIOR THERAPY

In the 1960s, there were few behavior therapists in private practice, and those working in psychiatric hospitals and outpatient facilities were still encountering resistance from traditional psychotherapists. Even in academic settings, which typically are accepting and nurturing atmospheres for new ideas, behavior therapists often were isolated because their colleagues viewed behavior therapy as a radical departure from mainstream psychology.

To overcome these barriers to acceptance and growth, behavior therapists in the late 1950s and early 1960s spent considerable time gathering evidence that behavior therapy was a viable alternative to traditional psychotherapy. This effort included the publication of demonstration projects, such as Ayllon's, that showed that a wide array of clinical problems could be treated successfully in a relatively brief period with behavior therapy techniques.[43]

Linda A. Cicero/Stanford News Service

Albert Bandura

In the 1960s, while already-established behavior therapy procedures (such as token economies and systematic desensitization) were being refined, another major approach to behavior therapy was born. Psychologist Albert Bandura at Stanford University developed a social learning theory that included not only principles of classical and operant conditioning but also *observational learning*[44]—the process of changing one's own behaviors by viewing the behaviors of another person (a model). In addition, Bandura's *social learning theory*[45] emphasized the critical role that cognitions (such as thoughts, images, and expectations) play in psychological functioning, including their role in the development and treatment of psychological disorders. Indeed, Bandura now calls his theoretical approach *social cognitive theory*.[46]

Making cognitions a legitimate focus of behavior therapy was antithetical to Watson's behaviorism because cognitions are not directly observable. Watson's behaviorism may have been a useful position for early behavior therapists to adopt, because it countered the deeply entrenched psychoanalytic perspective emphasizing unconscious forces that, of course, cannot be observed directly. Today, most behavior therapists believe that dealing only with directly observable behaviors is too restrictive.[47] After all, humans *do* think, expect, plan, and imagine, and these cognitive processes clearly influence how people act.

During the 1960s, several prominent behavior therapists created *cognitive-behavioral therapy*, which changes clients' maladaptive cognitions that contribute to psychological disorders. Independently, Aaron Beck at the University of Pennsylvania developed *cognitive therapy*,[48] and Albert Ellis, in private practice in New York City, designed *rational emotive therapy*[49] (which he renamed *rational emotive behavior therapy* in 1993[50]). Both therapies seek to modify the negative and illogical thoughts associated with many psychological disorders, such as depression and anxiety. Donald Meichenbaum (pronounced MIKE-en-baum), at the University of Waterloo in Ontario, developed cognitive-behavioral treatment packages, such as *self-instructional training* and *stress inoculation training* that are used to treat a wide range of psychological problems, including impulsive behaviors, anxiety, anger, and pain.[51] Meichenbaum was among the first to apply cognitive-behavioral interventions to children. Initially, cognitive-behavioral therapies served as supplements to existing behavior therapy procedures, but they rapidly evolved as a major approach in the field. Indeed, today, a majority of behavior therapists use cognitive-behavioral therapies.

In 1966, the Association for Advancement of Behavior Therapy was established in the United States. Cyril Franks, who previously had worked with Eysenck and Rachman at the Institute of Psychiatry in London, was its first president. It has become the major professional organization that advocates for behavior therapy and facilitates the field's further development. Additionally, by 1970 four major professional journals were devoted exclusively to behavior therapy.

Still, some critics voiced the opinion that behavior therapy would soon fade into oblivion, along with a host of other "faddish" therapies that arose in the 1960s, such as encounter groups and primal scream therapy. However, developments in the 1970s clearly showed that behavior therapy was much more than a passing fancy. Behavior therapy was beginning to be acknowledged as an acceptable form of treatment, and even a *treatment of choice* (that is, an optimal treatment) for certain psychological problems.

Courtesy of Cyril Franks

Cyril Franks

EMERGENCE OF BEHAVIOR THERAPY

In the 1970s, behavior therapy emerged as a major force in psychology and made a significant impact on psychiatry, social work, and education. The principles and techniques of behavior therapy also were adapted to enhance the everyday functioning of people in areas as diverse as business and industry,[52] child rearing,[53] ecology,[54] and the arts.[55] Applications included improving athletic performance,[56] increasing people's willingness to take prescribed medications,[57] enhancing the quality of life of nursing home residents and geriatric patients,[58] and more efficiently teaching young children to play musical instruments.[59] Examples of larger-scale behavioral interventions included promoting energy conservation,[60] preventing crimes,[61] providing individual instruction for large college classes,[62] and influencing entire communities to engage in behaviors that lower the risk of cardiovascular disease.[63]

During the 1980s, two important developments in the field of behavior therapy increased its applicability and acceptance. First, cognitive-behavioral therapy emerged as a major force. Second, behavior therapy began to make significant contributions to the field of *behavioral medicine*, which involves the treatment and prevention of medical problems.[64]

By 1990, the Association for Advancement of Behavior Therapy was a quarter of a century old and had grown in membership from 18 (in 1966) to approximately 4,000. Today, the organization is known as the Association for Behavioral and Cognitive Therapies and has almost 5,000 members. The new name simultaneously acknowledges the inclusion of both traditional behavioral and cognitive-behavioral approaches and that the field consists of many different therapeutic techniques.

Also by 1990, behavior therapy societies had been founded in other countries, including Argentina, France, Germany, Great Britain, Israel, Japan, Mexico, the Netherlands, and Sweden.[65] More than 20 major journals devoted solely to behavior therapy were being published, and empirical research on behavior therapy filled the leading clinical psychology journals as well as many prestigious publications in psychiatry, social work, and education. Although behavior therapy had its origins in South Africa, Great Britain, and North America, today it is practiced around the world in such diverse countries as Russia,[66] Poland,[67] Argentina,[68] Puerto Rico,[69] Italy,[70] Japan,[71] Singapore,[72] New Zealand,[73] and Cuba,[74] to name a few.

The field of behavior therapy continues to grow and evolve in the present. The end of the 20th century and the beginning of the 21st has seen two major trends. One is an increased emphasis on establishing the empirical validity of behavior therapies. The other is the development of therapies that alleviate clients' suffering through very different approaches that use mindfulness and acceptance strategies (which you'll read about in Chapter 14).

One indication of the increasing maturity of the field of behavior therapy is that beginning in the 1980s, its strongest critics have been its proponents rather than its opponents. In effect, the field of behavior therapy had reached the point where convincing skeptical outsiders was no longer a priority.[75] Instead, behavior therapists began to scrutinize their own therapy methods and the impact they were having on clients and on the broad field of psychotherapy.[76]

Behavior therapy is about change, and it should be clear to you after reading this chapter that change also aptly describes the field of behavior therapy in its relatively short history.

SUMMARY

1. Behavioral principles have been used for thousands of years to change people's problematic behaviors. However, only in the past 60 years have they been applied systematically.

2. There are a number of historical accounts of treatment procedures that resemble those of contemporary behavior therapy. However, the origins of behavior therapy lie in experimental research on learning conducted in the early part of the 20th century. This included the work of Pavlov, who conceptualized classical conditioning; Watson, who founded behaviorism, an approach that only dealt with observable behaviors; Jones, who designed an early learning-based treatment of fear; and the Mowrers, who designed the bell-and-pad treatment for bedwetting, based on classical conditioning.

3. Contemporary behavior therapy began in the 1950s, in part because of a growing discontent with psychoanalysis. It started simultaneously in North America, South Africa, and Great Britain. In the United States, Lindsley used the operant conditioning principles developed by Thorndike and Skinner to influence the behaviors of patients with psychiatric disorders, and Ayllon and Azrin developed the first token economy. In South Africa, Wolpe developed systematic desensitization, and Lazarus broadened its application. Rachman brought behavior therapy from South Africa to England and collaborated with Eysenck, an advocate for behavior therapy and critic of psychoanalytic therapy.

4. Early behavior therapy efforts were met with strong criticism and resistance from traditional psychotherapists. Initially, behavior therapists had to focus on demonstrating that behavior therapy could be effective.

5. Early ethical criticisms of behavior therapy, which proved to be unfounded, arose because of a heightened concern about the possible dangers of external control and because of confusion about what constitutes behavior therapy.

6. In the 1960s, Bandura developed a social learning theory that combined observational learning with classical and operant conditioning. The theory emphasized the critical role that cognition (thinking) plays in psychological functioning—a drastic departure from Watson's behaviorism.

7. Also in the 1960s, Ellis, Beck, and Meichenbaum developed the first cognitive-behavioral therapies that change clients' cognitions that maintain psychological disorders. Cognitive-behavioral therapy began as a supplement to existing behavior therapy procedures but rapidly evolved into a major behavior therapy approach.

8. In the 1970s, behavior therapy emerged as a major force among psychotherapy approaches.

9. The Association for Advancement of Behavior Therapy (today known as the Association for Behavioral and Cognitive Therapies) was established in 1966 in the United States to advocate for behavior therapy and has served as its major professional organization.

10. Although behavior therapy had its origins in South Africa, Great Britain, and North America, today it is practiced in many diverse countries.

REFERENCE NOTES

1. Franks & Wilson, 1973.
2. Franks, 1963.
3. Arnarson, 1994; Fell, 1975.
4. Itard, 1962.
5. Lovaas, 1977.
6. Kazdin, 1978.
7. Pitts, 1976.
8. Stewart, 1961.
9. Lewis, 1875; Rosen & Orenstein, 1976.
10. Franks, 1969.
11. Pavlov, 1927.
12. Kazdin, 1978.
13. Watson, 1914.
14. Jones, 1924; compare with Kornfeld, 1989.
15. Kazdin, 1978.
16. Mowrer & Mowrer, 1938.
17. Thorndike, 1911, 1931, 1933.
18. Jacobson, 1929, 1934.
19. Yates, 1970.
20. Sobell, 1994.
21. Eysenck, 1952.
22. For example, Cartwright, 1955; Luborsky, 1954; Smith & Glass, 1977.
23. Skinner, 1953.
24. Lindsley, 1956, 1960, 1963; Skinner, 1954; Skinner, Solomon, & Lindsley, 1953; Skinner, Solomon, Lindsley, & Richards, 1954.
25. Skinner, Solomon, & Lindsley, 1953.
26. For example, Ayllon, 1963, 1965; Ayllon & Michael, 1959.
27. Freud, 1909/1955.
28. Haughton & Ayllon, 1965.
29. Haughton & Ayllon, 1965, pp. 97–98.
30. Ayllon & Azrin, 1968.
31. Wolpe, 1958.
32. Wolpe, 1990.
33. Lazarus, 1959, 1961; Lazarus & Abramovitz, 1962.
34. Lazarus, 1966, 1967, 1976.
35. Rachman, 1959, 1967, 1972.
36. For example, Shapiro, 1957, 1966.
37. Skinner, 1953.
38. Davison & Stuart, 1975, p. 756.
39. Franks & Wilson, 1978.
40. Turkat & Feuerstein, 1978.
41. Reimringer, Morgan, & Bramwell, 1970.
42. Woolfolk, Woolfolk, & Wilson, 1977.
43. Ullmann & Krasner, 1965.
44. Bandura, 1969, 1977b, 1986b; Bandura & Walters, 1963.
45. Bandura & Walters, 1963.
46. Bandura, 1986b, 1997, 2008.
47. For example, Cloitre, 1995.
48. Beck, 1963, 1972, 1976.
49. Ellis, 1962, 1970.
50. Ellis, 1993.
51. Meichenbaum, 1974, 1975, 1977; Meichenbaum & Cameron, 1972, 1973.
52. Hermann, de Montes, Dominguez, Montes, & Hopkins, 1973; New tool, 1971; Pedalino & Gamboa, 1974.
53. For example, Becker, 1971; Christophersen, 1977; Patterson & Gullion, 1976.
54. Kazdin, 1977b.
55. Madsen, Greer, & Madsen, 1975.
56. For example, Rachman & Hodgson, 1980; Rachman & Teasdale, 1969; Rushall & Siedentop, 1972.
57. For example, Epstein & Masek, 1978; Lowe & Lutzker, 1979.
58. For example, Libb & Clements, 1969; Sachs, 1975.
59. Madsen, Greer, & Madsen, 1975.
60. Kazdin, 1977b.
61. For example, McNees, Egli, Marshall, Schnelle, Schnelle, & Risley, 1976; Schnelle et al., 1978.
62. For example, Keller, 1968.
63. Maccoby, Farquhar, Wood, & Alexander, 1977.
64. Arnkoff & Glass, 1992; Glass & Arnkoff, 1992.
65. Kazdin, 1978.
66. Lauterbach, 1999.
67. Kokoszaka, Popiel, & Sitarz, 2000.

68. Torres-Martinez & Spinetta, 1997.
69. Martinez-Taboas & Navas-Robleto, 2000.
70. Sanavio, 1999.
71. Sakuta, 1999.
72. Banarjee, 1999.
73. Blampied, 1999.
74. Dattilio, 1999.
75. Nezu, 1996.
76. For example, Baer, Hurley, Minichiello, Ott, Penzel, & Ricciardi, 1992; Kazdin & Wilson, 1978; Spiegler, 2005; Stolz & Associates, 1978.

3

The Behavioral Model

To appreciate the nature of behavior therapy, you must understand the model on which it is based. This chapter describes the general model of human behavior that forms the basis of behavior therapy. Then, Chapter 4 outlines the principles of behavior therapy derived from the model. Together, Chapters 3 and 4 present the core of behavior therapy.

WE ARE WHAT WE DO: PREEMINENCE OF BEHAVIOR

How do we define who a person is? What makes a person unique? According to the behavioral model, each of us is defined by our **behaviors**—in other words, by what we *do*. *We are what we do.*

Overt and Covert Behaviors

There are two broad categories of behaviors: overt and covert. **Overt behaviors** are *actions* that other people can directly see or hear; in a sense, they are public behaviors. Examples include eating, walking, talking, kissing, driving a car, writing a sentence, cooking, laughing, and singing.

Covert behaviors are private behaviors, things we do that others cannot directly observe; however, we usually are aware of them when we ourselves engage in them. There are three categories of covert behaviors: *cognitions* including thinking, expecting, attributing, and imagining; *emotions* (feelings); and *physiological responses* such as muscle tension, heart rate, blood pressure, and respiratory rate.

Overt behaviors, cognitions, emotions, and physiological responses constitute the four **modes of behavior** that are assessed and treated in behavior therapy. Participation Exercise 3-1 can help you distinguish between overt and covert behaviors.

| **PARTICIPATION EXERCISE 3-1** | **Distinguishing Between Overt and Covert Behaviors**[a] |

Distinguishing between overt (public) and covert (private) behaviors is easy. If you can directly observe other people engaging in the behavior, it is overt. If you cannot directly observe the behavior, it is covert.

Number from 1 to 20 on a sheet of paper, and for each of the behaviors listed, write O for overt behaviors and C for covert behaviors. Then, check the answers in your Student Resource Manual.

1. Singing
2. Thinking
3. Smiling
4. Learning
5. Eating
6. Remembering
7. Liking
8. Staring

[a]You should complete this Participation Exercise before you continue reading.

9. Enjoying
10. Writing
11. Listening
12. Observing
13. Speaking
14. Dreaming
15. Drinking
16. Smoking
17. Hoping
18. Touching
19. Concentrating
20. Sighing

Covert Behaviors: Special Considerations

Covert behaviors are no less important than overt behaviors. Indeed, many behaviors that supposedly set us apart from our relatives in the animal kingdom are covert, including complex thinking and reasoning. Although behavior therapists deal with both overt and covert behaviors, this was not always the case. Early behavior therapists followed the tradition of Watson's behaviorism and dealt only with overt behaviors (see Chapter 2).

Assessing overt behaviors is relatively straightforward because they are directly observable. In contrast, assessing covert behaviors is more complicated. Each of us has direct knowledge of our own covert behaviors, but we only have indirect knowledge of other people's covert behaviors.

The covert behaviors of others are inferred from their overt behaviors. (An exception is physiological responses that can be measured by instruments, such as a stethoscope and a polygraph.) Most often we learn of others' covert behaviors when they tell us about their thoughts and feelings. *Talking* about one's private experiences is an *overt* behavior.

The other way we learn about someone's covert behaviors is by observing what the person does and *inferring* from his or her overt actions what is "going on inside" the person. For instance, if you see someone smiling and laughing, you are likely to conclude that the individual is feeling happy. You could say that you have "anchored" a covert behavior with an overt behavior.[1] Look at Table 3-1, which gives examples of overt behaviors that could serve as anchors for common covert behaviors. Notice that some of the overt behavioral anchors could easily be indicative of other covert behaviors (for example, "missing an appointment" might be an overt behavioral anchor for what other covert behaviors than forgetting?).

Behavioral Versus Trait Descriptions

Before reading further, take 2 minutes to do a simple demonstration. Think of someone you know well. Write a brief description of that person so that someone who doesn't know the person could get a feel for what he or she is like. When you have finished, continue reading.

When describing someone, as you just did, most people refer to the individual's traits rather than to their behaviors. *Traits* are personality characteristics

TABLE **3-1**

Examples of Overt Behaviors That Serve as Anchors for Covert Behaviors

Overt Behaviors	Covert Behaviors
Telling others what's "on your mind"	Thinking
Missing an appointment	Forgetting
Staring, wrinkling one's brow, remaining motionless	Concentrating
Trembling, pacing, biting one's nails	Feeling frightened
Hugging, kissing, saying "I love you"	Feeling in love
Applauding, thanking	Appreciating

that we *attribute* to others and ourselves, such as friendly, smart, interesting, and honest. Traits are theoretical constructs that do not actually exist, but they are convenient ways of describing people. Traits are inferred from behaviors. For example, when we observe someone holding the door open for people and stopping to let other motorists enter the flow of traffic (behaviors), we infer that the person is *courteous* (trait). It is important to note that traits are abstract concepts, not covert behaviors.

Trait descriptions *appear* to provide a great deal of information about a person, but they actually provide generalizations rather than specific information. Consider the following example. When her friends are upset, Juanita tries to comfort them, whereas Juan respects his friends' privacy and leaves them alone. Both Juanita and Juan can be considered *caring*. However, referring to either of them as *caring* does not tell us how each will behave.

To understand what is meant by a trait for a particular person, you have to refer to the person's behaviors that led to the inference of the trait in the first place, which is circular reasoning. First, you observe a person's behavior; then, you infer a trait from the behavior you've observed; finally, to explain what is meant by the trait (for the particular person), you return to the behavior you observed. If one begins and ends at the observed behaviors, the use of traits is superfluous.

In contrast, the behavioral model simply describes people in terms of their behaviors. Behavioral descriptions are specific and much more detailed than trait descriptions. On the downside, they are lengthier (compare the inference "Lillian is conscientious" with the observation "Lillian studies at least four hours a day, plans her work carefully, and usually finishes her assignments ahead of time"). However, the accuracy—and therefore the usefulness of the behavioral description—outweighs its disadvantage of being lengthier.

There are several interrelated advantages of describing clients' problems in terms of behaviors rather than traits. Behavioral descriptions are more precise, and they promote individuality. In contrast, trait descriptions classify clients' problems into broad categories (such as depression and schizophrenia). Further, behavioral descriptions provide the detailed information needed to design a treatment plan tailored to each client's unique problem.

Being able to distinguish behaviors from traits is important for understanding the behavioral model. Descriptions that concern what people *do* refer to behaviors; descriptions that concern what people *are* or characteristics that they *possess* refer to traits. Participation Exercise 3-2 provides a check of your understanding of this distinction.

PARTICIPATION EXERCISE 3-2

Distinguishing Between Traits and Behaviors[b]

See if you can differentiate between traits and behavioral descriptions in the following paragraph. On a sheet of paper, number from 1 to 20. Then, write the letter *T* for trait or *B* for behavior for each of the numbered statements.

(1) Ramon is extremely perceptive. (2) He notices even small changes in others' emotions and (3) accurately tells them how they are feeling. (4) He reads a great deal and (5) is very knowledgeable about many topics. (6) He is very intelligent, and (7) he can recall facts he learned years ago. (8) Ramon is a warm, sincere, good-natured person. (9) He is a good friend, (10) goes out of his way to help other people, and (11) is generous. (12) He always dresses neatly. (13) Ramon works hard and (14) he is a dedicated worker. (15) He is a good athlete. (16) He swims during the summer and ice skates during the winter. (17) He is an active person (18) who is very energetic. (19) Although he is gregarious, (20) Ramon frequently spends time alone.

You can check your answers in your Student Resource Manual. Look at the descriptions you mislabeled and apply the following rule: What a person *does* is a behavior; what a person *is* or *possesses* is a trait.

[b]You should complete this Participation Exercise before you continue reading.

Behavior therapists deal with clients' behaviors, not their traits. However, clients often describe themselves and their problems by using traits (for example, "I'm shy and withdrawn"). Thus, behavior therapists must "translate" traits into behaviors. This involves identifying the unique behaviors that are associated with clients' trait descriptions. The key question the therapist asks is, *"What specific things do you do that lead you to describe yourself as [the trait]?"* As you can see in Table 3-2, a trait description may be associated

TABLE **3-2**
Examples of Overt Behaviors That Might Indicate Particular Traits

Behaviors	Trait
Smiling, laughing, talking about feelings of joy	Happy
Crying, sitting alone, moving slowly, saying that one is depressed ("down" or unhappy)	Depressed
Greeting people, smiling at others	Friendly
Arriving on time to appointments, carrying out assigned tasks, keeping secrets	Trustworthy
Volunteering to help others, frequently paying for the check when dining with others	Generous

with a variety of specific behaviors. Participation Exercise 3-3 will give you experience in translating traits into behaviors.

Translating Traits into Behaviors[c]

Translating trait descriptions into behavioral descriptions involves finding behaviors that could be indicative of particular traits. On a sheet of paper, list several behaviors that might help describe individuals with the following traits. The behaviors you list should be activities individuals *do* (in other words, behaviors) that most people would agree indicate the particular trait.

1. Sociable
2. Hostile
3. Helpful
4. Thrifty
5. Dependable
6. Smart
7. Patient
8. Healthy

You will find sample behaviors for each trait in your Student Resource Manual.

[c]You should complete this Participation Exercise before you continue reading.

WHY DO WE BEHAVE THE WAY WE DO?

How often have you asked, "Why did I do that?" or "Why did so-and-so act that way?" People are fascinated by "why questions" about human behavior, and psychologists have developed theories or models to explain human behavior. According to the behavioral model, *a person's behaviors are caused by present events that occur before and after the behaviors have been performed.* **Antecedents** are events that occur or are present *before* the person performs the behavior. **Consequences** are events that occur *after* and *as a result of* the behavior. For example, feeling tired is an antecedent for sleeping, and feeling rested the next day is a consequence of sleeping.

The ABC Model

The **ABC model** describes the temporal sequence of antecedents, behavior, and consequences (see Figure 3-1). The specific antecedents and consequences that cause an individual to perform a behavior are its **maintaining conditions.** Not all antecedents and consequences of a behavior are its maintaining conditions. Only a relatively small number of antecedents and consequences *maintain* (influence or cause) a behavior, and we refer to these as **maintaining antecedents** and **maintaining consequences.**

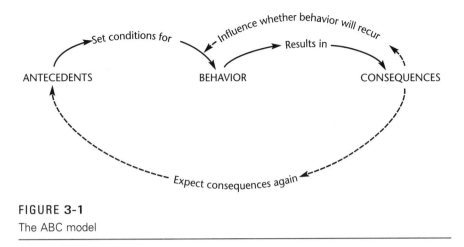

FIGURE 3-1
The ABC model

Maintaining Antecedents

There are two categories of maintaining antecedents—*prerequisites* and *stimulus control*—and both can occur naturally or can be introduced intentionally to change a behavior.

To engage in a behavior, you must first have the requisite knowledge, skills, and resources. For example, *going to the movies* requires knowing where the theater is located and what time the movie starts, being able to get to the theater, and having enough money to pay for a ticket. If these prerequisites seem trivial, consider whether you could go to a movie without them (sneaking in isn't allowed).

Stimulus control involves cues or conditions that "set the stage" for behaviors to occur. There are two types of stimulus control: *prompts* and *setting events*. **Prompts** are *cues* to perform a behavior, such as when a parent says, "Go wash your hands," to a child before dinner. **Setting events** are environmental *conditions* that elicit a behavior; they are broader and more complex than prompts. Setting events may include who is present and what they are doing, the time of day, and the physical arrangement of the environment. For example, you are more likely to study for a test if you are in a quiet room with others who are studying than if you were in a room where people are socializing.

Think about how your behavior differs when you are in class, at a party, with close friends, and with strangers. Each of these setting events elicits different behaviors. People frequently alter setting events in their daily lives to influence their own behaviors. For instance, a woman wishing to lose weight and improve her health might remove all high-fat foods from her house and keep healthful foods prominently displayed. Behavior therapists use both prompts and setting events in therapy to change clients' problem behaviors.

Maintaining Consequences

Whereas maintaining antecedents are responsible for a behavior's being performed in the first place, *maintaining consequences determine whether the*

IN THEORY **3-1**

It's Where You Are (Not Who You Are) That Counts: Behavior Is Situation Specific

Our predictions about how people in our lives will act often are correct because people generally behave *consistently.* Many theories have been developed to explain the source of this consistency. According to the behavioral model, the consistency is determined by the situation in which the behavior is performed. *Situation* refers to the context, including where we are, whom we are with, and what is happening. Setting events indicate which behaviors are typically expected or appropriate in the particular circumstances and therefore are likely to result in positive consequences. Setting events also may tell us which behaviors are inappropriate and likely to result in negative consequences.

Because the cues in each situation in which we find ourselves influence our behavior, how we act is likely to be consistent in the same or similar situations. The most reliable information we have to predict another person's behaviors is the context in which those behaviors occur. Thus, we say that behavior is **situation specific.**[2]

A simple example will illustrate what is meant by situation specificity. Wilberto is a college student who typically sits quietly in each of his lecture classes, usually talks at a moderate volume whenever he eats with friends at the cafeteria, and yells at basketball games until he becomes hoarse. In each instance, the social expectations and restrictions associated with the specific context influence how loudly Wilberto speaks. Wilberto's speech volume is consistent in similar situations, but it varies in different situations. Further, although Wilberto sits quietly in all his lecture classes, he often speaks up in seminars and discussion sections, where the demands of the situation are different from those in lecture classes.

By way of contrast, the major alternative to the situation-specificity explanation of the consistency of behavior is to attribute the consistency to a person's traits. We might call Wilberto quiet or loud. However, both these descriptions are inaccurate because *quiet* does not predict Wilberto's behavior at basketball games and *loud* does not predict Wilberto's behavior in lecture classes. Thus, describing Wilberto's behavior in different situations is more accurate than referring to traits he might have.

CALVIN AND HOBBES © 1990 Watterson. Dist. by UNIVERSAL PRESS SYNDICATE. Reprinted with permission. All rights reserved.

behavior will occur again. In general, when the consequences of performing a behavior are favorable, the individual is more likely to repeat the behavior. Unfavorable consequences make it less likely that the person will engage in the behavior in the future. Consequences include what happens directly to the person, to other people, and to the physical environment as a result of the behavior. Consequences can be immediate or delayed, and they can be short term or long term.

You may be wondering how events that occur *after* a behavior has been performed can influence that behavior. In fact, the actual consequences of a behavior can influence only the future occurrence of the behavior. However, a person's *expectations* about the probable consequences influence whether a person will perform a behavior in the present (see Figure 3-1). These expectations are *antecedents*. In other words, a person's prediction about what is likely to happen as a result of performing a particular behavior is one factor that determines whether the person will perform the behavior. Our expectations about the maintaining consequences of our actions are largely a product of the consequences we have experienced for similar behaviors in the past. *Maintaining consequences for today's actions are the maintaining* antecedents *of tomorrow's actions.* For example, if Julius's dinner guests praised his Caesar salad last week, he will be tempted to make one this week. His guests' praise was a consequence of making the salad last week, but it becomes an antecedent of the same behavior this week. Clearly, remembering the consequences of a behavior is necessary if the consequences are to affect the future occurrence of the behavior.[3]

Identifying Maintaining Antecedents and Consequences

Contrary to the popular misconception, behavior therapy does not *directly* change symptoms or problem behaviors. *Behavior therapy treats problem behaviors by directly changing their maintaining conditions.* And, before the maintaining conditions can be changed, they first must be identified. This process begins by identifying all antecedents and consequences of the behavior, some of which are its maintaining conditions. Participation Exercise 3-4 will give you some practice doing this.

As we have said, not all the antecedents and consequences of a behavior are its maintaining conditions. In behavior therapy, the therapist and client identify those antecedents and consequences that are likely to be influencing (causing) the problem behavior. It is these **probable maintaining conditions** of a behavior that are changed to modify the problem behavior.

An example may help clarify the concept of maintaining antecedents and maintaining consequences and their roles in determining behaviors. Consider the behavior you are engaging in right now—reading a chapter in your textbook. What prerequisites, prompts, and setting events have led to your reading the chapter? What are the likely consequences of reading the chapter? Take a moment to write down these antecedents and consequences, and then look at the examples in Figure 3-2 on page 41.

Identifying Antecedents and Consequences[d]

This exercise contains a list of six specific behaviors and the details surrounding each. From the details, list the antecedents and consequences of each designated behavior. Include all the antecedents and consequences actually mentioned in the scenario, but do not assume any that are not mentioned. When you have finished, check your answers with those in your Student Resource Manual.

Behavior 1: *Calling the police.* One hot summer evening, Mrs. Kriegel was sitting in her second-floor apartment. As she looked out the window, she saw two young men attack an elderly woman and then run off with the woman's purse. She immediately called the police. The police thanked her and then rushed to the scene of the crime. Mrs. Kriegel realized she had done the right thing.

Behavior 2: *Going to a play.* Quanisha read about a new play in town that had received especially good reviews. She knew she could get a student pass to see it and that she could earn extra credit for her English class if she saw the play. As it turned out, she was disappointed in the play and felt it was a waste of time. The extra credit, however, did boost her grade.

Behavior 3: *Getting up late.* Al did not go to bed until after 3 A.M., and he was so drunk he forgot to set his alarm clock. He awoke 2 hours late the next morning and missed the last bus to the office. When he finally arrived at his office, he discovered that he had missed two important appointments with clients.

Behavior 4: *Cooking a fancy meal.* Brendan's parents were coming for a visit, and he wanted to make a good impression. It was the perfect opportunity for him to try out a new recipe, and besides, he enjoyed preparing a fancy meal. Although his efforts turned the kitchen into a complete disaster area, the meal itself was a success and his parents enjoyed the dinner. Brendan also enjoyed the dinner and was satisfied with the evening as a whole.

Behavior 5: *Shopping for new clothes.* Jane needed new clothes, and she had saved enough money during the summer to go shopping. She got directions to the new shopping mall and borrowed the family car. Jane came home with a comfortable and stylish new wardrobe. She felt good about her new clothes, and her mother and friends commented on how good she looked in them.

Behavior 6: *Pulling a fire alarm.* Manny spotted a fire alarm box at the corner. He wanted to impress his friends and thought of all the excitement that would occur if he pulled the alarm. After reading the instructions on the fire alarm and checking to see that no one was around, he pulled the alarm. Fire trucks raced to the scene within minutes, and a crowd quickly gathered. The angry fire chief announced that it was a false alarm. The fire marshal began an investigation, while the crowd slowly dispersed and the fire trucks returned to the station.

[d]The Participation Exercise can be completed before you continue reading or later.

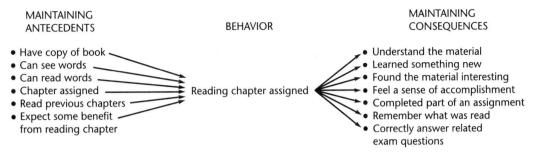

FIGURE 3-2

Some of the possible maintaining antecedents and maintaining consequences of performing a specific behavior: reading an assigned chapter

---

IN THEORY **3-2**

The Myth of Symptom Substitution

In the early days of behavior therapy—the 1950s and early 1960s—psychoanalysts used the concept of symptom substitution to argue that behavior therapy was an incomplete treatment.[4] *Symptom substitution* refers to the notion that treating behaviors—rather than their so-called "underlying causes"—will result in another maladaptive behavior (symptom) replacing (substituting for) the treated behavior. A hypothetical example would be a client's developing a fear of undressing in locker rooms after successfully being treated for fear of public speaking. A psychoanalyst

might argue that this occurred because the underlying cause of the public speaking anxiety, such as an unconscious conflict about exposing oneself in public places, was not treated. Although the client no longer is afraid of speaking in public, the unconscious conflict still exists, and it manifests itself in another symptom, fear of undressing in locker rooms.

The symptom substitution criticism of behavior therapy is fallacious for two reasons. First, it is based on the *mistaken* premise that behavior therapy treats symptoms (problem behaviors).[5] As you have

just learned, behavior therapy *directly* treats the maintaining conditions—which are the *causes*—of problem behaviors (symptoms). Second, and most important, there is no empirical support for symptom substitution's occurring in behavior therapy.[6] In studies in which evidence for symptom substitution was specifically sought, none has been found; clients do not develop maladaptive substitute behaviors.[7] Nonetheless, the myth of symptom substitution apparently still exists among some mental health professionals who are unfamiliar with behavior therapy.[8]

Present Maintaining Conditions Versus Past Originating Conditions: A Critical Distinction

According to the behavioral model, *present* conditions cause our current behaviors. What role do our past experiences play in determining our current behaviors? The answer is that past events only indirectly influence present behaviors. The factors that directly cause present behaviors are occurring now, in the present.

Let's look at a personal example. When was the last time you dressed yourself? Unless you are lounging at home in your pajamas, the answer probably is "sometime earlier today." In fact, you dress yourself one or more times a day, every day. What are the maintaining conditions of *dressing yourself*? The maintaining antecedents may include knowing how to dress yourself, having clothes, waking up in the morning, and anticipating going somewhere outside your home. The maintaining consequences may include feeling properly dressed, being complimented on your attire, and not getting arrested for indecent exposure.

Do you recall your first attempts to dress yourself as a child? You may have resisted dressing yourself initially. After all, you had been used to having others dress you, and dressing yourself was difficult and frustrating. Nonetheless, you learned to dress yourself. What conditions influenced your learning to dress yourself? The major maintaining antecedent probably was your parents' telling you to get dressed. The maintaining consequences probably included praise from your parents and permission to engage in some desirable activity (such as going outside to play) that required being dressed.

This example illustrates that the same behavior—dressing yourself—is maintained today by conditions that are very different from the conditions in which it originated. This is the essence of the crucial distinction between present maintaining conditions and *past originating conditions.*

Past events can have an *indirect* influence on current behaviors, as when the memory of previous events affects how you act now.[9] For instance, *recalling* how pleasant it was to be comforted by your mother when you cried can help maintain your crying years after you received your mother's sympathy. However, note that the comfort your mother provided is not influencing your current behavior. Rather, the *memory* of being comforted is serving as a maintaining condition—and memories are *present* events.

To summarize, behavior therapists assume that present conditions directly influence behaviors occurring in the present. In other words, *present behaviors are maintained by present maintaining conditions.* Thus, the way to change a present behavior is to change its present maintaining conditions. In Theory 3-3 continues the discussion of the role of past events on current behaviors.

Environment and Learning Versus Biology and Heredity

All our behaviors—including the abnormal behaviors treated by behavior therapy—develop and are maintained by both biological/hereditary factors and environmental/learning factors. *Learning* is the process by which environmental factors influence behaviors. The **environment** comprises all external influences on behaviors, including the physical setting and conditions as well as the people who are present. The proportion of influence of biological versus environmental factors varies with different behaviors, but even those behaviors that have a significant biological component are also influenced by environmental factors. For example, considerable evidence shows that intellectual behaviors (such as comprehension, reasoning, and problem solving)

IN THEORY 3-3

Don't Look Back: The Role of Past Events on Current Behaviors

The idea that past events have only a weak and indirect influence on our present behaviors may seem contrary to the widely held view that our past, especially early childhood, has a profound effect on our current lives. The notion that "the child is parent to the adult" is rooted in psychoanalysis, and like other psychoanalytic concepts, it has become part of our everyday belief system.

The behavioral and psychoanalytic views are not completely contradictory. Both hold that adults are products of their previous experiences. The two perspectives differ, however, in how they view the nature of that influence. Psychoanalysis postulates that early experiences have a direct and permanent effect on later behaviors, implying that current circumstances have little influence on adult (or later childhood) behaviors. The

behavioral model holds that the behaviors that result from early experiences can, with appropriate learning, change so that the early experiences exert little or no influence on later behaviors.

Looking to the past for the determinants of present behaviors can be problematic. Examining past events is difficult and involves gathering information that is *retrospective*, which often is inaccurate. Not only do we forget the specifics of past events, but we also inevitably reconstruct history, as when we fill in missing details or modify apparent inconsistencies in our recollections. Moreover, even if it were possible to collect reliable accounts of past events, there is no way to know whether particular events that occurred in the past caused a behavior because we cannot go back in time and test such hypotheses.

In contrast, the *current* factors that are influencing the way we behave are considerably easier to assess. First, because they are occurring in the present, obtaining accurate information is possible. Second, unlike past conditions, those in the present can be systematically modified and the effect of these changes on the behaviors can be evaluated. Thus, it is possible to test the validity of hypotheses about the influence of current (but not past) factors on behaviors.

All that being said, in practice, behavior therapists may inquire about the circumstances in which a client's problem may have started for the purpose of elucidating the nature of its current maintaining conditions. But, the focus of treatment will be on those current conditions.

Viewing the past from the present has its limitations.

have a strong genetic component.[10] Within the broad limits established by one's genetic endowment, however, environmental factors can substantially enhance (as with a stimulating environment) or inhibit (as with minimal stimulation) intellectual behaviors.[11]

Learning can influence behaviors that have biological or heritable components.[12] For instance, the self-injurious behaviors of individuals with Cornelia de Lange syndrome (a rare congenital condition involving delay of physical and psychological growth) are associated with specific setting events, such as whether the individuals are alone or with others.[13] Learning can change psychological disorders that seem to have substantial heritable or biological origins, such as autistic disorder, depression, and schizophrenia.[14] Although genetic and neurobiological factors play a dominant role in the development of Tourette's syndrome,[15] behavior therapy techniques that operate on the behavioral level are successful in significantly reducing tics[16] (as you will read about in Chapter 16). Moreover, successful behavior therapy can result in measurable central nervous system changes. For example, normalization of brain circuits has been shown to occur in clients successfully treated for spider phobia,[17] and other central nervous system changes that occur with medication for obsessive-compulsive disorder also occur with successful behavior therapy.[18]

IN THEORY **3-4**

Freedom in Reciprocal Determinism

According to the behavioral model, environmental factors play a major role in determining how people behave. If you interpret this statement as your "being controlled by the environment," then you will view it as limiting your options.

However, just the opposite is true. There are reciprocal or give-and-take relationships among the environment, overt behaviors, and covert behaviors. Each of these factors influences and is influenced by the other two—in other words,

they are *reciprocally determined* (as Figure 3-3 depicts).[19] Table 3-3 gives examples of how the environment, covert behaviors, and overt behaviors might reciprocally influence one another in the case of writing a paper.

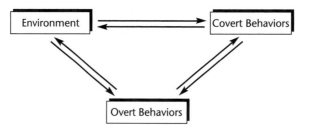

FIGURE 3-3

According to the principle of reciprocal determinism, the environment, overt behaviors, and covert behaviors each influence and are influenced by the two other factors

TABLE **3-3**

Examples of How the Environment, Covert Behaviors, and Overt Behaviors Might Reciprocally Determine One Another in the Case of Writing a Paper

ENVIRONMENT influences OVERT BEHAVIOR

When Chung writes in a quiet place, he gets more writing done.

OVERT BEHAVIOR influences ENVIRONMENT

When Megan starts to write in her dorm room, her understanding roommates lower the volume on the stereo.

COVERT BEHAVIOR influences OVERT BEHAVIOR

When Joan thinks that a particular topic is interesting, she spends more time writing about it.

OVERT BEHAVIOR influences COVERT BEHAVIOR

When Carlos successfully completes a difficult paper, he feels competent as a student.

ENVIRONMENT influences COVERT BEHAVIOR

When Manny waits until the night before the due date to write a paper, he gets anxious.

COVERT BEHAVIOR influences ENVIRONMENT

When Indiana is concentrating on writing a paper, her roommate stops talking to her.

The concept of reciprocal determinism has important implications for personal freedom. How we behave is not rigidly determined by external forces. We can alter or create the factors that influence our behaviors. For instance, a woman who rarely exercises can join a health club, which will increase the chances that she will exercise regularly. Likewise, a man who thinks poorly of himself because he is unsuccessful in his work can select a job at which he can succeed, which, in turn, will influence his thoughts about himself. A key to personal freedom lies in understanding the factors that influence our behaviors and accepting responsibility for controlling them.

SUMMARY

1. The behavioral model defines people in terms of their behaviors.
2. Behavior is anything a person does. Overt behaviors are actions that other people can directly observe. Covert behaviors are private behaviors, consisting of cognitions, emotions, and physiological responses. Covert behaviors are inferred from overt behaviors, with the exception of physiological responses, which can be measured by instruments.

3. The most common way of describing people is in terms of traits. The problem with trait descriptions is that they are general rather than specific. Behavioral descriptions are more precise than trait descriptions and preserve individuality.

4. The ABC model describes the temporal sequence of antecedents, behavior, and consequences. The specific antecedents and consequences that cause an individual to perform a behavior are its maintaining conditions. Maintaining antecedents establish the conditions for the behavior to occur and consist of prerequisites, prompts (cues to perform the behavior), and setting events (environmental conditions that elicit the behavior). Maintaining consequences determine whether the behavior will occur again.

5. Behavior therapy treats problem behaviors by directly changing their maintaining conditions, not symptoms or problem behaviors themselves. Confusion regarding this distinction leads to the mistaken notion of symptom substitution, the idea that treating behaviors rather than their underlying causes will result in a replacement maladaptive symptom.

6. The past originating conditions of a behavior—those conditions that account for its initial development—have only an indirect influence on our present behaviors.

7. Our behaviors are situation specific. They are consistent in the same or similar situations and vary in different situations.

8. Although behavior therapy manipulates learning/environmental factors to change problem behaviors, it is applicable to changing problem behaviors that are predominantly caused by biological/hereditary factors.

9. One's environment, covert behaviors, and overt behaviors are reciprocally determined; each factor influences and is influenced by the two other factors.

REFERENCE NOTES

1. Craighead, Kazdin, & Mahoney, 1976.
2. Mischel, 1968, 1973.
3. Compare with Greene, 2001.
4. Cahoon, 1968; Ullmann & Krasner, 1965.
5. For example, Sahakian & Charlesworth, 1994.
6. For example, Bandura, 1969; Kazdin & Wilson, 1978; Sloane, Staples, Cristol, Yorkston, & Whipple, 1975.
7. Paul, 1966.
8. Otto, 2006.
9. For example, Sahakian & Charlesworth, 1994.
10. Willerman, 1979.
11. For example, Lee, 1951; Skeels, 1966.
12. For example, Iwata, 1994; Otto & Pollack, 1994; Schwartz, Stoessel, Baxter, Martin, & Phelps, 1996.
13. Moss, Oliver, Hall, Arron, Sloneem, & Petty, 2005.
14. O'Leary & Wilson, 1975.
15. McCracken, 2000.
16. Cook & Blacher, 2007; Himle, Wood, Piacentini, & Walkup, 2006; Peterson, 2007.
17. Paquette et al., 2003.
18. Baxter et al., 1992; Schwartz, Stoessel, Baxter, Martin, & Phelps, 1996.
19. Compare with Bandura, 1986a, 1986b.

4

The Process of Behavior Therapy

The behavioral model you have just read about in Chapter 3 is the basis for behavior therapy. In this chapter, we provide an overview of how that model is applied in behavior therapy. We begin with a classic case published in 1965. The senior therapist was Arnold Lazarus, a prominent early behavior therapist. The case illustrates many of the principles of the behavioral model. It also provides examples of some of the defining themes and common characteristics of behavior therapy described in Chapter 1. As you read the case, see if you can identify those themes (scientific, active, present focus, learning focus) and characteristics (individualized therapy, stepwise progression, treatment packages, brevity) that are clearly evident. The title we've given this case is intended to be a humorous counterpoint to Freud's (1909/1955) classic case, "The Analysis of a Phobia in a Five-Year-Old Boy."[1] The similarity between the two cases ends with the titles.

CASE **4-1**

The Behavioral Analysis of a Phobia in a 9-Year-Old Boy[2]

At the beginning of the fourth grade, Paul (age 9) was intensely afraid of school. Initially, he hid in the coatroom and subsequently began spending less time at school each day. When he was referred to therapy, Paul had been absent from school for 3 weeks. Paul had also avoided school at the beginning of kindergarten and second grade.

During the 4 years preceding Paul's beginning fourth grade, a series of specific traumatic events had occurred in his life: nearly drowning, undergoing surgery with critical complications, and witnessing a drowning that had upset him considerably. Upon entering fourth grade, a close family friend died suddenly, and Paul's father was experiencing considerable stress at work. Finally, Paul was intimidated by a warning from his eldest sister that fourth grade was especially difficult.

From the initial interview, it became clear that Paul's school phobia was the most pressing problem of a "generally bewildered and intimidated child" who had a history of familial tensions and situational crises, including multiple traumatic events.

Paul lived two and a half blocks from his school. He typically walked to school leaving home at 8:30 A.M., and walked home when school ended at 3:30 P.M. When therapy began, Paul "was extremely surly and dejected in the mornings, refused breakfast, rarely dressed himself, and became noticeably more fearful toward 8:30." His parents' attempts to comfort him and coax him to go to school only led to Paul's sobbing and withdrawing.

The therapy was administered by two therapists and involved a series of increasingly more difficult behaviors related to his school phobia. Treatment began on a Sunday afternoon. The therapists accompanied Paul as he walked to school and allayed his anxiety through distraction and humor. At 8:30 A.M. on the following 2 days, Paul walked from his house into the schoolyard with one of the therapists. The therapist helped reduce Paul's anxiety by encouraging him, instructing him to relax and think of pleasant images, and playing with him in the schoolyard. After 15 minutes in the school yard, they returned home. Next, after school hours, the therapist persuaded Paul to enter his classroom and sit at his desk, at which point part of the normal school routine was playfully enacted. For the next three mornings, the therapist accompanied Paul into the classroom with the other children, and after chatting with his teacher, Paul and the therapist left.

A week later, Paul spent the entire morning in his class with the therapist in the classroom. The therapist smiled approvingly at Paul whenever he interacted with his classmates or the teacher. Two days later, Paul lined up with his classmates outside the classroom while the therapist waited for him inside the classroom.

While still walking to school with the therapist each morning, Paul began staying in his classroom without the therapist, who spent the day in the school library adjacent to Paul's classroom. Paul then agreed that the therapist would leave 1 hour before school ended. Gradually, the therapist was able to leave Paul alone at school for increasingly longer periods. Paul's school attendance without the therapist's presence was achieved by providing specific reinforcers, including comic books and tokens that could eventually be exchanged for a baseball glove. Paul's mother was recruited to emphasize the importance of school attendance to Paul, a role that the therapists had been playing. When Paul had earned sufficient tokens to get his baseball glove, he decided with his parents that the specific reinforcers were no longer necessary.

Paul's therapy was carried out over 4½ months, during which time there were a number of setbacks. However, at the end of treatment, Paul was not only attending school regularly but, according to his mother's reports, his behavior had improved outside of school. For example, Paul had become less moody, more willing to participate in household chores, more congenial in interacting with his peers, and more self-sufficient. Ten months after the termination of therapy, Paul's mother reported that Paul had not only maintained the positive changes but also had progressed further.

DEFINING THEMES AND COMMON CHARACTERISTICS OF BEHAVIOR THERAPY IN CASE 4-1

Many features of the treatment for Paul's school-phobic behaviors are typical of behavior therapy. The *scientific* approach taken in Paul's case is evident in the precision of the assessment and treatment. For example, highly specific details regarding the circumstances surrounding the problem behaviors, such as exact times, were gathered. Treatment focused on a specific and clearly defined overt behavior: school attendance.

The therapist encouraged Paul to engage in *active* procedures that helped reduce his fear and increase his school attendance and positive feelings about being in school. Further, Paul's therapy took place in vivo; the therapists worked directly with Paul in the school setting, where the problem was occurring. Because a therapist had to be at school with Paul for many hours, multiple therapists were employed. Using multiple therapists is not typical, but with children it is common to enlist the aid of parents and teachers to implement specific aspects of the treatment, as was done with Paul. And, consistent with the *collaborative nature* of behavior therapy, the therapists consulted Paul about a variety of treatment decisions even though he was only 9 years old.

The focus of therapy was in the *present*. Paul had a difficult, even traumatic childhood before he developed the problem that resulted in his parents seeking therapy for him at the beginning of the fourth grade, and these events no doubt affected Paul. However, treatment for his school avoidance (a present problem) focused on current conditions because they were the factors maintaining his problem.

Although standard therapy procedures were employed, they were *individualized* to fit Paul's unique case (for example, reinforcers were matched to Paul's interests). Paul's treatment involved a *stepwise progression* in which Paul was gradually exposed to increasingly more anxiety-evoking situations. Finally, a variety of behavior therapy procedures were combined in a *treatment package*.

THE PROCESS OF BEHAVIOR THERAPY: AN OVERVIEW

Behavior therapy proceeds via a series of interrelated steps, shown schematically in Figure 4-1. The steps are:

1. Clarifying the client's problem
2. Formulating initial goals for therapy
3. Designing a target behavior (the specific behavior that will be changed)
4. Identifying the maintaining conditions of the target behavior
5. Designing a treatment plan (specific therapy procedures) to change the maintaining conditions
6. Implementing the treatment plan
7. Evaluating the success of the treatment plan
8. Conducting follow-up assessments

Additionally, measurement of the target behavior begins immediately after the target behavior has been designed (step 3) and continues through the evaluation of therapy (step 7).

If the therapy has successfully changed the target behavior, then the therapy either is terminated or the process is begun again with another target behavior. If the therapy procedures have not succeeded, the therapist and client return to the step where the process broke down. For instance, the target

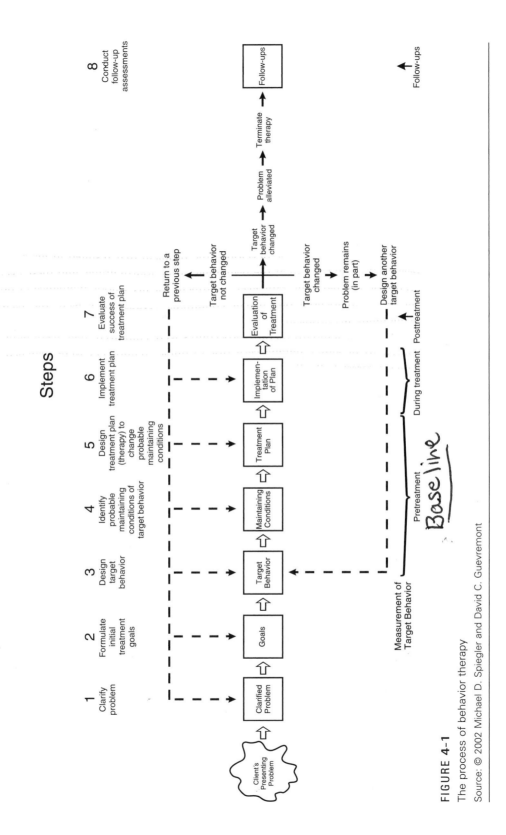

FIGURE 4-1

The process of behavior therapy

Source: © 2002 Michael D. Spiegler and David C. Guevremont

behavior may not have been defined precisely enough or the therapy procedures may not have been implemented correctly.

STEP 1: CLARIFYING THE PROBLEM

Clients usually describe their problems in broad, vague terms (for instance, "I'm unhappy much of the time" or "I can't seem to cope with my job"). The first step in behavior therapy is to clarify the client's *presenting problem*, the problem for which therapy is sought. For example, for a client whose presenting problem is "I'm stressed out a lot," specifying what the client means by "stressed out" and "a lot" is crucial.

Clients often come to therapy with multiple problems. Behavior therapy begins by narrowing the client's complaints to one or two problems to be worked on initially. Treating one problem at a time has three advantages. First, clients can focus their attention more easily on one task than on multiple tasks. Second, concentrating on a single problem often results in relatively quick change, which may motivate the client to continue working on other problems. Third, problems may be related to one another, so alleviating one problem may reduce or even eliminate others.[3] Thus, treating one problem at a time is efficient in the long run.

As an example, a 38-year-old man who had suffered from schizophrenia for 8 years had been minimally responsive to a variety of anti-psychotic medications.[4] In addition to persecutory delusions and hallucinations that were directly related to his schizophrenia, he had a fear of dogs and avoided going out in public places. Although the focus of treatment was on these two fears which were successfully treated through in vivo desensitization (Chapter 9), there was a marked improvement in his schizophrenic symptoms, especially regarding his persecutory delusions.

STEP 2: FORMULATING INITIAL TREATMENT GOALS

Once the client's problem has been clarified, the client and the therapist formulate initial goals for therapy, which will direct subsequent steps in the treatment process. Clients always enter therapy with some goals, but often they are general and vague (for instance, "getting help with my problem" or "feeling better"). Clarifying the client's problem allows more specific goals to be formulated.

The client is given the major responsibility for deciding on the specific goals he or she wants to achieve, and the therapist helps the client clarify expectations about the outcome of treatment. The therapist takes a more active role in goal setting in two circumstances: (1) when the client's goals are clearly unrealistic (for example, never getting angry at my children); or (2) when the goals are likely to have negative consequences for the client or others (for instance, a high school senior's wanting to lose 20 pounds in the 2 weeks before her prom). Once goals have been established, the therapist helps the client state them so that they are specific, unambiguous, and measurable.

Clients' goals may be reevaluated and changed during the course of therapy. For example, clients may raise or lower their expectations about the degree to which their target behavior might change, based on its ongoing assessment.

STEP 3: DESIGNING A TARGET BEHAVIOR

After treatment goals have been formulated, the next step is to design a target behavior. A **target behavior** is a narrow, discrete aspect of the problem that can be clearly defined and easily measured. So, rather than attempting to treat the client's problem in its entirety, one component of the problem is focused on at a time. As you will see later, the target behavior can be something the client is presently doing that needs to be eliminated (such as overeating) or something the client is not doing that the client needs to begin doing (such as regular exercise).

In Case 4-1, a series of target behaviors were designed for Paul, and each was dealt with in sequence, starting with the easiest and least anxiety-evoking behavior. For example, the first target behavior was, "Walking from his house to the school with the therapist on a nonschool day"; a later target behavior was, "Spending the morning in his classroom with the therapist present." Notice the specificity of these target behaviors and how their clarity makes it unambiguous as to whether the target behaviors were performed. Although Paul had a series of target behaviors, each one was worked on separately. The same advantages that focusing on one or two problems have also hold for treating one or two target behaviors at a time.

Characteristics of Good Target Behaviors

Target behaviors should meet four requirements:

1. *Narrow in scope.* The target behavior usually addresses one part of the problem rather than the entire problem. For example, "going out with close friends" might be a target behavior for a client whose problem is pervasive social anxiety. Further, the definition of the target behavior may include a specific time when and place where engaging in it is appropriate (for example, "making one's bed before leaving the house").
2. *Unambiguously defined.* A target behavior that is defined precisely can be assessed reliably. In the case of an overt behavior, knowing the definition of the target behavior should allow anyone observing the client to determine whether the client is engaging in the target behavior.
3. *Measurable.* Whenever possible, the target behavior should be quantified. Discrete numbers are more precise than qualitative categories (such as "improved" versus "unimproved"). The measurements can be of (1) *frequency* (how often), (2) *duration* (length of time), (3) *intensity* (strength), or (4) *amount of by-product* of the target behavior (for example, the amount of liquid soap remaining in a soap dispenser as an indication of hand washing[5]). Table 4-1 describes these measures and provides examples. The type of measure employed depends on such factors as the

TABLE **4-1**

Types of Measures Used to Assess Target Behaviors

Type	Description	Examples
FREQUENCY	Number of times the behavior occurs	1. Number of days child attends school 2. Number of cigarettes smoked
DURATION	a. Length of time spent engaging in target behavior	1. Hours child spends in school 2. Minutes spent smoking
	b. Latency (length of time to begin a target behavior)	1. Minutes to enter school after being dropped off by parents 2. Minutes to light up after sitting down at desk
	c. Interval between responses (length of time between the occurrence of instances of the target behavior)	1. Number of days preceding an absence 2. Minutes between cigarettes smoked
INTENSITY	Strength of the target behavior	1. How anxious (on scale of 1–10) child feels while in school 2. Strength of inhalation
AMOUNT OF BY-PRODUCT	Number of by-products of engaging in the target behavior	1. Number of punches in lunch meal ticket 2. Number of cigarette butts left in ashtray

nature of the target behavior, the treatment goals, and practical considerations (such as ease of measurement).

4. *Appropriate and adaptive.* The target behavior must fit the client's unique problem and be adaptive for the client. This requirement includes not causing other problems (for instance, in the treatment of obesity, smoking as a substitute for snacking results in health hazards). The target behavior also must suit the particular client's circumstances and abilities. For example, running 5 miles a day would not be an appropriate target behavior for a person who is 100 pounds overweight.

Two Types of Target Behaviors: Acceleration and Deceleration

There are two types of target behaviors. **Acceleration target behaviors** are increased, and **deceleration target behaviors** are decreased. Acceleration target behaviors are used for **behavioral deficits**, which are adaptive behaviors that clients are not performing often enough, long enough, or strongly enough (for instance, paying attention in class and standing up for one's rights). Deceleration target behaviors are used for **behavioral excesses**,

Huny Baby (handwritten)

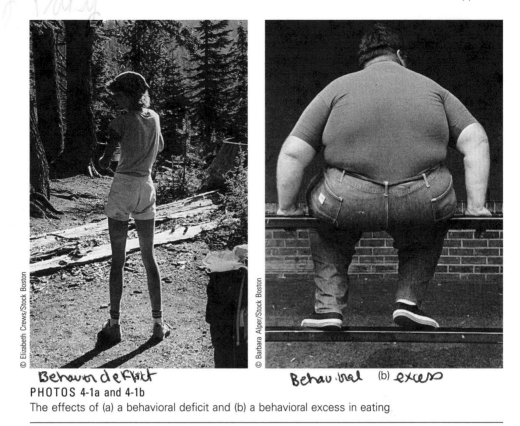

Behavior deficit (handwritten)   *Behavioral* (b) *excess* (handwritten)

PHOTOS 4-1a and 4-1b
The effects of (a) a behavioral deficit and (b) a behavioral excess in eating

which are maladaptive behaviors that clients are performing too often, for too long a time, or too strongly (for example, fighting and smoking).

Dealing with acceleration target behaviors is simple and straightforward. Behavior therapy procedures are used to increase the acceleration target behavior directly. For example, if social interaction was the acceleration target behavior for a hospitalized client who was depressed, the nurses might praise the client each time they saw the client interacting with someone. Dealing with deceleration target behaviors is more complicated.

Special Considerations for Deceleration Target Behaviors

Two basic strategies are used to treat deceleration target behaviors. One is to decrease the deceleration target behavior directly, as parents often try to do by punishing a child's misbehavior. This simple strategy often results in an incomplete solution. When a problem behavior is eliminated or substantially decreased, a void is created in the person's life. No matter how disruptive the problem behavior was, it served some function for the person and filled time. As a man who was struggling to give up drinking alcohol put it, "There's just this kind of hole in my life where drinking used to be."[6]

The preferred strategy for treating deceleration target behaviors is to *replace a deceleration target behavior with an acceleration target behavior.*

Take away problem behavior — Replace w/ positive behavior — positive Reinfor (handwritten)

This strategy fills the functional and temporal void with an appropriate adaptive behavior. For instance, if the deceleration target behavior is "criticizing friends," then "complimenting friends" would be a suitable acceleration target behavior. Often, the therapist implements both decelerating strategies simultaneous—this is, the deceleration target behavior is decreased at the same time that an appropriate substitute acceleration target behavior is increased.

An acceleration target behavior used as a substitute for a deceleration target behavior must meet three requirements. First, it must serve the same general function (compliments and criticisms, for example, are both ways of communicating feedback). Second, it should be adaptive; nothing is gained by substituting one maladaptive behavior for another. Third, the acceleration target behavior should be a **competing response**, meaning that it should be difficult to perform both at the same time (as is true of complimenting and criticizing).

Substituting an acceleration target behavior for a deceleration target behavior works because the more the client performs the acceleration target behavior, the fewer opportunities the client has to engage in the deceleration target behavior. It is standard practice in behavior therapy to include an acceleration target behavior in treatment plans that involve a deceleration target behavior. Table 4-2 gives examples of deceleration target behaviors and suitable competing acceleration target behaviors. After looking at the table, complete Participation Exercise 4-1 before you continue reading.

TABLE **4-2**

Examples of Acceleration Target Behaviors That Compete with Deceleration Target Behaviors

Deceleration Target Behavior	Competing Acceleration Target Behavior
Studying in front of the television	Studying in the library
Biting fingernails	Keeping hands in pockets or at sides
Driving home from parties drunk	Taking a taxi home
Staying up until 3 A.M.	Getting into bed and turning out the lights at 1 A.M.
Talking to "voices" (that is, hallucinating)	Talking to other people
Criticizing others	Praising others

PARTICIPATION EXERCISE 4-1

Competition Can Be a Good Thing: Finding Competing Acceleration Target Behaviors for Deceleration Target Behaviors

For each undesirable behavior listed, write one or more acceleration target behaviors that compete with it—in other words, behaviors that, when performed, make it unlikely that the undesirable behavior will occur. Be sure each of your acceleration target behaviors meets the requirements for a good target behavior (described earlier in the chapter).

1. Eating junk food between meals
2. Cramming for exams
3. "Blowing" an entire paycheck
4. Using foul language
5. Leaving lights on that are not in use
6. Wasting time
7. Being late for classes
8. Procrastinating in paying bills
9. Littering

Examples of appropriate competing acceleration target behaviors are given in your Student Resource Manual.

Dead Person Rule

Whereas acceleration target behaviors indicate what a client is expected to do, deceleration target behaviors indicate only what the client should *not* do, which poses a problem. Consider a typical scene in an elementary school classroom. Heather is disrupting the class by talking to Nigel when the teacher wants the class to read silently. If the teacher tells Heather, "Don't talk to Nigel" (a deceleration target behavior), all Heather knows is that she is *not* allowed to talk to Nigel. She could obey her teacher by talking to Katie or another classmate or by dancing in the aisle. It would be more useful if the teacher told Heather, "Work on your assignment," which is the acceleration target behavior the teacher wants Heather to engage in.

When dealing with behavioral excesses, it often is easier, but less beneficial, to specify what a client should *not* do than what the client should do. To avoid making this mistake, behavior therapists follow the **dead person rule**: *Never ask a client to do something a dead person can do.* Only dead people are capable of *not* behaving! "Don't talk" violates the dead person rule because dead people "cannot talk." Applying the dead person rule means that the client is asked to do something *active*. "Work on your assignment" follows the dead person rule because dead people can't work on assignments.

Ironically, the dead person rule violates itself. "Never ask a client to do something a dead person can do" is something a dead person *could* do. The general principle could be rephrased as a *live person rule*: "Always ask a client to do something that only a live person can do." However, the purpose of the dead person rule is to remind therapists to formulate target behaviors that clients can actively perform, and this function is better served by the catchy dead person rule. Participation Exercise 4-2 gives you a chance to apply the dead person rule to common violations of the rule.

Courtesy of Michael D. Spiegler

PARTICIPATION
EXERCISE 4-2

Resurrecting the Dead: Identifying and Correcting Dead Person Behaviors[a]

The dead person rule often is violated in everyday life. This exercise will make you aware of common violations of the rule and give you practice in rephrasing dead person behaviors as live person behaviors.

Part I: Changing Dead Person Behaviors to Live Person Behaviors

A series of frequently heard or seen instructions is listed in Table 4-3. Each instruction is a request to perform a dead person behavior. For each instruction, write a *live person behavior* that is appropriate for the situation. When you have finished, compare your answers with those in your Student Resource Manual.

Part II: Identifying Common Dead Person Behaviors

Over the next few days, look for violations of the dead person rule you hear or see in verbal and written instructions to others. Briefly note the situation or context (following the models in Table 4-3), then write the

[a]You should complete Part I of the Participation Exercise before you continue reading, but you will need to do Part II later.

instruction that calls for a dead person behavior, and finally rephrase the instruction so that it refers to a live person behavior. You may be surprised at the number of dead person behaviors that are commonly requested.

TABLE **4-3**
Everyday Violations of the Dead Person Rule

Situation/Context	Instruction
Parent to child	"Don't be impolite."
Sign in park	DO NOT LITTER
Teacher to student	"No running in the hallway."
Sign on one of two side-by-side doors	DO NOT ENTER
Parent to young boy having trouble tying his shoe	"Don't cry; big boys don't cry."
Parent to child at dinner table	"Don't eat with your fingers."
Sign at petting zoo	DO NOT FEED THE ANIMALS
Parent to child being put to bed	"I don't want to hear another word out of you."
Traffic sign at fork in road	NO LEFT TURN
Teacher to student	"Don't look at other students' tests."
Instructions on a written form	DO NOT WRITE BELOW THE RED LINE
Lifeguard to swimmer	"No diving off the side."
Parent to child	"Don't hit your sister when she takes your toy."

MEASURING THE TARGET BEHAVIOR

Measurement of the target behavior begins as soon as it has been designed and before therapy begins. This initial measurement provides a **baseline**, which consists of the repeated measurement of a target behavior as it occurs naturally—that is, before treatment. A baseline provides a standard for evaluating how much a target behavior changes after treatment has begun.[7] Measurement of the target behavior continues throughout the remainder of the therapy process as an ongoing check of the client's progress.

STEP 4: IDENTIFYING MAINTAINING CONDITIONS

Identifying the maintaining conditions of the target behavior is a crucial step because it is these conditions that will be changed in order to change the target behavior.[8] A variety of behavioral assessment procedures (covered in depth in Chapter 5) are employed to pinpoint maintaining antecedents and maintaining consequences.

The assessment typically begins with an interview in which the therapist questions the client in detail about the antecedents and consequences of the target behavior.[9] Examples of the questions are, "In what situations do you engage in the target behavior most frequently and least frequently?" "What are you thinking and how are you feeling right before you perform the target behavior?" "What happens right after you perform the target behavior?" "What are the long-term effects of engaging in the target behavior?"

The retrospective information gathered in interviews may be checked out with other assessment procedures.[10] The therapist may ask the client to keep a record of when the target behavior occurs during the week and to note the antecedents and consequences in each case. Parents may be instructed to observe the circumstances in which their child engages in the target behavior. Sometimes the therapist sets up a simulated situation in which possible maintaining conditions are systematically introduced and removed and the effects on the target behavior are noted.[11] For example, a child who has trouble concentrating on schoolwork might be asked to work on an assignment with and without an adult present.

STEPS 5 AND 6: DESIGNING AND IMPLEMENTING A TREATMENT PLAN

Target behaviors are changed indirectly by directly changing their maintaining conditions. A **treatment plan** specifies the therapy procedures that will be used to change the maintaining conditions of the target behavior, including the specifics of how they will be individualized for the particular client. In Case 4-1, for example, Paul's acceleration target behavior—school attendance—occurred infrequently because its consequences (anxiety) were negative. Accordingly, the treatment plan for Paul involved increasing his attending school by gradually exposing him to being in school (in vivo desensitization) while making the consequences of school attendance positive (reinforcement), which included the support and friendship of the therapists and specific tangible reinforcers.

Most behaviors are maintained by multiple antecedents and consequences. For example, among the common maintaining consequences of self-injurious behaviors (such as head banging) associated with severe developmental disorders are social attention, direct sensory stimulation, and removal of clients from frustrating tasks.[12] Generally, it is not feasible or necessary to change all the maintaining conditions in order to change the behavior because the maintaining conditions of a behavior tend to be interrelated. Behavior therapists select for change those maintaining conditions (1) that appear to exert the greatest control over the target behavior and (2) that available behavior therapy procedures are most likely to modify efficiently.

Although behavior therapists are the experts in the methods used to change target behaviors, it is clients who will undergo the treatment. Accordingly, clients in behavior therapy play a role in selecting the particular therapy procedures to be used. In most cases, several different behavior therapies are likely to be effective for the client's problem. The therapist describes each viable alternative therapy procedure to the client, including (1) the underlying rationale, (2) what the therapy entails, (3) what the client is expected to do, (4) an estimate of how long the therapy will take to work, and (5) the general success rate of the therapy for the client's problem. Finally, the therapist describes the advantages and disadvantages of each therapy.

Once the client and therapist decide on the therapy procedures, the treatment plan is implemented. The target behavior continues to be measured to assess progress during treatment. When problems or setbacks arise, which is common, the treatment plan is revised.

STEPS 7 AND 8: EVALUATING THE SUCCESS OF THERAPY AND FOLLOW-UP ASSESSMENT

Evaluating the success of therapy first involves determining whether the target behavior has changed significantly from the baseline—that is, from before the therapy was implemented. If the target behavior has not changed, then it is necessary to return to one of the previous steps and correct any mistakes made (for example, not having correctly identified the maintaining conditions of the target behavior). If the target behavior has changed, the next question is: Have the treatment goals been met and has the problem been alleviated? The answer is not always yes, because a target behavior deals with part of the problem. It may be necessary to change one or more additional target behaviors before the problem is fully alleviated (as in Case 4-1, in which a series of target behaviors were treated one at a time).

When the treatment goals have been met, therapy is terminated. However, the therapist and client may set up periodic checks (for example, in 3 months, 6 months, and 12 months) to ascertain whether the client's treatment gains have been maintained over time. This is called **follow-up assessment** (or **follow-up**, for short). If the follow-up reveals the clients' treatment gains have not been maintained, additional treatment is provided.

BEHAVIOR THERAPY RESEARCH) *Grad School*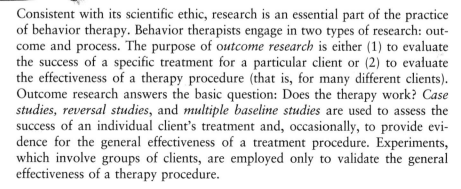

not covering

Consistent with its scientific ethic, research is an essential part of the practice of behavior therapy. Behavior therapists engage in two types of research: outcome and process. The purpose of *outcome research* is either (1) to evaluate the success of a specific treatment for a particular client or (2) to evaluate the effectiveness of a therapy procedure (that is, for many different clients). Outcome research answers the basic question: Does the therapy work? *Case studies, reversal studies,* and *multiple baseline studies* are used to assess the success of an individual client's treatment and, occasionally, to provide evidence for the general effectiveness of a treatment procedure. Experiments, which involve groups of clients, are employed only to validate the general effectiveness of a therapy procedure.

Process research answers the question: Why is a therapy successful? or How does it produce change?[13] Process research can use any of the quantitative methods employed in outcome research as well as qualitative methods (such as content analyses of therapy sessions). Although it might seem that whether a therapy works is more important to know than why it works, both questions are important. An understanding of the mechanisms of change that underlie the success of a therapy can contribute to refining the therapy procedures and increasing their effectiveness. Regrettably, compared to the number of outcome studies on behavior therapy, only a small number of process studies are conducted.[14]

(Case Studies)

A **case study**, such as Case 4-1 at the beginning of this chapter, is a detailed description of what transpires during the treatment of a specific client.[15] Besides documenting the success of therapy for individuals, case studies also are useful for describing new therapy procedures and novel applications of existing therapies.[16] Case studies can also demonstrate the feasibility of the delivery of a therapy technique—for a particular population or problem or in a particular setting—which lays the groundwork for further empirical testing using the research methods described in the next sections.[17] Finally, case studies are used for teaching purposes to provide a behind-the-scenes look at the practice of behavior therapy, as in this book. (Be aware that the sections in this book designated "Case" include reversal studies, multiple baseline studies, and experiments as well as case studies.)

The major limitation of case studies is that generalizations to other clients cannot be made because a single case cannot be considered representative. Sometimes, however, a series of case studies that evaluate the effectiveness of a therapy procedure with a number of clients is used to document its effectiveness.[18] Another limitation of case studies is that they cannot rule out the possibility that factors other than the treatment may have contributed to the changes obtained. For example, variations in a client's life circumstances that occur concurrently with therapy—such as beginning a new job—may be responsible for changing the client's problems.

(Reversal Studies)

Reversal studies systematically introduce and withdraw a therapy and examine what happens to the client's target behavior. Reversal studies always involve a minimum of three phases: baseline, treatment, and reversal. In the first phase, a *baseline* (pre-treatment) level of the target behavior is obtained to provide a basis for comparison.

In the second phase, the *treatment* is introduced and the target behavior continues to be assessed. If the therapy is effective, the client's target behavior will change from the baseline level. An acceleration target behavior will increase, and a deceleration target behavior will decrease. Figure 4-2 shows the typical change for an acceleration target behavior between baseline (A) and treatment (B).

Baseline –
Treatment
Reversal

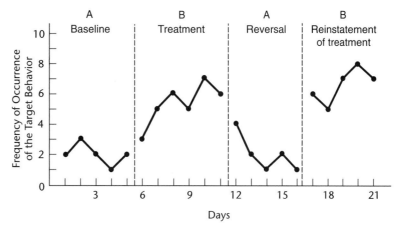

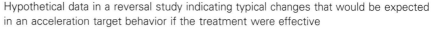

FIGURE 4-2

Hypothetical data in a reversal study indicating typical changes that would be expected in an acceleration target behavior if the treatment were effective

Change in the target behavior from the baseline to the treatment phase is not necessarily caused by the therapy. Some unaccounted-for factors in the client's life may have caused the change. To determine whether the therapy was influencing the change in the target behavior, a third phase of the study is introduced. The therapy is terminated, but the target behavior continues to be assessed. This is called a **reversal phase** because the conditions are reversed to the baseline conditions where the target behavior was only assessed. If the therapy was responsible for the change in the target behavior, then the target behavior will return to near baseline levels when the therapy is withdrawn (as depicted in Figure 4-2).

These three phases—baseline, treatment, and reversal—make up an **ABA study**. *A* stands for no therapy (assessment only)—in the baseline and reversal phases—and *B* stands for treatment. An ABA study provides evidence that the therapy was responsible for changes in the target behavior. However, ending with the reversal phase means that the client is not benefiting from the treatment. Thus, a fourth phase, *reinstatement of treatment*, is added so that the client can continue to benefit from the therapy. The study thus becomes an **ABAB study**, with the second *B* standing for the reinstatement of treatment. If the therapy is effective, the target behavior will again change in the desired direction (see Figure 4-2). The second B phase provides additional evidence that the therapy is responsible for the change in the target behavior. Compared with an ABA study, an ABAB study, by virtue of its additional confirming evidence, provides greater confidence that change is the result of the therapy. Table 4-4 summarizes the phases of an ABAB reversal study.

Reversal studies have three major limitations. First, it is not legitimate to generalize from the success of a single client's therapy to clients in general. As with case studies, this limitation can be overcome to some degree by

TABLE **4-4**

Phases of a Reversal Study

	PHASES			
	A **Baseline**	**B** **Treatment**	**A** **Reversal**	**B** **Reinstatement** **of Treatment**
Procedure	Measure target behavior	Introduce treatment; measure target behavior	Withdraw treatment; measure target behavior	Reinstate treatment; measure target behavior
Purpose	Assess normal level of target behavior	Change target behavior	Check whether treatment is responsible for change in target behavior	Reinstate change in target behavior
Expectation	None	Target behavior will change in desired direction	Target behavior will return to baseline level	Target behavior will change in desired direction

conducting a *series* of reversal studies on a particular therapy procedure for the same problem with multiple clients.[19]

Second, reversal studies cannot be used to evaluate the success of therapy with all types of target behaviors. Reversal studies are appropriate when target behaviors are maintained by external factors, such as privileges given to a teenage girl for studying and getting good grades. Reversal studies are inappropriate when intervention would be likely to bring about enduring changes in the target behavior, as when the therapy teaches a client a behavior that, once learned, will be retained (for example, study skills).

Third, withdrawing therapy in reversal studies may be unethical. For instance, if a treatment reduces a client's self-destructive behavior, such as driving while intoxicated, then it would be unethical to remove the treatment during a reversal phase (even though it is important to assess the effectiveness of the treatment). Multiple baseline studies circumvent the second and third limitations of reversal studies, and, to some degree, the first limitation.

(Multiple Baseline Studies)

A **multiple baseline study** evaluates the effects of a therapy for multiple target behaviors, clients, or settings—depending on the purpose of the study. One purpose is to ascertain whether the therapy is effective for multiple target behaviors; a second purpose is to determine whether the therapy is effective with different clients; and a third purpose is to assess whether the therapy is effective in different settings (such as at home and at work). If the therapy is responsible for the changes in a target behavior, then change should occur *only when the therapy is introduced* and not before. Table 4-5 summarizes the differences between the three types of multiple baseline studies.

TABLE **4-5**

Variables That Change and Remain Constant in Three Types of Multiple Baseline Studies

	VARIABLE		
Type of Study	Target Behaviors	Clients	Settings
Across target behaviors	Different	Same	Same
Across clients	Same	Different	Same
Across settings	Same	Same	Different

We'll illustrate the rationale and basic procedures of multiple baseline studies by examining a hypothetical example of a multiple baseline study that examined the effectiveness of a particular therapy on three different acceleration target behaviors, for the same client and in the same setting. (The same basic procedures would be used for evaluating the effect of a treatment for multiple clients or multiple settings).

As you can see in Figure 4-3, following 5 days of baseline, the therapy was introduced for behavior 1 but not for behaviors 2 and 3, for which baseline assessment just continued. Notice that only the target behavior being treated (behavior 1) increased, which is what would be expected if the therapy was responsible for the change because the therapy was not applied to the other behaviors.

When the therapy was introduced for behavior 2 on day 10, it changed, and behavior 1 maintained its changes because both behaviors were being treated. However, behavior 3 remained unchanged, which would be expected because it was not being treated.

Finally, the therapy was applied to behavior 3 on day 14. As with the other two target behaviors, behavior 3 increased when the therapy was introduced. Because each target behavior changed *only* after the therapy was applied to it, and because the client and setting were held constant, it is reasonable to conclude that the changes were attributable to the therapy and not to other factors.

Both reversal studies and multiple baseline studies provide more information about the causal effects of the therapy than case studies because of the systematic comparisons they make between treatment and no treatment. However, determining the general effectiveness of a particular therapy typically requires evidence from experiments with groups of clients.

Experiments

Experiments study groups of clients, all of whom are dealt with in the same way except that some clients receive the therapy being evaluated and others do not. Experiments are the primary research method used to evaluate the general effectiveness of a treatment, as opposed to its specific effectiveness in a particular case. Experiments address the question, "Is the therapy responsible for the

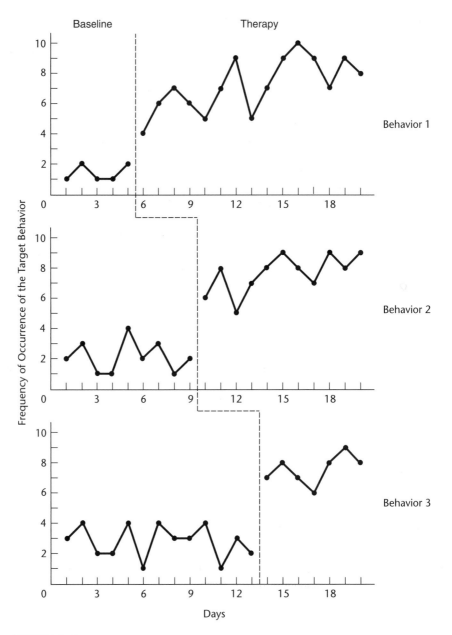

FIGURE 4-3

Hypothetical data in a multiple baseline study indicating typical changes that would be expected in three different acceleration target behaviors if the therapy were effective

changes in clients' target behaviors?" This question can be answered with some surety because experiments *control*, or account for, the influence of *extraneous factors*—that is, factors other than the therapy that are likely to affect clients' problems (such as motivation to change and beneficial changes in one's life).

In the simplest experiment, researchers randomly assign clients to one of two groups. *Random assignment* means that each client has an equal chance of being assigned to each group. The **treatment group** receives the therapy, whereas the other group does not, and so it serves as a comparison or **control group** (see Table 4-6 for examples of different kinds of control groups).

TABLE **4-6**

Types of Control Groups Commonly Used in Behavior Therapy Outcome Experiments

Control Group	Description	Purpose	Example
NO TREATMENT	Clients receive no therapy. Target behaviors are assessed at the same time that clients in the therapy group receive pretherapy and posttherapy assessments.	To control for improvements in clients' problems that are due to factors other than the specific therapy procedures	A young child was referred for therapy because of aggressive behaviors. The child's aggressive behaviors were assessed and then reassessed 10 weeks later.
WAIT-LIST	Clients initially receive no therapy. Target behaviors are assessed at the same time that clients in the therapy group receive pretherapy and posttherapy assessments. After the therapy group's final assessment, clients receive therapy.	To control for the influence of clients' expectations that they will receive therapy	Couples seeking help for their marital conflict had their marital relationship assessed and then reassessed two months later. They then participated in two months of marital therapy, after which their marital relationship was assessed again.
NO CONTACT	Clients receive no therapy. Target behaviors are assessed without the clients' being aware that they are part of a therapy study and without direct contact with the therapist or researcher.	To control for improvements in clients' problems that are due to being participants in a therapy study rather than to the specific therapy procedures	All people between the ages of 21 and 35 in a community were mailed a questionnaire to complete about their anxiety 3 days after an earthquake struck and then again 5 months later.
ATTENTION	Clients meet with a therapist for the same amount of time as clients in the therapy condition but receive no therapy.	To control for improvements in clients' problems that are due to the therapists' attention rather than to the specific therapy procedures	College students with severe test anxiety met with a therapist once a week for 12 sessions and discussed theories of the development and course of test anxiety.
PLACEBO	Clients receive a therapy-like procedure that they are led to believe is highly effective but in fact has no proven efficacy.	To control for improvements in clients' problems that are due to clients' expectations that the therapy they are receiving will be effective rather than to the specific therapy procedures	Clients who were depressed were told that listening to a specially prepared audiotape of rhythmic clicking sounds before they went to sleep for 3 weeks would result in dramatic improvements in their mood.

IN THEORY **4-1**

Behavior Therapy as an Experiment

Behavior therapy is analogous to an experiment. An experiment begins with a hypothesis that a particular *independent variable* (a condition that is directly varied) influences a particular *dependent variable* (the behavior being studied). To test the hypothesis, a researcher introduces the independent variable and measures the dependent variable to see if it changes—while controlling extraneous factors that might change the dependent variable. If the dependent variable changes when the independent variable is introduced,

the hypothesis is supported. In other words, the experiment has produced evidence that the independent variable has a causative effect on the dependent variable.

You can see the parallels between an experiment and the process of behavior therapy if you substitute the terms *maintaining conditions* for independent variable and *target behavior* for dependent variable. The behavior therapist hypothesizes that certain conditions are maintaining the target behavior. The therapist tests the hypothesis by

changing the maintaining conditions in therapy and by observing whether the target behavior changes. If the target behavior changes (in the desired direction), then the hypothesis is supported and the therapy is successful. If the target behavior does not change (in the desired direction), the hypothesis is not supported and the treatment is unsuccessful. Table 4-7 details the parallels between behavior therapy and an experiment.

TABLE **4-7**

Parallels Between Behavior Therapy and an Experiment

Step	Behavior Therapy	Experiment
1. *Define what is to be changed*	Target behavior	Dependent variable*
2. *Assess baseline level*	Pretherapy measurement of target behavior	Preexperiment measurement of dependent variable
3. *Search for influential factors*	Identify maintaining antecedents and maintaining consequences of target behavior	Decide on independent variable*
4. *Formulate hypothesis*	"If correct maintaining conditions have been identified, then modifying them will change the target behavior."	"If the independent variable does influence the dependent variable, then varying the independent variable will result in the dependent variable changing."
5. *Test hypothesis*	Implement therapy (that is, modify maintaining conditions)	Carry out experiment (that is, vary independent variable)
6. *Examine outcome*	Posttherapy measurement of target behavior	Postexperiment measurement of dependent variable
7. *Draw conclusions when*		
a. *Change is in expected direction*	Therapy successful	Hypothesis confirmed
b. *No change or change is in unexpected direction*	Reassess maintaining conditions (that is, return to step 3)	Find other independent variable (that is, return to step 3)

*In an experiment, the condition that is directly varied is called the *independent variable*. The object of an experiment is to observe the influence of the independent variable on subjects' behaviors. The specific behavior under investigation is called the *dependent variable* because it is hypothesized to depend on or be influenced by the condition varied by the experimenter (that is, the independent variable).

There is one major difference between behavior therapy and an experiment. In an experiment, control procedures prevent factors other than the independent variable from influencing the dependent variable. Accordingly, experiments can establish cause-and-effect relationships with a high degree of certainty. This is less true for behavior therapy. If the hypothesized maintaining conditions are changed and the target behavior changes, then therapy is successful. However, there is no way to know whether modifying the hypothesized maintaining conditions caused the change because in therapy extraneous variables are not controlled. For example, changes in a client's life that occur during therapy may have a beneficial effect on the problem (such as recovering from an illness). Not knowing definitively what accounts for the success of therapy usually is acceptable in clinical practice because the goal is to alleviate a client's problem.

The two groups are made equivalent with respect to extraneous factors in two ways. First, random assignment usually ensures that, overall, clients in one group do not differ from clients in the other group in terms of preexisting characteristics (such as age, education level, and marital status). Second, the two groups are dealt with in the same way (for instance, they are given the same assessment measures), except for the presence or absence of therapy. Thus, if clients in the treatment group improve significantly more than clients in the control group, then we can confidently conclude that the improvement was caused by the therapy and not by extraneous factors.

Once the effectiveness of a therapy has been demonstrated in relation to suitable control groups, researchers may carry out additional experiments to assess its relative effectiveness compared with other therapies. In such experiments, the comparison groups consist of clients treated by other therapies and a control group itself may not be necessary.

The findings of experiments are more generalizable than the findings of case studies or reversal studies because the results of experiments represent averages for a number of clients. However, the accuracy of generalizations to other clients depends on how similar the clients and their problems in the experiments are to the clients to whom the generalizations are made.

WHAT CONSTITUTES EFFECTIVE BEHAVIOR THERAPY?

Four *outcome measures,* or criteria, are used to evaluate the effectiveness of behavior therapy: meaningfulness of change, transfer and generalization of change, durability of change over time, and acceptability of the therapy. These outcome measures are applicable both to research that evaluates a therapy for clients in general and for a particular client in clinical practice.

Meaningfulness of Change

Effective therapy should result in a change that is meaningful, that clearly makes a difference for the client, which is known as **clinical significance**.[20][b]

[b]Clinical significance is not statistical significance, which refers only to the reliability of an outcome. A statistically significant outcome means that there is a high probability that the outcome would occur again if the therapy were applied in other cases, but it implies nothing about how important the outcome is. For example, suppose a treatment for smoking cessation results in an average reduction of cigarettes smoked from 36 to 33 per day. Given a sufficient number of clients in the treatment group, this outcome could be statistically significant, which would indicate that there is a high probability that the treatment would reduce the number of cigarettes smoked in other studies. However, because three fewer cigarettes per day would not improve the clients' health, the results of the study are not clinically significant because they have no pragmatic import.

Clinical significance is usually assessed by two criteria: relevant norms[21] and social validity. Consider the hypothetical case of Mai Lee, a 5-year-old girl who interacts with her peers only 5% of the time that she is with other children at her preschool. Suppose that after therapy, Mai Lee is spending 35% of her time at preschool interacting with other children. Although 35% clearly is a substantial change, if the norm for social interaction for 5-year-old girls were 55%, then the therapy outcome would not be considered clinically significant with respect to relevant norms.

Social validity,[22] the second criterion for clinical significance, refers to the generally accepted standards for adaptive and acceptable functioning. Social validity is assessed by having appropriate people judge whether the client's behaviors following therapy are adaptive and acceptable.[23] Using the example of Mai Lee, in addition to assessing the amount of peer interaction she engaged in, Mai Lee's teacher might be asked to observe her peer interactions and rate them in terms of how appropriate they are (for her age).

Another aspect of meaningfulness of change is the degree to which the clinical changes have increased clients' quality of life. Therapeutic success is usually measured by symptom reduction; given that clinical symptoms are maladaptive and distressing, it would be expected that their diminution would make clients' lives better. But whether this is the case must be assessed.[24]

Transfer and Generalization of Change

The purpose of therapy is to bring about changes in the client's everyday life. Obviously, then, effective treatment requires that changes that are achieved in therapy *transfer* to the client's life. **Transfer** occurs when what is learned and practiced in therapy carries over to other settings. Take the example of a man who has trouble controlling his anger when frustrations arise in his family life. In therapy, he is taught to use self-instructions to cope with frustrations and avoid becoming angry, and he is able to do so while role playing with his therapist. For the therapy to be effective, however, the man must use the self-instructions in his home situation.

In most cases, the therapeutic benefits should also impact behaviors and aspects of the client's life other than those that were specifically addressed in treatment, a process called **generalization.**[25c] The man in the previous example might use self-instructions to deal with his excessive drinking and work-related stress in addition to his anger as a response to frustration.[26]

On a broader level, when a therapy has been demonstrated to be effective for a particular disorder (for example, phobias), it cannot be assumed that it will also be effective in treating other disorders (for example, panic disorder). How well it works with other problems must be empirically validated separately.

Transfer and generalization of change are not always a natural outcome of successful treatment, so it often is necessary to include specific procedures that promote transfer and generalization in the treatment plan. For instance,

---

[c]Both transfer and generalization are forms of generalization, stimulus generalization and response generalization, respectively. We have chosen to use the term transfer to avoid confusion between the two forms of generalization.

with children who are socially withdrawn, social skills training can be carried out with multiple peers (to enhance generalization) and in a variety of settings (to enhance transfer).[27]

Durability of Change/ *Things need to last —*

Changes that result from therapy must endure long after the treatment has ended. Endurance of therapeutic effects typically is referred to as **long-term maintenance** (or **maintenance**, for short).

Maintenance of treatment effects is determined by assessing the client's functioning at various time intervals after therapy—optimally, extending for several years.[28] Such follow-up assessments have become standard in behavior therapy outcome research. Typically, the results of follow-up assessments are reported in the research literature using phrasing such as "the treatment gains were maintained up to 2 years." Such phrasing can be misleading. What is meant is that at a 2-year follow-up, the treatment gains were maintained, and not that the treatment effects only lasted 2 years or less. The major practical obstacle to obtaining follow-up assessments is keeping track of clients' whereabouts and inducing clients to undergo additional assessment procedures.[29]

Maintenance of treatment gains, like transfer and generalization, is not guaranteed by a successful therapy outcome immediately following therapy. Specific procedures may need to be included during and after therapy to ensure durability over time. For example, in a residential program for treating antisocial behaviors, teenage clients are reinforced for socially appropriate behaviors with spending money. As clients are nearing the end of the program, the reinforcers are switched to verbal praise because outside the program appropriate behaviors are more likely to be reinforced by praise than money. Additionally, significant people in the clients' lives, such as parents and teachers, are trained to continue the social reinforcement of appropriate behaviors. These procedures help insure that clients will continue to perform the behaviors after they have left the program.

Long-term maintenance is, in part, dependent on transfer and generalization. Maintenance is an issue only if the changes transfer to the client's everyday life. Further, the more situations to which therapeutic changes transfer and the more behaviors to which the changes generalize, the greater is the likelihood that the behaviors will be maintained.

Acceptability of the Therapy/ *How palatable therapy procedures are to the client.*

A final outcome measure concerns the acceptability of the treatment procedures to the client and sometimes to significant others, as in the case of children.[30] In this context, **acceptability** refers to how palatable the therapy procedures are. It does not refer to whether the client believes the therapy is effective.[31] Acceptability is typically assessed using standardized measures, such as the Satisfaction with Therapy Questionnaire.[32]

Some forms of behavior therapy are more likely to be acceptable than others. As with many treatments for medical problems, behavior therapies vary in terms of how pleasant they are, how much they intrude in clients' life styles, and how much time and effort they require. These variables influence how acceptable or tolerable different behavior therapies are to clients. And, clients clearly have individual preferences for different therapies.[33] All other things being equal, therapy procedures that are acceptable to clients are more useful because clients are more likely to seek therapy and remain in treatment.[34] Conversely, clients tend to drop out of treatments that have low acceptability.[35] Not surprisingly, there also is evidence that acceptability of treatment is associated with treatment effectiveness.[36]

In addition to the general acceptability of a treatment procedure, acceptability may depend on demographic variables, including age, educational level, and culture.[37] Modifications in standard procedures may have to be made to make them more acceptable for certain groups of clients, such as using examples and metaphors that are culturally specific.[38]

Acceptability of treatments also applies to therapists because if a therapist does not find a treatment acceptable, the therapist will not use it. This might occur for many reasons independent of the demonstrated usefulness of a particular therapy, ranging from the therapist's misunderstandings about a therapy[39] to the therapist finding a therapy difficult or boring to administer. Similarly, nonprofessional change agents, such as parents and teachers,[40] are more likely to continue administering therapy procedures that they find acceptable and discontinue or inconsistently employ procedures that they find unacceptable.[41] The bottom line is that even the most effective therapies can be helpful only if they are used, which partly depends on their being acceptable first to the clinician who recommends and administers the treatments and then to the client who must undergo them.

META-ANALYTIC STUDIES

In order to make general statements about the effectiveness of a given behavior therapy, it is necessary to examine relevant studies and draw conclusions from them. This can be a daunting task, given the large number of studies and the different methodologies they employ. Fortunately, there is a statistical procedure known as **meta-analysis** that integrates and compares empirical findings from multiple studies regarding a specific research question, such as "Is therapy X an effective treatment for disorder Y?"[42] Instead of asking this question in a single study, a meta-analytic study asks it about a group of studies.

The first step in a meta-analysis involves deciding on a set of criteria for the studies that will be included, such as the quality of the methodology, the assessment measures used, and the length of follow-up assessments. Then, an extensive search for published studies that ask the research question and meet the inclusion criteria is made.

In order to compare the findings from the studies that meet the criteria, a common numerical index is calculated for each study. This index, called an *effect size*, indicates the degree of change that clients experience as a result of the treatment.[43] The meta-analysis takes the effect sizes from all the studies and statistically averages them. The averages are usually weighted for number of clients and sometimes for quality of the study; studies with more clients and higher quality are given more weight.[44] The end result is an *average effect size* that is a measure of the degree of change clients experienced across all the studies.

Meta-analysis provides a more comprehensive answer to the question of whether a given therapy is effective in treating a particular problem than a single study because it is based on multiple, and usually high-quality, studies. Additionally, a meta-analysis may identify important common variables across the individual studies that refine the research question.[45] For example, the meta-analysis might reveal that although therapy X is generally effective in treating disorder Y, it is more effective with twice-weekly therapy sessions than weekly sessions or that it works better for children than for adolescents.

Increasingly, meta-analyses are being conducted to evaluate the effectiveness of behavior therapies. The strength of meta-analysis is that it combines research from a number of studies and thus includes many clients—strength in numbers, if you will. However, the downside of amalgamating many studies is that because the studies often use diverse methodologies, their comparability may be questionable. Additionally, although the result of a meta-analysis is quantitative and objective, interpretation of the overall effect size is subjective.

The generally accepted values indicating different levels of meaningfulness of change have been arbitrarily determined. For the most commonly used statistic for effect size, Cohen's d, .2 means a small change, .5 a moderate (and clinically significant) change, and .8 a large change.[46][d] However, the interpretation of the effect size depends on the context of the therapy. For example, small effect sizes can be clinically significant when there are small changes in a disorder that is extremely difficult to change. And, small effect sizes for therapies that are very efficient and cost-effective may be meaningful because some change has occurred with little expenditure of time or effort.[47] In sum, meta-analysis is a useful but imperfect method for assessing therapy effectiveness.

IN THEORY **4-2**

Evaluating the Efficacy and Effectiveness of Behavior Therapies

Using both the terms *efficacy* and *effectiveness* in the title of this In Theory may seem redundant, because in everyday language, they are synonymous. However, in scientific research they have different meanings. **Efficacy** refers to the success of therapy when it is assessed under "perfect" conditions—in research settings using standardized procedures and rigorous controls. **Effectiveness** refers to the success of therapy in "real" clinical settings (such as community-based clinics

and private practices), where rigorous controls and standardization may be lacking. It is important for therapies to be both efficacious and effective. (Bear in mind, this discussion concerns providing empirical support for a particular therapy procedure in general and not for its success in treating an individual client.)

Efficacy studies are usually conducted in a research, rather than a clinical, context. The participants all have the same, single reliably

diagnosed disorder, and they either receive the treatment free or they are paid for their participation. The specific therapy being evaluated is extensively defined in a **treatment manual** (or **protocol**) that provides detailed, session-by-session procedures for the therapist to follow,[48] and usually the number of sessions is prescribed. Thus, all the participants receive the same treatment.[49] Extraneous factors other than the therapy itself that could result in change are controlled for (such as

(continued)

---

[d]An effect size of zero indicates no change, and a negative effect size indicates worsening of clients' problems.

the client–therapist relationship). Most efficacy studies are experiments, and participants who receive the therapy are compared to equivalent participants who are in a no-treatment control group, an alternative treatment group, or a placebo control group. The participants are randomly assigned to groups, and such studies are called *randomized clinical trials*.[50] Because of the highly controlled conditions in efficacy studies, if participants who receive the therapy being tested improve compared to participants in a control group, it is possible to definitively attribute the improvement to the therapy itself (rather than to other factors).

The major limitation of efficacy studies is that they are artificial in that the conditions do not replicate those in the "real" world of clients' seeking and being treated in therapy.[51] For example, in efficacy studies, clients who have the same disorder are recruited, randomly assigned to treatments, do not pay for treatment, the treatment follows standardized procedures, and the therapists are skilled in implementing the therapy. By contrast, *effectiveness studies* take place in actual clinical facilities; clients often have multiple disorders, choose the type of therapy they receive, and pay for the treatment; and therapists, who may not be skilled in the specific therapy, are free to alter treatment procedures as the need arises (rather than strictly following the procedures in a treatment manual).

Because of these differences, whether an efficacious treatment will prove effective in everyday clinical practice is not known until effectiveness studies are carried out.[52] Effectiveness studies—which can be experiments, reversal studies, multiple baseline studies, or case studies—usually do not have the same rigorous standards and controls as efficacy studies; but they are methodologically sound and have the advantage of testing the therapy under "treatment as usual" conditions.

Although the logical progression is to test a therapy first in efficacy studies and then in effectiveness studies, this practice often does not occur. In fact, only a minority of studies evaluating behavior therapies are efficacy studies, and the preponderance of empirical support for behavior therapies comes from effectiveness studies. One reason is that efficacy studies are extremely expensive, time-wise and monetarily; efficacy studies often are multisite and multiyear investigations with follow-ups, and the cost can be several million dollars. Also, testing behavior therapies in efficacy studies is a relatively new practice, and so many established behavior therapies developed before the advent of efficacy studies have only been validated in effectiveness studies.

Finally, a note on the terminology we will use in this book in discussing the success of behavior therapies. We will use *effective/effectiveness* as a generic term to refer to a treatment leading to a favorable outcome and reserve *efficacy/efficacious* when referring to the results of efficacy studies.

SUMMARY

1. The process of behavior therapy involves eight basic steps: clarifying the client's problem, formulating goals, designing a target behavior, identifying the maintaining conditions of the target behavior, designing a treatment plan to change the maintaining conditions, implementing the treatment plan, evaluating its effectiveness, and conducting follow-up assessments. Assessment begins after the target behavior has been designed and continues through the course of therapy and after therapy is terminated.

2. Only one or two problems are treated simultaneously. Each problem is defined as a target behavior, an aspect of the problem that is relatively small, discrete, and measurable. A good target behavior is narrow in scope, unambiguously defined, measurable, and appropriate and adaptive for the client and the problem.

3. Acceleration target behaviors are increased and are used for behavioral deficits, which are adaptive behaviors clients are not performing enough. An acceleration target behavior is treated by increasing it directly. Deceleration target behaviors are decreased and are used for behavioral

excesses, which are maladaptive behaviors clients are performing too much. A deceleration target behavior can be decreased directly. However, the preferred strategy is to decrease it indirectly by increasing an adaptive acceleration target behavior that competes with the deceleration target behavior.

4. The dead person rule, "Never ask a client to do something a dead person can do," reminds therapists to specify target behaviors that clients can actively perform.

5. Once a target behavior has been selected, its probable maintaining conditions are identified. A treatment plan is then developed to change the maintaining conditions, which will change the target behavior.

6. The effectiveness of the treatment plan is evaluated in terms of the treatment goals. If the plan was successful, therapy is terminated and periodic follow-up assessments are conducted. If the treatment plan has not alleviated the problem, then additional target behaviors are designed and treated.

7. Outcome research evaluates whether therapy is effective, both for individual clients and for a therapy procedure in general. Process research investigates why a therapy is successful and how a therapy produces change.

8. Case studies are detailed, descriptive accounts of what transpired in the treatment of individual clients. Case studies are limited in terms of the generalizability of their findings to other clients and in terms of determining whether the therapy itself caused the changes in the target behavior.

9. Reversal studies systematically introduce and withdraw the therapy to assess its effects on the client's target behavior. In multiple baseline studies, a particular therapy procedure is introduced sequentially for different target behaviors, clients, or settings.

10. Experiments study groups of clients and control for the effects of extraneous variables. In a simple experiment, clients are randomly assigned to one of two groups. One group receives therapy and the other does not, the latter serving as a control or comparison group. Experiments can indicate whether the therapy has caused the changes in clients' target behaviors, and their results can be generalized.

11. Behavior therapy can be viewed as a scientific experiment in which hypotheses about the causes of the client's target behaviors are tested.

12. Four outcome measures are used to evaluate the effectiveness of behavior therapy: meaningfulness of change, transfer and generalization of change, durability of change, and acceptability of the therapy.

13. Meta-analytic studies integrate and compare empirical findings from multiple studies regarding a specific research question. The effect sizes of the individual studies are averaged and weighted, resulting in an average effect size that indicates the degree of change across all studies.

14. Efficacy refers to the success of therapy assessed under "perfect" controlled conditions (with the limitation of artificiality). Effectiveness refers to the success of therapy in "real" clinical settings (where rigorous controls and standardization may be lacking). It is important for therapies to be both efficacious and effective.

REFERENCE NOTES

1. Freud, 1909/1955.
2. Lazarus, Davidson, & Polefka, 1965.
3. For example, Rosales-Ruiz & Baer, 1997; Voeltz & Evans, 1982.
4. Dudley, Dixon, & Turkington, 2005.
5. Finney, Miller, & Adler, 1993.
6. Bryson, 1999, p. 257.
7. Barlow & Hersen, 1984.
8. For example, Derby et al., 1992; Iwata, Vollmer, & Zarcone, 1990.
9. O'Neill, Horner, Albin, Storey, & Sprague, 1990.
10. For example, Storey, Lawry, Ashworth, Danko, & Strain, 1994.
11. For example, Chapman, Fisher, Piazza, & Kurtz, 1993.
12. For example, Smith, Iwata, Vollmer, & Zarcone, 1993.
13. For example, Ablon & Marci, 2004; Doss, Thum, Sevier, Atkins, & Christensen, 2005; Garratt, Ingram, & Rand, 2007; Weersing & Weisz, 2002.
14. Kazdin, 2008.
15. For example, Campbell & Lutzker, 1993.
16. For example, Cautela & Kearney, 1993; Davison & Lazarus, 1995.
17. Borckardt, Nash, Murphy, Moore, Shaw, & O'Neil, 2008; Soroudi et al., 2008.
18. For example, Perlis et al., 2000; Wolpe, 1958.
19. For example, Guevremont, Osnes, & Stokes, 1986a, 1986b.
20. Kazdin, 1977a, 1999; Kendall, 1999.
21. Kendall & Sheldrick, 2000; Jacobson, 1988.
22. Kazdin, 1977a; Wolf, 1978.
23. For example, Bellini & Akullian, 2007a; Clarke & Dunlap, 2008; Dunlap, Ester, Langhans, & Fox, 2006.
24. Diefenbach, Abramowitz, & Norberg, 2007.
25. Risley, 1995.
26. Belchic & Harris, 1994.
27. For example, Beidel & Turner, 1998; Beidel, Turner, & Morris, 2000.
28. For example, Foxx & Faw, 1990.
29. For example, Heimberg, Salzman, Holt, & Blendell, 1993.
30. For example, Borrego, Ibanez, & Spendlove, 2007; Jones, Eyberg, Adams, & Boggs, 1998; Miller & Kelley, 1992.
31. For example, Johnston, Hommersen, & Seipp, 2008.
32. Beck, Wright, Newman, & Liese, 1993.
33. For example, Pemberton & Borrego, 2007; Renfrey, 1992.
34. Meichenbaum, 1991.
35. For example, Callahan & Leitenberg, 1973; Smith, Marcus, & Eldredge, 1994; Wilson & Tracey, 1976.
36. For example, MacKenzie, Fite, & Bates, 2004.
37. For example, Borrego, Ibanez, Spendlove, & Pemberton, 2007; compare with Miles, Peters, & Kuipers, 2007.
38. For example, Otto & Hinton, 2006.
39. For example, Becker, Zayfert, & Anderson, 2004; Feeny, Hembree, & Zoeliner, 2003.
40. For example, Eng, 2008.
41. McConnachie & Carr, 1997.
42. Neill, 2008.
43. Neill, 2008.
44. Graziano & Raulin, 2007.
45. Konstantopoulos & Hedges, 2006.
46. Cohen, 1988.
47. Neill, 2008.
48. Carroll & Rounsaville, 2008.
49. Nezu & Nezu, 2008.
50. Kendall, Holmbeck, & Verduin, 2004; Ollendick, King, & Chorpita, 2006.
51. Depp & Lebowitz, 2007; McEvoy, 2007.
52. For example, Scheeres, Wensing, Knoop, & Bleijenberg, 2008.

5

Behavioral Assessment

Behavioral assessment is to behavior therapy what a banana is to a banana split—indispensable. Behavioral assessment procedures are used to gather information relevant to clarifying clients' problems, setting goals, selecting and designing target behaviors, identifying the maintaining conditions of the target behaviors, designing a treatment plan, and monitoring clients' progress.

We will discuss the eight most frequently used behavioral assessment methods: interview, direct self-report inventory, self-recording, checklist/ rating scale, systematic naturalistic observation, simulated observation, role-playing, and physiological measurement (see Table 5-1).[1] The first three methods—interviews, self-report inventories, and self-recording—provide information from clients' reports about themselves. The next four methods— checklists and rating scales, naturalistic observations, simulated observations, and role-playing—employ other people to assess clients' behaviors. Finally, physiological measurements rely primarily on instrumentation to provide information. In subsequent chapters, you will see each of the basic methods of behavioral assessment used in behavior therapy.

TABLE **5-1**

Most Frequently Used Methods of Behavioral Assessment

Rank	Method	Percentage of Behavior Therapists Using Frequently
1	Interview	90
2	Direct self-report inventory	63
3	Self-recording	56
4	Checklist or rating scale	51
5	Systematic naturalistic observation	30
6	Simulated observation	23
7	Role-playing	20
8	Physiological measurement	19

*Percentage of behavior therapists indicating that they used the method with six or more clients in the past year.
Source: Based on data from Guevremont & Spiegler, 1990.

MULTIMETHOD AND MULTIMODAL ASSESSMENT

In practice, more than one method of assessment generally is used to gather information about a client.[2] **Multimethod assessment** leads to a more comprehensive assessment than does employing a single method. It provides corroborative evidence from different assessment procedures, which increases the reliability and validity of the assessment. Also, each method has its particular strengths and limitations, so using multiple methods yields a balanced assessment.

In behavioral assessment, information about more than one *mode* of behavior usually is obtained.[3] **Multimodal assessment** is important because psychological disorders generally involve more than one mode.[4] Depression, for example, may consist of reduced activity (overt behavior), thoughts of hopelessness (cognition), sadness (emotion), and weight loss (physiological response).

The particular modes of behavior assessed and the methods used depend on the nature of the problem and on practical considerations. Table 5-2 provides examples of how anger and aggressive behaviors might be assessed using each of the eight most common behavioral assessment methods for each of the four modes of behavior. As the table indicates, certain methods of assessment are optimal for each mode of behavior, and not all methods are appropriate for each of the modes.[5] In assessing a client's thoughts, for example, interviews, self-report inventories, and self-recordings are the optimal methods, and role-playing could possibly be used; however, the remaining four assessment methods are not applicable. In practice, the most efficient and least costly methods of assessment typically are chosen, which is one reason why behavioral interviews and self-report inventories are used most frequently.

TABLE **5-2**

Examples of Behavioral Assessment Methods Used to Assess *Anger* and *Aggressive Behaviors* (examples of commonly used methods are printed in **boldface**)

Method	Modes of Behavior			
	Overt Behaviors	Cognitions	Emotions	Physiological Responses
Interview	"Describe what you do when you get angry at your wife."	"What thoughts go through your mind when you get angry at your wife?"	"How are you feeling when you hit your wife?"	"What specific bodily reactions do you have when you get angry at your wife?"
Direct self-report inventory	True or false: "I often use physical violence to get my way."	True or false: "When I get angry, I think about attacking someone."	True or false: "When I am angry, I feel like I am going to explode."	True or false: "When I get angry, I start to sweat."
Checklist and rating scale	Parents check the specific aggressive acts a teenager engaged in last week.	Not used	Teacher rates the severity of a student's anger using a 5-point scale.	Mother checks off possible physiological responses (such as sweating and shaking) she observes in her son that may indicate anger.
Self-recording	Client keeps diary of incidents of aggressive acts.	Client keeps diary of thoughts before, during, and after incidents of anger and aggressive behaviors.	Client records occurrences of angry feelings during the day.	Client records pulse when provoked to anger.

(continued)

TABLE **5-2**   (*continued*)

Method	Overt Behaviors	Cognitions	Emotions	Physiological Responses
		Modes of Behavior		
Systematic naturalistic observation	**Therapist observes parent–child interactions at home, coding examples of parental verbally and physically aggressive behaviors.**	Not used	Therapist observes overt behaviors (such as shaking fist or making threatening remarks) that may indicate client feels angry.	In client's home, therapist observes overt signs of physiological reactions (for example, face flushing and rapid breathing).
Simulated observation	**Therapist deliberately provokes client and notes client's overt responses.**	Not used	Therapist deliberately provokes client and notes client's overt behaviors (such as shaking fist or making threatening remarks) that may indicate client feels angry.	Therapist deliberately provokes client and notes overt signs of physiological reactions (for example, face flushed and rapid breathing).
Role-playing	**Scenario is presented of client's boss' criticizing client for being late. Therapist role-plays boss, and client responds to boss's criticism. Therapist observes what client says.**	Scenario is presented of client's boss' criticizing client for being late. Therapist role-plays boss and client responds to boss's criticism. Client describes thoughts while responding to criticism.	Scenario is presented of client's boss' criticizing client for being late. Therapist role-plays boss, and client responds to boss's criticism. Therapist observes client's overt responses (such as grimaces) that may indicate anger.	Scenario is presented of client's boss' criticizing client for being late. Therapist role-plays boss, and client responds to boss's criticism. Therapist observes client's overt signs of physiological reactions (such as face flushing).
Physiological measurement	Not used	Not used	Heart rate and blood pressure, signs of arousal that may indicate anger, are measured while client thinks about frustrating situations.	**A father's heart rate, blood pressure, and galvanic skin response are measured before, during, and after he watches a video of his children's misbehaving.**

CHARACTERISTICS OF BEHAVIORAL ASSESSMENT

In a sense, behavioral assessment is defined independently of the methods used. Whether assessment is behavioral in nature depends on *how* it is implemented and used. For instance, the interview is hardly unique to behavioral

TABLE **5-3**

Comparison of Behavioral and Traditional Assessment

	Behavioral	Traditional
Aims	To identify target behaviors	To describe personality functioning
	To identify maintaining conditions	To identify etiology (origin)
	To select appropriate treatment	To diagnose or classify
	To evaluate and revise treatment	
Assumptions		
1. Role of behavior	Sample of client's typical behaviors in specific situations	Sign of client's personality (for example, traits and intrapsychic dynamics)
2. Role of past	Unimportant (present behavior caused by present events)	Crucial (present behavior caused by past events)
3. Consistency of behavior	Consistent in the same situation	Consistent in different situations
Interpretation		
1. Direct or indirect	Direct (sample)	Indirect (sign)
2. Degree of inference	Low (behavior to behavior)	High (behavior to personality)

Source: Adapted from Barrios, 1988.

assessment. However, the emphases in a behavioral interview (such as focusing on current circumstances) distinguish it from interviews in other types of assessment. Some of the general differences between behavioral and nonbehavioral (traditional) approaches to assessment are summarized in Table 5-3.

Behavioral assessment procedures share five characteristics. Behavioral assessment ① is individualized, ② focuses on the present, ③ directly samples relevant behaviors, ④ has a narrow focus, and ⑤ is integrated with therapy. These emphases are consistent with the behavioral model and overlap with the defining themes and common characteristics of behavior therapy described in Chapter 1.

Individualized

Behavioral assessment is used to gather unique, detailed information about a client's problem and its maintaining conditions.[6] Thus, the assessment methods are chosen with the particular client and the client's problem in mind, and standard tests and procedures may be customized as needed. These practices are consistent with behavior therapy's individualized approach.

IN THEORY **5-1**

Is There a Place for Diagnosis in Behavior Therapy?

Diagnosis involves classifying clients' problems into discrete categories of disorders. The American Psychiatric Association developed the standard diagnostic categories used today, and they are available in the 1994 publication of the *Diagnostic and Statistical Manual of Mental Disorders* (4th edition),[7] which is referred to as *DSM-IV*, and in a minor text revision published in 2000 *(DSM-IV-TR).*[8]

Philosophically, diagnosis is antithetical to fundamental premises of behavior therapy and behavioral assessment.[9] In contrast to the individualized approach, diagnosis groups clients' problems into categories.[10] For example, rather than dealing with a client's particular problem behaviors, DSM-IV views the client as having a specific disorder. The client's individual problem behaviors now are indistinguishable from the problems of all people whose behaviors have the same diagnosis. This often results in two false assumptions: (1) that all individuals with the same disorder display the same behaviors and (2) that an individual whose problem has been given a particular diagnosis displays all, or even most, of the symptoms that are supposedly characteristic of the diagnosis. Thus, based on a diagnosis, one may attribute characteristics to a client that the client does not possess.

Assigning discrete diagnoses also assumes that clients' problems will fall into a particular category. More often, however, clients' problems involve characteristics or symptoms of more than one

category. The recent growing recognition of such overlap has led to the development of *transdiagnostic* approaches,[11] such as viewing anxiety and depression as the same basic *emotional disorder* with common features and maintaining conditions,[12] and similarly considering anorexia nervosa and bulimia nervosa as being the same basic *eating disorder.*[13]

Diagnosis is a trait concept, which is another basic way in which diagnosis runs counter to the behavioral approach. Strictly speaking, a diagnosis refers to people's behaviors rather than to the people themselves. Unfortunately, this fact is often forgotten. The client becomes the diagnosis, which leads to viewing the client as a *schizophrenic* rather than as an *individual with schizophrenia*, for example. This error results in people's being stigmatized and discriminated against. Further, in the case of some disorders, it is assumed that, once diagnosed, the person always has the disorder, although the symptoms may not always be present.[14] This unsupported assumption accounts for the common expression "Once an alcoholic, always an alcoholic," which, incidentally, epitomizes the regrettable common practice of equating the person with her or his diagnosis. From the behavioral perspective, clients are viewed as *having* disorders, rather than *being* the disorder (or being disordered).

Accurate diagnosis may steer a behavior therapist toward general strategies for treatment. However, diagnosis does not specify (1) the specific behaviors that are

problematic for an individual client; (2) the conditions under which they are problematic; (3) their frequency, intensity, and duration; and, most important for developing a specific treatment plan, (4) the maintaining conditions of the problem behaviors.

Does this mean behavior therapists do not use diagnostic labels in referring to their clients' problems? No, it does not. In fact, most behavior therapists do assign DSM-IV diagnoses. In clinical practice, the major reason for doing so is that official diagnoses are required by clinics, hospitals, schools, and social service agencies before treatment and services can be offered and by health insurance companies before treatment will be paid for. Another potential benefit of diagnosis is that it provides a common language for clinicians to communicate about disorders, and it allows different researchers to assume that they are studying the same *basic* clinical phenomena.

The behavioral alternative to diagnosis is a detailed description of a client's unique problem and the antecedents and consequences that are maintaining it. On one hand, the end product of a thorough behavioral assessment is much lengthier and makes comparisons between clients (such as for research) much more difficult than diagnostic categorization. On the other hand, behavioral assessment provides the necessary information for designing individualized treatment, which diagnosis does not.

Individualized behavioral assessment directly contrasts with the practice of diagnosing psychological problems, as you will see in Theory 5-1.

Present Focus

The focus of behavioral assessment, like behavior therapy, is on relevant information about the client's current functioning and life conditions. Isolating the causes of problem behaviors involves assessing the current maintaining conditions. Details about the client's past, especially early childhood, are considered relatively unimportant.

Directly Samples Relevant Behaviors

Behavioral assessment procedures examine *samples* of a client's behaviors to provide information about how the client typically behaves in particular situations. Suppose Josephine's parents are concerned about that their daughter is not socializing with her peers. They could observe her in various social situations and record the time she spends interacting with her peers and alone. If she interacts with her peers only 10% of the time, this would probably indicate that Josephine has a deficit in social behavior. Their assessment takes a direct approach: a sample of the person's behavior is used to generalize about that behavior. In contrast, nonbehavioral, traditional assessment is *indirect*. Behaviors are used as *signs* (of traits or psychological states), rather than samples, of something other than behavior. In our example of Josephine's spending a minimal amount of time interacting with her peers, this observation, from a traditional assessment perspective, might indicate that Josephine is an introvert (a trait that is indirectly inferred from the observation of her behavior).

Narrow Focus

Behavioral assessment deals with discrete behaviors and specific circumstances rather than a client's total personality or lifestyle, as traditional assessment does. This strategy is consistent with the fact that behavior therapy focuses on target behaviors, aspects of the client's problem. It also makes behavioral assessment more efficient.

Integrated with Therapy

Behavioral assessment is an integral and continuous part of therapy. Assessment of the client's problem and its maintaining conditions are initial steps in behavior therapy, and assessment continues throughout therapy to evaluate changes in the client's target behavior. In fact, often it is difficult to distinguish between behavior therapy and assessment.[15] In the treatment of obesity, for example, clients self-record all the food they eat. Besides providing valuable information, keeping food records makes clients aware of the food they consume and of their eating habits. Such awareness is a key component in the treatment of obesity, and it often results in eating less. Thus, clients' self-recording can be both assessment and treatment.

BEHAVIORAL INTERVIEWS

Generally, the first session of behavior therapy begins with an interview. In addition to assessment, initial interviews serve two functions. The first is for the therapist and client to begin building rapport, which involves developing a relationship of mutual trust. Listening attentively and nonjudgmentally and letting clients know that they are understood are among the ways in which the therapist builds rapport with the client. The second function of the initial interview is to provide clients with information about behavior therapy. The therapist describes the behavioral model and how it views psychological problems, as well as the general nature of behavior therapy (essentially a synopsis of what you read in Chapters 3 and 4). The therapist also explains the ethical and legal rules of confidentiality that are followed in psychotherapy.

As an assessment tool, the interview enables the therapist to gather information about the client's problem and its maintaining conditions.[16] Clients often describe their problems in vague, trait terms. They may say that they are "shy" or "hot-headed." The therapist questions the client to elicit the specific details of the client's unique problem. It is not enough to know that the client "has trouble in relationships with men," for example. Does "trouble" mean that she cannot approach men or that she feels uneasy in their company? Is the client referring to casual or intimate "relationships"?

Once the specifics of the problem have been delineated, the client and therapist can design a target behavior. The next step is to identify the probable maintaining conditions of the target behavior. The therapist asks about the antecedents and consequences of the target behavior. Specifically, *when* and *where* (under what circumstances) does the client get anxious with men? What happens to the client and to her interactions with men when she experiences anxiety? Does she attempt to "escape" from the situation or remain in it? Do the men attempt to "escape" from the situation?

The standard questions in a behavioral interview (as well as those implicitly asked by other behavioral assessment methods) are: *what, when, where, how,* and *how often?* These types of questions provide information concerning the specific nature of the problem and its maintaining conditions. In contrast, traditional assessment emphasizes "why questions" to gather information about the causes of the client's problem. One difficulty with "why questions" is that clients often are not aware of what causes their behaviors (which is one reason they have come to therapy). Further, according to the behavioral model, the causes of a behavior are its maintaining conditions, which are assessed by the standard behavioral interview questions (what, when, where, how, and how often?).

The focus in the behavioral interview is on the present rather than the past. Table 5-4 has examples of questions a behavior therapist typically asks in an initial interview. The therapist may also interview significant people in the client's life (such as a parent or spouse) to provide additional or corroborating information. Sometimes only other people are interviewed, as in the case where relatives and institutional staff can provide the most valid information (for instance, for very young children or people with severe intellectual deficits).[17]

Stay away why questions

TABLE **5-4**

Examples of Questions Behavior Therapists Typically
Ask in Initial Behavioral Interviews

1. What brings you here today?
2. When did the problem begin?
3. How often does the problem occur?
4. When (in what situations) does the problem occur?
5. What tends to occur before the problem (antecedents)?
6. What tends to occur after the problem, and how does the problem affect your life (consequences)?
7. What do you think about when the problem is occurring?
8. What do you feel when the problem is occurring?
9. What steps have you already taken to alleviate the problem, and with what results?

PARTICIPATION EXERCISE 5-1

What, When, Where, How, and How Often? Behavioral Questioning[a]

Clients typically describe their problems in vague, general terms. This exercise presents examples of descriptions that a client or a client's advocate might give. For each description, write five questions that you think would be helpful for a behavior therapist to ask to clarify the problem, select target behaviors, and identify probable maintaining conditions. Be sure the format of your questions is appropriate for a *behavioral* interview—that is, what, when, where, how, and how often questions. When you have finished, compare your questions with the examples in your Student Resource Manual to see if you thought of the same type of questions and to see what other questions you might have asked.

1. The father of a 9-year-old girl reports, "My daughter's self-concept is so poor and she has so little confidence that she fails at most things she tries."
2. A 37-year-old business executive says, "There has been so much pressure on me lately. Between work and family responsibilities, I feel like I'm just going to explode."
3. The mother of a 5-year-old boy reports, "My son can be an absolute monster. He has no respect for authority and always has to have things his own way or else he acts up."
4. Two college juniors, boyfriend and girlfriend, report, "We are either best friends or at each others' throats. We seem to have a Jekyll and Hyde relationship."
5. A 22-year-old woman says, "I have this habit of avoiding responsibility, and it makes me feel like a coward. I lost two jobs in the past 6 months because of my stupid attitude."

[a] This Participation Exercise can be completed before you continue reading or later.

DIRECT SELF-REPORT INVENTORIES

Direct self-report inventories are questionnaires containing brief statements or questions that require a simple response from the client, such as answering "yes" or "no" or rating how true a statement is on a 5-point scale. Behavioral self-report inventories are *direct* because they ask straightforward questions and because the answers are taken at face value. For instance, when a client responds "yes" or "often" to "I avoid going to parties," the answer provides information about a specific situation the client avoids. In contrast, the same answer might be used in traditional assessment to *indirectly infer* a trait of shyness.[18] This contrast illustrates how behavioral assessment is defined by the way in which assessment procedures are used rather than by the methods themselves.

One example of a self-report inventory is a **fear survey schedule**, which provides a list of events or stimuli that commonly evoke anxiety in people and asks clients to rate how fearful they are of each. A fear survey schedule for adults appears in Table 5-5.[19] Fear survey schedules for children include

TABLE **5-5**
Portion of a Fear Survey Schedule

Instructions: The items in this questionnaire are objects, experiences, or ideas that may cause fear, anxiety, or other unpleasant feelings. Using the scale below, write the appropriate number after each item to describe the degree to which the item causes you to feel fear, anxiety, or other unpleasant feelings.

$$1 = \text{Not at all}$$
$$2 = \text{A little}$$
$$3 = \text{A moderate amount}$$
$$4 = \text{Much}$$
$$5 = \text{Very much}$$

1. Open wounds	18. Cats	34. Going blind
2. Being alone	19. Being watched while working	35. Drowning
3. Public speaking		36. Examinations
4. Falling	20. Dirt	37. Cancer
5. Automobiles	21. Dogs	38. Fog
6. Being teased	22. Sick people	39. Being lost
7. Dentists	23. Fire	40. Police
8. Thunder	24. Mice	41. Talking on the telephone
9. Failure	25. Blood	
10. High places	26. Enclosed places	42. Death of a loved one
11. Receiving injections	27. Flying in airplanes	43. Pain
12. Strangers	28. Darkness	44. Suicide
13. Feeling angry	29. Lightning	45. War
14. Insects	30. Doctors	46. Going insane
15. Sudden noises	31. Losing control	47. Violence
16. Crowds	32. Making mistakes	48. Psychologists
17. Large open spaces	33. Older people	

Source: Developed by Spiegler & Liebert, 1970.

events that are likely to evoke fear in youngsters, such as being in the dark and being left alone.[20]

There are hundreds of direct self-report inventories that are used to assess the gamut of problem behaviors clients present, including fear and anxiety;[21] depressive behaviors;[22] social skills, including assertive behaviors;[23] health-related disorders, such as premenstrual syndrome, Type A behavior, and eating disorders;[24] sexual dysfunctions;[25] and marital problems.[26] Direct self-report inventories have been developed for adults[27] and children.[28] Table 5-6 provides examples of items that might appear on direct self-report inventories for different problem behaviors.

Direct self-report inventories are highly efficient, which is the major reason why they are used so frequently. Clients complete them on their own, and the inventories can be scored quickly. Because self-report inventories contain standard questions that pertain to people in general, they may not yield specific and detailed information about an individual client. Accordingly, self-report inventories are most useful for initial screening; subsequently, more individualized assessment, such as an interview or self-recording, can be conducted.

Self-report inventories that focus on a particular problem, such as the Beck Depression Inventory,[29] often are used as general measures of changes over the course of therapy. For example, it is standard practice in cognitive therapy for clients to complete the Beck Depression Inventory before each therapy session so that the therapist and client can evaluate changes since the previous session.

TABLE **5-6**

Examples of Items Used in Direct Self-Report Inventories
for Various Problems

Problem	Sample Item
Unassertive behavior	When the food you are served at a restaurant is not done to your satisfaction, you complain about it to the waiter or waitress. (*Agree* or *Disagree*)
Depression	I cry often. (*True* or *False*)
Anxiety/Fear	Enclosed spaces (Rate on scale from 1–5, with 1 being *no discomfort* and 5 being *extreme discomfort in the situation.*)
Obesity	I have one or more between-meal snacks each day. (*True* or *False*)
Sexual dysfunction	I become aroused by sexual fantasies. (*Agree* or *Disagree*)
Social skills	I often share my toys with other kids. (*Yes* or *No*)
Marital discord	My partner does not understand me. (*Usually, Sometimes,* or *Never*)

Are You in the Habit of Good Study Habits? Find Out with a Direct Self-Report Inventory[b]

What is it like to complete a direct self-report inventory? To see, write the numbers 1–15 on a sheet of paper, and then rate how often you engage in each of the 15 study habits, using the following scale.

3 = Consistently
2 = Usually
1 = Occasionally
0 = Rarely or never

1. I review my class notes each evening.
2. I study in a setting that is free of distractions.
3. I read assigned material before class but do not study it until shortly before the exam on the material.
4. I look up the meaning of words I do not know while I am reading.
5. I get a good night's sleep before important exams.
6. I use background music to relax me while I study.
7. I start studying for exams at least 3 days before the exam.
8. Before reading course material, I skim the reading to get an idea of what it includes.
9. While reading course material, I underline or highlight as many important points as possible rather than taking notes as I read.
10. I take practice tests (such as in a study guide) when they are available.
11. When I get back an exam, I make sure I know the correct answers to the questions that I got wrong.
12. If I do not understand something a teacher says in class, I write it in my notes and try to figure it out later.
13. I read the chapter summary before and after I read the chapter.
14. After completing a reading assignment, I write down the key ideas.
15. I read all my assignments at the same speed.

The major purpose of this exercise was to give you the experience of completing a direct self-report inventory. So, before checking "how you did," think about the experience. To what extent do you think the inventory adequately assessed your study skills? Were you completely honest in your responses? For instance, did you note any tendency to respond as you think you *should* study rather than how you *do* study? What advantages of self-report inventories emerged? What limitations did you become aware of?

If you'd like to score the inventory, first reverse the scoring of the items that describe poor study habits. For items 3, 6, 9, 12, and 15, change *3* to *0*, *2* to *1*, *1* to *2*, and *0* to *3*. Now add the scores for all 15 items. The higher the total (the closer to 45), the better are your study habits. You may find it helpful to consider changing the study habits that you assigned a *0* or a *1* (after reversing scores). Also, if you are unsure why a particular study habit is good or poor, consult with a teacher, your learning assistance center, or a book on study skills.

[b] This Participation Exercise can be completed before you continue reading or later.

SELF-RECORDING

With **self-recording** (or **self-monitoring**) clients observe and record their own behaviors. Self-recording capitalizes on the fact that clients almost always are available to observe and record their own behaviors. Compared with observations made by others, self-recording is time efficient, especially for infrequent behaviors (such as panic attacks) that would necessitate constant observation by another person.[30] Self-recordings can be made of both overt and covert behaviors, which can include emotions[31] and thoughts.[32] Clients' privacy is protected with self-recording, which is not the case when others make the observations.

In the simplest form of self-recording, clients record the behavior's frequency (number of times they engage in the behavior). This can be done, for example, by making tally marks on a small card or wrist band or by using an inexpensive golf or knitting counter (see Photos 5-1a, 5-1b, and 5-1c).[33] More elaborate recording devices exist,[34] such as a cigarette pack that indicates the number of cigarettes removed[35] and a pill-bottle cap containing a microchip that records bottle openings.[36]

What is recorded depends on the problem being treated. Records may include quantitative data, such as frequency and duration, as well as qualitative data, such as situation, time, mood, and thoughts. Clients are instructed to self-record relevant behaviors immediately after they occur.[37] The more retrospective the recordings are—even with a few minutes delay—the less accurate they tend to be.

Participation Exercise 5-3 provides an experience analogous to clients' self-recording overt behaviors. Because this exercise must be done over a number of days, you can't complete it now. However, read it now (and carry it out in the coming week) because some of the procedures involved in self-recording are discussed in the instructions.

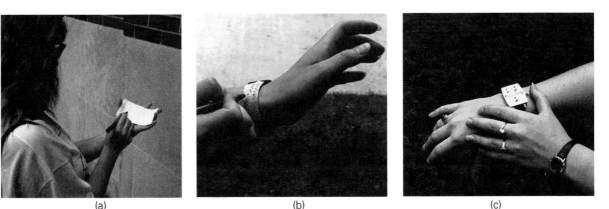

(a)   (b)   (c)

PHOTOS 5-1a, b, c

Examples of simple, inexpensive self-recording devices: (a) index card, (b) wrist band, and (c) golf counter

What Ya Doin'? Self-Recording

What is the experience of self-recording behaviors like for a client? Here's a chance to find out.

Before you begin self-recording, there are three preparatory steps.

1. First, choose a simple behavior to self-record. Examples might be reading, jogging, being late, day dreaming, text messaging, swearing, and listening to music. Whatever behavior you choose, be sure that (a) it is relatively easy to observe, (b) it can be quickly recorded without disrupting the behavior, and (c) it occurs at a moderate rate. If you perform the behavior very often (for example, blinking), it will be difficult to record; if you rarely engage in the behavior (for example, buying a new car), you will have nothing to record.
2. Decide on an appropriate unit of behavior (such as pages read, miles jogged, or minutes on the phone) and a unit of time (for example, per hour or per day) for the behavior.
3. Finally, devise a recording device. The simplest procedure is to divide a 3-by-5-inch index card into intervals and make a check mark each time you perform the behavior, as shown in Figure 5-1. At the end of your designated time period, total the number of check marks. Also include on your record brief notes about what is happening in your life while you are recording; they may help you understand variations in your rates of performing the behavior.

		Total Per Day
Mon.	☰☰ ☰☰ ☰☰ ☰☰ ☰☰ I	26
Tues.	☰☰ ☰☰ ☰☰ ☰☰ ☰☰ III	28
Wed.	☰☰ ☰☰ ☰☰ ☰☰ ☰☰ III	28
Thurs.	☰☰ ☰☰ ☰☰ ☰☰ ☰☰ ☰☰ ☰☰ ☰☰ ☰☰ ☰☰ ☰☰ I	56
Fri.	☰☰ ☰☰ ☰☰ ☰☰ ☰☰ ☰☰ ☰☰ ☰☰ ☰☰ ☰☰ ☰☰ II	57
Sat.	☰☰ ☰☰ ☰☰ ☰☰ ☰☰ ☰☰	30
Sun.		0
Sat. night big date		
Sun. slept till 1:30 PM		

FIGURE 5-1

Example of an index card record of pages read in a week

You are now ready to observe and record your behavior. Be sure you carry your index card (or other recording device) with you whenever you might be engaging in the behavior. Make your observations over the course of a week so that you can observe the behavior under various conditions.

When you have finished your observations, plot them on a graph on which the horizontal axis represents units of time and the vertical axis represents units of behavior (see Figure 5-2). The graph, along with your notes of what was happening during the recording, will provide a snapshot of the results of your self-recordings. For example, the graph in Figure 5-2 shows that the person read approximately the same number of pages (between 26 and 28) for the first 3 days. On Thursday the number of pages nearly doubled, and it remained the same on Friday. On Saturday the number of pages dropped to approximately the same rate as for Monday through Wednesday, perhaps because of a Saturday evening social engagement. And on the seventh day no pages were read (even God takes the seventh day off).

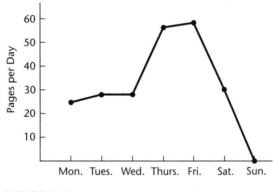

FIGURE 5-2
Graph of a week's reading

Your experiences in doing this exercise may have been similar to those of clients who are asked to self-record overt behaviors. For example, you may have found it inconvenient to record the behavior. Accordingly, you may have put off recording until later, which may have led to inaccurate recording or your forgetting to record altogether. You may have found that your behavior changed as a result of self-recording (which is called *reactivity*; see In Theory 5-2, page 94). Additionally, you may have learned something about your behavior, such as how often it actually occurs and the circumstances in which you engage in it more frequently and less frequently.

Self-recordings of covert behaviors, such as thoughts or feelings, are often brief qualitative descriptions of the behaviors and the circumstances in which they occur written in diaries or on simple forms,[38] such as the example in Figure 5-3. Covert behaviors also can be quantified, as in terms of frequency and duration. Intensity can be measured on a predetermined scale, such as the **Subjective Units of Discomfort scale** used to assess anxiety. The units of this scale, called **SUDs**, range from 0 to 100 (sometimes 0 to 10). Zero represents no anxiety; 100 represents the highest level of anxiety that the client can imagine.[39] As the word *subjective* implies, SUDs are relevant only for the individual client. Two people who report experiencing the same SUDs level are not necessarily experiencing equivalent degrees of discomfort; this means that comparisons between the two people cannot be made. However, the same person's SUDs levels can be compared at various times and in different situations. For instance, if a client reported experiencing 60 SUDs last week and 40 SUDs today in the same situation, then it is safe to conclude that the client is less anxious today. To see the usefulness of SUDs, complete Participation Exercise 5-4 over the next few days.

Date	Time	Place	Activity	Thoughts	Feelings
9/6	2:45 PM	home	watching TV	I'm wasting time. I'm lazy.	depressed helpless lonely
9/8	10:00 AM	work	on break	I'm going to have to stay late again to finish my work.	upset mad frustrated
9/13	7:30 PM	home	getting ready for a date	Will I look good enough? Will I say stupid things? What's going to happen at the end of the evening?	nervous anxious

FIGURE 5-3

Sample form used to record incidents of binge eating, including relevant environmental circumstances, thoughts, and feelings

Daily SUDsing

Choose a regularly occurring (at least daily) situation or experience in your life in which you generally feel uncomfortable. Whenever the situation occurs, rate your SUDs level (1–100), and record it on Work Sheet 5-1 (see your Student Resource Manual) along with a brief description of (1) your feelings and thoughts and (2) what is happening at the time. You can either have the work sheet with you all the time or a piece of paper to record the information on and transfer it to the work sheet later. Record a minimum of 10 instances of the situation you have chosen. Figure 5-4 shows a portion of a work sheet for a student who monitored her SUDs levels when she spoke up in her history class.

Situation: Speaking up in history class			
Date	**SUDs**	**Feelings and thoughts**	**What is happening**
9/4	80	Scared to death; I'm going to sound dumb	Professor asks our reasons for taking course
9/6	—		Didn't do anything
9/9	75	This is hard; butterflies	Answering questions from reading
9/11	70	Nervous; here I go again—better say something worthwhile	Joining discussion

FIGURE 5-4

A portion of a work sheet of SUDs levels, feelings and thoughts, and descriptions of what was happening each time a woman spoke up in her history class

After collecting your series of SUDs ratings, graph the ratings to provide an overall picture of how your level of discomfort varied. To account for the variations, consult your work sheet for particular circumstances that may have affected your level of discomfort.

Self-recording has three potential limitations. First, its usefulness depends on the client's ability and willingness to make careful and candid recordings. The accuracy of self-recording can be increased by simplifying recording procedures, recording as soon as possible after the observation is made, and having independent observers make occasional spot checks.

Second, self-recording interrupts ongoing activities. Clients usually must stop whatever they are doing, at least briefly, to record. If the target behavior occurs frequently, numerous interruptions will occur. Not surprisingly, clients may find self-recording irritating, which can result in their failing to record.

The third potential problem with self-recording is reactivity, where the act of self-recording a behavior influences the performance of the behavior, as In Theory 5-2 discusses.

might not be accurate —

IN THEORY **5-2** *Reacting to being observed — involves a behavior changing because its being observed.*

Reactivity

When clients are aware that their behaviors are being assessed, they may behave atypically. This phenomenon, known as **reactivity**, results in an inaccurate picture of the client's usual behaviors.[40] For example, when children self-monitor their remaining at an assigned task in the classroom, their on-task behaviors increase substantially.[41] Likewise, when clients monitor their self-destructive hair-pulling, the habitual behavior decreases dramatically.[42] Reactivity can occur whenever clients are aware that they are being assessed, which means it is a potential problem with naturalistic observation, simulated observation, and role-playing as well as self-recording, which we are focusing on here.

The consequences of self-recording may influence reactivity.[43] Clients may find recording their behaviors annoying and bothersome and thus self-recording becomes an aversive consequence, which reduces

its occurrence. Conversely, recording a behavior may serve as positive feedback if the behavior is one the client wants to increase, which will increase its occurrence.

Self-recording does not always result in reactivity, and some measures tend to be more reactive than others. For instance, self-recording caloric intake may result in weight loss for some clients, but self-recording eating habits is not likely to be associated with weight loss.[44] Thus, one way to reduce reactivity is to employ measures that tend to be less reactive.

On one hand, reactivity is a problem when accurate information about the current status of a client's target behavior is required, such as to establish a baseline level. On the other hand, if the client's self-recording changes the target behavior in the desired direction, why not harness reactivity in the service of therapy? In fact, self-recording

occasionally is used as a therapy procedure.[45] For example, in the treatment of panic disorder, self-monitoring of panic attacks focuses on the specifics of the experience, such as SUDs and the length of episodes. This specific self-monitoring creates *objective self-awareness* in contrast to global, exaggerated assessments (for example, "This is unbearable; I'm totally out of control") and thus lowers anxiety.[46] Self-monitoring also serves an essential therapeutic function in instances where clients are unaware of the extent of their problems, as with eating disorders[47] and nervous habits (such as tics).[48] In general, however, the changes produced through self-recording tend to be relatively small and short-lived.[49] Accordingly, self-recording as a therapy procedure typically is employed as one component of a treatment package rather than as the sole treatment.

THE FAR SIDE® By GARY LARSON

"Anthropologists! Anthropologists!"

All of the behavioral assessment methods we've looked at so far—interviews, self-report inventories, and self-recording—are *self-report* measures. Behavior therapists frequently use self-report measures because they have some distinct advantages over other methods of assessment. They also have distinct limitations. Both the pros and cons of self-report methods of behavioral assessment are the subject of In Theory 5-3.

IN THEORY **5-3**

The Boons and Banes of Self-Reports

By far the simplest and most efficient way for a behavior therapist to gather treatment-relevant information about clients is to ask them

directly. The information comes in the form of answers to interview questions, responses to a self-report inventory, or data collected through

self-recording. If the information is valid, it can be extremely useful in therapy; however, its validity depends on clients' ability and willingness to provide honest and accurate answers. This may not occur for various reasons, including the inclination to present oneself in a favorable light (for example, to please the therapist), the tendency to overestimate or underestimate one's own behaviors, and the frequent discrepancy between what people say and what they do.

Still, self-report measures are the major means of assessing clients' covert behaviors—how they are feeling and what they are thinking. Further, for some problems behaviors, subjective self-report is the standard measure of the success of therapy. This is the case with marital problems, where relationship satisfaction is paramount,[50] and sexual dysfunctions, where couple satisfaction with improvements is the best measure of success.[51]

Self-report measures are frequently used in behavior therapy because of their efficiency and the useful information they can provide. Whenever feasible, however, independent measures that do not rely on clients' self-reports are used to corroborate the findings from self-report measures. For instance, a man who indicates on a self-report inventory that he has difficulty asserting his desires could role-play situations with the therapist requiring such assertive behaviors, or a close friend could be asked to observe his reactions when such assertive responses are appropriate. If the information gathered from different methods of assessment is consistent, then the therapist can rely on it and use it to guide the client's therapy.

BEHAVIORAL CHECKLISTS AND RATING SCALES

Checklists and rating scales are similar in format to self-report inventories, but they are completed by someone other than the client, such as a parent, teacher, or spouse. Checklists and rating scales list potential problem behaviors. With a **checklist**, the informant checks off those behaviors that are problematic for the client. With a **rating scale**, the informant evaluates each behavior by indicating how frequently it occurs or how severe it is. Thus, rating scales provide more information than checklists.[52] Checklists and rating scales are both completed retrospectively; that is, they are based on the informant's recollections of the client's behaviors. For example, after school hours a teacher might complete a checklist of a student's behaviors that day.

Although checklists and rating scales typically are used to assess target behaviors, they also can be used to identify maintaining conditions. For example, using the Children's Headache Assessment Scale, parents rate environmental antecedents associated with their child's headaches.[53]

Many checklists and rating scales have been developed for both adults and children.[54] Some are broad, measuring problem behaviors in general; others are narrow, assessing specific problem areas. For example, the Child Behavior Checklist includes 113 common problem areas associated with childhood.[55] In contrast, the Children's Attention Profile is a rating scale designed specifically to assess inattention and hyperactivity in children within a classroom setting (see Figure 5-5).[56]

Checklists and rating scales are efficient ways to assess behaviors; most can be completed in less than 15 minutes (some take just a few minutes). Because they are completed retrospectively, reactivity is not a concern. Generally, checklists and rating scales are used for initial screening purposes and as global measures of change, and sometimes they are used to select target behaviors.[57]

The utility of checklists and rating scales depends on informants' accurately observing the client's behaviors and then making reliable ratings.[58]

CAP Rating Scale

Child's Name:	FOR OFFICE USE ONLY
Today's Date:	
Filled Out By:	

Below is a list of items that describes pupils. For each item that describes the pupil *now* or *within the past week*, check whether the item is Not True, Somewhat or Sometimes True, or Very or Often True. Please check all items as well as you can, even if some do not seem to apply to this pupil.

	Not True	Somewhat or Sometimes True	Very or Often True
1. Fails to finish things he/she starts	☐	☐	☐
2. Can't concentrate, can't pay attention for long	☐	☐	☐
3. Can't sit still, restless, or hyperactive	☐	☐	☐
4. Fidgets	☐	☐	☐
5. Daydreams or gets lost in his/her thoughts	☐	☐	☐
6. Impulsive or acts without thinking	☐	☐	☐
7. Difficulty following directions	☐	☐	☐
8. Talks out of turn	☐	☐	☐
9. Messy work	☐	☐	☐
10. Inattentive, easily distracted	☐	☐	☐
11. Talks too much	☐	☐	☐
12. Fails to carry out assigned tasks	☐	☐	☐

Please feel free to write any comments about the pupil's work or behavior in the last week.

FIGURE 5-5

The Children's Attention Profile

Source: Adapted from © 1986 Craig Edelbrock.

Reliability in general, refers to the consistency or dependability of observations. The specific type of reliability germane to checklists and rating scales is **interrater reliability**, which is the degree to which two or more raters agree. It is measured by comparing the responses of the raters and calculating the percentage of agreement.

Participation Exercise 5-5 gives you a chance to use a behavioral checklist—and probably have fun in the process.

PARTICIPATION
EXERCISE 5-5

Checking Out a Professor[c]

The checklist in this exercise, like most behavioral checklists, will take only a few minutes to complete. Table 5-7 contains a list of 40 behaviors in which professors might engage. Choose one of your current or past professors whose class you have been in for at least a month. Using Work Sheet 5-2 (see your Student Resource Manual), place a check mark next to each of the behaviors that the professor has performed on *at least one occasion*. Complete the checklist anytime you are not in the professor's class, which is analogous to how checklists are used in behavioral assessment.

To determine how reliable your responses to the checklist are, you will need the help of another student who has been in the professor's class. Ask this student to fill out the checklist using the duplicate copy of Work Sheet 5-2 (see your Student Resource Manual). Then compare your two checklists to obtain your interrater reliability. Count the number of times you both have responded the same way (either both of you checked a behavior or both of you left it blank). Divide the number of instances that you had the same response by 40 (the total possible agreements you could have), and multiply by 100. This percentage of agreement is a measure of your interrater reliability.

Doing this Participation Exercise should give you some insight into the checklist method. Obviously, it can be done quickly. Did you have any

TABLE **5-7**
Behaviors in Which a Professor Might Engage

Paces	Coughs	Drinks coffee in class
Fumbles with notes	Makes eye contact	Ridicules students
Arrives late	Speaks softly	Listens attentively to students
Speaks in monotone	Keeps class late	
Talks with hands	Picks nose	Gives hard exams
Smiles	Rubs eyes	Tells personal stories
Taps pen on desk	Strokes beard	Falls asleep
Pauses for long time	Tells jokes	Cracks knuckles
Plays with hair	Stutters	Uses blackboard
Talks rapidly	Loses train of thought	Talks to students before class
Hums		
Dismisses class early	Argues with students	Talks to students after class
Checks watch	Reads notes	
Sits on desk	Fiddles with clothing	Cancels class
	Repeats self	Takes attendance

[c]You should complete the checklist before you continue reading, but you will need to check your interrater reliability later.

problems completing the checklist? Were you clear about what each behavior referred to so that you could easily say whether you've noticed the professor engaging in each behavior? How reliable were your observations? Any ambiguity in what was meant by the behaviors on the checklist would lower interrater reliability. What other factors might account for your having less than 100% agreement?

most accurate method

SYSTEMATIC NATURALISTIC OBSERVATION

test

Systematic naturalistic observation consists of observing and recording a client's specific, predetermined overt target behaviors as the client naturally engages in them.[59] Precise definitions of the behaviors, including criteria for differentiating each target behavior from similar behaviors, are essential. Table 5-8 contains sample definitions of three different target behaviors along

TABLE **5-8**

Sample Definitions of Target Behaviors and Examples that Fit or Do Not Fit the Definitions, Which Would be Used for Behavioral Observations

---

PHYSICALLY AGGRESSIVE BEHAVIORS

Definition: The client physically strikes another person with any part of his or her body or with an object, with potential for inflicting pain on the other person.

Examples: Hitting, slapping, punching, tripping, tackling, pushing, biting, kicking, throwing an object at another person, hitting another person with a stick.

Nonexamples: Spitting, making faces, calling another person names, making verbal threats or threatening gestures at another person.

VERBALLY EXPRESSING ADMIRATION

Definition: The client verbally praises, compliments, expresses a liking or admiration for another person, or expresses a sense of awe about another person's behavior or accomplishment.

Examples: "You did a nice job," "I really like you," "You look very handsome," "How did you get that done so quickly?" "I enjoy talking with you very much," "Your fast ball is incredible."

Nonexamples: "Would you like to have dinner with me?" "How about a kiss?" "What do you know, he finally got a good grade" (a backhanded compliment), hugging, kissing, embracing, or any other physical show of affection without concomitant verbal affection.

INITIATING SOCIAL CONTACT

Definition: (1) The client initiates social contact by verbally greeting or *starting* an interaction with another person, (2) uses a neutral or pleasant tone of voice when talking to the person, (3) directly looks at the person when initiating contact, and (4) is within 15 feet of the other person at the time the social contact is begun.

(continued)

TABLE **5-8** (*continued*)

Examples: Introducing oneself to another person, asking another person a question (for example, "Can you please tell me where the exit is?"), calling another person by name, or starting a conversation with another person through a comment (for instance, "The team played well today").

Nonexamples: Yelling at or otherwise using an unpleasant tone of voice, talking to another person *only* after that person initiated the contact, talking to someone without looking at the person, or initiating social contact from a distance of greater than 15 feet.

with examples of behaviors that are consistent and inconsistent with the definition.

The type of measure used—such as frequency, time, or strength—depends on the nature of the target behavior and the purpose of the assessment.[60] When observations are made *continuously* over a relatively brief time, such as an hour or two, considerable observer time is required. A more efficient procedure is *time sampling*, in which observations are restricted to specific time intervals, such as the first 5 minutes of each hour.[61] Devices used to make recordings range from simple to complex and include paper and pencil; clocks and counters; electromechanical devices, such as event recorders and keyboards; and audio and video recordings.

Training observer—who are often nonprofessionals, such as parents, teachers, and psychiatric technicians—is essential.[62] Observers first study the definitions of the behaviors and familiarize themselves with the recording system. They then practice making observations until their observations are highly accurate, which is determined by **interobserver reliability** (the equivalent of interrater reliability). The minimum level of acceptable agreement among observers usually is between 80% and 90%.[63]

Systematic naturalistic observation has three potential problems: reactivity, observer error or bias, and impracticality.

Reactivity is a common occurrence when clients are observed by others, just as it is for people in everyday circumstances. Sometimes our performance is enhanced by others observing our behavior, as when children in a race run faster because their parents are watching. In other instances, we may perform less well because we are being watched, such as when we are trying to write a paper and someone is looking over our shoulder as we type.

The fundamental principle used to reduce reactivity during naturalistic observation is to minimize clients' awareness that they are being observed. This involves making *unobtrusive observations*, such as when the observer is out of sight or a hidden camera records the behavior.

When unobtrusive observations are not possible, reactivity may be minimized by an **adaptation period** in which clients become accustomed to the observation procedures before the actual observations begin.[64] In this way, they may ignore or forget about the fact that their behavior is being observed.

PHOTO 5-2

Systematic naturalistic observation of a 4-year-old child interacting with her peers in a preschool playground. Following an adaptation period, the children have become accustomed to the observer's presence.

For example, if a child were being observed in a classroom, the observer might simulate recording observations (for example, by taking notes on a clipboard) in the room for short periods over the course of a few days before starting the actual observations. It is likely that the children will adapt to the observer's presence, much as we tend to stop noticing a new piece of furniture after it has been in a room for a while.

Most observational errors occur because the behaviors being observed are not clearly and unambiguously defined. Even when the behaviors are clearly defined, observers' personal biases may make the observations invalid. For example, observers' expectations about how the target behaviors are likely to change as a result of therapy are a major source of bias.[65] Failure to take into account the cultural context of behaviors is another source of bias. Consider the following interaction observed in an African-American family.[66]

Adolescent: I thought you were my friend.

Parent: I am no pal to you.

European-American observers recorded this interaction as "harsh discipline." However, African-American observers, who were familiar with the cultural context, recorded it as "constructive discipline." Cultural issues must be considered when using standard observational codes because codes developed for one population may not apply to other populations.[67]

Assessment through systematic naturalistic observations often is impractical.[68] Considerable observer time is required, such as for training, travel to the client's natural environment, and the actual observations. If the client performs the target behavior infrequently, an observer may spend an inordinate amount of time waiting for it to occur. Further, naturalistic observation may not be possible because it invades a client's privacy, as would be the case in a client's home or professional office. When these practical or ethical limitations make systematic naturalistic observation impractical, simulated observation is an alternative.

SIMULATED OBSERVATION

In **simulated observation**, conditions are set up to resemble the natural environment in which the client's problem is occurring.[69] The observation often takes place in a room that allows observers to see and hear the client through a one-way mirror and intercom (see Photo 5-3). Having the observers out of sight generally minimizes reactivity. Simulated observation is more efficient than systematic naturalistic observation in terms of the observers' time.[70]

Using simulated observations, behavior therapists can test hypotheses concerning external maintaining conditions by systematically varying them and observing changes in the client's target behavior.[71] For example, suppose the therapist suspects that a couple communicates least effectively when they talk about financial matters. To test this hypothesis, the therapist can observe

Cary Wolinsky/stock, Boston

PHOTO 5-3

Observing a child's aggressive behaviors from behind a one-way mirror the couple interacting while they attempt to solve problems concerning money and a variety of other issues.[72]

A **behavioral approach** (or **avoidance**) **test** is a simulated observation procedure used to assess fear.[73] The therapist asks a client to engage in a series of steps that involve progressively more fear-inducing behaviors. The number of steps the client can complete is used as a measure of fear. For example, to assess how fearful a client is of snakes, the therapist might ask the client to (1) approach a snake that is in a glass cage 20 feet away; (2) put on gloves and touch the snake; (3) then hold the snake for a moment; (4) next take off the gloves and touch the snake; (5) then hold the snake for a moment; and finally (6) pick up the snake, walk to a chair, and sit down with the snake in his or her lap.

Therapists sometimes use simulated observation procedures that have been previously developed and validated for particular problems. An example is the Restricted Academic Situations Test, which assesses children's ability to pay attention while working independently on written assignments in the classroom.[74] The child is seated at a desk in an observation room and told to complete a written assignment while remaining seated at the desk. From behind a one-way mirror, the therapist records the child's behaviors in 30-second intervals for 20 minutes. The specific behaviors recorded are leaving the seat, playing with objects around the desk, fidgeting in the seat, talking out loud, and looking away from the written work. The observer simply places a check mark in the appropriate behavior category if the client engages in the behavior during the 30-second interval. The proportion of time the child engages in each behavior provides data that can be used to pinpoint target behaviors and assess progress during and after therapy.

The primary limitation of simulated observation concerns the ability to generalize from observations made under a simulated condition to the client's natural environment. The more closely the simulation approximates the natural conditions, the greater will be the generalizability.[75]

ROLE-PLAYING

simulate the real world

In **role-playing** clients enact problem situations to provide the therapist with samples of how they typically behave in those situations. Role-playing is especially useful in assessing social skills, such as assertive behaviors.[76]

Role-playing is an efficient form of simulated observation. No special physical arrangements are needed because the relevant environmental conditions are imagined—clients act *as if* they were in the problem situation. With interpersonal problems, the therapist plays the roles of other people. For example, a client who reported difficulty in giving her secretary work was asked to make work-related requests of the therapist, who played the role of the secretary.

The more clients are able to behave *as if* they were in the actual situations, the more likely it is that the behaviors observed will be valid indications of how they typically act. Many clients initially feel uneasy or awkward engaging in role-playing. With practice, however, most clients can "get into" it. The therapist also must be able to play roles realistically, which requires *specific* knowledge of how other people interact with the client. This includes avoiding stereotypic concepts of role relationships, such as how fathers "typically" deal with sons. Reactivity is a potential problem in role-playing, as when clients act more appropriately during role-playing than they typically do in actual situations.

PHYSIOLOGICAL MEASUREMENTS

When physiological components of a target behavior are relevant to treatment, physiological responses are measured. The most frequent measures are heart rate, blood pressure, respiration rate, muscle tension, and skin electrical conductivity (a common measure of anxiety).[77] These responses are used to assess complex behaviors, such as feeling anxious[78] and being sexually aroused.[79] Physiological responses can be the sole target behavior, as when lowering a client's blood pressure is the aim of relaxation training for hypertension.

Physiological measurements most often are carried out in specially equipped research laboratories. The high cost of the instrumentation required to obtain accurate physiological measures precludes general application in most clinics or private offices. Ideally, physiological recordings should be made in clients' natural environments as their problems are occurring. Portable measurement devices can be used for this purpose, but they generally are less accurate than stationary laboratory apparatus.

Physiological measurements are no more valid than any other assessment method, although people sometimes give them more credence either because they seem to be "pure" measures or because hi-tech equipment is used.

One physiological measure that requires no equipment and that clients can easily assess themselves in their natural environments is heart rate (as indicated by one's pulse), which can be used to measure anxiety. If you'd like to monitor your heart rate and see how it changes in various situations, complete Participation Exercise 5-6 over the course of the next few days.

PARTICIPATION EXERCISE 5-6

Getting to the Heart of the Matter: Measuring Your Pulse

In this exercise you will compare your heart rate at rest and in anxiety-evoking situations in your daily life. Because people's normal or resting heart rates can differ widely, *changes* in heart rate from one's resting base rate are used, rather than the absolute rate.

Part I: Taking Your Pulse

You can easily take your pulse from either your radial artery or carotid artery. To locate the radial artery, remove anything you are wearing on your wrist and turn your palm upward. Place the three middle fingers of your other hand over the thumb side of your wrist, as shown in Photo 5-4. To locate the carotid artery, gently place the three middle fingers of one hand along the opposite side of your neck, as shown in Photo 5-5. Take your pulse from both your radial and carotid arteries, and use the one that is stronger.

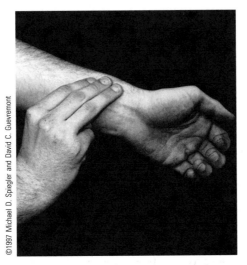

PHOTO 5-4
Placement of fingers for taking the radial pulse

PHOTO 5-5
Placement of fingers for taking the carotid pulse

Part II: Assessing Your Resting Heart Rate

To measure your resting heart rate, lie or sit comfortably and get relaxed. When you feel very relaxed, count your pulse for 15 seconds; then, continue to relax for another minute. Again, count your pulse for 15 seconds. Add these two counts, and multiply by 2 to get your resting heart rate.

(continued)

**PARTICIPATION
EXERCISE 5-6**
(continued)

Record your resting pulse in the upper left hand corner of Work Sheet 5-3 (see your Student Resource Manual).

Part III: Assessing Your Heart Rate In Vivo

Over the next few days, carry the work sheet with you. When you find yourself in a situation in which you feel some anxiety (for example, before an exam is handed out), take your pulse for 15 seconds and multiply by 4; write your pulse rate in the "Rate per minute" column of the work sheet. Then, rate your anxiety on a scale of 1 to 5, where 1 is calm and 5 is very anxious; write the number in the "Anxiety rating" column. Next, in the "Circumstances" column, write a brief description of the situation you are in at the time. Finally, subtract your resting pulse from your rate per minute, and write the difference in the "Change" column; use a minus sign if your rate per minute is less than your resting pulse. Check your pulse in at least five different situations in which you experience anxiety.

Part IV: Evaluation

Most likely, you will find that your heart rates for the anxiety-producing situations are higher (positive changes) than your resting pulse rate; however, some people's heart rates decrease when they are anxious, which is another reason that *change* rather than absolute rate is used. In either case, by comparing the numbers in the last two columns, you may see a correlation between your heart rate changes and your anxiety ratings.

Now that you have learned about each of the eight major methods of behavioral assessment, we can illustrate the multimethod/multimodal nature of behavioral assessment with the case of a woman who was treated for excessive anger and violent behaviors.

CASE **5-1**
Behavioral Assessment in a Case of Domestic Violence

Tina T. was a 36-year-old college graduate who worked as a computer sales representative. She had a 5-year history of violence toward her husband and 10-year-old daughter. Tina contacted a behavior therapist when her husband threatened to move to another city with their daughter if she did not seek help.

In the initial interview, Tina admitted that she had a serious problem, which she described as "uncontrollable fits of anger." The therapist asked Tina a series of questions to elucidate the nature of her problem and its maintaining conditions. The questions included:

1. When you have an "uncontrollable fit of anger," what do you do? How do you feel? What are you thinking? What bodily reactions do you experience?

2. What seems to precipitate your "anger fits"? Are they associated with something your husband or daughter says or does? Are there any situations that make you more prone to have a "fit"? Where do your "fits" usually occur? Who is there at the time? At what time of day and on which days of the week do they occur? What feelings and thoughts do you have right before an "anger fit"?

3. What happens after your "anger fits"? How do your husband and daughter react to your "fits"? What do they do and say? How long do their reactions last? What do you do after your "fits"? How do you feel and what thoughts run through your mind afterwards?

4. What strategies have you used to deal with your problem and how successful have they been?

In the initial interview, Tina told the therapist that her "anger fits" initially involved yelling and cursing, then throwing objects at her daughter and husband, and finally beating them with her fists and household objects. She became angry whenever she was frustrated about a situation she believed she could not handle (such as unreasonable demands from others). Her "fits" most often occurred shortly after returning home from work. A "fit," which rarely lasted more than 5 minutes, would gradually subside and become less violent as she "vented her anger." At that point, she would start to cry and beg for her family's forgiveness, which usually was forthcoming.

Other assessment procedures were instituted to confirm the accuracy of the information Tina gave in the interview and to provide additional data.

1. Tina filled out the Novaco Anger Inventory that assesses anger reactions in a wide array of situations.[80] The inventory contains descriptions of 80 situations, and clients rate the degree of anger they would expect to feel if the situation actually occurred.

2. Tina started an *anger diary* in which she (a) described each instance when she became angry, (b) rated the intensity of her anger (using a scale ranging from "no anger" to "rage"), (c) noted how she reacted to her own anger (including overt and covert behaviors), and (d) described the consequences of her reactions.[81] The anger diary provided the therapist with information about the situations that elicited Tina's anger, the ways in which she typically responded, and the consequences of her anger. It also helped Tina become more aware of her anger and her reactions to it. Tina continued to use the anger diary during therapy as an ongoing measure of her progress.

3. To directly observe her behaviors, the therapist visited Tina's house on three consecutive Tuesdays shortly after she had arrived home from work. Besides assessing Tina's aggressive acts toward her daughter and husband (for example, yelling and hitting), the therapist recorded positive behaviors (such as praising and physical affection). Using a modified Patterson Coding System[82] that listed 18 different aggressive and positive behaviors, the therapist recorded each of these behaviors that he observed Tina perform over the course of 30 minutes.

(continued)

CASE **5-1** (*continued*)

4. In the third therapy session, Tina and her therapist role-played several troublesome situations that the therapist learned about from her anger diary and the anger inventory. The therapist played the role of either her husband or daughter and observed Tina's reactions to provocations. Tina's heart rate and blood pressure were monitored during the role-playing and compared with baseline recordings taken when Tina was calm.

On the basis of the information gathered from these assessment procedures, the therapist and Tina designed a treatment plan for two related behaviors: positive interactions with family members and adaptive reactions to frustration. The systematic naturalistic observations in Tina's home had revealed that Tina rarely had positive interactions with her husband and daughter. Thus, one component of Tina's therapy involved teaching her specific ways to engage positively with her family. In both the home observations and role-playing, the therapist observed that Tina reacted to provocation impulsively. Accordingly, Tina was taught strategies to help her pause and think before reacting through self-instructional training (reminding herself to pause and think). From the interview, anger diary, and home observations, it became clear that a critical maintaining consequence of her anger and aggression was the sympathetic responses from her family to the remorse Tina expressed after a "fit." Consequently, Tina's husband and daughter were asked to withhold sympathy when Tina indicated that she was sorry about an "anger fit."

Tina's anger diary provided a continuous measure of her progress over the course of the 5½ months of her therapy, and it showed a steady improvement. Two home observations in the last weeks of therapy indicated that Tina now handled frustration and other potential provocations with restraint and often with prosocial responses. At the end of therapy, Tina again filled out the anger inventory; both the number of different situations that evoked anger and the intensity of the anger she experienced had decreased significantly. Additionally, role-playing with concurrent physiological recording during the last therapy session showed that Tina became less aroused to potentially provocative situations and that she responded in more socially appropriate ways than she had at the beginning of therapy. Two follow-up telephone interviews with Tina, 6 and 12 months after treatment, indicated that her anger and violence were no longer problematic for her or for her family.

Case 5-1 highlights the essentials of behavioral assessment. Assessment procedures supplied information to clarify the problem, design target behaviors, identify maintaining conditions, and then design a treatment plan and monitor the client's progress. The assessment proceeded in a stepwise fashion, by cumulatively gathering and substantiating data. Employing a multimethod/multimodal approach provided a comprehensive assessment. Finally, treatment and assessment were closely linked.

[handwritten: most valid method of assessment depends on the behavior being assessed.]

ALL THINGS CONSIDERED: BEHAVIORAL ASSESSMENT

[handwritten: they all have advantages and disadvantages]

If we liken behavior therapy to a pilot, behavioral assessment is the navigator. Behavioral assessment determines the direction in which therapy will proceed, provides the necessary course corrections along the way, and indicates when the destination has been reached.

Each behavioral assessment method has its strengths and limitations. Multimethod assessment helps overcome the limitations of single methods and provides more complete information about clients' problems. Multimodal assessment, because it examines different facets of the problem behavior, can result in more effective treatment. For example, anxiety may involve a client's thoughts, feelings, and actions. To assess only one of these modes might result in incomplete treatment. Different modes of a problem behavior may be optimally assessed by different methods because assessment methods vary in their ability to tap each mode of behavior[83] (as you saw in Table 5-2, pages 79–80). In addition, information gathered by one assessment method may be verified by other methods.

In this chapter, we have sketched a picture of behavioral assessment at the beginning of the new millennium. Behavioral assessment has evolved over the past 50 years, and its basic nature continues to change. For example, historically, behavioral assessment (and therapy) focused on overt behaviors. Behavior therapists considered systematic naturalistic observation the optimal method of assessment and viewed self-report measures as less valid.

Today, systematic naturalistic observation is no longer considered the sine qua non of behavioral assessment.[84] However, systematic naturalistic observation remains a highly desirable method for many target behaviors,[85] and it may be used in research.[86] Self-report methods, such as direct self-report inventories and self-recording, have become more popular both because of their efficiency and their ability to directly tap cognitive and emotional modes of behavior, which is not possible with systematic naturalistic observation.[87]

Although assessment has always been important in behavior therapy, advances in behavioral assessment have escalated in recent years, especially in the development of self-report inventories. There also has been an increased recognition of the need to design assessment techniques that are appropriate for clients from diverse cultural backgrounds.[88]

SUMMARY

1. Behavioral assessment is an indispensable part of behavior therapy. Behavioral assessment gathers information to clarify the problem, set initial goals, design target behaviors, identify maintaining conditions, and then design a treatment plan and monitor the client's progress.

2. Behavioral assessment is multimethod (using more than one method of assessment) and multimodal (assessing more than one mode of behavior).

3. Behavioral assessment procedures are individualized, focus on the present, directly sample relevant behaviors, are narrowly focused, and are integrated with therapy.

4. Generally, diagnosis of disorders is antithetical to the fundamental premises of behavioral assessment and behavior therapy. The behavioral alternative involves detailed descriptions of client's unique problems and their specific maintaining conditions.

5. Behavioral assessment procedures examine samples of a client's behaviors to provide information about how the client typically behaves in particular situations. This approach contrasts with traditional assessment in which the behaviors assessed are used as signs of traits or psychological states.

6. An interview is usually the first assessment method used. Besides their role in assessment, initial behavioral interviews are used to establish rapport with the client and to educate the client about the behavioral approach. To gather information about a client's problem and its maintaining conditions, behavioral interviews focus on the present and ask questions concerning what, when, where, and how often rather than why.

7. Direct self-report inventories are questionnaires containing brief statements or questions that require a simple response or rating. They are highly efficient and are often used for initial screening. Their validity depends on clients' responding honestly and accurately.

8. Self-recording involves clients' observing and keeping records of their own behaviors. It is time efficient and can be used to assess both covert and overt behaviors. Clients must be motivated to self-record and must make accurate recordings. Reactivity—a change in clients' behaviors because they know they are being observed—is a potential problem with most observational assessment procedures.

9. Behavioral checklists and rating scales contain lists of potential problem behaviors about which someone who knows the client well responds. With checklists, the informant indicates all the behaviors the client performs. With rating scales, the informant uses a scale of frequency or severity to evaluate the client on each behavior. Checklists and rating scales are efficient assessment methods.

10. Systematic naturalistic observations are made in the situations in which target behaviors normally occur. These observations are most accurate when the target behaviors are clearly defined and observers are well trained. The reliability of the observations is assessed by comparing the observations of two or more independent observers. Potential problems with systematic naturalistic observations are reactivity, observer error and bias, and impracticality.

11. Simulated observations are made under conditions set up to resemble the client's natural environment. A one-way observation mirror often is used. A potential limitation is the ability to generalize what is observed in the simulation to the client's natural environment.

12. In role-playing, a form of simulated observation, clients enact problem situations to provide the therapist with a sample of how they typically behave. Generalization to the natural environment can be limited because when clients role-play they may behave differently from the way they typically do.
13. Physiological measurements assess physiological responses associated with the target behavior.
14. Each behavioral assessment method has its strengths and limitations. Multimethod/multimodal assessment helps overcome the limitations of single methods and provides more complete information about clients' problems.
15. Initially, behavioral assessment focused on overt behaviors and systematic naturalistic observations. Today, direct self-report inventories and self-recording that can tap cognitive and emotional modes of behavior frequently are employed.

REFERENCE NOTES

1. Guevremont & Spiegler, 1990; compare with Swan & MacDonald, 1978.
2. King, Ollendick, Murphy, & Tibge, 1997; Schwartz, Houlihan, Krueger, & Simon, 1997.
3. Eifert & Wilson, 1991; Kazdin, 1992; Peterson & Bell-Dolan, 1995.
4. Compare with Jorgensen & Carey, 1994; Lazarus, 1989a.
5. For example, Wilfley, Schwartz, Spurrell, & Fairburn, 1997.
6. Goldfried & Sprafkin, 1974.
7. American Psychiatric Association, 1994.
8. American Psychiatric Association, 2000a.
9. Tryon, 1999.
10. Compare with Kutchins & Kirk, 1995.
11. Harvey, Watkins, Mansell, & Shafran, 2004.
12. Allen, McHugh, & Barlow, 2008.
13. Fairburn, 2008: Fairburn, Cooper, Shafran, & Wilson, 2008.
14. For example, Rosenhan, 1973.
15. Goldfried & Sprafkin, 1974.
16. For example, Storey, Lawry, Ashworth, Danko, & Strain, 1994.
17. For example, McGill, Teer, Rye, & Hughes, 2005.
18. Liebert & Spiegler, 1994.
19. For example, Geer, 1965; Spiegler & Liebert, 1970; Wolpe & Lang, 1964.
20. McCathie & Spence, 1991; Ollendick, 1983; Ramirez & Kratochwill, 1990.
21. Beidel, Turner, & Morris, 1995; Glass & Arnkoff, 1994; Nietzel, Bernstein, & Russell, 1988.
22. Beck & Steer, 1993; Rehm, 1988.
23. Becker & Heimberg, 1988.
24. Williamson, Davis, & Prather, 1988.
25. McConaghy, 1988.
26. For example, Margolin, Michelli, & Jacobson, 1988; Snyder, 1997.
27. For example, Peters, 2000; Sedlar & Hansen, 2001.
28. For example, Burham & Gullone, 1997; Reitman, Hummel, Franz, & Gross, 1998.
29. Beck & Steer, 1993.
30. For example, Craske & Barlow, 2008.
31. For example, Allen, McHugh, & Barlow, 2008.
32. Franklin & Foa, 2008.
33. Lindsley, 1968.
34. Schwitzgebel & Schwitzgebel, 1973.
35. Azrin & Powell, 1968.
36. Chamberlin, 2008.
37. For example, Fairburn, Cooper, Shafran, & Wilson, 2008.
38. For example, Allen, McHugh, & Barlow, 2008; Miklowitz, 2008.
39. Wolpe & Lazarus, 1966; see also Spiegler & Agigian, 1977, p. 100.
40. For example, Johnson & Bolstad, 1973; Kirby, Fowler, & Bear, 1991.
41. Reid, 1996.

42. Rothbaum, 1992.
43. Kazdin, 1974e.
44. Green, 1978.
45. For example, Clees, 1994–1995; Critchfield & Vargas, 1991; Maletzky, 1974.
46. Craske & Barlow, 2008.
47. Fairburn, Cooper, Shafran, & Wilson, 2008.
48. Miltenberger, Fuqua, & McKinley, 1985.
49. Thoresen & Mahoney, 1974.
50. Christensen, Atkins, Yi, Baucom, & George, 2006.
51. Rosen, Goldstein, & Huang, 2007.
52. Aiken, 1996.
53. Budd, Workman, Lemsky, & Quick, 1994.
54. Gross & Wixted, 1988; Morrison, 1988.
55. Achenbach, 1978.
56. For example, Guevremont, DuPaul, & Barkley, 1990.
57. Gross & Wixted, 1988.
58. Glaser, Kronsnoble, & Worner Forkner, 1997; Smith, Pelham, Gnagy, Molina, & Evans, 2000.
59. For example, Cook, Peterson, & DiLillo, 1999; Hummel & Gross, 2001.
60. Foster, Bell-Dolan, & Burge, 1988.
61. For example, Davis & Chittum, 1994.
62. For example, Barton & Ascione, 1984; Hartmann & Wood, 1982.
63. Hartmann, 1982.
64. Haynes, 1978.
65. Kent & Foster, 1977; Rosenthal, 1969.
66. Cauce, 1995.
67. Markman, Leber, Cordova, & St. Peters, 1995.
68. Wade, Baker, & Hartmann, 1979.
69. Jones & Friman, 1999.
70. Foster, Bell-Dolan, & Burge, 1988.
71. For example, Guevremont & Dumas, 1996.
72. For example, Burman, Margolin, & John, 1993.
73. For example, Buchanan & Houlihan, 2008.
74. Guevremont, DuPaul, & Barkley, 1990.
75. Bellack, Hersen, & Turner, 1979; Foster & Cone, 1980.
76. For example, Blumberg et al., 1997; Eisler, Hersen, Miller, & Blanchard, 1975.
77. Sturgis & Gramling, 1988.
78. Nietzel, Bernstein, & Russell, 1988.
79. Wincze, Bach, & Barlow, 2008.
80. Novaco, 1975.
81. For example, Bornstein, Hamilton, & Bornstein, 1986; Nomellini & Katz, 1983; Novaco, 1975.
82. Patterson, Ray, Shaw, & Cobb, 1969.
83. Tryon & Pinto, 1994.
84. Guevremont & Spiegler, 1990; Jacobson, 1985.
85. Cone, 1998; Foster & Cone, 1986.
86. Cone, 1993.
87. Jensen & Haynes, 1986; Kendall, 1987.
88. Ollendick & Greene, 1998.

PART TWO

Behavior Therapies

Now that we've whetted your appetite, you are ready for the elaborate main course: behavior therapy with all the trimmings. We'll begin by presenting relatively simple therapy procedures and proceed to more complex ones. The presentation of therapies is cumulative, so that you'll have to have tasted previously discussed therapies to fully appreciate and understand the discussion of each new group of therapies.

Chapter 6 deals with stimulus control and reinforcement procedures that increase clients' adaptive behaviors. Chapter 7 covers deceleration behavior therapies that decrease clients' maladaptive behaviors. Token economy, contingency contract, and behavioral parent training—the topics of Chapter 8—are treatment packages based on the procedures and principles presented in Chapters 6 and 7. Exposure therapies, covered in Chapters 9 and 10, treat anxiety disorders and other emotional problems by safely exposing clients to threatening stimuli. Chapter 11 covers vicarious extinction and skills training that are modeling-based treatments that foster adaptive behaviors and alleviate maladaptive behaviors. Chapters 12 and 13 discuss cognitive-behavioral therapies which change clients' cognitions that maintain their psychological disorders. Finally, Chapter 14 covers so-called "third generation behavior therapies"—new behavior therapies that introduce acceptance and mindfulness strategies.

Now that you've seen the entrée choices (we hope you'll choose them all), you are invited to really bite into behavior therapy.

6

Acceleration Behavior Therapy
Stimulus Control and Reinforcement

To treat clients' problems, behavior therapies modify maintaining antecedents, maintaining consequences, or both. In this chapter, we first explore therapy procedures that elicit or initiate target behaviors through antecedent control and then turn to therapy procedures that change the reinforcing consequences of target behaviors.

STIMULUS CONTROL: ANTECEDENTS THAT ELICIT BEHAVIORS

Antecedents, the *A* in the ABC model (discussed in Chapter 3), "set the stage" for behaviors to occur. In some cases, a client may not be performing a desirable behavior because there are no antecedents that elicit it; for such acceleration target behaviors, stimulus control procedures introduce antecedents to initiate the desirable behavior. In other cases, existing antecedents elicit an undesirable behavior; for such deceleration target behaviors, stimulus control procedures change the antecedents. These interventions involve either *prompts* or *setting events*, the two broad categories of stimulus control.

Prompting

test

Driving down the road, you see a sign for the street you're looking for and you slow down. Your friend, sitting next to you, tells you to turn left onto the street. You change lanes and turn left because you have been prompted to do so by the street sign and your friend's instructions. **Prompting** provides people with cues (prompts) that remind or instruct them to perform a behavior or indicate that it is appropriate to perform a behavior. Every day we rely on prompts to guide our behaviors, such as when we stop at a red light or check our appointment book. There are four types of prompts—verbal, environmental, physical, and behavioral—each of which can be used alone or in combination with other types of prompts.[1]

4 types of prompts and examples

① Verbal prompts involve telling clients what they are expected to do. For example, adolescents with moderate to severe mental retardation (IQs of 20–55) who were students in a community-based vocational training program were

Verbal Instruction

HAGAR © KING FEATURES SYNDICATE

given a series of verbal prompts through an MP3 player to remain on task. This intervention worked as effectively as or better than reinforcement for on-task behaviors.[2] In an unusual application of prompting, children were taught to prompt their teacher to praise the teacher's appropriate behaviors.[3] For example, children would approach the teacher with a completed assignment and say, "I finished all my math problems," to remind the teacher to praise them. Behavior therapists often use verbal prompts together with modeling and reinforcement. However, verbal prompts can also be effective on their own in such diverse applications as increasing seat belt use[4] and taking free condoms at a substance abuse clinic.[5]

Environmental prompts are cues in the environment, such as signs, that remind clients to perform behaviors. Some examples are alarms to remind older adults to take their medications,[6] written cue cards to prompt adults with mild disabilities to perform home maintenance tasks,[7] pictorial signs to remind children with autistic disorder to perform daily living skills (such as getting dressed),[8] and written notes for people with diabetes to remind them to self-monitor their blood glucose levels.[9]

With *physical prompts* (also called *physical guidance*), a client is physically directed to perform a behavior. An example is teaching a child to write by holding the child's hand and helping the child make the required movements. Physical prompts are used extensively to teach self-care skills to individuals with developmental disabilities, such as training children who are both deaf and blind in self-feeding skills.[10]

© 1997 Michael D. Spiegler and David C. Guevremont

PHOTO 6-1
How many different types of environmental prompts can you identify in this picture?

④ With *behavioral prompts*, one behavior cues another. For example, a husband in marital therapy learned to use his wife's crying as a signal to respond with sympathy rather than annoyance. An individual's own behavior can serve as a prompt to engage in another behavior, as when parents use their feeling angry at their child as a cue to leave the room to "cool off."

Guidelines for administering prompts include the following: ① administer the prompt just before it is appropriate to perform the target behavior, ② make the prompt salient so that the client is aware of it, ③ make the prompt specific and unambiguous, ④ have the prompt remind clients about the consequences of engaging in the desired behavior (such as a sign reading, "Taking Your Medication Will Make You Feel Better"), and ⑤ follow up prompts with reinforcement for engaging in the prompted behavior.[11]

Prompting usually is a temporary measure. As the client performs the behavior more frequently (because it is reinforced), prompts become less necessary and are gradually withdrawn—a process called **fading**. Prompting is a standard procedure for eliciting behaviors that a client rarely performs. Teaching language and social interaction skills to children with autistic disorder is a prime example.[12] To teach the names of objects, for instance, the therapist points to the object and says, "What is this? *Pencil.*" (The therapist's saying the word *pencil* is a verbal prompt.) As the child begins to imitate the prompt, the therapist fades the prompt by saying it at successively lower volumes. Eventually, the therapist whispers the prompt, then merely mouths it, and finally asks the child, "What is this?" without any prompt.

Setting Events

Setting events are environmental conditions that influence the likelihood that certain behaviors will be performed. When a setting event is identified as a maintaining antecedent of a target behavior, it is modified to create the desired change in the behavior. Consider the case of a boy with autistic disorder who behaved aggressively toward his baby sibling.[13] A detailed behavioral assessment showed that one of the setting events for the boy's aggressive behaviors was the noise the sibling made when eating from a metal plate. The sibling's metal plate was replaced with a plastic one that made little noise. This simple yet potent intervention reduced the client's aggressive behaviors.

Changing setting events, like prompting, is usually a component in a treatment package aimed at changing more than one maintaining condition of a target behavior.[14] However, when a target behavior is maintained primarily by a setting event, simply changing the setting event may be sufficient, as in the previous example. In another case, modifying setting events was the sole treatment for two boys with attention deficit hyperactivity disorder who interacted inappropriately during play.[15] The boys' inappropriate social interactions (such as calling each other names and refusing to share toys) occurred in a playroom containing 12 different toys and where there were no rules or adult supervision. A dramatic decline in antisocial behaviors and an increase in positive social interactions occurred when the therapist rearranged the playroom so that there were only two toys, specific rules for behaving were established, and an adult supervisor was present.

Teachers often change setting events to increase on-task behaviors and to reduce or prevent problem behaviors of children in classrooms.[16] Examples include rearranging seating (for example, placing a student who is disrupting the class close to the teacher), removing distractions (such as lowering window shades so children cannot look outside),[17] and modifying work (for instance, reducing the number of problems assigned to make the assignment more manageable).

Changing setting events is also used to treat adult problem behaviors, such as to facilitate weight loss,[18] reduce pathological gambling,[19] promote cholesterol-lowering diets,[20] and treat trichotillomania (compulsively pulling out one's hairs).[21] Changing setting events is used extensively in the treatment of insomnia in adults, as you will learn about in Chapter 16.

Stimulus Control in Perspective

Stimulus control procedures typically are part of a treatment package, although they can serve as the sole intervention. In the former case, the role stimulus control plays often is not assessed (in other words, the treatment package is shown to be effective without looking at the specific contributions of the treatment components). Accordingly, there is less direct empirical support for stimulus control procedures than for many other behavior therapies. When stimulus control is the primary intervention, the effectiveness of the techniques has been empirically validated. For example, the treatment of insomnia by simply modifying setting events is highly effective.[22]

Compared with other behavior therapy interventions that accelerate adaptive behaviors, stimulus control procedures can be very efficient because they can be easily implemented with little time and effort. Instructing a client to do something and posting a sign that reminds the client to perform a particular behavior are examples of efficient prompts. Making simple changes in setting events also can be effective, as when alcohol is removed from the home of a person who has a drinking problem.

Another advantage of stimulus control interventions is that they can prevent maladaptive behaviors. When the setting events that promote an undesirable behavior have been identified, those conditions can be systematically modified to prevent the behavior. For example, if a client trying to quit smoking is tempted to smoke when at bars that allow smoking, the client could patronize only establishments that prohibit smoking.

Similarly, using **planned activity scheduling**, behavior change agents arrange for clients to engage in *active* desirable behaviors in situations likely to elicit problem behaviors; this reduces opportunities for misbehavior.[23] For instance, in anticipation of sulking and sibling conflicts on a long-distance car trip, parents can provide a variety of activities for their children, such as having them play favorite games. Planned activity scheduling generally is employed with children, but it has been effectively used in treating adults with head injuries and adults with schizophrenia.[24]

When serious deceleration target behaviors are maintained by both antecedents and consequences, it sometimes is possible to intervene primarily through stimulus control. For instance, if a teenage boy often gets into fights after playing violent video games, his access to video games could be limited to those that are nonviolent. The advantage of treating the behavior by modifying antecedents rather than consequences is that effective consequential interventions may involve the use of aversive consequences. In general, behavior therapists avoid using aversive procedures whenever possible because of humanitarian and practical problems (that you will read about in Chapter 7).

The purpose of stimulus control procedures is to get clients to perform a target behavior. Ultimately, however, for the behavior to continue, it must be reinforced.

REINFORCEMENT: CONSEQUENCES THAT ACCELERATE BEHAVIORS

Teachers motivate students to learn by awarding high grades for good test performance. Parents get children to do chores by letting them watch TV if they complete their chores. Employers ensure continued work output by paying employees. These are common examples of the use of reinforcement in everyday life. People have always reinforced other people's behaviors (and their own) to get others (and themselves) to act in particular ways. Behavior therapists did not invent the concept of reinforcement. What behavior therapists have done, however, is to systematically apply the basic principles of reinforcement to reliably change behaviors.

What Is Reinforcement?

Test

To reinforce is to strengthen. The term *reinforcement* refers to strengthening a behavior so that the person will continue to perform it. Formally, **reinforcement** occurs when the consequences of a behavior increase the likelihood that the person will repeat the behavior. This is an *empirical definition* because it is based on the *observation* that the behavior recurs.

The reinforcing consequence is called a **reinforcer**. An individual receives the reinforcer only if he or she engages in the behavior—in other words, the reinforcer is *contingent* upon the behavior being performed.

Whether a consequence is a reinforcer depends on its effects on the behavior, not on the person's subjective evaluation of the pleasantness or desirability of the consequence. Reinforcers are defined by their accelerating effects on the behaviors they follow. However, in most cases, reinforcers are pleasant or desirable consequences for the person, and our discussion of them will assume that is the case.

Reinforcers differ from rewards. *Rewards* are pleasant or desirable consequences of a behavior that do *not necessarily* make it more likely that the person will perform the behavior again.[25] Receiving your driver's license is an example. You are rewarded for passing the driving test, but the reward does not result in your taking additional driving tests.

Behavior therapists do not assume that a consequence will serve as a reinforcer. A *potential* reinforcer is identified and then made contingent on the client's engaging in the target behavior. If the behavior increases, then the therapist assumes the consequence was a reinforcer.

Besides increasing the likelihood that the behavior will recur, reinforcers have a second function: providing *positive feedback*, which informs people that they are engaging in appropriate behaviors and are performing them properly.[26] When you receive an *A* for a poem in a writing class, the grade tells you that you have written a good poem.

Positive and Negative Reinforcement

Reinforcement always *increases* the frequency of a behavior. This accelerating effect can come about in two ways. When a pleasant or desirable stimulus is *presented* (added) as a consequence of a person's performing a behavior, it is known as **positive reinforcement**, and the consequence is a **positive reinforcer**. For instance, you hold the door open for your friend who is behind you, and your friend says, "Thank you." If hearing "thank you" makes you more likely to hold the door for your friend (or other people) in the future, then "thank you" is a positive reinforcer and positive reinforcement has occurred.

The other way that a behavior is accelerated through reinforcement occurs when an unpleasant or undesirable event is *removed, avoided,* or *escaped from* (subtracted) as a consequence of a person's performing a behavior. This is **negative reinforcement**, and the consequence is a **negative reinforcer**. Many everyday behaviors are maintained by negative reinforcement. For example, taking aspirin is reinforced by relief from pain, napping is reinforced by decreasing fatigue, turning in a paper on time is reinforced by avoiding a loss of points, and driving at the speed limit is reinforced by avoiding a ticket. In each instance, we avoid or escape from something undesirable. Such was the case with a 19-year-old man with autistic disorder who had been stealing and ingesting pills whenever and wherever he could find them.[27] In searching for the maintaining conditions of this dangerous behavior, his therapist learned that when the man ingested pills, he immediately was taken away from his job, which he disliked. Apparently, leaving work was negatively reinforcing his potentially life-threatening behavior.

Although negative reinforcement plays an important role in maintaining people's behaviors, behavior therapists only occasionally use it as an intervention.[28] Accordingly, this chapter deals almost exclusively with positive reinforcement.

Negative Reinforcement Versus Punishment

Equating negative reinforcement with punishment is a common mistake.[29] **Punishment** occurs when the consequences of a behavior *decrease* the likelihood that the person will repeat the behavior, and the consequence is called a **punisher**. Thus, punishment has the opposite effect of negative reinforcement because punishment *weakens* rather than strengthens a behavior. **Positive punishment** involves *presenting* (adding) an unpleasant or undesirable consequence. **Negative punishment** involves *removing* (subtracting) a pleasant or desirable consequence. Punishment always decelerates the behavior, whether positive or negative, and likewise punishers are defined by their ability to decelerate behaviors, rather then their pleasantness or desirability for the client. However, we will assume that punishers are subjectively unpleasant

PROCESS

	Add (+)	Subtract (−)
Strengthen	POSITIVE REINFORCEMENT **Consequence:** Store coupons given *Contingent upon* **ATB:** Remaining abstinent	NEGATIVE REINFORCEMENT **Consequence:** Job suspension removed *Contingent upon* **ATB:** Successfully completing therapy
Weaken	POSITIVE PUNISHMENT **Consequence:** Verbal reprimand given *Contingent upon* **DTB:** Missing therapy appointment	NEGATIVE PUNISHMENT **Consequence:** Home visits forfeited *Contingent upon* **DTB:** Resuming drug use

E F F E C T (vertical label at left)

FIGURE 6-1

Examples of how substance abuse can be treated by changing the consequences of an acceleration target behavior (ATB) with reinforcement and a deceleration target behavior (DTB) with punishment

Source: Based on Higgins & Silverman, 2008.

or undesirable, as they *usually* are for the client. Punishment will be discussed in the next chapter, but we've introduced the concept here to make the important distinction between negative reinforcement and punishment.

To distinguish the difference between reinforcement and punishment and what is meant by positive and negative, you just have to remember two things: (1) reinforcement involves *strengthening (accelerating)* and punishment involves *weakening (decelerating)* the behavior; (2) for positive, think " + " *(add)*; for negative, think " − " *(subtract)*. You can see this depicted in Figure 6-1, which gives examples of how a particular problem behavior (substance abuse) can be treated by positive and negative reinforcement and by positive and negative punishment.

Before reading any further, take just 2 minutes to make a list of consequences that you think would serve as reinforcers for you—in other words, that would increase the future likelihood of your performing a behavior. Save this list to use later in Participation Exercise 6-2.

Types of Positive Reinforcers

Positive reinforcers can be grouped into four major categories: tangible reinforcers, social reinforcers, token reinforcers, and reinforcing activities. Some reinforcers fit into more than one category.

Tangible Reinforcers

Tangible reinforcers are material objects. Food, clothes, electronic gadgets, jewelry, CDs, books, and recreational equipment are examples of tangible items that are reinforcers for many adults.[30] It is common to associate reinforcers exclusively with tangible reinforcers, and many of your own potential reinforcers that you listed a moment ago were probably tangible reinforcers. However, they are only one type of reinforcer.

Social Reinforcers

Social reinforcers consist of attention, praise, approval, and acknowledgment from other people.[31] They are administered verbally (for example, "Great job!"), in writing (for instance, a thank-you note), physically (as with a pat on the back), and through gestures (such as smiling).[32] Attention, a potent social reinforcer, can result in rapid and dramatic changes in clients' behaviors, as you can see in Figure 6-2; the graph shows the number of items of clothing a 6-year-old girl left lying on her bedroom floor before and after her mother began giving her attention for putting her clothes away.[33]

Social reinforcers have four advantages. First, they are easy to administer. All that is needed is another person. Second, social reinforcers don't cost anything, and people have a limitless supply of social reinforcers to give to others. Third, social reinforcers generally can be administered immediately after the person has performed the target behavior, which increases the effectiveness of a reinforcer. Fourth, social reinforcers are **natural reinforcers**—consequences that people receive as a regular part of their daily lives. Using social reinforcers during therapy increases the chances that the target behavior will be maintained after therapy has ended because the reinforcers will continue to be available.[34]

Social reinforcers are among the most powerful consequences for initiating and maintaining behaviors. People of all ages, including very young children, actively seek attention, affection, and praise from others for engaging

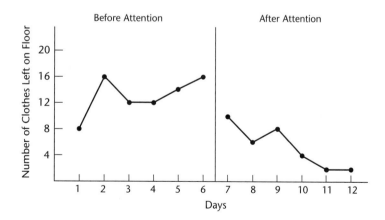

FIGURE 6-2

Number of items of clothes a 6-year-old girl left on her bedroom floor before and after her mother began giving her attention for putting her clothes away

Source: Hall & Hall, 1998b.

in desirable behaviors.[35] Think about how your own daily behaviors (such as the way you dress) are influenced by other people's approval and attention. Social reinforcement was the major component used in Case 6-1 to treat a patient whose legs were paralyzed due to psychological rather than physical causes, which is known as *conversion disorder*.

CASE **6-1**

Treatment of Conversion Disorder by Social Reinforcement[36]

On admission to a psychiatric hospital, a 42-year-old married man was bent forward at the waist, unable to straighten his body or move his legs. For 15 years, he had complained of lower back pain, despite two orthopedic surgeries. Every 4 to 6 weeks, he had episodes (lasting for 10 to 14 days) of being totally unable to walk, which he referred to as "drawing over." The patient had been hospitalized numerous times and treated with heat and muscle relaxants.

Orthopedic and neurological evaluations revealed no abnormalities. Behavioral assessment, however, indicated that the patient received considerable attention from family members for his physical complaints.

Treatment began in the hospital, where it was administered by an attractive young female assistant. The assistant asked the patient to leave his wheelchair and to stand and walk as far as possible, and she praised his efforts (for example, "You're standing very well today" and "I'm very proud of you").

In Phase 1, only standing was socially reinforced. As Figure 6-3 shows, this resulted in minimal walking. When both standing and walking were reinforced in Phase 2, walking increased. To check whether social reinforcement specifically for walking was responsible for the increase, a 5-day reversal period, in which only standing was reinforced, was instituted in Phase 3. The patient did not increase his walking distance, except on day 11. When reinforcement for both standing and walking was reinstated in Phase 4A, walking further increased. The social reinforcement for both standing and walking led to additional increases when a walker was substituted for the wheelchair (Phase 4B) and then when the walker was taken away (Phase 4C). By day 18, the patient was walking normally and was discharged from the hospital. Four weeks later, the patient had increased his walking to an average of 350 yards a day.

Immediately after the follow-up assessment (see Figure 6-3), the patient had a severe "drawing over" episode and was readmitted to the hospital, unable to walk. The therapist learned that the patient's family had reinforced his "sick-role" behaviors with social attention.

The patient began walking again when social reinforcers were reintroduced for standing in Phase 5 (see Figure 6-3). His walking dramatically

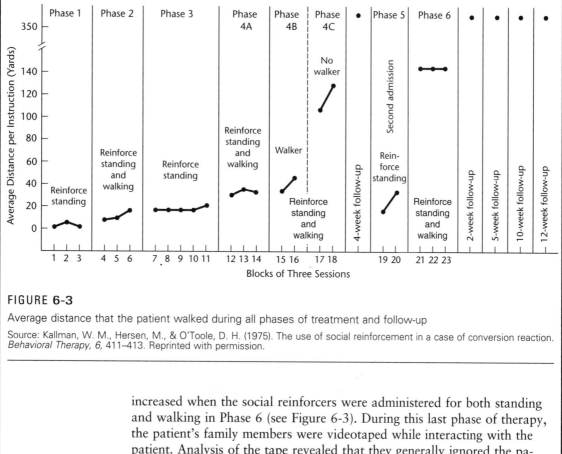

FIGURE 6-3

Average distance that the patient walked during all phases of treatment and follow-up

Source: Kallman, W. M., Hersen, M., & O'Toole, D. H. (1975). The use of social reinforcement in a case of conversion reaction. *Behavioral Therapy, 6*, 411–413. Reprinted with permission.

increased when the social reinforcers were administered for both standing and walking in Phase 6 (see Figure 6-3). During this last phase of therapy, the patient's family members were videotaped while interacting with the patient. Analysis of the tape revealed that they generally ignored the patient when he was standing and walking. Accordingly, the family was taught to socially reinforce the patient's attempts to stand and walk and to ignore his physical complaints. The social reinforcement procedures previously used by the assistant in the hospital were modeled for family members. After his second hospital discharge, the patient again increased his daily walking to an average of 350 yards. Follow-up assessments over the next 12 weeks indicated that he continued to walk normally.

Case 6-1 illustrates the potency of social reinforcement. Initially, the patient's physical complaints seemed to be exacerbated by the attention he received from family members. Later, the attention and praise of a hospital assistant accelerated the patient's walking. The case also points out that changes achieved in therapy do not automatically transfer to the person's natural environment. Usually, specific procedures must be implemented to ensure the transfer of treatment effects. This was accomplished in Case 6-1 by making certain that the reinforcement contingencies used in therapy continued in the patient's home environment.

Token Reinforcers

Token reinforcers, a third type of positive reinforcer, are symbolic items that have value because of what they can be exchanged for or what they stand for. Token reinforcers become *conditioned reinforcers*—that is, they acquire reinforcing properties because of their association with already-established reinforcers. Money, the most ubiquitous token reinforcer, has become a conditioned reinforcer in our society due to its association with the valued goods and services it can be exchanged for.[37] Other everyday examples of token reinforcers include good grades and merit pay.

Reinforcement is most effective when the reinforcer immediately follows the behavior.[38] However, often it is impractical to provide the reinforcer immediately. For instance, Kavitha's parents want to use bike riding after school as a reinforcer for her making her bed in the morning. When Kavitha makes her bed in the morning, her parents immediately place a sticker of a bicycle on the calendar for the current day, which indicates that she may ride her bike that afternoon. The sticker is a token reinforcer that serves the important function of bridging the time between the behavior and the substantive reinforcer.

Token reinforcement has been used in the treatment of substance abuse disorders.[39] For instance, drug abstinence has been reinforced with food and gas coupons and with points and vouchers used to purchase retail items.[40] In a controlled study of 70 outpatients who were dependent on cocaine, reinforcing cocaine-free urinalyses with vouchers exchangeable for retail goods resulted in abstinence during treatment and at a 1-year follow-up.[41] Similarly, for clients who were dependent on marijuana, receiving vouchers for retail items contingent on abstinence enhanced the effects of learning coping skills to deal with urges and avoid high-risk situations.[42]

Other examples of token reinforcers are stickers to increase school attendance in children with severe anxiety[43] and paying attention in children with autism,[44] and coupons for fast food to promote cooperation among disruptive adolescents in an inner city school.[45] In the business world, a recent use of token reinforcement involved providing employees with electronic codes for meeting periodic performance objectives.[46] The codes were used to play online games in which the workers could win bonuses of up to $50 or benefits such as time off from work. One large company reported that the intervention resulted in increased revenues and enhanced retention of workers. The most extensive use of token reinforcers is in token economies, which you will read about in Chapter 8.

Reinforcing Activities

Engaging in activities is the fourth type of positive reinforcer. Examples of activities that serve as reinforcers for many people include shopping, watching TV, listening to music, surfing the Internet, playing computer games, getting a massage, socializing with friends, talking on the telephone, sleeping late, and going out to eat.[47]

Reinforcing activities usually are pleasurable. However, activities in which a person frequently engages—but does not necessarily enjoy—can serve as reinforcers, which is the basis of the Premack principle.

(**Premack Principle**) *Par #5*

Know defir probility

Kaj, like many of us, turns on the radio every time she starts her car. She does not fasten her seat belt, however. What do you think would happen if Kaj could turn on her car radio *only after* she had put on her seat belt? Most likely, Kaj would start wearing her seat belt.

Forty-five years ago, David Premack discovered that higher probability (more frequent) behaviors—whether they are considered enjoyable or not—can serve as reinforcers for lower probability (less frequent) behaviors. This has come to be called the **Premack principle**.[48] In behavior therapy, the *relative frequency of occurrence* of a behavior is typically used as a measure of probability because frequency is easy to measure and approximates probability.

Acceleration target behaviors often are low-probability behaviors—that is, they occur infrequently, which is why they need to be accelerated. Thus, high-probability behaviors can be used as reinforcers for many acceleration target behaviors.[49] Although the high-probability behaviors need not be pleasurable to serve as reinforcers, high-probability behaviors that are *aversive* to the individual generally do not function as reinforcers.[50] Additionally, the high-probability behaviors must not be occurring so often that they lose their effectiveness in motivating clients to engage in the low-probability target behavior. As the familiar adage tells us, too much of a good thing can be bad.[51] Within these parameters, any high-probability behavior can serve as a reinforcer for a low-probability behavior. For example, providing children with attention deficit hyperactivity disorder with the opportunity to engage in vigorous activity (a high-probability behavior for people with ADHD) has significantly increased their being calm and paying attention (a low-probability behavior for people with ADHD).[52]

Employing high-probability behaviors as reinforcers is especially useful with clients for whom other potential reinforcers are difficult to identify, such as hospitalized patients with chronic psychiatric disorders for whom tangible and social reinforcers may be ineffective.[53] If we observe such patients' daily activities, we note such typical behaviors as standing, staring out the window, pacing, and sleeping in a chair. These simple, mundane activities (that might erroneously be labeled "doing nothing") are high-probability behaviors. Thus, they can serve as reinforcers according to the Premack principle, as Case 6-2 illustrates.

CASE **6-2**

Increasing Social Interaction with the Premack Principle[54]

B. H. was a 44-year-old female patient in a psychiatric hospital who rarely interacted with other patients or staff members. She responded to questions by nodding or giving one-word answers. The staff reported that they had "never observed B. H. enjoying anything." She spent almost all her waking hours sitting in a specific chair in the day room. The ward staff decided to use this high-probability behavior to reinforce social interactions, which clearly were low-probability behaviors for B. H.

(continued)

CASE **6-2** (*continued*)

The ward psychologist informed B. H. that she would be permitted to sit in her favorite chair only after she had interacted with another patient or staff member. Initially, 2 minutes of social interaction was required for 30 minutes of sitting. B. H. nodded that she understood, at which point the psychologist immediately reinforced their interchange by permitting her to sit in her chair for 30 minutes. The psychologist made the contingency explicit by specifically telling B. H. that she had just earned sitting time by listening and communicating that she understood what the psychologist had said.

At the end of the first 30-minute period, a staff member approached B. H. and suggested that they have a cup of coffee together, reminding B. H. that she had to spend 2 minutes interacting with others in order to sit in her chair. B. H. reluctantly accepted the invitation. For the rest of the day, one of the ward staff approached B. H. after each 30-minute period of sitting and suggested some minimal social activity that would allow her to continue sitting.

On each successive day, the number of minutes required for 30 minutes of sitting was gradually increased. As B. H. progressed, the staff gave her fewer and fewer suggestions about how she might socialize (fading verbal prompts) and made B. H. responsible for deciding how she wanted to spend time with others, drawing on the examples the staff had initially provided. By the 12th day, B. H. was getting up from her chair after 30 minutes without having to be prompted by a staff member.

Within 3 weeks, B. H. was spending more than the criterion time socializing and less than 30 minutes sitting in her chair. For example, she often played dominoes with a particular patient. Initially, she would get up in the middle of the game as soon as she had accumulated the required socializing time to sit in her chair. After a while, she would finish a game first, which took more than 30 minutes. Eventually, B. H. was spending the majority of each day in some social activity.

In using the Premack principle to accelerate B. H.'s social behaviors, the ward staff did not assume that she enjoyed sitting in her chair. All they knew was that sitting in the chair had a higher probability of occurring than social interaction. From the increases observed in B. H.'s social behaviors, it appeared that sitting in the chair was a reinforcer. The Premack principle will work for you as well, as you'll find out when you complete Participation Exercise 6-1. It needs to be carried out over the course of a couple of weeks, but you should read it now because it further describes the application of the Premack principle.

Behavioral Activation

Low levels of reinforcing activities are the nexus of a behavioral theory of depression posited by Charles Ferster[55] and Peter Lewinsohn in the 1970s.[56] In brief, the theory holds that people who are depressed avoid unpleasant environmental events; this alleviates their distress in the short term but also decreases the likelihood of their coming into contact with pleasurable events in the long term.

Doing What Comes Unnaturally: Applying the Premack Principle

You can easily see how well the Premack principle works by using it to accelerate one of your own low-probability behaviors. Choose a behavior that *you "should" be doing at least once a day but that you rarely do*. For many people, examples might be washing dishes right after meals, flossing their teeth, making their bed, cleaning their room, and exercising (although these may not be examples for you). Keep a record for a week of the number of times each day you perform the low-probability behavior you chose, which will provide a baseline.

Next, make a list of your routine high-probability behaviors, those you perform at least once a day without fail. These might include such routine behaviors as taking a shower, shaving, putting on makeup, combing your hair, eating breakfast, and checking your e-mail (or whatever your regular behaviors are). You do not have to consider the routine behaviors enjoyable.

Select one of these high-probability behaviors as a reinforcer. It must generally occur *after* you would engage in the low-probability behavior. For example, if your low-probability behavior were making your bed before leaving the house in the morning, then you could reinforce it with any high-probability behavior that you typically do after leaving the house, such as listening to the car radio or stopping for a cup of coffee.

After a week of recording a baseline, implement the Premack principle by following the rule: *Engage in the high-probability behavior only after you have performed the low-probability behavior.* Continue to record the number of times you perform the low-probability behavior each day for one week. At the end of the week, compare the frequency of your low-probability behavior during baseline with the frequency when you followed the Premack principle. Did you notice an increase?

This theory is the basis of a treatment for depression called **behavioral activation**. The therapy first identifies clients' avoidance behaviors and potential reinforcing activities. Then, it sets up activation strategies that are consistent with clients' life goals to get them to engage in reinforcing activities and decrease avoidance behaviors.[57] For example, a recently divorced man engaged in avoidance behaviors, such as alienating himself from his children (because contact with them was a painful reminder of the family breakup) and not attending social events with friends (which are usually attended by couples). Because the man's life goals included improving his relationship with his children and maintaining former friendships, the therapist suggested activation strategies that included planned encounters with his children and attending social events with friends. Alternative potentially reinforcing activities related to life goals such as beginning to date again or finding rewarding hobbies were also explored.

Initial evaluations of behavioral activation for the treatment of depression are encouraging[58] and indicate that it may be especially useful for some severe cases of depression that are not helped by cognitive therapy, the most effective cognitive-behavioral treatment for depression (see Chapter 12).[59] A brief form of behavioral activation[60] involving only nine sessions also has been successful in alleviating depression,[61] including with cancer patients.[62] Behavioral activation may prove to be particularly effective with adult Latino clients. It focuses on environmental events and changes overt behaviors rather than thoughts and beliefs, which is consistent with the focus on external factors in Latino cultures.[63] Behavioral activation also is being applied to other problems, such as anxiety,[64] suicidal behaviors associated with borderline personality disorder,[65] and posttraumatic stress disorder.[66]

Identifying Reinforcers

Reinforcers are most effective when they are individualized for each client. *Potential* reinforcers are first identified and then tested to see if they indeed accelerate the target behavior. Behavior therapists use a variety of methods to identify potential reinforcers, including directly questioning the client, selecting from generalized reinforcers, and observing the clients' routine behaviors.

Questioning Clients

Asking clients about potential reinforcers is the easiest and most frequently used procedure. The therapist might start with a general question (such as "What things do you find enjoyable or rewarding?"). Then, the questions would get more specific, asking about narrow categories of reinforcers (for example, "What do you like to do in the evenings?" or "If you had some extra money, what would you buy with it?").

Directly questioning clients to identify potential reinforcers has its limitations. For instance, it does not work for clients with severely limited intellectual and verbal abilities, and clients who are suffering from depression often cannot think of reinforcers because nothing seems pleasant or worthwhile to them. In such cases, the therapist can question people who know the client.

Exposing Clients to Generalized Reinforcers

Consequences that are reinforcing for many people are called **generalized reinforcers**.[67] Common examples include food, money, and social attention. Generalized reinforcers vary with clients' demographic characteristics, such as age, gender, and cultural background.[68] For example, food is a generalized reinforcer for most people. However, the specific food is likely to be different for young children and adults as well as for Hispanic and Japanese individuals. Similarly, generalized reinforcers may vary with specialized clinical populations. For instance, the privilege of taking methadone at home rather than at a clinic is a generalized reinforcer for clients who are being treated for heroin dependence.[69]

One method of identifying potential reinforcers is to expose clients to an array of generalized reinforcers and asking them to select those that they think would serve as reinforcers for them. For example, children can be taken to a toy store and asked to pick out toys they would like to have. Adults might make selections from a merchandise catalogue or the entertainment section of the Sunday newspaper. Special procedures have been developed for clients who are intellectually and verbally challenged.[70] For instance, clients with severe mental impairments spent time in a room containing 16 potential reinforcers, including a fan, juice, and a swing.[71] Reinforcer preference was determined by the frequency with which clients approached each of the objects. Whether these preferred items would serve as reinforcers was tested empirically by seeing if they accelerated target behaviors.

Behavior therapists have developed standardized lists of generalized reinforcers. For adults, the Reinforcement Survey Schedule is a direct self-report inventory that lists common generalized reinforcers (such as watching TV, shopping, and solving problems).[72] Clients rate the degree to which they enjoy each on a 5-point scale ranging from "not at all" to "very much." With the Pleasant Events Schedule, clients rate an extensive list of behaviors on two dimensions: (1) how often they engage in each behavior (frequency of occurrence) and (2) the amount of pleasure they experience from engaging in it.[73]

For children who cannot read, reinforcement menus such as the one shown in Figure 6-4 allow them to point to pictures of generalized reinforcers they prefer.[74] With the Children's Reinforcement Survey Schedule,[75] an adult checks off preferred generalized reinforcers for the child (for example, playing games, eating sweets, going on family outings, and playing with friends).

FIGURE 6-4

Part of a reinforcement menu

Source: Adapted from Daley, 1969, p. 44.

Identifying Your Own Potential Reinforcers[a]

Earlier, you made a list of your potential reinforcers. Now, you can compile a more complete list, using two of the methods you have just read about for identifying potential reinforcers.

Part I: Direct Questioning

As you answer the following questions, keep a running list of potential reinforcers that are elicited by the questions, eliminating duplicates. Some of the questions directly identify reinforcers, whereas others are designed to cue areas in your life in which you may find potential reinforcers.

1. What things do you like to use? Buy? Consume (for example, what kind of food)?
2. What would you like as a gift?
3. What items do you see in stores, ads, or catalogues that draw your attention?
4. What activities do you enjoy?
5. What do you like to do in your spare time?
6. What do you like to do most in your work?
7. What do you consider a fun night out? Night at home? Weekend? Vacation?
8. What accomplishments give you satisfaction?
9. What are you doing when you feel happy? Alive? Useful? Important?
10. What types of social events do you like? What types do you go to?
11. What do you like other people to do for you? Say to you?
12. What do you like to happen when you finish doing something well?

Part II: Identifying Pleasant Activities

Table 6-1 contains 50 activities that are potential reinforcers. Rate each item twice. First, answer the question, "How often have I engaged in the activity during the past 30 days?" For each item, use the following scale.

1 = *Not at all* in the past 30 days

2 = *A few times* (*1–6*) in the past 30 days

3 = *Often* (7 or more) in the past 30 days

Write the number in the Frequency column of Work Sheet 6-1.[b]

After rating the frequency of the 50 activities, read each item again and using the following scale, answer the question, "How pleasant, enjoyable, or rewarding was the activity during the past month?"

1 = This activity was *not* pleasant. (It was either unpleasant or neutral.)

2 = This activity was *somewhat* pleasant. (It was mildly or moderately pleasant.)

3 = This activity was *very* pleasant. (It was strongly or extremely pleasant.)

[a]You will need to complete this Participation Exercise later, but you should read it now.
[b]You will find this work sheet in your Student Resource Manual.

TABLE **6-1**
Common Activities That are Potential Reinforcers

Attending a club meeting	Listening to radio talk shows
Attending a concert	Playing video games
Being alone	Playing sports
Being with my parents	Playing a musical instrument
Complimenting or praising someone	Playing with a pet
Cooking	Reading fiction
Dancing	Reading the newspaper
Dating	Riding a bike
Daydreaming	Saying prayers
Doing art work	Sending and receiving emails
Doing volunteer work	Shopping
Driving	Sleeping late
Eating out	Staying up late
Eating snacks	Straightening up (house or car)
Exercising	Surfing the Internet
Getting dressed up	Taking a nap
Getting or giving a massage or back rub	Taking a shower
Getting up early in the morning	Taking a walk
Going on vacation	Talking on the telephone
Going to a mall	Telling stories and jokes
Going to a party	Watching a TV program
Going to the movies	Watching a video
Helping someone	Watching people
Listening to music	Watching sports events
Listening to or watching the news	Writing letters

Source: Adapted from MacPhillamy and Lewinsohn, 1971.

Write the number in the Pleasantness column of the work sheet. If you've engaged in an activity more than once in the past month, make an average pleasantness rating. If you have not engaged in an activity during the past month, rate it according to how enjoyable you think it *would have been*.

When you have rated the activities twice, multiply the frequency and pleasantness ratings for each activity and write the product in the Frequency × Pleasantness column of the work sheet. Higher products indicate more frequent and more pleasant activities and are more likely to be reinforcers. Add the activities with the highest products to your list of potential reinforcers that you compiled in Part I, eliminating duplicates. Remember that an activity is an *actual* reinforcer only if it accelerates a behavior that it follows.

Observing Clients' Routine Behaviors

A third method of identifying reinforcers is to observe clients in their natural environments and note the behaviors they engage in most frequently and spend the most time doing. These high-probability behaviors can serve as reinforcing activities following the Premack principle.

Alternatives to Identifying Reinforcers

Sometimes it is difficult to identify potential reinforcers, especially ones that are practical as well as potent. In such instances, behavior therapists may draw from generalized reinforcers that are appropriate for the particular client's demographic characteristics. The odds are good that some of them will work for the client.

It also is possible to create a reinforcer by making a generalized reinforcer desirable and valuable to a particular client. With **reinforcer sampling**, clients are first given a generalized reinforcer noncontingently—that is, without having to do anything to obtain it.[76] The aim is to "hook" the client on the

© 2008 Michael D. Spiegler

PHOTO 6-2

Offering free samples of food products in supermarkets to entice shoppers to buy them is analogous to reinforcer sampling.

generalized reinforcer. When the client begins to enjoy the reinforcer and wants more of it, the client is then required to perform the target behavior to obtain the reinforcer. For example, to get him to clean his room, a mother taught her son a new game that they played together each night for a week. The boy came to enjoy the game and to look forward to playing it. At that point, the mother made playing the game contingent on the boy's cleaning his room. Reinforcer sampling had established the game as a reinforcer, as evidenced by the fact that the boy began to clean his room. Businesses use an analogous strategy when they offer customers free samples to induce them to buy a product. For instance, supermarkets allow shoppers to taste new food products hoping that they will enjoy the products and purchase them.

Another way to create reinforcers is to expose the client to other people (models) who are partaking of the reinforcer and who clearly are enjoying it. What we find enjoyable or valuable is determined in part by what we observe others enjoying and valuing. Humor is a good example of this phenomenon. The next time you watch a comedy show on TV, check to see if your laughter coincides with the laugh track (an indispensable feature of TV sit-coms).

Administering Reinforcers

After identifying a client's potential reinforcers, the next step is to design procedures for administering them when the client performs the target behavior.

Sources of Reinforcers

Reinforcers can be administered (1) by other people and (2) by clients themselves, and reinforcers also can be (3) a natural consequence of the behavior. In behavior therapy, other people most often dispense reinforcers for a client. These **reinforcing agents** include therapists,[77] parents,[78] teachers,[79] spouses,[80] siblings,[81] and peers.[82] Adults usually reinforce children's behaviors, but sometimes the reverse occurs, such as when a 6-year-old girl's display of joy at seeing her parents when they pick her up on time from school increases her parents' coming on time.[83]

Clients can reinforce their own behaviors, which is called **self-reinforcement**.[84] Self-reinforcement has a number of advantages over reinforcement provided by others. The reinforcing agent is always present, and reinforcement usually can occur immediately after the target behavior is performed and when clients are alone.[85] Self-reinforcement is likely to increase transfer, generalization, and long-term maintenance of the target behavior. It also has the advantage of making clients responsible for changing their own behaviors. The major limitation of self-reinforcement is that clients may be less reliable at administering reinforcers than other people (for example, clients often forget to reinforce themselves).

Besides coming from reinforcing agents, reinforcers may occur as a natural result of engaging in the target behavior. For instance, increased endurance and energy are natural reinforcers of regular aerobic exercise.

Continuous Versus Intermittent Reinforcement

A *reinforcement schedule* is a rule that specifies which occurrences of a target behavior will be reinforced, and reinforcers are administered on two basic

schedules. On a **continuous reinforcement schedule**, a behavior is reinforced *every time* a person engages in it. On an **intermittent reinforcement schedule**, only *some* of the occurrences of the target behavior are reinforced. When an intermittent schedule of reinforcement is based on a specified interval of *time*, it is an *interval schedule*—as when a reinforcer is given after every 5-minute interval in which the individual performs the behavior one or more times. When the schedule is based on the *number* of times the behavior must be performed for it to be reinforced, it is a *ratio schedule*—as when a reinforcer is given after every five times the individual performs the behavior.

Continuous reinforcement is most useful when the client is first learning to perform a target behavior. Once the behavior is established, the client is usually switched to an intermittent schedule. Intermittent reinforcement is more economical than continuous reinforcement. Both the cost of reinforcers (such as with tangible reinforcers) and the time required to reinforce behaviors are less. The most important advantage of intermittent reinforcement is that it enhances transfer, generalization, and long-term maintenance of the target behavior.[86] Intermittent reinforcement simulates what occurs in clients' natural environments, where behaviors are only reinforced some of the time. To appreciate just how powerful intermittent reinforcement can be in maintaining behaviors over prolonged periods, consider what happens in compulsive gambling. Although gamblers are reinforced (by winning) only occasionally, they will continue to place countless bets after their last payoff.

Individual Versus Group Contingencies

Reinforcers most often are administered through **individual contingencies** in which the consequences a person receives (or fails to receive) depend only on his or her behavior. An example would be: Any student who scores at least 80 on a quiz gets 5 extra minutes of recess. In contrast, with a **group contingency** all members of a group receive (or fail to receive) the same consequences, depending on the performance of the group.

In one type of group contingency, each group member must meet a specified performance criterion for all the group members to receive the reinforcer. For instance, if all students get 80 or higher on a quiz, then the whole class receives 5 extra minutes of recess. Another type of group contingency depends on the total or average performance of all the group members to determine whether the entire group receives the reinforcer.[87] For example, if the average of all the students' quizzes is 80, the entire class gets extra recess.

The decision to use individual or group contingencies when a group of clients is being treated varies with the particular application.[88] For instance, using a group contingency requires that all members of the group are able to perform the target behavior.[89] Potential advantages of group contingencies include the fact that group members are more likely to reinforce one another's appropriate behaviors and the development of implicit or explicit group pressure to perform the target behavior. Potential disadvantages of group contingencies include group members' using excessive pressure or coercion to influence others—the downside of group pressure; one or more members' of the group intentionally sabotaging the program; and the unfairness of withholding reinforcers from individuals whose behavior was appropriate.[90]

Guidelines for Administering Reinforcers and Fostering Long-Term Maintenance

Behavior therapists have developed guidelines for administering reinforcers and fostering the long-term maintenance of target behaviors. The following are seven important guidelines.

1. *Reinforcers should be contingent on the client's performing the target behavior.*[91] The reinforcer is administered only *after* the client has performed the target behavior. Providing a potential reinforcer *before* the client engages in the target behavior will not accelerate it.

2. *The reinforcer should be administered immediately after the client performs the target behavior.* Immediate reinforcement is more effective than delayed reinforcement, especially when the client is initially learning a target behavior.

3. *Reinforcers should be administered consistently.* All of the people reinforcing the client's target behavior should use the same criteria for determining when a reinforcer should be administered, and they should administer the reinforcers each time they are earned.

4. *The client should be made aware that the reinforcer is a consequence of the target behavior.* The simplest way to do this is to tell the client the reason that the reinforcer is being administered (as was done in Case 6-2). This makes the contingency between the target behavior and the reinforcer explicit and helps the client remember the consequence, which is important because reinforcement affects the future performance of a behavior.[92]

5. *Continuous reinforcement should be used initially, followed by intermittent reinforcement.* Continuous reinforcement is optimal for initially accelerating a target behavior, and intermittent reinforcement facilitates long-term maintenance, transfer, and generalization.[93]

6. *Natural reinforcers should be used in therapy.* Employing reinforcers that the client is likely to receive outside therapy also enhances transfer, generalization, and long-term maintenance.[94]

7. *Reinforcers should be kept potent.* Reinforcers can lose their effectiveness with repeated use because clients satiate on them (as we become satiated with food after Thanksgiving dinner). Conversely, the more a client is deprived of a specific reinforcer, the greater is that reinforcer's potency (as when we don't eat before Thanksgiving dinner). The internal states of satiation and deprivation that can change the potency of reinforcers are called *establishing operations* because they establish how reinforcers will operate on (influence) clients' target behaviors.[95] Procedures for maintaining the potency of reinforcers include (1) using reinforcers to which clients have not had access recently,[96] (2) dispensing reinforcers in small amounts, (3) using reinforcers that are less likely to lead to satiation (for example, praise rather than food), and (4) switching reinforcers periodically.[97]

Shaping

Do you remember playing the game "hot and cold" as a child? One child has to locate a particular object while a playmate directs the child toward the object by saying "hot" when the child gets closer and "cold" when the child starts to move farther away from the object. The game is a variation of a reinforcement procedure known as *shaping*.[98]

With **shaping**, the _components_ of a target behavior are reinforced rather than the complete target behavior. Successively closer approximations of the total behavior are reinforced so that finally the complete behavior is being reinforced.

Shaping involves reinforcing successive steps required for a complex behavior.

Therapists use shaping to accelerate target behaviors that a client rarely performs, which means that there are very few opportunities to reinforce them. Shaping also is used to accelerate behaviors that are especially difficult or complex for a client, such as in teaching emergency fire-exiting skills to children.[99] The therapist breaks down the total behavior into its logical component parts or steps and then reinforces each component as it occurs. The process is cumulative: each component plus all preceding components are reinforced. Suppose a therapist was teaching a child to say the sentence, "I want milk." The therapist would first reinforce "I," then "I want," and finally "I want milk." Shaping generally is part of a treatment package and often is combined with prompting.

Shaping was used in the treatment of a 3-year-old girl who had to be fed through a gastronomy tube because she refused to eat.[100] Jenny's parents were taught to praise her and briefly engage in a game (such as pat-a-cake) for each bite of food she accepted. An assessment of the foods Jenny would and would not tolerate revealed that the more solid a food was, the less Jenny would tolerate it. Accordingly, the intervention began with baby food that was soft and watery and gradually increased in thickness and texture as Jenny began to eat. Jenny showed significant increases in the amount of food she consumed at home, and these results transferred to her preschool. By the end of the intervention, Jenny frequently fed herself a jar of baby food. A similar shaping procedure was used with three girls ages 5–7 who had severe feeding problems due to anatomical disorders of the digestive system which rendered normal eating by taking food through the mouth physically unpleasant.[101] Over the course of 7 months of treatment, the children learned to consume foods of varying taste and texture in a normal time.

Case 6-3 illustrates the details of the use of shaping and prompting to accelerate talking in a man who had not spoken for 19 years.

CASE **6-3**

Shaping and Prompting Used to Institute Speech in a Patient with Long-Standing Selective Mutism[102]

A 40-year-old male patient in a psychiatric hospital had been completely mute and virtually unresponsive during 19 years of hospitalization. For example, in group therapy he remained impassive, staring straight ahead even when he was offered a cigarette, which other patients were accepting. During one group therapy session, the therapist accidentally dropped a package of chewing gum, and the patient momentarily moved his eyes toward it. This response was chosen as a starting point to shape the patient's speaking.

Individual therapy sessions were held three times a week. The therapist began by holding a stick of gum in front of the patient's face and waited until he looked at it, at which point the patient was given the gum. When the patient consistently looked at the gum, the therapist waited for any lip movement before reinforcing the response with gum, and then looking at the gum, lip movements, and any sound were required for the reinforcer. Next, the therapist used the prompt, "Say *gum, gum,*" and made the reinforcer contingent on closer and closer approximations of saying "Gum."

At the end of the 18th therapy session, the patient spontaneously said, "Gum, please." This breakthrough was accompanied by other verbal responses, such as answering questions about his name and age. Thereafter, the patient responded to other questions the therapist asked, but he did not respond to other staff members. To generalize his responding to other people, a nurse was brought into the therapy sessions. After a month, the patient was responding to the nurse's questions. Finally, the patient's verbal requests were shaped and generalized by having all the staff members with whom the patient had contact do things for the patient only when he specifically asked them to.

Employing shaping to initiate speech in a man who had been mute for essentially all his adult life is an impressive demonstration of shaping. Case 6-3 illustrates that shaping may involve reinforcing tiny and subtle components (such as a brief, momentary eye movement). It also illustrates the use of specific procedures to generalize the patient's speaking to people other than his therapist.

Functional Analytic Psychotherapy

Shaping is the major treatment component of **functional analytic psychotherapy**, a behavior therapy that accelerates clients' appropriate and adaptive interpersonal behaviors as they occur in the client–therapist relationship.[103] Functional analytic psychotherapy, which was developed by Robert Kohlenberg and Mavis Tsai, capitalizes on the fact that the client–therapist relationship is a social environment in which clients' interpersonal problems may be reproduced.[104]

In the therapy sessions, the therapist looks for *clinically relevant behaviors*, which is what instances of the client's habitual interpersonal problems are called. When the client engages in clinically relevant behaviors, the therapist reinforces alternative adaptive behaviors. Consider the case of Ethel whose presenting problem was an inability to make and sustain friendships. During the initial therapy sessions, the therapist noticed that Ethel did not make eye contact with him and did not pay attention to what he said. The therapist identified Ethel's lack of eye contact and inattention as clinically relevant behaviors that were likely to be maintaining her lack of friends. The therapist shaped Ethel's eye contact and paying attention in the therapy sessions by reinforcing successive approximations of those adaptive behaviors. For instance, when Ethel turned in the direction of the therapist while talking or made momentary eye contact, the therapist leaned toward her or smiled. When Ethel commented on something the therapist had said, the therapist verbally reinforced her paying attention by saying, "Yes, you've got the point." The advantage of having the therapist shape clients' adaptive behaviors in the therapy session is that reinforcement is most effective when it is administered immediately and consistently. Therapists are competent at doing this, whereas reinforcement is less likely to be administered immediately and consistently when clients perform the adaptive behaviors in their everyday lives.

Shaping requires careful observation of the client's actions to make fine discriminations among the components of the target behavior (as you saw in Case 6-3). Participation Exercise 6-3 can help you appreciate the subtle skills required for effective shaping. Although you probably will want to complete the exercise at a later time, you should read it now as you are learning about shaping.

PARTICIPATION EXERCISE 6-3

Shaping Your Shaping Skills

You will need another person to do this exercise, so first ask a friend to assist you for about 20 minutes.

Choose a behavior that is (1) simple, (2) brief (taking less than 30 seconds), and (3) easily broken down into component parts or steps. Examples of suitable behaviors are opening and closing a book, removing the top of a pen and replacing it, standing up and sitting down, opening and closing a window, and talking about a particular topic (such as schoolwork or a social activity).

List the major components of the behavior in their appropriate order. Table 6-2 lists the major components of two simple behaviors as examples. Refer to your list as you shape your friend's behavior. However, your friend may not perform each component and is likely to perform some

TABLE **6-2**
Major Components of Two Simple Behaviors

Opening and closing a book

1. Movement of either hand
2. Movement of either hand in the direction of the book
3. Touching the book with the hand
4. Opening the book partially
5. Opening the book fully
6. Closing the book partially
7. Closing the book fully

Criticizing

1. Any verbal utterance
2. Any statement (as opposed to a question)
3. Any negative statement
4. Any negative statement that is a criticism

steps that fall between the major components you've identified. The key to effective shaping is to be able to notice differences among responses so that you are *always reinforcing closer approximations to the behavior.*

When your friend arrives, say something like the following:

> I am going to try to get you to perform a simple behavior—nothing embarrassing. I'll do this by saying "good" every time you get closer to performing the behavior. I can't give you any hints about what I want you to do. But, I will let you know when you are getting closer to performing the behavior by saying "good."

Your friend may appear quizzical or skeptical ("You want me to do something, but you won't tell me what?"). Just be sure your friend understands the instructions. If at any time your friend asks a question such as, "What do you want me to do?" answer, "Just get me to say 'good.'"

At first, your friend may remain motionless and speechless for several minutes (as he or she tries to figure out what to do or say). To get started, reinforce—by saying "good"—the first physical movement (or utterance if you are shaping a verbal behavior) your friend makes (as the therapist did in Case 6-3). Then, reinforce responses that are closer and closer to the complete behavior. It is crucial that you say "good" *immediately* after the component response is made. Otherwise, your friend may associate the reinforcer with some other response that he or she made at about the same time.

When your friend finally performs the behavior, congratulate him or her, describe the shaping procedure you were using, and ask your friend to comment on the process. Your friend may raise questions and issues that will enhance your understanding of shaping.

Reinforcement Therapy in Perspective

Reinforcement therapy is consistently effective in accelerating many different target behaviors for clients of all ages and intellectual and physical capabilities.[105] The keys to effective application of reinforcement are *consistently* administering *potent* reinforcers *immediately* following the behavior and using reinforcers that have been specifically *identified for the client.* After a client is successfully performing the target behavior, steps must be taken to ensure that the client will perform the behavior in different situations in his or her natural environment (if this is appropriate) and will continue to perform the behavior. Four strategies are employed to promote transfer, generalization, and long-term maintenance: (1) using natural reinforcers, (2) having natural reinforcing agents administer reinforcers, (3) using self-reinforcement, and (4) administering reinforcers intermittently. The first three strategies ensure that the target behavior will continue to be reinforced. The fourth procedure increases the chances that clients will continue to perform the behavior even when it is reinforced only occasionally in their natural environment, which is typically what will happen.

People will continue to perform a behavior only if the behavior is reinforced. Although this principle may appear obvious, many people harbor the illusion that once a person is engaging in a behavior, the behavior should magically continue—that is, without further reinforcement. In other words, reinforcement mistakenly is viewed as a one time cure, like taking an aspirin to relieve a headache. Behaviors must be reinforced at least occasionally (intermittently) if they are to continue being performed.

Reinforcement therapy is used to accelerate socially adaptive and desirable behaviors. Some critics have argued that clients should perform socially desirable behaviors without their having to be reinforced because the natural consequences of the behaviors are intrinsically worthwhile. However, if this were so, why don't the clients engage in these "intrinsically worthwhile" behaviors on their own? Apparently, the behaviors do *not* have intrinsic worth to the clients, which is why *extrinsic* reinforcers are needed to initiate and maintain many adaptive and socially desirable behaviors that clients are not performing.

There is a related ethical criticism of reinforcement: By fostering socially desirable behaviors, reinforcement therapy deprives clients of an aspect of their personal freedom—to act however they wish, which includes socially undesirable or nonconformist behaviors. In fact, clients who are not performing socially desirable behaviors either do not have these behaviors in their behavioral repertoire or do not have an incentive to engage in them. Reinforcement therapy both teaches clients new behaviors and provides incentives for engaging in them. Thus, clients now are in a position to engage in the socially adaptive behaviors if they choose to, which means that they have more personal freedom.

Another common criticism of reinforcement is that it is a form of bribery. *Bribery* refers to offering something valuable, such as money or a favor, to influence someone to act (usually dishonestly or illegally). Bribes are given *before* the behavior is performed, whereas reinforcers are always given *after* the behavior occurs. Receiving reinforcers for engaging in appropriate or adaptive behaviors is no more a form of bribery than being paid a salary for a day's work. Furthermore, reinforcers are not used in behavior therapy to accelerate dishonest or illegal behaviors.

Although reinforcement therapy is not a panacea, it is perhaps the most widely applicable behavior therapy, and its effectiveness has been demonstrated by a large body of empirical research. Accelerating desirable behaviors with reinforcement has no negative side effects, and clients consistently rate it as an acceptable treatment.[106] Reinforcement therapy provides clients with new, adaptive behaviors that are alternatives to their maladaptive problem behaviors. In doing so, reinforcement therapy increases clients' freedom by giving them more options for how to behave and enhances their dignity as human beings.

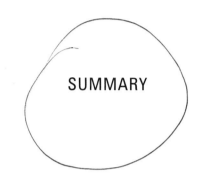

SUMMARY

1. Stimulus control procedures change antecedents that elicit behaviors. Prompting provides the cues that remind or instruct clients to perform target behaviors. Prompts can be verbal, environmental, physical, or behavioral. After the client is performing the behavior, prompts are faded (gradually withdrawn).

2. Setting events are environmental conditions that elicit behaviors. When a setting event is identified as a maintaining antecedent of a target behavior, it is modified to create the desired change in the behavior.

3. Reinforcement occurs whenever the consequences of a behavior increase the likelihood that the behavior will be repeated. Reinforcers usually are pleasant or desirable consequences, but whether a consequence is a reinforcer depends on its accelerating effects.

4. Reinforcers provide feedback that a behavior is being performed properly.

5. Reinforcement occurs when the consequences of a behavior increase the likelihood that a behavior will be repeated. Reinforcement can be positive or negative, depending on whether the consequence is added or subtracted, respectively. The term negative reinforcement often is used erroneously to refer to punishment.

6. Punishment occurs when the consequences of a behavior decrease the likelihood that a behavior will be repeated. Punishment also can be positive or negative, depending on whether the consequence is added or subtracted, respectively.

7. The four major types of positive reinforcers are tangible reinforcers, social reinforcers, token reinforcers, and reinforcing activities.

8. Social reinforcers are versatile because they are easy to administer, usually can be administered immediately, and are natural reinforcers.

9. The Premack principle uses high-probability behaviors as reinforcers for low-probability behaviors.

10. Behavioral activation is a treatment for depression that identifies clients' avoidance behaviors and potential reinforcing activities and then uses activation strategies to get clients to engage in reinforcing activities and decrease avoidance behaviors.

11. Reinforcers are identified by questioning clients, exposing them to generalized reinforcers, and observing their frequent activities.

12. Reinforcers can be created by reinforcer sampling and exposure to models' enjoying potential reinforcers.

13. Reinforcers are administered by other people and by clients themselves, and they can occur as a natural consequence of the behavior.

14. Continuous reinforcement is used to teach behaviors initially; intermittent reinforcement fosters long-term maintenance as well as transfer and generalization.

15. With groups of clients, reinforcers can be administered in a group contingency. All members of the group receive or fail to receive the reinforcers, depending on the performance of the group.

16. Shaping involves reinforcing components of a target behavior in sequence until the full target behavior is performed. Shaping is used to accelerate target behaviors that rarely occur or that are difficult or complex.

17. Functional analytic psychotherapy uses shaping to accelerate clients' appropriate and adaptive interpersonal behaviors as they occur in the client–therapist relationship.

18. Reinforcement consistently has been effective in accelerating many different types of target behaviors for clients of all ages and intellectual and physical capabilities.

19. Behavior is maintained only if it is reinforced. Procedures for enhancing long-term maintenance as well as transfer and generalization employ natural reinforcers, self-reinforcement, natural reinforcing agents, and intermittent reinforcement.

REFERENCE NOTES

1. For example, Ninness, Ellis, & Ninness, 1999.
2. Cihak, Alberto, & Fredrick, 2007.
3. Hrydowy, Stokes, & Martin, 1984.
4. Austin, Alvero, & Olson, 1998; Cox, Cox, & Cox, 2000.
5. Kirby, Marlowe, Carrigan, & Platt, 1998.
6. Lemsky, 1996.
7. McAdam & Cuvo, 1994.
8. Pierce & Schreibman, 1994; Van Houten, 1998.
9. Wagner, 1998.
10. Luiselli, 1993.
11. Van Houten, 1998.
12. Lovaas, 1977; Zanolli & Daggett, 1998.
13. Koegel, Stiebel, & Koegel, 1998.
14. For example, Davis & Fox, 1999; Sasso, Mundschenk, Melloy, & Casey, 1998.
15. Guevremont & Dumas, 2002.
16. Davis & Fox, 1999.
17. Kern & Dunlap, 1998.
18. Grave, 1999.
19. Hodgins, Wynne, & Makarchuck, 1999.
20. Shah, Coyle, Kavanaugh, Adams-Huet, & Lipskey, 2000.
21. Rothbaum & Ninan, 1999.
22. Bootzin & Perlis, 1992; Espie, Lindsay, Brooks, Hood, & Turvey, 1989; Lichstein & Riedel, 1994.
23. Bigelow & Lutzker, 1998; Close, 2000; Lutzker, Huynen, & Bigelow, 1998.
24. Lutzker, Huynen, & Bigelow, 1998.
25. Kazdin, 1989; Luman, Oosteriaan, Hyde, van Meel, & Sergeant, 2007.
26. For example, Babcock, Sulzer-Azaroff, Sanderson, & Scibak, 1992; Pollack, Fleming, & Sulzer-Azaroff, 1994.
27. Chapman, Fisher, Piazza, & Kurtz, 1993.
28. For example, Buckley & Newchok, 2006; DiGennaro, Martens, & McIntyre, 2005; Iwata, 1987; Kitfield & Masalsky, 2000.
29. Guevremont & Spiegler, 1990; McConnell, 1990.
30. For example, Cooper et al., 1999; McCain & Kelley, 1993.

31. For example, Griffiths, Feldman, & Tough, 1997; Hall & Hall, 1998b.
32. For example, Luiselli, 1993.
33. From the author's (DCG) case files.
34. For example, Stark et al., 1993.
35. For example, Borrego & Urquiza, 1998; Grandy & Peck, 1997; McConnachie & Carr, 1997.
36. Kallman, Hersen, & O'Toole, 1975.
37. For example, Ninness, Ellis, & Ninness, 1999.
38. For example, DuPaul & Weyandt, 2006.
39. Higgins, Silverman, & Heil, 2008.
40. Budney, Higgins, Radonovich, & Novy, 2000; Higgins, Wong, Badger, Ogden, & Dantona, 2000; Lussier, Heil, Mongeon, Badger, & Higgins, 2006.
41. Higgins, Wong, Badger, Ogden, & Dantona, 2000.
42. Budney, Higgins, Radonovich, & Novy, 2000.
43. Hagopian & Slifer, 1993.
44. Tarbox, Ghezzi, & Wilson, 2006.
45. Brigham, Bakken, Scruggs, & Mastropiere, 1992.
46. Win prizes online at work!, 2007.
47. For example, Axelrod & Hall, 1999; Hall & Hall, 1998a.
48. Premack, 1965.
49. For example, Carrington, Lehrer, & Wittenstrom, 1997; Danaher, 1974; Homme, C'de Baca, Devine, Steinhorst, & Rickert, 1963; Horan & Johnson, 1971; Wasik, 1970.
50. Watson & Tharp, 1972.
51. Timberlake & Farmer-Dougan, 1991.
52. Azrin, Ehle, & Beaumont, 2006; Azrin, Vinas, & Ehle, 2007.
53. Spiegler & Agigian, 1977.
54. From the author's (MDS) case files.
55. Ferster, 1973.
56. Lewinsohn, 1974.
57. Martell, Addis, & Jacobson, 2001.
58. Dimidjian et al., 2006; Dobson et al., 2008.
59. Coffman, Martell, Dimidjian, Gallop, & Hollon, 2007.
60. Hopko, Lejuez, Ruggiero, & Eifert, 2003.
61. Hopko, Lejuez, LePage, Hopko, & McNeil, 2003; Lejuez, Hopko, LePage, Hopko, & McNeil, 2001.
62. Hopko, Bell, Armento, Hunt, & Lejuez, 2005.
63. Santiago-Rivera, Kanter, Benson, Derose, Illes, & Reyes, 2008.
64. Hopko, Hopko, & Lejuez, 2004.
65. Hopko, Sanchez, Hopko, Dvir, & Lejuez, 2003.
66. Mulick & Naugle, 2004; Wagner, Zatzick, Ghesquiere, & Jurkovich, 2007.
67. Bandura, 1969.
68. Axelrod & Hall, 1999.
69. Schmitz, Rhoades, & Grabowski, 1994.
70. For example, Bigelow, Huynen, & Lutzker, 1993; Fox & DeShaw, 1993a, 1993b.
71. Pace, Ivancic, Edwards, Iwata, & Page, 1985.
72. Cautela & Kastenbaum, 1967.
73. MacPhillamy & Lewinsohn, 1971.
74. Daley, 1969; Homme, 1971.
75. Phillips, Fischer, & Singh, 1977.
76. For example, Bigelow, Huynen, & Lutzker, 1993; Steed, Bigelow, Huynen, & Lutzker, 1995.
77. For example, Kallman, Hersen, & O'Toole, 1975.
78. For example, Wahler, 1969.
79. For example, Stark, Collins, Osnes, & Stokes, 1986.
80. For example, Stuart, 1969, 1980.
81. For example, James & Egel, 1986.
82. For example, Solomon & Wahler, 1973; Strain, 1981.
83. For example, Graubard, Rosenberg, & Miller, 1974.
84. For example, Ajibola & Clement, 1995; Christian & Poling, 1997.
85. For example, Rokke, Tomhave, & Jocic, 2000; Solomon et al., 1998.
86. For example, Ducharme & Holborn, 1997; Esveldt-Dawson & Kazdin, 1998.
87. For example, Brigham, Bakken, Scruggs, & Mastropiere, 1992; Davis & Chittum, 1994.
88. For example, Pigott & Heggie, 1986; Shapiro, Albright, & Ager, 1986.
89. Axelrod, 1998.
90. For example, Axelrod, 1998; Kazdin & Geesey, 1977.
91. For example, Lamb, Morral, Kirby, Javors, Galbicka, & Iguchi, 2007.
92. Compare with Greene, 2001.
93. Esveldt-Dawson & Kazdin, 1998; Zanolli & Daggett, 1998.
94. Baer, 1999; Esveldt-Dawson & Kazdin, 1998.
95. Powell, Symbaluk, & Honey, 2008.
96. Michael, 2000.
97. Lindberg, Iwata, Roscoe, Worsdell, & Hanley, 2003.
98. Morgan, 1974.
99. Bigelow, Huynen, & Lutzker, 1993.
100. Gutentag & Hammer, 2000.
101. de Moor, Didden, & Tolboom, 2005.
102. Isaacs, Thomas, & Goldiamond, 1960.
103. Kohlenberg & Tsai, 1991.
104. Kohlenberg, Kanter, Bolling, Wexner, Parker, & Tsai, 2004.
105. Kazdin & Wilson, 1978; Rachman & Wilson, 1980.
106. For example, Jones, Eyberg, Adams, & Boggs, 1998; Miller & Kelley, 1992.

Deceleration Behavior Therapy
Differential Reinforcement, Punishment, and Aversion Therapy

Reinforcement therapy is used to accelerate adaptive and desirable behaviors. To decelerate maladaptive and undesirable behaviors, behavior therapists employ a number of strategies. In this chapter, we discuss three major deceleration strategies: differential reinforcement, punishment, and aversion therapy.

DIFFERENTIAL REINFORCEMENT: INDIRECTLY DECELERATING UNDESIRABLE BEHAVIORS

The preferred strategy for decelerating an undesirable behavior is to reinforce an acceleration target behavior that is an alternative to the deceleration target behavior, a procedure called **differential reinforcement**. For example, to reduce a client's criticism of people, the client might be reinforced for complimenting others. As this example shows, differential reinforcement changes the deceleration target behavior (criticizing) *indirectly* by directly reinforcing the alternative acceleration target behavior (complimenting).

Differential reinforcement works because the more the client engages in the alternative behavior, the less opportunity the client has to engage in the deceleration target behavior. Consider the case of a young girl with severe mental retardation who frequently hit herself.[1] To reduce her self-destructive behavior, she was reinforced for using her hands to play with a puzzle. Differential reinforcement was effective because while her hands were engaged in playing with the puzzle, she could not hit herself.

The four major types of differential reinforcement, in order of most to least effective, are differential reinforcement of (1) incompatible behaviors, (2) competing behaviors, (3) any other behaviors, and (4) a low frequency of the undesirable behavior.

Differential Reinforcement of Incompatible Behaviors

The best strategy for decelerating undesirable behaviors is to reinforce acceleration target behaviors that are incompatible with them—that is, **differential reinforcement of incompatible behaviors**. *Incompatible* means that the acceleration and deceleration target behaviors cannot occur simultaneously. Thus, while a person is performing the acceleration target behavior, it is *impossible* for the person to perform the deceleration behavior. For example, differential reinforcement of incompatible behaviors was used as part of a treatment package to reduce excessive crying associated with infant colic.[2] The parents played music and attended to the infant (such as by making eye contact with and gently touching the infant) whenever the infant was quiet and alert for 30 seconds or more. This procedure reduced the infant's crying by 75%.

Designing acceleration target behaviors that are incompatible with undesirable behaviors involves ingenuity and is even more challenging than devising *competing* acceleration target behaviors, which you did in Participation Exercise 4-1. You will get a feel for this process by taking a few minutes to complete Participation Exercise 7-1 before you read about the next form of differential reinforcement.

Finding Incompatible Acceleration Target Behaviors to Substitute for Undesirable Behaviors

For each undesirable behavior that follows, write an *incompatible* acceleration target behavior. Be sure the acceleration target behavior meets the standards for a good target behavior described in Chapter 4 (pages 53–54), including making the target behavior appropriate and realistic. You will know you have selected an incompatible behavior if it is *impossible* to *simultaneously* engage in the undesirable behavior while engaging in the acceleration target behavior.

1. Biting one's nails
2. Interrupting others during conversations
3. Sleeping in class
4. Making self-deprecating statements (such as "I'm just no good")
5. Leaving clothes on the floor

Differential Reinforcement of Competing Behaviors

Although reinforcing incompatible behaviors is the optimal strategy for reducing undesirable behaviors, finding appropriate incompatible behaviors often is not possible. The next best strategy is **differential reinforcement of competing behaviors**. Engaging in a competing acceleration target behavior reduces, but does not eliminate, the opportunity to simultaneously engage in the undesirable behavior.[3] Jogging competes with snacking, but it is still possible to snack while on the run.

Differential Reinforcement of Other Behaviors

Reinforcing an incompatible or competing behavior has the advantage that an adaptive behavior is substituted for a maladaptive behavior. However, this strategy is not possible when an alternative acceleration target behavior cannot be easily identified. If a target behavior is seriously maladaptive, it may be necessary to reinforce *any other* behavior to decrease the maladaptive behavior quickly; this is known as **differential reinforcement of other** (or **alternative**) **behaviors.**

Differential reinforcement of other behaviors is employed primarily for high-frequency behaviors that are either dangerous to others (such as hitting people[4]) or self-injurious (such as head banging[5]). In such cases, engaging in virtually any other behavior is preferable to engaging in the deceleration target behavior. For example, a child who frequently hurled objects at other people was reinforced for throwing objects at anything but a person. Although throwing things at inanimate objects is undesirable, it is *less* undesirable than injuring people. Differential reinforcement of other behaviors is occasionally used to reduce less severe maladaptive behaviors, such as preschoolers' noncompliance,[6] nervous habits (such as vocal tics),[7] and geriatric patients' wandering.[8]

Differential Reinforcement of Low Response Rates

Occasionally, it is unreasonable to expect that a client can completely stop engaging in the maladaptive behavior (go "cold turkey," so to speak), as when the rate of performing the behavior is very high. In such cases, the client can be reinforced for performing the deceleration target behavior less often, which is called **differential reinforcement of low response rates**.[9] This strategy was used with an adolescent boy who frequently talked out inappropriately in a special education class.[10] The teacher told the boy that she would spend extra time with him if he talked out inappropriately three or fewer times during a class period. This contingency lowered the rate of the boy's talking out from an average of more than 30 times a class period to an average of fewer than 3 times a period.

Differential reinforcement of low response rates can eliminate a behavior completely if the criterion for reinforcement is gradually decreased to zero. For example, first the client might be reinforced for 10 or fewer responses, then for 5 or fewer, next for 2 or fewer, and finally, for no responses.[11]

Variants of Differential Reinforcement

Both differential reinforcement of other behaviors and of low response rates are often used to treat severely maladaptive behaviors. Noncontingent reinforcement and functional communication training are two variants of differential reinforcement that are also used for such problem behaviors.

Noncontingent Reinforcement

With **noncontingent reinforcement**, the reinforcer identified as maintaining a problem behavior is administered on a frequent fixed-interval reinforcement schedule (for example, every 15 seconds), regardless of whether the client engages in the deceleration target behavior.[12] The client still receives the reinforcer but *usually* not after performing the target behavior, which means that the reinforcer is not contingent on the client's performing the behavior. Noncontingent reinforcement can be thought of as partial differential reinforcement of other behaviors (*partial* because occasionally the reinforcer may follow the deceleration target behavior).

The reductions in behavior following noncontingent reinforcement therapy are believed to be related to satiation and extinction.[13] Because the reinforcer is administered frequently, the client becomes satiated on it, which decreases its effectiveness. Extinction (which you will read about shortly) involves withholding the reinforcer for the problem behavior, which results in a decrease in the behavior.

Noncontingent reinforcement as a treatment for serious maladaptive behaviors is a relatively new intervention. However, an increasing number of studies have demonstrated that it can successfully reduce aggressive, self-injurious, and disruptive behaviors, particularly when social attention maintains them.[14]

Functional Communication Training

Sometimes clients engage in aggressive and disruptive behaviors to obtain desired reinforcers. For example, when 6-year-old Ari becomes frustrated with a task at school, he bangs loudly on his desk; this behavior results in his being permitted to take a break or do some other task. Ari's disruptive behavior is negatively reinforced by escaping from the frustrating task. Such a scenario is likely when the client lacks appropriate communication skills and therefore communicates desires inappropriately.

Functional communication training teaches clients to use acceptable ways of communicating their desire for a reinforcer rather than their typical unacceptable means of communicating the same message.[15] For instance, Ari might be taught to say "break" or make the hand gesture for "cut" (side of the hand across the throat) to communicate that he wants to terminate a frustrating task.

The first step in functional communication training is to identify the reinforcer maintaining the problem behavior. Next, the client is taught to use an appropriate communication behavior that will result in the client's obtaining the reinforcer. Because the training often is used with clients with severe developmental disabilities, a wide range of acceptable communication responses are employed, including simple phrases (for example, "Please watch me") and manual signs, gestures, and picture cards that indicate what the client wants. Typically, clients are taught to use several different communication responses.[16] Finally, the alternative, acceptable ways of communicating are reinforced by the client's obtaining the desired reinforcer for using them, and the reinforcer is withheld (extinction) for unacceptable communication behaviors. Thus, functional communication training is a specialized form of differential reinforcement of competing behaviors because appropriate communication competes with inappropriate communication.

Functional communication training has been used to treat aggressive, self-injurious, and disruptive behaviors of children and adults who have very limited communication skills, such as people with developmental disabilities and autistic disorders.[17] It has even been used with toddlers.[18] Functional communication training reduces problem behaviors relatively quickly, and studies have found that the effects of the training persist for at least 2 years.[19] Although it typically is part of a treatment package, functional communication training can be effective as the sole intervention[20] and can be successfully carried out by parents at home.[21]

In contrast to standard differential reinforcement procedures, the alternative behavior that is reinforced in functional communication training is specifically taught to clients, which means that it does not have to already be in their behavioral repertoires. In addition, clients in functional communication training determine when the alternative behavior will be reinforced by appropriately communicating their need or desire for the reinforcer.

DECELERATION BEHAVIOR THERAPY: DIRECTLY DECELERATING UNDESIRABLE BEHAVIORS

Differential reinforcement does not always reduce maladaptive behaviors sufficiently or fast enough. This is most likely to happen in three circumstances.

First, sometimes it is difficult to find a suitable acceleration target behavior. With substance abuse, for example, few alternative behaviors are as immediately satisfying as the physical effects of drugs.

Second, increasing the acceleration target behavior may only partially decrease the deceleration target behavior. For instance, accelerating *complimenting* may not result in an acceptable decrease in *criticizing* because a person can compliment and criticize someone in the same breath, as with sarcasm.

Third, differential reinforcement typically decreases the deceleration target behavior *gradually*, which may not be fast enough. This would be the case with behaviors (1) that are potentially dangerous to the client (for instance, self-mutilation) or to other people (such as physically aggressive acts) and (2) that infringe on others' rights (for example, destroying someone's property).

Two forms of deceleration behavior therapy are used to reduce undesirable behaviors *directly*. Punishment *changes the consequences* of the maladaptive target behavior. **(Aversion therapy)** associates *the maladaptive target behavior with something unpleasant*. Punishment is more broadly applicable and is used much more frequently than aversion therapy.

Both forms of deceleration therapy can be used in conjunction with procedures that accelerate alternative desirable behaviors. Indeed, treating an acceleration target behavior along with a deceleration target behavior is standard practice in behavior therapy.

PUNISHMENT

Punishment decelerates undesirable or maladaptive behaviors through one of two processes. With *negative punishment*, a pleasant or desirable consequence is removed, which makes it unconducive for the client to continue performing the deceleration target behavior. In practice, this is done by *eliminating reinforcement* for the target behavior, as in extinction and time out from positive reinforcement. The other process is *positive punishment*, in which an unpleasant or undesirable consequence, a punisher, is introduced, which also makes it unconducive for the client to engage in the behavior. In practice, positive punishment involves *administering an unpleasant or undesirable consequence*, as in response cost, overcorrection, and physically aversive consequences. We begin our discussion of punishment with negative punishment, eliminating reinforcement to decelerate undesirable behaviors.

Extinction

All behaviors are maintained by reinforcement. When the reinforcers maintaining a behavior are no longer administered, the person eventually stops performing the behavior. The process of withdrawing or withholding reinforcers is called **extinction**. Case 7-1 is a classic example.

CASE **7-1**
Eliminating Bedtime Temper Tantrums by Extinction[22]

The client was a 21-month-old boy who engaged in prolonged temper tantrums at bedtime. When his parents put the boy to bed and left the room, he screamed and cried. The parents responded by remaining in the room until he fell asleep (from ½ hour to 2 hours). Thus, it appeared that the boy's parents' attention was reinforcing his temper tantrums.

(continued)

CASE **7-1** (*continued*)

The therapist suggested an extinction procedure. The parents put the boy in his bed as usual. However, after remaining in the boy's bedroom for a short time, they left the room and did not return, even when he cried. As you can see from the solid line in Figure 7-1, after the boy cried for 45 minutes the first night of extinction, the length of crying quickly declined to zero. By the 10th night, the boy even smiled when his parents left his bedroom, and he continued to fall asleep without incident for the next week.

At this point, an unfortunate event occurred. His aunt put the boy to bed, and when he cried as she began to leave the room, she stayed in his bedroom until he fell asleep. This positively reinforced the tantrum behavior that had been eliminated. In fact, this single reinforcer increased the boy's crying to its pretreatment level.

The parents instituted the extinction procedures again. The broken line in Figure 7-1 shows that the boy's crying reached zero by the seventh night of the second extinction attempt, indicating that the procedures were successful. At a 2-year follow-up, the parents reported that no additional bedtime temper tantrums had occurred.

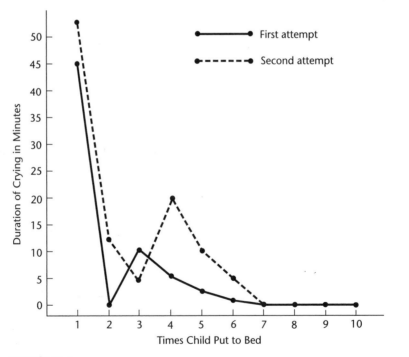

FIGURE **7-1**

Results of two attempts to eliminate a 21-month-old boy's bedtime temper tantrums through extinction

Source: Adapted from Williams, 1959, p. 269.

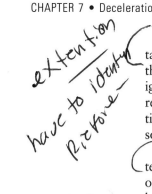

For extinction to work, the reinforcer that is maintaining the deceleration target behavior must be identified.[23] In Case 7-1, social attention was reinforcing the child's bedtime temper tantrums, so extinction appropriately involved ignoring the behavior. Extinction often is used to reduce behaviors that are reinforced by social attention. You have probably used extinction yourself from time to time, such as when you ignore (that is, withhold social attention) someone's obnoxious behavior.

Ignoring as an extinction procedure is appropriate *only* when social attention is maintaining the deceleration target behavior. Consider the example of a 9-year-old boy who regularly stole money from his mother's purse. The boy's mother decided to ignore her son when she saw him take money from her purse. She believed she was using extinction. However, her son's stealing continued because the behavior was reinforced by the money rather than by social attention. Thus, she was not using extinction because she was not withholding the reinforcer that was maintaining the behavior.

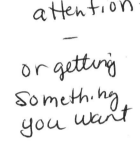

Extinction can be effective as the sole treatment (as in Case 7-1). Generally, however, it is more effective when it is combined with other therapies, such as differential reinforcement.[24]

Extinction has four potential problems. First, in some (but certainly not all) cases, extinction may work relatively slowly. This is a problem with target behaviors that must be decelerated rapidly, such as self-injurious behaviors.[25]

Second, in one of every four cases, extinction results in an *extinction burst*, an initial intensification of the target behavior before it begins to decrease.[26] And, for certain target behaviors, such as self-injurious behaviors where extinction bursts are especially undesirable,[27] extinction bursts occur in as many as half the cases treated with extinction.[28] Extinction bursts are reduced when extinction is combined with other deceleration procedures, such as differential reinforcement.[29]

Third, the effects of extinction may not transfer from the specific circumstances in which the extinction was carried out. This may have occurred in Case 7-1. The boy had not cried for a week and a half with his parents, who had administered the extinction procedure. However, when his aunt put him to bed, the circumstances changed and he cried.

The fourth potential problem with extinction is that the target behavior may recur temporarily after it has been eliminated, which is known as *spontaneous recovery*. Spontaneous recovery is not an indication that extinction has been ineffective. In fact, the intensity of the deceleration target behavior generally is weaker during spontaneous recovery than it was before extinction was implemented, and the target behavior soon begins to decline again. When using extinction, the therapist should tell the client and other people involved that the deceleration target behavior may recur temporarily.[30]

Extinction also has two practical limitations. First, the reinforcer maintaining the target behavior must be identified, which is not always possible. Second, for extinction to be most effective, the reinforcer generally must be *completely* withheld.[31] As you saw in Case 7-1, even a single, isolated exception can reinstate the deceleration target behavior and maintain it for a considerable time thereafter. When the boy's aunt stayed in the room when he cried, his crying was reinforced on an intermittent schedule, which increased the durability of the behavior.

Time Out from Positive Reinforcement

Time out from positive reinforcement (or **time out**, for short) involves *temporarily* withdrawing a client's access to generalized reinforcers immediately after the client performs the deceleration target behavior. When parents have their child stand in a corner for several minutes following a socially inappropriate behavior, they are using time out. In part, time out is time-limited extinction. However, in contrast to extinction, the actual reinforcer for the deceleration target behavior is not identified. In fact, what is temporarily denied is access to a range of generalized reinforcers.[32] Technically, then, the term *time out from positive reinforcement* is a misnomer, and the procedure should be called *time out from generalized reinforcers*.

Typically, time out requires that the client, usually a child, leave the situation in which the undesirable behavior occurs and spend a specified amount

PHOTO 7-1

Having a child spend a few minutes in a corner is a common way that time out from positive reinforcement is implemented

of time in a designated time-out area. This may be an isolated corner or a special **time-out room** that does not allow access to generalized reinforcers (such as windows to look out of or interesting objects to play with).[33]

Practical considerations often make it impossible to completely eliminate generalized reinforcers during the time-out period. For example, in a school setting, a time-out room may not be available, so children are put in a remote corner of the classroom for time out. Although many of the previously available generalized reinforcers have been removed (such as interacting with other children), the child still has access to some generalized reinforcers (such as observing other children, albeit from a distance).[34] Such "partial" time out tends to be less effective than "total" time out, in which all generalized reinforcers are removed.[35]

Time out from positive reinforcement is most effective when the following six conditions are met.

1. *The client should be aware of the reason for time out and its duration.* For instance, "For speaking disrespectfully, you have a 3-minute time out."

2. *The duration of time out should be brief.* Usually, 5 minutes or less is sufficient. For children up to age 5, a rule of thumb is 1 minute for each year of the child's age.[36] Relatively short periods are effective, and lengthening the time period does not necessarily increase the effectiveness of time out.[37]

3. *No reinforcers should be present or introduced during the time-out period.* Adults should not give children attention when they are in time out (as by answering their questions), and the time-out area should not contain generalized reinforcers (which makes most children's bedrooms inappropriate for time out).

4. *Time out should be terminated only when the specified time has elapsed.* If the child is removed from time out beforehand, the time out may be less effective in the future.

5. *Time out should be terminated only when the child is behaving appropriately,* which means the child is not engaging in any undesirable behaviors. This provision ensures that an undesirable behavior, such as screaming, is not inadvertently negatively reinforced by termination of time out or positively reinforced by once again gaining access to generalized reinforcers.

6. *Time out should not allow clients to escape or avoid situations they find unpleasant.* If a child dislikes schoolwork, for example, then removing the student from the classroom for time out allows the child to avoid schoolwork.[38] In such instances, time out serves as a negative reinforcer for the deceleration target behavior.

Time out from positive reinforcement is usually used with children, sometimes with adolescents, and occasionally with adults. Target behaviors have included self-injurious behaviors of children with autistic disorder,[39] inappropriate table manners and eating habits of institutionalized children with mental retardation,[40] verbal and physical aggression of children and adolescents,[41] disruptive social behaviors of adults with psychiatric disorders,[42] and alcohol consumption by clients with a history of substance abuse.[43]

Outside of therapy, many parents apply time out when their young children do not comply with instructions or rules,[44] and elementary school teachers use time out as a standard discipline procedure.[45] When applied correctly, time out is highly effective and efficient. Children easily learn the time-out routine and generally comply with it. Furthermore, merely the threat of time out can serve as a deterrent for future misbehaviors (for example, "The next time you eat with your fingers, you'll have a time out").

An interesting positive side effect of time out used with children is that it gives adults a "time out" of sorts—not from generalized reinforcers but from aversive elements of the child's misbehavior. The brief respite may lessen the chances that the adults will become overly upset and even abusive.

Although correctly applied time out from positive reinforcement is effective with most children, it does not work well with all children. For example, children with attention deficit hyperactivity disorder may not remain in time out for even a minute or two.[46] In such cases, undesirable consequences for failure to stay in time out may be added to the time-out procedure.

Extinction and time out from positive reinforcement are examples of negative punishment because they operate by removing reinforcers for the target behavior. They may also involve receiving undesirable consequences (positive punishment) because clients generally experience removal of reinforcers as unpleasant. However, this is a side effect of the primary operation of extinction and time out: removing reinforcers. By contrast, response cost, overcorrection, and physically aversive consequences clearly involve positive punishment because they operate by administering unpleasant or undesirable consequences.

Response Cost

The undesirable consequence in **response cost** is the removal of a valued item or privilege that the client possesses or is entitled to.[47] Many everyday behaviors are influenced by response cost, including fines (such as for illegal parking and failure to return library books), the loss of points for turning in school assignments late, and the loss of TV time or a favorite dessert for misbehavior. In each case, there is a cost for performing a particular behavior.

In behavior therapy, one way of implementing response cost is for the client to deposit items of value with the therapist (for example, favorite CDs). If the client performs the deceleration target behavior, the therapist or the client permanently disposes of one of the items. In practice, clients usually forfeit very few valuables because the *threat* of response cost often is sufficient incentive to eliminate the maladaptive behavior.[48]

Ogden Lindsley developed a response cost procedure for reducing the number of personal items that his family left lying around the house.[49] Whoever found an item in an inappropriate place (such as a jacket on the piano bench) put it in a large box, called the Sunday Box. The owner was not permitted to retrieve the item until the following Sunday. Lindsley discovered the power of his response cost procedure the day he left his briefcase on the coffee table.

© 2008 Michael D. Spiegler

PHOTO 7-2

Parking fines are an all-too-familiar form of response cost

He had to live without the briefcase and its contents until the beginning of the next week, which was a hardship, given that he was a professor. You can discover for yourself how well the Sunday Box works—without necessarily repeating Lindsley's experience—by completing Participation Exercise 7-2 over the course of the next few weeks.

PARTICIPATION EXERCISE 7-2

Boxing Your Way to a Neater Room[50]

If you are a member of the Messy Room Club, this exercise, which is a variation of the Sunday Box technique, is for you. Simply follow the six steps.

1. Make a list of your personal items that are frequently out of place in one room in your house (your bedroom is a good choice). Knowing the possible fate of the items you list, you may be reluctant to include items that you "cannot live without." However, remember that the more valuable the items, the more likely it is that the procedures will help you keep them in their proper places.

2. Next to each item on your list, write the precise location in which it belongs (for example, "on bookshelf," "on hook in bathroom," or "top dresser drawer").

(continued)

**PARTICIPATION
EXERCISE 7-2**

(*continued*)

3. Find a cardboard box or other suitable container large enough to hold all the items on your list.
4. Specify a particular time each day for inspecting the room. A good time is when you return home in the afternoon or evening.
5. Every day at the inspection time, place all the items on your list that are out of their designated locations in the box, and *leave them there until the predetermined retrieval time* (see step 6). An alternative procedure is to have a friend inspect the room each day and put out-of-place items in the box. (Roommates who would like your common living space to be neater may be delighted to assume this responsibility.)
6. Every fourth day, at the designated inspection time, count the number of items in the box and record this number. Then, remove all the items. They are yours to keep—for at least the next 24 hours until your next inspection time.

Follow these steps for at least 3 cycles (12 days). A declining number of items in your box in successive 4-day cycles will indicate that the response cost is working. You may even lose your membership in the Messy Room Club.

Response cost has been used extensively with children in schools.[51] Its effectiveness can be equal to or greater than that achieved by using reinforcement procedures.[52] For example, in the treatment of attention deficit hyperactivity disorder, loss of token reinforcers (response cost) was more effective than access to token reinforcers in improving accuracy on an arithmetic task.[53] Therapists have taught similar procedures to parents to decrease children's misbehaviors at home,[54] and parents consider response cost to be a highly acceptable treatment procedure.[55]

CALVIN AND HOBBES © 1986 Watterson. Dist. by UNIVERSAL PRESS SYNDICATE. Reprinted with permission. All rights reserved.

To treat problems of inattention in the classroom, a battery-operated device has been developed for administering response cost combined with reinforcement.[56] The student earns a point automatically, once per minute, as long as the student continues to pay attention to his or her work. A small box on the student's desk displays the cumulative points the student has earned (reinforcement), and the student can exchange the points later for desired reinforcers. The teacher deducts points (response cost) using a handheld remote-control device whenever the child is observed not paying attention to a task. When a point is deducted, a red light on top of the box on the student's desk comes on for 15 seconds. These procedures have significantly improved attention to schoolwork in boys with attention deficit hyperactivity disorder.[57] One reason the procedures have been effective is that they simultaneously accelerate a desirable behavior (on-task behavior) and decelerate an undesirable behavior (off-task behavior).

Response cost can be a highly effective procedure for decelerating a variety of target behaviors with children, adolescents, and adults. It even can be effective for severely aberrant behavior. For example, a 33-year-old woman with mental retardation showed an 87% reduction in self-injurious and aggressive behaviors after being treated with response cost (such as being deprived of music for 30 seconds).[58] The effects of response cost may endure when the procedure is terminated,[59] and most people view response cost as an acceptable deceleration therapy, which facilitates its application.[60]

Overcorrection

Overcorrection decelerates maladaptive behaviors by having clients correct the undesirable effects of their actions and then intensively practice an appropriate alternative behavior.[61] Richard Foxx and Nathan Azrin originally developed overcorrection[62] to treat behaviors that harm and annoy others or that are destructive.[63] Overcorrection also is used for behaviors that have negative consequences primarily for the client, including self-injurious behaviors,[64] bedwetting,[65] excessive and stereotypic behaviors (such as walking in circles),[66] and persistent eating of nonnutritive substances, such as dirt, paper, and buttons.[67]

Overcorrection consists of two phases: (1) *restitution*, in which the client makes amends for the damage done, and (2) *positive practice*, in which the client repeatedly performs an appropriate adaptive behavior in an exaggerated fashion. Case 7-2 illustrates both phases of overcorrection.

CASE **7-2**
Reducing Object Throwing by Overcorrection[68]

A 62-year-old woman, who had been a patient in a psychiatric hospital for 43 years, engaged in a number of inappropriate and dangerous behaviors, including throwing objects from the floor at people. Overcorrection was instituted to decelerate object throwing.

(continued)

CASE **7-2** (*continued*)

In the restitution phase, a staff member instructed the patient to apologize to individuals who had been hit. If the patient refused, the staff member apologized on the patient's behalf and prompted her to nod in agreement.

Positive practice consisted of 5 minutes of picking up trash on the floor and putting it into a garbage can. Initially, the patient refused to do this positive practice, so the staff member physically guided her through the clean-up activity. The physical prompting was discontinued when, after several sessions, the patient began to perform the positive practice voluntarily.

Before the overcorrection procedure was instituted, the patient threw objects at others an average of 13 times a day. After 2 weeks of overcorrection, the frequency of the target behavior decreased to an average of less than one incident per day. The frequency remained at or below that level for 4 months, at which point observations were terminated.

Sometimes only one phase of overcorrection is employed. When restitution alone is used, it may involve an exaggerated or augmented form of making amends.[69] This procedure was used for 34 hospitalized adults with mental retardation who frequently stole from one another, especially food at mealtimes or snack times.[70] Before the augmented restitution was instituted, staff members had the clients return the food (or what was left of it) to its owner. This intervention was not potent enough, and the stealing continued at a high rate (see Figure 7-2).

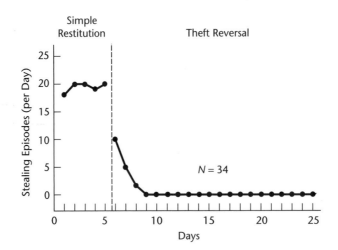

FIGURE 7-2

Daily stealing episodes for 34 institutionalized adults with mental retardation during simple restitution and theft reversal (exaggerated restitution)

Source: Azrin & Wesolowski, 1974.

For more over correction

Accordingly, the staff tried **theft reversal**, an overcorrection procedure consisting of augmented restitution in which the offender not only returns stolen items but also buys similar items for the victim (additional food in this case). As you can see in Figure 7-2, theft reversal dramatically reduced the number of thefts.

When a maladaptive behavior results in a consequence that cannot easily be corrected, as with behaviors that do not affect others or the environment, positive practice is used without restitution.[71] For example, children in a classroom had problems with speaking out and leaving their seats at inappropriate times.[72] During their recess period, the children were asked to practice appropriate classroom behaviors, such as raising their hands and asking permission to leave their seats. They practiced these behaviors repeatedly for 5 minutes. Compared with response cost (losing recess time), this positive practice markedly decreased the inappropriate classroom behaviors.

Two general issues concerning the practice of overcorrection are worth noting. First, although overcorrection generally is applied immediately after the target behavior is performed,[73] it also appears to be effective when it is delayed, as in the example just described.[74] Second, increasing the duration of positive practice does not result in greater reductions in maladaptive behaviors, and sometimes very brief periods are effective. For example, positive practice lasting 30 seconds was as effective as positive practice durations of 2 and 8 minutes in reducing the self-stimulatory behaviors (such as repetitive rocking) of adults with severe developmental disabilities.[75]

In one study, overcorrection was comparable to time out from positive reinforcement for treating sibling conflicts.[76] Restitution consisted of making an apology to the sibling, and positive practice involved complimenting or giving toys to the sibling. Positive practice was continued for a period comparable to time-out durations, which was set at 1 minute for each year of the child's age. Time out and overcorrection were *equally* effective in reducing sibling conflicts, and the children's parents rated both as acceptable deceleration strategies.

Overcorrection can augment other deceleration strategies.[77] For instance, with a group of clients who had developmental disabilities and were deaf and blind, differential reinforcement of other behaviors alone was ineffective in reducing self-injurious behaviors and hitting others. Adding overcorrection to differential reinforcement rapidly reduced the maladaptive behaviors.[78] In contrast to other deceleration therapies that only decelerate the maladaptive behavior, overcorrection that includes positive practice has the distinct advantage of accelerating an alternative adaptive behavior.[79]

Overcorrection is more limited in its range of applications than other therapies that involve punishment. Overcorrection is appropriate primarily for behaviors that have correctable adverse effects. Under these conditions, overcorrection procedures have been demonstrated to be effective in decelerating a variety of maladaptive behaviors, especially when both phases are employed.[80] Because overcorrection is viewed as an acceptable treatment, there is little resistance to using it.[81] However, not surprisingly, parents consistently rate overcorrection as less acceptable than positive reinforcement procedures for changing their children's behaviors.[82]

Designing Novel Overcorrections[a]

In this exercise, you will design procedures for novel applications of over-correction to common undesirable behaviors. In the process, you may discover some useful ideas for reducing some of your own unwanted behaviors. At the very least, you will check your understanding of over-correction.

For each of the behaviors in the list that follows, describe one or more procedures for restitution and for positive practice. Then, compare your procedures with the samples in your Student Resource Manual.

1. Littering in a park
2. Misspelling words in a paper
3. Leaving clothes in inappropriate places
4. Arriving late for classes or appointments
5. Trashing the neighbor's lawn
6. Leaving unnecessary lights on at home
7. Putting dishes in the sink without washing them

[a] This Participation Exercise can be completed before you continue reading or at a later time.

Overcorrection procedures have applications outside of therapy. For example, some consumer protection laws mandate that businesses that are found negligent automatically pay the consumer several times the amount of loss or damage. Community service as an alternative to fines or incarceration for people convicted of crimes also is a form of overcorrection.

Physically Aversive Consequences

Physically aversive consequences are stimuli that result in unpleasant physical sensations, including pain. Most people associate deceleration behavior therapy with physically aversive consequences, as when a parent spanks a child. In fact, physically aversive consequences are used infrequently in behavior therapy.[83] A number of potential undesirable side effects as well as ethical and humanitarian objections are associated with their use, and these will be discussed later in the chapter.

Time out from positive reinforcement, response cost, and overcorrection are effective and do not involve physically aversive consequences. However, these therapy procedures often take longer to work than do physically aversive consequences. Thus, when rapid deceleration of a maladaptive behavior is required, physically aversive consequences may be the treatment of choice.

Self-injurious behaviors (such as head banging and slapping oneself) are the major target behaviors treated by physically aversive consequences. These behaviors can result in serious physical harm and, in extreme cases, death. They occur most frequently with clients who have severe psychological problems, such as autistic disorder.

Ironically, mild electric shock often is an effective and efficient means of significantly reducing self-injurious behaviors.[84] The duration of the shock is only a second or two. It results in a sharp, stinging sensation that lasts for no more than a few minutes, and no permanent tissue damage occurs.[b] The use of shock may be justified by a cost-benefit analysis,[85] as you will see in Case 7-3.

CASE **7-3**
Eliminating Dangerous Climbing with Contingent Shock[86]

A 6-year-old girl with diffuse brain damage and no verbal communication skills frequently was found climbing to dangerously high places. "Her body bore multiple scars from past falls, her front teeth were missing, having been imbedded in molding from which she had fallen while climbing outside the second story of her house."

The initial behavioral assessment revealed that her mother's attention was probably maintaining the girl's climbing. Time out from positive reinforcement, extinction, and differential reinforcement of competing behaviors (such as sitting at a table) were tried to no avail. At this point, because of the seriousness of the problem, the therapist, in consultation with the girl's parents, decided to use contingent electric shock.

The room in which therapy was conducted had a small table and chairs in the center and a high bookcase next to the door. Each therapy session began with the therapist and girl seated at the table. Whenever the girl climbed on the bookcase, the therapist shouted, "No!" and immediately applied a 1-second shock to her calf or lower thigh. The therapist then returned to his chair. The shock was delivered by a handheld, battery-powered device resembling a long flashlight. The pain lasted only for the 1-second duration of the shock, and there were no aftereffects (such as redness, swelling, tingling, or aching).

The contingent shock rapidly reduced the girl's climbing, as you can see in Figure 7-3. In the first session, the girl climbed nine times; in the second, three times; and thereafter, only twice in the next 18 sessions.

Although the girl stopped climbing in the therapy sessions, she continued to climb at home, which indicated that the treatment effects were specific to the therapy room and to the therapist. Accordingly, the girl's mother—who had observed the therapy sessions from behind a one-way mirror—began to implement treatment at home. When her daughter began to climb, the mother shouted, "No!" and applied the shock as the therapist had done. She then resumed whatever she had been doing without further interaction with her daughter.

In the 16 days before the therapy was instituted at home, the mother had observed that her daughter had climbed an average of 29 times a day. Within 4 days after therapy began at home, the rate of climbing declined to an average of twice a day. After 33 days, the number of climbing incidents decreased to zero and, with one exception, did not recur in the next 15 days, at which point the therapy was terminated.

(continued)

---

[b] The shock used in deceleration therapies is not the same as that used in electroconvulsive therapy (ECT). ECT is a medical treatment primarily used for severe depression that has not responded to psychotherapy and medication. It involves passing electricity through the brain while the patient is sedated; this leads to a convulsion, temporary unconsciousness, and amnesia for the experience. ECT is not a behavior therapy.

CASE **7-3** (*continued*)

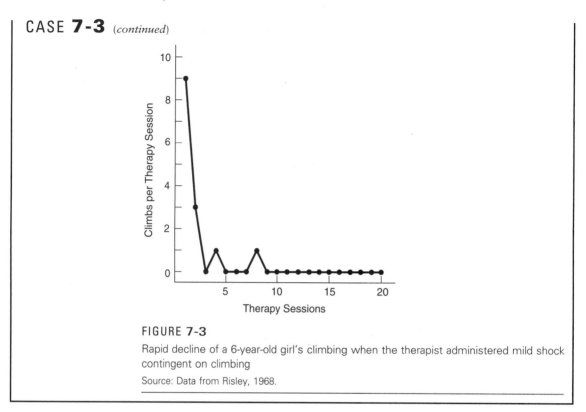

FIGURE 7-3

Rapid decline of a 6-year-old girl's climbing when the therapist administered mild shock contingent on climbing

Source: Data from Risley, 1968.

Sophisticated and precise means of monitoring self-injurious behaviors and administering electric shock have been developed. The Self-Injurious Behavior Inhibiting System (SIBIS; pronounced sEYE-biss), for example, is a lightweight device that a client wears on the part of the body that is subject to injury (see Photo 7-3).[87] The device measures the impact of the blow and automatically delivers a mild electric shock whenever the force of the impact exceeds a preprogrammed level (which is based on the intensity of the impact that will cause physical damage). The strength of the shock is like that of a rubber band snapped on the arm. The SIBIS can detect self-injurious behaviors and administer contingent electric shock more precisely and consistently than a therapist can. Another advantage of the SIBIS is that the client does not develop negative associations with the person who directly administers the shock. A small number of studies have evaluated the effectiveness of the SIBIS. Although it can result in rapid and dramatic decreases in self-injurious behaviors,[88] its effectiveness varies considerably with individual clients.[89]

Electric shock is a good aversive stimulus for four reasons. First, it is easily administered. Second, it can be activated instantaneously (at the press of a switch). Third, its intensity can be precisely controlled. Ease and precision of administration are important because physically aversive consequences are most potent when delivered immediately after the client performs the target behavior. Fourth, most clients experience electric shock as aversive.

The Johns Hopkins University Applied Physics Laboratory

PHOTO 7-3
A child with autistic disorder wearing the Self-Injurious Behavior Inhibiting System (SIBIS)

Many people, including some behavior therapists, consider electric shock an unacceptable treatment (for example, because they think it is too harsh).[90] A number of less innocuous physically aversive stimuli have been employed to treat a variety of problem behaviors, and some of these are listed in Table 7-1.

TABLE **7-1**

Examples of "More Acceptable" Physically Aversive Consequences than Electric Shock

Aversive Consequence	Problem Behavior
Rubber band snapped on wrist	Trichotillomania (pulling out hair)
Noxious odor	Self-stimulating behaviors
Cigarette smoke	Compulsive eating
Lemon juice	Head banging
Bitter substance	Nail biting
Mild mouthwash	Biting other children
Water mist sprayed in face	Face slapping
Loud noise	Bruxism (teeth grinding)
Bright light	Dangerous nocturnal rocking

Potential Negative Side Effects of Physically Aversive Consequences

Negative side effects of physically aversive consequences actually occur infrequently. In general, they occur less often when they are combined with procedures that accelerate alternative adaptive behaviors than when they are used alone.[91] Also, the milder the physically aversive consequences are, the fewer are the undesirable side effects.[92] Most negative side effects fall into three categories: avoidance behaviors, emotional responses, and perpetuation effects.

Avoidance Behaviors The application of physically aversive consequences may lead clients to develop negative associations toward the therapy situation, including the therapist and anyone else administering the treatment (such as a parent or teacher). The result is that clients may avoid therapy.[93] Children may run away from the person who administers the treatment, and adults may not show up for therapy sessions.

Avoidance behaviors can be minimized by having more than one person administer the therapy (for example, both parents) and by varying the setting in which the treatment takes place. The people administering the aversive consequences also should provide positive consequences for alternative behaviors (so that these individuals are not seen solely as "bearers of bad news"). This is especially important when these people have ongoing relationships with the client (as with parents).

Emotional Responses Clients treated with physically aversive consequences sometimes exhibit disruptive emotional responses, such as crying, tantrums, soiling and wetting their clothes, and fear.[94] Occasionally, clients become physically aggressive toward the person administering the treatment[95] or toward themselves.[96] Besides creating additional psychological problems for clients, these emotional responses interfere with the treatment by making the procedure more difficult to use, and they may add to clients' negative associations with the therapy situation.

Perpetuation Effects A third possible negative side effect of physically aversive consequences is that clients may learn to use this strategy as a means of controlling other people's behaviors. One revealing finding is that children whose parents use physically aversive consequences are more likely to behave aggressively[97] and changing such disciplinary tactics can reduce children's aggressive behaviors.[98]

A related side effect is that the use of physically aversive consequences may be reinforced in the change agent, especially in nonprofessionals such as parents.[99] Physically aversive consequences often lead to a rapid reduction of the deceleration target behavior. Thus, their use is negatively reinforced by the relief the change agent experiences when the client stops performing the target behavior. The result is that nonprofessionals are more likely to use physically aversive consequences in the future.

Guidelines for the Effective Use of Punishment

Behavior therapists have developed guidelines for administering all punishment procedures (that is, not just the use of physically aversive consequences).

1. *The punisher* (removal of reinforcers or introduction of undesirable consequences) *should occur immediately after the target behavior is performed.* The closer in time the punisher is to the target behavior, the greater is its effectiveness because the client is more likely to associate the punisher with the target behavior.
2. *The punisher should be administered every time the target behavior occurs.* Greater suppression results from the continuous (that is, for each occurrence) and consistent (that is, by all change agents involved) administration of the punisher, especially at the beginning of treatment.
3. *The client should be aware of the contingency between the target behavior and the punisher.* The client should be explicitly told and reminded about the contingency (for example, "When you hit other kids, you will get a time out").
4. *Reinforcement should not closely follow the delivery of the punisher.* If a potential reinforcer is administered shortly after a punisher, the punisher signals the client that a reinforcer is forthcoming and the deceleration target behavior may *increase* because the reinforcer is associated with the target behavior. A common example is when a parent comforts a child who is crying after being reprimanded for a misbehavior (as by hugging the child and saying, "You know I love you").
5. *The punisher should be preceded by a warning cue.* After the cue (for example, "No!") becomes associated with the punisher, the cue alone may decelerate the target behavior.

IN THEORY **7-1**

Punishment: What's in a Name?

Is using physically aversive consequences a punishment technique? Of course it is. Are extinction, time out from positive reinforcement, response cost, and overcorrection also punishment techniques? Yes, but until you read this chapter, you might not have thought so because most people only associate punishment with the administration of physically aversive consequences. Certainly, there are legitimate humanitarian objections to the use of physically aversive consequences; even when justified, they have a bad public reputation. And,

because the term *punishment* is primarily associated with the administration of physically aversive consequences, all punishment procedures become guilty by association.

What we call something strongly affects how we view it and our attitude toward it. Shakespeare's Juliet was wrong when she said that "a rose by any other name would smell as sweet." Similarly, punishment by any other name would not smell as sour. *Response cost*, for example, clearly does not have the same negative

connotation as *punishment*. In fact, response cost gets high marks on acceptability.[100]

It is fortunate that the general public does not think of extinction, time out from positive reinforcement, and response cost as punishment because of the term's negative connotations. We hope that you have not let the stereotypical negative bias associated with the term *punishment* taint your view of it, because punishment techniques can be effective, efficient, and ethical interventions.

6. *An adaptive behavior that competes with the undesirable target behavior should be reinforced in conjunction with decelerating the maladaptive behavior.* Engaging in a competing adaptive behavior decreases the opportunities the client has to engage in the maladaptive target behavior.
7. *If physically aversive consequences are employed, their potential negative side effects should be looked for and minimized if they occur.*

AVERSION THERAPY

Clockwork orange movie sample of Avesion Therapy

With physically aversive consequences, an unpleasant event is administered immediately *after* the client performs the deceleration target behavior. In contrast, in *aversion therapy* an aversive stimulus is introduced *while* the client is engaging in the deceleration target behavior, and it is terminated as soon as the client stops performing the behavior. The objective is for the client to *associate* performing the target behavior with the aversive stimulus so that performing the behavior becomes aversive. This is the same process that accounts for the development of common avoidance behaviors. For example, a person may get airsick when a plane encounters turbulence. Subsequently, the individual may avoid traveling by plane, which is associated with the unpleasantness of airsickness.

Aversion therapy primarily has been used to treat two classes of maladaptive behaviors: substance abuse and *paraphilias*, which are sexually deviant behaviors such as exhibitionism and pedophilia.

Basic Procedures

Maladaptive behaviors can be paired with any stimulus that the client finds aversive (that is, unpleasant, distasteful, or painful). Shock[c] and nausea-producing drugs are the most frequently used physically aversive stimuli; occasionally, noxious odors as well as hot air and smoke (to decelerate cigarette smoking) are employed. Psychologically aversive stimuli include feelings of humiliation and unpleasant thoughts.

The aversive stimulus used may depend on the target behavior. For example, nausea generally is more effective than shock in treating abuse of alcohol[101] and crack cocaine.[102] The client determines the strength of the stimulus. For the therapy to be effective, the client must honestly tell the therapist the intensity at which the stimulus becomes aversive. Clients for whom aversion therapy is successful must experience genuine pain or discomfort. Accordingly, clients who are being treated by aversion therapy must be highly motivated to change their maladaptive behavior.

The aversive stimulus is associated with the target behavior in one of three ways. Ideally, the association is created as the client is (1) *actually engaging* in the target behavior. Because this is not always possible or efficient, the client can be (2) *symbolically exposed* to the target behavior, as by viewing pictures of the target behavior or listening to a verbal description of it, or by (3) *imagining performing* the target behavior.

---

[c] The shock in aversion therapy is the same as that which is used in punishment and shares the same advantages described earlier (page 164).

Case 7-4 is an example of an adult who wanted to change a long-standing sexual habit that had recently become personally distressing to him. The case illustrates how clients can be exposed symbolically to the target behavior and the use of drug-induced nausea as the aversive stimulus.

CASE **7-4**

Treatment of Transvestic (Cross-Dressing) Behaviors by Aversion Therapy[103]

A 22-year-old married truck driver reported that he had experienced the desire to dress as a woman since he was 8 years old. From the age of 15 and through his military service and marriage, he had derived erotic pleasure from dressing in female clothes and viewing himself in a mirror. At the same time, he maintained a good sexual relationship with his wife. He was strongly motivated to seek therapy because of his fear of being seen wearing women's clothes and at the urging of his wife, who had just recently learned of her husband's cross-dressing.

The therapist prepared slides of the client in various stages of female attire and had the client prepare an audio tape that described these activities. The client then looked at the slides and listened to the tape to assess whether they induced sexual excitement, which they did.

The treatment involved pairing the transvestic experience with nausea, produced by injection of the drug apomorphine. As soon as the injection began to take effect, the slides and tape were presented, and they were terminated only after the client began to vomit. The treatment was administered several times a day for 6 days, which was sufficient to completely eliminate the client's desire to dress in women's clothes. Follow-up over a 6-month period, including interviews with both the client and his wife, indicated that the client no longer cross-dressed.

The effects of aversion therapy may not be durable because the association between the maladaptive behavior and the aversive stimulus does not last. To deal with this problem, clients are asked to return periodically (such as every couple of months) for additional therapy sessions called **booster treatments**.[104] Re-exposing the client to the target behavior and the aversive stimulus keeps that association "active." For example, booster treatments for alcohol abuse significantly increase the chances of continued abstinence.[105] Also, as with punishment, it is essential for clients to adopt new adaptive behaviors that substitute for the maladaptive behavior that has been decelerated. For instance, it is likely that, following his successful treatment, the client in Case 7-4 who no longer was cross-dressing had come to derive erotic pleasure in other ways, such as through his sexual relations with his wife.

Covert Sensitization

In **covert sensitization,** the therapist verbally describes both the client's engaging in the deceleration target behavior and the concomitant aversive stimulus, usually nausea. The following description was used with a college professor who wanted to stop smoking.

> You are preparing your lectures. . . . As soon as you start reaching for the cigarette, you get a nauseated feeling in your stomach . . . like you are about to vomit. You touch the pack of cigarettes and bitter spit comes into your mouth; when you take the cigarette out of the pack some pieces of food come into your throat. Now you feel sick and your stomach cramps. As you are about to put the cigarette in your mouth, you puke. . . . The cigarette in your hand is very soggy and full of green vomit. There is a stink coming from the vomit. Snot is coming from your nose. Your hands feel all slimy and full of vomit. . . . Your clothes are all full of puke. You get up from your desk and turn away from the . . . cigarettes. You immediately begin to feel better being away from the . . . cigarettes.[106]

Covert sensitization has four advantages over other aversion therapies: (1) no equipment, such as a shock apparatus, is needed; (2) unlike some drug-induced aversion, covert sensitization can be safely carried out without medical supervision; (3) with an aversive *image*, clients can easily self-administer covert sensitization in vivo; and (4) clients may consider it more acceptable, which is an important consideration because of the high dropout rate with aversion therapy.[107]

Developed by Joseph Cautela,[108] covert sensitization most frequently has been used to treat paraphilias,[109] overeating,[110] alcohol abuse,[111] and smoking,[112] and it is used almost exclusively with adults.[113] Support for the effectiveness of covert sensitization is tenuous, however. Most of the research has been case studies,[114] and some of the few controlled studies have yielded equivocal findings.[115]

DECELERATION BEHAVIOR THERAPIES FOR ADDICTIVE BEHAVIORS

A number of deceleration behavior therapies are used to treat addictive behaviors, such as abuse of alcohol and cigarette smoking. To conclude the topic of deceleration behavior therapies, we will discuss the application of differential reinforcement of competing behaviors, response cost, aversion therapy, and covert sensitization to treating addictive behaviors. The discussion illustrates the variety of behavior therapies that are often available for treating a particular problem.

With differential reinforcement of competing behaviors, clients are reinforced for behaviors that compete with drug-abusing behaviors. In one study, clients attending a methadone clinic for opiate dependence earned up to $15 each week in vouchers for goods and services contingent on their completing specific tasks that competed with drug-abusing behaviors, such as applying for a job and receiving vocational training. The program resulted in significant reductions in illicit drug use.[116]

An example of response cost to decelerate substance abuse involved an African-American man who was abusing amphetamines. He gave his therapist $50 checks made out to the Ku Klux Klan (understandably the man's least favorite organization), with the understanding that the therapist would automatically mail a check to the Klan each time he took amphetamines. The therapist had to send only one check to the Klan, and at a 15-month follow-up, the client reported that he had not used amphetamines since that one incident.[117]

Aversion therapy has been used to decelerate cigarette smoking. One technique, called **rapid smoking**, has clients (1) smoke at the rate of one puff every 6 seconds, (2) inhale normally, and (3) continue smoking rapidly until they cannot tolerate it anymore. In some cases, the aversion created by rapid smoking can have long-lasting effects in decreasing smoking,[118] although such results have not been obtained consistently.[119] Because rapid smoking can cause temporary cardiovascular stress,[120] it is used infrequently.

Covert sensitization is yet another technique used to decelerate addictive behaviors. Earlier in the chapter you read about the college professor who wanted to quit smoking. The simultaneous verbal description of the client's engaging in cigarette smoking and of the intensely unpleasant sensations related to this experience reduced his smoking.

The problem with using these behavior therapies to treat addictive behaviors is that they may be effective only in the short run. All too often, clients relapse—that is, revert to their addictive behaviors—after therapy has ended. In addition to the need for booster treatments, *relapse prevention*, which you will read about in Chapter 13, provides an alternative strategy that specifically deals with this problem.[121]

ETHICAL ISSUES IN THE USE OF AVERSIVE THERAPIES

Physically aversive consequences and aversion therapy are the behavior therapies that have come under closest scrutiny regarding ethical concerns. Because these treatments involve physical discomfort and sometimes pain, they have the *potential* of infringing on clients' fundamental human rights. Some people believe that aversive treatments should not be used at all, especially not with clients who are vulnerable to abuse and unable to make informed decisions about their own treatment, such as clients institutionalized for schizophrenia and mental retardation.[122]

As you consider the ethicality of aversive procedures, keep three points in mind. First, the aversive stimulus is relatively brief and has no long-term ill effects. For example, shock is administered for only a second or two. The stinging sensation lasts no more than a few minutes, and no permanent tissue damage results. Second, there is nothing inherently unethical about treatment that involves pain or discomfort. Consider receiving an injection, doing painful physical therapy exercises, and having chemotherapy that involves extreme discomfort. Because the benefits of these treatments outweigh their unpleasantness, we do not consider them unethical. Third, ethical issues generally do not arise when clients freely volunteer to receive aversive procedures, as did the man who wished to stop cross-dressing in Case 7-4. Ethical issues are much more likely to arise when aversive procedures are used with clients who are *required* to be in therapy, such as adults committed to institutions.

The potential for harm by aversive procedures has been exaggerated due to the widely held misconception that aversive procedures are used extensively in behavior therapy. Indeed, some people even think of aversive procedures as synonymous with behavior therapy. In fact, aversive procedures constitute a small proportion of behavior therapy techniques, and they are employed infrequently.[123] One reason for their limited use is that aversive procedures generally are relatively weak treatments, especially for producing lasting change.

Principle of Utility

Aversive techniques usually are instituted as a last resort, when other therapy procedures have failed to decelerate serious debilitating behaviors. In each case, a cost-benefit analysis is made. Does the potential outcome of therapy outweigh the potential negative effects of the aversive procedure, such as temporary discomfort or mild pain? This question addresses the *principle of utility*, which holds that an action is morally right if, when compared with alternative actions, it produces more benefit than harm.[124]

The following description addresses the question: "Do the ends justify the means?" with respect to using physically aversive consequences to reduce self-destructive behaviors.[125] As you read it, consider the ethical issues it raises.

A colleague . . . showed us a deeply moving film. The heroine was an institutionalized primary-grade girl. She . . . [frequently engaged in head banging], so a padded football helmet was put on her head. Because she could take it off, her hands were tied down in her crib. She kept tossing her neck and tore out her hair at every opportunity. She accordingly had a perpetually bruised face on a hairless head, with a neck almost as thick as that of a horse. She was nonverbal. My colleague and his staff carefully planned a program for her, using all kinds of reinforcers . . . but [she] persisted in her typical behavior. In desperation, the ultimate weapon was unwrapped. When she tossed her head, my colleague yelled "Don't!" simultaneously delivering a sharp slap to her cheek. She subsided for a brief period, tossed again, and the punishment was delivered.

My colleague reports that less than a dozen slaps were ever delivered and the word "Don't!" yelled even from across the room . . . [became] effective. Its use was shortly down to once a week and was discontinued in a few weeks. In the meantime, the football helmet was removed and the girl began to eat at the table. She slept in a regular bed. Her hair grew out, and she turned out to be a very pretty little blonde girl with delicate features and a delicate neck. In less than a year, she started to move toward joining a group of older girls whose behavior, it was hoped, she would [imitate]. She smiled often.

[When the girl's] . . . parents discovered that she had been slapped . . . , they immediately withdrew her from the custody of my colleague's staff. The last part of the film shows her back at the institution. She is strapped down in her crib. Her hands are tied . . . . She is wearing a football helmet. [Once again] her hair is torn out, her face is a mass of bruises and her neck is almost as thick as that of a horse.[126]

There is no doubt that the therapist violated ethical guidelines by not completely informing the girl's parents about the treatment procedures. When this case occurred more than 35 years ago, behavior therapists were not as sensitized as they are today to the importance of fully disclosing treatment procedures and obtaining consent for their use.

The case also raises another critical ethical question. Given the self-destructive nature of the girl's behaviors, was the treatment ethically justified? Alternatively, was it ethical to terminate the treatment? Was the principle of utility violated? How would you answer these questions?

Finally, consider a more recent case of a 31-year-old man with a severe developmental disability who engaged in life-threatening voluntary vomiting.[127] Because alternative nonaversive treatments could not be found, two behavior therapists recommended that short-term contingent shock be used. After a court ruled against this recommendation, the man was subjected to an intrusive medical procedure (permanent nasogastric intubation) that required hospitalization and intensive nursing care for the next year.

How would you evaluate the ethicality of the court's decision in terms of the principle of utility? How would you compare the ethicality of short-term contingent shock versus a permanent intrusive treatment and the year-long restrictive environment the treatment required?

The principle of utility may also be applicable when clients voluntarily seek treatment for psychological problems that seriously interfere with their living normal lives. In the treatment of paraphilias and substance abuse, aversion therapy can be an important component of a treatment package that includes procedures to accelerate alternative, socially desirable and adaptive behaviors. The brief discomfort experienced in aversion therapy is minimal compared with the extensive disruption of work and family life, the social ostracism, and the self-deprecation that result from longstanding socially unacceptable and personally maladaptive behaviors.[128]

Misuse, Abuse, and Safeguards

Aversive procedures occasionally are misused and abused. Misuse is usually perpetrated by nonprofessional change agents who have had minimal training and experience with the procedures. For example, aversive consequences often need be applied only briefly to be effective.[129] Inexperienced change agents may continue the aversive consequences long after they have had their desired effect. This practice is unlikely to produce a further decrease in the target behavior, and it is likely to produce negative side effects, such as aggressive behaviors. Moreover, such treatment justifiably would be considered harsh.

Abuses of aversive techniques are more likely to arise when the deceleration target behavior is disturbing to others, as with a patient on a psychiatric ward who disrupts the ongoing activities with inappropriate outbursts. Overburdened hospital staff may apply aversive procedures because they are, in the short run, more efficient. Generally, it is easier to devise an aversive consequence to stop disturbing behaviors immediately than to identify and then gradually accelerate alternative, competing prosocial behaviors.

A variety of guidelines have been proposed to promote the ethical use of aversive procedures, including the following.

1. Aversive procedures should be considered only after it is clear that nonaversive alternatives will not work effectively and efficiently.[130]
2. When possible, deceleration therapies that are not *physically* aversive should be tried before physically aversive procedures are employed.
3. If a physically aversive procedure is used, a physician should be consulted to assure that it will be medically safe for the client.
4. The client or the client's legal guardian must be made aware of the nature of the treatment and agree to it—that is, *informed consent* must be obtained.
5. The procedures should be implemented only by a competent professional.
6. Aversive techniques should be used along with procedures that simultaneously accelerate alternative behaviors to take the place of the behaviors being eliminated.
7. Clear-cut measures of the target behavior should be collected before, during, and after therapy to document changes.

These guidelines for the *ethical* use of aversive procedures supplement the guidelines for the *effective* use of punishment in general presented earlier in the chapter (page 167).

ALL THINGS CONSIDERED: DECELERATION BEHAVIOR THERAPY

Deceleration behavior therapies are an important part of the behavior therapist's armamentarium. They can be effective and efficient in treating maladaptive behaviors. In general, success rates for punishment have been higher than for aversion therapy. This difference is due, at least in part, to the fact that the primary targets of aversion therapy—substance abuse and paraphilias—are highly resistant to treatment of any kind.[131]

It is obvious that therapies that accelerate adaptive behaviors enhance clients' personal freedom by increasing the number of alternative behaviors they can choose to engage in. Therapies that decelerate undesirable behaviors also serve this function. A woman whose excessive drinking has been alleviated by aversion therapy is freer because now she has many more options in her life. She can engage in activities once impaired by intoxication, including holding a job and interacting with family and friends. With either acceleration or deceleration behavior therapy procedures, the client has more options for behaving after successful treatment than before treatment.

With both punishment and aversion therapy, the reduction of the target behavior may be only temporary, which can be a major limitation of these treatments.[132] However, in some cases, such as self-injurious and highly disruptive behaviors, even temporary suppression of the target behavior is desirable, especially when no other treatments have been effective. Moreover, temporary suppression provides the opportunity to reinforce alternative adaptive behaviors, which is the optimal strategy for creating durable change.

Besides the ethical issues discussed earlier regarding deceleration behavior therapy, two other concerns militate against its application: undesirable side effects and practical problems. The potential undesirable side effects of physically aversive consequences we discussed earlier are relevant to aversion therapy as well. However, to put this concern in perspective, the undesirable side effects are not inevitable. In fact, they are the exception rather than the rule; when they do occur, they are usually temporary and decline over the course of therapy.[133] Nonetheless, behavior therapists must be alert for their possible occurrence.

Practical problems also are associated with deceleration therapy procedures. These approaches are less acceptable to both clients and therapists than other behavior therapies. Clients generally do not want to subject themselves to discomfort or pain, or even to the loss of reinforcers. Additionally, some therapists find it distasteful to administer aversive therapies.

A related problem concerns the client's motivation to change. High motivation is necessary to enter and remain in treatment that has distinctly negative aspects. Clients who are not highly motivated to change are less likely to cooperate with the therapy procedures and more likely to drop out of therapy.[134]

In sum, deceleration behavior therapy procedures can be effective means of treating maladaptive behaviors, especially when time is of the essence. Otherwise, deceleration therapy should be used after more acceptable therapies have been tried. Finally, deceleration therapy techniques always should be part of a treatment package that includes procedures for accelerating alternative adaptive behaviors.

SUMMARY

1. The preferred strategy for decelerating an undesirable behavior is to reinforce an acceleration target behavior that is an alternative to the deceleration target behavior. This differential reinforcement can be of incompatible behaviors, of competing behaviors, of any other behaviors, and of low response rates of the target behavior. Two variants of differential reinforcement are noncontingent reinforcement and functional communication training.

2. The two strategies that decrease maladaptive behaviors directly are punishment, which changes the consequences of maladaptive behaviors, and aversion therapy, which associates unpleasant events with maladaptive behaviors.

3. Extinction and time out from positive reinforcement are examples of negative punishment because they remove the reinforcers maintaining the deceleration target behavior.

4. Extinction does this by permanently removing or withholding the reinforcers that maintain the behavior.

5. Time out from positive reinforcement involves immediately and temporarily removing the client's access to generalized reinforcers. Time out always is brief and often is implemented in a special area, such as a time-out room.

6. Response cost, overcorrection, and physically aversive consequences are examples of positive punishment because they introduce undesirable consequences to decelerate maladaptive behaviors.

7. Response cost removes a valued item or privilege when a maladaptive behavior is performed.

8. Overcorrection decelerates maladaptive behaviors by having clients correct the effects of their actions (restitution) and then intensively practice an appropriate alternative behavior (positive practice).

9. Physically aversive consequences can decelerate undesirable behaviors rapidly. Painful but harmless shock frequently serves as the aversive consequence. Physically aversive consequences are rarely used in behavior therapy because they have potential negative side effects—avoidance behaviors, emotional responses, and perpetuation effects—and because of ethical and humanitarian objections.

10. Punishment refers to any procedure that decelerates a behavior by changing its consequences, although people often erroneously associate punishment only with the use of physically aversive consequences.

11. In aversion therapy, an unpleasant or painful stimulus is introduced while the client is engaging in the deceleration target behavior. The client comes to associate the target behavior with the unpleasant stimulus (most often shock or nausea). The association can occur while the client is performing the behavior, is symbolically exposed to the behavior, or is imagining performing the behavior. Aversion therapy is used primarily to treat substance abuse and paraphilias. Because the effects of aversion therapy may be temporary, booster treatments may be necessary to increase its durability.

12. In covert sensitization, the client imagines both the target behavior and the aversive stimulus, which is usually nausea created by the therapist's vivid descriptions of disgusting events.

13. Addictive behaviors can be treated by a variety of deceleration behavior therapies, including differential reinforcement of competing behaviors, response cost, aversion therapy, and covert sensitization.

14. Aversive procedures have come under the closest scrutiny regarding ethical violations. In fact, aversive procedures constitute a small proportion of behavior therapy techniques and are used infrequently. When aversive procedures are used, a cost-benefit analysis is performed for each case.

15. Misuses and abuses of aversive procedures most often are perpetrated by change agents who have limited experience with the procedures and who employ them because they are easier to implement than alternative therapy approaches.

16. Deceleration therapies can be effective and efficient. Success rates have been higher for punishment than for aversion therapy. Deceleration therapies, like acceleration therapies, increase clients' freedom by expanding

their options for behaving. A major limitation of deceleration therapies is that their effectiveness may be only temporary, which is one reason for simultaneously accelerating alternative adaptive behaviors. Three issues that militate against the use of deceleration behavior therapy are ethical and humanitarian objections, undesirable side effects, and practical problems.

REFERENCE NOTES

1. Nunes, Murphy, & Ruprecht, 1977.
2. Larson & Ayllon, 1990.
3. For example, Deitz, Repp, & Deitz, 1976; Shafto & Sulzbacher, 1977.
4. For example, Foxx & Meindl, 2007; Hegel & Ferguson, 2000.
5. For example, Foxx & Garito, 2007; Thompson, Iwata, Conners, & Roscoe, 1999; Vollmer, Roane, Ringdahl, & Marcus, 1999.
6. Goetz, Holmberg, & LeBlanc, 1975.
7. Leitenberg, Burchard, Burchard, Fuller, & Lysaght, 1977; Wagaman, Miltenberger, & Williams, 1995.
8. Heard & Watson, 1999.
9. For example, Lennox, Miltenberger, & Donnelly, 1987; Poling & Ryan, 1982.
10. Deitz & Repp, 1973.
11. Deitz, 1977.
12. Tucker, Sigafoos, & Bushell, 1998.
13. Hagopian, Crockett, van Stone, DeLeon, & Bowman, 2000.
14. For example, Butler & Luiselli, 2007; Doughty & Anderson, 2006; Gouboth, Wilder, & Booher, 2007; Rasmussen & O'Neill, 2006; Wilder, Normand, & Atwell, 2005.
15. Carr & Durand, 1985; Carr, Levin, McConnachie, Carlson, Kemp, & Smith, 1994; Durand, 1999.
16. Brown et al., 2000; Kahng, Hendrickson, & Vu, 2000.
17. Harding, Wacker, Berg, Barretto, & Ringdahl, 2005; Kurtz et al., 2003; Mancil, Conroy, Nakao, & Alter, 2006.
18. Dunlap, Ester, Langhans, & Fox, 2006.
19. Derby et al., 1997.
20. Casey & Merical, 2006.
21. Dunlap, Ester, Langhans, & Fox, 2006.
22. Williams, 1959.
23. For example, Ducharme & Van Houten, 1994; Magee & Ellis, 2000.
24. For example, Coe et al., 1997; Mazaleski, Iwata, Vollmer, Zarcone, & Smith, 1993.
25. For example, Lerman & Iwata, 1996; Neisworth & Moore, 1972.
26. Cooper, Heron, & Heward, 1987; Lerman & Iwata, 1996.
27. For example, LaVigna & Donnellan, 1986; Lerman, Iwata, & Wallace, 1999.
28. Lerman, Iwata, & Wallace, 1999.
29. Ducharme & Van Houten, 1994; Kazdin, 1994; Lerman & Iwata, 1995.
30. Ducharme & Van Houten, 1994.
31. For example, Lawton, France, & Blampied, 1991.
32. Ducharme & Van Houten, 1994.
33. For example, Bloxham, Long, Alderman, & Hollin, 1993.
34. Kazdin, 1994.
35. Costenbader & Reading-Brown, 1995; Twyman, Johnson, Buie, & Nelson, 1994.
36. Barkley, 1987.
37. For example, Barton, Guess, Garcia, & Baer, 1970; White, Nielson, & Johnson, 1972.
38. Everett, Olmi, Edwards, Tingstrom, Sterling-Turner, & Christ, 2007.
39. For example, Tate & Baroff, 1966.
40. Barton, Guess, Garcia, & Baer, 1970.
41. For example, Kendall, Nay, & Jeffers, 1975.
42. Cayner & Kiland, 1974.
43. For example, Bigelow, Liebson, & Griffiths, 1974; Griffiths, Bigelow, & Liebson, 1974.
44. For example, Forehand & McMahon, 1981; Rortvedt & Miltenberger, 1994.
45. Marlow, Tingstrom, Olmi, & Edwards, 1997.
46. For example, McNeil, Clemens-Mowrer, Gurwitch, & Funderburk, 1994.
47. Kazdin, 1972.
48. For example, Mann, 1972, 1976.
49. Lindsley, 1966.
50. Spiegler, 1989, 2000.

51. For example, McCain & Kelley, 1994; Reynolds & Kelley, 1997.
52. For example, Sullivan & O'Leary, 1990.
53. Carlson, Mann, & Alexander, 2000; Carlson & Tamm, 2000.
54. Barkley, 1987.
55. Pemberton & Borrego, 2007.
56. Polaha & Allen, 2000.
57. DuPaul, Guevremont, & Barkley, 1992; Evans, Ferre, Ford, & Green, 1995.
58. Keeney, Fisher, Adelinis, & Wilder, 2000.
59. Armstrong & Drabman, 1998; Sullivan & O'Leary, 1990.
60. Blampied & Kahan, 1992; Jones, Eyberg, Adams, & Boggs, 1998; Reynolds & Kelley, 1997.
61. MacKenzie-Keating & McDonald, 1990.
62. Foxx & Azrin, 1972.
63. Foxx & Garito, 2007; Foxx & Meindl, 2007.
64. For example, Harris & Romanczyk, 1976.
65. Azrin, Sneed, & Foxx, 1973.
66. Rojahn, Hammer, & Kroeger, 1997; Rollings, Baumeister, & Baumeister, 1977.
67. For example, Ellis, Singh, Crews, Bonaventura, Gehin, & Ricketts, 1997; Singh & Bakker, 1984.
68. Foxx & Azrin, 1972.
69. Tremblay & Drabman, 1997.
70. Azrin & Wesolowski, 1974.
71. Azrin & Besalel, 1999.
72. Azrin & Powers, 1975.
73. Axelrod, Brantner, & Meddock, 1978; Ollendick & Matson, 1978.
74. Azrin & Powers, 1975.
75. Cole, Montgomery, Wilson, & Milan, 2000.
76. Adams & Kelley, 1992.
77. For example, Testal, Francisco, Ortiz, Angel, Santos, & Dolores, 1998.
78. Sisson, Van Hasselt, & Hersen, 1993.
79. Carey & Bucher, 1981, 1986.
80. Axelrod, Brantner, & Meddock, 1978; Ollendick & Matson, 1978.
81. Jones, Eyberg, Adams, & Boggs, 1998.
82. Jones, Eyberg, Adams, & Boggs, 1998; Miller, Manne, & Palevsky, 1998.
83. Guevremont & Spiegler, 1990; Spiegler & Guevremont, 1994, 2002.
84. For example, Bucher & Lovaas, 1968; Prochaska, Smith, Marzilli, Colby, & Donovan, 1974.
85. Salvy, Mulick, Butter, Bartlett, & Linscheid, 2004.
86. Risley, 1968; quotation from p. 22.
87. Linscheid, Iwata, Ricketts, Williams, & Griffin, 1990.
88. Linscheid, Hartel, & Cooley, 1993; Linscheid, Iwata, Ricketts, Williams, & Griffin, 1990; Salvy, Mulick, Butter, Bartlett, & Linscheid, 2004.
89. Linscheid, Hartel, & Cooley, 1993; Ricketts, Goza, & Matese, 1993; Williams, Kirkpatrick-Sanchez, & Crocker, 1994.
90. Kazdin, 1980.
91. For example, Carey & Bucher, 1986.
92. Kazdin, 1989.
93. For example, Azrin & Holz, 1966.
94. For example, Azrin & Wesolowski, 1975; Carey & Bucher, 1981.
95. For example, Knight & McKenzie, 1974; Mayhew & Harris, 1978.
96. For example, Azrin, Gottlieb, Hughart, Wesolowski, & Rahn, 1975; Rollings, Baumeister, & Baumeister, 1977.
97. Kazdin, 1987, 2008; Timberlake, 1981.
98. Reid, Patterson, & Snyder, 2002.
99. Kazdin, 1989.
100. For example, Borrego, Ibanez, Spendlove, & Pemberton, 2007.
101. Nathan, 1976.
102. Bordnick, Elkins, Orr, Walters, & Thyer, 2004.
103. Lavin, Thorpe, Barker, Blakemore, & Conway, 1961.
104. Rachman & Teasdale, 1969.
105. Voegtlin, Lemere, Broz, & O'Hollaren, 1941.
106. Cautela, 1972, pp. 88–89.
107. For example, Callahan & Leitenberg, 1973; Wilson & Tracey, 1976.
108. Cautela, 1966, 1967.
109. For example, Barlow, 1993; Dougher, 1993; Krop & Burgess, 1993a; Maletzky, 1993.
110. For example, Cautela, 1966; Janda & Rimm, 1972; Stuart, 1967.
111. For example, Anant, 1968; Ashem & Donner, 1968; Cautela, 1970; Hedberg & Campbell, 1974; Smith & Gregory, 1976.
112. For example, Lawson & May, 1970; Sipich, Russell, & Tobias, 1974; Wagner & Bragg, 1970.
113. Compare with Cautela, 1982.
114. For example, Cautela & Kearney, 1993.
115. Rachman & Wilson, 1980.
116. Iguchi, Belding, Morral, Lamb, & Husband, 1997.
117. Boudin, 1972.
118. Lichtenstein, Harris, Birchler, Wahl, & Schmahl, 1973; Lichtenstein & Rodrigues, 1977.

119. For example, Lando, 1975; Raw & Russell, 1980.
120. Horan, Hackett, Nicholas, Linberg, Stone, & Lukaski, 1977; Lichtenstein & Glasgow, 1977; Poole, Sanson-Fisher, German, & Harker, 1980.
121. Marlatt & Donovan, 2005; Marlatt & Gordon, 1985; Witkiewitz & Marlatt, 2007.
122. Tustin, Pennington, & Byrne, 1994.
123. Spiegler & Guevremont, 2002.
124. Beauchamp & Walters, 1978.
125. For example, Lovaas & Simmons, 1969.
126. Goldiamond, 1974, pp. 62–63.
127. Mudford, 1995.
128. Bandura, 1969.
129. For example, Cole, Montgomery, Wilson, & Milan, 2000; Lovaas & Simmons, 1969; White, Nielson, & Johnson, 1972.
130. Carr & Durand, 1985; Emerson, 1993.
131. Kazdin & Wilson, 1978.
132. Compare with Linscheid, Hartel, & Cooley, 1993.
133. Kazdin, 1989.
134. For example, Callahan & Leitenberg, 1973; Wilson & Tracey, 1976.

8

Combining Reinforcement and Punishment

Token Economy, Contingency Contract, and Behavioral Parent Training

Now that you are familiar with the basic principles and procedures of reinforcement and punishment, we can explore their application in three standard treatment packages: token economy, contingency contract, and behavioral parent training. A wide array of acceleration and deceleration problem behaviors have been modified with these treatment packages, as you will see.

TOKEN ECONOMY

Even if you are unfamiliar with the term *token economy*, you are familiar with the concept. Every day you participate in an elaborate token economy—our monetary system.

What Is a Token Economy?

A token economy is a system for motivating clients to perform desirable behaviors and to refrain from performing undesirable behaviors.[1] Clients earn **tokens**—token reinforcers such as poker chips or points—for adaptive behaviors and lose tokens for maladaptive behaviors. The clients exchange tokens for actual reinforcers called **backup reinforcers**. Clients are made aware of what they have to do to earn or forfeit tokens and how they can spend them on backup reinforers. Token economies are used more often for groups of clients than for individuals, so most of our discussion deals with group programs.

Modern token economies have some highly innovative historical precursors. In Chapter 2, you read about Maconochie's point system for prisoners in Australia at the beginning of the 19th century.[2] At about the same time in England, Joseph Lancaster set up an elaborate token reinforcement system to motivate students' learning.[3] Because the school had a large number of students and few teachers, students who excelled academically tutored other students in small groups. The students, as well as their tutors, received token reinforcers based on the students' performance. By the late 19th century, a number of school systems in the United States were using token reinforcement to promote learning and foster appropriate classroom behaviors (such as arriving on time for school).[4] The token economy as we know it today began with a program for hospitalized patients with chronic psychiatric disorders, developed by Teodoro Ayllon and Nathan Azrin in 1961 at Anna State Hospital in southern Illinois.[5]

Basic Elements

A token economy consists of four basic elements:

1. *A list of acceleration and deceleration target behaviors, including the number of tokens that clients can earn or lose for performing each.* Token economies primarily deal with acceleration target behaviors that vary with clients' problems. For a 10-year-old with mental retardation, dressing might be a target behavior, whereas for a 10-year-old 5th-grader with attention deficit hyperactive disorder, completing an assignment might be a target behavior.

2. *A list of backup reinforcers, including the token cost of each.* The list of backup reinforcers is general for all the clients in the token economy, and it includes reinforcers that will motivate each of the clients.

Courtesy of Teodoro Ayllon

Teodoro Ayllon

Courtesy of Nathan Azrin

Nathan Azrin

3. *The type of token.* Tokens can be tangible or symbolic. Tangible tokens include poker chips (different colors for different values), metal washers, specially designed paper currency, stickers, stars on a chart, and money itself. Points are symbolic tokens.

4. *Specific procedures and rules for the operation of the token economy* (for example, indicating when clients can exchange tokens for backup reinforcers). Such rules are crucial when a small staff must administer the program with a large number of clients.

Token economies are used to treat diverse problem behaviors and client populations.[6] To show how token economies function, we will describe two token economies in detail: the Community Training Center (a program for patients with chronic psychiatric disorders) and Achievement Place (a home-style program for juveniles who have committed minor legal offenses). We also will briefly review the application of token economies to people with mental retardation, children in classrooms, and individuals and families.

The Community Training Center: A Token Economy for Patients with Chronic Psychiatric Disorders

The Community Training Center, a day treatment program for individuals previously hospitalized for chronic psychiatric disorders (predominantly schizophrenia), was developed by Michael Spiegler and Haig Agigian at the Palo Alto (California) Veterans Administration Hospital.[7] The goal of the program was to prepare the patients, called *trainees*, for independent living in the community. The trainees had been hospitalized for an average of more than 8 years. Most trainees were male, and their average age was 45. They lacked the self-care, home management, interpersonal, and community interaction skills necessary to live independent lives. To treat these behavioral deficits, the Community Training Center was run as a school that offered classes in which the skills were taught, such as social communication, problem solving, money management, health and hygiene, social customs, and current events. This innovative program ushered in the use of social skills training for treating serious psychiatric disorders (a treatment you'll read about in Chapter 11).

For the most part, trainees had little desire to learn the skills taught. They were frightened of independent living and, through years of hospitalization, had grown accustomed to acting dependently. To motivate the trainees to develop independent living skills, a token economy, named the *credit system*, was used.

Credits and Credit Cards

The units of exchange in the credit system were points called *credits*. Each day, trainees received a new *credit card* on which the number of credits they earned and spent that day were recorded (see Figure 8-1). Trainees filled out their own credit cards, and staff members validated transactions to prevent cheating (see Figure 8-1). By recording what they had done to earn credits (such as attending a class) and the number of credits they had earned, trainees were made aware of the contingency between their behaviors and the reinforcers. It also gave the trainees practice in self-reinforcement, which is important for independent living.

Michael Spiegler

Haig Agigian

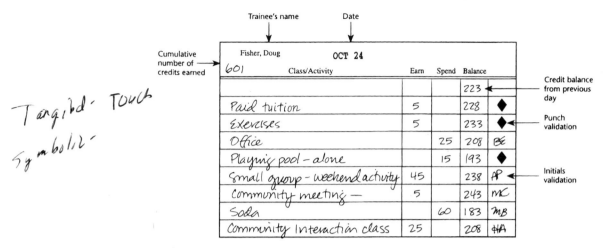

Tangibd - Touch

Symbolic-

FIGURE 8-1

Example of a credit card used by trainees in the Community Training Center credit system (token economy)

Source: Adapted from Spiegler & Agigian, 1977, p. 119.

Earning Credits

Trainees earned credits for learning skills, which were assessed by written and oral quizzes and behavioral tests (such as role-playing). They also earned credits for doing homework, which was an integral part of many classes. Most homework assignments involved practicing daily living skills in the community (for instance, taking a friend to lunch).

The procedures for administering credits during classes were based on four principles, which are important in all token economies. (1) The criteria for earning credits were clearly defined. (2) The staff made trainees aware of the criteria (as by posting them in the classroom). (3) Staff members awarded credits as soon as possible after a target behavior was performed. (4) The program paired earning credits with social reinforcers (such as praise from a class instructor and other trainees in the class).

Generally, each target behavior resulted in earning a specified number of credits. Occasionally, however, the staff individualized the credit values for trainees, depending on the relative difficulty of that behavior for the trainee. For example, trainees who rarely spoke to others received substantially more credits for commenting on another trainee's performance in class than did trainees who had little difficulty speaking up.

Backup Reinforcers

Trainees spent their credits on a variety of backup reinforcers that fell into two categories: reinforcing activities and tangible reinforcers. During the design of the credit system, trainees were interviewed to determine potential reinforcers. Trainees also were observed for several weeks to assess how they spent their time during the day. Activities in which they frequently engaged became potential backup reinforcers, consistent with the Premack principle.

Table 8-1 lists examples of reinforcing activities that trainees could purchase with credits. Notice that the credit costs reflected the relative therapeutic benefit of the activities. The more beneficial an activity, the lower was its cost, which encouraged trainees to spend credits on more beneficial activities. For example, activities with other people (such as playing table games) provided opportunities to practice social communication skills, and trainees paid less for social activities than for solitary activities. For example, whereas trainees had to pay 15 credits to play a game of pool alone, the cost was only 10 credits when they played with one or two other trainees and 5 credits when they played with three other trainees.

The Reinforcement Room was a large area in which trainees could engage in various pleasurable activities, such as playing pool, darts, and pinball; watching TV; listening to music; and reading magazines. These reinforcers could be purchased in two ways. Trainees could spend their credits for specific activities,

TABLE **8-1**

Examples of Reinforcing Activities and Their Credit Costs at the Community Training Center

Activity	Credit Cost
Travel club	10/hour
Photography	10/hour
Short films	10/hour
Feature films	50/film
Pool	
Playing alone	15/game
Playing with 1 or 2 others	10/game
Playing with 3 others	5/game
Ping-pong	
Singles	10/game
Doubles	5/game
Bowling	10/hour
Table games	10/hour
Ceramics	10/hour
Cooking	10/hour
Reading	15/hour
Sitting	25/hour

Source: Adapted from Spiegler & Agigian, 1977, p. 127.

or they could purchase a block of time in the Reinforcement Room and engage in whatever activities they chose during that period.

The Crediteria was a store where trainees used their credits to purchase a variety of tangible reinforcers (such as drinks, snacks, toiletries, and hobby items). Posters advertising items sold in the Crediteria were displayed around the Community Training Center. The posters encouraged trainees to spend their credits. In a token economy, exchanging tokens for backup reinforcers is important because it reinforces the adaptive behaviors for which the tokens were earned.

Decelerating Maladaptive Behaviors

The major function of the credit system was to accelerate adaptive social and daily living skills by reinforcing them, initially with credits and later with backup reinforcers. Trainees' maladaptive behaviors were treated primarily by reinforcing competing adaptive behaviors.

Maladaptive behaviors sometimes were decelerated directly by having trainees pay credits for engaging in them (response cost). Table 8-2 lists examples of undesirable behaviors for which trainees paid credits. Notice that the credit costs for engaging in maladaptive behaviors are considerably higher than the credit costs for engaging in reinforcing activities listed in Table 8-1. The high credit cost for the undesirable behaviors discouraged trainees from engaging in them. For instance, missing a class and sleeping in class, which were the most expensive undesirable behaviors, were rarely purchased—which means that trainees rarely engaged in these behaviors.

TABLE **8-2**

Examples of Undesirable Behaviors and the Average Number of Credits Trainees at the Community Training Center Paid to Engage in Them

Undesirable Behavior	Average Credit Cost
Sleeping in class	75
Smoking in class	50
Leaving class early (unexcused)	50
Cutting class	100
Being late to class	15
Coming to class without having done the homework	50
Pacing in class	20
Having an unbalanced credit card	10
Making a mess (for example, flicking ashes on the floor)	25
Begging	20

Source: Adapted from Spiegler & Agigian, 1977, p. 132.

Evaluation of the Community Training Center Program

A number of studies have demonstrated the effectiveness of the Community Training Center program.[8] One experiment compared a sample of graduates from the program with a comparable sample of patients not in the program. The two groups were matched for age, diagnosis, length of hospitalization, type of hospital treatment, and time spent in the community. The groups were compared on eight different measures of personal adjustment. As you can see in Figure 8-2, the Community Training Center graduates had significantly higher functioning on all but one of the outcome variables.

Rehospitalization is a critical measure of the effectiveness of treatment for previously hospitalized patients. The Community Training Center program resulted in consistently lower rehospitalization rates than comparable programs. For example, during the first 2 years of the Community Training

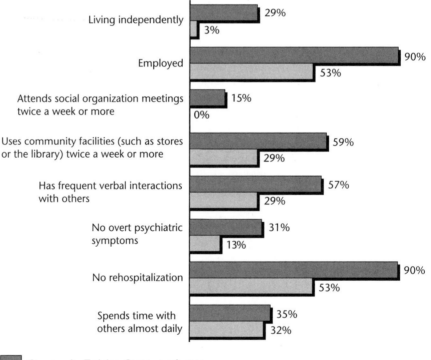

■ Community Training Center graduates

▨ Comparable outpatients

FIGURE 8-2

Comparison of personal adjustment between Community Training Center graduates and a comparable sample of outpatients. The Community Training Center graduates showed higher functioning than the comparison outpatients on all but one measure of personal adjustment.

Source: Data from Spiegler & Agigian, 1977.

Center operation, the rehospitalization rate was 11%; during the comparable period for the previous day treatment program, the rate was 73%. In another comparison, during a 6-month period, the Community Training Center rehospitalization rate was 5%, in contrast to 22% and 31% for two day treatment programs with comparable clients using different forms of treatment.

Achievement Place: A Token Economy for Juveniles in Trouble with the Law

© Sandra Wolf

Montrose Wolf

Achievement Place is the prototype of the *teaching family model* for rehabilitating juveniles in trouble with the law. Achievement Place was established in Lawrence, Kansas, in 1967 by Montrose Wolf and his colleagues;[9] it has since inspired more than 200 other similar programs.[10] A token economy is central to the operation of Achievement Place. To illustrate its use, we will describe the original program for boys. (Most of the teaching family programs have been for boys, but there have been a few for girls.[11])

Achievement Place served as a residence for six to eight boys, 10 to 16 years of age, from lower socioeconomic backgrounds. They had been court referred for committing minor crimes, such as petty theft and fighting. Achievement Place was set up in a large house in the boys' community. It was run by two *teaching parents*, a married couple trained in behavior therapy.[12]

The boys earned points for appropriate social behaviors (such as using proper manners), academic performance (for example, good grades), and daily living behaviors (for instance, personal hygiene). They lost points for inappropriate behaviors in these areas. Table 8-3 lists some of the behaviors for which points were earned or lost.

The token economy was divided into three systems or levels. Initially, the boys were placed on a *daily system*, in which the points they earned were exchangeable each day for backup reinforcers. This arrangement helped them learn

TABLE **8-3**

Examples of Behaviors for Which Boys at Achievement Place Earned or Lost Points

Behaviors That Earned Points	Points
Watching news on television or reading the newspaper	300 per day
Cleaning and maintaining neatness in one's room	500 per day
Keeping neat and clean	500 per day
Reading books	5 to 10 per page
Aiding houseparents in various household tasks	20 to 1000 per task
Doing dishes	500 to 1000 per meal
Being well dressed for an evening meal	100 to 500 per meal
Doing homework	500 per day
Obtaining desirable grades on school report cards	500 to 1000 per grade
Turning out lights when not in use	25 per light

(continued)

TABLE **8-3** (*continued*)

Behaviors That Lost Points	Points
Failing grades on the report card	500 to 1000 per grade
Speaking aggressively	20 to 50 per response
Forgetting to wash hands before meals	100 to 300 per meal
Arguing	300 per response
Disobeying	100 to 1000 per response
Being late	10 per minute
Displaying poor manners	50 to 100 per response
Engaging in poor posture	50 to 100 per response
Using poor grammar	20 to 50 per response
Stealing, lying, or cheating	10,000 per response

Source: Phillips, 1968, p. 215.

how the token economy operated. After the boys became familiar with the token economy, they were switched to a *weekly system*, in which the points they earned were exchanged for backup reinforcers once a week. For example, a boy could purchase snacks and television time for the entire week. Table 8-4 shows a comparison of the points needed to purchase different privileges on the daily and weekly systems. Most boys were on the weekly system for the 9 to 12 months

TABLE **8-4**
Privileges That Could Be Earned with Points on the Daily
and Weekly Point Systems at Achievement Place

Privilege	Price in Points	
	Daily System	Weekly System
Hobbies and games	400	3000
Snacks	150	1000
Television	50	1000
Allowance (per $1)	300	2000
Permission to leave Achievement Place (home, downtown, sports events)	NA	3000
Bonds (savings for gifts, special clothing, etc.)	150	1000
Special privileges	NA	Variable

NA = not available.
Source: Adapted from Phillips, Phillips, Fixsen, & Wolf, 1971, p. 46.

they typically lived at Achievement Place. Because ample opportunities to earn points existed, the boys usually could buy all the privileges they wanted.

The final level in the token economy, the *merit system*, was reserved for boys who were ready to leave Achievement Place in the near future. Under the merit system, a boy would not earn or lose points, and he would not have to pay points for any backup reinforcers—as long as he continued to demonstrate a high level of appropriate social, academic, and daily-living behaviors. Instead, the teaching parents merely praised the boy for appropriate behaviors. The merit system prepared boys for returning to their home environments where no point system existed.[13]

A Day at Achievement Place

A typical weekday at Achievement Place began when the boys arose at about 6:30 A.M., washed and dressed, and cleaned their rooms. Morning chores were followed by breakfast, and then the boys were off to school.

Each day, one boy served as *manager* and was paid points to hold this prestigious position. As one of his responsibilities, the manager assigned cleanup jobs, supervised their completion, and awarded points to other boys for doing the jobs. The manager earned points according to how well the boys performed the household chores.[14]

Academic achievement was a major goal of the program. Each boy attended the same school he had gone to before coming to Achievement Place. The teachers and school administrators worked closely with the teaching parents, providing them with systematic feedback about each boy's school performance through daily or weekly report cards. The boys earned or lost points based on how well they were doing at school.[15]

After school, the boys returned to Achievement Place, had a snack (purchased with points), and then began their homework or other point-earning activities, such as house chores. Later, they engaged in various recreational activities (such as bike riding or playing games), for which they paid points.

After dinner, a "family conference" was held. The boys and the teaching parents discussed the day's events, evaluated the manager's performance, discussed problems with the program, and decided on consequences for specific rule violations. The conferences allowed the boys to actively collaborate in their treatment program. The boys spent the rest of the evening, until bedtime at 10:30 P.M., in group or individual activities.

Evaluation of Achievement Place and Other Teaching Family Programs

Numerous controlled studies have evaluated the effectiveness of Achievement Place and other teaching family programs.[16] These studies have shown that the programs are effective in reducing delinquent and other inappropriate behaviors (such as acting aggressively and using poor grammar when speaking) and increasing appropriate prosocial behaviors (such as being on time, completing homework, and saving money). Favorable attitudinal changes also have occurred for program participants, including increased self-esteem and optimism about having control over their lives.[17]

These positive changes were observed while boys were in the program and were maintained for a year or so afterward, but no longer.[18] Poor long-term maintenance of treatment gains is not completely surprising, however. The teaching family group home environment is very different from the home environments from which the boys came and, most important, to which they returned. Most of the boys were from home environments where they received little reinforcement for prosocial behaviors and ample reinforcement for antisocial behaviors from their peers—just the opposite of the contingencies in the teaching family home.[19] Thus, when the boys left the teaching family home, the reinforcement contingencies changed: prosocial behaviors were no longer reinforced, which resulted in their eventual decline. Given the less-than-ideal home environments of most youths in teaching family programs, specific procedures must be used to promote long-term maintenance of changes. One approach is to provide aftercare in specially developed foster homes, where the foster parents continue to reinforce prosocial behaviors and discourage antisocial behaviors.[20] Another approach is to give parents behavioral parent training (described later in this chapter).[21]

Token Economies for Training Individuals with Mental Retardation

Individuals institutionalized because of mental retardation display many of the same behavioral deficits as patients hospitalized for psychiatric disorders. For example, they frequently lack basic self-care and daily living skills (such as dressing appropriately and preparing simple meals). Token economies are effective in teaching such skills and motivating their consistent practice.[22] In addition to accelerating adaptive behaviors, token economies are used to decelerate various socially inappropriate behaviors (such as eating with one's fingers) and personally maladaptive behaviors (such as refusing to brush one's teeth) among institutionalized people with mental retardation.[23]

Language skills often are target behaviors for children, adolescents, and sometimes adults with mental retardation.[24] Because of the complexity of language and speech skills, token reinforcement programs for such target behaviors usually are administered individually and are part of a treatment package that includes modeling, prompting, and shaping.

Token economies are effective in increasing the quantity and quality of job-related tasks performed by individuals with mental retardation.[25] In one sophisticated program, young adults with moderate mental retardation earned tokens for jobs on three levels.[26] The lowest level involved janitorial-type tasks; the middle level consisted of jobs with more responsibility (such as operating machines and checking attendance); and the highest level required more skill, responsibility, and independence (such as sorting and distributing mail and serving as a teacher's aide). The clients advanced through the levels by meeting specified performance criteria. They exchanged tokens for a variety of backup reinforcers, including favorite snacks, money, and access to pleasurable activities. Some of the highest-level clients were placed into community-based jobs after they completed the program.

In another program, residents of a group home for adults with mental retardation received tokens for various tasks involved in running the home and for socializing with other residents and staff members.[27] They also earned tokens for attending recreational activities in the community and for behaviors leading to gainful employment, such as contacting prospective employers and going on job interviews. Once residents were working in the community, their employers were asked to participate in the token economy program. The employers provided the staff with feedback about residents' performance on the job so that the residents could receive tokens for appropriate work behaviors.[28]

Token Economies in the Classroom

Token economies have been used in preschool, elementary, and secondary classrooms across the gamut of educational levels (special education, remedial, and mainstream). These programs, which teachers rate as highly acceptable interventions,[29] have focused on classroom conduct and academic performance.

Classroom Conduct

Token economies have modified a variety of undesirable behaviors that interfere with classroom learning, including problems associated with attention deficit hyperactivity disorder.[30] Examples are aggressive behaviors, talking out of turn, being out of one's seat, disregarding instructions, throwing objects, destroying property, and disturbing others.[31] Three basic strategies are used to treat classroom conduct problems: (1) earning tokens for engaging in competing acceleration target behaviors, (2) losing tokens for performing inappropriate behaviors, and (3) both earning and losing tokens. Earning and losing tokens appear to be equally effective in modifying classroom conduct (as well as academic behaviors).[32]

Backup reinforcers in classroom token economies have included tangible reinforcers (such as toys, snacks, and school supplies) and reinforcing activities (such as extended recess time and field trips). As children grow older, in-class backup reinforcers become less potent than reinforcers available at home (such as playing video games); accordingly, arrangements are made for children to exchange tokens earned at school for backup reinforcers at home.[33]

Academic Performance

The ultimate purpose of decreasing disruptive classroom behaviors is to enhance students' academic performance. Attention and proper conduct in the classroom are necessary but not sufficient conditions for promoting academic skills and learning.[34] Thus, token economies also are used to directly increase learning.

Token economies have successfully improved children's academic performance in basic subject areas, such as arithmetic and reading, as well as in more complex skills, such as creative writing.[35] These programs not only have increased students' skill levels, but they also have been associated with higher grades and fewer suspensions from school.[36]

One illustrative program was designed to increase writing skills.[37] Elementary school students earned points for the number of different adjectives, verbs, and beginnings of sentences they wrote in stories. The class was divided into two teams, and a group contingency was employed. Backup reinforcers included candy and early recess. As Figure 8-3 shows, an increase in the number of different sentence parts (such as adjectives) occurred when, and only when, points were given for the specific sentence parts. For example, the average number of adjectives used increased during the 4 days that adjectives were reinforced with points, but not on the following 4 days when only verbs were reinforced. When all three sentence parts were reinforced, an increase in each sentence part was observed. Moreover,

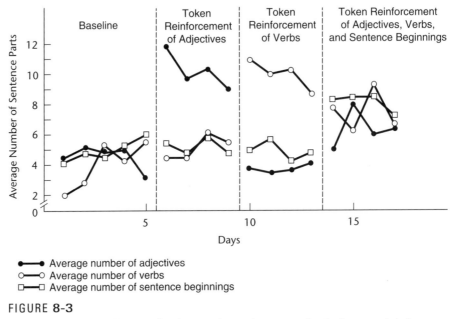

Average number of adjectives
Average number of verbs
Average number of sentence beginnings

FIGURE 8-3

Average number of different adjectives, verbs, and sentence beginnings used during baseline and token reinforcement phases in a class designed to increase elementary school students' writing skills

Source: Adapted from Maloney & Hopkins, 1973, p. 429.

people who were unfamiliar with the procedures used in the class rated the students' stories written during the token reinforcement days as more creative than those written during the baseline period, when no token reinforcers were administered.

Token Economies for Individuals and Families

Token economies are used for individuals and small groups (such as families) as well as with large groups of clients. Individual token economies are most often employed with children for such problems as stuttering, inappropriate table manners, reading difficulties, poor attention to schoolwork, failure to do household chores, and noncompliance with parental instructions.[38] Stickers placed on a wall chart (see Photo 8-1) are frequently used as tokens that can be exchanged for reinforcers listed on a reinforcement menu. Individual token economies occasionally are used with adults—in particular, adults with mental retardation and with senior citizens, such as in Case 8-1.

If you'd like to experience the process of setting up and being motivated by a token economy (and also receive some personal benefits), complete Participation Exercise 8-1 (page 194) over the next couple of weeks.

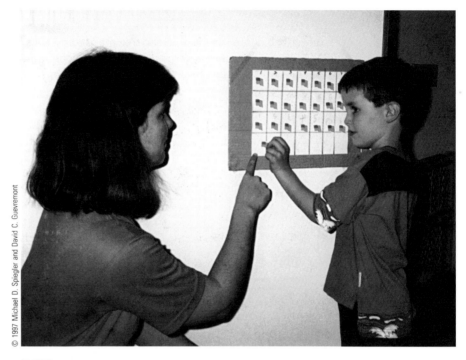

PHOTO 8-1

Parents can be trained to administer simple token economy programs for their children at home. Stickers, which are placed on a chart, may be used as tokens and exchanged for backup reinforcers.

CASE **8-1**

Increasing Adherence to a Medical Regimen with an Individual Token Economy[39]

Mr. A. was an 82-year-old retired longshoreman who had suffered a massive heart attack. His physician told him to exercise, to eat foods high in potassium, and to take his medication, but he failed to follow these instructions. Mr. A.'s granddaughter, who lived with him, agreed to administer a token economy in which Mr. A. earned poker chips for walking, drinking potassium-rich orange juice, and taking his medication. He exchanged the poker chips for the privilege of choosing what he wanted for dinner at home or going out to eat at a restaurant of his choice.

The token economy significantly increased each of the three target behaviors from their baseline levels. When the tokens were temporarily withdrawn in a reversal period, the target behaviors declined to baseline levels, and reinstating the token economy immediately brought the behaviors back to the treatment level (see Figure 8-4 as an example of one of the

(continued)

CASE **8-1** (*continued*)

target behaviors). Instituting the token economy also appeared to improve Mr. A.'s relationship with his family by reducing arguments, especially about Mr. A.'s adherence to his medical regimen.

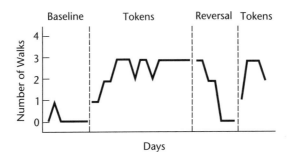

FIGURE 8-4

Number of walks per day Mr. A. took under baseline and token reinforcement conditions

Source: Dapcich-Miura, E., & Hovell, M.F. (1979). Contingency management of adherence to a complex medical regimen in an elderly heart patient. *Behavior Therapy, 10*, 193–201. Reprinted with permission.

PARTICIPATION EXERCISE 8-1

More than a Token Gesture: Designing and Implementing an Individual Token Economy

This exercise provides directions for setting up a simple token economy to motivate you to do those everyday chores that you'd rather not do.

Step 1: In the Chore column of Work Sheets 8-1 and 8-3 list four chores that you "must" do but dislike doing (for example, cleaning the bathroom and taking out the garbage).[a]

Step 2: To establish a baseline, over 5 consecutive days, place a check mark in the Frequency column on Work Sheet 8-1 each time you do one of the chores. After 5 days, add the number of check marks for each chore and record it in the Sum column of Work Sheet 8-1, and then put the total at the bottom of the column.

Step 3: Rank order the four chores from most unpleasant to least unpleasant and write them *in that order* in column A (Chores) on the top half of Work Sheet 8-2. Column B (Points Earned) contains the points you will receive for doing each of the chores. Note that the more unpleasant the chore is, the higher the number of points you will earn for doing it (from most to least unpleasant: 40, 30, 20, and 10).

Step 4: Choose four activities (1) that you both *enjoy* and *engage in regularly* (for example, listening to music, talking on the phone, watching

[a]You will find all the work sheets for this exercise in your Student Resource Manual.

TV, reading for pleasure, and surfing the Internet) and (2) that you are *willing to temporarily forgo* (if you do not earn sufficient points to engage in them when the token economy is in effect).

Step 5: Rank order the four activities from most enjoyable to least enjoyable and write them in that order in column C (Activities) on the bottom half of Work Sheet 8-2. Column D (Point Cost) lists the points you will pay for each backup reinforcer. The more enjoyable the activity, the higher is its cost (from most to least enjoyable: 25, 20, 10, and 5).

Step 6: Begin the token economy on the same day of the week on which you started your baseline and continue it for 5 consecutive days. Each time you complete a chore, place a check mark in the Frequency column of Work Sheet 8-3 next to the chore and then write the number of points you earned for doing that chore (refer to Work Sheet 8-2, column B) in the Points Earned column of Work Sheet 8-4.

Step 7: Use the points you earn to engage in your backup reinforcing activities; record their cost (refer to Worksheet 8-2, column D) in the Points Spent column of Work Sheet 8-4. Maintain a running balance in the Point Balance column of Work Sheet 8-4 by adding points earned and subtracting points spent (as balancing a check book). For the token economy to be effective in motivating you to do the chores, you must engage in the backup reinforcing activities. While your token economy is in effect, you may engage in the reinforcing activities *only* if you have purchased them with points. If you don't have sufficient points, you must wait until you have earned sufficient points to engage in the activity. If you violate this rule, the token economy will not accelerate your doing the chores.

Step 8: After 5 days of the token economy, add the number of check marks for each chore and record it in the Sum column of Work Sheet 8-3, and then put the total at the bottom of the column. Now compare the total number of chores you did during the baseline (bottom right of Work Sheet 8-1) and during the token economy (bottom right of Work Sheet 8-3). If the token economy was effective, you should have done more chores while the token economy was in effect than during baseline. If this did not occur, you may have to increase the point values earned for each chore or select more enjoyable backup reinforcers.

Token Economy in Perspective

Since the first major token economy was developed 45 years ago,[40] numerous token economies have been implemented to treat diverse target behaviors, ranging from simple self-care skills to complex interpersonal problems that develop in marital relations. Clients of all ages—from children to elderly individuals—with a wide range of intellectual capacities have been treated. Token economies have been used in many different settings—in classrooms, group living situations, hospitals, outpatient facilities, work environments, and homes.

Clients enter token economy programs because they have deficits of adaptive behaviors and/or excesses of maladaptive behaviors. In their natural environments, adaptive behaviors were not reinforced and maladaptive behaviors were reinforced. The token economy reverses these reinforcement contingencies, which often results in impressive (and sometimes immediate) changes, as demonstrated in reversal and multiple baseline studies.[41] However, when clients leave the token economy and return to their previous natural environments, the contingencies usually revert to their pretreatment state—that is, the conditions that had been instrumental in maintaining the clients' problem behaviors.

The most obvious solution to this dilemma is for clients to remain in the token program. Occasionally, this solution may be viable, as when token economies have been instituted in clients' natural environments and it is feasible to operate them indefinitely. This was the case with token economies that were set up to promote safety practices in two mines and were continued for more than 11 years.[42] Mining is a hazardous occupation resulting in many injuries and deaths every year, and these two mines had especially poor safety records. Miners earned trading stamps that they exchanged for a wide selection of merchandise. Each month, miners who suffered no injuries resulting in lost time or compensation earned a specified number of trading stamps, and they earned bonus stamps for making safety suggestions that were subsequently implemented. There also was a group contingency in which miners were awarded trading stamps if all the members of their work group remained injury-free during the month. The token economies resulted in large reductions in injuries. For example, the number of days lost from work due to injuries changed from eight times the national average to one-fourth of the national average at one mine and from three times to one-twelfth of the national average in the other mine.

In most cases, however, token economies are only temporary treatment procedures. To assure long-term maintenance of treatment gains, clients must be reinforced in their natural environments for the same behaviors that were reinforced in the token economy. Sometimes it is possible to change the environment to which clients return after leaving a token program. For instance, parents can be trained to reinforce their child's adaptive behaviors at home. Alternatively, rather than return to their homes, clients can go to a living situation that continues the adaptive contingencies, such as a specialized foster home in which the foster parents are trained in behavior therapy procedures.

Long-term maintenance as well as transfer and generalization also require shifting clients from token reinforcers to reinforcers that are available in the their natural environments. Toward this end, social reinforcers such as praise are generally administered along with tokens. Further, the use of tokens may be withdrawn gradually while clients are still in the token economy. This allows natural reinforcers (such as feeling good after completing a task) to assume an increasingly important role in maintaining the adaptive behaviors instituted in the token economy. One way to gradually withdraw token reinforcers is for clients to move through levels within the token economy, such as the daily, weekly, and merit systems at Achievement Place.[43] Clients also may be reinforced with tokens on an intermittent reinforcement schedule.[44]

Critics have voiced ethical and humanitarian objections to token economies. For example, token economies have been described as demeaning, especially for adults. The argument is that token reinforcement is appropriate for children but not for adults, who are supposedly "above" receiving tokens for

behaving appropriately. Interestingly, the same people who think token reinforcement is inappropriate for adults forget that they participate in a large-scale token economy every time they earn or spend money. The token economy also has been mistakenly viewed as a form of bribery (an argument we rebutted in Chapter 6, page 142).

In fact, there is evidence that token economies enhance clients' dignity by increasing their self-esteem, self-respect, pride, and sense of worth. Consider the following evaluation of an early token economy at a psychiatric hospital. "The program's most notable contribution to patient life is the lessening of staff control and putting the burden of responsibility, and thus more self-respect, on the patient."[45] Or, consider the virtually identical comments made by two very different people in two separate token economies. The first was made by a female patient with Down syndrome who was in the Anna State Hospital token economy. The woman approached a visitor and, with obvious pride in her accomplishments that day, pointed to the card on which her points were recorded and said, "Look, I got 120 points today." The second comment was made by a 40-year-old male trainee with superior intelligence at the Community Training Center. He approached the program director and also feeling good about what he had accomplished that day said, "Doctor, I earned 85 credits today."[46] These expressions of pride sound very much like a sales executive's telling her husband at dinner, "I earned a bonus today for closing the deal," or a college student's telling his roommate, "I got an A on that paper I worked so hard on." Another common positive side effect of token economies is that once clients' behaviors improve and become more prosocial, clients' relationships with family members and other people in their lives improve (as with Mr. A. in Case 8-1).

CONTINGENCY CONTRACT

A **contingency contract** is a written agreement that specifies the relationship between target behaviors and their consequences for a particular client. The essential components of a contingency contract are clear, unambiguous statements of

Effective dates: From : 2-10-02   To : 3-9-02

Jerry agrees to:

1. Go to school each day

His parents agree to:

Reward: Give Jerry $10 spending money per week (on Sunday)

Penalty: Subtract $2 from a possible $10 for each school day that Jerry fails to attend

2. Arrive home each day after school by 4 p.m. to check in with his parents

Reward: Allow Jerry to stay out until 10 p.m. on Saturday night

Penalty: Subtract 1 hour from a 10 p.m. curfew on Saturday for each day Jerry fails to check in by 4 p.m.

3. Come home each day no later than 6 p.m. to have dinner with the family

Reward: Allow Jerry to play video games for 45 minutes

Penalty: Lose access to video games for the day

Bonus: Each time Jerry goes 4 weeks with fewer than six infractions, his parents will give him money to purchase one compact disk (maximum of $18 per purchase).

Penalty: Each time Jerry has more than six infractions, he will be grounded (remain in the house and not be able to watch television, talk on the telephone, or use the computer) for the entire day on Saturday.

I, Jerry Michaelson, agree to the terms of the above contract.

_____
Signature   Date

I, Mrs. Michaelson, agree to the terms of the above contract.

_____
Signature   Date

I, Mr. Michaelson, agree to the terms of the above contract.

_____
Signature   Date

FIGURE 8-5

Contingency contract with individual contingencies for each target behavior used with a 15-year-old boy

Source: © 2002 Michael D. Spiegler and David C. Guevremont.

(1) the target behaviors, (2) the consequences for performing (or failing to perform) them, and (3) the precise contingency between each target behavior and its consequences (for example, "If the client does X for 3 consecutive days, then the client will receive Y").[47]

The contract in Figure 8-5 illustrates other features of contingency contracts. They specify the responsibilities of the client and the other people

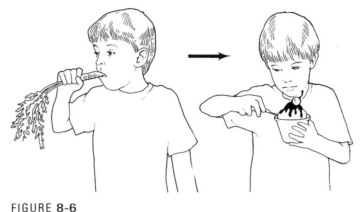

FIGURE 8-6

Pictorial contingency contract showing the target behavior and the reinforcer

involved in the treatment, each of whom signs the contract. With deceleration target behaviors, contracts can include both reinforcement and punishment. For clients who cannot read, the contract can be presented pictorially, such as the simple contract in Figure 8-6.

Rather than being a treatment itself, a contingency contract is used to formalize a treatment plan. For example, contingency contracts were part of an effective substance abuse treatment program for adolescents and young adults.[48] Clients contracted to engage in specific overt behaviors that competed with drug abuse, such as attending school, complying with an early curfew, and notifying their families of their whereabouts when they were not at home, school, or work. The contracts specified the roles of the client, family members, and the therapist and were reviewed weekly. Family members administered immediate and delayed reinforcers.

Using contingency contracts to formalize treatment plans has a number of benefits. Contingency contracts minimize disagreements about the conditions of the plan. The contract is the final authority, which underscores the importance of stating the terms of the contract unambiguously. Signing the contract increases the commitment of the people involved to fulfill their roles specified in the contract. The process of designing a contingency contract makes clients active participants in their treatment. When relational problems are being addressed in therapy (as between spouses or child and parents), it is helpful for the parties involved to jointly develop a contingency contract, which may benefit the relationship by providing structure for their negotiations and opportunities to practice cooperating and negotiating.

Contingency contracts are used for clients of all ages.[49] Examples of behaviors treated with contingency contracts include disruptive classroom behaviors,[50] school attendance,[51] school and homework performance,[52] setting learning goals,[53] antisocial behaviors,[54] sibling cooperation,[55] studying,[56] physical exercise,[57] smoking,[58] overeating,[59] undereating,[60] problem drinking,[61] and marital discord.[62] Contingency contracts sometimes are used to increase compliance with behavior therapy homework assignments, such as getting parents who physically abuse their children to practice using positive reinforcement procedures with them.[63]

Relatively few studies have examined the essential features of contingency contracts.[64] It is clear, however, that specifying the contingency between the target behavior and the consequence is essential.[65]

Outside of therapy, contingency contracts apparently appeal to teenagers as a way of securing access to favorite Web sites, which often is a bone of contention between children and parents. A recent article in the *Wall Street Journal* described three examples of teens' initiating the idea of a written contract that clearly spells out the rules of their Web site access and the penalties for failing to follow them.[66] One parent's comments about his son's contract highlighted the benefits of contingency contracts described earlier: "The good thing about the contract is that it's all been thought out beforehand, and it's all on paper, and everyone agrees to it and knows what is expected."

BEHAVIORAL PARENT TRAINING

One-third of all referrals of children for psychotherapy involve noncompliance with parental requests and rules as well as disruptive behaviors (such as aggressive acts and temper tantrums).[67] When such behaviors occur occasionally, as they do with most children, they are considered normal ("growing pains" or "just a stage"). However, when they are frequent, long-lasting, or intense, parents appropriately may seek professional assistance.

One approach to dealing with children's noncompliant and disruptive behaviors is for the child to receive individual psychotherapy. However, around 1960 it became clear that traditional psychotherapy with children exhibiting such problems was largely ineffective.[68] The reason may be that the problem does not reside within the child, as is assumed in traditional psychotherapy. Rather, the problem may lie with the parent–child interactions. Parents who seek help for their child's noncompliant and disruptive behaviors interact differently with their child than parents who are not reporting such problems. Specifically, extensive observations have revealed that parents who are experiencing difficulty with their children's problem behaviors (1) give more vague and inconsistent instructions; (2) use more negative, threatening, and angry warnings in an attempt to modify the child's behaviors; (3) administer inconsistent and ineffective consequences for undesirable behaviors; and (4) provide fewer positive consequences for their child's prosocial, desirable behaviors.[69]

These observations led two prominent behavior therapists—Gerald Patterson[70] at the Oregon Social Learning Center and Rex Forehand[71] at the University of Georgia—to develop **behavioral parent training** (also called *behavioral child management training* and *parent management training*) to teach parents (most often mothers[72]) behavior therapy procedures to effectively manage their children's behavioral problems.[73] A number of variations of this basic model exist,[74] and our discussion will include them.

The primary goals of behavioral parent training are to increase parents' use of (1) clear, direct, and age-appropriate instructions to their children; (2) consistent reinforcement for prosocial, desirable child behaviors; and (3) consistent and appropriate punishment for children's noncompliant and disruptive behaviors. Positive reinforcement, including differential reinforcement,

Gerald Patterson

Rex Forehand

and time out from positive reinforcement are the major therapy procedures that therapists teach parents. They may also teach parents to use contingency contracts, home token economies, and response cost.[75]

Parents initially learn to notice and reinforce their children's desirable behaviors. Therapists teach them to use a variety of reinforcers, including enthusiastic praise (for instance, "What a great job. You came the first time I called you!"), physical affection (a hug, for example), and the provision of privileges (such as staying up 15 minutes past bedtime). Next, parents are taught how to differentially reinforce behaviors that compete with serious undesirable behaviors (such as hitting siblings) and to extinguish (often by ignoring) minor undesirable behaviors (such as whining). Parents learn to give clear-cut instructions calmly and to refrain from angry, indirect negative instructions (such as "Wait until your father gets home!"). They also learn to use time out from positive reinforcement in a consistent and effective manner.

Planned activity scheduling is another procedure taught in behavioral parent training.[76] Parents learn to change setting events in anticipation of their child's behavior problems to prevent the problems from occurring in the first place.[77] A common strategy is to provide children with an active task that they enjoy and that is appropriate for the situation. In the case of a child who is disruptive while waiting in a doctor's office, for example, parents might bring some of the child's favorite games or toys to the doctor's office. Planned activity scheduling has been shown to be an effective treatment for families whose members have developmental disabilities[78] and for parents who abuse their children,[79] as well as for families whose children have common behavior problems.[80]

Behavioral parent training is conducted with a single family or in small groups containing 4 to 10 sets of parents. Parents rehearse the behavior therapy procedures in the training sessions and receive feedback from the therapist. The practice involves role-playing, with the therapist or another parent playing the role of the child. Occasionally, parents will practice with their own child during training sessions.[81] Homework between sessions is an integral part of the training.[82] For example, parents may be asked to self-monitor and self-reinforce their use of the behavioral skills they have learned.

Behavioral parent training has been applied to a variety of child behavior problems, including noncompliance with instructions and rules;[83] oppositional, aggressive, and antisocial behaviors;[84] Asperger's syndrome;[85] attention deficit hyperactivity disorder;[86] childhood sleep problems;[87] separation anxiety;[88] eating behavior of undernourished children with cystic fibrosis;[89] and completion of homework.[90] The training has been successful with parents who physically abuse their children,[91] parents with mild mental retardation,[92] and even with parents who are reluctant to participate in the training.[93] However, sometimes parents who have significant psychological problems of their own may have difficulty learning and implementing the child management skills.[94] Finally, behavioral parent training is more effective when administered by trained mental health practitioners than when parents learn the procedures by following exercises in a workbook.[95]

Meta-analytic studies have demonstrated that behavioral parent training is effective in changing children's noncompliant and disruptive behaviors.[96]

In one study, children whose parents received behavioral parent training showed a 63% reduction in problem behaviors compared to a 17% reduction for children whose parents received a nonbehavioral (control) treatment.[97] Another study demonstrated that behavioral parent training was more effective than the typical, eclectic treatment offered by community mental health clinics for children with disruptive behavior problems.[98]

Behavioral parent training can result not only in children's becoming compliant with their parents' instructions but also in their becoming more compliant than children who have no significant behavior problems.[99] Besides changing children's behaviors, behavioral parent training modifies parents' interactions with their children[100] and may reduce parents' stress.[101] And recently, behavioral parent training has been part of a multicomponent intervention for preventing serious conduct problems in school-age youth.[102]

The positive effects of behavioral parent training are consistently maintained over time, as demonstrated in follow-up studies ranging from 4 to 10 years.[103] However, following successful behavioral parent training, transfer to other settings (such as from home to school)[104] and generalization to untreated behaviors[105] may not occur. Additional specific interventions to promote transfer and generalization may be required. One interesting finding is that behavioral parent training specifically for dealing with one child sometimes decreases problem behaviors of siblings.[106]

[handwritten marginal note: lasting up to 10 years]

SUMMARY

1. A token economy is a system for motivating clients to perform desirable behaviors and to refrain from performing undesirable behaviors. Clients earn token reinforcers for the former and lose them for the latter. Tokens can be tangible, such as poker chips, or symbolic, such as points. Clients exchange tokens for backup reinforcers. Token economies most often are used for groups of clients.

2. The basic elements of a token economy are (1) a list of target behaviors, including the number of tokens clients can earn or lose for performing each, (2) a list of backup reinforcers, including the token cost of each, (3) the type of token used, and (4) specific procedures and rules for running the token economy.

3. The Community Training Center, a day treatment program for individuals previously hospitalized for chronic psychiatric disorders, employed a token economy to motivate learning daily living and social skills needed for independent living. The Community Training Center was run as a school in which the skills were taught in classes. The program was shown to be superior to other comparable day treatment programs.

4. Achievement Place was a home-style, residential rehabilitation program for juveniles in trouble with the law that employed a token economy. Points were earned for appropriate social behaviors, academic performance, and daily living behaviors; points were lost for inappropriate behaviors. The program was effective while the clients were in treatment and up to a year afterward.

5. Token economies have been applied to teach self-care and daily living skills to clients with mental retardation and to modify classroom conduct and academic performance in schoolchildren.

6. Token economies have been used with both individuals and small groups, such as families.

7. Evidence from reversal and multiple baseline studies clearly shows that token economies can modify clients' target behaviors. However, treatment gains often decline rapidly when token reinforcement is discontinued unless specific procedures to foster durability of change are instituted. Such procedures include gradually withdrawing tokens while increasing natural reinforcers, using intermittent reinforcement, and establishing the same reinforcement contingencies used in the token program in clients' natural environments.

8. A contingency contract is a written agreement that specifies the relationship between target behaviors and their consequences for a particular client and responsibilities of all the participants in the contract.

9. Behavioral parent training involves teaching parents behavior therapy procedures to effectively change their children's noncompliant and disruptive behaviors. The major therapy procedures taught are positive reinforcement, differential reinforcement, and time out from positive reinforcement.

REFERENCE NOTES

1. For example, Franco, Galanter, Castaneda, & Paterson, 1995.
2. Barry, 1958; Maconochie, 1848.
3. Kaestle, 1973; Lancaster, 1805.
4. For example, Ulman & Klem, 1975.
5. Ayllon & Azrin, 1968.
6. Kazdin, 1977c; Milan, 1987.
7. Spiegler & Agigian, 1977.
8. Spiegler & Agigian, 1977.
9. Phillips, 1968.
10. Braukmann & Wolf, 1987.
11. Minkin et al., 1976; Timbers, Timbers, Fixsen, Phillips, & Wolf, 1973.
12. Fixsen, Phillips, Phillips, & Wolf, 1976; Phillips, Phillips, Fixsen, & Wolf, 1971.
13. Phillips, Phillips, Fixsen, & Wolf, 1971.
14. Phillips, Phillips, Wolf, & Fixsen, 1973.
15. Bailey, Wolf, & Phillips, 1970.
16. Braukmann, Wolf, & Kirigin Ramp, 1985; Fixsen, Phillips, Phillips, & Wolf, 1976; Kirigin [Ramp], Braukmann, Atwater, & Wolf, 1982; Maloney, Fixsen, & Phillips, 1981.
17. Eitzen, 1975.
18. For example, Bailey, Timbers, Phillips, & Wolf, 1971; Phillips, 1968.
19. Compare with Wilson & Herrnstein, 1985.
20. For example, Jones & Timbers, 1983; Meadowcroft, Hawkins, Trout, Grealish, & Stark, 1982.
21. Reid, Eddy, Bank, & Fetrow, 1994.
22. For example, Horner & Keilitz, 1975; Hunt, Fitzhugh, & Fitzhugh, 1968.
23. For example, Peniston, 1975.
24. For example, Baer & Guess, 1971, 1973; Guess & Baer, 1973; MacCubrey, 1971.
25. For example, Hunt & Zimmerman, 1969; Zimmerman, Stuckey, Garlick, & Miller, 1969.
26. Welch & Gist, 1974.
27. Asylum on the front porch, 1974; Clark, Bussone, & Kivitz, 1974; Clark, Kivitz, & Rosen, 1972.
28. Clark, Bussone, & Kivitz, 1974.
29. McGoey & DuPaul, 2000.
30. McGoey & DuPaul, 2000; Reid, 1999; Roberts, White, & McLaughlin, 1997.
31. Cavalier, Ferretti, & Hodges, 1997; McGoey & DuPaul, 2000.
32. Sullivan & O'Leary, 1990.
33. Kelley, 1990.
34. For example, Ferritor, Buckholdt, Hamblin, & Smith, 1972; Harris & Sherman, 1974. See also O'Leary, 1972; Winett & Winkler, 1972.

35. For example, Dolezal, Weber, Evavold, Wylie, & McLaughlin, 2007; McGinnis, Friman, & Carlyon, 1999; McLaughlin, 1982.
36. For example, Bushell, 1978; Heaton & Safer, 1982.
37. Maloney & Hopkins, 1973.
38. Gannon, Harmon, & Williams, 1997; Heward, Dardig, & Rossett, 1979; Jason, 1985; Moore & Callias, 1987; Strauss, 1986.
39. Dapcich-Miura & Hovell, 1979.
40. Ayllon & Azrin, 1965, 1968.
41. For example, Glynn, 1990.
42. Fox, Hopkins, & Anger, 1987.
43. For example, Paul & Lentz, 1977; Phillips, Phillips, Fixsen, & Wolf, 1971.
44. For example, Rosen & Rosen, 1983.
45. Atthowe & Krasner, 1968, p. 41.
46. Spiegler, 1983.
47. See Hall & Hall, 1982; O'Banion & Whaley, 1981.
48. Azrin et al., 1994.
49. Kazdin, 1994.
50. White-Blackburn, Semb, & Semb, 1977.
51. Vaal, 1973.
52. Kahle & Kelley, 1994; Newstrom, McLaughlin, & Sweeney, 1999.
53. Self-Brown & Mathews, 2003.
54. Stuart, 1971; Stuart & Lott, 1972.
55. Guevremont, 1987.
56. Bristol & Sloane, 1974.
57. Wysocki, Hall, Iwata, & Riordan, 1979.
58. Spring, Sipich, Trimble, & Goeckner, 1978.
59. Mann, 1972.
60. Donahue, Thevenin, & Runyon, 1997.
61. Miller, 1972.
62. Jacobson & Margolin, 1979; Stuart, 1969.
63. Wolfe & Sandler, 1981.
64. Kazdin, 1994.
65. Spring, Sipich, Trimble, & Goeckner, 1978.
66. Opdyke, 2008.
67. Forehand & McMahon, 1981.
68. Levitt, 1957, 1963.
69. For example, Patterson, 1982; Patterson, Reid, & Dishion, 1992.
70. Patterson, 1982.
71. Forehand & McMahon, 1981.
72. For example, Fabiano, 2007.
73. Wells, 1994.
74. For example, Brinkmeyer & Eyberg, 2003.
75. Barkley, Guevremont, Anastopolous, & Fletcher, 1992; Robin & Foster, 1989.
76. O'Reilly & Dillenburger, 1997.
77. Bigelow & Lutzker, 1998; Close, 2000.
78. Lutzker & Steed, 1998.
79. Bigelow & Lutzker, 1998; Close, 2000.
80. Lutzker, Huynen, & Bigelow, 1998.
81. Greene, Kamps, Wyble, & Ellis, 1999.
82. For example, Barkley, 1989; Wells, Griest, & Forehand, 1980.
83. For example, Long, Forehand, Wierson, & Morgan, 1993.
84. For example, Kazdin 2003, 2005.
85. Sofronoff & Whittingham, 2007.
86. Fabiano, 2007; van den Hoofdakker, van der Veen-Mulders, & Sytema, 2007.
87. For example, Wolfson, Lacks, & Futterman, 1992.
88. Pincus, Santucci, Ehrenreich, & Eyberg, 2008.
89. For example, Stark et al., 1993; Stark, Powers, Jelalian, Rape, & Miller, 1994.
90. For example, Anesko & O'Leary, 1982.
91. Lundquist & Hansen, 1998; Wolfe & Wekerle, 1993.
92. Bakken, Miltenberger, & Schauss, 1993.
93. Smagner & Sullivan, 2005.
94. Forehand & Long, 1988; Wahler & Graves, 1983; Wells, 1994.
95. Sanders, Markie-Dadds, Tully, & Bor, 2000.
96. McCart, Priester, Davies, & Azen, 2006; Maughan, Christiansen, Jenson, Olympia, & Clark, 2005.
97. Patterson, Chamberlain, & Reid, 1982.
98. Taylor, Schmidt, Pepler, & Hodgins, 1998.
99. Forehand & King, 1977; Wells & Egan, 1988.
100. For example, Peed, Roberts, & Forehand, 1977.
101. Danforth, 1998.
102. Slough, McMahon, & Conduct Problems Prevention Research Group, 2008.
103. For example, Forehand & Long, 1988; Hood & Eyberg, 2003.
104. For example, Breiner & Forehand, 1981.
105. Brestan, Eyberg, Boggs, & Algina, 1997.
106. For example, Humphreys, Forehand, McMahon, & Roberts, 1978; Patterson, 1974.

9

Exposure Therapy
Brief/Graduated

When something makes you anxious or fearful, the last thing you want to do is reexperience it. But often that is the best way to reduce the anxiety or fear—the common wisdom of getting back on the horse that has just thrown you. **Exposure therapies** are used to treat anxiety, fear, and other intense negative emotional reactions (such as anger) by exposing clients—under carefully controlled and safe conditions—to the situations or events that elicit the emotional reactions.

We will use the terms *anxiety* and *fear* interchangeably to refer to intense, inappropriate, and maladaptive reactions that are characterized by uneasiness, dread about future events, a variety of physical responses (such as muscle tension, increased heart rate, and sweating), and avoidance of the feared events.[a] (Incidentally, the word *anxiety* comes from the Latin *anxius*, which means constriction or strangulation.)

Some strong fears are realistic and adaptive, such as the fear of walking alone at night in high-crime neighborhoods. Further, mild anxiety can be adaptive when it motivates us to act. For example, most students require some anxiety about an upcoming exam to get them to study.

Anxiety becomes problematic when its intensity is disproportionate to the actual situation and it interferes with normal, everyday functioning. Anxiety disorders are the most prevalent psychological problem in the United States; between 24–42% of the population will suffer from an anxiety disorder in their lifetime, and, in any given year, more than 18% of the population do.[1]

The goal of exposure therapies is to reduce clients' anxiety to a level that allows them to function effectively and feel comfortable.

VARIATIONS OF EXPOSURE THERAPY

When ordering in some restaurants, you start with a basic dish. Then, you customize it by specifying how you want it cooked (for example, grilled) and for how long (for instance, medium-rare) and by picking and choosing toppings and sides. Even the basic dish may be a variation involving "holding" an ingredient (such as no cheese on your cheeseburger) or changing a main component (such as substituting turkey for corned beef in a Reuben sandwich). As you are about to see, exposure therapy involves an analogous process. The customization involves four variables (which are depicted in Figure 9-1).

1. *Paradigm of exposure.* There are two basic paradigms of exposure therapy. **Brief/graduated exposure therapy** exposes the client to threatening events (a) for a short period (ranging from a few seconds to a few minutes) and (b) incrementally, beginning with aspects of the events that produce minimal anxiety and progressing to more anxiety-evoking aspects. Graduated exposure is a prime example of the stepwise progression that characterizes many behavior therapy procedures. In contrast, **prolonged/intense exposure**

---

[a]Early theorists made a distinction between fear and anxiety. *Fear* referred to apprehension concerning a tangible or realistic event, whereas *anxiety* referred to apprehension about something intangible or unrealistic. Some theorists have considered fear to be emotional and anxiety to be cognitive in nature (for example, Beck & Emery, 1985). In general, behavior therapists have not found it useful to distinguish between the two concepts (for example, Rachman, 1990), which is the position we have adopted in this book.

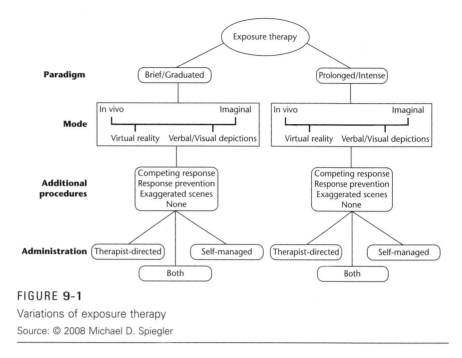

FIGURE 9-1

Variations of exposure therapy

Source: © 2008 Michael D. Spiegler

therapy exposes the client to threatening events (a) for a lengthy period (usually 10 to 15 minutes at a minimum and sometimes more than an hour) and (b) at a high intensity from the outset.

Although many applications of exposure therapy fit neatly into one of the two paradigms, often they do not. For instance, a client may be exposed to anxiety-evoking stimuli for an extended period but the stimuli are introduced incrementally; this means that it is prolonged/graduated exposure, a hybrid.

2. *Mode of exposure.* The mode of exposure in both paradigms can occur in four basic ways that fall on a continuum. At one end is *in vivo exposure*—actually encountering the event (such as taking a flight, in the case of fear of flying). At the other end is *imaginal exposure*—vividly imagining the event, as one does in a daydream (for example, visualizing taking a flight). Close to the in vivo end of the continuum, *virtual reality* technology now allows clients to be exposed to anxiety-evoking events through interactional computer simulations that appear almost real.[2] Toward the imaginal end, clients can listen to detailed *verbal descriptions*[3] (read by the therapist or client) or view *visual* (video) *depictions*[4] of anxiety-evoking events.

3. *Additional procedures.* Exposure therapies may use one or more additional procedures, with the three most common being:

- *Competing response*: During exposure, the client engages in a behavior that competes with anxiety, such as relaxing muscles while visualizing an anxiety-evoking event.
- *Response prevention*: During treatment, the client is kept from engaging in the maladaptive avoidance or escape behaviors he or she typically uses to reduce anxiety, such as repeatedly washing one's

hands because of the possibility of having touched something containing germs.

- *Exaggerated scenes*: To heighten the intensity or vividness of imaginal exposure, the depiction of the event may be exaggerated. For example, a therapist might ask a client who is afraid of snakes to imagine being in a pit with hundreds of snakes.

4. *Administration of exposure.* The exposure can be either *therapist-administered* in therapy sessions[5] or *self-managed* by the client outside of the therapy sessions.[6] Or, both methods can be used, beginning with therapist-administered exposure (as you will see in Case 9-4 later in the chapter).

If the variety of paradigms, modes, and other procedures that make up exposure therapies is slightly overwhelming, have no fear. You will be gradually exposed to examples of exposure therapy procedures that mix and match these variables, and in context, their use will become clear.

So let's see what exposure therapy looks like in practice. We begin with the brief/graduated paradigm (which includes systematic desensitization and in vivo desensitization) because they were the first to be developed; in the next chapter we turn to the prolonged/intense paradigm (in vivo flooding, imaginal flooding, and implosive therapy).

SYSTEMATIC DESENSITIZATION

Joseph Wolpe

Systematic desensitization, developed by Joseph Wolpe more than 50 years ago, was the first exposure therapy and the first major behavior therapy.[7] In **systematic desensitization**, the client imagines successively more anxiety-arousing situations while engaging in a behavior that competes with anxiety (such as skeletal muscle relaxation). The client gradually (systematically) becomes less sensitive (desensitized) to the situations. The therapy involves three steps:

1. The therapist teaches the client a response that competes with anxiety.
2. The specific events that cause anxiety are ordered in terms of the amount of anxiety they engender.
3. The client repeatedly visualizes the anxiety-evoking events, in order of increasing anxiety, while performing the competing response.

Progressive Relaxation as a Competing Response to Anxiety

Deep muscle relaxation is the most frequently used competing response in systematic desensitization (we'll discuss other competing responses later). Muscle relaxation counters some of the physiological components of anxiety, including increased muscle tension, heart rate, blood pressure, and respiration.

Edmund Jacobson

Training in **progressive relaxation** involves relaxing various skeletal muscle groups: arms, face, neck, shoulders, chest, abdomen, and legs. (Progressive relaxation used in systematic desensitization is an abbreviated version of Edmund Jacobson's original procedures, which required as much as 200 hours of training.[8]) Clients first learn to differentiate relaxation from tension by tensing and then releasing each set of muscles (see Photo 9-1). Later they

PHOTO 9-1

Progressive relaxation teaches clients to relax their skeletal muscles by first tensing and then relaxing various muscle groups. Clenching the fist results in tension in the hand, wrist, and forearm.

learn to induce relaxation without first tensing their muscles.[9] While the client is sitting or reclining comfortably, the therapist guides the client through the relaxation process. Clients practice progressive relaxation at home, often with a prerecorded tape of the relaxation instructions. The following is an excerpt from relaxation instructions:

> Close your eyes, settle back comfortably. . . . Let's start with your left hand. I want you to clench your left hand into a fist, clench it very tightly and study those tensions, hold it . . . (5-second pause) and now release the tension. Relax your left hand and let it rest comfortably. Just let it relax . . . (15-second pause). Once again now, clench your left hand . . . clench it very tightly, study those tensions . . . (5-second pause) and now release the tension. Relax your hand and once again note the very pleasant contrast between tension and relaxation.

Progressive relaxation training alone can be effective in treating anxiety disorders and in some cases is as effective as exposure therapy.[10] It also is used to treat a host of psychological and physical problems, including asthma, eczema (skin inflammation), headaches, hypertension, pain, side effects of chemotherapy, postsurgical distress, and insomnia.[11]

If you'd like to learn progressive relaxation, Participation Exercise 9-1 will guide you through the process. It involves practice over several days, but you should read through it now so that you will understand what is involved when clients learn this technique.

<table>
<tr><td>

PARTICIPATION EXERCISE 9-1

</td><td>

Progressively Making a Difference in Your Life with Progressive Relaxation

</td></tr>
</table>

Progressive relaxation can benefit your psychological and physical well-being. In this exercise, you will learn progressive relaxation in two phases. In the first phase, you will tense each muscle group before relaxing it. This procedure will make you aware of the sensations associated with muscle tension and with relaxation and will teach you to differentiate between these two sensations. In the second phase, you will relax your muscles without first tensing them.

Preparation

A recliner is often used for learning and practicing progressive relaxation, but any comfortable, firm surface on which you can lie down, such as a rug, mat, or bed will do. Find a location free of distractions, and then assure that you won't be interrupted by turning off your phone and placing a "Do Not Disturb" sign on the door. If you are interrupted, just resume where you left off.

Place this book, opened to Table 9-1, next to you so that you can read the specific relaxation instructions for each muscle group. Loosen tight clothing and remove your shoes and any articles of clothing or jewelry that might interfere with the relaxation exercises. Lie on your back with your legs slightly apart and your arms at your sides. Adjust your body so that you are comfortable. To remove visual distractions, keep your eyes *lightly* shut (except to read the relaxation instructions in Table 9-1).

TABLE **9-1**

Tensing Instructions for Learning Progressive Relaxation

Muscle Group	Tensing Instructions
1. Dominant hand and forearm (right hand if you're right-handed)	1. Make a tight fist.
2. Dominant biceps	2. Push your elbow down against the floor (or bed), and simultaneously pull the elbow inward toward your body.
3. Nondominant hand and forearm	3. Follow instruction 1.
4. Nondominant biceps	4. Follow instruction 2.
5. Upper part of face (forehead and scalp)	5. Lift your eyebrows as high as you can. (Alternative: Make an exaggerated frown.)[a]
6. Central part of face (upper cheeks and nose)	6. Squint your eyes tightly, and simultaneously wrinkle up your nose.
7. Lower part of face (jaw and lower part of cheeks)	7. Clench your teeth together, and pull the corners of your mouth back. *Caution:* Do not clench your teeth very hard—just enough to feel tension in your jaw and cheeks.

[a]Use the alternative tensing strategy only when the first one presented does not create tension in the appropriate muscle group.

Muscle Group	Tensing Instructions
8. Neck and throat	8. Pull your chin down toward your chest, and simultaneously try to keep you chin from touching your chest. (You should feel a small amount of trembling or shaking in your neck.)[a]
9. Chest, shoulders, and upper back	9. Take a deep breath and hold it; at the same time pull your shoulders back as if you were trying to make your shoulder blades touch each other. (Alternative: Pull your shoulders upward as if you were trying to touch your shoulder blades to your ears. It may help to imagine that puppet strings are attached to your shoulders, which are being pulled upward.)[a]
10. Abdomen	10. Make your stomach hard, as if you were bracing before being hit in the stomach. (Alternatives: Pull your stomach in as far as it will go. Or push your stomach out as far as it will go.)[a]
11. Dominant thigh (upper leg)	11. Keeping your leg straight, lift it a few inches off the floor.
12. Dominant calf (lower leg)	12. Pull your toes upward toward your head (without moving your legs).
13. Dominant foot	13. Point your toes downwards, turn your foot inward, and curl your toes downward (as if you were burying them in the sand). *Caution:* Do not tense these muscles very hard or very long—just enough to feel the tightness under your arch and the ball of your foot for about 3 to 5 seconds. (You may also feel some tension in your calf.)
14. Nondominant thigh	14. Follow instruction 11.
15. Nondominant calf	15. Follow instruction 12.
16. Nondominant foot	16. Follow instruction 13.

Before you begin, remember two things. First, concentrate on the sensations associated with tension and with relaxation; when your mind wanders, just refocus on the sensations in your muscles. Second, do not fall asleep while practicing. (However, once you learn progressive relaxation, you can use it to help you fall asleep.)

Phase 1: Tension and Relaxation

When you are ready to begin, take a few deep breaths. Start with the first of the 16 muscle groups (instruction 1 in Table 9-1). *Tense those muscles tightly for about 5 seconds without straining them* (count to yourself, "one-thousand-one, one-thousand-two," and so on). You should definitely feel tension in your muscles, but it should not hurt. As you tense your muscles, concentrate on the physical sensations you experience.

(continued)

After 5 seconds of tensing, say "relax" or "calm" to yourself and *gradually* relax the muscles you have just tensed. *Make your muscles loose; smooth them out.* Pay attention to the sensations of relaxation, *noting the difference between relaxation and tension.* Continue relaxing your muscles for at least 30 seconds until they feel quite relaxed. Now repeat the tension–relaxation sequence for the same muscle group (instruction 1). Next, proceed to the next muscle group (instruction 2) and go through the tension–relaxation sequence twice. Continue until you have gone through the tension–relaxation sequence twice for each of the muscle groups (instructions 1 through 16). This should take about 45 minutes at first, and less time as you practice.

After you have tensed and relaxed each of the muscle groups twice, remain in a relaxed state for several minutes. If you feel tension in any of your muscles, relax away that tension by making your muscles loose and smooth.

To conclude your practice sessions, slowly count backward from 5 to 1, following these instructions for each number:

- At 5 begin to move your legs and feet.
- At 4 move your arms and hands.
- At 3 move your head and neck.
- At 2 open your eyes.
- At 1 stretch (as you do when you wake up in the morning).

When you reach 1, *you should feel relaxed and calm, as if you had just awakened from a restful sleep.* Sit up slowly. When you are ready, stand up.

You should devote at least three practice sessions to tensing and relaxing each of the muscle groups (instructions 1 through 16); try more practice sessions if you still are feeling tension in any of your muscles at the end of a session.

Phase 2: Relaxation Only

In this phase of training, you will just relax your muscles (without any initial tensing). Begin with the first muscle group, and relax those muscles as deeply as you can. Even when you think your muscles are completely relaxed, it is always possible to relax them a bit more. Proceed through each of the muscle groups, relaxing each for at least 30 seconds until they are completely relaxed. When you have relaxed all of the muscle groups, follow the same procedure described earlier for concluding the practice session. Remember: Now you are *only relaxing* your muscles; do not tense them first.

Spend a minimum of two sessions relaxing each of the 16 muscle groups. Many people find that a few of their muscle groups are especially hard to relax, so you may need to spend more time practicing relaxing "troublesome" muscles.

Anxiety Hierarchy Construction

An **anxiety hierarchy** is a list of specific events that elicit anxiety in the client, ordered in terms of increasing levels of anxiety. To construct an anxiety hierarchy, clients, often with their therapist's assistance, identify a number of specific, detailed *scenes* that would make them anxious and then order the scenes from highest to lowest anxiety evoked. Once in order, it is useful to assign a SUDs (subjective units of discomfort; see Chapter 5) rating to each hierarchy scene. Optimally, there will be approximately equal intervals of SUDs between the scenes. If there is a particularly large interval, compared with the average interval, additional scenes need to be added so that the transition between scenes is gradual.

Anxiety hierarchies generally consist of events that share a common theme (see Table 9-2). When a client is anxious about more than one class of situations, multiple hierarchies are constructed. Completing Participation Exercise 9-2 will give you the experience of constructing an anxiety hierarchy. You can do the exercise before you continue reading (it will take about 10 minutes) or at a later time, but you should read it now.

TABLE **9-2**

Two Examples of Anxiety Hierarchies

Item		SUDs	Item		SUDs
	DEATH			FLYING	
19.	Death of a close friend or loved one	100	20.	Plane is flying in rough weather	100
18.	Death of strangers in a dramatic fashion	85	19.	Plane is touching down on runway	95
17.	Watching horror movies	80	18.	Pilot turns on seatbelt sign and announces turbulence ahead	90
16.	Seeing others in dangerous situations	75	17.	Plane is banking	85
15.	Hearing about a fatal and especially gruesome disease	70	16.	Plane is descending for landing	80
14.	Being around guns	60	15.	Announcement of preparation for final descent and landing	75
13.	Swimming in the ocean at night	55	14.	Plane is taking off	65
12.	Riding as a passenger in a car on the highway	50	13.	Plane is taxiing to the runway	60
11.	Flying in an airplane	48	12.	Plane is climbing to cruising altitude	55
10.	Driving a car on the highway	45	11.	Plane is cruising in good weather	50
9.	Thoughts of fire	43	10.	Sitting down and fastening seatbelt	45
8.	Climbing on high objects	40	9.	Announcement that the plane is ready for boarding	40
7.	Being alone in a house at night	38	8.	Boarding the plane	35
6.	Thinking about auto crashes	35	7.	Waiting to board the plane	30
5.	Thoughts of earthquakes	25	6.	Checking in at the airport	25
			5.	Driving to the airport	22

(continued)

TABLE **9-2** (*continued*)

Item		SUDs	Item		SUDs
	DEATH			FLYING	
4.	Thinking of witches and ghosts	20	4.	Calling the airport to find out if the flight is on time	20
3.	Swimming in a pool at night	15	3.	Packing for the trip	15
2.	Seeing a snake	10	2.	Purchasing ticket 10 days before flight	10
1.	Hearing a siren	5	1.	Making reservations 3 weeks before flight	5

PARTICIPATION EXERCISE 9-2

Constructing an Anxiety Hierarchy

From Table 9-3, choose a situation in which you could easily imagine yourself feeling anxious. Alternatively, choose a situation that actually makes you anxious. Then, complete the following steps in order:

TABLE **9-3**

Hypothetical Situations to Be Role-Played for Constructing Anxiety Hierarchies

1. You receive a letter in your mailbox instructing you to make an appointment with the dean before the end of the week to discuss "concerns" about your academic standing. You know that you have not been doing as well as you would like in your classes, but you didn't know your academic standing was in jeopardy.
2. You have a dentist appointment next week to have several cavities filled. You always have hated going to the dentist, and you have put off this visit for months.
3. You got into an automobile accident with your parents' car after borrowing it for the weekend. The accident was your fault, and the damages are estimated at $2800. You have not yet told your parents, but you are supposed to return the car in an hour.
4. You have a final exam in 2 days. The exam is in your most difficult subject this semester. You need a high grade on the exam to pass the course. You haven't started studying for the exam yet, and you have two other final exams before the one you are dreading most.
5. You have to give an oral presentation in one of your classes in 2 days. You have always had difficulty speaking in public, and this is a particularly large class. One-third of your grade is based on this oral presentation.

1. Assume the role of a person who is experiencing anxiety related to the situation.
2. Write eight brief descriptions of scenes related to the situation that would cause you to experience varying levels of anxiety. Be sure you include one scene that would elicit very high anxiety and one that would elicit very little anxiety.
3. Assign SUDs to each scene (using a scale of 1 to 100).
4. Write the numbers 8 through 1 in descending order on a sheet of paper. List the scenes from lowest anxiety (SUDs) to highest anxiety (SUDs), with number 1 being lowest.
5. Optimally, the six scenes between your lowest and highest will be approximately spaced at even intervals of SUDs levels. For example, if your lowest scene was rated 5 and your highest 95, then the six intermediate scenes should be *roughly 15* SUDs apart. If you find that you have large gaps, fill them in with additional scenes that you would assign intermediate SUDs levels.

You have now constructed an anxiety hierarchy that could be used in systematic desensitization.

THE FAR SIDE BY GARY LARSON

© 1987 FarWorks, Inc. All Rights Reserved/Dist. by Creators Syndicate

The Far Side® by Gary Larson © 1987 FarWorks, Inc. All Rights Reserved. The Far Side® and the Larson® signature are registered trademarks of FarWorks, Inc. Used with permission.

"Now relax. ... Just like last week, I'm going to hold the cape up for the count of 10. ... When you start getting angry, I'll put it down."

Desensitization

Desensitizing anxiety-evoking events begins as soon as the client has learned progressive relaxation (or another competing response) and has constructed an anxiety hierarchy. The therapist instructs the client, who is seated or reclining comfortably, to relax all of his or her muscles. The therapist then describes scenes from the anxiety hierarchy for the client to imagine, starting with the lowest item on the hierarchy. The scenes are described in detail and are specific to the client. For example, "initially greeting a date" might be elaborated as follows:

> You arrive at your date's apartment and knock on the door. There is no immediate answer and the waiting seems endless. Finally, your date opens the door, smiles, and says, "Hi!"

The client imagines each scene for about 15 seconds at a time. Whenever the client experiences anxiety or discomfort, the client signals the therapist, usually by raising a finger. When this occurs, the therapist instructs the client to "stop visualizing the scene and just continue relaxing"; thus, the client visualizes anxiety-evoking scenes *only when relaxed*. The aim is for relaxation to replace the anxiety previously associated with the scene. Each scene in the hierarchy is presented repeatedly until the client reports little or no discomfort. Typically, clients use SUDs to report the degree of anxiety they feel while visualizing scenes. When the anxiety associated with a scene has reached a low level, the next highest scene in the hierarchy is visualized. Case 9-1 illustrates the desensitization process.

CASE **9-1**
Systematic Desensitization for Severe Test Anxiety[12]

A 24-year-old female art student entered therapy complaining of severe test anxiety that had caused her to fail a number of tests. When she discussed her anxiety with the therapist, the therapist discovered that other situations also made her anxious. Accordingly, the client and therapist constructed four different anxiety hierarchies: taking tests, witnessing discord between other people, being scrutinized by others, and being devalued by others.

The desensitization process began with the therapist's instructing the client to become deeply relaxed. Then, the therapist said:

> I am now going to ask you to imagine a number of scenes. You will imagine them clearly and they will generally interfere little, if at all, with your state of relaxation. If, however, at any time you feel disturbed or worried and want to attract my attention, you will be able to do so by raising your left index finger. First I want you to imagine that you are standing at a familiar street corner on a pleasant morning watching the traffic go by. You see cars, motorcycles, trucks, bicycles, people, and traffic lights; and you can hear the sounds

associated with all these things. *(Pause about 15 sec.)* Now stop imagining that scene and give all your attention once again to relaxing. If the scene you imagined disturbed you even in the slightest degree, I want you to raise your left index finger *now. (Client does not raise finger.)* Now imagine that you are at home studying in the evening. It is the 20th of May, exactly a month before your examination. *(Pause of 5 sec.)* Now stop imagining the scene. Go on relaxing. *(Pause of 10 sec.)* Now imagine the same scene again—a month before your examination. *(Pause of 5 sec.)* Stop imagining the scene and just think of your muscles. Let go, and enjoy your state of calm. *(Pause of 15 sec.)* Now again imagine that you are studying at home a month before your examination. *(Pause of 5 sec.)* Stop the scene, and now think of nothing but your own body. *(Pause of 5 sec.)* If you felt any disturbance whatsoever to the last scene raise your finger. *(Client does not raise finger.)* If the amount of disturbance decreased from the first presentation to the third, do nothing, otherwise again raise your finger. *(Client does not raise finger.)* Just keep on relaxing. *(Pause of 15 sec.)* Imagine that you are sitting on a bench at a bus stop and across the road are two strange men whose voices are raised in an argument. *(Pause of 10 sec.)* Stop imagining the scene and just relax. *(Pause of 10 sec.)* Now again imagine the scene of these two men arguing across the road. *(Pause of 10 sec.)* Stop the scene and relax. Now I am going to count up to 5 and you will open your eyes, feeling very calm and refreshed.

A total of 17 sessions were required for the client to report no anxiety while visualizing the highest scene in each hierarchy. Following therapy, the client successfully passed a series of examinations, which demonstrated that the anxiety reduction transferred from the imagined scenes to the actual situations.

Three features of Case 9-1 are typical of systematic desensitization. First, before presenting scenes from the hierarchy, the therapist assessed if the client was deeply relaxed by presenting a neutral scene (standing on a street corner)—a scene not expected to elicit anxiety. Second, scenes from more than one hierarchy were visualized in the same session. Third, the therapy was relatively brief.

Essential and Facilitative Components of Systematic Desensitization

Therapies usually have both essential and facilitative components. An *essential component* is a procedure that is necessary for the therapy to be effective; the therapy will not work without it. A *facilitative component* is a procedure that is not always necessary but that may enhance the therapy's effectiveness and efficiency. Researchers isolate the essential components by systematically omitting components and then comparing the abbreviated treatment with the full treatment.[13] If an abbreviated treatment is shown to be as effective as the complete one, then the missing component is not essential.

The three major components of systematic desensitization are (1) *repeated safe exposure* to anxiety-evoking situations (2) in a *gradual manner*

(3) while engaging in a *competing response*. Research indicates that generally, desensitization can be effective when the client is exposed to the highest items in the hierarchy first[14] or only to the highest items,[15] and desensitization with and without relaxation training can be equally effective.[16] The only essential component is *repeated exposure to anxiety-evoking situations without the client experiencing any negative consequences.*[17] However, there are exceptions.

The facilitative components—gradual exposure and engaging in a competing response—are more likely to be beneficial when the client's anxiety is severe. For example, in a study with cancer patients, both gradual exposure and relaxation were *necessary* to alleviate nausea that patients experienced in anticipation of chemotherapy.[18] One effect of the facilitative components of desensitization may be to render the therapy more acceptable (less disturbing) to clients, which in turn may motivate clients to fully participate in their treatment and to remain in therapy.

Variations of Systematic Desensitization

The standard systematic desensitization procedures just described are still widely used. Since Wolpe developed them, a number of variations have been devised, including competing responses other than muscle relaxation, target behaviors other than anxiety, group treatment, a coping model of systematic desensitization, and interoceptive exposure.

Other Competing Responses

Deep muscle relaxation is not always the most appropriate competing response. Some clients, especially young children but also some adults, have difficulty learning progressive relaxation. **Emotive imagery** employs pleasant thoughts to counter anxiety and often is used with children.[19] It was part of the treatment of Paul's school-phobic behavior in Case 4-1. Other examples of competing responses include eating, listening to music, behaving assertively, and becoming sexually aroused.

Appreciating humor and laughing also can compete with anxiety.[20] Indeed, research in psychology and medicine has demonstrated the effectiveness of humor and laughter in treating a wide array of problems,[21] including coping with AIDS.[22] One advantage that humor and laughter have over progressive relaxation is that the client does not have to learn the response. Thus, with laughter as the competing response, it is possible to carry out "crisis" desensitization in a single session, as Case 9-2 illustrates.

CASE **9-2**

One-Session Systematic Desensitization for Fear of Humiliation[23]

A 20-year-old woman contacted a behavior therapist with a pressing problem. She was distressed about having to attend a banquet that evening because she feared that she might be embarrassed by her former boyfriend and his new girlfriend. The client and the therapist constructed an anxiety hierarchy of humiliating situations that might arise at the banquet. The scenes were presented to the client with details that elicited laughter. In one scene, for example, the client pictured herself sitting at the banquet and seeing her old flame enter the room. In describing the scene, the therapist added that the man was dressed in tights. The client found the recast scenes quite humorous, and she completed the hierarchy in a single therapy session. Several hours later, she attended the banquet and experienced only minor discomfort.

Other Target Behaviors

Anxiety is, by far, the most frequent problem treated by systematic desensitization. However, systematic desensitization as a general model of treatment is applicable to diverse problems, including anger,[24] complicated grief,[25] asthmatic attacks,[26] insomnia,[27] motion sickness,[28] nightmares,[29] problem drinking,[30] sleepwalking,[31] speech disorders,[32] and body image disturbances.[33] Even racial prejudice can be influenced by desensitization. In a racially integrated high school in the South, White students who reported anxiety related to unwanted prejudicial feelings received 3 months of biweekly desensitization sessions.[34] Following treatment, not only did the students report less racial-related anxiety, but they also acted in ways that indicated that their prejudice had declined (for example, attending social functions involving predominantly African Americans, which they would not have done before the treatment).

Case 9-3 illustrates the application of systematic desensitization to the treatment of anger, using laughter as a competing response. The woman's anger was intense and sometimes resulted in her physically abusing her child and husband.

CASE **9-3**

Systematic Desensitization for Anger with Laughter as the Competing Response[35]

A 22-year-old woman referred herself for treatment because of her reported inability to control her extreme anger toward her husband and 3-year-old son. She described her son as "a very active child whose almost constant misbehavior appeared to be attempts to antagonize his mother and gain her attention." Behavioral observations of the mother and child supported this description. The client reported that she generally reacted to her son's misbehavior by "screaming at the top of her voice, jumping up and down, smashing things, and physically attacking [him]." She said she could not control these responses. The client also reported that, when angry, she screamed at her husband and berated him, and she occasionally physically assaulted him. At the time of her self-referral, the client indicated that she had been contemplating suicide because "my temper makes everyone, including me, miserable."

After seven sessions of systematic desensitization using muscle relaxation as the competing response, little progress was made. Because of the

(continued)

CASE **9-3** (*continued*)

strength of the client's anger responses, she was able to imagine only the most innocuous scenes involving her son or husband without experiencing anger. At this point, it was decided to try laughter as a competing response. When the client signaled that a scene evoked anger, the therapist introduced and emphasized humorous aspects of the situation—generally in the form of slapstick comedy—such as in the following scene.

> As you're driving to the supermarket, little Pascal the Rascal begins to get restless. Suddenly he drops from his position on the ceiling and trampolines off the rear seat onto the rear view mirror. From this precarious position, he amuses himself by flashing obscene gestures at shocked pedestrians. As you begin to turn into the supermarket . . . , Pascal alights from his perch and lands with both feet on the accelerator. As the car careens through the parking lot, you hear Pascal observe, "Hmm, . . . 25–80 in 2 sec . . . not bad." But . . . your main concern is the two elderly . . . women that you're bearing down upon. [They are] . . . limping toward the door of the supermarket clutching their little bargain coupons. One, who is clutching a prayer book in the other hand, turns and, upon seeing your car approaching at 70 mph, utters a string of profanities, throws her coupons into the air, and . . . sprints out of the way and does a swan dive into a nearby [ditch]. The other [elderly woman] . . . nimbly eludes your car and takes refuge in a nearby shopping cart, which picks up speed as it rolls downhill across the parking lot.

The client reacted to the scenes with laughter and amusement, and rarely reported experiencing anger to any of the scenes in the hierarchy. Subsequently, she reported major reductions in the frequency and intensity of her anger responses to her son and husband. She also reported that she was able to remain calm in situations that previously had infuriated her. The client's self-reports were confirmed by relatives and by comparing behavioral observations of playroom interactions with her son before and after treatment. Moreover, the client reported that she no longer experienced depressive episodes and suicidal thoughts.

Group Systematic Desensitization

Groups of clients can be treated using systematic desensitization by making slight modifications in the standard procedures.[36] Progressive relaxation is simultaneously taught to the entire group. When the clients share a common problem (such as public speaking anxiety), a **group hierarchy** is constructed, which combines information from each client.[37] When a group hierarchy is not appropriate, individual hierarchies are used; the hierarchy items are written on cards to which each client refers during desensitization.

When one of the clients signals that he or she is experiencing anxiety, the scene is terminated and then repeated for all group members. Although this procedure is inefficient for some group members, it does not decrease the effectiveness of the treatment. Compared with individually administered desensitization, group desensitization requires less therapist time, and sharing similar problems and solutions can be beneficial for clients.

Marvin Goldfried

Coping Desensitization

In standard desensitization, anxiety associated with specific events is replaced with a competing response. In **coping desensitization**, a variation developed by Marvin Goldfried, the *bodily sensations* of anxiety are used to cue the client to engage in a coping response, such as muscle relaxation.[38] For example, when a client signals that a scene is producing anxiety, the therapist instructs the client to "stay with the scene and use relaxation to cope with the anxiety"—rather than terminating the scene and just relaxing (as in standard desensitization). In addition, the client continues visualizing the anxiety-evoking scene while thinking such thoughts as, "I'm handling things; I don't have to be anxious." Muscle relaxation is just one possible coping response clients might use while visualizing a scene that elicits anxiety. Other examples include visualizing themselves approaching the feared stimulus or acting assertively. For religious clients, praying has been used as a coping response.[39] A hybrid form of coping desensitization called *active-imaginal exposure* has clients physically perform coping responses while imagining the feared stimulus.[40] For instance, walking in a nonthreatening, friendly manner toward an imagined feared dog.

In coping desensitization, the anxiety hierarchy need not have a common theme, as it often does in standard desensitization. Because bodily sensations generally associated with anxiety are desensitized, rather than specific anxiety-producing events, the hierarchy items only must result in increasing levels of anxiety. This feature makes coping desensitization applicable to non-specific anxiety (generalized anxiety disorder).[41]

Coping desensitization is a prime example of the self-control approach that is inherent in many behavior therapies.[42] First, clients practice reducing their anxiety while visualizing anxiety-evoking scenes by imagining themselves actively coping with the situation. Then, they use bodily sensations associated with anxiety as reminders to use coping skills whenever they experience these sensations in their daily lives.

Although few studies have evaluated the effectiveness of coping desensitization, it appears to be at least as effective as standard desensitization in reducing anxiety.[43] Additionally, there is some evidence that the coping skills generalize to unrelated anxiety-evoking events other than the ones specifically treated in therapy.[44]

Anxiety Management Training, originally developed by Richard Suinn and Frank Richardson,[45] is a variant of coping desensitization in which clients learn to use feelings of anxiety as cues to begin relaxing or to use emotive imagery. Anxiety Management Training is highly structured and brief (six to eight sessions)[46] and does not employ an anxiety hierarchy. Although Anxiety Management Training typically is used to treat anxiety disorders,[47] it has been applied to other negative emotions, including anger associated with road rage.[48]

Interoceptive Exposure for Panic Attacks

Panic disorder is characterized by repeated, unexpected, and sudden attacks of intense apprehension and terror, which are accompanied by physical symptoms, such as shortness of breath, dizziness, heart palpitations, and chest

David Barlow

pain. Clients with panic disorder are hypersensitive to bodily sensations that can trigger a panic attack (for example, misinterpreting mild chest pain as a heart attack). David Barlow and his colleagues have developed a specific treatment package for panic attacks.[49] The novel treatment component is **interoceptive exposure**, in which the bodily sensations associated with panic attacks are artificially induced while the client visualizes panic-evoking events. (*Interoceptors* are specialized nerve receptors that respond to sensations in internal organs.) For example, increased heart rate and dizziness can be artificially induced by rapid stair climbing and spinning in a chair; other inductions involve hyperventilating (abnormally fast or deep respiration), breathing through a straw, and using a tongue depressor.[50] During the interoceptive exposure, clients cope with their anxiety by viewing the situation and sensations in a less threatening manner. Clients are also taught to use *breathing retraining*, which involves diaphragmatic breathing that results in slow, steady inhalations and exhalations to combat hyperventilation that is often associated with panic attacks.

This treatment package has been found to be highly effective in treating panic disorder in both individual and group treatment[51] as well as social phobia and generalized anxiety disorder.[52] It also has been found to be at least as effective as medication[53] and significantly more effective than medication for long-term maintenance.[54] Recently, interoceptive exposure has been incorporated into treatment packages for posttraumatic stress disorder[55] and substance abuse.[56] It also has been successfully modified to fit the cultural beliefs and culture-specific symptom interpretations of Cambodian refugees who have been severely traumatized.[57]

Systematic Desensitization in Perspective

Fifty years after Wolpe developed systematic desensitization, it remains a versatile and highly effective and efficient treatment that is still widely practiced.[58] However, it is not applicable to all clients suffering from anxiety. Young children, for example, have difficulty carrying out the procedures.[59] Techniques more suitable for children include emotive imagery, in vivo desensitization (covered later in this chapter), flooding (see Chapter 10), and modeling therapy (see Chapter 11).

When anxiety is maintained by a skill deficit, systematic desensitization is not an appropriate treatment. For instance, people who have problems with dating often do not know how to act appropriately while on a date. The anxiety they experience in dating situations may be a by-product of the skill deficit rather than the primary maintaining condition of the problem. Thus, the appropriate treatment is skills training (see Chapter 11). When both a skill deficit and anxiety are maintaining conditions of a problem, as is often the case with social anxiety, treatment must address both maintaining conditions.[60]

Clients find systematic desensitization an acceptable treatment. It does not involve much discomfort because clients are gradually and symbolically exposed to anxiety-evoking situations. Further, clients control the process by proceeding at their own pace and terminating exposure when they begin to feel anxious.

Efficiency of Systematic Desensitization

Systematic desensitization is efficient in three ways. First, exposure to problematic situations in one's imagination is less time consuming (for both client and therapist) than in vivo desensitization, which involves venturing into the actual anxiety-provoking situations. In addition, clients do transfer the anxiety reduction they experience with imagined scenes to the real-life situations. Second, compared with traditional psychotherapies that treat anxiety disorders, systematic desensitization requires relatively few sessions. Third, the procedures can be adapted for groups of clients.

Desensitization can be automated by using tape-recorded instructions,[61] written instructions,[62] or computer programs.[63] Self-managed desensitization obviously reduces the amount of time therapists need to spend with clients. In some instances, such procedures can be as effective as therapist-administered treatment.[64] However, self-administered desensitization is used infrequently because it has limitations, especially for clients who are extremely anxious or who have problems following the standard procedures (such as difficulty visualizing scenes).[65] When the treatment is therapist-administered, the therapist can modify standard procedures on the spot to handle unexpected problems that arise (as in Case 9-3, where the therapist introduced humorous scenes) and can provide support and encouragement for the client.[66]

Effectiveness of Systematic Desensitization

There is no doubt that systematic desensitization is an effective procedure for treating a variety of anxiety disorders. The findings of hundreds of studies assessing the effectiveness of systematic desensitization over the past 50 years are overwhelmingly positive.[67] As early as 1969, a review of the controlled outcome studies of systematic desensitization concluded that "for the first time in the history of psychological treatments, a specific treatment . . . reliably produced measurable benefits for clients across a broad range of distressing problems in which anxiety was of fundamental importance."[68] Seven years and many studies later, another comprehensive review concluded, "Systematic desensitization is demonstrably more effective than both no treatment and every psychotherapy variant with which it has so far been compared."[69] Moreover, the treatment effects are relatively durable. For example, one study found that 70 clients with dental phobias still were maintaining regular dental checkups between 1 and 4 years after being treated by systematic desensitization.[70]

IN VIVO DESENSITIZATION

In vivo desensitization essentially is systematic desensitization except that the client is exposed to the actual feared event rather than imagining it. The exposure is brief and graduated, and the client has the option of terminating the exposure if it becomes too uncomfortable.

During in vivo desensitization, clients often employ muscle relaxation to compete with their anxiety as they progress through their anxiety hierarchy. Because clients are using a variety of muscles to actually engage in the behaviors in their hierarchy, they cannot relax all of their skeletal muscles, as in systematic desensitization.[71] However, it is possible for clients to relax all their muscles that are not needed to engage in the actions they are performing and to tense the required muscles only as much as is needed. This procedure is known as **differential relaxation**.[72] For example, standing requires some tension in the neck, back, and leg muscles, but facial, arm, chest, and abdominal muscles do not have to be tensed. Other competing responses used for in vivo desensitization include pleasant images, laughter, and sexual arousal. Sometimes merely the therapist's presence—which is reassuring and calming to the client—competes with anxiety. Case 9-4 illustrates the basic procedures of in vivo desensitization.

CASE **9-4**

Fear of Leaving Hospital Grounds Treated by
In Vivo Desensitization[73]

A 36-year-old man, who had been hospitalized for 7 years for a serious psychiatric disorder, was intensely afraid of venturing outside the hospital. Spending increasing amounts of time outside the hospital grounds was established as an acceleration target behavior.

> After several relaxation sessions in the office, the relaxation sessions were continued while the patient was seated in an automobile. Each week the automobile was driven by the therapist closer to the gate of the hospital grounds, and then farther and farther away from the hospital, until a five mile drive took place during the third session in the car. During each trip outside the hospital, the patient was let out of the car for increasing lengths of time, going from one minute to a half-hour in three weeks. Concomitant with therapy sessions outside the hospital grounds, the patient was encouraged to go on trips with other patients. By the seventh week, the patient had been to a country fair in the neighboring state, an art show across the river, a local fireman's carnival, and a fishing trip. The art show was the only trip on which the therapist accompanied the patient, and even then, he was alone for half of the two hour show. After the seventh session it was no longer necessary to encourage the patient to go out on day passes, since he signed up for passes and outside activities on his own. At the end of seven in vivo [exposure] . . . sessions, the patient felt comfortable enough to venture outside the hospital without the support of the therapist [or other patients].

Case 9-4 is a "textbook case" of in vivo desensitization. Exposure was graduated both *spatially*, by increasing the distance the patient ventured from the hospital, and *temporally*, by increasing the time he spent outside the car. Differential relaxation was employed as a competing response.

In an unusual application of in vivo desensitization to anorexia nervosa, a 24-year-old man was treated for his pronounced anxiety related to consuming high-fat/high-calorie foods.[74] At the time of treatment, the client reported that in the past year he had lost approximately 100 pounds through diet and exercise. The anxiety hierarchy consisted of foods that made the client anxious and that he routinely avoided, ranging from a plain bagel to pizza and cookies. The client brought foods listed in his hierarchy to the therapy session, where, encouraged by the therapist, he ate them in hierarchical order. The therapist's support served as a competing response for the client's anxiety.

By the 10th session, the client was able to consume as many as 2500 calories a day. By the end of treatment (34th session), he had integrated more foods into his diet and no longer had an intense fear of high-calorie foods.

Self-Managed In Vivo Desensitization

Although self-managed systematic desensitization is used occasionally, self-managed in vivo desensitization is used more frequently. Self-managed in vivo desensitization was part of a treatment package for a 28-year-old teacher suffering from *body dysmorphic disorder*[75] (preoccupation with a perceived physical defect that is not noticeable to others[76]). The teacher was convinced that she had a "bad" complexion. She repeatedly checked her face in the mirror looking for blemishes, which significantly interfered with her work and home life. Self-managed in vivo desensitization involved having the client gradually apply less makeup and get physically closer to people at work when she talked to them (which she had avoided because of her "bad" complexion). After the 11th session, the therapist instructed her to wear no makeup at all and to expose herself to a broader range of people in stores and restaurants. By the end of the treatment, she was spending no time checking for physical defects, in contrast to 4 hours a day before treatment.

Self-managed exposure clearly is more efficient than therapist-administered exposure. Moreover, clients may be less likely to drop out of therapy when they fully control their own exposure.[77] Self-managed treatment at home can be implemented through the use of treatment manuals written for clients and with the assistance of family members.[78] The therapist may make occasional home visits to ensure that the client is carrying out the exposure correctly.[79] It even is possible for clients to carry out self-managed in vivo desensitization with guidance from the therapist via telephone calls.[80] Telephone-administered therapy has obvious advantages for clients who are housebound or who live far from available therapists. Case 9-5 is an example of self-managed in vivo desensitization that illustrates the flexibility of the procedure.

CASE **9-5**

Self-Managed In Vivo Desensitization for Fear of Dogs[81]

A man sought the help of a behavior therapist to deal with his overwhelming fear of dogs. Between the first and second therapy sessions, a fortuitous incident occurred. A friend told the client that his dog had just had puppies, and he jokingly asked the client (who he knew was afraid of dogs) if he wanted one of them. After consulting with his therapist, the client decided to take one of the dogs because he believed he could tolerate a *puppy* in his home.

The situation contained all the essential ingredients for self-managed in vivo desensitization. The client would be exposed to a dog that gradually became larger. Moreover, his exposure to the dog would be in the context of happy interactions with his children and the accompanying pleasure would serve as a competing response to his fear of dogs. After 6 months of raising the puppy, the client no longer reported any fear of dogs.

Self-Managed In Vivo Desensitization in the Treatment of Sexual Dysfunctions

Self-managed in vivo desensitization is especially useful when the therapist's presence is inappropriate, such as in the treatment of sexual dysfunctions.[82] *Sexual dysfunctions* include diminished sexual desire, problems achieving orgasm, and pain during intercourse. Typically couples, rather than individuals, are treated because sexual dysfunctions are most usefully viewed in the context of a sexual relationship and not as a problem of one of the partners and because the treatment requires a partner.[83]

Anxiety often is a primary maintaining condition of sexual dysfunctions, and in vivo desensitization typically is part of a treatment package for such problems. At home, the couple is instructed to gradually engage in physically intimate behaviors, which are arranged in an anxiety hierarchy. For example, at the bottom of the hierarchy might be holding hands and at the top might be sexual intercourse. The couple's physical intimacies produce sexual arousal (often mild at first), which competes with their anxiety. The couple proceeds up the hierarchy, stopping whenever one partner begins to experience anxiety and his or her sexual arousal starts to diminish. Only when both partners feel comfortable engaging in a particular sexual behavior is the next behavior in the hierarchy attempted. Sexual performance, including intercourse and orgasm, is not a goal of the treatment. Couples are instructed to follow the rule that pleasurable physical contact alone is the goal of each in vivo desensitization session. In such a *nondemand situation*, couples learn to enjoy sexual activity by gradually coming to feel comfortable and sexually aroused.

In Vivo Desensitization in Perspective

In vivo desensitization, like systematic desensitization, can be used to treat many different anxiety disorders.[84] For example, in vivo desensitization is at least as effective as medication in treating clients with panic attacks.[85] It is superior to other psychological interventions (such as educational information-based approaches and social support) and behavior therapies (such as cognitive restructuring and relaxation training) in reducing anxiety associated with social phobias.[86] The versatility of in vivo desensitization is illustrated by its successful application to a 71-year-old man who was suffering from a delusional disorder.[87] The man believed that electricity caused cancer and therefore he avoided anything having to do with electricity, which, understandably, significantly interfered with his daily life.

In vivo desensitization can reduce both overt behavioral and cognitive components of anxiety. For instance, clients treated by in vivo desensitization for public speaking anxiety showed fewer overt behavioral signs of anxiety (such as pacing while talking) and reported fewer cognitive indications of anxiety (such as worrying about others' negative evaluations of them).[88]

In vivo desensitization has three advantages over systematic desensitization. First, in vivo desensitization can be effective for clients who have difficulty imagining scenes, which occasionally occurs with adults and often with young children.[89] Second, the exposure to the anxiety-evoking events can be monitored directly with in vivo desensitization; this is not possible with systematic desensitization because the therapist does not have access to the client's mental images.[90] Third, in some instances in vivo desensitization is more effective than systematic desensitization because the therapy often takes place directly in the anxiety-evoking situation, which eliminates the need for transfer from the imagined to the actual situation.

In vivo desensitization has three limitations. First, because it frequently involves going to the actual environment where the client's anxiety occurs, considerable therapist time is required. For instance, two therapists were required to implement the in vivo desensitization for Paul's school phobia in Case 4-1. Self-managed in vivo desensitization is one way to deal with the problem of inordinate demands on therapists' time. A second limitation is that in vivo desensitization is not feasible with certain anxiety-evoking events (for example, natural disasters such as floods and earthquakes). Third, some clients cannot tolerate being in the actual threatening situation, even when exposure is graduated and the client is engaging in a competing response. Imaginal exposure in systematic desensitization may be all that the client can tolerate, at least initially. A promising strategy for dealing with children's resistance to in vivo desensitization incorporates behavioral parent training.[91] The parents are taught to use child management techniques (such as prompting and shaping) to facilitate their children's exposure to anxiety-evoking situations.

VIRTUAL REALITY EXPOSURE THERAPY

Reaping the advantages of in vivo desensitization without its disadvantages may seem like having one's cake and eating it too. In fact, this may be possible by exposing clients to anxiety-evoking stimuli through computer-generated virtual reality technology.[92] Clients wear a head-mounted display that provides a computer-generated view of a virtual reality environment (see Photo 9-2).[93] Electromagnetic sensors placed on the client's head and arms monitor movements so that the client is able to "interact" with objects in the virtual environment. For example, clients treated for fear of flying virtually sit in the window seat of a commercial airliner. As clients move their heads, they look out the window or inside the plane. Not only are visual cues simulated, but sounds, vibrations, and odors can be also. Clients are gradually exposed to increasingly more anxiety-evoking scenes and sensations, such as sitting on a plane with its engines off, sitting on a plane with its engines running, taxiing, taking off, cruising in smooth air, flying around a thunderstorm with turbulence, and landing.

As is implied by the term *virtual reality*, what clients experience is almost as real as if they were in the actual situation,[94] as the following incident illustrates. Before an early test of the effectiveness of virtual reality for fear of heights, the therapists who developed the therapy exposed themselves to the virtual reality scenes before exposing clients to them. One of the scenes was an open elevator door with only space below. Despite the fact that the

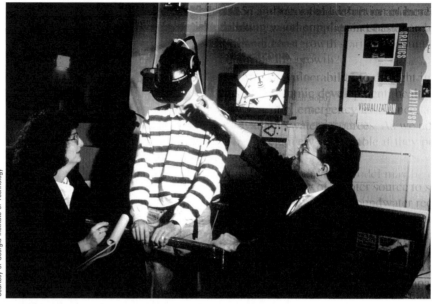

Courtesy of Georgia Institute of Technology

PHOTO 9-2

Client with fear of heights undergoing exposure therapy using virtual reality technology

therapists knew that they were in a virtual environment, they would not "walk off the elevator into midair" without being prompted to do so and being reassured that it was perfectly safe.[95]

Virtual reality exposure therapy has been used to treat a variety of phobias, including fear of flying,[96] fears of heights,[97] fear of spiders,[98] claustrophobia (fear of enclosed spaces),[99] and social phobia.[100] After September 11, 2001, it was used to treat posttraumatic stress disorder related to the terrorist attacks on the United States,[101] and a virtual reality environment is being developed for victims of bus bombings in Israel.[102]

Various virtual reality environments are being tested for posttraumatic stress disorder in military personal who have served in combat.[103] Virtual Iraq presents clients with typical scenes they would have encountered while stationed in Iraq, including a marketplace, old buildings, desolate streets, and mosques as well as combat situations (see Photo 9-3 for an example). The therapist adds or subtracts various elements depending on the needs of the client. For example, vehicles and civilian and military personnel can move about the streets. The client can be positioned inside a HUMVEE as driver, passenger, or in the turret position; the number of other soldiers in the vehicle can be varied, and they can be wounded in attack scenarios.

Courtesy of Albert Rizzo/USC Institute for Creative Technologies

PHOTO 9-3

Combat scene used in virtual reality exposure therapy with veterans of the Iraq war suffering from PTSD

Clients can navigate the environment using a gamepad controller or a thumb-mouse that is part of a replica of an M4 weapon. The therapist can manipulate the time of day and weather as well as introduce in real time a variety of visual, auditory, tactile, and olfactory stimuli.[104]

Exposure therapy through Virtual Iraq for posttraumatic stress disorder is still in the developmental stage. Although results from case studies[105] and an ongoing clinical study are encouraging,[106] it remains to be seen whether it is an effective treatment. If it proves to be, one advantage of Virtual Iraq as a treatment for combat veterans is that it can be advertised as "post-combat reintegration training" rather than therapy. This might help to overcome the stigma of seeking treatment that exists in the military.[107]

There is a growing body of controlled studies that demonstrates the effectiveness of virtual reality exposure therapy for a variety of anxiety-related disorders.[108] Virtual reality exposure therapy seems to be as effective or more effective than in vivo treatment,[109] which may indicate that virtual reality scenes are equivalent to actual scenes. Its potential benefits are exciting to consider, including the ability to expose clients to anxiety-evoking situations that they could not be exposed to in vivo for practical and ethical reasons (such as actual combat) and the savings in time compared with in vivo desensitization.

IN THEORY **9-1**
Why Does Brief/Graduated Exposure Therapy Work?

Why does brief/graduated exposure reduce anxiety? A number of theoretical explanations have been advanced, and we will describe the five most common: counterconditioning, reciprocal inhibition, extinction, cognitive factors, and nonspecific factors.

Counterconditioning

Wolpe's original theory involved a *counterconditioning process* in which an adaptive response (feeling relaxed, for example) is substituted for a maladaptive response (anxiety) to a threatening stimulus.[110] To understand this process, it is helpful to first see how anxiety may develop according to a classical conditioning model of learning. Anxiety develops when a neutral event (a conditioned stimulus) that does not elicit anxiety

is associated with an event that naturally causes anxiety (an unconditioned stimulus). Consider the simple example diagrammed in Figure 9-2. You *speak up in a class* and *students laugh at you*. Being laughed at (unconditioned stimulus) typically results in feeling embarrassed and humiliated (unconditioned response). If you are laughed at on a number of occasions when you speak in class, speaking in class will come to be associated with feeling embarrassed and humiliated and this behavior becomes a conditioned stimulus. The result is that you now become anxious (conditioned response) when you have to speak in class (conditioned stimulus) because you anticipate being embarrassed and humiliated.

Brief/graduated exposure counters this conditioning by associating the anxiety-evoking event with relaxation or another anxiety-competing response (see Figure 9-3). One problem with the counterconditioning explanation is that brief/graduated exposure without a competing response can be effective.

Reciprocal Inhibition

In theorizing about the process of systematic desensitization, Wolpe also posited a more basic, neurophysiological explanation. Our physiological responses associated with anxiety (for example, increased heart rate and sweating) are largely controlled by the autonomic nervous system, which is divided into two branches:

Before conditioning	Speaking up in class (conditioned stimulus)	────────────────▶		No negative emotional reaction
Conditioning	Speaking up in class (conditioned stimulus)	‐ ‐ ‐ ‐ ‐ ‐	Other students laugh (unconditioned stimulus) ────▶	Anxiety (unconditioned response)
After conditioning	Speaking up in class (conditioned stimulus)	────────────────▶		Anxiety (conditioned response)

────▶ "results in"

‐ ‐ ‐ ‐ ‐ ‐ "paired with"

FIGURE 9-2

Development of anxiety through classical conditioning

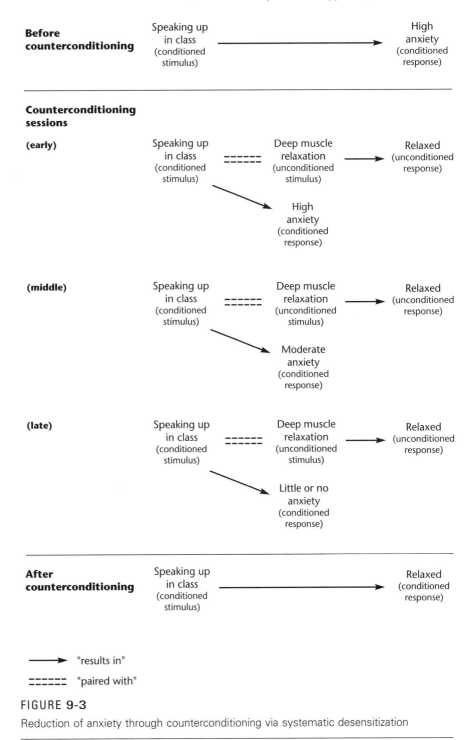

FIGURE 9-3

Reduction of anxiety through counterconditioning via systematic desensitization

(continued)

IN THEORY 9-1 (*continued*)

sympathetic and parasympathetic. The physical symptoms of anxiety are primarily sympathetic functions, whereas relaxation is primarily a parasympathetic function. At any given moment, either our sympathetic or the parasympathetic system predominates. Thus, during brief/graduated exposure therapy, the client's anxiety (sympathetic) is *inhibited* by a *reciprocal* or opposite physiological response, relaxation (parasympathetic). This process is known as *reciprocal inhibition*. One potential problem with this explanation is that sympathetic activity and parasympathetic activity are only partially independent because both branches of the autonomic nervous system always are active to some degree.

Extinction

Another explanation of how brief/graduated exposure works suggests that extinction is the basic underlying mechanism.[111] The extinction explanation, like Wolpe's counter-conditioning explanation, assumes that anxiety develops by classical conditioning. Extinction involves terminating reinforcement. In classical conditioning, *reinforcement* specifically refers to the unconditioned stimulus being presented after the occurrence of the conditioned stimulus. This pairing is broken in brief/graduated exposure when the client is repeatedly exposed to the conditioned stimulus (speaking in class) *in the absence* of the unconditioned stimulus (being laughed at). Recently, basic research on the underlying mechanisms of extinction of fears reveals that biochemical changes occur during the process, which may result in fear reduction.[112]

Cognitive Factors

There are at least three ways in which changes in clients' thought processes might explain the effectiveness of brief/graduated exposure therapy. One explanation is that the safe exposure to anxiety-arousing situations may result in clients' *thinking about the situations more realistically*,[113] which renders the situations less threatening. Relaxation, or another competing response, may help clients think more objectively about their reactions to anxiety-evoking situations and see that they are exaggerated or otherwise inappropriate.[114]

A second cognitive explanation suggests that brief/graduated exposure leads clients to *expect that they will be less anxious* than they had assumed they would be when exposed to anxiety-evoking events. This explanation is consistent with the finding that when people are led to believe that they are less afraid (as through false feedback), they actually feel less afraid.[115]

The first two cognitive explanations are indirectly supported by research which indicates that anxiety disorders seem to be maintained by people's faulty appraisals of threat. Specifically, people with anxiety disorders exhibit judgment biases, such as anticipating an unrealistically high probability of harm or exaggerated negative consequences associated with feared stimuli.[116] And, research has revealed an association between successful treatment of social anxiety and reduction of these judgment biases.[117]

A third cognitive explanation holds that brief/graduated exposure may *strengthen clients' beliefs that they are capable of coping with their anxiety*.[118] This belief would be expected to develop from clients'

repeated successes during treatment—that is, they repeatedly are exposed to anxiety-provoking situations without experiencing negative consequences, including feeling anxious.

Nonspecific Factors

Finally, the effects of brief/graduated exposure may be explained by *nonspecific factors*, which are elements common to all forms of therapy. For example, the attention a therapist gives the client is a generic nonspecific factor. Research studies have controlled for therapist attention to assess its effect on treatment outcome. This is done by comparing clients who receive brief/graduated exposure with clients in an attention-control condition in which clients spend time with the therapist but receive no therapy. Studies evaluating the effects of nonspecific factors such as therapist attention indicate that they can play a role in the success of brief/graduated exposure.[119] However, the studies also show that nonspecific factors alone do not account for the effectiveness of the therapy.[120]

Obviously, there are many answers to the question: Why does brief/graduated exposure therapy work? We have presented the most prominent theoretical explanations; a variety of other explanations have been proposed, including those based on shaping and modeling.[121]

In the next chapter, we turn to the other paradigm of exposure therapy, prolonged/intense. The extinction, cognitive, and nonspecific factors explanations of brief/graduated exposure therapies just described also may explain why prolonged/intense exposure therapies work.

ALL THINGS CONSIDERED: BRIEF/GRADUATED EXPOSURE THERAPY

The first exposure therapies to be developed were brief and graduated, starting with systematic desensitization and then in vivo desensitization. These early exposure therapies all employed a competing response for anxiety, usually muscle relaxation. In more recent applications of brief/graduated exposure, a competing response sometimes is omitted, which is legitimate given that a competing response is not an essential component of the treatment.[122]

Increasingly, imaginal and in vivo desensitization are being combined for clients,[123] which is consistent with current practice in behavior therapy to use treatment packages to enhance therapy effectiveness and bring about change more quickly.[124] Another trend has been to supplement visualization of anxiety-evoking scenes with their verbal descriptions during imaginal exposure and for the descriptions to be audiotaped and used during homework practice.[125]

The results from hundreds of studies evaluating brief/graduated exposure therapies clearly indicate that they are effective treatments for a variety of anxiety and related disorders. Justifiably, then, relatively few outcome studies of these therapies have been done in recent years.[126] However, brief/graduated exposure therapies are still widely used in clinical practice.[127] There even has been a trend toward using a graduated exposure component in exposure therapies that are more consistent with the prolonged/intense paradigm (the topic of the next chapter).[128]

When exposure is brief and graduated, the distress clients experience is minimized. This probably accounts for the finding that clients generally evaluate brief/graduated exposure as more acceptable than prolonged/intense exposure, and clients are more likely to enter and less likely to drop out of brief/graduated exposure therapies.

SUMMARY

1. Exposure therapies are used to treat anxiety, fear, and other intense negative emotional responses by exposing clients to the events that evoke the negative emotions.

2. There are two paradigms of exposure therapy. With brief/graduated exposure, the client is gradually exposed to increasingly threatening events for a short period. With prolonged/intense exposure, the client is exposed all at once to highly threatening events for a lengthy period. In both paradigms, the client can be exposed to the threatening events imaginally or in vivo (or a combination of the two). The exposure can be therapist-administered or self-managed by the client. Procedures that may be used to augment exposure include the use of a competing response to anxiety, response prevention, and exaggerated scenes.

3. In systematic desensitization, the client is exposed imaginally to successively more anxiety-arousing situations while engaging in a response that competes with anxiety. First, the client learns the competing response, most often muscle relaxation. Second, the client and therapist construct an anxiety hierarchy, which is a list of events ordered in terms of

increasing levels of anxiety they elicit. Third, the client visualizes the anxiety-evoking events in the hierarchy, beginning at the low end, while performing the competing response. If the client experiences anxiety while visualizing a scene, the client stops visualizing it and relaxes.

4. The essential component of systematic desensitization is repeated exposure to anxiety-evoking situations without experiencing any negative consequences. Gradual exposure and a competing response are facilitative components.

5. Variations of systematic desensitization include using competing responses other than muscle relaxation (such as thinking pleasant thoughts and laughing); target behaviors other than anxiety (such as anger); group desensitization; and coping desensitization, in which clients use bodily sensations of anxiety as cues to relax and cope with an anxiety-evoking event. Interoceptive exposure is a treatment package that artificially induces the bodily sensations the client experiences while gradually visualizing panic-inducing events.

6. Systematic desensitization was the first exposure therapy to be developed, and it is still widely used. It is both effective and efficient, and clients consider it an acceptable treatment.

7. With in vivo desensitization, clients are exposed to the actual feared events. The competing response is usually differential relaxation, which involves clients' relaxing all nonessential muscles. The exposure is brief and graduated. Self-managed in vivo desensitization is efficient and useful when it is impractical or inappropriate for the therapist to be present, such as in the treatment of sexual dysfunctions.

8. In vivo desensitization is a versatile procedure that sometimes is superior to systematic desensitization. Its limitations include the extensive amount of therapist time required, its not being applicable to some anxiety-evoking events, and the inability of some clients to tolerate being in the actual threatening situation.

9. Virtual reality exposure therapy exposes clients to anxiety-producing stimuli through computer-generated virtual reality technology. It is a promising new method of treatment for a variety of anxiety disorders, including phobias and posttraumatic stress disorder.

10. Brief/graduated exposure can be explained in terms of learning (counter-conditioning and extinction), physiological processes (reciprocal inhibition), cognitive variables, and nonspecific factors. The learning explanations are predicated on anxiety being developed and maintained through classical conditioning.

REFERENCE NOTES

1. American Psychiatric Association, 2000a; Hansell & Damour, 2008.
2. For example, Rothbaum & Hodges, 1999; Rothbaum, Hodges, Smith, Lee, & Price, 2000.
3. For example, Fecteau & Nicki, 1999; Foa et al., 2005; Tolin & Foa, 1999.
4. For example, Coldwell, Getz, Milgrom, Prall, Spadafora, & Ramsay, 1998; Schwartz, Houlihan, Krueger, & Simon, 1997; Tolin & Foa, 1999.
5. For example, Williams, Dooseman, & Kleifield, 1984.
6. For example, Fecteau & Nicki, 1999; Marks, 1978.

7. Wolpe, 1958.
8. Jacobson, 1929.
9. Compare with Lucic, Steffen, Harrigan, & Stuebing, 1991.
10. For example, Bernstein, Borkovec, & Hazlett-Stevens, 2000; Lukins, Davan, & Drummond, 1997; Öst & Breitholz, 2000.
11. For example, Bernstein, Borkovec, & Hazlett-Stevens, 2000; de L. Horne, Taylor, & Varigos, 1999; McCallie, Blum, & Hood, 2006; Means, Lichstein, Eppereson, & Johnson, 2000.
12. Wolpe & Lazarus, 1966, quotation from p. 81.
13. Lang, 1969.
14. For example, Krapfl, 1967; Richardson & Suinn, 1973.
15. For example, Goldfried & Davison, 1994; Walker, Hedberg, Clement, & Wright, 1981.
16. For example, Miller & Nawas, 1970; Nawas, Welsch, & Fishman, 1970.
17. Bandura, 1969; Lang, 1969.
18. Morrow, 1986.
19. Lazarus & Abramovitz, 1962.
20. Nevo & Shapira, 1988.
21. Cousins, 1979, 1989.
22. Seligson & Peterson, 1992.
23. Ventis, 1973.
24. For example, Rimm, DeGroot, Boord, Heiman, & Dillow, 1971.
25. Boelen, de Keijser, van den Hout, & van den Bout, 2007.
26. For example, Moore, 1965.
27. For example, Steinmark & Borkovec, 1974.
28. Saunders, 1976.
29. For example, Shorkey & Himle, 1974.
30. For example, Hedberg & Campbell, 1974.
31. For example, Meyer, 1975.
32. For example, Walton & Mather, 1963.
33. Fisher & Thompson, 1994.
34. Cotharin & Mikulas, 1975.
35. Smith, 1973; quotations from pp. 577–578.
36. For example, Anton, 1976; Lazarus, 1961; Paul & Shannon, 1966; Taylor, 1971.
37. For example, Spiegler, Cooley, Marshall, Prince, Puckett, & Skenazy, 1976.
38. Goldfried, 1971.
39. Tan, 2007.
40. Rentz, Powers, Smits, Cougle, & Telch, 2003.
41. Borkovec & Costello, 1993; Borkovec & Whisman, 1996.
42. For example, Borkovec & Costello, 1993; Borkovec & Whisman, 1996.
43. Spiegler, Cooley, Marshall, Prince, Puckett, & Skenazy, 1976.
44. Borkovec & Mathews, 1988.
45. Suinn & Richardson, 1971.
46. Suinn, 2001; Suinn & Deffenbacker, 2002.
47. Suinn, 2001; Thom, Sartory, & Johren, 2000.
48. Deffenbacker, Filetti, Lynch, & Dahlen, 2000; Deffenbacker, Huff, Lynch, Oetting, & Salvatore, 2000.
49. Barlow, 1988.
50. Antony, Ledley, Liss, & Swinson, 2006.
51. Galassi, Quercioli, Charismas, Niccolai, & Barciulli, 2007.
52. Barlow, Gorman, Shear, & Woods, 2000; Gould & Otto, 1995; Gould, Otto, & Pollack, 1995; Stuart, Treat, & Wade, 2000.
53. Otto, Pollack, Sachs, Reiter, Meltzer-Brody, & Rosenbaum, 1993; Pollack, Otto, Kaspi, Hammerness, & Rosenbaum, 1994.
54. Barlow, Gorman, Shear, & Woods, 2000; Otto & Gould, 1995; Otto, Gould, & Pollack, 1994.
55. Otto & Hinton, 2006; Wald & Taylor, 2005, 2007.
56. Tull, Schulzinger, Schmidt, Zvolensky, & Lejuez, 2007; Watt, Stewart, Birch, & Bernier, 2006; Zvolensky, Lejuez, Kahler, & Brown, 2003.
57. Otto & Hinton, 2006.
58. Guevremont & Spiegler, 1990; Spiegler & Guevremont, 2002.
59. For example, Silverman & Rabian, 1994.
60. For example, Herbert, Gaudiano, Rheingold, Myers, Dalrymple, & Nolan, 2005.
61. For example, Evans & Kellam, 1973; Lang, Melamed, & Hart, 1970.
62. For example, Rosen, Glasgow, & Barrera, 1976.
63. For example, Bornas, Fullana, Tortella-Feliu, Llabrés, & de la Banda, 2001; Chandler, Burck, & Sampson, 1986.
64. For example, Evans & Kellam, 1973; Rosen, Glasgow, & Barrera, 1976.
65. For example, Bernstein, Borkovec, & Hazlett-Stevens, 2000; Carlson & Bernstein, 1995.
66. For example, Goldfried & Davison, 1994; Walker, Hedberg, Clement, & Wright, 1981.
67. For example, Kazdin & Wilson, 1978; Masters, Burish, Hollon, & Rimm, 1987.
68. Paul, 1969, p. 159.
69. Leitenberg, 1976, p. 131.
70. Liddell, DiFazio, Blackwood, & Ackerman, 1994.
71. For example, McCarthy & Craig, 1995; McGlynn, Moore, Rose, & Lazarte, 1995.

72. Goldfried & Davison, 1994.
73. Weidner, 1970; quotation from p. 80.
74. Boutelle, 1998.
75. Neziroglu & Yaryura-Tobias, 1993.
76. Thompson, 1992.
77. For example, Barlow, O'Brien, & Last, 1984; Jannoun, Munby, Catalan, & Gelder, 1980.
78. Barlow, O'Brien, & Last, 1984; Munby & Johnston, 1980.
79. For example, Mathews, Gelder, & Johnston, 1981; Mathews, Teasdale, Munby, Johnston, & Shaw, 1977.
80. Lovell, Fullalove, Garvey, & Brooker, 2000; Swinson, Fergus, Cox, & Wickwire, 1995.
81. Goldfried & Davison, 1994.
82. Masters & Johnson, 1970.
83. For example, Kaplan, 1974, 1975; Masters & Johnson, 1970; Wolpe & Lazarus, 1966.
84. For example, Antony, McCabe, Leeuw, Sano, & Swinson, 2001; de Jong, Vorage, & van den Hout, 2000; Franklin, Abramowitz, Kozak, Levitt, & Foa, 2000; Öst, Thulin, & Ramnerö, 2004.
85. Clum, Clum, & Surls, 1993.
86. Donohue, Van Hasselt, & Hersen, 1994.
87. Townend, 2002.
88. Newman, Hofmann, Trabert, Roth, & Taylor, 1994.
89. Hill, 1989; Morris & Kratochwill, 1983; Ollendick & Cerny, 1981.
90. Chambless, 1985.
91. Silverman, Kurtines, Ginsburg, Weems, Lumpkin, & Carmichael, 1999; Silverman, Kurtines, Ginsburg, Weems, Rabian, & Serafini, 1999.
92. Glantz, Rizzo, & Graap, 2003; Wiederhold & Wiederhold, 2005.
93. Hodges et al., 1994.
94. Hodges et al., 1994; Kalawsky, 1993; Rothbaum, Hodges, Kooper, Opdyke, Williford, & North, 1995b.
95. Hodges et al., 1994.
96. Rothbaum, Anderson, Zimand, Hodges, Lang, & Wilson, 2006; Rothbaum, Hodges, Anderson, Price, & Smith, 2002.
97. Emmelkamp, Krijn, Hulsbosch, de Vries, Schuemie, & van der Mast, 2002; Rothbaum & Hodges, 1999; Rothbaum, Hodges, Kooper, Opdyke, Williford, & North, 1995a, 1995b.
98. Carlin, Hoffman, & Weghorst, 1997; Garcia-Palacios, Hoffman, Carlin, Furness, & Botella, 2002.
99. Botella, Baños, Perpiña, Villa, Alcañiz, & Rey, 1998.
100. Anderson, Rothbaum, & Hodges, 2003.
101. Difede et al., 2007; Difede, Cukor, Patt, Goisan, & Hoffman, 2006; Difede & Hoffman, 2002.
102. Josman, Somer, Reisberg, Weiss, Garcia-Palacios, & Hoffman, 2006.
103. Gamito et al., 2007; Rothbaum, Hodges, Ready, Graap, & Alarcon, 2001; Wood et al., 2007.
104. Rizzo, Reger, Gahm, Difede, & Rothbaum, 2008.
105. Gerardi, Rothbaum, & Ressler, 2008; Gerardi, Rothbaum, Ressler, Heekin, & Rizzo, 2008; Rizzo et al., 2008.
106. Rizzo, Reger, Gahm, Difede, & Rothbaum, 2008.
107. Rizzo, Reger, Gahm, Difede, & Rothbaum, 2008.
108. Parsons & Rizzo, 2008; Powers & Emmelkamp, 2008.
109. Powers & Emmelkamp, 2008.
110. Wolpe, 1958.
111. Kazdin & Wilcoxon, 1976.
112. Davis, 2006; Davis, Myers, Chhatwal, & Ressler, 2006; Myers & Davis, 2007.
113. For example, Borkovec & Whisman, 1996.
114. Beck, 1976.
115. Lick, 1975; Valins & Ray, 1967.
116. Foa, Huppert, & Cahill, 2006.
117. For example, Hofmann, 2004; McManus, Clark, & Hackmann, 2000.
118. Bandura, 1977a, 1978, 1984.
119. Compare with Strupp, 1995.
120. Kazdin & Wilcoxon, 1976.
121. Kazdin & Wilcoxon, 1976.
122. de Jong, Vorage, & van den Hout, 2000.
123. For example, Abramowitz, 2001; Tolin & Foa, 1999.
124. For example, Tolchard, Thomas, & Battersby, 2006.
125. For example, Fecteau & Nicki, 1999; Tolin & Foa, 1999.
126. For example, McGlynn, Smitherman, & Gothard, 2004.
127. Spiegler & Guevremont, 2002.
128. For example, Tolin & Foa, 1999.

10

Exposure Therapy
Prolonged/Intense

We introduced exposure therapy in the previous chapter by likening it to getting back on the horse that has thrown you. In fact, brief/graduated exposure is more like getting back on an old mare, whereas prolonged/intense exposure is more like mounting a wild stallion. Brief/graduated exposure minimizes anxiety during treatment by presenting clients with small doses of anxiety-evoking stimuli that gradually become more intense. In contrast, prolonged/intense exposure *maximizes* clients' anxiety with large doses of anxiety-evoking stimuli that are intense from the outset. The exposure can occur in vivo or imaginally.

Because prolonged/intense exposure therapies reduce anxiety by initially increasing it, they are sometimes called **anxiety-induction therapies**. In a sense, these therapies fight anxiety with anxiety. **Flooding** is the generic name for prolonged/intense exposure because the client is flooded with anxiety[1] for a prolonged period (sometimes for more than an hour).[2] Although the client experiences significant anxiety during exposure, the feared negative consequences do not actually occur—a characteristic of all exposure therapies.

Occasionally, people inadvertently find themselves in circumstances that are analogous to flooding and can use them to overcome a strong and even long-standing fear, as is illustrated in Case 10-1.

CASE **10-1**
Debugging a Cockroach Phobia: A Case of Informal Self-Managed Flooding[3]

Early in his first year of graduate school, V. W., a world-renowned entomologist (insect specialist), was given a lab assignment to draw blood from a cockroach. For someone who was about to embark on a career studying insects, this seemingly innocuous task created intense anxiety for V. W. Although he had been fascinated with insects from an early age, he detested cockroaches. His aversion to cockroaches began when he first encountered them in his home as a child. Although his repulsion to and avoidance of cockroaches had persisted into adulthood, it had not generalized to other insects.

To complete his lab assignment, V. W. had to go with other students in his class to an underground passageway and secure a blood sample from the thousands of cockroaches that could be found there. He went to the passageway feeling intensely anxious. As his classmates nonchalantly picked up cockroaches and returned to the lab, V. W. stood there frozen, not knowing what he would do. At that moment, he realized that if he could not complete this lab assignment, he would have to drop out of graduate school. Although he was terrified, he reached out and grabbed a cockroach. Almost immediately his anxiety began to diminish. By the time he reached the lab holding the cockroach, the anxiety was completely gone. More than 60 years later, V. W. has remained free of his former intense aversion to cockroaches.

IN VIVO FLOODING

In vivo flooding involves prolonged/intense exposure to *actual* anxiety-producing stimuli. It is used to treat an array of problems, including phobias,[4] obsessive-compulsive disorder,[5] posttraumatic stress disorder,[6] anorexia nervosa,[7] and body dysmorphic disorder.[8] Case 10-2 illustrates the basic procedures of in vivo flooding, including the essential component: *exposure to a highly anxiety-evoking situation long enough for the client's discomfort to peak and then start to decline.*[9] In the case description, you will see that before the therapy began, the therapist explained in vivo flooding to the client, including telling her that the treatment would cause some discomfort.

CASE **10-2**

Fear of Riding on Escalators Treated by In Vivo Flooding[10]

The patient was a 24-year-old female student with an intense fear . . . of escalators. She had developed this phobia about 7 years previously. She had ascended an escalator with some of her immediate family with relative ease, but had expressed fear of descending because of the apparent height. The relatives had jokingly forced her on to the escalator, and ever since she had experienced an aversion toward escalators, always taking the stairs or the elevator. . . . On one occasion she had unexpectedly come upon an escalator while shopping, and had become so overwhelmed with anxiety that it was only with great difficulty that she had prevented herself from vomiting. Whenever she was in the company of anyone who proposed riding an escalator to another floor, she would experience a quickening of the pulse and would bluntly refuse. Before [entering therapy] . . . , she had made some unsuccessful attempts to overcome the fear by attempting, in the company of friends, to get on to an escalator. On those occasions when she could bring herself to stand at the foot of the escalator, she would not step on [because she feared] . . . that by holding on to the hand rail she would be pulled downward and so miss her step.

At the single session during which the history of the disorder was obtained, the in vivo flooding procedure was explained to the patient. She was told that the technique had been successfully employed in the treatment of numerous phobias and was almost certain to work in her case. She was also informed that she would experience some emotional distress but was assured that [the therapist] would be with her throughout the experience to ensure no resulting adverse effects. [The therapist] then arranged to meet her at a large department store with four levels of escalators. Initially, the patient manifested an intense anxiety reaction when requested to approach the escalator, and it was only through much coaxing, reassurance, and physical [prompting] . . . that she finally stepped on to it. She then threatened to vomit and seemed at the verge of tears, all the time clinging tightly to [the therapist's] shirt. Getting on to the second flight of the escalator was much easier, but she still manifested the same signs of anxiety. After 27 minutes of riding up and down the escalator, she was approaching it with increasing readiness and reported a dramatic decrease in anxiety. She was then instructed to ride the escalator alone, and did so with relative ease. When she felt that there was no need for further treatment

(continued)

CASE **10-2** *(continued)*

the session was terminated, after 29 minutes. Six months later the patient reported that she still experienced no anxiety on escalators except on rare occasions when descending.

Nesbitt, E. B. (1973). An escalator phobia overcome in one session of flooding in vivo. *Journal of Behavior Therapy and Experimental Psychiatry, 4,* 405–406. Reprinted with permission.

The woman in Case 10-2 clearly was motivated to rid herself of her intense fear. Before seeking therapy, she had been unsuccessful in her attempts to overcome her fear on her own. In the single session, the woman experienced considerable initial anxiety during the flooding procedure, followed by a rapid decrease in anxiety. Although flooding occasionally can involve just a few sessions of intense exposure, as in Case 10-2, typically more sessions are required.

The description of the development and maintenance of the patient's fear of riding on escalators in Case 10-2 is worth noting. Her intense fear began with a single, traumatic experience. From that time on, she avoided going on escalators, which reduced her fear and reinforced her avoidance behaviors. This sequence of events is consistent with the two-factor learning theory described in In Theory 10-1.

IN THEORY **10-1**

The Two-Factor Theory of the Development and Maintenance of Fear

The two-factor learning theory of how debilitating fear develops and is maintained involves both classical and operant conditioning.[11] Fear initially develops through classical conditioning (see Figure 9-2, page 230). A neutral event (conditioned stimulus)—one that does not elicit fear—is associated with a threatening event (unconditioned stimulus), which elicits fear. Because of the association between the conditioned and unconditioned stimuli, the previously neutral event comes to evoke fear. For instance, a man who previously had no fear of being in an automobile may develop an

intense fear of driving in cars after being in an automobile accident. Being in an accident naturally results in fear. Through the association of being in a car and having an accident, just being in a car comes to elicit fear.

Once a person's fear has developed, it is maintained through operant conditioning. The person learns to engage in a fear-reducing response whenever he or she is faced with the fear-evoking event. Usually, this response involves avoiding or escaping from the fear-evoking event. The response continues and is strengthened because it is negatively

reinforced—that is, it terminates the unpleasant experience of fear. For example, when the man who is afraid of driving in cars refuses an offer of a ride, his fear declines because the threatening situation is avoided. On one hand, the avoidance behavior serves the function of keeping the man from feeling fearful. On the other hand, the behavior is maladaptive because the man never learns that driving in a car can be safe, which is important in our automobile-dependent world. Fortunately, exposure therapy can facilitate such learning.

In vivo flooding is a versatile therapy, which the following atypical case illustrates. Not only was the client an infant, but the flooding was carried out at home by the child's parents.

CASE **10-3**

Parental Treatment of Acute Traumatic Stress in an Infant through In Vivo Flooding[12]

Following a major surgical procedure (cranial remodeling), 5-month-old Michael began to exhibit a number of emotional and physical symptoms that were in all likelihood due to the physical and emotional traumas he had experienced as part of the surgery. He exhibited a change in sleep and feeding patterns, increased crying, night terrors, regression in motor skills, fear of strangers, and terror when lying on his back. The last symptom was made the target of in vivo flooding. Before surgery, Michael loved to lie on his back while his diaper or clothes were changed. After surgery, he screamed in terror, flailed his arms, and kicked his legs when he was placed on his back. Michael's parents were taught how to use in vivo flooding to reduce Michael's terror responses when he lay on his back.

One week after surgery, the parents began treatment. When Michael exhibited the terror responses after being put on his back, the parents left him on his back, but stayed close enough to him so that he could touch their faces. They touched him, talked lovingly to him, and occasionally held him and then laid him down again. This procedure did not diminish his terror responses. However, after an extended period, as long as an hour, Michael spontaneously ceased crying and became calm.

After eight flooding sessions during the first month after surgery, Michael no longer exhibited terror responses while in the supine position and showed the same delight of spending prolonged periods in that position that he had shown before surgery. At a 2-month follow-up, none of his emotional and physical symptoms remained, and he was symptom free at a 1-year follow-up.

Response Prevention

In vivo flooding often includes **response prevention**, which involves specifically preventing clients from engaging in their typical maladaptive anxiety-reducing responses. (Response prevention sometimes is used with in vivo desensitization.[13]) Safety-seeking behaviors, which response prevention eliminates during treatment, are ubiquitous to anxiety disorders. Avoiding an anxiety-evoking event is the most common safety-seeking behavior. It is crucial to prevent such behaviors because they interfere with exposure therapy.[14]

Response prevention is an essential component of in vivo flooding for *obsessive-compulsive disorder*, in which a person is preoccupied (obsessed) with particular anxiety-evoking events and alleviates the resulting anxiety by performing maladaptive ritualistic behaviors (compulsions).[15] *Ritual prevention*, as the technique is referred to in the treatment of obsessive-compulsive disorder, keeps the client from performing the ritualistic behaviors, as you will see in Case 10-4.

CASE **10-4**

Home Treatment of Obsessive-Compulsive Behaviors by In Vivo Flooding"[16]

A 45-year-old divorced woman suffered from an obsessive-compulsive disorder that consisted of washing and cleaning rituals whenever she came in contact with objects that she thought might be even remotely associated with death. For example, holding a newspaper article about someone who had been killed would make her intensely anxious. The disorder first occurred at the time of her mother's death, when the client was 15.

When the client entered treatment, she was to be remarried in 2 weeks. She was experiencing panic attacks and heart palpitations related to her fear of contamination almost daily. As time passed, the number of objects she considered potentially contaminated increased. Because her fiancé was a widower, he became a "carrier" of contamination by association with his dead wife. The client did not think she could deal with marriage in her present condition. In vivo flooding was indicated because the client wanted to alleviate her problem within 2 weeks and because her high motivation for treatment allowed her to undergo the discomfort of an anxiety-induction therapy.

The client chose to be treated in her home environment, but the in vivo flooding began in a hospital mortuary. There, the client and the therapist became "contaminated" by handling a corpse, which made the client intensely anxious. Later, the therapist and the client completely "contaminated" the client's apartment with objects associated with death (such as a newspaper photograph of a man shot to death in the street). The therapist instructed the client to refrain from engaging in her typical rituals of washing and cleaning, which would reduce her anxiety during flooding. That evening and the next morning, she successfully resisted engaging in her rituals. During daily hour-long therapy sessions, the therapist gave her various "contaminated" objects, encouraged her not to resort to her rituals, and praised her for complying. By the third day of flooding, she was not performing the rituals. However, when the client's fiancé brought some groceries from his house to her apartment, the client was unable to touch them, fearing that they were contaminated by association with his deceased wife. She called the therapist, and over the phone, the therapist guided her through a flooding session that consisted of "contaminating" her entire apartment by placing the groceries throughout the apartment.

After 12 days of therapy, the client reported that she had made considerable progress with her problem, and she was married the next day. She continued to have periodic episodes of tension over the next 8 months, but she no longer felt the urge to engage in her compulsive rituals.

Although the client engaged in many hours of flooding, the entire therapy was accomplished within 12 days. The therapist directed each of the in vivo flooding sessions, including one by telephone. The therapist's presence and guidance no doubt makes it easier for clients to undergo in vivo flooding. In contrast to self-managed in vivo desensitization (described in Chapter 9), in which the exposure is brief and gradual, self-managed in vivo flooding is especially difficult for clients. Nonetheless, it is occasionally successfully employed, such as in the treatment of social phobias where the therapist's presence in the client's actual social circumstances is impractical.[17]

Case 10-4 is an example of a relatively severe obsessive-compulsive disorder. The woman's anxiety was intense, as evidenced by her panic attacks. Moreover, her obsession was extensive because virtually any object she touched in the course of the day could potentially be associated with death. Given the level of her anxiety, it is not hard to understand how difficult the prolonged/intense exposure might have been for the woman. Like most clients who decide to undergo in vivo flooding, she was highly motivated to alleviate her problem behaviors.

Antidepressant medication such as Prozac is frequently prescribed for obsessive-compulsive disorder. However, in vivo flooding can be as effective as medication, and it has a lower relapse and dropout rate;[18] moreover, clients may view in vivo flooding as more effective than medication.[19]

In vivo flooding with response prevention also is used to treat body dysmorphic disorder. In one treatment study, clients went to public places where perceived bodily imperfections could potentially be easily observed by others.[20] The clients were asked to make eye contact with others, talk to strangers, and ask salespeople for assistance. From the outset of therapy, they were instructed to refrain from using any tactics that would minimize their perceived flaws, such as wearing special clothing or makeup. (Compare this prolonged/intense exposure and response prevention with the brief/graduated in vivo desensitization treatment of body dysmorphic disorder described in Chapter 9, page 225.) Additionally, half the clients in the study also received specific training in dealing with relapses, including information about the nature of relapse, self-managed exposure exercises, and a contingency contract specifying that they attend emergency sessions with the therapist to address relapse. All the clients in the study showed a significant reduction in body dysmorphic perceptions and in avoidance of situations that had previously triggered intense anxiety (such as being seen in public). However, those who participated in the relapse prevention component were better at managing minor relapses that occurred over time and had significantly lower self-reported depression and anxiety.

Cue Exposure

Cue exposure is a specialized form of exposure with response prevention used to treat substance-related disorders. The client is exposed to cues associated with addictive behaviors but is prevented from using the drug. For example, a client with a drinking problem might spend time in a bar. There, the client would experience the visual cues (such as seeing other people drinking), auditory cues (such as hearing people order drinks), and olfactory cues (such as smelling alcohol) associated with drinking. However, the client would refrain from drinking alcohol (see Photo 10-1). The cues can be presented in vivo (as in the previous example), by exposure to pictures and imagery, and through virtual reality.[21] Repeated exposure to the conditioned stimuli (cues) in the absence of the unconditioned stimuli (consuming the drug) eliminates reinforcement which results in extinction of cravings for the drug (see In Theory 10-1, page 240).

Cue exposure by itself can be effective in reducing clients' cravings for the addictive substance.[22] However, it is more effective when combined with coping strategies, such as differential relaxation, to deal with cravings.[23] In essence, clients learn to substitute coping strategies for their habitual addictive behaviors when they encounter the salient cues that previously have prompted the addictive behaviors. Cue exposure has been used to treat a number of different substance-related disorders, including those involving alcohol,[24] nicotine,[25] and opiates[26] (the last with mixed results[27]) as well as the addictive-like behaviors of bulimic binge eating and vomiting.[28]

© Michael D. Spiegler and David C. Guevremont

PHOTO 10-1

In cue exposure, a client is exposed to cues associated with an addictive behavior, but the client refrains from engaging in the addictive behavior. Here, the client (far right) interacts with others who are drinking in a bar, but he himself does not drink.

IMAGINAL FLOODING

Imaginal flooding follows the same basic principles and procedures used with in vivo flooding except that exposure occurs in the client's imagination. One advantage of imaginal exposure is that there are no restrictions on the nature of the anxiety-evoking situations that can be treated. This feature has proved useful in the application of imaginal flooding to help victims of traumatic experiences, such as natural disasters and physical assault. Such people may suffer from posttraumatic stress disorder, which is characterized by highly disturbing recurrent recollections of the event (such as nightmares and flashbacks), avoiding any stimuli associated with the event (for example, refusing to go to the neighborhood where one was assaulted), and a variety of emotional and cognitive symptoms, including anxiety, depression, and an inability to concentrate.

Exposure to the actual traumatic events generally is not possible (as with a tornado) or is inappropriate for ethical reasons (as with rape).[29] Imaginal flooding is well suited for recreating the circumstances of the trauma safely—that is, without the actual negative consequences occurring.[30] Imaginal flooding was first used to treat posttraumatic stress disorder in Vietnam War veterans,[31] and it is frequently used today to treat military casualties stemming from the recent wars in Iraq and Afghanistan.[32] It now is being applied to stress disorders stemming from rape,[33] nonsexual assault,[34] war-related traumas in civilians,[35] and natural disaster-related traumas.[36] Case 10-5 illustrates the procedures used in imaginal flooding.

CASE **10-5**

Treatment of an Adolescent's Posttraumatic Stress Disorder by Imaginal Flooding[37]

A 14-year-old Lebanese boy was referred for evaluation by his school principal because of academic and behavioral problems. Six months earlier, the client had been abducted in Beirut by the Lebanese militia for 2 days. At the time of the evaluation, the client was experiencing anxiety related to recollections of his traumatic experience. He also reported avoiding the area where he had been abducted, having difficulty concentrating and remembering information, and being depressed. The client had not experienced these problems before he was abducted.

The therapist described the pros and cons of imaginal flooding and systematic desensitization, and the client and his parents chose flooding. To assess the client's level of anxiety and functioning, before therapy began the client completed a number of direct self-report inventories (of general anxiety and depression) and cognitive measures (of memory and concentration). The client also was given a 12-step behavioral approach test that included leaving his home, walking to the area of his abduction, entering a store, making a purchase, and walking home by another route.

(continued)

CASE **10-5** (continued)

During the test, two assistants unobtrusively observed the client through a store window and by following the client at a distance. Finally, during flooding, the client reported his level of discomfort using a SUDs scale.

The client was asked to imagine four different scenes (described in Table 10-1) in detail, including what he saw, heard, thought, and felt (for example, the location of the abduction, the voices of the abductors, thoughts he had of being executed, and discomfort caused by the blindfold). Each of the six therapy sessions involved 60 minutes of flooding, which was preceded and followed by 10 minutes of relaxation exercises.

TABLE **10-1**
Scenes Used in Imaginal Flooding for a 14-year-old Boy with Posttraumatic Stress Disorder

Scene Number	Content
1	Approaching the area where the abduction occurred and being stopped, forced into a car at gunpoint, blindfolded, and driven away
2	Walking into a building while blindfolded, being questioned and accused, and listening to the militia argue over the merits of his execution
3	Being interrogated, responding, receiving repeated blows to the head and body, and experiencing intermittent periods of isolation
4	Learning that he was going to be released and not trusting the militia to keep its word

Source: Saigh, 1987, p. 148.

Scenes 1, 2, and 4 were each successfully treated in the course of a single therapy session, and scene 3 required three sessions. The client's anxiety and depression decreased, and his memory and concentration increased. This improvement was evident immediately after treatment and was maintained at a 4-month follow-up. Also, immediately after treatment and at the follow-up, the client completed all 12 steps of the behavioral approach test, compared with only 4 steps before therapy.

Because the area in Beirut where the client had been abducted remained a dangerous locale, he generally continued to avoid going there. However, after the termination of therapy, he did visit the area several times out of necessity. He reported that he experienced no abnormal anxiety on these occasions. Finally, the client expressed satisfaction with the flooding treatment, and he commented that the success of the therapy was adequate compensation for the discomfort he experienced during the flooding sessions.

Case 10-5 illustrates all the basic elements of imaginal flooding. Clear and detailed visualization of scenes is critical, so the client was asked to use multiple senses. Exposure to these cues was both prolonged (60 minutes) and intense (highly anxiety-inducing).

Another means of enhancing the vividness of traumatic scenes in imaginal flooding is to have clients verbally describe, in detail and in the present tense, the scenes they are imagining.[38] Consistent with flooding, this is done for prolonged periods, sometimes with the therapist's prompting the client about omitted details.

The versatility and efficiency of imaginal flooding was demonstrated in its use in treating victims of an earthquake in Turkey who suffered from posttraumatic stress disorder.[39] The initial therapy sessions were used to assess the particular problems each client was having (for example, fear of earthquakes, avoidance behaviors, re-experiencing the trauma), explain the treatment and its rationale (which focused on gaining a sense of control), develop target behaviors, and provide clients with self-exposure instructions. Clients carried out the self-exposure at home on their own. Subsequent sessions involved reviewing progress, troubleshooting, reinforcing progress, and giving new homework. The length of the treatment varied, depending on the number of sessions as needed to obtain clinically significant improvement, which occurred in 76% of cases after a single session and 88% after two sessions. Not only was the treatment highly effective, but given that a minimal amount of therapist time was required (the mean number of sessions was 4.3), it was also efficient and allowed a large number of earthquake victims to be treated.

Imaginal and in vivo flooding are often used in combination, as the following case illustrates.

CASE **10-6**

Religious-Related Obsessions and Compulsions Treated by In Vivo and Imaginal Flooding[40]

R. H., a 36-year-old Catholic man, had a 14-year history of religious-related obsessions and compulsions. He obsessed about being "damned to hell" because he had said or done things that he mistakenly believed were against Catholic doctrine (such as laughing at a tasteless joke). To alleviate his guilt about his assumed transgressions, R. H. compulsively sought reassurance that he had not sinned, such as by mentally reviewing the events or by talking to a priest. He spent more than 8 hours a day preoccupied with his obsessional doubts and seeking reassurance about his religious failings.

To expose R. H. to events that triggered anxiety, the therapist instructed R. H. to deliberately behave in ways that he considered sinful (for example, telling a tasteless joke). Response prevention entailed refraining from engaging in any behaviors he had previously used to reduce his

(continued)

CASE **10-6** (*continued*)

uncertainty about the sinfulness of his behaviors. Imaginal flooding also was used to expose R. H. to the consequences he feared would occur for his "sinful" acts. Figure 10-1 shows the expected peaking and subsequent decline of anxiety during R. H.'s imaginal flooding.

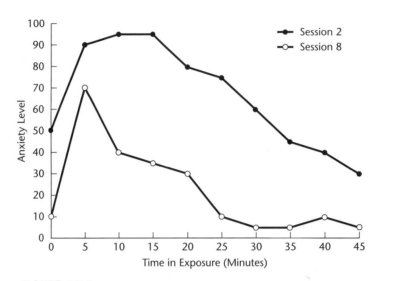

FIGURE **10-1**

Client's levels of anxiety during imaginal flooding for religious obsessions and compulsions, showing the expected peaking and declining of anxiety in an early session (2) and a session (8) at the end of therapy

Source: Adapted from Abramowitz, 2001

At home, R. H. engaged in daily in vivo and imaginal flooding (using audiotapes of in-session imaginal exposure). At the end of 8 weeks of treatment, R. H.'s obsessions and compulsions had decreased significantly and remained at that level through a 6-month follow-up. Additionally, R. H. reported being more hopeful about his life and more interested in engaging in social and recreational activities that had not been part of his life prior to treatment.

In the report of R. H.'s case, the therapist commented on the unique challenges of treating religious obsessions and compulsions, which generally requires consultation with clergy.

Differences between normal and pathological religious practices must be clarified and . . . [clients] should understand that the purpose of treatment is to restore normal religiosity. Moreover, a clear explanation of how exposure is consistent with this goal seems crucial for fostering a successful therapeutic relationship and maintaining high motivation.[41]

Thomas Stampfl

Donald Levis

Implosive Therapy

Implosive therapy is an imaginal prolonged/intense exposure therapy developed by Thomas Stampfl and Donald Levis.[42] Three procedures during scene presentation distinguish implosive therapy from other imaginal flooding treatments: (1) the use of hypothesized anxiety-producing cues, (2) the exaggeration of scenes to heighten anxiety, and (3) the elaboration of scenes as they are presented. These differences are highlighted in Table 10-2.

The therapist adds hypothesized cues to the client's description of the threatening situation based on the client's problem and personal characteristics.[43] With bulimia, for example, the therapist might incorporate cues of striving for perfection and fear of abandonment, which are often associated with the disorder.[44] Other hypothesized cues are based on psychoanalytic interpretations. For instance, the therapist might speculate that a man with a dental phobia also would fear castration (according to psychoanalytic theory, tooth extraction symbolizes castration). The hypothesized cues are assumed to be relevant if the client shows strong emotional responses when the therapist introduces them.[45]

The scenes are exaggerated, sometimes with fantasy-like details, to heighten the client's anxiety. The following is an example of an exaggerated scene used with a client who was afraid of flying insects:

Insects are flying around your head. First there is one, then a few, then dozens. They just keep flying around you, more and more of them, until you are surrounded by hundreds of flying insects. They are getting bigger and bigger by the moment. Huge bugs, the size of birds, are flying so close to you that you can feel the vibrations of their wings against your skin. And now they begin to touch your skin, to bite you while moving up from your ankles and legs to your groin. Now they are boring into you and flying into your mouth and down your esophagus. You can feel them tearing up your insides.

For each scene, the therapist begins by describing what appear to be the salient cues (actual and hypothesized) that make the client anxious. Then, the therapist questions the client about his or her reactions ("How does that

TABLE **10-2**

Differences Between the Nature of the Scenes Presented in Implosive Therapy and in Imaginal Flooding

	Implosive Therapy	Imaginal Flooding
CUES INCORPORATED IN SCENE	Client-reported cues and therapist-hypothesized cues	Client-reported cues only
DESCRIPTION OF SCENE	Exaggeration of reported scenes	Actual reported scenes (unexaggerated)
CONSTRUCTION OF SCENE	Scenes evolve as they are presented	Scenes constructed before they are presented

make you feel?" "What are you thinking?"). Based on the client's feedback, the therapist can further refine and embellish the scene. Case 10-7 shows how hypothesized cues are presented and their relevance is tested as well as how role-playing is used during scene presentation.

CASE **10-7**

Excerpts from an Implosive Therapy Session[46]

A young college professor reported first experiencing intense anxiety attacks shortly after she and her husband moved to another city. The move furthered her husband's career, but it interfered with the client's professional development. The client's anxiety appeared to be elicited by the situational cues of being in the presence of other people and her imagining being unable to speak, losing control, and fainting. In addition, the therapist hypothesized that the client was afraid of her own unexpressed anger toward her husband. To test this hypothesis, the therapist presented a relevant scene for the client to imagine and assessed her reaction to it.

Therapist: . . . See yourself getting up in the morning. Your husband has gone to work. Another day faces you sitting around the apartment doing nothing but wasting time. You really feel bored, unproductive. What is going through your mind?

Client: I need to find a job. I have to do something with my life.

Therapist: That's right. You don't want to waste your time. This morning you set out to find a job. You go down to the employment bureau. See yourself there. You're filling out forms. But no jobs are available for you. Next, you look through the want ad section of the newspaper, but nothing in your area is advertised. You already tried the colleges in the area but they are not hiring. How do you feel?

Client: Depressed.

Therapist: That's right. Feel the depression. You had a good teaching job. People liked you. You had friends. But you moved and your life has become worthless, empty, and unproductive. You now think about your husband. He likes his job. He is moving up the ladder of success. How do you feel?

Client: I feel angry.

Therapist: Try to feel the anger toward your husband.

Client: No, it is not his fault. We both agreed to the move.

Therapist: Whether it is his fault or not, try to imagine that all he is really concerned about is his work and his needs. Your needs and aspirations are not important. See him, get a clear image. Ask him to go back to his former job so you can return to your old job. Verbalize it.

Client: "Can we go back to [couple's former residence]?"

Therapist:	Put some feeling into the request.
Client:	"Can we?"
Therapist:	He looks at you in a cold, rejecting manner. "No. You agreed to come here. I am making more money. You will find something here. Stop feeling sorry for yourself." Feel that concern. Try and communicate to him so he will understand.
Client:	"Please. I can't stand it here."
Therapist:	"Stop acting like a baby. Grow up." How do you feel?
Client:	Mad.
Therapist:	Tell him off, express your anger. Tell him you hate him.
Client:	"I hate you."
Therapist:	Say it with feeling.
Client:	"I hate you. I hate you. I hate you."

After this scene, the client was asked to imagine being back in high school, a period when she had felt alone and rejected (note the psychoanalytic emphasis on the past). At that time, she had not felt any anger toward her peers who rejected her. A series of scenes involving rejection in high school were described to the client. The therapist augmented successive scenes with new material provided by the client. Eventually, the client was able to feel considerable anger and hostility toward the people who had rejected her. The therapist continued to present each scene, with embellishments, until the client experienced a high degree of upset (anxiety, anger, and depression) and the negative feelings began to diminish.

Levis, D. J. (1980). Implementing the technique of implosive therapy. In A. Goldstein & E. B. Foa (Eds.), *Handbook of behavioral interventions: A clinical guide* (pp. 92–151). New York: Wiley. Dialogue reprinted with permission.

Much of the evidence for the effectiveness of implosive therapy comes from case studies rather than controlled experiments.[47] Although there is research indicating that implosive therapy can reduce anxiety,[48] many of the studies contain methodological flaws.[49] Some studies indicate that implosive therapy is not more effective than control conditions.[50] Moreover, implosive therapy generally has not been shown to be superior to other therapies, such as systematic desensitization.[51] In sum, no definitive statements about the effectiveness of implosive therapy can be made.

As you have seen, implosive therapy incorporates psychoanalytic themes and explores past events, which is inconsistent with the theory and practice of behavior therapy and makes implosive therapy a highly controversial behavior therapy.[52] Implosive therapy was developed in the very early stages of behavior therapy. Psychoanalytic elements may have been deliberately included to make the therapy more acceptable at a time when psychoanalytic therapy predominated. As it turns out, implosive therapy with little or no psychoanalytic imagery can be successful.[53]

Eye Movement Desensitization and Reprocessing

Eye movement desensitization and reprocessing (EMDR) is a relatively new and somewhat controversial exposure-based treatment that Francine Shapiro developed to treat upsetting memories and thoughts about traumatic experiences.[54] EMDR is a hybrid imaginal exposure therapy in that it does not cleanly fit into either the prolonged/intense or the brief/graduated paradigm. Although clients visualize anxiety-evoking scenes for relatively brief periods, the scenes often engender intense anxiety. The treatment consists of three basic phases that involve assessment and preparation, imaginal flooding, and cognitive restructuring.

In the *assessment and preparation* phase, clients (1) identify a traumatic image (memory) that results in anxiety or distress, (2) identify the bodily sensations associated with the anxiety (such as tension in the chest), (3) assess the level of anxiety they are experiencing using a 0 to 10 SUDs scale, (4) identify a maladaptive belief that is strongly associated with the event (for example, in the case of a rape image, "I should have run away"), and (5) construct an adaptive belief that would alleviate the distress associated with the traumatic event (for instance, "I did the best I could") and rate how personally believable the adaptive belief is on scale of 1 to 7.

Next, in the *imaginal flooding* phase, the client visualizes the traumatic image while verbalizing the maladaptive belief and concentrating on his or her physical sensations associated with the trauma. During this process, the client is asked to visually track the therapist's index finger as it is moved rapidly and rhythmically back and forth across the client's line of vision (from left to right, twice per second, 12 to 24 times). (Shapiro theorizes that the eye movements produce a neurological effect—similar to what occurs during rapid eye movement sleep which is associated with intense dreaming—that facilitates the processing of emotionally charged, stress-related material.[55]) After the period of eye movements, the client is instructed to block out the experience momentarily, take a deep breath, and then report what he or she is imagining, thinking, and feeling and rate the experience using SUDs.

When the client's SUDs rating has been reduced to 0 or 1, the client is ready for the final phase of treatment that involves *cognitive restructuring* (described in detail in Chapter 12). The client again is asked to imagine the traumatic image (which now elicits little, if any, anxiety), but this time while thinking about the adaptive belief. The aim is to associate the traumatic image with the adaptive belief so that the image no longer results in emotional distress and maladaptive thinking. The believability of the adaptive belief and the client's anxiety level are reassessed at this time. If the client can generally accept the adaptive belief as believable and experiences little anxiety, therapy is terminated. If either criterion has not been met, then additional exposure with eye movements is required.

Following Shapiro's first published account of EMDR in 1989,[56] a slew of reports about the procedure were published in professional journals, and EMDR was touted in the popular media.[57] It was suggested that EMDR

Francine Shapiro

results in rapid and dramatic improvement in trauma-based anxiety problems (such as complete elimination of symptoms in a single session[58]).[59] However, these claims are misleading[60] because most of the early evidence for the effectiveness of EMDR came from studies with serious methodological flaws.[61]

More recently, the quality of the research has improved. There is now empirical evidence that demonstrates that EMDR can be an effective treatment for posttraumatic stress disorder. However, it is no more effective than other exposure therapies[62] and, in some cases, it is less effective.[63] In its favor, EMDR is a relatively efficient treatment for PTSD, often requiring fewer sessions and less homework than other exposure therapies.[64] Finally, the role of lateral eye movements has yet to be clearly demonstrated; the evidence so far indicates that the eye movement component is not essential.[65]

ALL THINGS CONSIDERED: PROLONGED/INTENSE EXPOSURE THERAPY

Prolonged/intense exposure therapy is most often used to treat anxiety-related disorders, including phobias,[66] obsessive-compulsive disorder,[67] posttraumatic stress disorder,[68] and agoraphobia.[69] Other problems treated include bulimia,[70] complaints of cardiac-like symptoms,[71] psychogenic urinary retention,[72] and agitated depression.[73]

Outcome studies indicate that flooding, in vivo and imaginal, is an effective treatment. Although some studies have found in vivo flooding to have more striking results,[74] no general statement can be made about the superiority of one mode over the other.[75] In specific cases, one mode of presentation may be superior (for example, imaginal flooding is necessary when the threatening event cannot actually be reproduced).[76] In vivo and imaginal flooding sometimes are combined, as for clients with intense social phobias[77] and with severe trauma-based anxiety.[78] The use of imaginal flooding prior to in vivo flooding may actually facilitate subsequent in vivo flooding for clients who initially are unable to tolerate exposure to the actual threatening events.[79] Studies comparing the efficacy of flooding with that of systematic desensitization also have not found either of these two exposure therapies to be clearly superior.[80] Besides being effective, flooding is an efficient means of reducing clients' anxiety, often in a relatively brief time (as in Case 10-4) and occasionally in a single session (as in Case 10-2).[81] Group treatment using imaginal flooding for anxiety disorders is an effective and efficient alternative to individual treatment.[82]

One of the consequences of the recent extended deployment of U.S. troops into battle conditions in Iraq and Afghanistan is an alarming number of soldiers who are developing debilitating posttraumatic stress disorder. The military's standard one-session debriefing (Critical Incident Stress Management) has been ineffective in preventing PTSD.[83] A promising, but as not yet properly tested, treatment involves repeated imaginal and in vivo flooding administered in four therapy sessions over a 5-week period.[84]

One major drawback of flooding is the discomfort it produces.[85] In one study, clients were treated for test anxiety with flooding, modeling, or systematic desensitization.[86] Nearly all the clients who received modeling and about half who had received systematic desensitization indicated satisfaction with their treatment. In contrast, clients who had undergone flooding said they would not recommend the treatment because of the discomfort they had experienced—even though the flooding had significantly reduced their anxiety! Moreover, clients may be more likely to refuse to enter therapy or drop out of therapy that involves flooding, compared with less upsetting exposure therapies.[87] These potential drawbacks may be specific to the problem being treated. In a comparison of 25 controlled studies of the treatment of posttraumatic stress disorder, no differences in dropout rates were found among exposure therapy (including EMDR), cognitive therapy (Chapter 12), and stress inoculation training (Chapter 13).[88]

In an effort to make flooding more palatable for clients, prolonged exposure that includes response prevention occasionally is presented *gradually*.[89] In other words, the client is exposed to increasingly more anxiety-evoking events, rather than the very highest anxiety-evoking events initially. However, the exposure is for a prolonged period and is terminated only when the client's anxiety begins to diminish.

Some therapists have considered the possibility that flooding might be made less aversive for clients if the exposure occurred with the presence and assistance of a family member.[90] Three studies have systematically examined this possibility, and only one demonstrated additional benefits of family-assisted exposure beyond those achieved with therapist-administered or self-managed exposure.[91] When the relationship between the client and the relative is marked by conflict or overdependence, the relative's presence actually may diminish the effectiveness of the therapy.[92] Despite procedures aimed at making prolonged/intense exposure more tolerable, the fact remains that clients often experience discomfort. As a consequence, clients may not elect such treatment, even though it may be the treatment of choice for their problem.

One concern with prolonged/intense exposure is that clients may become even more anxious or fearful than before therapy as a result of the treatment. This possibility exists because prolonged/intense exposure therapies induce anxiety in order to reduce it. Fortunately, serious negative side effects appear to be rare. In a survey of behavior therapists who had used prolonged/intense exposure therapies, serious negative side effects were reported in only 0.26% of the clients treated (9 out of 3493).[93] The major exception to this general finding is the use of prolonged/intense exposure therapy for posttraumatic stress disorder with clients who have a history of other serious psychiatric disorders.[94] In such cases, the chances of being retraumatized and experiencing increased anxiety and other adverse reactions to the treatment are substantially increased.[95]

The major ethical or humanitarian objection to prolonged/intense exposure therapy is that it increases clients' anxiety. The question is: Should already traumatized clients, such as victims of rape or incest, be subjected to therapy procedures that further disturb them?[96] Such treatment runs counter to the ethical principle "First, do no harm." However, the following two caveats should be kept in mind. First, clients have prior knowledge about the process of prolonged/intense exposure therapy, and they consent to undergo the *temporarily* stressful treatment. Second, discomfort often is a necessary part of psychotherapy; for example, many psychotherapies require clients to confront disturbing events in their lives.

Ultimately, the decision to use prolonged/intense exposure therapy should be based on a cost-benefit analysis of the discomfort associated with the treatment and its practical advantages. For example, sometimes prolonged/intense exposure can bring about a marked reduction in anxiety in a few sessions and occasionally in a single session, which is generally quicker than brief/graduated exposure therapies.[97] More rapid treatment has obvious practical, ethical, and humanitarian advantages for distressed clients. In some cases, only a limited time may be available for treatment (such as in Case 10-4, where the woman wanted relief from her obsessive-compulsive disorder before getting married in 2 weeks).[98]

Another factor that enters into the choice of therapy is that clients differ in their tolerance for discomfort.[99] Some clients find that getting the treatment over with quickly compensates for the distress they experience. For example, the teenage boy who was treated for recurring disturbing thoughts about his abduction in Case 10-5 reported that the success of his treatment was adequate compensation for the unpleasantness he experienced during the flooding sessions.

ALL THINGS CONSIDERED: EXPOSURE THERAPY

All exposure therapies share the common procedural element of *exposure to anxiety-evoking stimuli without actual negative consequences occurring*. Exposure therapies differ with respect to the basic paradigm into which they fit (brief/graduated or prolonged/intense), the mode of exposure (ranging from in vivo to imaginal), whether the exposure is therapist-administered or self-managed, and whether additional features are employed (such as a competing response, response prevention, and exaggerated scenes).

Systematic desensitization, the parent of exposure therapies, is a tried-and-true treatment that is broadly applicable. Because exposure is imaginal, the nature of the anxiety-evoking events is limited only by the client's imagination. Because the exposure is brief, graduated, and imaginal, systematic desensitization is the least distressing exposure therapy. It also has the practical advantage that it can be implemented in a therapist's office.

In vivo desensitization shares with systematic desensitization the advantages associated with brief/graduated exposure without the potential limitation of clients' inability to imagine scenes vividly. Exposure to the actual situations is likely to be more upsetting, but the treatment may be quicker and may transfer more readily to actual situations in the client's life. Therapist-administered in vivo exposure is always costly in terms of a therapist's time, but self-managed in vivo exposure, when viable, is highly cost-effective.[100] In vivo exposure now is recognized as one of the critical components in the treatment of *agoraphobia*. Agoraphobia involves intense fear and avoidance of public places or situations from which escape might be difficult or help might not be available should the individual experience incapacitating panic-like symptoms.

In vivo flooding can rapidly reduce fear, and it also is used to treat agoraphobia. It is the treatment of choice for obsessive-compulsive disorder,[101] and research has shown long-term maintenance for at least 5 years.[102] The studies that provide strong support for the effectiveness of in vivo flooding for obsessive-compulsive disorder predominantly have examined Caucasian clients. More recently, studies have included African-American clients and have obtained the same results.[103]

In vivo flooding is applicable to a wide range of clients, including elderly individuals.[104] With children (as young as 4 years old)[105] in vivo flooding is used more frequently than imaginal flooding. Two potential limitations of in vivo flooding are (1) that clients must be willing to subject themselves to the discomfort of prolonged/intense exposure to the actual situations that make them anxious; and (2) that therapist assistance generally is necessary, which is not always practical.

Imaginal flooding also can result in rapid reduction of fear and shares with systematic desensitization the advantages of imaginal exposure. Imaginal flooding does involve discomfort for the client, although usually to a lesser degree than in vivo flooding.

As these brief synopses of specific exposure therapies indicate, each is a viable treatment for some clients and some anxiety-related disorders. None, however, is useful in all cases. A similar conclusion can be drawn regarding mode of exposure (imaginal versus in vivo) and exposure paradigm (brief/graduated versus prolonged/intense).

Although some behavior therapists believe that exposure in vivo generally is superior to imaginal exposure,[106] there is reason to question this broad conclusion.[107] Studies involving clients with serious anxiety-related problems show that exposure in vivo has no clear-cut, general superiority to imaginal exposure. This is true when in vivo desensitization is compared with systematic desensitization[108] and when in vivo flooding is compared with imaginal flooding.[109]

When the actual feared events cannot be reproduced, imaginal exposure must be used. For some specific populations or disorders, either imaginal or in vivo exposure may be the superior treatment. For example, in vivo desensitization is generally more effective than systematic desensitization for treating childhood fears,[110] whereas imaginal flooding has been shown to be superior to in vivo flooding in preventing relapse for clients with obsessive-compulsive disorder who compulsively check (for example, whether they have locked their apartment door).[111] Nonetheless, the safest general conclusion that can be drawn about imaginal versus in vivo exposure is that both are useful and effective procedures.

The decision to employ brief/graduated or prolonged/intense exposure depends, in part, on the psychological disorder being treated, as there is no general superiority of either paradigm.[112] For instance, in vivo desensitization (brief/graduated) is particularly useful with agoraphobia, whereas imaginal flooding (prolonged/intense) is the treatment of choice for posttraumatic stress disorder.[113] In the case of obsessive-compulsive disorder, both types of exposure may be warranted because each affects different aspects of the disorder. Brief/graduated exposure reduces anxiety and avoidance behaviors, whereas prolonged/intense exposure reduces ritualistic acts.[114]

Other factors likely to influence the decision about the optimal paradigm of exposure include the severity of the complaint and the client's preference. The actual decision about which exposure therapy to employ is a joint one, drawing on the behavior therapist's knowledge and experience and the client's preference. In some cases, the therapist clearly can recommend one exposure therapy based on research findings regarding its relative effectiveness with the client's particular disorder. The therapist describes the procedures of each potentially beneficial therapy as well as its pros and cons. For example, both systematic desensitization and flooding may alleviate a client's fear of flying. Desensitization is likely to take longer and be less "painful," whereas the reverse is true for flooding. With exposure therapies, the issue of how much discomfort the client is willing to endure must be considered in addition to effectiveness and efficiency.

As a group, exposure therapies appear to be the single most potent behavior therapy for anxiety disorders[115] and can have long-lasting effects. This does not mean that exposure alone always is sufficient. Indeed, with severe and multifaceted disorders, the use of more than one type of therapy often is required. This is often the case with posttraumatic stress disorder. Besides the intense emotional distress and behavioral avoidance that is best treated by exposure therapy,[116] people suffering from posttraumatic stress disorder often have a variety of skills deficits and comorbid disorders, such as substance abuse, that need to be treated.[117]

Exposure Therapy for Culturally Diverse Clients

To date, the vast majority of research studies on exposure therapies have been conducted with clients from the majority White, European-American culture. Fortunately, evidence is accumulating for the applicability of exposure therapies to culturally diverse clients. For example, for the treatment of anxiety disorders, exposure therapies in both individual and group formats seem to be as effective with Latino-American youths as with European-American youths.[118] Flooding for obsessive-compulsive disorder has been demonstrated to be effective for African Americans and Caribbean Americans.[119]

Although minority clients may benefit from exposure therapies, the anxiety reduction they experience may not be as great as it is for European Americans.[120] One possible reason is that existing racial prejudice may interfere with the process, and hence with the outcome, of therapy. This can be seen in the following reconstructed dialogue between a European-American behavior therapist and her African-American client as they attempted in vivo flooding for anxiety about going to a shopping mall.[121]

Client:	I really don't want to do this today.
Therapist [thinking anticipatory anxiety was the issue]:	I know you are anxious about going there, but think of it as a chance to confront and overcome the fear.
Client:	No, you don't understand. I don't have any money with me. I can't buy anything.

Therapist: That's okay. You can window shop. A lot of people do that. For some people, it's a cheap way to have a good time.

Client: That's okay for you. White people can go into a store and just browse. But if a Black person does it, the store security people will watch her like a hawk. If I don't act like I'm really buying something, they'll think I'm stealing.

Clearly, behavior therapists must consider possible diversity factors—including racial, cultural, socioeconomic, gender, sexual orientation, and age factors—that may be relevant to the maintenance and treatment of problem behaviors. As another example, consider the case of a 39-year-old African-American physician suffering from a chronic and severe social phobia.[122] The client reported experiencing anxiety when she interacted with other medical professionals and in social situations, especially with strangers. Consequentially, she avoided such encounters whenever possible. Initially, imaginal and in vivo flooding resulted in a moderate reduction of her anxiety. However, the flooding achieved its greatest effectiveness only after her therapist discovered that interaction with European-American physicians was particularly troublesome for the client and introduced issues of race into the exposure situations.

IN THEORY **10-2**

Exposure Therapies or Therapy?

More than any other category of behavior therapy, exposure therapy mixes and matches approaches and procedures. In terms of treating individual clients, this practice clearly allows clients' treatment plans to be individualized to meet their specific problems and personal preferences. In research, the practice requires behavior therapists to specify the components that make up the exposure therapy being studied. Unfortunately, all too often this is not done. Behavior therapists have been notoriously inconsistent in their use of terms to describe exposure therapies, with the exception of systematic desensitization. In some cases the same term is used to designate more than one therapy, as you can see in Table 10-3. The inconsistency leads to confusion about the specific therapy procedures being employed. At the same time, it may reflect the current state

of affairs—namely, a genuine overlap among exposure therapy applications, which makes it difficult to categorize them.

To begin with, all of the exposure therapies share common theoretical explanations (see In Theory 9-1, page 230). Although the major exposure therapies differ in a variety of procedural aspects, in fact, they may share more similarities than differences. A simple example is that implosive therapy actually is a specialized form of imaginal flooding, which may account for the frequent use of the term *implosive (flooding) therapy* when referring to implosive therapy.[123] A more complex example of overlapping procedures is that whichever mode of exposure clients receive—in vivo or imaginal—they often indirectly receive the other mode. With in vivo flooding, clients have had experience with the exposure procedures

in previous sessions. Thus, it is likely that before an in vivo flooding session, clients think about (imagine) the exposure procedure, including the events to be presented; this process approximates imaginal flooding.[124] Likewise, imaginal flooding may involve in vivo flooding. Therapists may recommend that clients engage in self-managed in vivo flooding at home.[125] Even without this suggestion, clients may naturally undergo in vivo flooding when they encounter the threatening stimuli during the course of their daily activities.[126]

Another instance of procedural overlap is in the use of competing responses. It is standard practice to include a competing response in brief/graduated exposure therapies. Although a competing response is not standard practice in prolonged/intense exposure therapies, the presence and support of the

TABLE **10-3**
Terms Used to Designate Exposure Therapies

Most Common Term	Other Terms
Systematic desensitization	Desensitization
In vivo exposure	In vivo desensitization Graduated exposure Graded exposure Exposure
In vivo flooding	Flooding In vivo exposure Exposure Response prevention In vivo exposure with response prevention Rapid exposure
Imaginal flooding	Flooding In vitro flooding Fantasy flooding
Implosive therapy	Implosion Implosive (flooding) therapy Flooding

therapist may serve an equivalent function. It also is possible that clients spontaneously employ coping responses (such as reassuring themselves) that compete with the high levels of anxiety encountered in prolonged/intense exposure.

The similarities among exposure therapies raise the question of whether it would be more fruitful to classify such procedures as *exposure therapy with variations* than as different exposure therapies. Uncovering the similarities among exposure

therapies may increase our understanding of the fundamental nature of exposure as a treatment and help account for the effectiveness of seemingly different exposure procedures.

SUMMARY

1. Prolonged/intense exposure therapies, generally called flooding, expose clients for extended periods to anxiety-evoking stimuli that, from the outset, are intense. Exposure is continued until the client's anxiety peaks and then begins to decline.
2. In flooding, the exposure can be in vivo or imaginal. Flooding often includes response prevention, in which clients are kept from engaging in their typical anxiety-reducing but maladaptive behaviors. In vivo flooding is a treatment of choice for obsessive-compulsive disorder and involves

clients' engaging in anxiety-evoking behaviors without engaging in their typical compulsive rituals.

3. Cue exposure is a specialized form of response prevention used to treat substance-related disorders; clients are exposed to cues related to addictive behaviors, but they are not permitted to use the drug.

4. Imaginal flooding makes it possible to expose clients to any anxiety-evoking event. It can be used to treat posttraumatic stress disorder, for which it might be impractical and unethical to use in vivo flooding.

5. The development and maintenance of fear that often is treated by exposure therapies can be explained by a two-factor learning theory. Fear is initially learned by association of a neutral event with one that naturally elicits fear (classical conditioning). Then, the person's anxiety-reducing responses (avoidance) are maintained through negative reinforcement (operant conditioning).

6. Both in vivo and imaginal flooding are effective treatments. Because of the discomfort caused by prolonged/intense exposure therapies, clients may not choose these treatments, despite their effectiveness.

7. Implosive therapy involves imaginal prolonged/intense exposure in which the scenes are exaggerated and elaborated on with hypothesized cues (often psychoanalytically based) related to the client's fear.

8. Eye movement desensitization and reprocessing (EMDR) is a relatively new variant of exposure therapy that essentially involves imaginal flooding (including rapid, rhythmic eye movements) and cognitive restructuring.

9. Each of the major exposure therapies is a viable treatment for some clients and some anxiety disorders. Increasingly, evidence is accumulating for the applicability of exposure therapies to culturally diverse clients.

10. Although exposure therapies differ in a variety of procedural aspects, they overlap sufficiently to raise the question of whether they should be considered variations of a single therapy.

REFERENCE NOTES

1. For example, Agras, Kazdin, & Wilson, 1979; Chambless, Foa, Groves, & Goldstein, 1982.
2. Malleson, 1959.
3. From the author's (MDS) clinical files.
4. For example, de Jong, Vorage, & van den Hout, 2000; Kneebone & Al-Daftary, 2006.
5. For example, Roth & Fonagy, 1997; Tundo, Salvati, & Busto, 2007.
6. For example, Tolin & Foa, 1999.
7. Boutelle, 1998.
8. For example, McKay, 1999; McKay, Todaro, Neziroglu, Campisi, Moritz, & Yaryura-Tobias, 1997.
9. For example, Kozak, Foa, & Steketee, 1988.
10. Nesbitt, 1973, pp. 405–406.
11. Mowrer, 1960; Solomon, 1964.
12. Solter, 2007.
13. Franklin, Abramowitz, Kozak, Levitt, & Foa, 2000.
14. Powers, Smits, & Telch, 2004.
15. Franklin & Foa, 2008; Abramowitz, Foa, & Franklin, 2003.
16. Meyer, Robertson, & Tatlow, 1975.
17. Scholing & Emmelkamp, 1993a, 1993b.
18. Stanley & Turner, 1995.
19. For example, Van Balkom, Van Oppen, Vermeulen, Van Dyck, Nauta, & Vorst, 1994.
20. McKay, 1999.
21. For example, Lee et al., 2003; Lee, Kwon, Choi, & Yang, 2007.
22. For example, Lee & Oei, 1993; Monti, Abrams, Kadden, & Cooney, 1989.

23. For example, Monti et al., 1993.
24. For example, Lee, Kwon, Choi, & Yang, 2007; Loeber, Croissant, Heinz, Mann, & Flor, 2006.
25. For example, Lee et al., 2003.
26. For example, de Quirós Aragón, Labrador, & de Arce, 2005.
27. Marissen, Franken, Blanken, van den Brink, & Hendriks, 2005, 2007.
28. Martinez-Mallén et al., 2007; Toro et al., 2003.
29. Compare with Tolin & Foa, 1999.
30. For example, Frueh, 1995.
31. Foa & Rothbaum, 1989; Frueh, Turner, & Beidel, 1995.
32. Schnurr et al., 2007.
33. For example, Foa, Dancu, Hembree, Jaycox, Meadows, & Street, 1999; Foa, Rothbaum, Riggs, & Murdock, 1991.
34. For example, Foa, Dancu, Hembree, Jaycox, Meadows, & Street, 1999.
35. For example, Saigh, 1986, 1987.
36. For example, Başoğlu, Livanou, Şalcioğlu, & Kalender, 2003.
37. Saigh, 1987.
38. Rothbaum, Meadows, Resick, & Foy, 2000.
39. Başoğlu, Livanou, Şalcioğlu, & Kalender, 2003.
40. Abramowitz, 2001.
41. Abramowitz, 2001, pp. 83–84.
42. Levis, 1980; Stampfl, 1961; Stampfl & Levis, 1967, 1973.
43. Stampfl, 1970.
44. Johnson, Corrigan, & Mayo, 1987.
45. Levis, 1980; Levis & Malloy, 1982.
46. Levis, 1980; quoted therapeutic dialogue from pp. 125–126.
47. Saper, Blank, & Chapman, 1995.
48. Hogan & Kirchner, 1967; Levis & Carrera, 1967; Stampfl, 1966.
49. Morganstern, 1973.
50. For example, Hodgson & Rachman, 1970; Willis & Edwards, 1969.
51. For example, Borkovec, 1970, 1972; Mealiea & Nawas, 1971.
52. Levis, 1988.
53. Hogan, 1968, 1969.
54. Shapiro, 1989a, 1989b, 1995.
55. Shapiro, 1995; compare with Rosen, 1995.
56. Shapiro, 1989a, 1989b.
57. Bouhenie & Moore, 2000; Cowley, 1994; Oldenburg, 1994; Stone, 1994.
58. For example, Cocco & Sharpe, 1993.
59. For example, Forbes, Creamer, & Rycroft, 1994; Kleinknecht, 1993; Sanderson & Carpenter, 1992.
60. Bouhenie & Moore, 2000.
61. Spiegler & Geuvremont, 2003.
62. For example, Bradley, Greene, Russ, Dutra, & Weston, 2005; Davidson & Parker, 2001; Rothbaum, Astin, & Marsteller, 2005; Seidler & Wagner, 2006.
63. For example, Devilly & Spence, 1999; Taylor, Thordarson, Maxfield, Fedoroff, Lovell, & Orgodniczuk, 2003.
64. For example, Jaberghaderi, Greenwald, Rubin, Dolatabadim, & Zand, 2004; Lee, Gavriel, Drummond, Richards, & Greenwald, 2002; Rothbaum, Astin, & Marsteller, 2005.
65. Davidson & Parker, 2001; Resick, Monson, & Rizvi, 2008; compare with MacCulloch, 2006.
66. For example, Butler, 1985; Kneebone & Al-Daftary, 2006.
67. Abramowitz, 1996; Steketee, 1994; Van Balkom, Van Oppen, Vermeulen, Van Dyck, Nauta, & Vorst, 1994.
68. For example, Foa et al., 2005; Meichenbaum, 1994; Otto, Penava, Pollock, & Smoller, 1995.
69. Chambless, 1985; Swinson & Kuch, 1989; Trull, Nietzel, & Main, 1988.
70. For example, Leitenberg, Gross, Peterson, & Rosen, 1984; Schmidt, 1989.
71. For example, Stambaugh, 1977.
72. Glasgow, 1975; Lamontagne & Marks, 1973.
73. Hannie & Adams, 1974.
74. For example, Emmelkamp & Wessels, 1975; Watson, Mullet, & Pillay, 1973.
75. James, 1986.
76. For example, Saigh, 1986, 1987.
77. For example, Turner, Beidel, & Jacob, 1994.
78. Richards, Lovell, & Marks, 1994.
79. Steketee, 1994.
80. For example, Boulougouris, Marks, & Marset, 1971; Home & Matson, 1977; Suarez, McCutcheon, & Adams, 1976.
81. For example, Kneebone & Al-Daftary, 2006.
82. Fals-Stewart, Marks, & Schafer, 1993; Steketee, 1994.
83. Nathan, 2005.
84. Cigrang, Peterson, & Schobitz, 2005.
85. Cox, Fergus, & Swinson, 1994.
86. Home & Matson, 1977.
87. For example, Richard, 1995; Smith, Marcus, & Eldredge, 1994.
88. Hembree, Foa, Dorfan, Street, Kowalski, & Tu, 2003.
89. For example, Ollendick, Hagopian, & King, 1997; Tarrier et al., 1999; Tolin & Foa, 1999.

90. For example, Emmelkamp, De Haan, & Hoogduin, 1990; Mehta, 1990.

91. Steketee & Lam, 1993.

92. Emmelkamp, De Haan, & Hoogduin, 1990.

93. Shipley & Boudewyns, 1980.

94. Meichenbaum, 1994.

95. For example, Allen & Bloom, 1994; Pitman et al., 1991.

96. Kilpatrick & Best, 1984.

97. For example, Marshall, Gauthier, Christie, Currie, & Gordon, 1977; Rychtarik, Silverman, Landingham, & Prue, 1984.

98. For example, Rychtarik, Silverman, Landingham, & Prue, 1984.

99. For example, Rothbaum, Meadows, Resick, & Foy, 2000.

100. For example, Van Oppen, De Hann, Van Balkom, Spinhoven, Hoogduin, & Van Dyck, 1995.

101. Franklin & Foa, 2008; Rowa, Antony, & Swinson, 2000.

102. McKay, 1997; Rowa, Antony, & Swinson, 2000.

103. For example, Williams, Chambless, & Steketee, 1998.

104. Beck & Stanley, 1997; Calamari, Faber, Hitsman, & Poppe, 1994.

105. Ollendick, Hagopian, & King, 1997.

106. For example, Öst, 2001.

107. James, 1985, 1986.

108. James, 1985.

109. James, 1986.

110. King, Muris, & Ollendick, 2005.

111. Foa, Steketee, Turner, & Fischer, 1980.

112. For example, Öst, Brandenberg, & Alm, 1997.

113. For example, Glynn et al., 1999; Keane, Fairbank, Caddell, & Zimering, 1989; compare with Tolin & Foa, 1999.

114. Foa, Rothbaum, & Kozak, 1989.

115. For example, Berman, Weems, Silverman, & Kurtines, 2000; Foa, 2000.

116. Foa, 2000; Lombardo & Gray, 2005.

117. For example, Coffey, Schumacher, Brimo, & Brady, 2005; Turner, Beidel, & Frueh, 2005.

118. Pina, Silverman, Fuentes, Kurtines, & Weems, 2003.

119. Friedman et al., 2003.

120. Chambless & Williams, 1995; Williams & Chambless, 1994.

121. Williams & Chambless, 1994, p. 159.

122. Fink, Turner, & Beidel, 1996.

123. For example, Keane, Fairbank, Caddell, & Zimering, 1989; Levis, 1993.

124. Marshall, Gauthier, & Gordon, 1979.

125. Barlow, O'Brien, & Last, 1984; Mathews, Teasdale, Munby, Johnston, & Shaw, 1977.

126. For example, Mathews, Johnston, Lancashire, Munby, Shaw, & Gelder, 1976.

11

Modeling Therapy
Vicarious Extinction and Skills Training

Just shy of 4 months after two hijacked airliners were deliberately flown into the World Trade Center in New York City on September 11, 2001, 15-year-old Charles Bishop intentionally flew a stolen small private plane into a bank building in Tampa, Florida. He carried a note in which he expressed sympathy for Osama bin Laden, the alleged mastermind of the terrorist attacks on the World Trade Center. Although the reasons for Bishop's suicidal act are unknown, there is no doubt where he got the idea for ending his life as he did. In the same vein, ever since two students at Columbine High School in Littelton, Colorado went on a shooting rampage on April 20, 1999, there have been other shootings as well as numerous plots by teenagers to murder students and teachers in their own schools.

Learning by observing and then imitating other people's behaviors is a pervasive part of our lives. Fortunately, most of the time such learning and imitation is prosocial. We learn language, attitudes and values, preferences, standards for how to act, mannerisms, emotional responses, and countless skills by observing the behaviors of others. We borrow many of our habits, such as verbal expressions and body language, from people we know well, such as our parents or older siblings. Think about some of your own mannerisms, favorite expressions, and even your general ways of dealing with everyday situations. Do these behaviors remind you of anyone you know?

Modeling can play a role in the development and maintenance of psychological and physical disorders. For example, the aggression people have observed in their families of origin correlates with the amount and type of aggression in their own marriages.[1] How we experience pain seems to be influenced by how significant people in our lives have dealt with pain.[2] There even is evidence that observing mass media depictions of suicide, actual or fictional, may lead to imitation; suicide rates typically rise following such media presentations.[3] Fortunately, the same basic modeling processes can be used to allieviate problem behaviors, as you will see shortly.

DO WHAT I DO: BASICS OF MODELING

The basic ingredients for modeling are simple: a **model** who engages in a behavior and an **observer** who attends to the model. Observing a model provides two pieces of information: (1) what the model did and (2) what happened to the model as a result of the model's actions. The consequences of a model's behaviors—known as **vicarious consequences**—are important because they indicate the consequences observers are likely to receive for imitating the model. When the model's behavior is reinforced—**vicarious reinforcement**—the observer is more likely to imitate the model; when the model's behavior is punished—**vicarious punishment**—the observer is less likely to imitate the model. Consider whether you'd be more or less likely to speak up in class if your professor praised (vicarious reinforcement) or ridiculed (vicarious punishment) other students who spoke up in class.[4]

Up to this point in our discussion, we've not defined *imitation* because it is a common term. Formally, **imitation** occurs when someone observes a model and then behaves like the model. However, observing a model does not necessarily result in imitation, as In Theory 11-1 describes.

IN THEORY **11-1**

Three Stages of Observational Learning

Observational learning is the process by which people are influenced by observing others' behaviors. The process involves three sequential stages: exposure, acquisition, and acceptance (see Figure 11-1).[5] Assuring that each of these stages occurs is crucial for the success of modeling therapy.

The first stage is *exposure* to (observation of) the model's behaviors. The second stage is *acquisition* of (learning) the model's behaviors. Acquisition requires that the observer pay attention to and remember what the model does. Vicarious consequences are one of the factors that influence acquisition because the consequences a model receives enhance paying attention to the model. In effect, when there are consequences (either reinforcing or punishing) for the model's behavior, the observer is more likely to attend to what the model did than if there were no (or neutral) consequences.

The third and final stage of observational learning is the observer's *acceptance* of the model's behaviors as a guide for her or his own actions. Four types of acceptance are possible. Table 11-1 contains everyday examples of the possible outcomes in the acceptance stage. Acceptance can involve imitation or counterimitation, each of which can be either specific or general.

Imitation involves behaving *like* the model, and *counterimitation* involves behaving *differently than* the model. In *specific imitation*, the observer engages in the *same* behavior as the model; in other words, the observer copies the model. In *specific counterimitation*, the observer does *exactly the opposite* of what the model did. In *general imitation*, the observer

behaves *similarly* (but not in precisely the same way) to the model. In *general counterimitation*, the observer behaves *differently* (but not in the directly opposite manner) than the model. Finally, an observer may be exposed to a model and remember what the model did but may not be influenced by the model, which is called *nonacceptance*.

Exposure and acquisition are necessary but not sufficient conditions for modeling to influence an observer. The observer also must accept the model's behaviors as a guide for his or her own behaviors. The form of acceptance is largely determined by the vicarious consequences that occur. Vicarious reinforcement generally leads to imitation, whereas vicarious punishment generally results in counterimitation.

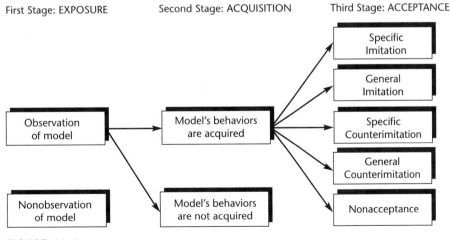

First Stage: EXPOSURE   Second Stage: ACQUISITION   Third Stage: ACCEPTANCE

FIGURE 11-1

Three stages of observational learning and the possible outcomes in each stage

(continued)

IN THEORY **11-1** *(continued)*

TABLE **11-1**

Examples of the Five Possible Outcomes in the Acceptance Stage of Observational Learning

Modeled Behavior: Miri observes her roommate's frequently making charitable donations	
Acceptance Outcome	**Example of Miri's Behaviors**
SPECIFIC IMITATION	Miri puts coins in a beggar's cup.
GENERAL IMITATION	Miri shares her belongings with her friends.
SPECIFIC COUNTERIMITATION	Miri walks past the beggar without putting coins in the cup.
GENERAL COUNTERIMITATION	Miri does not share her belongings with her friends.
NONACCEPTANCE	Miri is unaffected by observing her roommate's donating behaviors.

For modeling therapy to be effective, all three stages of observational learning must occur. Thus, the therapist must assure that the client observes the model (exposure). Then, the client must accurately remember and later recall what the model did (acquisition). The therapist may facilitate exposure and acquisition through verbal prompts (for example, "Watch the model carefully," or "Remember what the model did"). Finally, the client must use the model's behavior as a guide for her or his own behavior (acceptance). To enhance the chances of acceptance, reinforcers can be given for imitating or counterimitating the model.

There are two types of models. A model who is actually present ("in person") is known as a **live model**; a model who is observed indirectly is called a **symbolic model**. We often are exposed to symbolic models on television, in books and movies, and through oral descriptions (such as when we are told about what someone has done). Myths and fairy tales are time-honored sources of culturally shared symbolic models.[6] Hansel and Gretel are models of courage, and Beauty (in "Beauty and the Beast") is a model of compassion. **Covert modeling** is a familiar form of symbolic modeling in which people *imagine* how someone would perform a particular.[7] For instance, a child might imagine how a favorite cartoon character would handle a difficult or feared situation.[8]

Table 11-2 describes the five functions that modeling can serve for observers: teaching, prompting, motivating, reducing anxiety, and discouraging.[9] Modeling therapies often serve multiple functions. Social skills training, for example, involves teaching, prompting, and motivating clients to engage in socially adaptive behaviors. Although the discouraging function of modeling has potential for treating deceleration target behaviors in behavior therapy,[10] it is rarely used.[11]

TABLE **11-2**

Five Functions of Modeling

Function	Description	Example
TEACHING	Observer learns a new behavior by observing a model	Children's learning language by hearing adults speak
PROMPTING	Observer is cued (reminded) to perform a behavior after observing a model engage in the behavior	People's laughing when they hear other people laugh, as with laugh tracks on TV sitcoms
MOTIVATING	Observing a model's behavior and the favorable consequences it receives (vicarious reinforcement) serves as an incentive for an observer to engage in the same behavior	Students' volunteering to read aloud when they observe other students' reading aloud and the teacher's responding favorably
REDUCING ANXIETY	Observing a model safely engage in an anxiety-evoking behavior reduces an observer's anxiety	People's overcoming their anxiety about going swimming by watching other people who are enjoying swimming
DISCOURAGING	Observing a model's behavior and the unfavorable consequences it receives (vicarious punishment) decreases the likelihood that the observer will imitate the model's behavior	Children who see peers punished for hitting others are less likely to engage in the same or even a similar behavior

Self-Modeling

© Tony Foster

Peter Dowrick

Similarity between a model and the observer tends to enhance imitation.[12] With children, for example, peer models are usually more effective than adult models.[13] Similarity is maximized by **self-modeling**, in which clients serve as their own models of adaptive functioning.[14] *Covert self-modeling*, in which clients imagine themselves performing the target behavior, is the simplest application. *Video self-modeling therapy*, developed by Peter Dowrick,[15] has clients view videos that show their performing acceleration target behaviors. For example, self-modeling was used to teach a 9-year-old boy with Asperger's syndrome to recognize and understand emotions by watching himself express a variety of emotions.[16] Outside of therapy, video self–modeling has been applied to such diverse endeavors as sports instruction[17] and parenting education for first-time fathers.[18]

Making self-modeling videos requires clever editing techniques, including deleting errors and off-camera prompting. When the target behavior has multiple components, the client can be taped performing each one separately; when each component has been performed correctly, they can be combined so that the full behavior appears to have been performed fluidly. Another technique involves taping clients as they engage in the target behavior in a neutral (nonthreatening) situation and then superimposing the performance on scenes of the problematic situation. The standard procedures used in self-modeling therapy are illustrated in Case 11-1.

CASE **11-1**
Modifying Inappropriate Social Behaviors by Self-Modeling[19]

Ten-year-old Chuck, a resident of a treatment center for patients with bronchial asthma, spent most of his time alone. His peers rebuffed his attempts to interact with them by calling him "boob" and "baby." Chuck would respond by retreating to his room and having a temper tantrum. Chuck also displayed inappropriate behaviors with adults, such as giggling constantly, attempting to tickle them, and jumping onto their laps during interviews.

To deal with these problems, a self-modeling video was prepared. Chuck and two other boys enthusiastically agreed to make a "television film." In one self-modeling sequence, Chuck came into an adult's office and seated himself in a chair (rather than on the adult's lap).

After Chuck viewed the self-modeling tape daily for 4 weeks, the frequency of Chuck's socially appropriate behaviors in his daily interactions increased substantially. After treatment ended, Chuck maintained his appropriate social behaviors for the remaining 6 months that he was at the center. It is noteworthy that many of the reports of Chuck's improved behaviors came from staff members who were unaware that Chuck had received the self-modeling therapy.

Not only does self-modeling provide demonstrations of skills, but it also shows people succeeding. As one student pilot commented while watching a video of his landings, "I can see what I did right and what I did wrong, but mostly I can see that I *did* it."[20]

Self-modeling can also highlight the possibility of future success by depicting clients' acting adaptively in challenging situations that they will encounter.[21] This *video futures* technique was used with an Alaska Native man ("Albert") in his late 20s with intellectual disabilities; Albert had a history of pedophilic behaviors, and he was trained to engage in self-control behaviors that competed with his pedophilic behaviors.[22] The competing behaviors involved avoiding children when he encountered them in his daily activities. Albert watched the 2-minute self-modeling tape he had made once every other day for 10 days. He quickly began to perform the self-control behaviors and transferred them to other situations. These gains were maintained at a 9-month follow-up.

Self-modeling therapy has been applied to clients across the age spectrum[23] for such diverse problems as social, daily living, and academic skills deficits;[24] selective mutism;[25] stuttering;[26] tic disorders;[27] aggressive behaviors;[28] hyperactivity;[29] problematic classroom behavior;[30] public speaking anxiety disorders;[31] depression;[32] sexual unresponsiveness;[33] and inappropriate sexual behaviors.[34] Self-modeling can create rapid, clinically significant changes, sometimes requiring as little as 12 minutes of self-observation.[35] A recent meta-analysis of video self-modeling with children and adolescents with autism spectrum disorder revealed that the skills that they had learned transferred across people and settings and were maintained over time.[36]

The Nature of Modeling Therapy

Modeling procedures generally are combined with other behavior therapies, such as prompting, shaping, reinforcement, in vivo desensitization, and **behavior rehearsal**, in which clients practice performing acceleration target behaviors and coping skills. Although modeling often is part of a treatment package, it can be highly effective by itself, as you will see in Case 11-2.

CASE **11-2**

Accelerating a Prescribed Oral Hygiene Practice Through Modeling[37]

Julie was a 25-year-old married woman who recently had had oral surgery for serious, progressive gum disease. The dentist had instructed Julie to use a Waterpik, a device that squirts water to clean between the teeth. She had bought a Waterpik months before her surgery, but she had never used it. The dentist warned that if she did not use the Waterpik daily, her gum condition would regress.

Several months after Julie's surgery, her husband, Art, became concerned because Julie was not using the Waterpik, and he mentioned this to her. Julie said she would start using it. Another month passed, and the Waterpik remained unused. Art became increasingly concerned and began to remind Julie to use the Waterpik. Julie became annoyed at Art's nagging and told him to stop worrying about *her* teeth.

At this point Art called the dentist. The dentist suggested that Art use the Waterpik himself on a daily basis and record the times that his wife used it to see if his modeling made a difference. The results of Art's modeling were striking. As Figure 11-2 shows, Julie had not used the Waterpik once in the 30 weeks before Art's modeling. During the first week of modeling, Julie used the Waterpik 6 of 7 days; the next week she used it every day; after a drop to 5 times in the third week, she used the Waterpik every day for the next 3 weeks.

No modeling or recording took place during the next 2 weeks because Art was out of town on business. The day he returned from his trip, he called the dentist to report on the success of the dentist's advice. The dentist suggested that Art discontinue his modeling and just continue to record how often Julie used the Waterpik. During the next 5 weeks, Julie used the Waterpik an average of 5 times per week (see Figure 11-2). This was a vast improvement from her baseline rate, which was zero. Moreover, the outcome of the informal modeling therapy was clinically significant because 5 times a week was sufficient to keep her gums healthy.

(continued)

CASE **11-2** (*continued*)

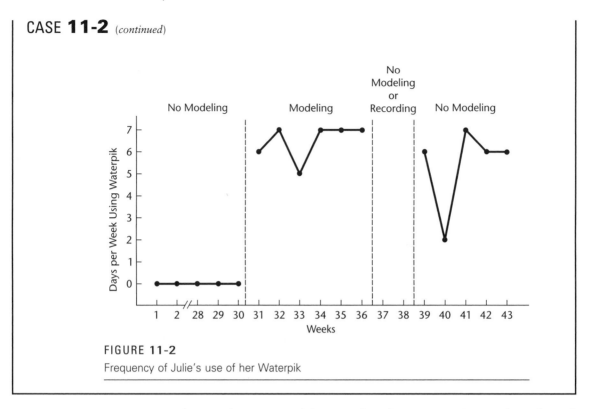

FIGURE **11-2**
Frequency of Julie's use of her Waterpik

In the preceding case, modeling was the sole treatment. Art merely performed the target behavior, which Julie could observe. No prompting to pay attention to the modeling or reinforcement for imitating was used, as often is done, which illustrates the potency of modeling itself.

Case 11-2 also illustrates the *subtleness* of modeling, which can be advantageous when clients resist direct instructions from others to change their behaviors. Julie did not use the Waterpik when Art reminded her; in fact, Art's prompts probably made Julie more resistant to using the Waterpik. Children often resist parents' telling them what to do ("Mom, I'd rather do it myself!") but will respond to more subtle prompts. For example, parents bring their own plates and silverware to the sink after a meal; this modeling may be more effective in getting their children to do so than reminding them each time. Similarly, modeling therapy is useful with clients from cultures in which subtlety and self-determination are valued (for example, Cambodian, Native American, and Slavic cultures).[38]

Modeling therapies have been used primarily to reduce fear/anxiety and alleviate skills deficits, and we will describe a variety of modeling therapy procedures used to deal with these problems.

VICARIOUS EXTINCTION: REDUCING FEAR BY MODELING

Fear or anxiety is maintained by the anticipation of negative consequences (such as expecting to be turned down when asking for a date) and by skills deficits (such as not knowing how to ask for a date). Modeling can treat both of these maintaining conditions simultaneously when a model demonstrates the anxiety-evoking behaviors without incurring negative consequences, a process known as **vicarious extinction**.

Vicarious extinction typically employs a **coping model**—a model who is initially fearful and incompetent and who gradually becomes more comfortable and skilled performing an anxiety-evoking behavior.[39] Coping models are appropriate because clients are initially fearful and incompetent, so the use of a coping model increases model–observer similarity. In contrast, a **mastery model** is an expert who shows no fear and is competent from the outset.[40] Mastery models are more suitable for precise skill development, such as learning to physically defend oneself from sexual assault.[41]

Live Modeling to Reduce Fear

Live models have been used to treat a variety of anxiety disorders, such as specific phobias (for example, fear of small animals),[42] test anxiety,[43] social phobia,[44] and obsessive-compulsive disorder.[45] Case 11-3 is an unusual application of parental modeling and in vivo desensitization to reduce a child's fear of dental treatment.

CASE **11-3**

Planned and Unplanned Treatment of Fear of Dental Procedures by Parental Modeling and In Vivo Desensitization[46]

Four-year-old S. Z. needed restorative dental work, but she was intensely afraid of the dentist. In the six attempted visits to the dentist, S. Z. would "scream, cry, [and] shake violently as [she] walked to the dentist, was short of breath and would adamantly refuse to cooperate." S. Z.'s mother reported that she too was terrified of dentists, and she believed that her daughter had learned to fear dentists from her.[47] Although S. Z.'s mother did not want to be treated for her own fear, she did agree to serve as a model for her daughter.

In the first five weekly visits to the dentist's office, S. Z. and her mother viewed a video depicting various dental procedures (modeling) and spent time in the office with no dental procedures being performed (in vivo desensitization). During the sixth visit, the therapist and the mother both modeled experiencing a 1-minute dental checkup. Playing the role of coping models, they exhibited initial hesitancy; then, they cooperated with the dental procedures and commented that it "wasn't that bad at all." The mother was able to do this despite her own fear. During the seventh session, S. Z. received dental treatment while her mother was present to provide reassurance.

The eighth and final session served as a posttherapy assessment. The dentist performed two procedures on S. Z. under local anesthesia. S. Z. sat by herself in the chair and showed no overt signs of fear. Before therapy and during the final session, S. Z.'s mother used a 100-point scale to rate her daughter's overt signs of disturbance regarding 10 dentistry-related

(continued)

CASE **11-3** (*continued*)

behaviors, which ranged from "telling S. Z. about a dental appointment" to "the dentist's using the drill." During the final session, the average rating was 6, compared with 78 before therapy. Over the next 6 months, S. Z. received considerable dental treatment. At a 6-month follow-up, S. Z.'s average rating of disturbance was 3. A 1-year telephone follow-up with both the mother and the dentist indicated that S. Z. continued to display little or no fear of dental procedures.

S. Z.'s mother was not specifically treated for her own dental fears. However, she had participated in S. Z.'s in vivo desensitization, and her modeling for S. Z. constituted self-modeling and behavior rehearsal for her. Apparently, this indirect therapy was sufficient to almost eliminate her own fear.[48] The mother's pretherapy, posttherapy, and 6-month follow-up average disturbance ratings were 54, 3, and 7, respectively. A year later, the mother and her dentist reported that she was experiencing very little fear about dental visits.

Participant Modeling

In **participant modeling**, the therapist models the fear-evoking behavior for the client and then verbally encourages and physically guides the client's practicing the behavior. Developed by Brunhilde Ritter,[49] participant modeling combines modeling, verbal and physical prompting, behavior rehearsal, and in vivo desensitization. Participant modeling also is known as *contact desensitization*[50] or *guided participation*,[51] for reasons that will become apparent shortly. The three basic steps in participant modeling are:

1. *Modeling*: The therapist first models the fear-evoking behavior for the client.
2. *Prompting, Behavior Rehearsal, Shaping*, and *In Vivo Desensitization*: The therapist verbally prompts the client to imitate the behavior she or he has just modeled. The therapist physically prompts the client to perform the behavior (such as by actually holding a client's hand while petting a dog) and reinforces the client as she or he successfully completes a task. Besides guiding the behavior, the physical contact between the therapist and client reassures and calms the client, which competes with fear.
3. *Fading Prompts*: The therapist gradually withdraws the verbal and physical prompts. The client begins to perform the behavior with the therapist present but without physical contact, and finally without the therapist present.

The behaviors that are modeled and practiced are arranged in a hierarchy, and treatment proceeds from the least to the most threatening behaviors. The rate of exposure is determined by the client's level of fear, as with in vivo desensitization. Case 11-4 illustrates the basic steps in participant modeling; Ritter was the therapist.

CASE **11-4**

Fear of Crossing Streets Treated by Participant Modeling[52]

Mrs. S. was a 49-year-old widow who had been intensely afraid of crossing streets for 10 years. Her fear had caused her to withdraw from social contacts almost completely, and her resulting despair had led her to attempt suicide. Participant modeling proceeded as follows:

A low-traffic location in which a narrow street intersected with a moderately wide street was chosen. The counselor walked across the narrow street for about one minute while Mrs. S. watched. Then the counselor firmly placed her arm around Mrs. S.'s waist and walked across with her. This was repeated . . . until Mrs. S. reported she was fairly comfortable at performing the task . . . . Street crossing was then continued while physical contact between counselor and Mrs. S. was gradually reduced until the counselor only lightly touched the back of Mrs. S.'s arm . . . [and] walked slightly behind her. Contact was then eliminated completely, with the counselor first walking alongside Mrs. S. as the street was crossed and then slightly behind her. The counselor subsequently followed Mrs. S. approximately three-fourths of the way across the street and allowed her to go the remaining distance alone. Gradually the counselor reduced the distance she accompanied Mrs. S. until eventually Mrs. S. was able to cross the street entirely alone.

These procedures then were applied on increasingly wider and busier streets, and Mrs. S. was given more responsibility for her therapy, including planning and carrying out her own homework assignments. Mrs. S. had set four specific goals for therapy, including independently crossing the four streets of a busy intersection. She accomplished all four goals in less than 7 weeks.

Participant modeling has been used to treat a variety of anxiety disorders, including small animal phobias,[53] fear of dental treatment,[54] public speaking anxiety,[55] fear of water,[56] fear of heights,[57] and agoraphobia.[58] In some studies, participant modeling has been shown to be superior to live modeling,[59] film modeling,[60] and in vivo desensitization.[61] The potency of participant modeling may be due to its being a treatment package consisting of modeling, prompting, behavior rehearsal, and in vivo desensitization. Clients' fears are reduced both by what they "see" (observe) and by what they do.[62]

Film/Video Modeling to Reduce Fear

Fear of medical and dental procedures can have far-reaching consequences because it can keep people from seeking regular health checkups and obtaining necessary treatment. Film/video modeling has been highly successful in reducing such fear and avoidance behaviors. One survey indicated that 37% of all pediatric hospitals in the United States use film/video modeling to prepare children for hospitalization and surgery.[63] We will describe film/video modeling therapies for reducing fear of surgery and related medical procedures. Parallel modeling therapies have proven effective in reducing fear of dentistry in children and adults.[64]

Barbara Melamed

Barbara Melamed spearheaded the use of films to reduce children's anxiety about hospitalization and medical procedures with *Ethan Has an Operation*, a 16-minute modeling film depicting the experiences of a 7-year-old boy hospitalized for a hernia operation (see Photo 11-1).[65]

> This film . . . consists of 15 scenes showing various events that most children encounter when hospitalized for elective surgery from the time of admission to the time of discharge, including a child's orientation to the hospital ward and medical personnel such as the surgeon and anesthesiologist; having a blood test and exposure to standard hospital equipment; separation from the mother; and scenes in the operating and recovery rooms. In addition to explanations of the hospital procedures provided by the medical staff, various scenes are narrated by the child, who describes his feelings and concerns at each stage of the hospital experience. Both the child's behavior and verbal remarks exemplify the behavior of a coping model, so that while he exhibits some anxiety and apprehension, he is able to overcome his initial fears and complete each event in a successful and nonanxious manner.[66]

Compared with children who viewed a control film (depicting a boy on a nature trip), children who viewed *Ethan Has an Operation* had less postoperative anxiety and fewer conduct problems at home.[67]

An 18-minute film was developed to minimize children's fear of receiving injections.[68] At the moment the child in the film receives the injection, a close-up shot of the child's upper body and face shows the child's wincing, exclaiming, "Ouch," and frowning, which is a realistic reaction to the injection.

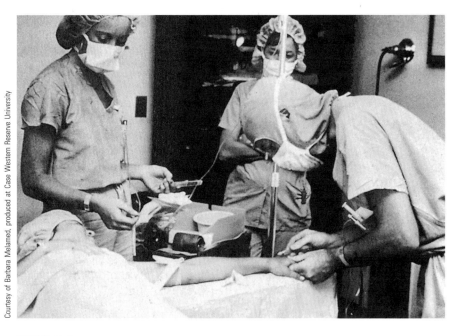

PHOTO 11-1

Scene from the film *Ethan Has an Operation*, showing Ethan in the operating room as the surgeon inserts an intravenous needle

Children (ages 4 to 9) viewed the film at home 36 hours before receiving their preoperative injections. These children, who had seen the realistic coping model, were compared with children who saw the same basic film, except that the patient-model did not show any signs of pain or discomfort. Such behavior is unrealistic because injections do hurt. Another group of children saw no movie at all. Children who had seen the realistic film indicated experiencing the least pain when they received their injections; those who had viewed the unrealistic film reported experiencing the most pain.[69]

Modeling films have been combined with other behavior therapies to reduce children's fear of medical procedures. For example, a 12-minute modeling film, *Joy Gets a Bone Marrow and Spinal Tap*, was part of a treatment package for reducing the distress of children with cancer (ages 3 to 7) undergoing two very painful treatments: bone marrow aspiration and spinal tap.[70] Joy, the model in the film, is a 6-year-old leukemia patient who comes to the clinic for treatment.

> She describes her thoughts and feelings . . . . As a coping model, Joy admits she is scared about the procedures, exhibits some signs of distress, but then copes effectively . . . . Joy explains *why* she has to have the procedures and she illustrates *what* happens at each point in the procedures.[71]

The treatment package successfully reduced the distress for each of the children in the study.

Modeling films to treat adults' fear and distress that they experience *during* medical procedures also are beneficial.[72] Sexual anxiety in women is yet another target behavior that has been treated with video modeling.[73]

IN THEORY 11-2

Self-Efficacy as a General Explanation of the Effects of Modeling and Other Behavior Therapies

Perceived self-efficacy refers to the belief people have that they can be successful at a task.[74] The self-efficacy is *perceived* because it totally depends on how the individual views his or her chances of success, independent of the external odds. A person can have high perceived self-efficacy for an impossible task, such as swimming across the Pacific Ocean, and low self-efficacy for a relatively easy task, such as swimming across a pool.

According to Bandura's theory of perceived self-efficacy, people's level of self-efficacy determines (1) whether they will attempt a task, (2) the effort they will expend to complete the task, and (3) the time

they will spend on the task.[75] The stronger one's perceived self-efficacy, the more vigorous and persistent one tends to be in the face of obstacles and setbacks.[76] Self-efficacy is situation specific—it varies with the particular task.[77] For example, people's self-efficacy expectations about their ability to stop smoking predict success in smoking cessation but not in remaining on a diet.[78]

Bandura has speculated that modeling and other behavior therapies (as well as other forms of psychotherapy) are effective because they create and strengthen a client's perceived self-efficacy.[79] Recall that one of the

cognitive theoretical explanations of exposure therapies is that they heighten clients' belief that they are capable of handling their anxiety (see In Theory 9-1, page 230).

Self-efficacy is strengthened by information provided by four sources:

1. *Performance accomplishments*: Direct experience in succeeding at a task may be the most powerful source of self-efficacy.
2. *Vicarious experience*: Observing models succeed at tasks helps clients believe

(continued)

IN THEORY **11-2** *(continued)*

that they themselves can succeed.

3. *Verbal persuasion*: Telling or logically proving to clients that they can succeed is the most common source of self-efficacy in verbal psychotherapies and also plays a role in behavior therapies, especially cognitive-behavioral therapies (as you will see in Chapters 12 and 13).

4. *Emotional arousal*: People's levels of emotional arousal influence their perceived self-efficacy. Generally, high arousal is associated with anxiety and doubt and hence low self-efficacy; low arousal tends to be associated with calm and confidence and hence high self-efficacy. Thus, therapies that lower clients' arousal levels (such as progressive relaxation) can enhance clients' perceived self-efficacy.

Table 11-3 presents examples of behavior therapies that provide clients with each of the four sources of self-efficacy.

TABLE **11-3**

Examples of Behavior Therapies That Provide Clients with Each of the Four Sources of Self-Efficacy (numbers in parentheses refer to chapters in which the therapies are discussed)

Self-Efficacy Source	Behavior Therapies
PERFORMANCE ACCOMPLISHMENTS	Reinforcement therapies (6) Token economy (8) In vivo desensitization (9) In vivo flooding (10) Behavior rehearsal (11) Participant modeling (11) Stress inoculation training (13) Problem-solving therapy (13) Acceptance and commitment therapy (14) Dialectical behavior therapy (14)
VICARIOUS EXPERIENCE	Vicaroius extinction (11)
VERBAL PERSUASION	Rational emotive behavior therapy (12) Cognitive therapy (12) Self-instructional training (13)
EMOTIONAL AROUSAL	Systematic desensitization (9) Imaginal flooding (10) Implosive therapy (10) Eye movement desensitization and reprocessing (10) Mindfulness-based cognitive therapy (14)

Note: The sources of self-efficacy categories are not mutually exclusive; for a given therapy, self-efficacy may come from more than one source

Storytelling to Reduce Fear and Other Negative Emotions

Storytelling is another form of symbolic modeling used to treat fear. For example, a story told through a puppet show depicting a teddy bear's going through a typical hospital visit has been shown to be as effective as films, including the benchmark *Ethan Has an Operation*.[80] Many commercially available books and pamphlets describing various diagnostic and treatment procedures, such as those found in physicians' offices, include modeling in that they describe the experiences of actual or hypothetical patients. For instance, one page in *My Tonsillectomy Coloring Book*[81] is a picture of a young boy on a gurney moving toward the open doors of the operating room where the surgeon is waving to him; the caption reads: "With Joe and the nurse, Tim drove to a room and met a doctor there/Who wore a mask upon his face and a funny cap to hide his hair." Another page shows Joe lying on the operating table with an anesthesia mask over his mouth and nose; the caption reads: "The doctor let him breathe through it and that was quite a treat./He felt just like an astronaut and drifted into sleep."

Uncle Lightfoot is an 85-page book designed to reduce children's fear of the dark.[82] Michael, a young boy who is afraid of the dark, visits his Uncle Lightfoot, who teaches him fun games to play in the dark, such as making shadow puppets on the wall. As a coping model, Michael learns to deal with progressively more threatening situations in the dark. The games have been adapted so that children can engage in behavior rehearsal with their parents after reading the book.

Covert modeling can be used to treat anxiety-related problems, such as social anxiety,[83] specific phobias,[84] anxiety anticipatory to surgery,[85] and obsessive-compulsive disorder.[86] Covert modeling implicitly is part of storytelling because the observer imagines the characters' actions.

Parents and teachers frequently use stories, rather than direct instructions, to influence children's behaviors and emotions. For example, stories and comic strips that model adaptive ways of dealing with potentially stressful events can be customized for a child, as by using the child's name. Such modeling stories have been used with children and adolescents suffering from autism spectrum disorder, Asperger's syndrome, and mild–moderate disabilities.[87] Modeling can be more effective than instructions because modeling provides *suggestions* rather than directives, which gives children a greater sense of independence. Consider the following example. A 7-year-old girl told her father that she was intimidated by a bully at school. Rather than directly suggest how she might handle the situation, the father wisely chose to give her vicarious advice by telling her a story about the way he handled a bully when he was a child.[88] In the same vein, to reduce children's fears in the wake of the 9/11 terrorist attacks, parents were advised to expose their children to stories depicting similar-age models coping with fear. For young children, *Sesame Street* produced a segment in which Elmo, the furry red monster, is a coping model who deals with his fear after a fire in his neighborhood.

SKILLS TRAINING

Skills deficits are often maintaining conditions of clients' problems. To perform a skill, a person must (1) know how to perform the skill, (2) be proficient at the skill, (3) know when it is appropriate to use the skill, and (4) be adequately motivated to perform the skill. Thus, a client's skill deficit maybe due to a deficiency in *knowledge, proficiency, discrimination,* and *motivation* (see Table 11-4). Clients may be deficent in one or more of these four components that are prerequisites for performing a skill.

TABLE **11-4**

Types of Skills Deficits

Type	Description	Example
KNOWLEDGE	Client does not know how to perform the skill	A college student who has never learned to use email
PROFICIENCY	Client is not competent at performing the skill because of inadequate practice	Psychiatric patient who has been hospitalized for many years is not used to managing money
DISCRIMINATION	Client does not know the conditions (time and place) in which it is appropriate to perform the skill	Student who initiates conversations with classmates while the professor is lecturing
MOTIVATION	Client does not have adequate incentives to perform the skill	Nursing home resident who has no desire or reason to engage in self-care skills

Skills training refers to treatment packages designed to overcome clients' skills deficits.[89] The training focuses on the specific deficient components (knowledge, proficiency, discrimination, or motivation) that are maintaining the client's problem. Modeling is a key component in skills training, which also may involve direct instruction, prompting, shaping, reinforcement, behavior rehearsal, role-playing, and corrective feedback.[90] Modeling is an essential component because direct instruction often is insufficient to communicate the subtleties of performing complex skills, and prompting and shaping alone may be insufficient.[91] The client may need to "see" the behavior performed.[92] The major components of skills training are illustrated in the following excerpt from a social skills training session with a high school student who was having difficulty asking girls on dates over the phone.

Therapist: Suppose you wanted to ask Cornelia to go to a party. What might you say?

Client: Well, I'm not exactly sure. I guess I'd just ask her if she wanted to go.

Therapist: Why don't you pretend that you are calling Cornelia and actually say what you might say on the phone to her?

Client: Okay, but don't expect much.

Therapist: Remember, we are only practicing. Just give it a try. *[prompting]*

Client: "Hello, Cornelia, this is Clint. How y'all doin'? Listen, if you've got nothing better to do, would you want to go to Grace's party with me?" *[role-playing]*

Therapist: That's a reasonable start. *[feedback, shaping]* Let's see if you can do even better. For one thing, you don't want to make it sound like going to the dance with you is a last resort. *[direct instruction]* Let me demonstrate one way you might continue the conversation after you've said hello. Listen, and see if you can hear a difference. *[prompting]* "Grace is having a party Saturday night, and I'd like to take you if you're not busy." *[modeling]*

Client: Yeah, I can hear the difference.

Therapist: Why don't you try to say something like that.

Client: "Grace told me about her party on Saturday, and I was wondering if you'd like to go with me." *[behavior rehearsal]*

Therapist: Very good. *[reinforcement]* That's much better. Just a straightforward statement of what you'd like. *[feedback]*

An early application of skills training targeted the enormous skills deficits that children with autistic disorder have.[93] Language skills are a prime example, and modeling is a critical component in teaching such children to speak. Most children learn to imitate in the course of normal development by being reinforced for emulating the behaviors of others, but children with autism usually do not. The ability to imitate is a social skill called **generalized imitation**,[94] and if it is not learned naturally, it can be specifically taught through shaping. This is done by initially reinforcing *any* behavior the child imitates, whether or not it is an adaptive behavior, so that the child begins to imitate. Once generalized imitation is established, modeling can be used to teach children with autistic disorder the host of adaptive behaviors they have never learned to perform (see Photo 11-2).

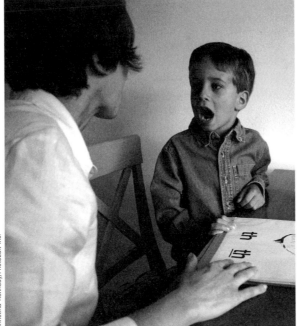

Christina Kennedy/PhotoEdit Inc.

PHOTO 11-2

Modeling is a key component in language training for children with autistic disorder. The therapist models the correct mouth and tongue positions and the sound for the child to imitate.

Other groups of clients who may suffer from major skills deficits and who have benefited from skills training include clients with mental retardation,[95] learning disabilities,[96] head injuries,[97] posttraumatic stress disorder,[98] and bipolar disorder.[99] Skills training has been employed to alleviate a wide array of specific skills deficits, including cognitive,[100] problem solving,[101] self-appraisal,[102] stress management,[103] academic,[104] consumer,[105] employment,[106] and child management.[107] Particularly innovative treatment packages have been developed to teach children skills for preventing abduction and sexual abuse.

Preventing Abduction and Sexual Abuse Through Skills Training

Child abduction is a serious problem in the United States and other countries. Only 10% to 17% of abductors use force to lure their victims.[108] Typically, the abductor attempts to develop a relationship with the child or to verbally entice the child, and children usually are unskilled at resisting abductors' inducements.[109]

Skills training interventions for teaching children to protect themselves from abduction was spearheaded by Cheryl Poche.[110] In one of her studies, three preschool children, who were at risk for being abducted, were taught abduction prevention skills.[111] Potential susceptibility was assessed by having an adult male role-play an abductor who approached the child and asked the child to leave the preschool with him. The "abductor" used three strategies commonly employed to lure children, which are described in Table 11-5.

The children were taught an appropriate response to each of the three common lures through modeling, behavior rehearsal, feedback, and social reinforcement. (A fully appropriate response was succinctly telling the "abductor" that he or she will not go with him [for example, saying, "No, I have to ask my teacher"] and running away within 3 seconds.) Before training, the appropriateness of the children's responses, based on a rating from 0 to 6,

TABLE **11-5**

Lures Used in Naturalistic Role-Played Assessment of Children's Ability to Avoid Abduction

Type of Lure	Definition	Role-Played Scenario
SIMPLE	Simple request to go with the "abductor"	"Abductor" approaches child, says "Hello" or "Hi, there," and engages in small talk (for example, saying "Nice day, isn't it?"). Then "abductor" says, "Would you like to go for a walk?"
AUTHORITY	Request with the implication that an authority figure (such as a parent or teacher) approves	After small talk, "abductor" says, "Would you like to go with me for a walk? Your teacher won't mind."
INCENTIVE	Request with the promise of an incentive	After small talk, "abductor" says, "I've got a nice surprise in my car. Would you like to see it?"

Source: Based on Poche, Brouwer, & Seraringen, 1981.

PHOTO 11-3

In child-abduction prevention training, children practice self-protection skills (such as yelling "No" and running away) in response to an adult who role-plays an abductor.

was near 0. After training, the appropriateness was near 6, and the responses transferred to a different setting in the community. A 12-week follow-up for the two children who remained at the preschool demonstrated that the treatment effects were maintained.

The same treatment components were incorporated in a 20-minute interactive video in which child models demonstrated two safety rules: (1) saying, "No, I have to go ask my teacher [or parent]," and then (2) quickly running to the teacher [or parent]. After each enticement scene, the narrator asked viewers if the child had done and said the right things.[112] After a pause, the narrator praised appropriate responses and corrected inappropriate ones by saying, "If you said ____, you're right, good listening! If you said ____, then I've fooled you. Watch again."[113] The video also provided an opportunity for behavior rehearsal of the skills that the children learned through the video. For children ages 5 to 7, the combination of viewing the video modeling and behavior rehearsal was more effective than just the modeling. This finding, and more recent research,[114] makes it clear that direct practice, particularly in a real-life setting, is important in teaching children to protect themselves from potential abductors.

In a skills training program developed by Sandy Wurtele, children as young as 4 learned to discriminate between situations in which it is appropriate and inappropriate for "bigger people" to touch children's "private parts," as well as what to say and do if an adult tried to abuse them.[115] The program effectively increased children's knowledge of sexual abuse and skills for protecting themselves from abuse without upsetting the children,[116] which is an important consideration given the frightening nature of sexual abuse.[117]

Similar skills training packages have been used to prevent sexual abuse among adult women with mental retardation.[118] Research evaluating these treatment packages demonstrated not only that the women learned protective skills but also that they were able to use them when they encountered inappropriate sexual advances.[119] The latter finding was ascertained by having adult male assistants, whom the clients did not know, make inappropriate sexual solicitations toward the women while other assistants unobtrusively observed the women's responses.

Social Skills Training

Social skills, the interpersonal competencies necessary to successfully interact with others, are essential for normal living. Their absence is correlated with a host of adjustment problems throughout the life span.[120] For example, in childhood and adolescence, social skills deficits are associated with social isolation, poor academic achievement, and delinquency;[121] in adulthood, social skills deficits are associated with depression, social anxiety, and schizophrenia.[122] Not surprisingly, many clients treated in psychotherapy have social skills deficits. Skills training has been extensively used to teach social skills to both children[123] and adults,[124] including specific social interaction skills related to social isolation,[125] anger control,[126] couple relationships,[127] and sexual behaviors.[128]

Social Skills Training with Children and Adolescents

Children who exhibit low levels of social interaction with peers are prime candidates for social skills training. Film modeling has proved effective with nursery school children.[129] One such modeling film, 23 minutes in length,

> portrayed a sequence of 11 scenes in which children interacted in a nursery school setting. In each of these episodes, a child is shown first observing the interaction of others and then joining in the social activities, with reinforcing consequences ensuing. The other children, for example, offer him play material, talk to him, smile, and generally respond in a positive manner to his advances into the activity. The scenes [are] graduated on a dimension of threat in terms of the vigor of the social activity and the size of the group. The initial scenes involve very calm activities such as sharing a book or toy while two children are seated at a table. In the terminal scenes, as many as six children are shown gleefully tossing play equipment around the room.[130]

Viewing such modeling films once or twice has been sufficient to increase children's social interactions to a normal level, and these gains have been maintained over time.[131] Film modeling is highly efficient, compared with other procedures such as shaping.[132] Live peer modeling also is effective in increasing children's social interactions.[133] In one case, two sixth-grade boys with poor social skills were taught to conduct social skills training with two kindergarten boys with low rates of peer interaction.[134] Not only did the kindergarten boys show an increase in positive social interactions with peers following the intervention, but so did their sixth-grade trainers. The latter finding illustrates the potential reciprocal effects of live modeling—by modeling a behavior, the model is engaging in behavior rehearsal (as with the mother who modeled comfort with dental procedures for her daughter in Case 11-3). To prevent children from developing their parents' fears, they may force themselves to engage in fear-evoking behaviors, such as skiing and speaking in public.

Poor social interaction skills are a serious handicap for adolescents, for whom socializing is so important. Case 11-5 illustrates the use of social skills training for this problem.

CASE **11-5**
Social Skills Training with a Young Adolescent[135]

Fourteen-year-old Sherman interacted with children who were 5 to 8 years younger. He had no friends his own age and had difficulty engaging in even simple conversations with peers.

Social skills training for Sherman was conducted twice weekly for 20 to 30 minutes. The training focused on (1) asking appropriate questions, (2) making positive or acknowledging comments, (3) maintaining appropriate eye contact, and (4) acting in a warm and friendly manner. For each skill, the therapist provided Sherman with a rationale for learning it and modeled each component of the skill. Then, Sherman rehearsed each of the skills with the therapist. After demonstrating proficiency in the skills with the therapist, Sherman practiced them with peers of both sexes for 10 minutes at a time. The therapist prompted Sherman to use the four conversational skills and gave him feedback. Sherman also practiced his new conversational skills at home and at school.

Whereas Sherman rarely had engaged in the four targeted social skills before therapy, after social skills training he showed significant increases in each. To assess the social validity of Sherman's behavior changes, 10 peers who attended a different school and did not know Sherman rated videos of Sherman's conversations before and after training. The peer ratings consistently indicated that Sherman's social skills had improved considerably. Ratings made by Sherman's parents and teachers after training also indicated significant improvements in Sherman's overall social adjustment, ability to make friends, ease of interacting with peers, and involvement in extracurricular activities. A telephone follow-up 16 months after treatment revealed that Sherman's improved social skills and peer relations had been maintained. Sherman had classmates to his home, he had begun to date, and he was trying out for a school athletic team.

Social skills training has been beneficial with children and adolescents who engage in aggressive and disruptive behaviors. Examples include adolescents' being treated for sexual offenses,[136] youths hospitalized for conduct disorder (habitual violation of others' rights),[137] juveniles who are incarcerated,[138] inner-city minority children,[139] and children with attention deficit hyperactivity disorder.[140]

Social skills training also has been successfully extended to children and adolescents with special needs. For example, children diagnosed with cancer who received social skills training reported receiving greater social support from classmates and teachers.[141] Likewise, adolescents with language and hearing disabilities benefited from social skills training and then were able to use self-control strategies (such as self-reinforcement) to maintain their use of the newly acquired skills.[142]

Social skills training is not just appropriate for children and adolescents. Elderly people have benefited from training in specific social skills,[143] such as conversational skills to decrease feelings of loneliness and the fundamentals of reinforcement and extinction to influence people in their lives.[144] Another population for which social skills training has been applied extensively is adults with schizophrenia.

Social Skills Training for Adults with Schizophrenia

Social withdrawal and social skills deficits are hallmarks of schizophrenia.[145] Even when disabling symptoms such as hallucinations and delusions are absent (usually as a result of medication), significant social impairment often continues to be problematic.[146] Moreover, the rate of relapse and rehospitalization is higher for clients who are socially isolated and who cannot function effectively within the community.[147] Using skills training in the treatment of schizophrenia was first introduced by Michael Spiegler in 1970 at the Community Training Center program you read about in Chapter 8.[148]

The goals of social skills training for clients with schizophrenia are (1) to increase social interactions, (2) to teach the specific social skills needed to function in the community (such as talking to neighbors), and (3) to reduce stress by teaching clients to cope with problematic social situations that arise in their daily lives.[149]

The specific skills taught depend on the severity of the client's social deficits. For clients with the most severe deficits, social communication skills might include basic nonverbal behaviors, such as appropriate eye contact, facial expressions, posture, and proximity to others. Clients who are able to perform basic skills are trained in holding a conversation, behaving assertively, interviewing for a job, asking for a date, and general social problem solving that can be applied to any interpersonal problem in daily living.[150]

Although social skills training has been effective in teaching social skills to clients with schizophrenia, and the clients often transfer the skills from therapy sessions to their hospital living setting, transfer outside the hospital is a major challenge.[151] Assigning and prompting homework carried out in clients' natural environments and reinforcing clients for engaging in social skills at home enhance transfer to different settings and to people other than the trainers.[152] Other ways to enhance transfer of training are covered in the next section.

Social skills training for people with schizophrenia reduces social anxiety and improves hospital discharge rates.[153] It moderately reduces relapse rates in comparison with other forms of psychological treatment (such as family education and family therapy), particularly within the first 3 to 6 months after treatment.[154] Teaching clients general problem-solving skills that can be applied to diverse social situations may enhance the durability of behavior changes following social skills training.[155]

Skills training relying heavily on modeling also has been used to teach clients with schizophrenia daily living skills, such as personal hygiene, self-care, self-administration of medication, personal recreation skills, food preparation, home maintenance, vocational skills, job finding, use of public transportation, management of personal finances, and assertive behaviors.[156]

Promoting Transfer of Social Skills Training

Transfer of social skills from the training environment to the client's natural environment is not an inevitable outcome of social skills training. Often clients will only use the social skills they have learned in the training setting and with their specific trainers.[157] This is especially true for clients with significant handicapping conditions,[158] as in the case of people with schizophrenia and attention deficit hyperactivity disorder.[159] Accordingly, active strategies to promote transfer may be necessary. They include:

- Providing a sufficient number and variety of examples during training[160]
- Using intermittent reinforcement during training, which simulates the natural environment where behaviors are not continually reinforced[161]
- Using the same physical and social stimuli that exist in the client's natural environment in the training setting[162]
- Providing prompts in the natural environment[163]
- Using natural reinforcers, such as praise[164]
- Providing opportunities to practice newly acquired skills[165]
- Teaching general, self-control skills (such as problem solving) that can be applied in novel social situations[166]

Assertion Training

Assertive behaviors are actions that secure and maintain what one is entitled to in an interpersonal situation without infringing on the rights of others, which includes expressing desires and feelings.[a] Deficits in assertive behaviors are extremely common[167] and, in some cases, can result in dire consequences, such as not being forthright about wanting to practice safer sex.[168] Assertive behaviors fall into five categories that are relatively distinct, as Table 11-6 describes.[169]

Assertive behaviors are, for the most part, situation specific, which has three important implications.[170] First, a person should not be characterized as assertive or unassertive. Rather, a person's *behavior* in a particular

---

[a]*Assertive behavior* has been variously and vaguely defined and even equated with socially adaptive behavior. Our definition is an attempt to combine widely accepted but restrictive definitions (for example, Alberti & Emmons, 2001; Lazarus, 1971; Wolpe, 1990).

TABLE **11-6**

Five Relatively Distinct Types of Assertive Behavior

Type of Assertive Behavior	Example
ASKING FOR WHAT YOU ARE ENTITLED TO	Correcting the mistake when you receive incorrect change
STANDING UP FOR YOUR RIGHTS	Objecting when a person steps ahead of you in line
REFUSING UNREASONABLE OR INAPPROPRIATE REQUESTS	Saying no when a friend asks to borrow money you can't spare
EXPRESSING OPINIONS AND FEELINGS (EVEN WHEN THEY ARE UNPOPULAR OR NEGATIVE)	Voicing your conservative views in a group of liberals
EXPRESSING DESIRES AND REQUESTS	Telling your sexual partner what you enjoy

situation or class of situations could be assertive or unassertive. And, it is true that some people typically act assertively or unassertively in many situations (but not likely all). Second, training in one type of assertive behavior may not generalize to other types.[171] For example, refusing unreasonable requests and expressing one's desires usually requires separate training. Third, assertive behaviors are not always appropriate or adaptive.[172] How appropriate or adaptive they are is determined by the consequences, for oneself and others, of being assertive in a particular situation.[173] For example, if a waiter overcharges you by a small amount, you can act assertively and bring it to the waiter's attention. If you are in a rush, however, you may decide to pay the higher amount, which would be an unassertive but adaptive response under the circumstances.

The appropriateness of acting assertively varies in different cultures.[174] Assertive behaviors generally are considered admirable and appropriate in Western cultures, in which individualism and independence are valued. In contrast, in cultures that value collectivism and interdependence (such as Japanese and Puerto Rican cultures), assertive behaviors are likely to be seen as socially inappropriate. In some cultures, appropriate assertive behavior involves subtle nuances that must be incorporated into assertion training (for example, the need to demonstrate respect for others in Latino cultures).[175]

Even in cultures that do consider asserting one's rights to be socially desirable (such as mainstream United States), fostering assertive behaviors should not be considered a goal for all people and in all situations. This caveat is consistent with the practice in behavior therapy of providing individualized treatment and for clients to set their own treatment goals. Thus, if a behavior therapist thinks that a client would benefit from behaving more assertively in certain situations but the client does not, assertion training would not be part of the client's treatment plan.

TABLE **11-7**

Comparison of Assertive, Aggressive, and Unassertive Responses to Common Situations

Situation	Assertive Response	Aggressive Response	Unassertive Response
You don't drink alcohol. At a party someone offers you a drink.	"No, thank you."	"No! I don't want any alcohol; just get it away from me."	"Oh . . . thanks but . . . I guess it won't hurt me."
You are rushing off to class and don't want to be late. A friend stops you and asks you to help move furniture in his room right then.	"Sorry, I'm on my way to class. If you still need help this evening, let me know."	"You must be kidding! I'm on my way to class. Find someone else."	"Well, I'm on my way to class, but I guess I could give you a hand for just a few minutes."

Assertive and aggressive behaviors are not the same. Although they may result in the same end—obtaining what one wants or is entitled to—they differ in the *means* by which they accomplish the goal.[176] Assertive behaviors achieve their goal without violating others' rights, whereas aggressive behaviors do so at someone else's expense. Table 11-7 compares examples of assertive, aggressive, and unassertive behaviors.

Assessing Assertive Behavior Deficits

Clients' deficits in assertive behaviors are assessed by a variety of methods, including interviews, direct self-report inventories, self-monitoring, systematic naturalistic observations, and simulated observations, including role-playing.[177] Assessment provides information about the specific details of the client's assertive skills deficits as well as the type(s) of skills deficits the client has (that is, in knowledge, proficiency, discrimination, or motivation), which is crucial for selecting the most appropriate treatment.

Two types of direct self-report inventories are used to assess deficits in assertive behavior. With one type, clients rate the degree to which they engage in various assertive behaviors (see Participation Exercise 11-1).[178] The second type has clients indicate how they would respond to a situation (described in writing) by choosing one of several responses provided. Figure 11-3 shows an item from the Conflict Resolution Inventory[179] that assesses one type of assertive behavior, refusing unreasonable requests.

Complete assessment of assertive behavior deficits usually requires behavioral observations. If feasible, systematic naturalistic observations are made of the client in the situations in which the client is having difficulty behaving assertively. However, simulated observations are more typical because they are easier to arrange. Generally, the simulated observations involve the client's role-playing responses to hypothetical situations that call for assertive behaviors.

Behavioral observations, either naturalistic or simulated, make it possible to assess the stylistic components of the client's attempts to act assertively, such as voice tone and body posture (see Table 11-8), which are critical components of effective assertive behaviors.[180]

A person *you do not know very well* is going home for the weekend. He or she has some books that are due at the library and asks if you would take them back so they won't be overdue. From where you live, it is a 25-minute walk to the library, the books are heavy, and you hadn't planned on going near the library that weekend.

_____ 1. I would *refuse* and would not feel uncomfortable about doing so.

_____ 2. I would *refuse* but would feel uncomfortable doing so.

_____ 3. I would *not refuse* even though I might prefer to, but would feel uncomfortable because I didn't.

_____ 4. I would *not refuse* even though I might prefer to, but would not feel particularly uncomfortable because I didn't.

_____ 5. I would *not refuse*, because it seems to be a reasonable request.

FIGURE 11-3

Item on the Conflict Resolution Inventory

Source: McFall, R. M., & Lillesand, D. B. (1971). Behavior rehearsal with modeling and coaching in assertion training. *Journal of Abnormal Psychology, 77,* 313–323. Reprinted with permission.

PARTICIPATION EXERCISE 11-1

Assessing Your Assertive Behaviors by a Direct Self-Report Inventory[b]

In this exercise, you will respond to a brief self-report inventory for assessing assertive behaviors.[181] List the numbers 1 to 13 on a sheet of paper. Read each item, and write the number from the following scale that best describes your typical behavior. There are no right or wrong answers.

> 0 = Never
> 1 = Rarely
> 2 = Sometimes
> 3 = Usually
> 4 = Always

1. When someone is unfair to me, I call it to the person's attention.
2. When I am not receiving service to which I am entitled, I ask for it.
3. I speak up when someone steps ahead of me in line.
4. When a salesperson tries to sell me something that I do not want, I tell the salesperson I am not interested.
5. I freely speak up when I am in a group.
6. If a person has borrowed something from me (such as money or a book) and is late in returning it, I say something to the person.
7. I express my positive feelings to others.
8. I express my negative feelings to others.

[b]You should complete this Participation Exercise before you continue reading.

9. If food I have ordered in a restaurant is served improperly, I ask to have it corrected.
10. I return merchandise that I find to be defective.
11. I refuse unreasonable requests made of me.
12. I compliment and praise others.
13. If someone is disturbing me, I say something to the person.

Your responses to this inventory may make you aware of how you deal with various situations that generally call for assertive behaviors (in Western cultures). The higher the score for an item, the more assertive you tend to be in the particular situation described. However, it is not appropriate to add the scores to obtain a total assertiveness score because the items are related to different situations and assertive behaviors are situation specific.

TABLE **11-8**

Physical and Vocal Stylistic Components of Assertive, Unassertive, and Aggressive Behaviors

Stylistic Component	Assertive Behavior	Unassertive Behavior	Aggressive Behavior
EYE CONTACT	Looking at the person while talking	Looking away from the person while talking	Intently staring at the person while talking
FACIAL EXPRESSION	Appropriate to message	Sheepish or expressionless	Hostile no matter what the message is
GESTURES	Moderate; appropriate to message	None or inappropriate to message	Excessive; overenthusiastic
BODY POSTURE	Erect; at an appropriate distance; leaning slightly toward the person	Slouched; a bit too far from the person; leaning away from the person	Erect; either too close or too far from person; exaggerated leaning in either direction
VOICE QUALITY	Firm (confident); appropriate volume; appropriate expression	Apologetic; whisper; monotone	Overzealous; shouting; "soapbox" speech

Assertion Training Procedures

Assertion training refers to the specific social skills training procedures used to teach clients how and when to behave assertively. Modeling is especially valuable in teaching assertive behaviors because stylistic components that are difficult to describe verbally can be modeled for the client (for example, appropriate body posture, volume, and verbal expression to show confidence).

Homework assignments are routinely part of assertion training and proceed in a stepwise progression, as in graduated exposure (see Table 11-9). Feedback on the client's performance both in the therapy sessions and on homework assignments is an important aspect of the training. The therapist

TABLE **11-9**

Hierarchy of Assertive Behaviors Practiced by a Client Having Difficulty with Refusing Unreasonable Requests (in descending order)

9. Refusing an unreasonable request from a close friend when the request is very important to the friend

8. Refusing an unreasonable request from a close friend when the request is moderately important to the friend

7. Refusing an unreasonable request from an acquaintance when the request is very important to the acquaintance

6. Refusing an unreasonable request from an acquaintance when the request is moderately important to the acquaintance

5. Refusing an unreasonable request from a close friend when the request is relatively unimportant to the friend

4. Refusing an unreasonable request from an acquaintance when the request is relatively unimportant to the acquaintance

3. Refusing an unreasonable request from a stranger when the request is very important to the stranger

2. Refusing an unreasonable request from a stranger when the request is moderately important to the stranger

1. Refusing an unreasonable request from a stranger when the request is relatively unimportant to the stranger

Note: The rank ordering is an individual matter and will vary from client to client.

reinforces the client for acting assertively but not for obtaining a favorable outcome. The reason is that the outcome of an assertive behavior rarely is totally in the client's control (for instance, securing a day off from work may depend on the availability of other workers). Accordingly, clients are taught, through modeling and behavior rehearsal, how to react and cope when their appropriate assertive responses fail to obtain the desired outcome.

Modeling assertive behavior can be covert,[182] as was the case with a 7-year-old girl who had been sexually abused and responded with emotional outbursts and sexually inappropriate behaviors whenever she felt taken advantage of.[183] The therapist asked the girl to visualize scenes in which a peer model similar to the girl constructively dealt with her negative feelings, such as by saying something to a teacher who treated her unfairly.

Table 11-10 has examples of typical scenes used in covert modeling of assertive behaviors. Covert modeling may be supplemented with **covert behavior rehearsal**, in which clients imagine themselves performing target behaviors. We often do this informally to rehearse how we are going to act. For example, right before going to see a professor about getting an extension on a paper, you might mentally rehearse making the request.

The following case illustrates the nature of assertion training.

TABLE **11-10**
Covert Modeling Scenes Used in Assertion Training

Situation	Modeled Assertive Behavior	Vicarious Reinforcement
A woman is eating in a restaurant with friends. She orders a salad and tells the waiter to put the dressing on the side. When the salad arrives, it has the dressing directly on it.	The woman immediately turns to the waiter and says, "I asked for my salad with the dressing on the side. Please bring me another salad without dressing and the dressing in a separate dish."	A few minutes later the waiter returns with the salad correctly prepared and says that he is very sorry for the error and hopes that the woman enjoys the salad.
A man who is trying to stop smoking is at a party where most people are smoking. The host offers him a cigarette.	The man says, "No, thanks. But I would like something to eat."	The host replies, "Sure thing. The food is in the dining room."

CASE **11-6**
Assertion Training for Refusing Inappropriate Requests[184]

Amira, a 33-year-old woman from Yemen, had immigrated to the United States 3 years ago. She worked as an insurance agent in an office where there were only three female agents, and she was the newest agent. The male agents frequently asked Amira to do a variety of demeaning tasks, such as getting coffee for them. Because Amira had been raised with the traditional Yemenite value that serving men is appropriate, she acquiesced. However, as she became increasingly assimilated into the dominant U.S. culture, she became conflicted about being the "office housewife." The following is an excerpt from the initial assertion training session.

Client: I know that my traditional upbringing feeds into my complying with my colleagues' requests, but I don't think it's appropriate—this is not Yemen. It's the United States. They are taking advantage of me.

Therapist: You know, you can refuse to comply with their inappropriate requests.

Client: I've never done it before. It's scary.

Therapist: What we can do is to teach you appropriate assertive behaviors for the situation and then you can practice them with me. When you feel comfortable enough, you can gradually begin to use them in your office. What do you think?

Client: I guess so, but it goes against all I've known for most of my life.

Therapist: Well, let's just try a simple role-play and see how it goes.

(continued)

CASE **11-6** (*continued*)

Client: Okay.

Therapist: For the moment, let's role-play a typical situation for you. You pretend that you are one of your male co-workers, and I'll pretend I am you. You ask me to do something inappropriate, and I'll give you an example of a suitable assertive response. Let's try it. Ask me to do something that is an inappropriate request.

Client: All right. Bob might say, "Hey, Amira, you're not doing anything important. How about going to get us some coffee and donuts, like a good little girl." [role playing] He said something just like that yesterday.

Therapist: "I'd love some coffee, Bob, but I'm in the middle of working up a quote. Maybe you or someone else could get us all coffee." [modeling]

Client: I couldn't say that.

Therapist: Well, you certainly don't have to use my exact words. I'm just giving you an example. What would you feel comfortable saying for a start? Let's switch roles. You be yourself, and I'll be Bob. You respond to what I say. "Amira, some of us would like some coffee. How about getting it for us?" [role playing]

Client: "Oh, I guess so. But I am busy right now. As soon as I finish, I guess I could." [behavior rehearsal]

Therapist: Not bad. [shaping] It sure isn't totally giving in to the request; and you're not exactly saying that you will. [feedback] Do you think you could go one step further and tell Bob you don't want to get the coffee?

Client: What would I say?

Therapist: How about something like, "I'd rather not go for coffee." [modeling] Words to that effect make it clear that you don't want to but you aren't actually saying no, which may be hard for you to say at first. [direct instruction] Let's try again. "Amira, some of us would like some coffee. How about getting it for us?" [role playing]

Client: "I'm really busy, Bob, so this isn't a good time for me to get coffee." [behavior rehearsal]

Therapist: Very good. [reinforcement] Much better. [feedback] Your first response indicated you probably would get the coffee later. Now you are saying no, albeit indirectly. [shaping] Do you see the difference?

After seven sessions of assertion training, Amira felt comfortable enough to attempt responding assertively to inappropriate requests in everyday situations, but not at work. After 3 weeks of in vivo practice, she began to assert herself with her male co-workers.

Most people have some trouble refusing unreasonable or inappropriate requests in their daily lives. Participation Exercise 11-2 will help you hone those skills.

Assertion Training for Refusing Unreasonable Requests[c]

In this exercise, you will engage in assertion training consisting of symbolic modeling, behavior rehearsal, and feedback to teach you to appropriately refuse unreasonable requests. Table 11-11 contains four hypothetical situations in which requests are made in a letter. For each, read the letter, keeping in mind the particular situation. Assume that you have received the letter and write an appropriate reply. If the request is unreasonable, refuse the request; if the request is reasonable, agree to it.

TABLE **11-11**

Hypothetical Situations and Letters Requiring Responses

Situation	Letter to Respond to

1. You are invited to a party by a student who was in a class you took during the summer. She asks you to pick up someone you don't know, which will mean your driving 30 miles out of your way.	Dear Classmate,
	    How's it going? We're having a little party at my house next Thursday, and I'd like you to come. My cousin was coming, but he's having trouble getting a ride down. Do you think you can give him a lift? He lives about 45 minutes out of town so I've enclosed a map. See you on Thursday.
	        Regards,
	        Classmate

2. A CD company you recently joined has sent you four CDs you never ordered. In fact, you promptly returned the order card stating that you didn't want any CDs sent.	Dear CD Club Member,
	    We have, up to this time, sent you four CDs for a total of $59.80. We have not received any payment. Please send full payment immediately, plus shipping and handling costs, as indicated on the enclosed bill.
	        Thank you,
	        President,
	        Ripoff Recordings, Inc.

3. You receive a letter asking for a contribution to a religious group you have never heard of.	Dear Neighbor, In order for our organization to grow and to build new places of worship, it is essential that we receive financial backing from people like you. Please open your heart and send your check today. Return this card with your contribution so that we can continue

[c]This Participation Exercise can be completed before you continue reading or later.

(continued)

TABLE **11-11** *(continued)*

Situation	Letter to Respond to
	sending you news and information about our ministry. Most sincerely, President, United Affluent Church
4. A close friend writes you asking if you would pick up an important package for him at the local post office, which you pass every day, and pay the delivery charge.	Dear Friend, I won't be in the city until some time next week, but I'm expecting an important package to arrive at the main post office. I would really appreciate it if you could pick it up for me and pay the delivery charge. It should only be a few dollars. I'll pay you when I get back. Thanks, Your friend

Here are some general guidelines for writing an *appropriate* refusal to an unreasonable request:

1. Be polite.
2. Be direct; say what you mean. If you mean that you *don't want* to do something, say that directly (and politely) instead of saying that you are not sure whether you can do it. The former reply would be honest and unambiguous, whereas the latter would be dishonest and ambiguous.
3. Do not apologize excessively. It might, however, be appropriate to wish the writer luck in obtaining a positive response from others.
4. Tailor the letter to the degree of unreasonableness of the request. For example, a mildly unreasonable request should be responded to with mild refusal, such as, "Sorry that I can't help you out."
5. Consider your relationship, present and future, with the writer. If the relationship is important to you, you may want to tone down your reply.
6. In *some* cases it may be appropriate to compromise, which, in effect, would render the request more reasonable so that you feel comfortable doing part of what the writer requested.
7. Remember: You are entitled to refuse others' unreasonable requests— and even reasonable ones.

After you have replied to the first letter, look at Table 11-12 and read the modeled reply along with the explanation, which will give you feedback on what you have written. Your reply need not match the model, but it should contain the same basic elements. Repeat the process for each situation and letter. To benefit from the feedback provided in Table 11-12, refer only to the specific modeled reply (that is, don't read all the examples in Table 11-12) after writing each letter and before writing the next one.

TABLE **11-12**

Model Letters for Refusing Unreasonable Requests, with Explanations

Model Letter	Explanatory Note
1. Dear Classmate, Thanks for the invitation to the party. I'll sure be there, but I really won't be able to pick up your cousin. Thirty miles is just too far for me to go out of my way. I'm looking forward to seeing you at the party.	Polite and friendly; states what you will and will not do; ends on an upbeat note
2. Dear President: I did not order the four CDs you have sent. I promptly returned the order card and checked off that I did not want the CDs. Therefore, I refuse to pay for them, although I will return them at your company's expense.	Clearly explains situation; categorically says no; adds a compromise that demonstrates good faith
3. Dear President, I am not interested in your organization or in receiving any further news or information from you.	Very brief, formal reply, appropriate for the impersonal form letter received; unequivocally states your position
4. Dear Friend, I'll be glad to pick up the package for you. Give me a call when you get back in town, and we'll arrange for you to pick it up.	*Reasonable* request in this case

Assertion Training in Perspective

Hundreds of studies have demonstrated the effectiveness of assertion training for clients with diverse problems and across the age spectrum.[185d] For example, assertive behavior is especially important in preventing HIV infection among vulnerable populations, including women who are chronically hospitalized for schizophrenia and depression,[186] inner city low-income African-American men[187] and women,[188] people with mental retardation,[189] and high-risk adolescents such as those with other sexually transmitted diseases[190] and those with poor social skills with the opposite sex.[191] Assertion training with these populations has been effective in reducing the risk of contracting HIV as assessed by such measures as the number of sexual partners, the number of sexual contacts with strangers, and the use of condoms.

---

[d]Research on assertion training has decreased significantly over the past 20 years. This may be due, in part, to deficits in assertive behavior not being classified as a disorder in the *Diagnostic and Statistical Manual of Mental Disorders* (American Psychiatric Association, 1987, 1994, 2000a), which generally is necessary for research funding. It is not due to a decline in assertive behavior skills deficits in the population.

Research also has been directed at identifying the components of optimal assertive behavior. For example, people are considered competent and likable if their assertive responses are empathic[192] and complimentary.[193] An example would be: "You guys are doing a great job given how shorthanded you are; I just hope you'll be able to have my car fixed by the end of the day."

Assertion training is frequently used in conjunction with other behavior therapies. For example, assertion training was combined with cognitive therapy (used to identify and cope with negative thoughts) in a group setting to treat Iranian adolescents for shy behaviors.[194]

Although clearly a behavior therapy, assertion training also has been incorporated into many different kinds of psychotherapy (such as Gestalt therapy). Assertion training also has been a hot topic in "pop" psychology for many years. Consider the large number of books on the subject written for the general public, including "treatises … on the technique of how, when and why to say no; what to say no to; and why you should not feel guilty in saying no."[195]

ALL THINGS CONSIDERED: MODELING THERAPY

Modeling is effective in treating anxiety disorders and skills deficits.[196] Overall, modeling therapies have been found to be at least as effective as other behavior therapies with which they have been compared. For a number of specific applications, such as in reducing children's fears,[197] modeling procedures have been shown to be more effective.[198]

Modeling therapies are very efficient. Significant changes sometimes are obtained in one or two brief sessions.[199] One reason may be that modeling simultaneously teaches clients adaptive behaviors, prompts their performance, motivates their practice, and reduces anxiety about performing the behaviors. Symbolic modeling is highly cost-effective. Once produced, modeling films/videos and books do not require therapists' time. For example, modeling videos to reduce fear of dental procedures now are routinely shown in some dentists' offices. The major limitation of standard symbolic modeling presentations is that they are aimed at the "average" client, which means that they are not individualized. However, present technology makes it possible to customize symbolic modeling relatively easily. For instance, individualized modeling videos can be made using video recorders,[200] and written stories can be customized with a word processor by changing a few significant phrases (such as names and locations). Symbolic modeling also can be supplemented with individualized live modeling, in which case the live modeling may not have to be as extensive and time consuming because the client has already been exposed to symbolic modeling.

Modeling therapy can be administered in a variety of modalities—live, symbolic (primarily through films), and in combination with behavior rehearsal (participant modeling)—and each has its advantages. For example, for vicarious extinction of fears, generally participant modeling is most effective (perhaps because it incorporates behavior rehearsal), film modeling is least effective (perhaps because it is generic rather than individualized for the client), and live modeling is of intermediate effectiveness.[201]

Modeling therapies easily can be implemented in naturalistic settings by nonprofessional behavior change agents, which is another way in which modeling therapies are efficient. In one application, social skills training for preschoolers with low levels of peer social interaction consisted of modeling and prompting by teachers' aides, followed by behavior rehearsal.[202] The training significantly increased the children's social interactions in a short time.

Modeling can be highly cost-effective in another way. **Natural models**—people in clients' everyday environments who exhibit behaviors that clients need to learn and practice—are abundantly available, and clients can observe them on their own.[203] For example, a client who is fearful of speaking to people at social gatherings could go to a large party and observe how people speak to one another and what happens when they do (vicarious consequences). Parents and teachers naturally serve as models for children and adolescents, which can be used to therapeutic advantage. For instance, children who give up easily when tasks are difficult could benefit from observing adults in their lives who model appropriately coping with frustration.[204] Although the use of natural models is a potentially potent and efficient form of modeling therapy, the extent to which behavior therapists instruct clients to observe appropriate natural models is unknown.

Clients rate modeling as an acceptable therapy. It is subtle and unintrusive. Modeling indirectly influences clients merely by presenting an example of how one might behave, which may result in clients' feeling more in control of their behavior changes. This is important because behavior change is more effective when people believe that they are personally responsible for the change.

A related advantage of modeling is that it does not involve verbal instructions or the necessity of verbal communication between therapist and client. Clients can benefit solely from observing models engaging in adaptive behaviors. This is especially helpful for clients who have minimal verbal comprehension.

Modeling increases clients' personal freedom by providing them with alternative ways of behaving. This is equally true for the child with mental retardation who learns to ask for assistance and for the business executive who learns appropriate assertive behaviors to use in complex social interactions. Competency-based treatments that involve skills training can enhance self-efficacy, independent functioning, and the overall quality of life even for clients with serious, chronic psychiatric disorders.[205]

Modeling is intrinsically part of many behavior therapies. For example, modeling is part of in vivo desensitization and in vivo flooding when the therapist demonstrates the desired behavior for the client.[206] The therapist's modeling not only prompts the target behavior but also shows the client that no harm comes from performing it. Modeling also is a component of many cognitive-behavioral coping skills therapies (which you will read about in Chapter 13).

Besides being a treatment modality, modeling is used to teach therapy skills to therapists and nonprofessional change agents, including clients themselves.[207] For example, modeling is an essential component in behavioral parent training (as you saw in Chapter 8).[208] The therapist first models a behavior management procedure, such as shaping. Then, parents practice shaping their children's behaviors and receive feedback from the therapist.

Similar procedures are used to teach family members to care for elderly relatives with physical and psychological impairments.[209] Modeling also has potential for encouraging clients to seek therapy[210] and in preparing clients for psychotherapy.[211]

SUMMARY

1. Modeling requires two people: a model who demonstrates a behavior and an observer who attends to what the model does. Live models are actually present, and symbolic models are observed indirectly, as on TV. Observing a model provides information about what the model does as well as the consequences of the model's actions, which are called vicarious consequences (vicarious reinforcement or vicarious punishment).

2. Observational learning is the process by which people are influenced by observing a model's behaviors. It involves three stages: exposure (to the model), acquisition (of the model's behaviors), and acceptance (of the model's behaviors as a guide for one's own actions). The observer can be influenced by the model in four ways: specific imitation, specific counterimitation, general imitation, and general counterimitation.

3. Modeling serves five functions for observers: teaching, prompting, motivating, reducing anxiety, and discouraging.

4. Self-modeling, in which clients serve as their own models (in a video or their imagination), maximizes observer–model similarity, which enhances imitation.

5. Modeling generally is part of a treatment package, which often includes behavior rehearsal. However, modeling can be effective by itself.

6. Modeling therapies have been used primarily for two broad classes of problems—fear/anxiety and skills deficits.

7. Vicarious extinction involves reducing fear or anxiety by having a client observe a model performing the feared behavior without the model incurring negative consequences. A coping model is initially fearful and incompetent and then gradually becomes comfortable and competent performing the feared behavior. A mastery model shows no fear and is competent from the outset. Coping models are more appropriate for reducing fear.

8. In participant modeling, the therapist models the anxiety-evoking behaviors for the client, then verbally and physically prompts the client to perform the behaviors, and finally fades the prompts.

9. Film/video modeling has been used to treat fear of medical and dental procedures in both children and adults. Storytelling is another form of symbolic modeling used to reduce fear and other negative emotions in children.

10. Perceived self-efficacy is the belief that one will be successful at a task. Modeling and other therapies may be effective because they increase clients' self-efficacy through performance accomplishments, vicarious experiences, verbal persuasion, and emotional arousal.

11. Skills deficits can involve deficiencies in knowledge, proficiency, discrimination, and motivation. Skills training is a treatment package that may include modeling, direct instruction, prompting, shaping, reinforcement, behavior rehearsal, role-playing, and feedback. Occasionally, clients, such as children

with autistic disorder, may have to be taught generalized imitation—the ability to imitate—so that they will be able to imitate the model during treatment.

12. Social skills training, which can employ modeling films/videos and live modeling, often is used to increase social interactions. It is an important component in the treatment of clients with schizophrenia, where the major goals are to increase social interactions, to teach skills needed for functioning in the community, and to reduce stress by teaching clients how to cope with problematic social situations.

13. Specific procedures often must be used to promote transfer of skills learned in social skills training.

14. Assertive behaviors are actions that secure and maintain what one is entitled to in an interpersonal situation without infringing on the rights of others. Assertive behaviors are situation specific.

15. Assertion training begins by assessing the specific details of the client's assertive skills deficits and the type(s) of skill deficit the client has. Live or symbolic modeling and behavior rehearsal are the primary components of assertion training.

16. Modeling therapies are effective and efficient treatments for anxiety disorders and skills deficits. They simultaneously teach clients adaptive behaviors, prompt performance, motivate practice, and reduce anxiety about performing the threatening behaviors. Modeling is a subtle and unintrusive therapy and is acceptable to clients. It is a component of many behavior therapies because therapists often model adaptive behaviors. Modeling also is used to train therapists and other change agents.

REFERENCE NOTES

1. Kalmuss, 1984.
2. Craig, 1986.
3. Gould & Shaffer, 1986; Lester, 1987; Ostroff & Boyd, 1987; compare with Wasserman, 1984.
4. Compare with Strain, Shores, & Kerr, 1976; Wilson, Robertson, Herlong, & Haynes, 1979.
5. Liebert & Spiegler, 1994.
6. For example, Bly, 1990; Campbell, 1988; Constantino, Malgady, & Rogler, 1986.
7. Kazdin, 1974a, 1974b, 1974c.
8. Kendall, Chu, Pimentel, & Choudhury, 2000.
9. Bandura, 1971, 1977b.
10. Kazdin, 1979; Rosenthal & Steffek, 1991.
11. Compare with Maeda, 1985; Olson & Roberts, 1987; Owusu-Bempah & Howitt, 1985.
12. Bandura, 1986b.
13. For example, Barry & Overmann, 1977; Kazdin, 1974b; Kornhaber & Schroeder, 1975.
14. Meharg & Woltersdorf, 1990.
15. Dowrick, 1991, 1994.
16. Bernad-Ripoll, 2007.
17. Barker & Jones, 2006; Barzouka, Bergeles, & Hatziharistos, 2007; Ram & McCullagh, 2003.
18. Magill-Evans, Harrison, Benzies, Gierl, & Kimak, 2007.
19. Creer & Miklich, 1970.
20. Simmons, 1993, p. 161, emphasis in original.
21. Dowrick, 2007; Dowrick, Kim-Rupnow, & Power, 2006; Dowrick, Tallman, & Connor, 2005.
22. Dowrick & Ward, 1997.
23. Dowrick, 1999.
24. Buggey, 2005; Delano, 2007; Dowrick, 1999; Hitchcock, Dowrick, & Prater, 2003; Hitchcock, Prater, & Dowrick, 2004; McGraw-Hunter, Faw, & Davis, 2006; Sherer, Pierce, Paredes, Kisacky, Ingersoll, & Schreibman, 2001; Wert & Neisworth, 2003.
25. Kehle, Madaus, Baratta, & Bray, 1998; Kehle, Owen, & Cressy, 1990; Pigott & Gonzales, 1987.
26. Bray & Kehle, 1998, 2001.

27. Clarke, Bray, Kehle, & Truscott, 2001.
28. Dowrick, 1978.
29. Davis, 1979; Kehle, Clark, Jenson, & Wampold, 1986.
30. Bray & Kehle, 1998; Clare, Jenson, Kehle, & Bray, 2000; Possell, Kehle, McLoughlin, & Bray, 1999.
31. Rickards-Schlichting, Kehle, & Bray, 2004; Schwartz, Houlihan, Krueger, & Simon, 1997.
32. Kahn, Kehle, Jenson, & Clark, 1990; Prince & Dowrick, 1984.
33. Hosford & Brown, 1975.
34. Dowrick & Ward, 1997.
35. Bellini & Akullian, 2007a; Dowrick & Raeburn, 1995.
36. Bellini & Akullian, 2007b.
37. From the author's (MDS) clinical files.
38. Spiegler, 2008.
39. Meichenbaum, 1971.
40. Bandura, 1986b.
41. Ozer & Bandura, 1990.
42. For example, Öst, 1989.
43. For example, Sarason, 1975.
44. For example, Mattick & Peters, 1988.
45. For example, Silverman, 1986; Thyer, 1985.
46. Klesges, Malott, & Ugland, 1984; quotation from p. 161.
47. Milgrom, Mancl, King, & Weinstein, 1995.
48. Compare with Newman & Adams, 2004.
49. Ritter, 1968a, 1968b.
50. Ritter, 1968a, 1968b, 1969a, 1969b, 1969c.
51. For example, Bandura, 1976; Bandura, Jeffery, & Gajdos, 1975.
52. Ritter, 1969a; quotation from pp. 170–171.
53. For example, Minor, Leone, & Baldwin, 1984; Öst, 2001; Öst, Ferebee, & Furmark, 1997.
54. Klingman, Melamed, Cuthbert, & Hermecz, 1984.
55. Altmaier, Leary, Halpern, & Sellers, 1985.
56. Davis, Kurtz, Gardner, & Carman, 2007; Menzies & Clarke, 1993.
57. Davis, Kurtz, Gardner, & Carman, 2007.
58. For example, Williams & Zane, 1989.
59. Menzies & Clarke, 1993; Öst, Ferebee, & Furmark, 1997.
60. For example, Downs, Rosenthal, & Lichstein, 1988; Öst, Ferebee, & Furmark, 1997.
61. Williams, Dooseman, & Kleifield, 1984; Williams, Turner, & Peer, 1985; Williams & Zane, 1989.
62. Bandura, 1986b.
63. Peterson & Ridley-Johnson, 1980.
64. Kleinknecht & Bernstein, 1979; Klorman, Hilpert, Michael, LaGana, & Sveen, 1980; Melamed, 1979; Melamed, Hawes, Helby, & Glick, 1975.
65. Melamed & Siegel, 1975.
66. Melamed & Siegel, 1975, p. 514.
67. Melamed & Siegel, 1975.
68. Vernon, 1974.
69. Vernon, 1974.
70. Jay, Elliott, Ozolins, Olson, & Pruitt, 1985.
71. Jay, Elliott, Ozolins, Olson, & Pruitt, 1985, p. 516.
72. Allen, Danforth, & Drabman, 1989; Shipley, Butt, & Horwitz, 1979; Shipley, Butt, Horwitz, & Farbry, 1978.
73. Nemetz, Craig, & Reith, 1978; Wincze & Caird, 1976.
74. Bandura, 1997, 2001.
75. Bandura, 1977a, 1986b, 2001.
76. Cervone & Scott, 1995.
77. Cervone & Peake, 1986.
78. For example, Haaga, 1990.
79. Bandura, 1984.
80. Peterson, Schultheis, Ridley-Johnson, Miller, & Tracy, 1984.
81. My Tonsillectomy Coloring Book, 1969.
82. Mikulas & Coffman, 1989; Mikulas, Coffman, Dayton, Frayne, & Maier, 1985.
83. Dawe & Hart, 1986.
84. Cautela, 1993; Jackson & Francey, 1985.
85. A. J. Kearney, 1993.
86. Hay, Hay, & Nelson, 1977.
87. Glaeser, Pierson, & Fritschman, 2003; Pierson & Glaeser, 2005.
88. Author's (MDS) clinical files.
89. Farmer & Chapman, 2008.
90. For example, Matson, Bamburg, Smalls, & Smiroldo, 1997; Matson, Smalls, Hampff, Smiroldo, & Anderson, 1998; Miltenberger, 2000.
91. For example, Charlop & Milstein, 1989; Gambrill, 1995a.
92. For example, Star, 1986.
93. For example, Charlop & Milstein, 1989; Charlop, Schreibman, & Tryon, 1983; Lovaas, 1977, 1987.
94. Metz, 1965.
95. For example, Goldstein & Mousetis, 1989; Rietveld, 1983.
96. For example, Rivera & Smith, 1988; Smith & Lovitt, 1975.
97. For example, Foxx, Martella, & Marchand-Martella, 1989.

98. Coffey, Schumacher, Brimo, & Brady, 2005; Lombardo & Gray, 2005; Turner, Beidel, & Frueh, 2005.

99. Pavuluri, 2008.

100. Newman & Haaga, 1995.

101. O'Donohue & Noll, 1995.

102. Szymanski & O'Donohue, 1995.

103. Pierce, 1995.

104. Vargas & Shanley, 1995.

105. Haring, Breen, Weiner, Kennedy, & Bednerah, 1995.

106. Rusch, Hughes, & Wilson, 1995.

107. Barclay & Houts, 1995.

108. Groth, 1980.

109. For example, Poche, Brouwer, & Swearingen, 1981.

110. Miltenberger & Thiesse-Duffy, 1988; Poche, Brouwer, & Swearingen, 1981; Poche, Yoder, & Miltenberger, 1988.

111. Poche, Brouwer, & Swearingen, 1981.

112. Poche, Yoder, & Miltenberger, 1988.

113. Poche, Yoder, & Miltenberger, 1988, p. 255.

114. Johnson, Miltenberger, Egemo-Helm, Jostad, Flessner, & Gatheridge, 2005; Johnson et al., 2006.

115. Wurtele, Currier, Gillispie, & Franklin, 1991.

116. Wurtele, 1990; Wurtele, Currier, Gillispie, & Franklin, 1991; Wurtele, Marrs, & Miller-Perrin, 1987.

117. For example, Brazelton, 1987.

118. Lumley, Miltenberger, Long, Rapp, & Roberts, 1998; Miltenberger et al., 1999.

119. Miltenberger et al., 1999.

120. Frame & Matson, 1987.

121. Matson, Sevin, & Box, 1995.

122. Gambrill, 1995b; Trower, 1995.

123. For example, Matson, Sevin, & Box, 1995.

124. For example, Trower, 1995.

125. Gambrill, 1995b.

126. For example, Sukhodolsky, Golub, Stone, & Orban, 2005.

127. Gottman & Rushe, 1995.

128. Gold, Letourneau, & O'Donohue, 1995.

129. Ballard & Crooks, 1984; O'Connor, 1969; Rao, Moely, & Lockman, 1987.

130. O'Connor, 1969, p. 18.

131. O'Connor, 1969; Rao, Moely, & Lockman, 1987.

132. O'Connor, 1969.

133. For example, Star, 1986.

134. Gumpel & Frank, 1999.

135. Franco, Christoff, Crimmins, & Kelly, 1983.

136. For example, Graves, Openshaw, & Adams, 1992.

137. For example, Foxx, Faw, & Weber, 1991.

138. For example, Cunliffe, 1992.

139. For example, Middleton & Cartledge, 1995.

140. For example, Guevremont, 1990; Posavac, Sheridan, & Posavac, 1999.

141. Varni, Katz, Colegrove, & Dolgin, 1993.

142. Rasing, Coninx, Duker, & Van Den Hurk, 1994.

143. Gambrill, 1985; Garland, 1985.

144. Carstensen & Fisher, 1991.

145. Bellack, Morrison, Wixted, & Mueser, 1990; Spiegler & Agigian, 1977; Trower, 1995.

146. Emmelkamp, 1994.

147. For example, Bellack & Mueser, 1994.

148. Spiegler & Agigian, 1977.

149. For example, Liberman, Vaccaro, & Corrigan, 1995.

150. For example, Liberman, Wallace, Blackwell, Eckman, Vaccaro, & Kuehnel, 1993.

151. Emmelkamp, 1994.

152. Wong et al., 1993.

153. For example, Benton & Schroeder, 1990.

154. For example, Bellack & Mueser, 1994; Benton & Schroeder, 1990.

155. Liberman, Wallace, Blackwell, & Vaccaro, 1993.

156. For example, Bellack & Mueser, 1994; Spiegler & Agigian, 1977.

157. Herring & Northup, 1998; Miller & Cole, 1998.

158. Ducharme & Holborn, 1997; Huang & Cuvo, 1997; Pollard, 1998.

159. O'Callaghan, Reitman, Northup, Hupp, & Murphy, 2003.

160. For example, Beidel & Turner, 1998; Beidel, Turner, & Morris, 2000; Ducharme & Holborn, 1997.

161. For example, Ducharme & Holborn, 1997.

162. For example, Griffiths, Feldman, & Tough, 1997.

163. For example, Coyne, Faul, & Gross, 2000; Herring & Northup, 1998.

164. For example, Coyne, Faul, & Gross, 2000; Griffiths, Feldman, & Tough, 1997; Herring & Northup, 1998.

165. For example, Beidel & Turner, 1998; Beidel, Turner, & Morris, 2000.

166. For example, Griffiths, Feldman, & Tough, 1997.

167. Alberti & Emmons, 2001.

168. Kelly, St. Lawrence, Hood, & Brasfield, 1989; Powell, 1996.

169. For example, Bucell, 1979.

170. For example, Frisch & Froberg, 1987; Gambrill, 1995a.

171. Lazarus, 1973; Schroeder & Black, 1985.
172. Gambrill, 1995a.
173. Wilson & Gallois, 1993.
174. Spiegler, 2008.
175. Organista, 2006; Interian, Allen, Gara, & Esobar, 2008.
176. Alberti & Emmons, 2001; Gambrill, 1995a.
177. Blumberg et al., 1997; Gambrill, 1995a; St. Lawrence, 1987.
178. For example, Gambrill & Richey, 1975; Rathus, 1973.
179. McFall & Lillesand, 1971.
180. For example, Eisler, Hersen, & Miller, 1973; Hersen, Eisler, Miller, Johnson, & Pinkston, 1973; McFall & Lillesand, 1971.
181. Alberti & Emmons, 2001.
182. For example, Alberti & Emmons, 2001; Kazdin, 1974d, 1976; Maeda, 1985.
183. Krop & Burgess, 1993b.
184. From the author's (MDS) clinical files.
185. Gambrill, 1995a.
186. weinhardt, Carey, Carey & Verdecias, 1998.
187. Kalichman, Cherry, & Browne-Sperling, 1999.
188. Carey et al., 2000.
189. Miltenberger et al., 1999.
190. Metzler, Biglan, Noell, Ary, & Ochs, 2000.
191. Nangle & Hansen, 1998.
192. Kern, 1982; Kern, Cavell, & Beck, 1985.
193. Levin & Gross, 1984; St. Lawrence, Hansen, Cutts, Tisdelle, & Irish, 1985.
194. Shariatnia & D'Souza, 2007.
195. Franks & Wilson, 1976, p. 148.
196. Bandura, 1986b; Rachman & Wilson, 1980.
197. Graziano, DeGiovanni, & Garcia, 1979; Ollendick, 1979.
198. Rachman & Wilson, 1980.
199. For example, Allen, Danforth, & Drabman, 1989; Dowrick & Raeburn, 1995; Rao, Moely, & Lockman, 1987; Spiegler, Liebert, McMains, & Fernandez, 1969.
200. For example, Charlop & Milstein, 1989; Dowrick, 1991.
201. King, Muris, & Ollendick, 2005.
202. Storey, Danko, Ashworth, & Strain, 1994.
203. Spiegler, 1970.
204. Braswell & Kendall, 2001.
205. Hunter, 1995.
206. For example, Mattick & Peters, 1988; Silverman, 1986; Thyer, 1985.
207. For example, Duley, Cancelli, Kratochwill, Bergan, & Meredith, 1983; Nawaz, Griffiths, & Tappin, 2002.
208. For example, Webster-Stratton, 1981a, 1981b, 1982a, 1982b.
209. Pinkston, Linsk, & Young, 1988.
210. Park & Williams, 1986.
211. For example, Day & Reznikoff, 1980; Weinstein, 1988.

12

Cognitive-Behavioral Therapy
Cognitive Restructuring

Michael stood at the top of the black diamond (expert level) ski slope contemplating his fate. "Do you think I can make it?" Michael asked Daryl, his ski instructor. Daryl smiled and matter-of-factly said, "Whether you think you can, or whether you think you can't, you're right."

The way we think about events in our lives exerts a powerful and pervasive influence on how we act and feel.[1] *Cognitions* are thoughts—including beliefs, assumptions, expectations, attributions, and attitudes. *Cognitive-behavioral therapy*, which changes cognitions that play a role in maintaining a wide array of psychological disorders and problems, has proliferated during the past 30 years[2] and is at the forefront of behavior therapy.[3]

NATURE OF COGNITIVE-BEHAVIORAL THERAPY

Clients' cognitions are modified in two ways: directly through cognitive interventions and indirectly through overt behavioral interventions. Changing our actions in order to change what we think is the time-honored strategy for attitude change.[4] For example, arguing *for* a political position with which you *disagree* is likely to dispose you more favorably toward it. The emphasis on cognitive (direct) versus overt behavioral (indirect) change varies in different cognitive-behavioral therapies and for different problems; however, usually both cognitive and (overt) behavioral components are included, hence the hyphenated term *cognitive-behavioral therapy*.[5]

Cognitive-behavioral therapies fit into two basic models.[a] **Cognitive restructuring therapy**, one model, teaches clients to change distorted and erroneous cognitions that are maintaining their problem behaviors. **Cognitive restructuring** involves recognizing maladaptive cognitions and substituting more adaptive cognitions for them.[6] It is used when clients' problems are maintained by an *excess of maladaptive thoughts*.

Cognitive-behavioral coping skills therapy, the other model, teaches clients adaptive responses—both cognitive and overt behavioral—to deal effectively with problematic situations. When clients act adaptively, they begin to think differently about troublesome situations. This model is appropriate for problems that are maintained by a *deficit in adaptive cognitions*. Table 12-1 summarizes the two models. Cognitive restructuring therapy is covered in this chapter, and cognitive-behavioral coping skills therapy is the topic of Chapter 13.

Operationalizing Cognitions: Making Private Thoughts Public

Originally, behavior therapists focused on overt behaviors, which excluded covert behaviors such as thoughts, beliefs, and attitudes. With the advent of cognitive-behavioral therapy in the 1970s, that changed, and behavior therapists were faced with the dilemma of how to treat cognitions that could not be

---

[a]Our conceptualization of two models of cognitive-behavioral therapy is consistent with Kendall and Braswell's (1985) distinction between cognitive distortions and deficits, and it shares commonalities with the categories of mechanisms used to change cognitions proposed by Ross (1977) and Hollon and Beck (1986).

TABLE **12-1**

Comparison of the Two Models of Cognitive-Behavioral Therapy

	Cognitive Restructuring	Cognitive-Behavioral Coping Skills
TARGET OF THERAPY	Excess of maladaptive cognitions	Deficit of adaptive cognitions
GOAL OF THERAPY	Substituting adaptive cognitions for maladaptive cognitions	Using cognitive-behavioral coping skills
EXAMPLES OF THERAPIES	Thought stopping Rational emotive behavior therapy Cognitive therapy	Self-instructional training Problem-solving therapy/ training Stress inoculation training Cognitive-behavioral couple therapy

directly observed. You may discover the solution to this quandary by taking just a minute to complete Participation Exercise 12-1 before reading further.

Thinking About Thinking

Identify a problem that you must solve or deal with in the near future. The problem can be a major one (such as having to make a decision that will influence your future in a significant way) or it can be a minor one (such as planning what you should do next weekend). The only requirement is that the problem be detailed enough so that you can easily spend several minutes thinking about it.

Once you have chosen a problem, think about it for a minute. As you think about the problem, *be aware of your thoughts, particularly the form they take.* "Listen" to yourself thinking. After doing this for a minute, continue reading.

What form did your thoughts take? They probably included words, phrases, and perhaps full sentences. Much of our thinking involves the explicit use of language (see In Theory 12-1). Capitalizing on this fact, behavior therapists generally operationally define cognitions as **self-talk**, what people say to themselves when they are thinking. If you want to know what someone is thinking, the optimal question to ask the person is: *"What are you saying to yourself?"* Cognitions also include sensory images (including visual, auditory, and tactile), but the focus in cognitive-behavioral therapy is on inner, verbal language.[7]

We often are not aware of our inner speech because we do not think about our thinking. Thinking is a habitual, automatic process that goes on even when we are not specifically engaged in mental endeavors, such as when we are exercising and eating.

IN THEORY 12-1

Talking to Yourself Isn't Necessarily Crazy

The world is such and such or so-and-so only because we tell ourselves that it is the way it is…. You talk to yourself. You're not unique at that. Every one of us does that. We carry on internal talk…. In fact we maintain our world with our internal talk.[8]

This brief description, by cultural anthropologist and author Carlos Castaneda, sums up the salience of "inner speech" in our lives. More specifically, inner speech has been described as the soundless, mental speech, arising at the instant we think about something, plan or solve problems in our mind, recall books read or conversations heard, read and write silently. In all such instances, we think and remember with the aid of words which we articulate to ourselves. Inner speech is nothing but speech to oneself, or concealed verbalization, which is instrumental in the logical processing of sensory data, in their realization and comprehension within a definite system of concepts and judgments. The elements of inner speech are found in all our conscious perceptions, actions, and emotional experiences, where they manifest themselves as verbal sets, instructions to oneself, or as verbal interpretations of sensations and perceptions. This renders inner speech a rather important and universal mechanism.[9]

Only after clients can identify what they are saying to themselves can they change the cognitions that are maintaining their problems. Thus, the first step in cognitive-restructuring therapy is for clients to become aware of their self-talk, especially before, during, and after their problem behaviors occur.

This chapter is devoted primarily to two cognitive-behavioral therapies that make extensive use of cognitive restructuring: *rational emotive behavior therapy* and *cognitive therapy*. We will also briefly describe *thought stopping*, a simple technique that employs cognitive restructuring to reduce persistent, intrusive thoughts. However, first things first—that is, assessing cognitions, the initial step in cognitive restructuring therapy.

Assessing Cognitions

Four basic methods are used to assess clients' cognitions: *interview, self-recording, direct self-report inventory,* and *think-aloud procedures.* Each method elicits clients' self-reports of their cognitions, which is the only way to gain direct information about another's thoughts. The methods differ along five dimensions: (1) *timing* (for example, retrospective or concurrent), (2) *degree of structure* (for example, open-ended or forced choice), (3) *mode of response* (for example, written or oral), (4) *nature of the stimulus* (for example, written scenario or simulated situation), and (5) *source of evaluation* (for example, by the client or by the therapist).[10] Later in this chapter we will illustrate the application of interview techniques and self-recording. Here we will describe the use of self-report inventories and think-aloud procedures.

Direct self-report inventories for assessing cognitions consist of common self-statements related to a particular problem area.[11] Clients indicate how often they make each self-statement (or similar self-statements).[12] For example, the Social Interaction Self-Statement Test, developed by Carol Glass, lists 15 positive and 15 negative self-statements about problematic heterosocial dating interactions (see Table 12-2 for examples).[13] Adults rate each statement on a 5-point scale to indicate how frequently they have had each thought (from "hardly ever" to "very often"). Children's cognitions also can be assessed with self-report inventories. For instance, the Children's Negative Affectivity Self-Statement Questionnaire assesses maladaptive thoughts associated with anxiety.[14] Standardized self-report inventories are efficient methods for initial screening purposes. They give the therapist a general idea about the type of thoughts the client is having. Specific, individualized assessment requires other methods of assessing cognitions.

Think-aloud approaches have clients verbalize their thoughts (usually by talking into a tape recorder) while engaging in a simulated task or role-playing situation.[15] The Articulated Thoughts in Simulated Situations method, developed by Gerald Davison, is an example of a think-aloud procedure.[16] Clients listen to audiotaped scenarios designed to elicit different cognitions. A social criticism scenario, for instance, describes a person's overhearing two acquaintances talking about him or her in negative terms (such as ridiculing the person's choice of clothes). Clients are asked to imagine themselves in the situation and to "tune in" to their thoughts. Every 30 seconds, a tone prompts clients to say their thoughts aloud into a microphone. The therapist assures clients that there are no good or bad or right or wrong thoughts and encourages them to verbalize their thoughts without concern about whether the thoughts seem appropriate.

Think-aloud approaches to cognitive assessment have five distinct advantages over direct self-report inventories.[17] First, think-aloud approaches have an open-ended response format so that clients do not have to make forced choices from a predetermined and limited array of responses. Second, they tap clients'

TABLE **12-2**

Examples of Items on the Social Interaction Self-Statement Test (rated on a 5-point scale from "Hardly Ever" to "Very Often")

I hope I don't make a fool of myself.
She/he probably won't be interested in me.
This will be a good opportunity.
It would crush me if she/he didn't respond to me.
This is an awkward situation but I can handle it.
Maybe we'll hit it off real well.
What I say will probably sound stupid.

cognitions immediately following the simulated situation, which eliminates the problems associated with retrospective reporting, such as forgetting.[18] Third, think-aloud approaches can be customized for each client. Fourth, audiotaped simulated presentations of stressful stimuli may more readily elicit genuine emotional responses than written stimuli, resulting in a more realistic sampling of potentially maladaptive cognitions. Finally, children as young as 9 are able to respond to think-aloud approaches used to assess cognitions.[19]

Think-aloud procedures are designed for simulated situations rather than actual situations because talking into a tape recorder while engaging in everyday activities usually is not practical. Thus, an important potential limitation of think-aloud approaches is that they may miss highly relevant but low-frequency thoughts that are likely to occur only in vivo.

THOUGHT STOPPING

Thought stopping is designed to decrease the frequency and duration of persistent, intrusive thoughts by interrupting them and substituting pleasant thoughts for them.[20] Examples of the problems treated with thought stopping are obsessive ruminations (such as constantly worrying about being contaminated by germs), depressive ideas (for example, "Nothing seems to go right"), and self-deprecating thoughts (for instance, "I'm just not good at anything"). Thought stopping involves two phases: first (1) interrupting the disturbing thoughts and then (2) focusing on a competing adaptive thought.[b]

In the first phase, whenever disturbing thoughts occur, the client says, "Stop!" The word is said with a sharp, jolting expression, as if warning of imminent danger. Initially, clients say, "Stop!" aloud; then, they switch to saying "Stop!" silently to themselves. Although saying "Stop!" usually is the interrupting stimulus, another appropriate stimulus could be used, such as a loud noise or an image of a stop sign.[21]

Therapists sometimes introduce thought stopping to clients with a dramatic demonstration of its effect. The therapist asks the client to concentrate on the disturbing thought and to signal (as by raising a finger) when the thought is clear. As soon as the client signals, the therapist shouts, "Stop!" The client is then asked, "What happened?" Typically, clients report that they were startled and that the disturbing thought vanished.

Although "Stop!" momentarily eliminates the intrusive thought, the thought may reappear quickly if the person does not start thinking about something else. (As you know, trying *not to think* about something almost guarantees your thinking about it.) Thus, in the second phase of thought stopping, immediately after saying "Stop!" the client focuses on a prepared thought that competes with the disturbing thought. Therapists assist clients in selecting one or more adaptive competing thoughts that can be used in the second phase of thought stopping. The basic procedures of thought stopping can be seen in Case 12-1.

---

[b]Thought stopping should not be confused with *thought suppression*, which involves deliberate attempts *not* to think about something. Unlike thought stopping, thought suppression can result in either an immediate or delayed increase of the thoughts (Zeitlin, Netten, & Hodder, 1995).

CASE **12-1**

Eliminating Jealousy by Thought Stopping[22]

A 27-year-old man, K. F., discovered that the woman he was living with had had a brief affair a week before they had moved in together. After an initial period of feeling intensely hurt and angry, K. F. resolved to forget the incident. He wanted the relationship to continue, and he believed the woman's feelings for him had not changed. However, K. F. frequently thought about the woman's affair and became extremely upset whenever he imagined her being sexually intimate with the other man. These thoughts not only were disturbing, but they also prevented him from concentrating on whatever he was doing at the time.

Several years previously, K. F. had learned thought stopping as part of the treatment for another problem. Recalling the procedure, he applied thought stopping to his jealous thoughts. Whenever he began ruminating about the woman's affair, he yelled, "Stop!" to himself and then imagined one of two prearranged pleasant thoughts. One involved the woman's acting lovingly toward him. The other was completely unrelated to the woman or the relationship; it concerned his playing a good game of tennis, which was a source of personal satisfaction. Both pleasant thoughts successfully kept him from thinking of the woman's affair.

Before thought stopping, the distressing thoughts had lasted from several minutes to as long as an hour and had occurred on the average of 10 times a day. Thought stopping immediately reduced the duration of the intrusive thoughts to only a few seconds, and the frequency of the intrusive thoughts gradually declined. By the end of the second week, the thoughts occurred about 5 times per week; after a month, they occurred no more than once a week. Three months after K. F. initiated thought stopping, he was completely free of the disturbing thoughts, and they did not return during the 2-year span of his relationship with the woman.

The substitute thoughts that K. F. used in Case 12-1 were completely different from his jealous thoughts. Another technique, called *imagery rescripting*, has the client modify the disturbing thought, image, or belief so that it is more tolerable and even pleasant.[23] For example, a client experienced the frightful thought of falling from a great height and hearing his bones breaking as he hit the ground. He rescripted the thought to an image of hitting the ground and bouncing up in the air in a humorous cartoon-like manner. Another client who had been sexually abused as a child rescripted intrusive images of the abuse by creating a new scenario in which she visualized herself as an adult entering the scene to help herself as a child. Imagery rescripting may be particularly helpful for clients who experience recurrent distressing thoughts related to prior traumatic experiences, such as sexual victimization.[24]

Thought Stopping in Perspective

Thought stopping is a simple, straightforward procedure used to treat intrusive, disturbing thoughts. Such thoughts not only upset the individual but also result in a variety of serious problems that thought stopping has been successful in treating, including anxiety,[25] compulsive behaviors,[26] depression,[27] headaches,[28] excessive masturbation,[29] physical aggression,[30] and self-injurious behaviors.[31]

Clients can quickly learn and easily apply thought stopping on their own with little or no therapist supervision. As was illustrated in Case 12-1, thought stopping, like other cognitive-behavioral therapies, gives clients self-control skills that they can generalize to other problems.[32]

Thought stopping usually is part of a treatment package.[33] It is used relatively frequently, which seems to indicate that it is effective.[34] However, little controlled research has been done to validate its effectiveness.[35] Further, it is difficult to draw conclusions from the few existing outcome studies because the effects of thought stopping cannot be isolated from the other treatments with which it is combined or because the studies contain methodological weaknesses.[36] Although there is no definitive evidence for its effectiveness, no risks appear to be associated with clients' using thought stopping.

RATIONAL EMOTIVE BEHAVIOR THERAPY

Courtesy of Dr. Debbie Joffe Ellis

Albert Ellis

Rational emotive behavior therapy[37] **(REBT)** is a well-known treatment that primarily employs cognitive restructuring to change the irrational thoughts that cause psychological problems such as anxiety, depression, anger, and guilt.[38] Albert Ellis designed REBT almost 50 years ago.[39] The procedures follow from Ellis' theory of how psychological disorders develop and are maintained.[40] Before reading about his theory, take 2 minutes to complete Participation Exercise 12-2, which will help you understand Ellis' theory.

Rational Emotive Theory of Psychological Disorders

According to Ellis' rational emotive theory, psychological problems—negative emotions and maladaptive behaviors—are maintained by the *interpretations* people make of events in their lives. As the Greek Stoic philosopher Epictetus succinctly stated 2000 years ago, *people are disturbed not by things, but by the views they take of them.*

What is striking about this simple idea is that most people implicitly disagree with it. Generally, people believe that external events ("things") cause negative emotions. When someone takes the parking spot you are about to pull into, you get angry *because* someone took "your" spot. In the Participation Exercise that you just completed, did you answer the question, "What made you mad?" by attributing your upset to the situation or to the hostess?

In contrast, Ellis' theory holds that our *beliefs* about events—not the event themselves—are what make us angry (frustrated, annoyed, upset, etc.). The sequence always is the same: (1) Some event activates (2) an irrational belief that results in (3) negative consequences (negative emotions as well as maladaptive behaviors). In the parking spot example, your anger is likely to

What Are You Mad About?

First, get a paper and pen. Then, read the following scenario and picture yourself in the situation described—in other words, role-play it in your mind *as if it were happening to you.*

> You are taking a special friend out for a birthday celebration that you want to be especially nice. You have made a reservation at a fancy restaurant and have dressed up for the occasion. When you arrive at the restaurant, you give your name to the hostess, who goes to check the reservation book to see which table you've been assigned. As you are waiting, your friend remarks, with obvious appreciation, how elegant the restaurant is. When the hostess returns, she tells you that she cannot find your reservation, that they are fully booked for the evening, and that it will not be possible to seat you. Not surprisingly, you are mad!

Now write brief answers to the following two questions.

1. What has made you mad?
2. What are you saying to yourself?

be the *direct* result of irrational beliefs such as, "That was my parking spot," "It's not fair," and "That so-and-so *made* me late for my appointment." In Participation Exercise 12-2, was your self-talk related to similar beliefs?

Psychological problems are maintained by irrational beliefs that come from faulty reasoning or logical errors, such as absolute thinking, over-generalizing, and catastrophizing.[41] *Absolute thinking* is viewing an event in an all-or-none, black-or-white fashion, such as, "I must always do well" and "Others should treat me considerately and precisely in the manner I would like to be treated." *Overgeneralization* is drawing the conclusion that all instances of a situation will turn out a particular way because one or two did. For example, after having delivered one poor lecture, a professor told himself, "I'll never be a good lecturer." *Catastrophizing* involves seeing minor situations as disastrous. For instance, a woman who received a low grade on a quiz told herself, "This is the end of my college career."

Ellis identified two themes that often run through the irrational ideas that lead to psychological problems: personal worthlessness and a sense of duty. *Personal worthlessness* is a specific form of overgeneralization associated with failure. For example, a business executive decides that she is a "total failure" because she was unable to get all her work done by the end of the day.

To appreciate the second theme, *before* you continue reading, write down three things you *have* to do this week. Now read on.

A *sense of duty* is evident in the use of the words *must, have to, should,* and *ought to* in speech and thoughts. Ellis colorfully called the use of these words *musturbation.*[42] Musturbatory statements are irrational because, in fact, there are only a few behaviors that people *must* do. Consider what happens when you are physically ill and unable to attend to normal activities, such as the three things you *have* to do this week. At such times, all the tasks you *had* to get done do not, in fact, get done—yet somehow you survive, and the consequences rarely are catastrophic.

Insisting that you *must* do something is abdicating personal choice. It often may be convenient to blame an external source for what is actually a personal choice. When Juanita responds "I *have* to study" to her friends' invitation to go out for the evening, her friends readily accept her reason. However, they are likely to find it difficult to accept "I *want* to study." How can Juanita want to study and not want to go out with her friends? Something must be wrong with her! In fact, Juanita may want to go out with her friends, but she wants to study more because of the negative consequences of not studying, such as failing an exam the next day. Yet, however disagreeable those consequences, she still has the choice to study or go out with her friends. Participation Exercise 12-3, which is easy to do over the course of the next few days, will help you understand the degree to which you musturbate and how you can break the habit.

PARTICIPATION EXERCISE 12-3

Kicking the Musturbation Habit

Most people are unaware that they frequently use the words *must, have to, should*, and *ought to*. For example, students tell teachers, "I can't take the exam on Friday because I *have to* go home for a wedding"; teachers inform students, "You *must* turn in your papers by Friday." Countless times each day, people speak as if the world will end if they do not do one thing or another.

The purpose of this exercise is to make you aware of your own musturbation and to give you practice in the REBT technique of disputing irrational thoughts and substituting rational thoughts for them. Divide a lined sheet of paper into three equal columns, labeling the first column *Musturbatory Thoughts*, the second column *Rational Rebuttals*, and the third column *Rational Thoughts*.

Over the course of the next few days, write down examples of your use of the words *must, should, have to*, and *ought to* in your speech and thoughts. Record them in the first column of the work sheet you have prepared, skipping several lines between each. Because we generally are oblivious to our musturbatory thoughts, ask friends to point out your use of *must-type* words.

When you have 10 musturbatory statements, write a brief rebuttal of each in the second column of your work sheet. The rebuttal should explain why the statement is irrational. Finally, write a rational statement in the third column as an alternative to the irrational, musturbatory statement. The rational statement should reflect your taking responsibility for directing your actions. It should state what you *want* or *choose* to do rather than what you believe you must do. Part of a student's record sheet is shown in Figure 12-1 to give you examples of possible rebuttals and rational thoughts.

Musturbatory Thoughts	Rational Rebuttals	Rational Thoughts
I can't go to class because I have to study for next period.	I could go to class if I chose to. I just feel it's important to be well prepared for the exam.	I would rather miss class than risk not being prepared.
I must clean up my room before my parents visit this weekend.	My parents are going to be upset with a messy room, but they won't disown me if my room is a mess.	I'd like to get my room neat before my parents get here.
I have to get home in time to see my favorite TV program.	I sure do enjoy my favorite TV show, but my life won't end if I miss an episode.	I hope I can get home in time for my favorite TV show.

FIGURE 12-1

Excerpts from a student's record sheet used in Participation Exercise 12-3

Although irrational beliefs play an important role in maintaining psychological disorders, they are not the only maintaining conditions. Psychological disorders also are influenced by a complex interaction of biological, developmental, and environmental factors.[43] By changing clients' irrational beliefs, cognitive restructuring therapies modify an important—albeit not the only—class of maintaining conditions.

Process of Rational Emotive Behavior Therapy

The aim of REBT is to modify irrational beliefs, which is accomplished through three major procedures: (1) identifying thoughts based on irrational beliefs, (2) challenging the irrational beliefs, and (3) replacing thoughts based on irrational beliefs with thoughts based on rational beliefs.

First, to identify thoughts based on irrational beliefs, clients are asked about the specific self-statements they make when they feel upset (for example, depressed) or when they are engaging in maladaptive behaviors. As with other cognitive restructuring therapies, clients may have to learn to attend to their self-talk, such as by writing down their self-talk whenever their problems occur.

Once the client's self-talk associated with the problem has been identified, the therapist teaches the client to challenge irrational statements by stating why they are irrational.[44] For example:

Client: I feel awful because May wouldn't go out with me. I don't seem to attract women that I am attracted to.

Therapist: That doesn't make any sense. You are blowing up the situation, overgeneralizing. I'm sure you don't feel great being turned down, but it's not the end of the world. And, it certainly does not follow that just because May isn't interested in going out with you that you are not attractive to other women you like.

Active disputing of irrational beliefs is the key element that distinguishes REBT from other cognitive restructuring therapies.[45] As much as 90% of the therapy session may involve the therapist's challenging the rationality of the client's thoughts and debunking the client's myths about how the world "should be."[46]

Finally, the client learns to substitute rational thoughts for irrational thoughts. In the previous example, the therapist might suggest that the client tell himself, "I'm disappointed that May wouldn't go out with me, but she's not the last woman in the world." Table 12-3 presents an example of the changes in clients' thinking and emotional reactions that are expected over the course of REBT.

Case 12-2 presents part of an initial REBT session and illustrates many of the principles and procedures employed in REBT.

TABLE **12-3**

Example of the Changes in Client's Thinking and Emotional Reactions That Are Expected Over the Course of REBT

	Situation	Client's Self-Talk About Situation	Client's Emotional Reaction
BEFORE THERAPY	Failed course	(Unaware of or not focusing on self-talk)	Angry, depressed
DURING THERAPY	Failed course	1. "This is horrible." 2. "My parents will hit the roof." 3. "I am just plain stupid."	Angry, depressed
AFTER THERAPY	Failed course	1. "This sure won't help my average." 2. "My parents aren't going to be pleased, but they'll get over it." 3. "It's not the end of the world; I can make up the course."	Upset, disappointed

CASE **12-2**

Treatment of Depression by Rational Emotive Behavior Therapy[47]

The client was a college student in his second semester at a highly competitive university. He had not found high school particularly challenging, and he had earned high grades with little effort. He described himself as apathetic and depressed. The dialogue that follows is an excerpt from the first REBT session. It is annotated with comments about the process and procedures.

Therapist:	How long have you had these feelings of depression?	
Client:	Ever since the beginning of this quarter, I think.	
Therapist:	Can you tell me what is bothering you?	
Client:	Everything is ... I don't know ... a bunch of shit. I don't seem to care about anything anymore. I don't even care about school anymore, and that used to mean a lot to me.	
Therapist:	How are you doing in school, grade-wise?	*Therapist (T) asks about a possible activating event.*
Client:	Lousy. This quarter I've studied a total of two hours.	
Therapist:	Let's see. Fall quarter was your first at Stanford? How were your grades then?	
Client:	Shitty; had a 2.3 average. C average. And I worked hard, too. I feel like shoving the whole thing.	
Therapist:	Maybe this is part of what is getting you down.... What does that make you, in your eyes?	*T inquires about interpretations of external events.*
Client:	I'm a failure.... I'll never get accepted to a decent medical school with grades like that. I'll probably end up pumping gas in Salinas ... that's all I'm good for. I feel worthless.	*Client (C) draws an illogical conclusion, evoking the theme of personal worthlessness.*
Therapist:	Sounds like you've been saying to yourself, "I'm a failure ... I'm worthless" on account of your C average last quarter. That would be enough to depress anybody.	*T introduces idea of self-talk.*
Client:	It's true. I've got to do well and I'm not.	*Sense of duty and absolute thinking.*
Therapist:	So, you believe that in order for you to consider yourself a worthwhile person, you've got to succeed at something ... like making A's at Stanford?	*T makes C's irrational belief explicit.*

(continued)

CASE **12-2** (*continued*)

Client:	A person's got to be good at something to be worth a damn. School was the only thing I was ever much good at in the first place.	*C confirms the irrational belief.*
Therapist:	I'd like to point out that you're competing against some of the best students in the country, and they don't care very much about grading on a curve there. An average performance among outstanding people isn't really average, after all, is it?	*T introduces rational ideas to counter C's irrational ideas.*
Client:	I know what you are getting at, but that doesn't help too much. Any decent medical school requires at least a *B+* average, and I've got to get into medical school. That's been my goal ever since I was a kid.	*More sense of duty.*
Therapist:	Now, wait a minute! You say you *have* to go to medical school. Sounds like you think not going to medical school is against the law. Is that so?	
Client:	Well, not exactly. You know what I mean.	
Therapist:	I'm not sure. Do you really mean that you want very much to go to medical school? Because that is very different from believing that you *must* go to medical school. If you think you have to go to medical school, you are going to treat it like it's a life-or-death thing, which it isn't. But you believe that it is, and that is likely to be a major reason why you're depressed.	*T challenges the irrationality of C's "have to" and suggests the rational alternative "want to."* *T explains that irrational beliefs maintain depression.*
Client:	I can see your point, but even if I agreed with you, there's my family.... All my life my parents have been telling me that the whole family is counting on my being a doctor.	*A possible origin of C's irrational beliefs is revealed.*
Therapist:	OK, but that is their belief. Does it have to be yours?	*T disputes C's illogical assumption.*
Client:	I just can't let them down.	
Therapist:	What would happen if you did?	
Client:	They'd be hurt and disappointed. Sometimes I almost think they wouldn't like me any more. That would be awful!	*Catastrophizing.*
Therapist:	Well, the worst possible thing that could happen if you don't go to medical school is that your father and mother wouldn't like you, and might even reject you. You aren't	

even sure this would happen But, even if they did, does it follow that it would be awful? Could you prove that, logically, I mean?

T points out the lack of evidence.

T models logical analysis of thoughts and beliefs.

Client: It's lousy when your own family rejects you.

Therapist: I still can't see the logical connection between their rejecting you and things being awful or even lousy. I would agree that it wouldn't exactly be a pleasant state of affairs. You are equating rejection with catastrophe, and I'd like you to try and convince me one follows from the other.

T continues to challenge C's illogical thoughts.

Client: They wouldn't even want me around... like I was a worthless shit. And that would be rotten.

Therapist: Well, there you go again, telling yourself that because they would reject you, which means they wouldn't want you around, you are a worthless shit. Again, I don't see the logic.

Client: It would make me feel that way.

Therapist: No, I emphatically disagree...it's *you* who would make you feel that way. By saying those same things to yourself.

T directly confronts C's idea and introduces the basic premise of REBT.

Client: But I believe it's true.

Therapist: I'm still waiting for some logical basis for your belief that rejection means you are worthless, or not going to medical school means you're a shit.

Client: OK, I agree about the medical school bit. I don't *have* to go. But about my parents...that's heavy....I was thinking...where would I go over the holidays? But I don't spend that much time at home anyway, come to think of it. But, there is money...this place is damned expensive and I don't have a scholarship. If they cut off funds, that would be a disaster.

C begins to think rationally.

Therapist: There you go again...catastrophizing. Prove to me that it would be a disaster.

Client: Well, maybe I was exaggerating a bit. It would be tough, though I suppose I could apply for support, or get a job maybe. In fact, I know I could. But then it would take

(continued)

CASE **12-2** (*continued*)

> longer to get through school, and that would be shitty.
>
> *Therapist:* Now you are beginning to make a lot of sense. I agree that it would be shitty . . . but certainly not terrible.
>
> *Client:* You know, for the first time in weeks I think I feel a little better. Kind of like there is a load off my mind. Is that possible?
>
> *Therapist:* I don't see why not, but I'm wondering what would happen if you'd start feeling depressed tonight or tomorrow . . . how would you deal with it?
>
> At this point, the therapist suggested that the client rehearse identifying and challenging his irrational ideas and then do this at home.

Many of the characteristics of REBT are contained in the therapist–client dialogue in Case 12-2. The therapist actively challenges the client's irrational thoughts and models this process for the client so he can do it himself. The therapist's style is confrontational, almost argumentative. The client's task is to learn to identify and dispute irrational thoughts and beliefs and then to substitute rational thoughts for them. The client first rehearses these skills in the therapy sessions and then is asked to use them at home. Besides practicing identifying and disputing irrational beliefs, clients in REBT engage in a variety of homework assignments, including engaging in behavior rehearsal of skills learned in therapy sessions (such as appropriate assertive behaviors), keeping mood diaries, and reading material related to REBT principles.[48]

Rational Emotive Education

Rational emotive behavior therapy is used primarily with adults, who are more practiced at reasoning verbally. The basic format of disputing irrational beliefs is not as well suited for children, especially young children.[49] A few cases using standard REBT with children have been reported, but its effectiveness has not been evaluated.[50]

Rational emotive education is an adaptation of REBT for children and adolescents.[51] The curriculum includes (1) identifying emotions and differentiating them from thoughts; (2) learning how thoughts, rather than situations, influence emotions; (3) recognizing rational and irrational thoughts; and (4) dealing with common difficult situations (such as being teased) by using these concepts and skills. Children learn experientially, as through the Expression Guessing Game, which involves trying to guess the emotions pantomimed by other children. By playing the game, children discover for themselves that the most reliable way to know what other people are feeling is to ask them. Such user-friendly formats for children are increasingly being used in cognitive-behavioral approaches.[52]

Compared to the research literature on REBT, only a relatively small number of studies have evaluated rational emotive education. A recent meta-analysis of 26 studies indicates that rational emotive education reduces irrational beliefs and dysfunctional behaviors and has a moderate effect on decreasing negative emotions.[53] However, a number of these studies are based solely on self-report measures, which limits the strength of the evidence.[54] Potentially, rational emotive education could prevent psychological disorders;[55] however, longitudinal studies have not been carried out to evaluate this possibility.[56]

I Think, Therefore I Feel: Making the Connection[c]

Identifying the cognitions that are associated with our emotions and recognizing how our thoughts may influence the way we feel are essential goals of REBT and rational emotive education. This exercise can help you become more aware of how your thoughts influence your emotions.

Over the next few days, whenever you experience a strong emotion (positive or negative), be aware of what you are thinking at the moment—in other words, what you are saying to yourself. Immediately write the emotion and the associated cognitions on an index card or sheet of paper you carry with you. Divide the card into two columns: the first column for the *emotion* you are experiencing and the second for your *cognitions* at the time.

After you have collected a sample of different emotions and associated cognitions, consider the following questions: (1) What did you learn from this exercise? (2) Did you find yourself becoming more aware of your self-talk? (3) What were the basic differences between your cognitions associated with positive emotions and your cognitions associated with negative emotions? (4) Did your emotions seem to come from your thoughts or vice versa? Your answers to these questions can give you some insight into the basic assumptions and practices of REBT and cognitive restructuring therapies in general.

[c]You will need to complete this Participation Exercise later.

Rational Emotive Behavior Therapy in Perspective

Rational emotive behavior therapy is popular among therapists and clients for a number of reasons. Its focus on rationality makes sense! Ellis' theory of the development and maintenance of psychological problems is easy to understand. Further, the "direct, persuasive, and authoritative approach ... conforms to culturally sanctioned doctor–patient roles."[57] The notoriety of REBT has been enhanced by self-help books based on the REBT approach, many of which have been written by Albert Ellis.[58] Ellis, who died in 2007, was an outspoken advocate of REBT, and he drew attention to REBT because of his colorful personality,[59] which has been described as inspired and charismatic.[60]

Potentially, REBT could be used to treat any problem maintained by irrational beliefs.[61] Problems that have been treated include stress, generalized anxiety, agoraphobia and other phobias, unassertive behaviors, obsessions, anger, depression, antisocial behaviors, headaches, stuttering, sexual dysfunctions, obesity, Type A behaviors, and chronic fatigue syndrome.[62]

REBT has been applied to culturally diverse client populations. Self-defeating beliefs about mathematical ability in African-American high school students have been changed by REBT.[63] Components of REBT have been successfully employed in the treatment of Puerto Rican adolescents with depression.[64] REBT has been used with elderly clients who may become vulnerable to irrational thoughts and beliefs related to aging[65] (such as, "I must do as well as I did when I was younger or else I'm inadequate," "Other people must treat me kindly and fairly because of my age," and "I should have the good health I used to have and not be ill and disabled"). Although variations of REBT have been devised for children and adolescents,[66] REBT is more suitable for adults.

For clients with strong religious beliefs, REBT can capitalize on those convictions to challenge clients' irrational beliefs and reinforce the use of adaptive thoughts.[67] For example, using a Christian approach, clients are asked to examine what the Bible has to say about their beliefs.[68] One woman who believed that anger is always wrong or sinful was able to cognitively restructure this thought by considering that in the Bible, both God and Jesus were angry and their behavior was not sinful.

The reliance on direct confrontation of clients' beliefs, a hallmark of REBT, has some limitations. For example, direct confrontation may not work with clients with certain disorders, such as substance dependence, paraphilias, panic disorder, anorexia and bulimia, and obsessive-compulsive disorder.[69] REBT also may be inappropriate for clients from cultures that eschew direct confrontation (such as Native American and Japanese). There is even some evidence that confrontation in therapy generally is associated with clients' noncompliance with treatment procedures.[70]

Despite proponents' enthusiastic claims for the clinical effectiveness of REBT, its empirical support is only modest.[71] For example, although REBT for alcohol abuse results in changes in irrational thinking, there are limited changes in drinking.[72] Many of the studies that have evaluated the effectiveness of REBT were poorly designed, so their findings are inconclusive.[73] One major methodological weakness has been a failure to operationally define REBT.[74] Thus, it is unclear which specific therapy procedures were used in different studies. In general, REBT has been found to be superior to no-treatment and wait-list control groups,[75] but often REBT is only equivalent to or less effective than other behavior therapies (such as exposure therapies and progressive relaxation). Finally, few long-term follow-up studies have been conducted.

No systematic process research has been carried out to identify the essential components of REBT, which leaves important questions unanswered.[76] For example, is direct confrontation of the client's irrational beliefs a necessary component? Would the therapy work as well with a gentler exploration of the client's irrational beliefs?[77] These are crucial questions to answer because some clients and therapists feel uncomfortable with REBT's "tough-minded," confrontational approach.[78]

COGNITIVE THERAPY

Courtesy of the University of Pennsylvania Medical Center

Aaron Beck

Cognitive therapy is a cognitive restructuring therapy that emphasizes empirically testing the validity of maladaptive beliefs. Aaron Beck[79] conceived of cognitive therapy in the early 1960s, at the same time Ellis was developing REBT. Apparently, Beck and Ellis created their theories and therapy techniques independently.[80] Both therapies rest on the fundamental assumption that psychological disorders are maintained by distorted cognitions, and they share the goal of modifying these cognitions. Both involve challenging distorted, irrational beliefs, but the strategies they use to do this differ. Cognitive therapy has the client view beliefs as tentative hypotheses; the client then tests the validity of these hypotheses by gathering evidence that refutes (or supports) them.[81] In contrast, REBT primarily relies on direct instruction, persuasion, and logical disputation to challenge distorted beliefs. Another difference is that cognitive therapy is more empirically based, whereas REBT tends to be more philosophically based.[82] Table 12-4 summarizes the major differences between REBT and cognitive therapy.

Cognitive therapy evolved from Beck's research on the distorted thinking of clients suffering from depression,[83] and treating depression has been its primary focus. More recently, the scope of cognitive therapy has been widened to include anxiety disorders,[84] including panic attacks[85] and panic disorder,[86] phobias,[87] and obsessive-compulsive disorder;[88] personality disorders;[89]

TABLE **12-4**
Major Differences Between REBT and Cognitive Therapy

	Rational Emotive Behavior Therapy	Cognitive Therapy
BASIS OF APPROACH	Rationality	Empirical evidence
PROCEDURE	Instruction, persuasion, disputation	Empirical hypothesis testing
MECHANISM	Primarily cognitive restructuring	Combination of cognitive restructuring and overt behavioral interventions
ROLE OF THERAPIST	Model of rational thinking (recognizing and disputing irrational beliefs)	Coinvestigator seeking empirical test of client's beliefs
STYLE OF THERAPIST	Confrontational	Collaborative
ROLE OF HOMEWORK	Practice disputing irrational beliefs and cognitive restructuring	Gather evidence to establish validity of beliefs

marital distress;[90] anger;[91] suicidal behaviors;[92] anorexia;[93] bulimia;[94] obesity;[95] and schizophrenia.[96]

Cognitive Therapy Theory of Psychological Disorders

Beck's theory of the development and maintenance of psychological disorders shares the same fundamental premises as Ellis' theory. Differences emerge in the specific concepts each theory employs. To begin with, Beck refers to maladaptive (irrational) cognitions as **automatic thoughts**, a term that emphasizes how clients experience their distorted thinking.[97] Clients report that their distorted thoughts arise "reflexively," without prior reflection or reasoning. Automatic thoughts seem totally plausible and valid to the client, which may help explain their powerful influence on emotions and actions. According to Beck's theory, psychological disorders occur when people perceive the world as threatening.

> When this happens, there is a functional impairment in normal cognitive processing: Perceptions and interpretations of events become highly selective, egocentric, and rigid. The person has a decreased ability to "turn off" distorted thinking . . . to concentrate, recall, or reason. Corrective functions, which allow reality testing and refinement of global conceptualizations, are weakened.[98]

Thus, the person makes systematic errors in reasoning. For example, children who are anxious tend to misinterpret benign situations as hostile;[99] adults with panic disorder make catastrophic interpretations of their physical sensations (such as increased heart rate meaning a heart attack);[100] and people who are depressed tend to automatically view themselves, the world (including other people), and the future negatively (Beck's *cognitive triad*).[101] Beck has identified six common *cognitive distortions* or logical errors that frequently are found in the thoughts of people experiencing psychological distress; these cognitive distortions are described in Table 12-5. Not surprisingly, there is some overlap with the common forms of irrationality Ellis identified. Note that

TABLE **12-5**
Cognitive Distortions Associated with Psychological Distress

Cognitive Distortion	Definition	Example
ARBITRARY INFERENCE	Drawing conclusions without sufficient evidence, or when the evidence is actually contradictory	Believing that you have been laid off from a job because of personal incompetence, although the company has gone out of business
OVERGENERALIZATION	Drawing a general conclusion on the basis of a single incident	Concluding that you will never succeed after failing on the first attempt
SELECTIVE ABSTRACTION	Attending to a detail while ignoring the total context	Feeling rejected because a friend who was rushing to catch a bus did not stop to talk
PERSONALIZATION	Erroneously attributing an external event to yourself	Thinking that people who are laughing are laughing at you

(continued)

TABLE 12-5 *(continued)*

Cognitive Distortion	Definition	Example
POLARIZED (DICHOTO-MOUS) THINKING	Thinking in extremes, in a black-or-white or all-or-none fashion	Believing that you are a pauper after having lost your wallet
MAGNIFICATION OR MINIMIZATION	Viewing something as far more or less important than it is	Thinking that you are a poor writer after getting back a paper with several corrections or thinking that you are a great writer after getting back a paper with dozens of corrections

Source: Beck and Weishaar, 1989.

overlap also exists among the different types of cognitive distortions, so that distorted thoughts may consist of more than one type of cognitive distortion.

Process of Cognitive Therapy

The goals of cognitive therapy are to (1) correct clients' faulty information processing, (2) modify clients' dysfunctional beliefs that maintain maladaptive behaviors and emotions, and (3) provide clients with the skills and experiences that create adaptive thinking.[102] The therapist and client collaborate to identify the client's dysfunctional beliefs and challenge their validity. Cognitive therapy requires clients' active participation, including homework assignments that are considered an integral part of the treatment. Compliance with and the quality of homework assignments have been found to be positively correlated with the effectiveness of cognitive therapy.[103]

Because collaboration between the client and therapist is a key element in cognitive therapy, establishing a good therapeutic relationship is considered a prerequisite for effective treatment.[104] Toward this end, cognitive therapists focus on clients' ways of viewing the world in general as well as understanding their cognitive distortions.[105]

Cognitive therapists help clients recognize dysfunctional beliefs through *Socratic dialogue* (also called *guided discovery*). They ask clients a series of easily answerable questions that lead clients to recognize dysfunctional beliefs and automatic thoughts for themselves—rather than directly pointing out such beliefs to clients, as is done in REBT. This process is illustrated in the following excerpt from a cognitive therapy session with a college senior who was seriously abusing alcohol.[106]

Therapist: How are you going to deal with all the drinking that will occur at the party you and your roommates are throwing this weekend?

Client: There's no way I am going to not drink! I'll just have to deal with it afterwards.

Therapist: You're very adamant about that. What bothers you about not drinking at the party?

Client: I wouldn't be fun if I didn't drink.

Therapist:	So, if you weren't fun, what would be so bad about that?
Client:	People would ignore me.
Therapist:	If they ignored you, what would that mean?
Client:	They didn't like me?
Therapist:	So suppose people ignored you and that meant they didn't like you. What would be the consequences for you?
Client:	Well, I guess word would get out on campus, and I'd be a social outcast. I'd have no friends; no one to hang out with; no girl would want to date me.
Therapist:	And all of that would happen just because you weren't drinking at your own party?
Client:	Well, I guess that's a bit of an exaggeration.
Therapist:	It sure is. I think it is important for you to realize that one irrational belief builds on another and leads you to assume that the worst will happen—just because in this one instance you didn't drink.
Client:	I didn't realize that was what I was doing. Without analyzing it, it did seem catastrophic; but maybe it's not.

The therapist asks the client to view automatic thoughts as *hypotheses* that are subject to empirical verification rather than as "the way things are" (established facts). Then, the therapist and client design homework "experiments" to test these hypotheses, a process Beck calls **collaborative empiricism**.[107] For instance, a woman believed that a co-worker she found attractive disliked her because he did not talk to her. The therapist suggested that the woman check out the validity of this *hypothesis* by observing how frequently the man interacted with other women in the office. Much to her surprise, she found that the man rarely spoke to any of the women. Thus, her dysfunctional belief, which was based on arbitrary inference and personalization, was refuted with empirical evidence.

Notice that both cognitive therapy and REBT attempt to change faulty thinking, but they employ different strategies. Cognitive therapy uses *empirical* disputation based on observations of actual events to challenge faulty thinking. In contrast, REBT uses *rational* disputation, focusing directly on the illogical nature of the beliefs.

Once clients in cognitive therapy learn to challenge the validity of their dysfunctional beliefs, they are taught to replace them with adaptive beliefs. The woman in our previous example came to see the man she was attracted to as "uninterested in women in general." This view not only was more accurate but also was more adaptive because it allowed her to feel better about herself.

Sometimes testing the validity of a dysfunctional belief reveals that the belief is valid—that it is consistent with what actually is occurring. This would have been the case if the woman had discovered that the man was interacting with other women in the office, excluding only her. In such instances, the therapist helps the client view the situation in a way that fits the data but does not lead to maladaptive reactions. For example, the woman might have changed her thoughts to, "The man doesn't know what he is missing by not paying attention to me. It's his loss, not mine."

The specific techniques used in cognitive therapy to change clients' dysfunctional thinking fall into two categories: cognitive interventions and overt behavioral interventions.

Cognitive Interventions

Cognitive interventions, which are based on cognitive restructuring, change clients' cognitions directly. For example, to dispel unrealistic fear, the therapist and the client would *analyze faulty logic* the client is using, and the therapist might *provide relevant information* about what makes the fear unrealistic (for instance, people rarely are injured riding elevators).

Clients are asked to keep records of their automatic thoughts during the course of the day, including such information as the situation in which the thought occurs, their emotions at the time, the logical errors they are making, and rational responses to the situation.[108] Figure 12-2 shows an example of such a record, sometimes called a *three-column technique*.

Generating alternative interpretations is a crucial aspect of cognitive restructuring. For example, a student who is anxious about being one of the last to finish exams could counter the thought, "I must be stupid," with more adaptive thoughts, such as, "I knew the material well and had a lot to say," and "Writing good answers takes time." The therapist first models generating alternative interpretations of anxiety-evoking events, and then the client rehearses this skill.

Reattribution of responsibility is helpful when clients believe they have more control over potentially negative outcomes than they actually do. A

Situations	Automatic Thoughts	Logical Errors
Wearing new outfit for first time	People are going to laugh at me.	No evidence
Giving an oral report in class	I froze last time, and I'll freeze again.	Overgeneralization
	I'll die if I don't do well.	Magnification
Family moved away	They just don't want to be around me anymore.	Personalization
Rejected by date	My life is ruined.	Magnification
Getting a B on a paper	I just have no grasp of the material in this course.	Polarized thinking

FIGURE **12-2**

Example of a client's use of a three-column technique

young man who was highly anxious about an upcoming date feared that the woman would not have a good time. Through Socratic dialogue, the therapist helped the man accept that he could plan the evening and enjoy it himself, but he had no control over the woman's feelings.

Decatastrophizing is a specific form of reattribution that is useful when clients anticipate dire consequences, which is common in anxiety disorders. Through Socratic dialogue, the therapist guides the client to see the absurdity of highly unlikely consequences and to entertain more probable, noncatastrophic outcomes. For example, a headache is much more likely to be caused by fatigue, hunger, or stress than by a brain tumor.

PARTICIPATION EXERCISE 12-5

Turning Your Thinking Upside Down: Cognitive Restructuring[d]

You can use cognitive restructuring to cope with difficult or stressful situations in your daily life. In this exercise you will read brief descriptions of everyday situations followed by examples of negative self-statements someone faced with the situations might make. These self-statements are maladaptive because they present the consequences of the situation as so terrible that nothing can be done to cope with them. In fact, the situation may be unfortunate, but it is not necessarily disastrous.

Your task is to think of alternative self-statements that are positive, optimistic, and adaptive. The self-statements must also be realistic. For example, if your new car is stolen, it would be unrealistic to think, "I didn't need the car," because that is not likely to be true. For each situation and negative self-statement, write two possible alternative self-statements that are positive, optimistic, adaptive, and realistic. Then, compare your self-statements with the examples given in your Student Resource Manual.

Situation	Negative Self-Statement
1. Having to hand in a long, difficult assignment the next day	1. "There is just no way I can get this work done for tomorrow."
2. Getting into an automobile accident	2. "Oh no, my father will kill me."
3. Being asked to dance but not being a skillful dancer	3. "I can't dance; I'll make a fool of myself."
4. Losing your job	4. "I'll never get another job."
5. Moving to a new home, away from family and friends	5. "Everything I care about is left behind."
6. Having a roommate with whom you don't get along	6. "We'll never get along. What a horrible year this is going to be!"
7. Breaking up with the person you are in love with	7. "She (or he) was everything to me . . . my whole life. I have nothing else to live for."

---

[d]This Participation Exercise can be completed before you continue reading or later.

Overt Behavioral Interventions

Besides changing clients' cognitions directly, cognitive therapy changes clients' overt behaviors, which indirectly modifies their cognitions and emotions. In general, the more severe the client's disorder and cognitive distortions, the more reliance is put on overt behavioral interventions, at least at the beginning of therapy. For example, clients with severe depression generally have difficulty engaging in Socratic dialogue and generating alternative interpretations. From their perspective, "Everything is hopeless, so what's the use?" Further, their reasoning abilities may be too impaired to benefit from direct cognitive interventions. Thus, changing their overt behaviors may be the better strategy.[109]

Three particular overt behavioral interventions commonly are used in cognitive therapy: activity schedules, mastery and pleasure ratings, and graded task assignments.

Activity Schedules

An **activity schedule** is a written plan of a client's daily activities and is particularly useful for clients who are anxious or depressed. The client and therapist schedule activities for most hours of each day (see Figure 12-3). The activity schedule provides clients who are anxious with a sense of direction and control. It counteracts feelings of disorganization and being overwhelmed and serves to distract clients from anxiety-evoking thoughts. Clients who are depressed often are inactive and have difficulty doing even the simplest tasks. An activity schedule provides a structure that encourages clients to engage in active behaviors throughout the day.

Mastery and Pleasure Ratings

Clients suffering from depression and anxiety not only need to be active, but they also need to feel competent at and pleasure from what they are doing. The **mastery and pleasure rating** technique provides clients with feedback about the sense of accomplishment and pleasure they actually are experiencing. *Mastery* refers to a sense of accomplishment (though not perfection), and *pleasure* refers to feelings of enjoyment or satisfaction while performing a task. Clients rate each activity on their activity schedule for mastery and for pleasure using a 0 to 5 rating scale (with 0 representing no mastery/pleasure and 5 representing maximum mastery/pleasure).[110] Using a rating scale encourages clients to recognize *partial* accomplishments and *small* pleasures. Mastery and pleasure rating is especially useful for depression because it penetrates clients' "'blindness' ... to situations in which they are successful and their readiness to forget situations that do bring them some satisfaction."[111] The same clients who make statements such as, "I can't do anything right" and "Nothing is enjoyable," may rate specific activities with scale scores higher than zero. These partial successes and small pleasures can be used as empirical evidence to refute clients' beliefs that they can't accomplish anything and that nothing they do is at all enjoyable.

	Monday	Tuesday	Wednesday
8–9	Get out of bed, get dressed	Get out of bed, get dressed	Get out of bed, get dressed
9–10	Clean bathrooms	Do grocery shopping	Vacuum house
10–11	Go to museum	↓	Go to library
11–12	Exercise	Exercise	Exercise or take walk
12–1	Lunch	Lunch with friend	Lunch
1–2	Do therapy homework	↓	Clean bedrooms
2–3	Do laundry	Clean living room	Pay bills
3–4	Housework	Visit with mother	Attend therapy
4–5	Read newspaper	Read newspaper	Read newspaper
5–6	Fix dinner	Go out to dinner	Fix dinner
6–7	Eat dinner with family	Do therapy homework	Eat dinner with family
7–8	Clean kitchen	Take walk	
8–9	Watch TV, read novel	Work on computer	Watch TV, read novel
9–11	↓	Read novel	↓

FIGURE 12-3

Portion of an activity schedule for a 45-year-old man suffering from depression

Graded Task Assignments

A **graded task assignment** is a small sequential step that leads to a thera-peutic goal. The therapist encourages the client to perform a series of graded task assignments and thereby shapes the therapeutic goal. Case 12-3 illus-trates the impact that graded task assignments can have on a client who is de-pressed and whose activity level is minimal.

CASE **12-3**

Using Graded Task Assignments to Accelerate Walking in a Japanese-American Man with Somatic Complaints[112]

Makoto S. was a 42-year-old Japanese-American man who had been admitted to a hospital with multiple physical complaints. His attending physician had found no physical basis for his complaints. Somatic complaints often are key symptoms of depression in Japanese clients, which made depression the most likely diagnosis.

Because nonverbal communication is valued in Japanese culture, the therapist primarily used overt behavioral interventions. A series of graded task assignments were employed to get Makoto to walk. He claimed that he could not walk, and he was taken to his therapy sessions in a wheelchair. The therapist introduced the initial graded task assignment as follows.

Therapist: Why is it that you think you can't walk?

Client: I don't have the strength.

Therapist: What would happen if you tried?

Client: I'd fall.

Therapist: Are you sure of that?

Client: Yes.

Therapist: Well, you could be right. But you also might be mistaken. How about our testing that out?

Client: I know I can't walk.

Therapist: You may be right. People who are depressed often think that way, but they usually find that when they try to walk, they can. Do you think you could take just a few steps to the sofa?

Client: Suppose I fall.

Therapist: I'll walk with you and hold on to you.

At this point the therapist took Makoto's arm, and Makoto was able to walk to the sofa. The therapist pointed out that Makoto had done better than he had thought he could and suggested that Makoto try to walk to the office door. With much skepticism, Makoto attempted this and succeeded. Over the course of the next three therapy sessions, increasingly longer walks were achieved, which provided evidence to refute Makoto's automatic thought that he could not walk. As this occurred, Makoto's mood became more positive for a short time, which typically occurs with clients who are depressed.[113] This provided the motivation for Makoto to attempt increasingly more active behaviors. The more active Makoto became, the harder it was for him to tell himself that he was unable to engage in normal, everyday activities and the more positive his mood became.

The graded task assignments helped the client become more active and provided him with immediate experiences of success. The assignments served as informal investigations to test his hypothesis that he could not walk. When the client's experiences provided evidence that his belief about himself was invalid, he was able to view himself differently. In turn, this new perspective allowed him to attempt new behaviors that were consistent with the belief that he was healthy and capable of functioning. As a consequence, his depression—manifested in his somatic complaints—declined.

Cognitive Therapy for Anxiety-Related Disorders

Anxiety-related disorders are the second most frequent problem that cognitive therapy is used to treat. Although exposure therapies often are considered the treatment of choice for obsessive-compulsive disorder, cognitive therapy can be used to challenge and replace obsessive thoughts related to the need to be perfect, exaggerated views of responsibility (for instance, "If anything goes wrong, it is my fault"), and magical ideas (for example, "It is dangerous to step on the cracks on the sidewalk").[114] Posttraumatic stress disorder is another anxiety-related disorder for which cognitive therapy is employed with such diverse traumatic precipitants as war[115] and sexual assault.[116] Victims of sexual assault often perceive the world as dangerous and themselves as incapable of coping with stress. Cognitive therapy is well suited to addressing victims' maladaptive automatic thoughts related to fear (for example, "That man is going to attack me"), guilt and shame (for example, "I could have stopped my attacker"), anger and rage (for example, "Why me?"), and sadness (for example, "I'll never be the same again"). Cognitive therapy has been shown to be as effective as imaginal exposure in treating posttraumatic stress disorder.[117] Combined with exposure therapies, cognitive therapy is an effective treatment for social phobia and can be as effective as medication which is often prescribed for social phobia.[118] In treating clients with generalized anxiety disorder, cognitive therapy has been found to be as effective as relaxation training.[119]

Irritable bowel syndrome is a stress-related disorder that results in abdominal pain and discomfort associated with altered bowel function, including constipation and diarrhea. It is not caused by a specific organic condition, and psychological events, such as stress and anxiety, can contribute significantly to the symptoms. The general goal of cognitive therapy is to help clients reconceptualize their bowel-related symptoms.[120] Clients are taught to shift their view that their symptoms are all-encompassing and constitute an uncontrollable medical condition to the belief that the symptoms are subject to their mood and are therefore controllable. Other applications of cognitive therapy in stress management have been with gay men who are HIV-infected[121] and with women in treatment for early-stage breast cancer.[122]

Cognitive Processing Therapy for Stress Disorders

Cognitive processing therapy, developed by Patricia Resick, is an adaptation of cognitive therapy for clients who have experienced trauma and are suffering from stress disorders.[123] The therapy includes exposure and cognitive components,

Patricia Resick

is typically structured in 12 sessions, and can be administered individually or in groups.[124] Clients first write a statement that describes the impact of the trauma on their lives—that is, what the trauma means to them—which helps the therapist and client identify maladaptive thoughts and feelings related to the trauma. Then, clients are exposed to the traumatic event by writing a detailed account of it that includes thoughts, feelings, and sensory details. They read this account to the therapist and then reread it to themselves at home on a daily basis. The remainder and majority of cognitive processing therapy consists of challenging clients' maladaptive thoughts and beliefs concerning the trauma using Socratic questioning and replacing them with more adaptive cognitions. Initially, the focus is on thoughts and beliefs concerning irrational self-blame and attempts to change aspects of the traumatic event after the fact (for example, "It was my fault" or "If I only had run away"). The last five sessions cover common problem areas for trauma victims: safety, trust, control, esteem, and intimacy. For instance, victims of trauma may overgeneralize and believe that they are no longer safe in any circumstances, that no one can be trusted, or that they have no control over what happens to them. Clients are taught to challenge and cognitively restructure single maladaptive thoughts at first and later they apply these skills to broad, pervasive maladaptive themes in their thinking.

Cognitive reprocessing therapy was initially used to treat adult victims of rape,[125] and it also has been used to treat adult female survivors of childhood sexual abuse,[126] female victims of interpersonal violence,[127] men and women with military-related posttraumatic stress disorder,[128] and incarcerated adolescents with posttraumatic stress disorder.[129] A cultural adaptation of the therapy has been effective for Bosnian war refugees.[130] Single cases of cognitive processing therapy have been reported for the treatment of posttraumatic stress disorder in a survivor of the World Trade Center bombing;[131] acute stress disorder in a 30-year-old gay man following a homophobic assault;[132] and a complex case of trauma involving a 41-year-old woman with a history of childhood sexual, physical, and psychological abuse and multiple rapes in adulthood.[133] Preliminary data indicate that cognitive processing therapy may be particularly effective for dealing with trauma-related guilt.[134]

Cognitive Therapy for Delusions and Hallucinations

Delusions and hallucinations are the hallmark of schizophrenia, and they are occasionally seen in other disorders. They are very disturbing to the person experiencing them (as well as to other people) and seriously impair the person's functioning. Until recently, they were treated almost exclusively with antipsychotic medication. Over the past two decades, cognitive therapy has been used to treat these serious symptoms.[135]

Delusions are blatantly false beliefs people steadfastly hold in the face of contradictory evidence (for example, a client's believing that she is Joan of Arc). Cognitive therapy for schizophrenic delusions involves the same basic steps used to treat depression and anxiety. First, cognitive distortions are identified; then, evidence for their validity is sought; and finally, adaptive cognitions are substituted for the distorted cognitions. A few special procedures and precautions are required, however, because of the nature and severity of schizophrenic delusions and the fragility of the clients. For example, the client–therapist relationship is especially important because clients must trust their therapist if they are to talk about delusions that are frightening, threatening, and bizarre.[136] The therapist avoids directly challenging the delusions because such confrontation often meets with negative reactions.[137] This is especially likely with *paranoid delusions*, which involve thoughts that people are following, plotting against, and wanting to harm the client.

To help identify specific delusional beliefs, the client maintains a daily log of his or her delusions. The log includes a measure of the client's *strength of conviction* that the delusion is true, rated on a 0–100 scale.

Treatment of delusions proceeds in a stepwise fashion.[138] Initially, the focus is on beliefs having the lowest conviction ratings. As the client begins to feel more comfortable in therapy, more strongly held delusions are addressed.[139] Clients are encouraged to consider alternative interpretations of events.[140] For instance, a 22-year-old man believed that a "haggly witch" followed him around wherever he went.[141] Considering alternative interpretations of his delusion (such as, "Maybe I just have a wild imagination") dramatically decreased the frequency and strength of his delusions as well as his need for medication to control his delusional thoughts.

The client and therapist collaborate to empirically evaluate the evidence on which the client bases the delusions.[142] For example, a client believed that to avoid being physically attacked, he had to get angry and shout back at the voices he "heard."[143] The client agreed to refrain from becoming angry and shouting back at the voices and just to observe whether he was attacked. When the client discovered that he was not attacked, he was greatly relieved and became much less concerned about his safety. Such empirical investigations are useful because they allow clients to draw their own conclusions about the validity of their delusions.[144]

Hallucinations, the other core symptom of schizophrenia, are sensory perceptions without an external source which people experience as real. Auditory hallucinations predominate and typically involve hearing nonexistent voices that are extremely disturbing, such as a man who hears a voice that commands him to do penance by cutting himself.

According to the prevailing theoretical explanation of auditory hallucinations,[145] they arise from the client's thoughts, which are obviously internal, but the client attributes them to an external source. Further, clients' beliefs about the source of the voices influence how distressing the voices are; for example, condemnation by God is more distressing than condemnation by a preacher. On the basis of these formulations, cognitive therapy for auditory hallucinations involves challenging the interpretations and content of hallucinatory voices.[146]

To challenge clients' interpretations of the source of their voices, clients are asked to generate alternative explanations for their voices and to rate their believability (0% to 100%). Next, the evidence for each alternative explanation is examined, which may include homework assignments involving collaborative empiricism. In addition to these steps, which parallel standard cognitive therapy procedures, special techniques applicable to schizophrenic hallucinations are included. Clients are educated about the nature of hallucinations, stressors that tend to trigger them, and the prevalence of hallucinatory experiences in the general population (which helps to make them more normative). Therapists also help clients examine the advantages (such as increased attention from hospital staff) as well as the disadvantages of hearing voices.

Clients frequently use what voices say as "evidence" to support the source of the voices (for example, "It must be the CIA who has been telling me what to do because only the CIA could know so much about me"). If disconfirmatory evidence for the content can be found, then the source may be discredited. Thus, it also is necessary to challenge the content of the hallucinations, which involves the same basic procedures employed in challenging the client's interpretations of them.

The basic cognitive therapy procedures just described are augmented by providing clients with a variety of coping strategies,[147] such as the following.

- *Awareness training* helps the client attend to the onset of a delusion or hallucination and allows the client to engage in active coping strategies.
- *Attention switching* changes the client's focus from a delusion or hallucination to an alternative response (such as a pleasant scene).
- *Attention narrowing* restricts the client's focus and thereby reduces the stimulus overload often experienced in schizophrenia.
- *Self-instructions* involve specific adaptive self-statements (such as, "I don't need to be afraid").
- *Activity scheduling* increases the client's activity level, which is important because clients are more likely to experience delusions and hallucinations during periods of inactivity.

Meta-analyses of studies examining the benefits of cognitive therapy for delusions and hallucinations in conjunction with antipsychotic medication indicate that cognitive therapy is an effective treatment.[148] In a 5-year follow-up, the benefits of cognitive therapy have persisted.[149] However, to date, no studies have tested whether cognitive therapy alone can be effective, which is not surprising because most clients with schizophrenia are treated with medication, and taking clients off of their medication poses ethical problems.[150] An additional benefit of cognitive therapy for clients with schizophrenia is that it has been shown to significantly reduce thoughts of suicide, which is important because there is a high risk of suicide in schizophrenia.[151]

Clients treated with cognitive therapy for their delusions and hallucinations consider it an acceptable treatment, both immediately and 3 months after therapy. The extent to which clients believe that they have acquired specific skills and knowledge predicts their overall satisfaction.[152]

Schema-Focused Cognitive Therapy

So far, we have described the application of cognitive therapy to changing clients' discrete cognitive distortions that are maintaining conditions of their

Jeffrey Young

psychological disorders. Schema-focused cognitive therapy, spearheaded by Jeffrey Young, has extended traditional cognitive therapy to address the needs of clients with longstanding psychological problems, such as personality disorders, which often are maintained by maladaptive schemas.[153] A **schema** is a broad and pervasive cognitive theme about oneself, others, or the world.[154] Schemas often stem from childhood experiences and are further developed throughout one's lifetime. For example, a girl who received little nurturing, empathy, or protection from her parents had, as an adult, an "emotional deprivation" schema.[155] It involved an exaggerated theme of not being cared for or understood by others—which remained even in light of contradictory evidence—and it pervaded the woman's view of the world.

In contrast to a discrete cognitive distortion, a schema serves as a template for processing a wide range of experiences, is self-perpetuating, and is far more irrefutable and rigid, which makes it extremely resistant to change.[156] Table 12-6 lists five broad-based schemas that have been tentatively identified as core cognitive structures of clients with chronic, treatment-resistant psychological problems.[157]

Although schemas are long-standing, they are triggered by present experiences. A client's "abandonment" schema that developed in childhood may be triggered when his wife goes out of town for a business meeting. Once activated, schemas generate significant psychological distress, including depression, anxiety, feelings of intense loneliness, interpersonal conflicts, and addictive behaviors.

The assessment phase of schema-focused cognitive therapy involves four steps: (1) schema identification, (2) schema activation, (3) schema

TABLE **12-6**

Broad-Based Schemas That Have Been Tentatively Identified as Core Cognitive Structures of Clients with Chronic Treatment-Resistant Psychological Problems

Schema	Description
ABANDONMENT/INSTABILITY	The perceived instability or unreliability of others for support and stable, trustworthy relationships
MISTRUST/ABUSE	The expectation that others will intentionally hurt, abuse, humiliate, cheat, or manipulate you
EMOTIONAL DEPRIVATION	The expectation that others will not adequately meet your desire for emotional support, including nurturance, empathy, and protection
DEFECTIVENESS/SHAME	The feeling that you are defective, inferior, bad, or unlovable, which results in hypersensitivity to criticism, rejection, and blame as well as self-consciousness about perceived flaws
SOCIAL ISOLATION/ ALIENATION	The feeling that you are isolated from the rest of the world, different from others, and unconnected to any group or community

Source: Young, 1994.

Situation	Mood Intensity (1–10)	Automatic thought	Underlying assumption	Schema
Was not invited to Julie's party	depressed (7)	There's something wrong with me. I'm abnormal.	If I were normal, I'd be popular.	Defectiveness/ Shame
	depressed (5)	No one likes me. I'm the class outcast.	She didn't invite me because she doesn't like me.	Social Isolation/ Alienation

FIGURE 12-4

Example of an entry on the Schema Identification Worksheet

conceptualization, and (4) schema education. Schemas are identified from information gathered in a variety of ways, including self-report inventories,[158] interviews, and clients' self-recorded observations at home, such as filling out the Schema Identification Worksheet (see Figure 12-4).[159] From the data obtained, the therapist indentifies the underlying themes around which the client's automatic thoughts are organized.[160]

Once a client's specific schemas have been identified, the therapist intentionally activates them through imagery or role-playing (which might involve a painful childhood experience associated with the schema). The purpose of schema activation is to determine those schemas that elicit strong emotional responses; such schemas are considered critical schemas for the client and are dealt with during the change phase of therapy.

Next, the therapist formulates a schema conceptualization for the client. This includes the specific schemas impacting the client's life experiences, the situational cues that activate the schemas, and the specific cognitions, emotions, and actions the client displays when the schemas are activated. Finally, the therapist explains the schema conceptualization to the client, and the therapist and client formulate a treatment plan.

Schema-focused cognitive therapy employs the same basic cognitive and overt behavioral change techniques used in traditional cognitive therapy, but they may be modified for dealing with schemas. For instance, *life review* is a cognitive exercise in which therapists ask clients to provide evidence from their lives that supports and contradicts their schemas. This helps clients see how their schemas distort their perceptions and begins a process of distancing themselves from their schemas, rather than identifying with them. A graded task assignment in which clients gradually perform new behaviors that contradict their schemas is an example of an overt behavioral technique used in schema-focused cognitive therapy.

Experiential and interpersonal change techniques also are part of schema-focused cognitive therapy. *Schema dialogue* is an experiential technique. Clients role-play both the "voice" of the schema and the "voice" of their own healthy responses to the schema, while moving back and forth between two chairs, confronting and refuting the schema. Experiential techniques may be the most effective interventions in schema-focused cognitive therapy.[161]

Interpersonal change techniques are used because clients treated with schema-focused cognitive therapy often have core interpersonal problems, including difficulty establishing a relationship with the therapist. With *limited reparenting*, for example, the therapist provides a therapeutic relationship that counteracts maladaptive schemas. In the case of a client with a "rejection" schema who experienced extreme criticism as a child, the therapist would be as accepting as possible and praise the client frequently.[162]

Schema-focused cognitive therapy differs from traditional cognitive therapy in four important respects: (1) a greater use of the client–therapist relationship as a change vehicle, (2) the exploration of the earliest expression (often in childhood) of a schema to understand the nature of its current expression, (3) a greater emphasis on emotions and the use of experiential change strategies, and (4) a longer course of treatment. Schema-focused cognitive therapy has been shown to be effective in treating personality disorders, substance dependence, clients with histories of childhood abuse, eating disorders, and chronic pain, as well as in preventing relapse in depression and anxiety disorders.[163] However, conclusions about the relative effectiveness of schema-focused versus traditional cognitive therapy await controlled, clinical outcome studies.

Adaptations of Cognitive Therapy to Diverse Populations

Cognitive therapy primarily has been used with adults who are not hospitalized. However, increasingly, it is being adapted to other populations, including hospitalized clients[164] and elderly clients.[165] Adaptations of cognitive therapy for children have been particularly innovative.[166] For example, the Adolescent Coping with Depression program[167] uses popular cartoon strip characters (such as "Garfield") to illustrate how negative thoughts contribute to depression and how positive thoughts can improve mood. This therapy program has been modified to be relevant for African-American adolescents.[168] As another example, cognitive therapy has been adapted for Turkish children with test anxiety.[169]

Cognitive therapy, like all behavior therapies, is most effective when it is tailored to the particular characteristics of the client.[170] For example, a creative adaptation of cognitive therapy for religious clients treated for depression employed religious rationales for the therapy procedures and religious arguments to counter clients' irrational beliefs (similar to the use of REBT for religious clients described earlier in the chapter).[171] The religious-oriented cognitive therapy was more effective than standard cognitive therapy for this population.

Cognitive therapy that involves examining and correcting negatively biased maladaptive beliefs may be useful for gay clients who are having difficulty accepting their homosexual orientation.[172] Examples of such beliefs are, "A gay lifestyle means forgoing experiences that are only for heterosexuals" (such as having a stable relationship and rearing children), and "Being gay requires acting in certain ways that fit with mainstream stereotypes" (for instance, going to art galleries instead of sporting events). Through collaborative empiricism, gay clients can learn about the lives and habits of other gay men and collect data that refute their false assumptions. Clients can discover, for instance, that many homosexual couples have long-term relationships and that many gay men enjoy sports.

Cognitive Therapy in Perspective

Beck's studies of the distorted thinking of depressed clients led him to develop cognitive therapy 40 years ago.[173] Subsequently, it has become clear that distorted thinking also is associated with many other psychological disorders, and the general principles of cognitive therapy appear to be adaptable to a variety of disorders. Specialized cognitive therapy procedures have been designed to treat anxiety disorders,[174] personality disorders,[175] marital distress,[176] and schizophrenic delusions and hallucinations.[177] In some cases, such as in the treatment of sexual dysfunctions,[178] obesity,[179] and problem gambling,[180] therapists have employed cognitive therapy along with other behavior therapy procedures to deal with clients' cognitive distortions that are contributing to their problems.

There is a substantial body of research that clearly demonstrates the efficacy of cognitive therapy for the treatment of depression.[181] Although the majority of studies have been conducted with women, cognitive therapy appears to be equally effective with men suffering from depression.[182] The quality of studies has been especially high (in contrast to outcome research on REBT),[183] and many of the studies have been carried out with clinical populations. The specific interventions are well defined, so clinicians using cognitive therapy and researchers evaluating it are employing standard procedures (which is not the case with REBT[184]). Moreover, clients consider cognitive therapy to be highly useful for depression.[185]

Cognitive therapy is especially effective for acute episodes of major depression[186] and somewhat less effective for chronic depression.[187] Successful cognitive therapy for chronic depression may require more sessions and repetition, narrowing the focus to one or two pivotal problems, and enriching mastery and pleasure exercises.[188] Cognitive therapy also has been used to treat bipolar disorder, which is characterized by mood fluctuations between depression and manic states.[189]

It is especially noteworthy that cognitive therapy has been shown to be at least as effective in treating depression as medication, even in severe cases.[190]

Medication, the most common treatment for depression, has major drawbacks, including possible physical and psychological negative side effects. Moreover, cognitive therapy is a more cost-effective treatment than medication; for example, the use of Prozac may be 33% more expensive than individual cognitive therapy.[191]

Cognitive therapy also may prevent the recurrence of depression to a greater degree than other treatments, including medication.[192] For example, cognitive group therapy was used to prevent relapse/recurrence in a group of high-risk patients who had had repeated episodes of depression but whose depression was currently in remission. Recurrence of depression was assessed over 2 years. For the 77 clients (41% of the total sample) with five or more previous episodes of depression, eight weekly 2-hour cognitive therapy sessions reduced recurrence from 72% to 46%.[193] It is possible that cognitive therapy (1) sensitizes clients to the types of cognitions associated with depression and (2) provides them with coping skills to neutralize potential depression-evoking events (such as substituting adaptive thoughts for automatic thoughts). Thus, with cognitive therapy, "'People come away from treatment not only having their symptoms relieved, but learning something they can use the next time.'"[194] Process research has demonstrated that changes in clients' cognitions are associated with improvement in cognitive therapy.[195] Cognitive therapy might also prove useful in preventing relapse in other disorders for the same reasons. Another benefit of cognitive therapy related to depression is that it appears to decrease the risk of suicide.[196] (We will return to the prevention of relapse of depressive episodes in Chapter 14 when we discuss mindfulness-based cognitive therapy.)

The efficacy of cognitive therapy in treating depression and a host of other psychological disorders has strong empirical support based on hundreds of methodologically sound studies. However, most of these studies are carried out in research settings (such as hospitals) where the clients have been recruited (as through a newspaper advertisement). In contrast, the vast majority of clients treated with cognitive therapy have sought therapy, rather than enrolling in a treatment study, and the therapy occurs in community-based settings. Because there are essential differences between these two groups of clients, it is important to ascertain whether cognitive therapy is effective for self-referred clients in community settings. Evidence that indicates that it is effective in community settings for both depression and panic disorder has been accumulating.[197]

Cognitive therapy is a versatile treatment. Although typically implemented individually, cognitive therapy is effective in a group format,[198] which has been shown to be as effective as individual treatment.[199] Telephone-administered cognitive therapy is well suited to clients with physical illnesses and impairments as well as to elderly clients who cannot travel for therapy sessions. For example, cognitive therapy administered by telephone has been efficiently and effectively used to treat depression in patients with multiple sclerosis.[200]

Cognitive therapy integrates a variety of cognitive and overt behavioral interventions[201] and emphasizes a self-control approach.[202] Hypothesis-testing skills to examine one's beliefs and between-session practice of skills are two self-control components of cognitive therapy that are associated with its effectiveness.[203]

Cognitive therapy is popular with clients and therapists for some of the same reasons that REBT is—namely, the therapy procedures and their underlying theory are easy to understand. In addition, some clients like cognitive therapy because participating in collaborative empiricism and Socratic dialogue allows them to discover the distortions in their thinking for themselves. Indeed, clients report feeling more control over their thoughts and feelings and greater insight into their problems after completing cognitive therapy.[204]

ALL THINGS CONSIDERED: COGNITIVE RESTRUCTURING THERAPIES

The order in which we have presented the three cognitive restructuring therapies—thought stopping, rational emotive behavior therapy, and cognitive therapy—parallels the increasing complexity of the procedures they employ. That order also parallels an increasing reliance on overt behavioral interventions. Thought stopping is exclusively a cognitive technique, REBT is more cognitive than behavioral, and cognitive therapy clearly employs both cognitive and behavioral interventions.

Whereas the application of thought stopping is restricted to intrusive thoughts, REBT and cognitive therapy treat a wide range of problems and overlap in some of their specific procedures. Although REBT and cognitive therapy share the goal of promoting adaptive thought processes, they take two different approaches to attaining it: rational disputation versus collaborative empiricism, respectively. Using rational disputation in REBT, the therapist makes the client aware of dysfunctional thoughts through verbal persuasion—a "tell me" approach. The focus of collaborative empiricism in cognitive therapy is on the client's self-discovery of dysfunctional thinking through empirical hypothesis testing—a "show me" approach. Individual clients differ in their preferences for one of these two distinctive strategies, which is one reason for having both therapies available to clients. REBT and cognitive therapy both require clients to reason using better logic or data, so they are likely to exclude clients who have limited intellectual and communication skills (such as with severe mental retardation or serious brain damage).

Cognitive restructuring is a core procedure in thought stopping, REBT, and cognitive therapy. It also is a component of the cognitive-behavioral coping skills therapies that you will read about in Chapter 13. Changing our interpretations of life events can have a powerful effect on our overt behaviors, our emotions, and our overall life satisfaction and happiness.[205]

IN THEORY **12-2**

Constructivism: All in the Eye of the Beholder

The philosophical basis of cognitive restructuring is known as *constructivism*, which holds that people make (construct) their own realities (what is real and meaningful to them).[206] The interpretations we place on events—rather than the events themselves—determine the meaning of events. This idea applies both to external events (such as what other people do in relation to us) and internal events (such as how we are feeling physically).

To appreciate the usefulness of constructivism, consider how frequently the same event has different meanings for different people. On an unusually hot day in October, some people complain about the heat, while others rejoice about getting a few more days of summer weather. The frequently observed wide discrepancies among eyewitness accounts of accidents and crimes is another example.[207]

Clients construct the irrational thoughts that maintain their negative emotions and maladaptive behaviors. By the same token, they can *re*construct their thoughts—view situations differently—so that their cognitions lead to positive feelings and adaptive behaviors.

This process is illustrated by the case of M. H., a 44-year-old woman who had decided to leave her job at the end of the year, which was 4 months away.[208] She had been intensely unhappy at work because her supervisor, Wanda, seemed to be criticizing her constantly. Although M. H. felt good about her decision to leave, she increasingly found going to the office aversive. She dreaded the morning commute, felt "on edge" all day, and was relieved when she left work each day.

M. H.'s therapist suggested that she *reframe* (cognitively reconstrue) her interactions with Wanda in such a way that M. H. would come to view them positively. Specifically, the therapist suggested that she view Wanda's criticisms as validating her decision to leave her job. M. H. expanded on this general reframe on her own. Each time Wanda criticized her, M. H. told herself something like: "That was really nice of Wanda to show me, once again, how good my decision to leave was." Initially, such self-talk just made her chuckle or smile. However, by the second week, M. H. was viewing Wanda as her ally rather than her enemy. On one occasion, she told herself, "How wonderful it is to have a friend like Wanda who repeatedly reminds me of the wisdom of my decision to leave." Within 3 weeks, M. H. no longer dreaded going to work, remained relaxed while on the job, and left work feeling good. In essence, M. H.'s work situation had changed because she viewed it differently (reality is all in the eye of the beholder). As a result, she was able to finish out the year with relatively little stress in her reconstrued work situation.

SUMMARY

1. Cognitive-behavioral therapy changes cognitions that are maintaining conditions of psychological disorders in two ways. Cognitions are modified directly, by cognitive restructuring, and indirectly, by changing overt behaviors.

2. Cognitive-behavioral therapy consists of two basic models. Cognitive restructuring therapy teaches clients to change distorted and erroneous cognitions that are maintaining their problem behaviors by substituting more adaptive cognitions. Cognitive-behavioral coping skills therapy teaches clients adaptive responses—both cognitive and overt behavioral—to deal effectively with difficult situations they encounter.

3. Cognitions are operationally defined as self-talk. Four basic methods are used to assess clients' cognitions: interview, self-recording, self-report inventory, and think-aloud procedures.

4. Thought stopping decreases the frequency and duration of persistent, intrusive thoughts by interrupting them and then substituting adaptive competing thoughts.

5. Rational emotive behavior therapy (REBT) employs cognitive restructuring to change irrational thoughts. Ellis' rational emotive theory holds that it is beliefs about events in our lives, rather than the events themselves, that maintain psychological problems.

6. Maladaptive thoughts are illogical because they result from logical errors in thinking, including absolute thinking, overgeneralizing, and catastrophizing. Personal worthlessness and a sense of duty are two common themes found in irrational ideas that lead to psychological problems.

7. REBT identifies thoughts based on irrational beliefs, challenges the irrational beliefs, and substitutes thoughts based on rational beliefs. The therapist challenges the rationality of the client's thoughts, debunks the client's myths about how the world "should be," and persuades the client to recognize irrational thoughts and to think rationally.

8. REBT is used primarily with adults. Rational emotive education is an adaptation of REBT principles and procedures for children and adolescents.

9. Cognitive therapy is similar to REBT. Both assume that psychological disorders are maintained by distorted cognitions, and both use cognitive restructuring. However, cognitive therapy emphasizes empirical hypothesis testing as a means of changing existing beliefs—rather than disputation and persuasion, as in REBT.

10. The goals of cognitive therapy are to correct faulty information processing, to modify dysfunctional beliefs, and to provide clients with skills and experiences that create adaptive thinking. Cognitive therapy involves a collaborative effort between the client and therapist. Clients are taught to view automatic thoughts (maladaptive cognitions) as hypotheses subject to empirical validation, rather than as established facts. Clients test out the hypotheses in homework assignments, in which they make observations that can refute (or confirm) the hypotheses.

11. Cognitive therapy procedures that directly change clients' cognitions include analyzing faulty logic, obtaining accurate information,

self-recording automatic thoughts, generating alternative interpretations of events, reattributing responsibility about negative outcomes, and decatastrophizing exaggerated thoughts.

12. Cognitive therapy procedures that indirectly change clients' cognitions and emotions by changing overt behaviors include activity schedules, mastery and pleasure ratings, and graded task assignments.

13. Cognitive processing therapy is an adaptation of cognitive therapy for stress disorders and combines exposure therapy with cognitive therapy.

14. Treating schizophrenic delusions and hallucinations with cognitive therapy involves the same basic procedures employed with other problems along with special considerations and procedures that are necessary due to the severity of the cognitive distortions and the fragility of the clients.

15. Some clients' problems are maintained less by discrete, maladaptive cognitions and more by maladaptive schemas, which are broad and pervasive cognitive themes about oneself, others, and the world. Schemas often stem from childhood experiences and are developed throughout one's lifetime. Schema-based cognitive therapy employs specialized assessment procedures and cognitive therapy treatment procedures to change schemas.

16. Cognitive restructuring is based on constructivism, the philosophical position that people make their own realities. The interpretations we place on events—rather than the events themselves—determine the meaning of events.

REFERENCE NOTES

1. For example, Lazarus & Follkman, 1984.
2. Craighead, 1990.
3. Cottraux, 1990; Goldfried, Greenberg, & Marmar, 1990; Spiegler & Guevremont, 2002.
4. Festinger, 1957; Kelly, 1955.
5. Bandura, 1986a.
6. For example, Hartl & Frost, 1999; Reinecke, 2000; Rudd, Joiner, & Rajab, 2001.
7. Beidel & Turner, 1986; Beutler & Guest, 1989.
8. Castaneda, 1972, pp. 218–219.
9. Sokolov, 1972, p. 1.
10. Blankstein & Segal, 2001; Glass & Arnkoff, 1997.
11. Glass & Arnkoff, 1997.
12. Glass & Arnkoff, 1989.
13. Glass, Merluzzi, Biever, & Larsen, 1982.
14. Ronan, Kendall, & Rowe, 1994.
15. For example, Craighead, Kimball, & Rehak, 1979; Genest & Turk, 1981; White, Davison, Haaga, & White, 1992.
16. For example, Davison, Vogel, & Coffman, 1997; Feindler, Rathus, & Silver, 2003.
17. Davison, Vogel, & Coffman, 1997.
18. Davison, Navarre, & Vogel, 1995.
19. Lodge, Tripp, & Harte, 2000.
20. Wolpe, 1958; compare with Ellis, 1989b.
21. For example, Kenny, Mowbray, & Lalani, 1978.
22. Author's (MDS) clinical files.
23. Rusch, Grunert, Mendelsohn, & Smucker, 2000.
24. Smucker, Dancu, Foa, & Niederee, 1995.
25. Upper, 1993.
26. A. B. Kearney, 1993.
27. Peden, Rayens, Hall, & Grant, 2005.
28. Dewhurst, 1993.
29. Krop & Burgess, 1993a.
30. Groden, 1993.
31. Jurgela, 1993.
32. Newman & Haaga, 1995.
33. For example, Degotardi, Klass, Rosenberg, Fox, Gallelli, & Gottlieb, 2006; Peden, Rayens, Hall, & Grant, 2005; Trzepacz & Luiselli, 2004.
34. Freeman & Simon, 1989; Guevremont & Spiegler, 1990; Spiegler & Guevremont, 2002.
35. Tyron, 1979.
36. For example, Hackmann & McLean, 1975; Kenny, Mowbray, & Lalani, 1978; Rimm,

Saunders, & Westel, 1975; Stern, Lipsedge, & Marks, 1973.
37. Ellis, 1993, 1995, 1999.
38. Ellis & Dryden, 1993.
39. Ellis, 1962, 1994a; Hansen, 2001.
40. Ellis & Abrams, 2009.
41. Bernard & DiGiuseppe, 1989; Ellis & Bernard, 1985; Harris, Davies, & Dryden, 2006.
42. Ellis & Dryden, 1987.
43. Beck & Weishaar, 1989; Ellis, 1989a; Ellis & Abrams, 2009.
44. Ellis, 1970.
45. Ellis & Bernard, 1985.
46. Ellis, 1989a; Kopec, Beal, & DiGiuseppe, 1994; Lazarus, 1989b.
47. Rimm & Masters, 1979; dialogue is quoted from pp. 385–387; annotations are original to this text.
48. Broder, 2000.
49. For example, DiGiuseppe, 1981; Kendall, 1987.
50. For example, Ellis, 1959; Ellis & Bernard, 1983.
51. For example, Bernard & Joyce, 1984; Knaus, 1985; Knaus & Haberstroh, 1993; Omizo, Lo, & Williams, 1986.
52. Braswell & Kendall, 2001; Friedberg, Crosby, Friedberg, Rutter, & Knight, 2000; Kendall, 2000.
53. Trip, Vernon, & McMahon, 2007.
54. Gossette & O'Brien, 1993.
55. Joyce, 1995.
56. Haaga & Davison, 1989a.
57. Mahoney, Lyddon, & Alford, 1989, p. 87.
58. For example, Burns, 1980; Dyer, 1977.
59. Franks & Wolfe, 2008.
60. Mahoney, Lyddon, & Alford, 1989.
61. For example, Dryden & Hill, 1993; Ellis, 1994b, 1994c, 1994d, 1994e.
62. Abrams & Ellis, 1994; Alvarez, 1997; Balter & Unger, 1997; Greaves, 1997; Haaga & Davison, 1989a; Rieckert & Moller, 2000; Scholing & Emmelkamp, 1993a, 1993b.
63. Shannon & Allen, 1998.
64. Rossello & Bernal, 1999.
65. Dryden & Ellis, 2001; Ellis, 1999.
66. Bernard, 1990; Flanagan, Povall, Dellino, & Byrne, 1998.
67. Nielsen, 2001; Robb, 2001.
68. Tan, 2007.
69. Lazarus, 1989b.
70. Meichenbaum, 1991; Patterson & Forgatch, 1985.
71. Franks, 1995; Haaga & Davison, 1989a, 1989b; Hollon & Beck, 1986.
72. Terjesen, DiGiuseppe, & Gruner, 2000.
73. Solomon & Haaga, 1995.
74. Haaga & Davison, 1989a, 1989b, 1993; Kendall, Haaga, Ellis, Bernard, DiGluseppe, & Kassinove, 1995.
75. Lyons & Woods, 1991.
76. Haaga & Davison, 1993.
77. Compare with Goldfried, 1988; Haaga & Davison, 1989a.
78. Weinrach, 1995.
79. Beck, 1963, 1976, 2005.
80. Bernard & DiGiuseppe, 1989.
81. Hollon & Beck, 1986.
82. Padesky & Beck, 2003.
83. Beck, 1967, 1976.
84. For example, Alford, Freeman, Beck, & Wright, 1990; Beck, 1988; Beck & Emery, 1985.
85. Laberge, Gauthier, Cote, Plamondon, & Cormier, 1993.
86. Schmidt & Woolaway-Bickel, 2000.
87. Brown, Heimberg, & Juster, 1995.
88. Van Oppen, De Haan, Van Balkom, Spinhoven, Hoogduin, & Van Dyck, 1995; Whittal, Thordarson, & McLean, 2005.
89. Beck & Freeman, 1989; Leahy, Beck, & Beck, 2005; Young, 1999.
90. Baucom & Epstein, 1990; Beck, 1988; Dattilio & Padesky, 1990; Epstein & Baucom, 1989.
91. Deffenbacher, Dahlen, Lynch, Morris, & Gowen-Smith, 2000.
92. Beck, 1967; Freeman & White, 1989; Reinecke, 2000; Rudd, Joiner, & Rajah, 2001.
93. Edgette & Prout, 1989; Simon, 1994; Weishaar, 1996.
94. Leitenberg & Rosen, 1988; Leung, Waller, & Thomas, 2000.
95. Kramer & Stalker, 1989.
96. Alford & Beck, 1994; Morrison, Renton, French, & Bentall, 2008.
97. Beck, 1976.
98. Beck & Weishaar, 1989, p. 23.
99. Bell-Dolan, 1995.
100. Otto & Gould, 1995.
101. Beck, 1976.
102. Beck & Weishaar, 1989.
103. Addis & Jacobson, 2000; Burns & Sprangler, 2000; Schmidt & Woolaway-Bickel, 2000.
104. Beck & Emery, 1985; Beck & Freeman, 1989.
105. Burns & Nolen-Hoeksema, 1992.

106. Based on Beck, Wright, Newman, & Liese, 1993.
107. Beck & Weishaar, 1989.
108. For example, Beck, Wright, Newman, & Liese, 1993; Foa & Rothbaum, 1998.
109. Bowers, 1989.
110. Beck, Rush, Shaw, & Emery, 1979.
111. Beck, 1976, p. 272.
112. From the author's (MDS) clinical files.
113. Beck, Rush, Shaw, & Emery, 1979.
114. Freeston, Leger, & Ladouceur, 2001; Hartl & Frost, 1999.
115. Chemtob, Novaco, Hamada, & Gross, 1997.
116. Foa & Rothbaum, 1998.
117. Tarrier, Sommerfield, Pilgrim, & Faragher, 2000.
118. Coles, Hart, & Heimberg, 2001; Otto, Pollack, Gould, Worthington, McArdle, & Rosenbaum, 2000.
119. Öst & Breitholz, 2000.
120. Toner, Segal, Emmott, & Myran, 2000; Vollmer & Blanchard, 1998.
121. Antoni et al., 2000.
122. Antoni et al., 2001.
123. Resick & Schnicke, 1992, 1993.
124. Chard, 2005.
125. Resick, Nishith, Weaver, Astin, & Feuer, 2002.
126. Chard, 2005; House, 2006.
127. Resick, Monson, & Rizvi, 2008.
128. Monson, Schnurr, Resick, Friedman, Young-Xu, & Stevens, 2006.
129. Ahrens & Rexford, 2002.
130. Schulz, Huber, & Resick, 2006; Schulz, Resick, Huber, & Griffin, 2006.
131. Difede & Eskra, 2002.
132. Kaysen, Lostutter, & Goines, 2005.
133. Messman-Moore & Resick, 2002.
134. Nishith, Nixon, & Resick, 2005.
135. Alford & Beck, 1994; Bentall, Haddock, & Slade, 1994; Morrison & Renton, 2001.
136. Alford & Correia, 1994; Kingdon & Turkington, 2005.
137. Alford & Correia, 1994.
138. Alford & Beck, 1997; Morrison, Renton, French, & Bentall, 2008.
139. Alford & Beck, 1994.
140. Alford & Correia, 1994; Himadi, Osteen, Crawford, 1993.
141. Alford, 1986.
142. Chadwick & Lowe, 1990.
143. Tarrier, 1992.
144. Alford & Beck, 1994.
145. For example, Morrison, 1998.
146. Morrison & Renton, 2001.
147. Tarrier, 2008.
148. Rathod, Kingdon, Weiden, & Turkington, 2008; Wykes, Steele, Everitt, & Tarrier, 2008.
149. Turkington et al., 2008.
150. Kingdon, Rathod, Hansen, Naeem, & Wright, 2007.
151. Bateman, Hansen, Turkington, & Kingdon, 2007.
152. Miles, Peters, & Kuipers, 2007.
153. Young, Rygh, Weinberger, & Beck, 2008.
154. Riso, du Toit, Stein, & Young, 2007.
155. DeRubeis, Tang, & Beck, 2001.
156. Leahy, 2007.
157. Young, 1994.
158. For example, Schmidt, Joiner, Young, & Telch, 1995.
159. Tinch & Friedberg, 1998.
160. Persons, 1989.
161. McGinn & Young, 1996.
162. McGinn & Young, 1996.
163. McGinn, Young, & Sanderson, 1995; Weertman & Arntz, 2007; Young, Beck, & Weinberger, 1993.
164. Bowers, 1989; Thase & Wright, 1991.
165. Glanz, 1989.
166. DiGiuseppe, 1989.
167. Clarke, Hawkins, Murphy, Sheeber, Lewinsohn, & Seeley, 1995; Lewinsohn & Rohde, 1993.
168. Lewinsohn, Clarke, & Rohde, 1994.
169. Aydin & Yerin, 1994.
170. Vallis, Howes, & Standage, 2000; Whisman, 2008.
171. Propst, Ostrom, Watkins, Dean, & Mashburn, 1992.
172. Kuehlwein, 1992.
173. Beck, 1967; Beck, Rush, Shaw, & Emery, 1979.
174. Hollon & Beck, 1994; Otto & Gould, 1995; van Oppen & Arntz, 1994; van Oppen, de Hann, van Balkom, Spinhoven, Hoogduin, & van Dyck, 1995.
175. Beck & Freeman, 1989.
176. Abrahms, 1983; Baucom & Epstein, 1990; Beck, 1988.
177. Alford & Beck, 1994; Alford & Correia, 1994; Morrison, Renton, Williams, & Dunn, 1999.
178. McCarthy, 1989.
179. Kramer & Stalker, 1989.

180. Battersby, Oakes, Tolchard, Forbes, & Pols, 2008; Doiron & Nicki, 2007.
181. For example, Lewinsohn, Clarke, & Rohde, 1994; Shapiro, Rees, Barkham, Hardy, Reynolds, & Startup, 1995; Teasdale, Segal, & Williams, 1995.
182. Thase, Reynolds, Frank, Simons, McGeary, et al., 1994.
183. For example, Shapiro, Rees, Barkham, Hardy, Reynolds, & Startup, 1995.
184. Haaga & Davison, 1993; Kendall, Haaga, Ellis, Bernard, DiGiuseppe, & Kassinove, 1995.
185. For example, Friedberg, Viglione, Stinson, Beal, Fidaleo, & Celeste, 1999.
186. Antonuccio, Danton, & DeNelsky, 1995; Thase, Bowler, & Harden, 1991; Thase, Simons, Cahalane, & McGeary, 1991.
187. Sanderson, Beck, & McGinn, 1994; Thase, Reynolds, Frank, Simons, Garamoni, et al., 1994.
188. Thase, 1994.
189. Lam et al., 2000.
190. Antonuccio, Danton, & DeNelsky, 1995; Antonuccio, Thomas, & Danton, 1997.
191. Antonuccio, Thomas, & Danton, 1997.
192. Hollon, Shelton, & Davis, 1993; Hollon, Stewart, & Strunk, 2006; Teasdale, Segal, & Williams, 1995; Vittengl, Clark, Dunn, & Jarrett, 2007.
193. Bockting et al., 2005.
194. DeAngelis, 2008, p. 49.
195. Garratt, Ingram, & Rand, 2007.
196. Brown, Ten Have, Henriques, Xie, Hollander, & Beck, 2005.
197. Penava, Otto, Maki, & Pollack, 1998; Persons, Bostrom, & Bertagnolli, 1999; Stuart, Treat, & Wade, 2000.
198. For example, Deffenbacher, Dahlen, Lynch, Morris, & Gowensmith, 2000; Oei & Shuttlewood, 1997.
199. Vollmer & Blanchard, 1998.
200. Mohr, Hart, & Vella, 2007; Mohr et al., 2000.
201. Hollon & Beck, 1994.
202. Newman & Haaga, 1995; O'Leary & Rathus, 1993.
203. Robins & Hayes, 1993.
204. O'Leary & Rathus, 1993.
205. For example, Csikszentmihalyi, 1990; Csikszentmihalyi & Csikszentmihalyi, 1988.
206. Neimeyer, 2000; Neimeyer & Raskin, 2000, 2001.
207. Loftus, 1979.
208. From the author's (MDS) clinical files.

13

Cognitive-Behavioral Therapy
Coping Skills

Cognitive restructuring therapy, which you read about in the previous chapter, is appropriate for problems maintained by an *excess of maladaptive thoughts.* In contrast, cognitive-behavioral coping skills therapy—the other model of cognitive-behavioral therapy—is used to treat problems that are maintained by a *deficit of adaptive cognitions.* The focus is not so much on what clients are thinking as on what they are *not thinking.* As with cognitive restructuring therapy, cognitive-behavioral coping skills therapy changes both clients' cognitions and overt behaviors. We will discuss three cognitive-behavioral coping skills therapies that are broadly applicable—self-instructional training, problem-solving therapy/training, and stress inoculation training—and one therapy with a specific target, cognitive-behavioral couple therapy.

SELF-INSTRUCTIONAL TRAINING

The odds of surviving ejection from a jet fighter at 47,000 feet—nearly 9 miles above the Earth where the temperature, not counting wind chill, is 70 degrees below zero—are not favorable, to say the least. As horrific as that experience was for William Rankin, it was nothing compared to the next 40 minutes of his free fall, in which he alternately fell and rose through a thunderstorm with turbulence that could have disintegrated his abandoned F8U Crusader. Rankin may well owe his survival to what he remembers telling himself: *"Hang on! You might make it yet. You're thinking. You're conscious. You know what's going on. Just ride out this free fall and you've got it made."* [1]

Every day, in much less dramatic circumstances, when we are confronted with difficult situations, we tell ourselves what to do, what to think, and how to feel. "Go to the cleaners first because it may close early, and then stop by the bank on the way home." "Concentrate. I studied hard for this test, and I know this material." "Keep your eye on the ball, racket back, step in, follow through." *Self-instructions* are directed self-talk and serve six different functions, which are described in Table 13-1. Self-instructions can be phrased in a variety of ways, as you can see in Table 13-2.

TABLE **13-1**
Six Functions of Self-Instructions

Function	Example
PREPARING CLIENT TO USE SELF-INSTRUCTIONS	"Remember to use the self-instructions while you're working on the test."
FOCUSING ATTENTION	"Concentrate. Don't let your mind wander."
GUIDING BEHAVIOR	"All right. Now, check your answer one more time before going on."
PROVIDING ENCOURAGEMENT	"So far, so good. Keep on trying."
EVALUATING PERFORMANCE	"Good work. I got another one right."
REDUCING ANXIETY	"Stay calm. Just relax. I'm doing fine."

TABLE **13-2**

Forms of Self-Instructions

Form	Example
IMPERATIVE	"Sit and relax for a moment."
FIRST PERSON	"I'd better sit and relax for a moment."
SECOND PERSON	"You need to sit and relax for a moment."
NAME	"Megan, sit and relax for a moment."

Donald Meichenbaum

Donald Meichenbaum developed **self-instructional training** to teach people to direct themselves to cope effectively with difficult situations.[2] It has been used to treat a wide array of problems, ranging from deficits in academic skills of children[3] to the bizarre thoughts and speech of clients with schizophrenia.[4]

Self-instructional training was first used to treat children's impulsive behaviors.[5] Children who act impulsively do not think before acting, which has undesirable consequences for both them and other people. The general goal of self-instructional training for impulsive behaviors is to teach children to think and plan before acting—to "stop, look, and listen." Self-instructional training consists of five steps.

1. *Cognitive modeling.* An adult model performs a task while verbalizing aloud a deliberate strategy. As an example, while demonstrating a line copying task, the model said aloud,

   OK, what is it I have to do?... copy the picture with the different lines.... go slowly and carefully. OK, draw the line down, down, good; then to the right, that's it; now down some more and to the left. Good, I'm doing fine so far.[6]

2. *Cognitive participant modeling.* The child performs the task as the model verbalizes the instructions aloud.
3. *Overt self-instructions.* The child performs the task while verbalizing the instructions aloud.
4. *Fading of overt self-instructions.* The child performs the task while whispering the instructions.
5. *Covert self-instructions.* Finally, the child performs the task while saying the instructions to herself or himself.

Following these steps, the therapist initially teaches the client to use self-instructions with brief, simple tasks (such as connecting a series of numbered dots) and then with lengthier, more complex tasks (such as completing multi-step verbal math problems).[7] With young children, the training may be presented as a game and pictorial prompts are presented to remind the child to use self-instructions (see Figure 13-1). Case 13-1 illustrates self-instructional training with a preschool boy.

FIGURE **13-1**

Cue cards for prompting children to use self-instructions to solve problems

Source: Camp, B. W., & Bash, M. A. S. *Think Aloud: Increasing cognitive and social skills— A problem-solving program for children (Primary Level)*. Champaign, IL, Research Press, 1981. Reprinted by permission.

CASE **13-1**

Improving a Preschooler's Academic Skills Through Self-Instructional Training[8]

Five-year-old Peter attended a preschool for children with conduct and learning problems. Although he was bright and capable of doing his schoolwork, Peter often did not complete his assignments. He spent considerable time looking around the classroom and daydreaming. As time was running out, he would rush to complete his work.

The therapist met with Peter three times a week for 20 to 30 minutes in a room adjacent to his classroom. The therapist taught Peter to use four specific self-instructions: (1) "What do I have to do first?" (problem

(continued)

CASE **13-1** *(continued)*

definition); (2) "Circle all the words that begin with [a two letter sequence]" (attention focusing and response guidance); (3) "Did I find all the words on the line?" (self-evaluation and error correction); and (4) "Good job. I found all of them" (self-reinforcement). The therapist taught these self-instructions sequentially; only after Peter was using a self-instruction correctly was he taught the next one.

Two types of recordings of Peter's behaviors were made to assess the effectiveness of the training. First, videos of Peter during work periods provided a measure of the time he spent paying attention to his work. Second, a small microphone connected to a tape recorder was attached to Peter's work desk to record the self-instructions that Peter spoke aloud.

The average percentage of time Peter paid attention to his work increased from 31% before self-instructional training to 72% after training. The improved attention was reflected in an increase in the percentage of problems Peter correctly completed each day, from an average of 32% before training to an average of 79% after training. Thus, using self-instructions was associated with increased attention to and quality of schoolwork, and overt-self instructions resulted in more correctly completed problems.

There are advantages to clients' using both overt and covert self-instructions. Overt self-instructions can be monitored by others, as in Case 13-1. Further, overt self-instructions are likely to increase clients' attention to self-instructions because clients actually hear them aloud. Covert self-instructions do not disturb others, and clients are not embarrassed by others' hearing their self-instructions.

Enhancing the Effects of Self-Instructional Training

A number of factors appear to enhance the effectiveness of self-instructional training for academic problems. Children who are more actively involved in their training, as by helping to generate the self-instructions they use, show greater improvements than children who are passive recipients of training. Not surprisingly, a good client–therapist relationship is associated with better performance.[9] Involving natural change agents (such as parents and teachers) in the training[10] and increasing the number of training sessions[11] also result in greater improvements in children's academic and social behaviors.

Various procedures are used to help clients transfer their self-instructional training from the therapy sessions to the classroom setting. These procedures include making training materials (such as work sheets) similar to those the children will use in the classroom[12] and arranging training situations to simulate normal classroom conditions, such as conducting self-instructional training in the presence of other children.[13]

Generalization to different tasks is influenced by the types of self-instructions children are taught. General conceptual instructions that children can apply to many tasks (for instance, "I must go slowly and be careful") result in greater generalization than task-specific instructions (such as, "I have to circle the pictures that are the same").[14]

Before you continue reading, take a few minutes to generate self-instructions for everyday difficulties you encounter by following the directions in Participation Exercise 13-1.

PARTICIPATION EXERCISE 13-1

Being Your Own Boss: Using Self-Instructions

Using self-instructions can help you deal with many difficulties you encounter in your daily life. They can guide your behavior, reduce your anxiety, focus your attention, and encourage you.

For each of the following situations, write a self-instruction that you might find useful. When you have finished, compare your self-instructions with the examples in your Student Resource Manual.

1. It is Friday evening. You feel overwhelmed with all the studying and assignments you are supposed to complete by Monday.
2. You are tired during a long drive at night. You find that you are having trouble concentrating on driving. Several times you had to quickly steer the car back into your lane as the car wandered into an adjacent lane.
3. You are hurriedly packing for an overnight trip and don't want to forget your essential clothes.
4. You are on a diet, which involves not eating desserts. When you go out with friends after a movie and everyone is ordering pie or ice cream, your resolve is starting to weaken.
5. You are in the last mile of a 5-mile run. You are getting very tired and feel like quitting but you want to complete the run.
6. You are driving in an unfamiliar area. You stop for directions. The person tells you, "Make a right at the next traffic light. Go about a mile to a stop sign and turn left. Then, in a half mile or so, the road ends. Go left there. The restaurant is down about a quarter of a mile on the right."
7. You are about to go into a job interview. You feel confident and relaxed. In fact, you realize you are too relaxed and not at all "psyched" for the interview.
8. You want to ask a classmate for a date. You have gone to the phone, but you are not sure what to say.

Self-Instructional Training in Perspective

Self-instructional training has been used for 40 years for a wide array of problems, including impulsive behaviors,[15] schizophrenic behaviors,[16] social withdrawal,[17] anxiety,[18] anger,[19] personality disorders,[20] obesity,[21] bulimia,[22] poor body image,[23] and pain,[24] as well as deficits in assertive behaviors,[25] problem solving,[26] leisure skills,[27] creativity,[28] and cognitive and motor performance due to brain injuries.[29]

Although self-instructional training is primarily used with children, it also is used with adolescents and adults. For example, adolescents who frequently acted aggressively and displayed angry outbursts were taught coping self-instructions to deal with conflicts.[30] They learned self-instructions to *prepare* to act (for instance, "I'm not going to take it personally"), to *guide* their behaviors during conflicts (such as, "I've got to keep in control"), and to *evaluate* their actions afterward (for example, "I handled that pretty well").

Self-instructional training has been used to guide job-related tasks of adults with mental retardation.[31] The training has resulted in significant improvements in work-related on-task behaviors,[32] accuracy of performance,[33] completion of tasks,[34] and punctuality.[35] These findings are impressive because they indicate that self-instructional training can be applied successfully to improve the quality of life of individuals with significant intellectual impairment.

PROBLEM-SOLVING THERAPY/TRAINING

Problems are a ubiquitous part of life, and problem solving is a broadly useful skill for coping with many of life's difficulties.[36] Moreover, inadequate problem solving is associated with a host of psychological problems.[37]

In the present context, *problem solving* refers to a systematic process by which a person (1) generates a variety of potentially effective solutions to a problem, (2) judiciously chooses the best of these solutions, and (3) implements and evaluates the chosen solution.[38] Like reinforcement, problem solving was not invented by behavior therapists. However, over the past 40 years, behavior therapists—spearheaded by the work of Thomas D'Zurilla[39]—have been refining problem-solving procedures and adapting them to treat and prevent psychological problems.

Courtesy of Thomas D'Zurilla

Thomas D'Zurilla

Problem-solving therapy (also called *social problem-solving therapy*) is the application of problem solving to difficulties for which a client has specifically sought treatment. With adults, it is used to treat a variety of problems, including stress,[40] depression,[41] agoraphobia,[42] eating disorders,[43] smoking,[44] problem gambling,[45] marital discord,[46] child abuse,[47] and living skills of clients with schizophrenia and depression.[48] Problem solving also has helped with the difficulties families face in caring for relatives with schizophrenia[49] and cancer.[50] With children and adolescents, applications include anxiety,[51] migraine headaches,[52] obesity,[53] aggressive behaviors,[54] anger,[55] habitual gambling,[56] assertive social behaviors,[57] classroom behaviors,[58] school adjustment,[59] and parent–adolescent conflicts.[60]

Because problem solving is a broadly applicable coping skill, problem-solving therapy often serves a dual purpose. First, it treats the immediate problems for which clients seek treatment. Second, it prepares clients to deal with future problems on their own, which may help prevent psychological disorders from developing.[61]

Problem-solving training, in contrast to *therapy*, serves only the second function. It teaches problem-solving skills as a general coping strategy for dealing with problems that may arise in the course of daily life. The training often is provided for populations who have been identified as being at risk for developing psychological disorders (such as adolescents who have difficulties controlling anger) or at risk for relapsing (such as adults with chronic schizophrenia).[62] Prevention-oriented problem-solving training sometimes is incorporated into regular classroom curricula so that all children learn problem-solving skills.[63]

Most of our discussion of the problem-solving method is applicable to both problem-solving therapy and problem-solving training.

Basic Procedures

Problem-solving therapy divides the problem-solving process into stages or steps.[64] The basic seven stages are (1) adopting a problem-solving orientation, (2) defining the problem, (3) setting goals, (4) generating alternative solutions, (5) choosing the best solution, (6) implementing the solution, and (7) evaluating its effects (see Figure 13-2). The successful completion of each stage depends on skills and information learned in previous stages. Accordingly, if clients encounter difficulty in later stages, they may have to return to previous stages (as indicated by the dashed lines in Figure 13-2).

Stage 1: Adopting a Problem-Solving Orientation

Adopting a problem-solving orientation is a crucial stage of problem solving and may determine the outcome of the subsequent stages.[65] Clearly, it is necessary to recognize that a problem exists before one can attempt to solve it. For example, people who lose their jobs easily recognize that they will be facing a problem. However, when people view dilemmas in their lives as unsolvable, they may not consider them "problems," in the sense that they might be amenable to problem solving. Additionally, when individuals develop exaggerated or maladaptive reactions to difficult or unchangeable situations (such as the death of a loved one), they are less likely to recognize that a potentially solvable problem exists. In such cases, it is one's *reaction* to the situation that is the problem, not the situation itself.

Adopting a problem-solving orientation requires understanding that (1) it is necessary to identify problems when they occur so that appropriate action can be taken; (2) problems are a normal part of life, and people can learn to cope with them; and (3) effective problem solving involves carefully assessing alternative courses of action.

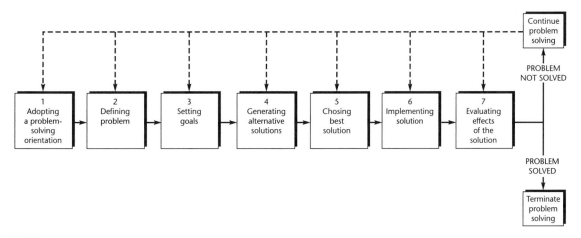

FIGURE 13-2

Schematic representation of seven stages of problem-solving therapy/training. Dashed lines indicate the possibility that difficulties at one stage may necessitate returning to prior stages.

Stage 2: Defining the Problem

In the second stage, the therapist helps the client precisely define the problem so that specific solutions can be generated. It would be difficult, for example, to generate solutions for the vaguely defined problem: "My roommate and I can't get along." In contrast, "My roommate likes to go to sleep early and wake up early, and I prefer just the opposite schedule" does lend itself to concrete solutions (see Figure 13-3, #1).

Problem-Solving Work Sheet

1. *Define the problem, including important details*:

   Background: My roommate likes to go to bed early and wake up early in the morning. I like to stay up late and sleep in. We are good friends but don't get a lot of time to talk or socialize because of our different schedules. Also, I have to limit myself to quiet activities in the evening because she has gone to bed. I would like to have other friends over in the evening, but this wouldn't be fair to my roommate. In the morning while I'm still sleeping, my roommate's getting up so early frequently wakes me up, and then I have trouble getting back to sleep.

   Specific problem situation: Our different schedules are beginning to interfere with our friendship and cause inconveniences for both of us. I would like to be able to socialize with friends in the evening and sleep in without being awakened by my roommate.

2. *Set specific goals (What must happen so that I no longer have the problem?)*: I have to be able to socialize with friends in the evening because I really enjoy doing this and not be awakened in the morning while my roommate prepares to leave the house.

3. *Generate alternative solutions (brainstorm)*:   4. *Chose best solution:*
                                                          (+ + = very good; + = good;
                                                          0 = neutral; – – = poor; – – – = very poor)

a. Just put up with the situation for the rest of the semester.   a. __– –__

b. Make plans to go over to other friends' places during
   the evening.   b. __+__

c. Move out of the apartment completely.   c. __–__

d. Ask some friends what they think I should do.   d. __–__

e. Rearrange the house a bit so that we don't interfere
   with each other in the morning and evening.   e. __+ +__

f. Start going to bed early and getting up early like
   my roommate.   f. __– –__

g. Take turns so that one day I follow her schedule and
   the next day she follows mine.   g. __+__

FIGURE 13-3
Sample problem-solving work sheet

Stage 3: Setting Goals

To set goals, the client must answer the question, "What must happen so that I no longer have the problem?" (see Figure 13-3, #2). The goals can focus on the (1) problem situation, (2) reactions to the problem situation, or (3) both.[66] *Situation-focused goals* are aimed at changing the problem situation itself (such as getting out of debt). *Reaction-focused goals* are aimed at changing one's emotional, cognitive, and overt behavioral reactions to the problem situation (such as feeling worthless because one is in debt). The nature of the problem—that is, how it is defined—determines the type of goal that is appropriate. For example, when the situation cannot be changed, only a reaction-focused goal is possible. The client's goals guide the generation of solutions in the fourth stage.

Stage 4: Generating Alternative Solutions

In the fourth stage, the client is taught to generate solutions (courses of action) that might solve the problem. The objective is to come up with as many alternative solutions as possible to maximize the chances of finding one that will be successful (see Figure 13-3, #3). Clients are encouraged to use *brainstorming*, a procedure in which any possible solution is entertained, no matter how impractical or outlandish it might appear. Although the "far out" ideas may not be viable themselves, they may lead to usable solutions by steering the client in a new direction. Using our roommate problem example, "murdering your roommate" clearly is not a viable solution, but its intended effect—getting rid of the roommate—might lead to a more workable solution, such as your moving out. Brainstorming counters the narrow, rigid thinking that clients in therapy often exhibit and may reveal solutions that clients might otherwise miss.

Brainstorming is a general strategy that is employed in different stages of problem solving.[67] For example, brainstorming can be used to generate alternative goals in the third stage and to identify different consequences of a particular solution in the fifth stage.

Stage 5: Choosing the Best Solution

In the fifth stage, the client chooses the best solution from among the alternatives generated in the fourth stage. This choice is made by examining the potential consequences of each course of action: what is likely to happen in the short and long run, for the client and for other people. Using a rating scale to evaluate the alternative solutions is helpful (as in the example in Figure 13-3, #4).

Stage 6: Implementing the Solution

In the sixth stage, the client implements the solution chosen in the previous stage. In one sense, this is the most critical stage because the best solutions can solve the problem only if they are implemented properly. This means that the client must have the requisite skills and opportunity to implement the solution and also be motivated to do so.

Stage 7: Evaluating the Effectiveness of the Chosen Solution

Finally, once the implemented solution has had time to take effect, the client evaluates how successful it has been. If the problem has been resolved, therapy is terminated. If the problem still exists, then the client repeats one or more of the previous stages. First, the client would choose another solution (Stage 5). If no acceptable alternatives remain, more solutions must be generated (Stage 4). Sometimes, the difficulty lies in the goals that were selected (Stage 3) or how the problem was defined (Stage 2), and it is necessary to repeat those processes.

Teaching Problem-Solving Skills to Clients

A variety of behavior therapy procedures are used to teach clients problem solving, including modeling, prompting, self-instructions, shaping, and reinforcement.[68] In the early stages, the therapist may employ *cognitive modeling* to demonstrate the problem-solving process. For example, the therapist might brainstorm aloud about a hypothetical problem to illustrate this uninhibited, open-ended procedure, as in the following cognitive-modeling scenario in which the therapist plays the role of a graduate student who is having difficulty completing her thesis.

> How am I going to get my thesis finished by the June deadline? I could put in more hours, which would mean giving up my daily jogging and TV... even sleeping. Don't evaluate; just come up with ideas. I could hire an assistant to do some of the literature search. Maybe I could get an English grad student to help with my writing. Of course, I could buy a thesis from one of those on-line companies that sells them... or I could bribe the dean.

During the fourth stage, the therapist *prompts* the client to use brainstorming and *reinforces* the client's ideas, both practical and outrageous ideas. If the client has difficulty with brainstorming, the procedure may need to be *shaped*. The therapist also teaches and encourages the client to remind him- or herself to engage in appropriate problem-solving behaviors with *self-instructions* and to use *self-reinforcement* for doing so. In the final stage, the therapist may have to use other behavior therapy procedures to facilitate the client's actions. For example, if the client feels anxious or inhibited in asking a friend for help, systematic desensitization and assertion training might be employed.

Problem-Solving Therapy/Training for Children

Problem-solving therapy/training, with minor procedural differences, is the same for both adults and children.[69] For example, hypothetical problem scenarios, such as those in Table 13-3, are used to teach problem-solving skills for interpersonal difficulties and aggressive behaviors.

Problem-solving therapy/training has been used with preschoolers,[70] preadolescents,[71] and adolescents,[72] both individually and in groups.[73] Problem-solving therapy is especially suitable for adolescents who resist unilateral adult decision and rule making.[74] For example, incorporating family problem-solving therapy into a traditional behavioral parent training program resulted in increased cooperation and compliance on the part of an adolescent boy who was defiant with adults.[75] Case 13-2 illustrates the use of problem-solving therapy with a preadolescent.

TABLE **13-3**

Hypothetical Problem Scenarios Used to Teach Problem-Solving Skills to Boys

---

You just get in from recess on a very hot day. You are standing in line to get a drink of water. A bunch of other kids are in line in front of you. After a 5-minute wait you are finally next in line. Just as you are about to have your turn, another boy in your class cuts in front of you.

You notice that some kids in your neighborhood are playing basketball. You think one of them goes to the same school as you, but you are not sure who the others are. You would like to play with them, but you are not sure they will let you.

After school, you notice some of your classmates smoking cigarettes behind the school building. They call you over and ask you if you want a cigarette. You don't really want to smoke, but you don't want them to dislike you either.

When you arrive at school, another boy in your class begins to laugh at you and tease you about the haircut you just had. You tell him to stop it, but he continues anyway. Soon several other kids begin to tease you also.

CASE **13-2**

Reducing Aggressive and Disruptive Behaviors in a Preadolescent Boy Using Problem-Solving Therapy[76]

Eleven-year-old Carl was referred for treatment by his teacher because of his aggressive and disruptive classroom behaviors and poor relationships with his classmates. Carl frequently drew attention to himself by engaging in a variety of inappropriate behaviors, such as burping loudly, humming, and leaving his seat. Carl wanted to have friends, but he was shunned by his peers, who found his behaviors rude and obnoxious. When faced with a conflict with his teacher or classmates, Carl often acted aggressively—threatening others, yelling obscenities, or storming out of the room. The therapist spoke with Carl's teacher about the specific types of situations that Carl handled ineffectively, and brief scenarios about each problem situation were constructed (similar to those in Table 13-3).

Carl and the therapist met for a total of 18 ½-hour sessions over 12 weeks in a private room at Carl's school. The therapist explained the rationale and benefits of "stopping and thinking" before acting as well as how the therapy could help Carl get along better with his peers and teacher. Carl was taught to think of as many solutions to the problem scenarios as he could. Next, Carl learned to select the best solutions, those that were both realistic and most likely to result in positive, or at least neutral, consequences. If Carl evaluated a solution unrealistically (for example, "If I hit him, he won't bother me anymore"), the therapist

(continued)

CASE **13-2** *(continued)*

reminded him of what the consequences actually were likely to be. Finally, Carl and the therapist discussed how he would implement the chosen solutions and assess their effectiveness.

In later sessions, Carl and the therapist role-played situations that might occur when Carl attempted the solutions. For example, Carl decided that he would ask another boy in his class to play with him at recess; the therapist assumed the role of the boy, and Carl practiced what he would actually say and do. The therapist provided Carl with feedback about how he was presenting himself and modeled alternative approaches when Carl had difficulty.

Carl learned each of the problem-solving skills, as evidenced by his applying them to the problem scenarios. More important, he was able to use the skills to change his behaviors at school. After problem-solving therapy had begun, his disruptive classroom behaviors decreased significantly. Before problem-solving therapy, Carl engaged in disruptive behaviors an average of 30% of the time, whereas at the end of therapy the time was cut in half.

Problem-Solving Therapy/Training in Perspective

Problem solving has been applied to diverse problems and populations.[77] It has its strongest empirical support in the treatment of adult depression[78] and as a maintenance strategy following behavioral weight-control programs.[79] It is also useful with mild depression in children,[80] elderly clients,[81] and people with schizophrenia.[82] Problem-solving therapy can help clients solve immediate problems and provide clients with skills for solving future problems—which exemplifies the self-control approach in behavior therapy. It is especially beneficial for problems that involve conflict or require a decision, such as deciding whether to have a baby, to change jobs, or to drop out of school. Deficits in problem-solving skills have been linked to hopelessness and suicide risk, and problem-solving therapy might be employed to help clients contemplating suicide consider alternatives to ending their lives.[83]

Some of the factors that appear to be important in effective problem-solving interventions are (1) a positive client–therapist relationship, (2) customizing procedures for the client, (3) the therapist's modeling problem-solving skills, (4) the client's doing homework assignments, and (5) the client's learning specific means of implementing solutions.[84]

The effectiveness of problem-solving therapy/training depends on three sequential outcomes: (1) learning problem-solving skills, (2) applying them to real-life problems, and (3) benefiting from their application—that is, actually solving problems. To evaluate the first outcome, clients' problem-solving skills are assessed before and after therapy/training, often using hypothetical problems. Clients' responses to the problems are recorded and later rated by the therapist. Table 13-4 contains abbreviated scoring guidelines for rating

TABLE **13-4**

Abbreviated Guidelines For Rating Children's Problem-Solving Skills

1. *Number of Solutions*
   Solutions are considered separate only if they differ in a significant way. For example, telling the teacher, telling the principal, and telling the playground supervisor all would be considered one solution—that is, telling an authority.

2. *Effectiveness of Solutions*
   The characteristics of an effective solution are that it (1) is nonaggressive, (2) is likely to resolve the problem, and (3) does not result in adverse effects for the child or others. Ratings are as follows:

   1–2 Physical aggression

   3–4 Verbal aggression

   5 Nonaggressive but passive and unlikely to resolve problem

   6–7 Nonaggressive, prosocial, and active attempt to solve problem

3. *Sophistication of Planning*
   Ratings from 1 to 7 are based on the number of the following categories the child's problem-solving skills demonstrate.

   1. Sensitivity to possible consequences
   2. Anticipation of obstacles
   3. Reference to social rules
   4. Goal setting
   5. Amount of detail
   6. Realistic
   7. Sequential

Source: Adapted from Guevremont & Foster, 1992.

children's problem-solving skills based on their responses to problem scenarios (such as those in Table 13-3, page 357). Alternatively, problem-solving ability can be assessed by paper-and-pencil measures, such as the Social Problem-Solving Inventory,[85] which has Spanish,[86] German,[87] and Chinese[88] versions for adults. The evidence is clear that adults and children can learn problem-solving skills, often very quickly.[89]

That being said, do clients apply and benefit from problem-solving therapy/training? Studies have not consistently found a relationship between children's acquisition of problem-solving skills and their behavioral adjustment.[90] Although children do learn problem-solving skills, changes in their problems at home and in school may not be clinically significant. Studies with adults have obtained similar findings.

What accounts for the disappointing general finding that clients do not consistently apply problem-solving skills they have learned to deal with actual problems in their lives? One possibility is that clients may not view difficulties in daily living as problems. This may be true particularly in cases in which reaction-focused goals are appropriate. One solution may be additional Stage 1 training in viewing life difficulties, including both situations and reactions to situations, as problems that can be solved or dealt with. Interestingly, one study found that a negative problem orientation was a strong predictor of depression and anxiety in adults.[91] *Negative problem orientation* refers to the general tendency to (1) appraise a problem as a threat, (2) doubt one's own problem-solving ability, (3) expect negative problem-solving outcomes, and (4) show a low tolerance for frustration when confronted with a problem.

Another reason why clients fail to apply problem-solving techniques consistently may be that they lack the specific skills required to implement solutions. For instance, clients may not have the requisite knowledge and proficiency to competently perform the behaviors specified by the solution. This would be the case for a client who decided to confront her boss about unfair treatment but who did not have the appropriate assertive skills to carry out this course of action. Or, clients may simply lack the motivation necessary to implement the solution, perhaps because it seems like too much effort.

Traditionally, problem-solving therapy/training has emphasized helping clients generate alternative solutions and selecting the optimal one. However, to get clients to apply problem-solving skills in their daily lives, more attention may need to be paid to adopting a problem-solving orientation and implementing solutions (Stages 1 and 6), which may be the most crucial stages.

PARTICIPATION EXERCISE 13-2

Solutions, Solutions, and More Solutions: Practicing Problem Solving[a]

Solving problems can be fun if you view the process as a challenge. In this exercise, you will practice two stages of problem solving: generating alternative solutions and choosing the best solution.

Begin by reading the description of Situation 1 and follow the directions for generating solutions and selecting the best solution.

Situation 1. Although the weather report predicts rain, you are skeptical and walk to the library without a raincoat or umbrella. When it is time to walk home, it is pouring. You live five blocks from the library and will get soaked walking home. *What could you do?*

Think of as many *different* solutions to the problem as you can; your goal is *quantity*, not quality. Brainstorm: List any and all solutions, no matter how impractical or "far out" they appear. Of course, don't omit practical or conventional solutions. Even if you find what seems to be the most obvious or optimal solution, don't stop thinking of additional solutions. Write down all the alternative solutions you think of.

When you have a sizable list of solutions, rate the overall potential consequences of each. Consider (1) how successful you expect the solution

[a] This Participation Exercise can be completed before you continue reading or later.

to be and (2) the consequences of the solution for you and others. Using the following scale, write the appropriate rating next to each solution.

$$5 = very\ good$$
$$4 = good$$
$$3 = neutral$$
$$2 = poor$$
$$1 = very\ poor$$

Next, look at all the solutions you've rated 5 (very good), or 4 (good) if none is rated 5. (If you have rated none of your solutions 4 or 5, generate some additional solutions.) From among your top-rated solutions, choose the best one—that is, the one you think would result in the most satisfactory consequences.

Now repeat the same steps for Situation 2.

Situation 2. You are treating a friend to dinner. When it comes time to pay the check, you discover that you left your wallet at home. *What could you do?*

Consider what you have learned by doing this exercise. Did brainstorming help you generate solutions? Were you surprised by the number of different solutions possible for each of the problems? Can you identify any "mental blocks," such as rigid thinking, that impeded your generating alternative solutions? How well do you think the process of selecting the best solution worked? Finally, you may find it interesting to compare your alternative solutions with another student who did the exercise.

STRESS INOCULATION TRAINING

People experience many life events—both large and small—as stressful. We have little control over many potentially stress-evoking events *(stressors)*, ranging from earthquakes and serious illness to academic examinations and flat tires. However, we can control how we *view* and *cope* with such events. *Stress* broadly refers to an array of negative psychological reactions, including anxiety, anger, frustration, and depression, and a variety of physical ailments, including headaches, insomnia, fatigue, ulcers, and hypertension.[92b]

Basic Procedures

In **stress inoculation training**, another therapy developed by Meichenbaum, clients learn to cope with stress-evoking events by acquiring coping skills and then practice using them while being exposed to stressors.[93] The therapy is divided into three phases: (1) conceptualization, (2) coping skills acquisition, and (3) application.

---

[b] In everyday usage, people use the term *stress* to refer both to *events* that precipitate adverse reactions and to the *reactions* themselves. This dualism is regrettable because it perpetuates the idea that events themselves cause adverse reactions. This idea is counter not only to cognitive-behavioral theorizing but also to the prevailing scientific conceptualization of stress (for example, Lazarus & Folkman, 1984). Using correct terminology, *stressor* refers to an event and *stress* refers to a negative reaction to the event.

Phase 1: Conceptualization

The first phase of stress inoculation training is educational. The therapist explains to the client that events themselves do not cause negative emotional reactions, such as anxiety or anger; rather, the negative reactions arise from how we perceive these events. Clients are told that they can learn coping skills that will allow them to reconceptualize and deal with potentially stress-evoking events without becoming emotionally upset. Clients are encouraged to view coping as a simple, five-step process:

1. *Preparing* for the potentially stress-evoking event (stressor)
2. *Confronting and coping with* the stressor
3. *Dealing with temporary difficulties* in coping
4. *Assessing one's performance* in coping with the stressor
5. *Reinforcing oneself* for successful coping

Phase 2: Coping Skills Acquisition

In the second phase of stress inoculation training, the client learns and rehearses coping skills. Although the specific coping skills depend on the nature of the client's problem, four general coping skills are employed most often: differential relaxation, cognitive restructuring, problem-solving self-instructions, and self-reinforcement/self-efficacy self-instructions.

Most clients who have stress-related problems experience muscle tension, which practicing *progressive relaxation* can alleviate. Similarly, clients typically have negative thoughts about potential stressors and about their ability to cope with them, and clients can use *cognitive restructuring* to deal with them. Examples of coping self-statements that clients might use include: "This anxiety is a reminder to use my relaxation exercises"; "Look for the positives and be optimistic"; "I have a right to get annoyed, but I can keep the lid on"; and "When the pain increases, I can switch to a different coping strategy."

Clients whose problems are being maintained, in part, by not knowing how to approach and solve problems can benefit from *task-oriented problem-solving self-instructions*. As the examples in Table 13-5 illustrate, these self-instructions put the problem in perspective and focus the client's attention on concrete problem-solving steps.

Clients will continue to perform coping skills only if they are reinforced. Natural consequences, such as accomplishing goals, cannot be relied on to maintain coping skills, especially when the client is first beginning to apply coping skills and may not be successful. Thus, clients are taught individualized *self-reinforcement/self-efficacy self-instructions*, such as the examples in Table 13-6.

In addition to these general coping skills that are applicable to diverse problems, clients also may be taught coping skills that are tailored to specific problems. For fear, the client might learn to gather accurate information about threatening events. For chronic pain, the client might learn to use self-distracting thoughts.

TABLE **13-5**

Examples of Task-Oriented Problem-Solving Self-Instructions Used in Stress Inoculation Training

Viewing the stressful situation as a problem

This is not the end of the world, just a problem to be solved.

It's okay to feel discouraged, but just remember that you can deal with this problem

Orienting to the stressful situation as a problem

Just think about what I can do about it.

Focus on the information I need to gather.

Breaking the stressful situation into smaller units

What are the steps I need to do?

How can I break this thing down so I can tackle one piece at a time?

Problem solving

Set up a plan of action. What is the first thing to do?

What's my goal? What would I like to happen?

Source: Based on Meichenbaum & Deffenbacher, 1988.

TABLE **13-6**

Self-Reinforcement/Self-Efficacy Self-Instructions Used in Stress Inoculation Training

Keep it up. You're doing great.

Hang in there. You're coping well.

I'm getting better and better at this.

That wasn't as bad as I expected. Next time it will be even easier.

I'm not doing as well as I would like, but I do feel good that I am continuing to try.

Phase 3: Application

In the first two phases of stress inoculation training, clients develop adaptive ways of viewing potentially stress-evoking events and learn coping skills to deal with them. In the third phase, clients apply their new outlooks and coping behaviors. Initially, this is done in therapy sessions by visualizing and role-playing potentially stress-evoking scenes. For example, a client who experiences panic attacks might be asked to visualize having an attack and coping with it (a variation of coping desensitization; see Chapter 9). Imagining the panic attack can be made more realistic by inducing hyperventilation, a common symptom in panic attacks,[94] as is done in interoceptive exposure (see Chapter 9).

A single session of stress inoculation training was used to help African-American children (average age 12 years) cope with pain associated with sickle cell anemia (a disease that only occurs in African-Americans).[95] The cognitive coping skills taught included abbreviated progressive relaxation, emotive imagery, and calming self-instructions. The therapist first described and modeled each skill for the clients. The clients then practiced each skill until they were proficient at it. Next, clients practiced the newly acquired coping skills while experiencing two trials of low-intensity laboratory-induced pain. The pain was created through the use of a pressure stimulator; a blunt plastic edge is applied at a continuous pressure to a finger to gradually produce a dull, aching pain. The clients were given homework assignments involving daily practice of the skills along with audiotaped instructions about how to perform the skills. The therapist also telephoned clients once during the week after treatment to prompt them to practice using their coping skills. In comparison to children in a standard care control group, those receiving stress inoculation training had lower levels of negative thinking and were less likely to report pain during the pain stimulation trials following treatment.

Anger management programs for children typically include stress inoculation training as a component.[96] First, the therapist teaches coping skills to the children in groups. Then, the children in the program are asked to role-play taunting and teasing each other for 30-second periods, which gives each client an opportunity to practice implementing anger control strategies. Clients are given feedback on their performance and reinforced for using appropriate coping skills.

In the preceding examples, the simulated stress-evoking events with which clients practiced coping closely resembled the events the clients were expected to encounter in their daily lives. However, the simulated stressors need not be the same as the actual events because clients usually are taught *general* coping skills applicable to a wide range of potential stressors (which parallels coping desensitization procedures; see Chapter 9).

When clients have become proficient in applying coping skills to simulated stressors during therapy sessions, the therapist gives them homework assignments that gradually expose them to increasingly more stress-evoking events in real life. The therapist also trains clients to deal with inevitable failures and setbacks that occur in coping with real-life stressors using relapse prevention procedures that are described in the next section.

Case 13-3 illustrates an innovative application of stress inoculation training to a serious problem that 4 years of psychoanalytic therapy (three times a week) had not successfully treated.

CASE **13-3**

Eliminating Self-Mutilating Behavior Through Stress Inoculation Training[97]

Donna was a 32-year-old mother of two children who was hospitalized because of severe self-mutilating behavior consisting of "savagely scratching the left side of her face, resulting in an extensive, deep and frequently bleeding scar." Donna had a 15-year history of self-mutilation.

Stress inoculation training was the major component of the treatment package that was designed for the client. During the conceptualization phase, Donna kept a daily written log of (1) situations in which she felt the urge to scratch, (2) duration of the urges, (3) thoughts and feelings prior to and during scratching, and (4) thoughts and feelings after scratching. From this information, three situations that triggered her scratching emerged: looking at herself in the mirror; thinking about the scar on her face; and thinking about her estranged husband, who often had humiliated her because of the scratching. The increased tension she felt in these situations was relieved only by vigorous scratching, lasting a few minutes to several hours.

Donna was taught four coping skills: (1) progressive relaxation, (2) self-instructions, (3) covert sensitization, and (4) self-administered

(continued)

CASE **13-3** *(continued)*

physically aversive consequences (slapping the hand that she used to scratch herself). She rehearsed these skills as she looked at herself in a mirror and as she visualized herself with her husband.

After six sessions over a 2-week period, Donna's scratching had declined and she went home for a visit. During the visit, she was unable to cope with a provocative encounter with her husband and reverted to scratching. After another six sessions of therapy, Donna again made a home visit. This time she was able to apply her coping skills to an anxiety-provoking incident involving her husband. This success experience was a turning point for Donna. Thereafter, she reported needing to rely on only two of the coping skills—progressive relaxation and self-instructions—and expressed confidence in her ability to cope.

After 18 sessions, Donna was no longer scratching herself. She was discharged from the hospital and continued to keep a daily log. One year after therapy, her scratching had not recurred, and she reported that she no longer had the urge to scratch and that her scar had healed. Further, she had held a full-time job for 6 months and had divorced her husband.

Case 13-3 illustrates how the successful treatment of one problem can have positive effects on other problems a client is experiencing, which is an advantage of treating one or two target behaviors at a time. After Donna's scratching had been eliminated, she was able to work full-time, which her self-mutilating behavior had previously precluded, and put her family life in order.

IN THEORY **13-1**

Stress Inoculation Training: Parallels with Biological Immunization

Stress inoculation training is a behavioral analogue to *biological immunization* such as a flu vaccination. Disease-causing microorganisms are introduced into the body at doses too small to produce the physical symptoms of the disease; however, the person's immune system releases antibodies that fight off or neutralize the microorganisms. The antibodies remain in the system and are available to combat the microorganisms in the future, which strengthens the body's immune system.

Ernest Poser[98] first proposed the idea of psychologically immunizing people to stress-evoking events that result in maladaptive behaviors. *Behavioral immunology* involves exposing people to stress-evoking events in small doses and under safe conditions before they encounter the full-blown events in real life. Presumably, individuals pre-exposed to minor stressors develop, *on their own*, coping strategies that they can employ with future stress-evoking events.

Stress inoculation training does not rely on clients' devising their own coping skills. Instead, clients are taught a variety of coping skills that they rehearse while being exposed to controlled doses of stress-evoking events. Coping skills can be thought of as "psychological antibodies" that increase one's resistance to stressors. The goal is for clients to be able to activate these stress-fighting coping skills as they encounter real-life stressors.

Relapse Prevention: A Variation of Stress Inoculation

Relapse prevention consists of specific procedures for handling the inevitable setbacks that occur in coping with real-life stressors.[99] It involves identifying high-risk situations in which relapse is most likely to occur and learning and rehearsing coping skills that can be used in these high-risk situations.

Courtesy of Alan Marlatt

Alan Marlatt

Alan Marlatt and his colleagues initially developed an approach for preventing the relapse of addictive behaviors (in substance-related disorders) *after* the behaviors have been successfully treated.[100] Central to the relapse prevention model is the distinction between a lapse and a relapse. A *lapse* refers to a single, isolated violation of abstinence, which does not necessarily lead to a *relapse*, which is a full-blown return to the addictive behavior (that is, to pretreatment levels of substance abuse). Relapse prevention teaches clients to view a lapse as an error and as an opportunity for additional learning. The treatment provides clients with the cognitive-behavioral coping skills necessary to prevent lapses from escalating into relapses. Relapse prevention consists of four components: (1) identifying high-risk situations, (2) learning coping skills, (3) practicing coping skills, and (4) creating a lifestyle balance.

Identifying High-Risk Situations

Relapses are most likely to occur in high-risk situations. Almost three-fourths of all relapses of addictive behaviors are associated with (1) negative emotional states (35%), including frustration, anxiety, depression, anger, and loneliness; (2) social pressure (20%), such as being coaxed to go to a bar; and (3) interpersonal conflicts (16%), such as arguments with a spouse.[101] Clients must become aware of the specific situations that are most likely to trigger their relapse episodes so that they will be prepared to deal with them.

Learning Coping Skills

The ability to engage in effective coping responses when faced with a high-risk situation decreases the probability of a relapse. Further, successful coping with one high-risk situation tends to increase one's self-efficacy about being able to cope with other high-risk situations.[102]

The cognitive-behavioral coping skills that clients are taught include (1) *assertive behaviors* to help clients deal with social pressures to engage in addictive behaviors, (2) *progressive relaxation* and *stress management* to reduce tension and discomfort associated with negative emotional states, (3) *social and communication skills* to manage interpersonal conflicts, (4) *problem-solving skills* to deal effectively with problems in their daily lives, and (5) *cognitive restructuring* to change maladaptive cognitions related to their addictive behaviors (see Table 13-7 for a description of the four types of cognitions most often associated with addictive behaviors[103]).

Practicing Coping Skills

Once clients have learned coping skills, they practice them in simulated high-risk situations. For example, the therapist and client might role-play a scenario in which a friend asks the client to go out drinking, and the client responds with an appropriately assertive refusal. The two aims of this behavior rehearsal

TABLE **13-7**

Four Types of Cognitions Most Often Associated with Addictive Behaviors

Cognitions	Descriptions	Examples
ANTICIPATORY BELIEFS	Expectation of a positive result from engaging in an addictive behavior	"They'll think I'm pretty cool if I get high with them."
RELIEF-ORIENTED BELIEFS	Expectation of reduced discomfort from engaging in an addictive behavior	"I need a cigarette so I can relax."
FACILITATING BELIEFS	Client's giving himself or herself permission to engage in an addictive behavior	"It's only pot. It's not like I'm doing drugs."
AUTOMATIC THOUGHTS	Brief, repetitive, spontaneous mental images related to an addictive behavior that result in urges or cravings	Imagining sipping a cold beer while socializing with friends

Source: Based on Liese, 1994.

are for the client (1) to learn to recognize high-risk situations and then (2) to "automatically" engage in well-rehearsed coping skills rather than "automatically" reverting to habitual addictive behaviors.

Creating a Lifestyle Balance

A common trigger of addictive behaviors occurs when clients perceive that there is an imbalance in their lives between their obligations (what they "should" do, such as go to work) and their desires (what they want to do, such as go to a ball game).[104] The obvious solution is to increase clients' access to their desires. However, in the case of clients recovering from addictive habits, their most salient desires are likely to involve addictive behaviors. For instance, a client might think, "I deserve a drink for all the work I did today."

Accordingly, clients are encouraged to develop a *lifestyle balance* between their obligations and desires. First, they self-monitor their obligations and desires daily to identify the degree and nature of the imbalance. Then, where imbalances exist, clients use an activity schedule to increase activities that are both enjoyable and adaptive, which implies that the desirable activities are not at all associated with their addictive habits. The process can be viewed as relearning joy or "rejoyment."[105]

Relapse Prevention in Perspective

Relapse prevention has been used as part of the treatment of various substance-related disorders, including those involving alcohol,[106] nicotine,[107] cocaine,[108] marijuana,[109] and opiates.[110] Relapse prevention typically is part of a treatment package. For example, it has been combined with cognitive-behavioral couple therapy when alcohol abuse is an issue,[111] with pharmacological treatment,[112] and even with the Alcoholics Anonymous Twelve-Step Recovery program.[113] Relapse prevention also is used for other types of problems, such as to prevent high-risk sexual activity[114] and to treat body dysmorphic disorder,[115] erectile dysfunction,[116] and child molestation.[117]

The evidence regarding the effectiveness of relapse prevention for addictive behaviors is mixed.[118] Some studies show relapse prevention to be more effective than alternative treatments and no-treatment control conditions. For example, clients receiving transdermal (through the skin) nicotine replacement patches plus relapse prevention training had higher rates of smoking cessation than clients who received only the pharmacological intervention.[119] Other studies indicate that relapse prevention is at least as effective as alternative therapy approaches.[120] Thus far, the strongest evidence for the effectiveness of relapse prevention is in the treatment of the abuse of alcohol and multiple drugs.[121] Relapse prevention may be effective in the treatment of alcohol abuse when it is self-administered, as through a guided self-help approach that includes self-monitoring, goal setting, and brief readings and homework assignments.[122] In addition to promoting long-term maintenance, relapse prevention may decrease the severity of relapses.[123]

Positive findings regarding the effectiveness of relapse prevention must be viewed cautiously. Some of the relevant studies contain methodological weaknesses, such as not employing control groups[124] and evaluating relapse prevention in the context of a larger treatment package,[125] which clouds the specific contribution of the relapse prevention component. Further, some studies are less supportive of the superiority of relapse prevention compared with other treatments, particularly for cigarette smoking.[126] Taken together, the cumulative evidence indicates that relapse prevention for addictive behaviors is a promising intervention, but the evidence remains inconclusive.

Stress Inoculation Training in Perspective

Stress inoculation training has been used to treat and prevent a wide array of problems in adults. The three most common problems have been anxiety,[127] anger,[128] and pain.[129] Specific problems treated include fear of flying,[130] presurgical anxiety,[131] coping with dental examinations,[132] reducing stress in cancer patients,[133] trauma-related stress (such as from terrorist attacks),[134] and child abuse by adults.[135] Stress inoculation training also can be used to help people in inherently stress-evoking situations reduce their emotional distress and impaired performance. As one example, first-year law students exhibited decreases on measures of stress and irrationality as well as enhanced academic performance after receiving stress inoculation training.[136] Stress inoculation training can be applied with groups of clients as well as individually.[137]

Although stress inoculation training most often has been used with adults, it occasionally has been applied with children and adolescents, such as for dealing with aggressive behaviors[138] and refusal to attend school.[139] However, controlled research on stress inoculation training applications to the problems of children and adolescents is lacking.[140]

Stress inoculation training recently has been used to treat posttraumatic stress disorder, especially with female victims of sexual and physical assault.[141] In one intensive treatment program involving nine biweekly individual sessions, therapists taught clients a variety of coping skills, including progressive relaxation, differential relaxation, thought stopping, cognitive restructuring, self-instructions, and covert modeling.[142] Clients practiced applying their coping skills to manage assault-related anxiety that arose during their daily activities. Stress inoculation training significantly reduced posttraumatic stress disorder symptoms and depression compared with clients in a wait-list control group, and clients maintained these gains at a 12-month follow-up. In some cases, stress inoculation training has been as effective as exposure therapy in treating posttraumatic stress disorder. Moreover, women who have been sexually assaulted consider stress inoculation training a palatable treatment.[143] Preliminary evidence also indicates that stress inoculation training was effective in treating posttraumatic stress disorder with 8- to 10-year-old girls and boys who were sexually abused.[144]

The stress inoculation model has potential for preparing people to deal with almost any stress-inducing event. For example, it may be useful for adolescents with gay, lesbian, and bisexual orientations who experience significant stress related to others' negative attitudes about homosexuality (homophobia); accepting one's sexual identity; disclosing one's sexual orientation to others; and developing relationships, both sexual and friendship-based.[145] Enhancing the psychological resiliency of military personnel to cope with the stressors in military service and to prevent posttraumatic stress disorder also has potential.[146]

Most controlled research studies evaluating stress inoculation training have indicated that it is an effective treatment.[147] Long-term maintenance of treatment effects have been found for anxiety, depression,[148] and dental phobia.[149] The essential treatment component in stress inoculation training appears to be *learning coping skills.*[150]

Stress inoculation training has not been as extensively evaluated as other cognitive-behavioral therapies.[151] One possible reason is that stress inoculation training is a treatment package consisting of components that have been evaluated independently, including relaxation training, cognitive restructuring, and self-instructions. It is tempting to assume that combining therapies that are known to be effective will produce a treatment that is more potent than any of its components. However, whether the whole is greater or even equal to one of its parts is an empirical question that research must answer.

COGNITIVE-BEHAVIORAL COUPLE THERAPY

Problems in couple relationships—in or out of marriage, between same-sex or opposite-sex partners—are among the most frequent reasons that adults seek psychological assistance. Because couple relationships are complex and multifaceted, therapy generally involves treatment packages that address different aspects of couple difficulties.

Traditional Behavioral Couple Therapy

Traditional behavioral couple therapy originally consisted of two basic components: *training in communication and problem-solving skills* and *increasing positive behavior exchanges*. In later variations, cognitive restructuring was also included.

Training in Communication and Problem-Solving Skills

Communication is the basis for any interpersonal relationship, and poor communication is a common denominator among distressed couples.[152] Communication skills emphasized in traditional behavioral couple therapy include listening, restating what the other person has said, expressing feelings directly, making requests, giving feedback, and arranging regular times to talk. Dealing with the numerous small and large problems all couples face also is necessary for maintaining a healthy relationship, and distressed couples typically have deficits in problem-solving skills. Both communication and problem-solving skills are taught to couples using standard skills training procedures (see Chapter 11).

Increasing Positive Behavior Exchanges

Distressed partners often do not feel especially loving toward one another, and not surprisingly, this is reflected in the negative ways they interact (for example, using sarcasm and doing things the other person dislikes). Accordingly, a general goal of traditional behavioral couple therapy is to increase partners' *positive behavior exchanges*.[153] One way to accomplish this goal is through the **caring-days technique**, developed by Richard Stuart, in which partners act *as if* they care for each other.[154] The therapist instructs partners to perform small, specific, positive behaviors for each other (consistent with Eliza Doolittle, in *My Fair Lady*, telling Professor Henry Higgins, "If you're in love, show me"). Each partner is asked to answer the question, "What could your partner do that would show you that he or she cares for you?" and compile a list of these *caring behaviors*. The therapist instructs each partner to perform a minimum number of caring behaviors from his or her partner's list, even if the partner has not done so. The partners keep records of the caring behaviors they perform, such as the example in Figure 13-4.

Another way to increase positive behavior exchanges is through the *Catch Your Partner Doing Something Nice* technique.[155] Each partner notices and acknowledges one pleasing behavior performed by the other each day. Contingency contracts also are employed to promote positive behavior exchanges and implement broader behavior changes in the relationship.[156]

Cognitive Restructuring

Discrepancies in partners' cognitions about aspects of their relationship often play a role in creating and maintaining couple problems. The discrepancies may be in (1) *perceptions* about what has occurred, (2) *attributions* about why a partner did something, (3) *expectations* about how things will be, or (4) *assumptions* about how things are or should be (see Table 13-8).[157] To deal with these discrepancies, couples use cognitive restructuring and other

Caring Behaviors Record

Week of June 16

Sandy _____ does for Shelly _____

	Su	Mo	Tu	We	Th	Fr	Sa
Ask how I'm feeling.		✓		✓	✓		
Play scrabble with me.	✓	✓					
Do the dishes.		✓	✓		✓	✓	✓
Make me a cup of coffee.	✓		✓		✓		
Kiss me when I leave or come home.		✓	✓	✓		✓	
Put the cap on the tooth paste.	✓		✓	✓	✓		✓
Turn lights off.	✓		✓	✓	✓		
Compliment me.	✓		✓	✓	✓	✓	
Say "good night" before going to sleep.	✓	✓				✓	✓
Say "good morning," when I first wake up.						✓	✓

Shelly _____ does for Sandy _____

	Su	Mo	Tu	We	Th	Fr	Sa
Kiss me spontaneously.			✓		✓		✓
Call me at work to say hello.			✓	✓		✓	
Compliment my appearance.		✓	✓		✓		✓
Flush the toilet after using it.		✓	✓		✓	✓	✓
Leave/send me short, loving notes.	✓	✓		✓			
Thank me for something I did.	✓	✓		✓			
Laugh at my jokes.	✓	✓			✓	✓	✓
Keep your dresser neat.	✓		✓	✓			
Ask how my day went.		✓		✓		✓	

FIGURE 13-4

Record of each partner's caring behaviors and their being performed

cognitive-behavioral therapy procedures. Couples are first taught to evaluate how valid or reasonable their cognitions are and then to modify biased or unrealistic thoughts by substituting more appropriate and adaptive ones.

Effectiveness of Traditional Behavioral Couple Therapy

A number of well-controlled studies have demonstrated that traditional behavioral couple therapy can effectively reduce couples' distress.[158] Further, for married couples it has been found to alleviate depression.[159] This is an important finding because almost half the clients who seek treatment for

TABLE **13-8**

Common Cognitive Discrepancies Held by Distressed Couples

Discrepancy	Description	Example
PERCEPTIONS	Partners "see" things differently	PAT: "We haven't talked in months." CHRIS: "We talked just last week."
ATTRIBUTIONS	One partner wrongly infers the cause of the other's behavior	PAT: "I've been waiting for a half hour. You just wanted to keep me waiting." CHRIS: "I'm late because I had a flat tire on the way here."
EXPECTATIONS	Partners anticipate different outcomes	PAT: "I was looking forward to making love tonight." CHRIS: "I was hoping to watch TV and just drift off to sleep."
ASSUMPTIONS	Partners hold different assumptions	PAT: "*You* are supposed to take care of the kids." CHRIS: "Taking care of *our* children is *our* responsibility."

depression have marital difficulties.[160] Traditional behavioral couple therapy also has shown particular promise in treating substance abuse.[161]

Unfortunately, traditional behavioral couple therapy is effective for only about two-thirds of couples treated. Moreover, of these couples, only two-thirds maintain their improvement over a 1- to 2-year period.[162] The net result is that less than half the couples treated with traditional behavioral couple therapy maintain the benefits after therapy. This sobering statistic was the impetus for developing integrative behavioral couple therapy.[163]

Integrative Behavioral Couple Therapy

Courtesy of Virginia Rutter

Neil Jacobson

Traditional behavioral couple therapy focuses on changing partner behaviors that are most upsetting to the other partner.[164] In contrast, Neil Jacobson and Andrew Christensen's **integrative behavioral couple therapy** establishes an alternative goal for distressed couples—namely, *emotional acceptance of one's partner's upsetting behaviors.*[165c] In couple therapy, emotional acceptance is sometimes the only realistic goal. In some cases, partners are not willing to change particular behaviors that upset their partner, such as giving up a job that requires working nights. In other cases, a partner may be willing to change, but achieving the desired change may be extremely difficult and take a long time, such as overcoming long-standing emotional inhibitions or modifying habitual ways of behaving. In some instances, partners have limitations that are unchangeable, such as when physical conditions preclude engaging in particular activities that the other partner enjoys. Finally, partners will always

---

^c*Acceptance* should not be confused with the *acceptability* of behavior therapy procedures to clients and therapists, one of the criteria of treatment effectiveness (see Chapter 4).

Andrew Christensen

have differences, which implies that acceptance may be a fundamental requirement for long-term satisfaction in a couple relationship.[166] At the risk of stating the obvious, when domestic violence is one of the presenting problems in couple therapy, acceptance is not a viable goal.

Acceptance does not mean resignation to a troubled relationship as it is. Accepting a partner's limitations or "unacceptable characteristics" can be a vehicle for promoting greater closeness and intimacy, which does change the nature of the relationship. Moreover, when acceptance is the goal of couple therapy there is an absence of pressure to change, and, paradoxically, the absence of pressure may create change.[167]

Acceptance as a goal in couple therapy is not a new idea. Until recently, however, concrete methods for promoting acceptance have not been available.[168] To promote acceptance, integrative behavioral couple therapy uses four strategies:

1. *Empathic joining* refers to the partners' learning to understand and appreciate each other's experience of emotional pain within the relationship. Empathic joining requires careful listening to a partner's description of what he or she is experiencing, not judging the experience, and attempting to view the experience from the partner's perspective. The therapist helps the couple understand that the way they view and react to their differences—not the mere fact that they have differences (which is inevitable)—is primarily responsible for their interpersonal distress.[169] Lack of empathy is often a problem for distressed couples with one partner who suffers from chronic physical pain, and integrative behavioral couple therapy may be a particularly useful treatment for them.[170]

2. *Detachment* fosters acceptance by having the partners distance themselves from their conflicts. The partners are encouraged to talk and think about their difficulties as an "it"—something external to each of them rather than part of them.[171] The "it" becomes a painful, common enemy that they share and cope with together rather than a problem that one partner creates or something that one does to the other. Couples may feel less upset when talking about "it," even though the problem itself has not been resolved.

3. *Tolerance building* involves learning ways to become less upset by a partner's behaviors. Through cognitive restructuring, partners come to view the other's so-called negative behaviors positively. For example, "moody" might be reconstrued as "thoughtful," "picky" as "careful," and "scatterbrained" as "free-wheeling." To effectively engage in such cognitive restructuring, the couple must understand that most behaviors are not inherently negative or positive. "Positive" and "negative" are evaluations we place on behaviors. Moreover, often the very behaviors that partners view as disturbing when they are experiencing conflict in their relationship are the same behaviors they found attractive in the past, particularly during courtship.[172] For instance, when they were dating, a man may have found a woman's willingness to do things on the spur of the moment refreshing and exciting. Several years into their marriage, however, the husband may complain that his wife is unpredictable and seems to change her mind all the time.

4. *Self-care* consists of each partner's developing ways to derive satisfaction and personal fulfillment independent of the relationship. This promotes less dependence on one another for some basic life needs. Couples are asked to facilitate each other's engaging in self-care activities.

At first glance, the idea of promoting acceptance in distressed couples may not seem particularly behavioral. On closer inspection, it turns out to be well grounded in behavior therapy principles and procedures.[173] In addition to using specific cognitive-behavioral procedures (such as cognitive restructuring) to foster acceptance, the general approach is action-oriented. Partners engage in specific behaviors to develop acceptance. This active approach differs from traditional views of acceptance as passive resignation. You will learn more about the use of acceptance in behavior therapy in Chapter 14.

Integrative Behavioral Couple Therapy in Perspective

In the largest efficacy study of couple therapy ever conducted, Christensen and his colleagues randomly assigned 134 seriously and chronically distressed couples in Los Angeles and Seattle to either integrative or traditional behavioral couple therapy.[174] Seven experienced clinical psychologists practicing in the community implemented the therapy. They were trained in both forms of couple therapy and followed a protocol contained in treatment manuals to provide the form of therapy each client was assigned to. Ratings of the therapists' adherence to the protocols and proficiency in implementing each therapy indicated that they had competently administered the treatments.

Immediately after treatment, a majority of the couples in both conditions showed clinically significant improvement.[175] For example, on a measure of marital satisfaction—the standard measure used to assess the success of couple therapy—71% of the couples in integrative behavioral couple therapy and 59% of the couples in traditional behavioral couple therapy reliably improved or recovered. At a 2-year follow-up of 130 of the 134 original couples, 69% of the couples in the integrative treatment and 60% of the couples in the traditional treatment showed clinically significant improvement.[176] Although the final outcomes of the two forms of behavioral couple therapy were similar, there were some noteworthy differences in the course of the change. Compared to couples in traditional behavioral couple therapy, couples in integrative behavioral couple therapy tended to report improvements in marital satisfaction earlier and couples who remained together had greater marital satisfaction and more stability throughout the follow-up period. These are encouraging findings, especially given that the couples in the study began treatment with serious, long-standing marital distress. Along with the findings of other studies that compared behavioral couple therapy to no treatment,[177] it is fair to say that behavioral couple therapy is a potent treatment.

Perhaps the most difficult couple problem to treat is infidelity. There are some initial indications that integrative behavioral couple therapy is a promising treatment for dealing with infidelity both in opposite-sex[178] and same-sex couples.[179]

Preventing Couple Relationship Problems

Couple relationship problems are difficult to treat because of their complex, multifaceted nature and because, over time, patterns of maladaptive interactions have been mutually reinforced. One way around these inevitable hurdles is to prevent such patterns from developing in the first place.[180] Toward this end, Howard Markman has developed the Prevention and Relationship Enhancement Program (aptly known as PREP) that parallels cognitive-behavioral couple therapy.[181] PREP teaches couples who are not in distress specific skills that are associated with successful relationships. The skills include communication, problem solving, negotiation of roles and responsibilities, and clarification of values and expectations related to sexuality and intimacy; in its most recent version, PREP also emphasizes commitment, friendship and positive connection, and forgiveness.[182] The relationship-enhancement skills training approach has led to improved relationship satisfaction and positive feelings about one's partner, lower levels of couple violence, and lower rates of separation.[183]

ALL THINGS CONSIDERED: COGNITIVE-BEHAVIORAL COPING SKILLS THERAPY

Cognitive-behavioral coping skills therapies are used to treat a wide array of problem behaviors. In contrast to cognitive restructuring therapies, which are primarily applicable to adults, most cognitive-behavioral coping skills therapies are also suitable for children and adolescents.

In general, the effectiveness of cognitive-behavioral coping skills therapy is well documented by research, especially for emotional problems such as anxiety and depression. However, the complexity of cognitive-behavioral coping skills therapies poses problems for evaluating their effectiveness. The therapy often involves a treatment package, and usually the specific contributions of the various components are not assessed. Further, the specific components employed can vary from study to study, even though the same name is used to designate the therapy in each study. These variations may account, in part, for occasional discrepant findings of research evaluating cognitive-behavioral coping skills therapies.

The self-control nature of cognitive-behavioral coping skills therapies requires clients to accept major responsibility for the success of treatment, especially in the transfer of the coping skills to their everyday lives. Whereas the general findings are that clients can and do learn the coping skills, clients often fail to implement the coping skills on their own when the skills are needed.[184] This is true for employing self-instructions, problem-solving strategies, and coping skills learned and practiced in stress inoculation training. Training in and transfer of the implementation phase of cognitive-behavioral coping skills therapies are important challenges that need to be addressed.

Cognitive-behavioral coping skills therapies have been used with ethnic minority clients,[185] including those with gay, lesbian, and bisexual orientations.[186] The emphasis on self-control may be especially well-suited for cultures that consider it shameful and embarrassing to seek help from others for personal problems.

Therapies that teach clients coping skills serve two functions. First, they enable clients to deal with the problems for which they have sought therapy. Second, clients may be able to apply the coping skills to future problems in their lives. For example, this is essential in treating *borderline personality disorder*, which is characterized by repeated unstable relationships, extreme mood changes, a negative self-image, and impulsive and often self-destructive behaviors. People with this debilitating disorder appear to have one crisis after another in their lives. Marsha Linehan developed *dialectical behavior therapy* specifically to treat borderline personality disorder (which you will read about in Chapter 14). A major component of dialectical behavior therapy is teaching clients cognitive-behavioral coping skills, including problem solving, progressive relaxation, cognitive restructuring, and the use of assertive behaviors for dealing effectively with stressors.[187]

ALL THINGS CONSIDERED:
COGNITIVE-BEHAVIORAL THERAPY

We conclude our discussion of cognitive-behavioral therapy, begun in Chapter 12, with some general comments on its current status. In 1968, a group of prominent behavior therapists suggested that "current [behavior therapy] procedures should be modified and new procedures developed to capitalize upon the human organism's unique capacity for cognitive control."[188] Clearly, this recommendation was heeded. Over the next decade, cognitive-behavioral therapy developed, with only minor opposition from those who believed that behavior therapy should deal only with overt behaviors.[189] By 1980, cognitive-behavioral therapy constituted a subfield of behavior therapy,[190] and today it is at the forefront of behavior therapy.[191] The cognitive-behavioral *Zeitgeist* (German for "spirit of the times") within behavior therapy parallels the "cognitive revolution" in psychology.[192] Bandura has argued that *all* behavior therapies are most usefully viewed as cognitive-behavioral.

> The field of psychological change is not well served by false dichotomies that there exist pure cognitive and pure [overt] behavioral treatments. One would be hard pressed to find a "behavioral" method that does not rely, at least in part, on cognitive conveyance [mediation], or a "cognitive" method that is devoid of any performance [overt behavioral] elements.[193]

To benefit from cognitive restructuring therapies, clients must possess the requisite cognitive skills, such as the ability to use language and to reason logically. These abilities are linked to cognitive development,[194] which is one reason that cognitive restructuring therapies are more suitable for adults than children and adolescents.

In contrast, cognitive-behavioral coping skills therapies have been effective with children and adolescents as well as clients with severe intellectual deficits. Because the treatment procedures are largely self-administered, successful treatment by cognitive-behavioral coping skills therapy requires clients to have relatively high motivation to change their behaviors. For instance, youngsters who are referred by adults for treatment of aggressive or impulsive behaviors generally have little motivation to change their behaviors. After all, it is the adults who want these children to behave differently. Thus, children may be capable of learning self-instructions and problem-solving skills, but they often cannot be relied on to apply them in their natural environments without additional interventions, such as prompting and reinforcement from adults.[195]

SUMMARY

1. Cognitive-behavioral coping skills therapy treats problems that are maintained by a deficit of adaptive cognitions by changing both cognitions and overt behaviors.

2. In self-instructional training, clients learn to direct themselves to cope effectively with difficult situations. Self-instructions serve six functions: preparing clients to use self-instructions, focusing attention, guiding behavior, providing encouragement, evaluating performance, and reducing anxiety.

3. The five steps of self-instructional training are cognitive modeling, cognitive participant modeling, overt self-instructions, fading of overt self-instructions, and covert self-instructions.

4. Problem-solving therapy/training teaches clients a systematic strategy for approaching problems. Problem-solving therapy serves the dual purpose of treating clients' immediate problems and preparing clients to deal with future problems on their own. Problem-solving training teaches problem-solving skills as a general coping strategy for dealing with problems that arise in the course of daily life.

5. The seven stages of problem solving are adopting a problem-solving orientation, defining the problem, selecting goals, generating alternative solutions, choosing the best solution, implementing the solution, and evaluating its effects. Problem-solving skills are taught to clients through cognitive modeling, prompting, self-instructions, and reinforcement.

6. Children and adults can learn problem-solving skills, often quickly. However, clients frequently do not apply the skills in their everyday lives.

7. Stress inoculation training helps clients cope with stress by teaching them coping skills and then having clients practice the skills while they are exposed to stress-evoking events. Stress inoculation training consists of three phases: conceptualization, coping skills acquisition, and application. Anxiety, anger, and pain are the most frequently treated problems. The essential component is learning coping skills.

8. Stress inoculation training is a behavioral analogue of biological immunization. The coping skills clients learn can be considered "psychological antibodies" that increase a person's resistance to potentially stress-evoking events.

9. Relapse prevention is a variant of stress inoculation that prepares clients who have completed treatment for addictive behaviors to deal with future relapses. Clients identify high-risk situations, develop coping skills, practice the coping skills before they are needed, and develop a lifestyle that balances obligations and desires.

10. The three basic components of traditional behavioral couple therapy are training in communication and problem-solving skills, increasing positive behavior exchanges, and training in cognitive restructuring. The usual

goal of cognitive-behavioral couple therapy is for each partner to change behaviors that are problematic for the other.

11. Integrative behavioral couple therapy employs the alternative goal of accepting one's partner's troublesome behaviors. To promote acceptance, four strategies are used: empathic joining, detachment, tolerance building, and self-care.

12. A preventive approach to the problem of couple distress, Prevention and Relationship Enhancement Program (PREP) teaches couples who are not experiencing relationship problems specific skills that are associated with successful relationships.

13. Cognitive-behavioral coping skills therapies are used to treat a wide array of problems and most are applicable to children and adolescents as well as adults. Although clients learn coping skills easily, the challenge is getting clients to implement them in their daily lives.

REFERENCE NOTES

1. Rankin, 1960.
2. Meichenbaum & Goodman, 1971.
3. For example, Camp & Bash, 1981; Camp, Blom, Herbert, & Van Doorwick, 1977; Spivack & Shure, 1974.
4. For example, Meichenbaum & Cameron, 1973; Meyers, Mercatoris, & Sirota, 1976.
5. For example, Guevremont, Tishelman, & Hull, 1985.
6. Meichenbaum & Goodman, 1971, p. 117.
7. Meichenbaum, 1977.
8. Guevremont, Osnes, & Stokes, 1988.
9. Kendall & Braswell, 1985.
10. For example, Guevremont, Tishelman, & Hull, 1985.
11. For example, Lochman, 1985; Lochman & Curry, 1986.
12. For example, Bryant & Budd, 1982; Guevremont, Osnes, & Stokes, 1988.
13. Burgio, Whitman, & Johnson, 1980.
14. For example, Kendall & Wilcox, 1980; Schleser, Meyers, & Cohen, 1981.
15. For example, Kendall & Finch, 1978; Meichenbaum & Goodman, 1971.
16. Bentall, Higson, & Lowe, 1987; Meichenbaum & Cameron, 1973; Meyers, Mercatoris, & Sirota, 1976.
17. Combs & Lahey, 1981.
18. Cradock, Cotler, & Jason, 1978; Glass, Gottman, & Shmurak, 1976; Holroyd, 1976; Kendall, 1994; McCordick, Kaplan, Finn, & Smith, 1979; Meichenbaum, Gilmore, & Fedoravicius, 1971; Ollendick, Hagopian, & King, 1997.
19. For example, Camp, Blom, Herbert, & Van Doorwick, 1977; Foreman, 1980.
20. Overhoser & Fine, 1994.
21. For example, Dunkel & Glaros, 1978.
22. For example, Kettlewell, Mizes, & Wasylyshyn, 1992.
23. Cash & Lavallee, 1997.
24. Gil, Carson, Sedway, Porter, Schaeffer, & Orringer, 2000.
25. For example, Jacobs & Cochran, 1982; Kaplan, 1982; Kazdin & Mascitelli, 1982.
26. For example, Labouvie-Vief & Gonda, 1976; Meichenbaum, 1974.
27. Keogh, Faw, Whitman, & Reid, 1984.
28. Meichenbaum, 1975.
29. O'Callaghan & Couvadelli, 1998; Suzman, Morris, Morris, & Milan, 1997.
30. Ecton & Feindler, 1990.
31. Rusch, Hughes, & Wilson, 1995.
32. For example, Rusch, Morgan, Martin, Riva, & Agran, 1985.
33. For example, Hughes & Rusch, 1989.
34. For example, Rusch, Martin, Lagomarcino, & White, 1987.
35. For example, Sowers, Rusch, Connis, & Cummings, 1980.
36. For example, D'Zurilla & Chang, 1995.
37. For example, Biggam & Power, 1999; D'Zurilla & Nezu, 2007; Frye & Goodman, 2000; McCabe, Blankstein, & Mills, 1999; Rudd, Joiner, & Rajab, 2001.
38. D'Zurilla & Nezu, 2007; Nezu, Nezu, & D'Zurilla, 2007.

39. D'Zurilla & Goldfried, 1971.
40. For example, D'Zurilla & Maschka, 1988.
41. For example, Alexopoulos, Raue, & Arean, 2003; Arean, Perri, Nezu, Schein, Christopher, & Joseph, 1993; Mynors-Wallis, Gath, Day, & Baker, 2000.
42. Kleiner, Marshall, & Spevack, 1987.
43. Black, 1987; Johnson, Corrigan, & Mayo, 1987.
44. Shaffer, Beck, & Boothroyd, 1983.
45. Bujold, Ladouceur, Sylvain, & Boisvert, 1994; Doiron & Nicki, 2007.
46. Jacobson, 1991; Jacobson & Margolin, 1979.
47. Dawson, De Armas, McGrath, & Kelly, 1986; MacMillan, Guevremont, & Hansen, 1989.
48. Hansen, St. Lawrence, & Christoff, 1985.
49. Falloon & Coverdale, 1994.
50. Varni, La Greca, & Spirito, 2000.
51. For example, Kendall & Gerow, 1995.
52. For example, Lascelles, Cunningham, McGrath, & Sullivan, 1989.
53. Braet & Winckel, 2000.
54. For example, Kazdin, Esveldt-Dawson, French, & Unis, 1987.
55. Lochman & Curry, 1986; Lochman, Nelson, & Sims, 1981.
56. Bujold, Ladouceur, Sylvain, & Boisvert, 1994.
57. Feindler, Ecton, Kingsley, & Dubey, 1986; Feindler, Marriott, & Iwata, 1984.
58. Frisby, 1990.
59. Shure & Spivack, 1980; Spivack & Shure, 1974.
60. Robin & Foster, 1989.
61. For example, Kendall & Gerow, 1995.
62. For example, Bushman, 2008; Tarrier, Kinney, McCarthy, Humphreys, Wittkowski, & Morris, 2000.
63. For example, Daunic, Smith, Brank, & Penfield, 2006.
64. For example, D'Zurilla & Nezu, 2007; D'Zurilla & Goldfried, 1971; Spivack & Shure, 1974.
65. D'Zurilla & Nezu, 2001.
66. Nezu, Nezu, D'Zurilla, & Rothenberg, 1996.
67. Nezu, Nezu, D'Zurilla, & Rothenberg, 1996.
68. Nezu, Nezu, D'Zurilla, & Rothenberg, 1996; Nezu, Nezu, & Houts, 1993; Watson & Kramer, 1995.
69. Braswell & Kendall, 2001; Spivack & Shure, 1974.
70. For example, Sharp, 1981; Spivack & Shure, 1974.
71. For example, Kazdin, Esveldt-Dawson, French, & Unis, 1987; Yu, Harris, Solovitz, & Franklin, 1986.

72. Feindler, Marriott, & Iwata, 1984.
73. Feindler, Ecton, Kingsley, & Dubey, 1986.
74. Grothberg, Feindler, White, & Stutman, 1991; Robin & Foster, 1989.
75. Nangle, Carr-Nangle, & Hansen, 1994.
76. Adapted from Guevremont & Foster, 1992.
77. Chang, D'Zurilla, & Sanna, 2004; Nezu, 2004.
78. D'Zurilla & Nezu, 2001.
79. D'Zurilla & Nezu, 1999.
80. Weersing, Gonzalez, Campo, & Lucas, 2008.
81. Arean, Perri, Nezu, Schein, Christopher, & Joseph, 1993.
82. Liberman, Eckman, & Marder, 2001.
83. Clum & Febbraro, 2004; D'Zurilla, Chang, Nottingham, & Faccini, 1998; Rudd, Joiner, & Rajab, 2001; Fitzpatrick, Witte, & Schmidt, 2005.
84. Nezu, Nezu, D'Zurilla, & Rothenberg, 1996; Nezu, Nezu, & Houts, 1993.
85. D'Zurilla, Nezu, & Maydeu-Olivares, 2002; Maydeu-Olivares & D'Zurilla, 1997.
86. Maydeu-Olivares, Rodriguez-Fornells, Gomez-Benito, & D'Zurilla, 2000.
87. Graf, 2003.
88. Siu & Shek, 2005.
89. For example, D'Zurilla & Nezu, 1982; Shure & Spivack, 1980; Spivack & Shure, 1974; Yu, Harris, Solovitz, & Franklin, 1986.
90. Yu, Harris, Solovitz, & Franklin, 1986; compare with D'Zurilla & Maschka, 1988.
91. McCabe, Blankstein, & Mills, 1999.
92. Cofer & Appley, 1964; Lazarus & Folkman, 1984.
93. Meichenbaum, 1977, 1985, 2007.
94. Barlow & Cerney, 1988.
95. Gil et al., 1997.
96. Lochman, 2003; Lochman, Whidby, & FitzGerald, 2000; Nelson & Finch, 2000.
97. Kaminer & Shahar, 1987; quotation from p. 289.
98. Poser, 1970; Poser & King, 1975; Spiegler, 1980.
99. Marlatt & Gordon, 1985.
100. Marlatt & Donovan, 2005; Marlatt & Gordon, 1985; Witkiewitz & Marlatt, 2007.
101. Marlatt & Barrett, 1994.
102. Marlatt & Barrett, 1994.
103. Liese, 1994.
104. Collier & Marlatt, 1995; Marlatt & Tapert, 1993.
105. Collier & Marlatt, 1995.
106. For example, Peterson & Lowe, 1992; Sobell, Sobell, & Leo, 2000; Somers & Marlatt, 1992.
107. For example, Dooley & Halford, 1992; Gruder et al., 1993.

108. For example, Maude-Griffen, Hohenstein, Humfleet, Reilly, Tusel, & Hall, 1998; Rohenow, Monti, Martin, Michalec, & Abrams, 2000.

109. For example, Stephens, Rottman, & Simpson, 1994.

110. For example, Chang, Carroll, Behr, & Kosten, 1992.

111. Wells, Peterson, Gainey, Hawkins, & Catalano, 1994.

112. For example, Irvin, Bowers, Dunn, & Wang, 1999; O'Farrell, 1994.

113. For example, Minneker-Hugel, Unland, & Buchkremer, 1992.

114. For example, Corrigan, Thompson, & Malow, 1992.

115. McKay, 1999,

116. McCarthy, 2001.

117. Gillies, Hashmall, Hilton, & Webster, 1992.

118. For example, Carroll, 1996; Carroll, Rounsaville, & Gawin, 1991; Hollon & Beck, 1994.

119. Minneker-Hugel, Unland, & Buchkremer, 1992.

120. For example, Ouimette, Finney, & Moos, 1997; Wells, Peterson, Gainey, Hawkins, & Catalano, 1994.

121. Irvin, Bowers, Dunn, & Wang, 1999.

122. Sobell & Sobell, 2000; Sobell, Sobell, & Leo, 2000.

123. Carroll, 1996; Wells, Peterson, Gainey, Hawkins, & Catalano, 1994.

124. For example, Mazur & Michael, 1992.

125. For eample, Chang, Carroll, Behr, & Kosten, 1992.

126. Carmody, 1992; Irvin, Bowers, Dunn, & Wang, 1999; Ockene et al., 2000.

127. Meichenbaum & Cameron, 1972; Suinn, 2001.

128. Cahill, Rauch, Hembree, & Foa, 2004; Novaco, 1975, 1977a, 1977b; Suinn, 2001.

129. García, Simón, Durán, Canceller, & Aneiros, 2006; Turk, 1975, 1976.

130. Meichenbaum & Deffenbacher, 1988.

131. For example, Wells, Howard, Nowlin, & Vargas, 1986.

132. For example, Getka & Glass, 1992; Liddell, Di Fazio, Blackwood, & Ackerman, 1994; Moses & Hollandsworth, 1985.

133. Elsesser, Van Berkel, Sartory, Biermann-Göcke, & Ohl, 1994.

134. Meichenbaum & Deffenbacher, 1988.

135. Meichenbaum & Deffenhacher, 1988.

136. Sheehy & Horan, 2005.

137. For example, Lochman, 2003; Lochman, Whidby, & FitzGerald, 2000; Nelson & Finch, 2000.

138. For example, Feindler, Ecton, Kingsley, & Dubey, 1986; Lochman & Curry, 1986.

139. King et al., 1998.

140. Maag & Kotlash, 1994.

141. Foa & Rothbaum, 1998; Rothbaum, Meadows, Resick, & Foy, 2000; Trzepacz & Luiselli, 2004; Veronen & Kilpatrick, 1983.

142. Foa, Dancu, Hembree, Jaycox, Meadows, Street, 1999.

143. Meadows & Foa, 1998; Muran & DiGiuseppe, 2000.

144. Farrell, Hains, & Davies, 1998.

145. Safren, Hollander, Hart, & Heimberg, 2001.

146. Thompson & McCreary, 2006.

147. Foa, Davidson, & Frances, 1999; Hembree & Foa, 2003; Meichenbaum, 1985; Meichenbaum & Deffenbacher, 1988.

148. Meichenbaum & Deffenbacher, 1988.

149. Liddell, Di Fazio, Blackwood, & Ackerman, 1994.

150. Horan, Hackett, Buchanan, Stone, & Stone, 1977; Vallis, 1984.

151. For example, Maag & Kotlash, 1994.

152. For example, Geiss & O'Leary, 1981.

153. For example, Jacobson & Margolin, 1979; Patterson & Reid, 1970.

154. Stuart, 1969, 1980.

155. O'Farrell & Fals-Stewart, 2000.

156. Baucom & Epstein, 1990; Jacobson & Margolin, 1979; O'Farrell & Fals-Stewart, 2000; Stuart, 1969, 1980.

157. Baucom & Epstein, 1990; Beck, 1989.

158. Baucom & Hoffman, 1986; Baucom, Shoham, Mueser, Daiuto, & Stickle, 1998; Hahlweg & Markman, 1988; Jacobson, 1989.

159. For example, Baucom, Shoham, Mueser, Daiuto, & Stickle, 1998; Beach & O'Leary, 1992.

160. Beach, Whisman, & O'Leary, 1994.

161. Epstein & McCrady, 1998; O'Farrell & Fals-Stewart, 2000.

162. Christensen, Jacobson, & Babcock, 1995.

163. Christensen, Jacobson, & Babcock, 1995.

164. For example, Stuart, 1980.

165. Baucom, Christensen, & Yi, 2005; Christensen, Jacobson, Babcock, 1995; Jacobson, 1991, 1992, 1993; Jacobson & Christensen, 1996.

166. Waller & Spiegler, 1997.

167. Jacobson, Christensen, Prince, Cordova, & Eldridge, 2000.

168. Waller & Spiegler, 1997.

169. Compare with Waller & Spiegler, 1997.

170. Cano & Leonard, 2006.

171. Compare with White, 1989, 1995.

172. Waller & Spiegler, 1997.

173. Jacobson, 1992.

174. Christensen, Atkins, Berns, Wheeler, Baucom, & Simpson, 2004.

175. Christensen, Atkins, Berns, Wheeler, Baucom, & Simpson, 2004.

176. Christensen, Atkins, Yi, Baucom, & George, 2006.

177. Baucom, Hahlweg, & Kuschel, 2003; Shandish & Baldwin, 2005.

178. Baucom, Gordon, Snyder, Atkins, & Christensen, 2006.

179. Martell & Prince, 2005.

180. Jacobson & Addis, 1993; Sullivan & Bradbury, 1996.

181. Markman, Floyd, Stanley, & Lewis, 1986; Markman, Renick, Floyd, Stanley, & Clements, 1993.

182. Markman, Stanley, Jenkins, Petrella, & Wadsworth, 2006; Markman, Williams, Einhorn, & Stanley, 2008.

183. Hahlweg & Markman, 1988; Markman, Floyd, Stanley, & Storaasli, 1988; Markman, Renick, Floyd, Stanley, & Clements, 1993; Stanley, Markman, St. Peters, & Leber, 1995.

184. For example, Peterson, Crowson, Saldana, Holdridge, 1999.

185. Hansen, Zamboanga, & Sedlar, 2000; Paniagua, 1998.

186. Safren, Hollander, Hart, & Heimberg, 2001.

187. Linehan, 1993a, 1993b; Linehan & Dexter-Mazza, 2008.

188. Davison, D'Zurilla, Goldfried, Paul, & Valins, 1968.

189. For example, Ledwidge, 1978, 1979; Locke, 1979; Zettle & Hayes, 1982.

190. Spiegler, 1983.

191. Kendall, 1987; Spiegler & Guevremont, 2002.

192. Dember, 1974.

193. Bandura, 1986a, p. 14.

194. Bernard & Joyce, 1984; Morris & Cohen, 1982; Schleser, Meyers, & Cohen, 1981.

195. For example, Kendall, 1993.

14

Third-Generation Behavior Therapy

Acceptance and Mindfulness-Based Interventions[a]

[a]This chapter was written in collaboration with John P. Forsyth and Sean C. Sheppard.

Some behavior therapists have conceptualized the development of behavior therapies in terms of three generations,[1] which are depicted in a behavior therapy family tree in Figure 14-1. First-generation therapies were initially developed during the 1950s and 1960s and include stimulus control, reinforcement and punishment, aversion therapy, exposure therapies, and modeling therapies (Chapters 6–11). These therapies emphasize treating clients' directly observable problem behaviors by changing the external environmental conditions that are influencing them.

Second-generation behavior therapies, which emerged in the mid-1960s, introduced cognitive factors as important determinants of problem behaviors. Cognitive-behavioral therapies (Chapters 12–13) modify clients' dysfunctional thoughts and beliefs using specific cognitive change procedures as well as first-generation therapy techniques.

In the 1990s, a third generation of behavior therapies developed.[b] The primary goal of first- and second-generation behavior therapies is to *eliminate or reduce* clients' problems. In contrast, the goal in third-generation therapies is for clients to actively *accept* various forms of *psychological discomfort and pain* (*problems* in first and second generation terms) as inevitable parts of their lives—instead of viewing them as obstacles to fulfilling their goals. In other words, clients learn to live with inevitable forms of pain and discomfort while doing what is important to them. An intriguing perspective, wouldn't you say? This alternative goal is achieved through an integration of first- and second-generation change strategies with acceptance and mindfulness interventions that help people live their lives according to their personal values.

All three generations are represented in the current practice of behavior therapy. They are to some degree cumulative and overlapping, with second-generation therapies using principles and procedures from first-generation therapies, and third-generation therapies using principles and procedures from the first and second generations. Each generation is a member of the behavior therapy family by virtue of its sharing the defining themes and common characteristics of behavior therapy (described in Chapter 1), especially a commitment to alleviating a wide range of human suffering through a scientific approach.[2]

Even from the very brief description of third-generation therapies you have just read, you are likely to have glimpsed some of the radical differences between them and first- and second-generation therapies. Third-generation behavior therapies are, in fact, controversial[3] (as were second-generation behavior therapies when they were originally proposed). This is not surprising considering some of the issues that are addressed by third-generation behavior therapies, such as mindfulness, acceptance, values, and the meaning and purpose of one's life. Indeed, learning about the third-generation approach may challenge not only your assumptions about the nature of behavior therapy but also your long-held assumptions about the nature of human suffering. So, to fully benefit from what you are about to read, keep an open mind.

---

[b]The term *third wave* has been used to characterize third-generation behavior therapies (Hayes, 2004b). We prefer the term *third generation* because it emphasizes tradition and continuity with the previous generations of behavior therapy, while leaving room for growth. Waves, by contrast, come and go, and this may not be an apt description of the future status of third-generation therapies. However, be mindful that the terms *third generation* and *third wave* tend to be used interchangeably in the behavior therapy literature.

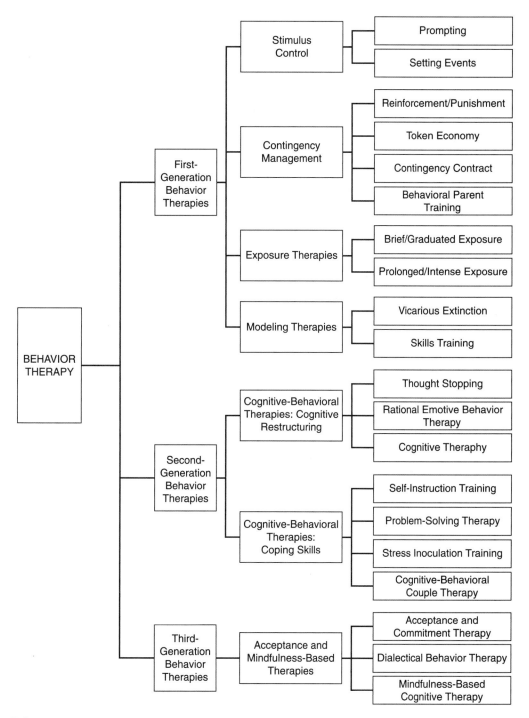

FIGURE **14-1**

Behavior therapy family tree with its three generations

Source: © 2008 Michael D. Spiegler

CORE THEMES OF THE THIRD GENERATION

Third-generation behavior therapies share five interrelated core themes: an expanded view of psychological health, a broad view of acceptable outcomes in therapy, acceptance, mindfulness, and the goal of a life worth living.[4]

Expanded View of Psychological Health

The primary goal of behavior therapy is to help people with psychological problems. The approach that first- and second-generation behavior therapies (and most other psychotherapies) take is to diminish clients' psychological distress. Certainly this makes sense; for one thing, it is what clients expect. The implicit assumption of first- and second-generation therapies is that psychological distress is bad and therefore should be eliminated or at least lessened.

The approach of third-generation behavior therapies is based on a radically different assumption: *Psychological pain and distress are assumed to be an inevitable, ubiquitous part of life, which means that they cannot be completely avoided or eliminated.* Not accepting this premise and fighting it may actually contribute to a person's distress and suffering. In the short term, efforts to control, minimize, or avoid discomfort can result in temporary relief, and those efforts are negatively reinforced. (For example, Steve, who is anxious in social situations, reduces his anxiety by avoiding activities that involve groups of people.) Yet, in the long term, such efforts may be detrimental because they demand enormous effort and time and can amplify the suffering people experience. (For instance, Steve is constantly making up excuses, which is stressful and results in his losing the respect of his friends and colleagues.) A growing body of research indicates that such efforts may be linked to diminished physical health, psychological distress, and above all, diminished quality of life.[5]

Third-generation behavior therapies build on this research and aim to change how people *respond* to painful aspects of their thoughts, memories, feelings, and physical sensations. Rather than avoid the pain, clients are encouraged *to experience it in a less engaging way and still do what they care about.* This approach leads to an expanded view of treatment targets and acceptable outcomes in therapy.

Broad View of Acceptable Outcomes in Therapy: Focusing on Second-Order Change

Clients enter therapy with problem behaviors—such as test anxiety, difficulty focusing, and depression—that are interfering with the quality of their lives. First- and second-generation behavior therapies work to directly alleviate these problem behaviors so that people can accomplish what is important to them, such as getting good grades, accomplishing work tasks, or even getting out of bed. This is known as **first-order change**.

Third-generation behavior therapies take a different stance. They focus on **second-order change** by employing interventions that change the *function* of the problem behavior, without necessarily changing its *form*.[6] For example, a person could experience a thought such as, "I am a loser and nobody will like me," and, over the course of therapy, learn to see this as just a thought, even a painful thought. The person could still interact with people instead of attempting to change or eliminate the thought itself (that is, the form of the behavior).

What defines first- and second-order change is not the therapy itself, but the goal of the therapy. For example, from a first-order change perspective, the goal of traditional exposure therapy (Chapters 9–10) is to teach clients to *think and feel better* (in the sense of being less fearful or distressed). In the context of second-order change, the same exposure procedures can also be used to teach clients to be *better at thinking and feeling* (in the sense of connecting with thoughts and feelings as they are) in the service of living well. Rather than viewing "problems" as interfering with achieving life goals, clients develop ways of achieving their goals despite their experiencing discomfort. This means, for example, that one can do well on tests even though one is anxious while studying for or taking them. To experience how second-order change might work, take 2 minutes to do Participation Exercise 14-1.

PARTICIPATION EXERCISE 14-1	## "I Can't Touch the Wall": Applying Second-Order Change

To complete this exercise you simply need to be in a room with a chair. Read the following two directions, and then carry them out.

1. While sitting in the chair, repeat aloud the following thought: "I can't get up and touch the wall." Do this for at least 15 seconds.
2. While continuing to repeat, "I can't get up and touch the wall," stand up and move toward a wall, reach out, and touch it.

If you succeeded in touching the wall while still saying, "I can't get up and touch the wall," congratulations! You have just applied a second-order change strategy to alter your thought, "I can't get up and touch the wall." Notice that you didn't have to change the *form* of the thought, which you would have done had you said, "I *can* get up and touch the wall." You didn't make the thought occur less often or stop it altogether. You did, however, change the *function* of the thought from being a potential barrier to what you "wanted to do" (get up and touch the wall) to allowing the behavior to occur despite your thought.

This exercise demonstrates that you can move with your thoughts and do what you choose to do, even when your thoughts say otherwise—as often occurs in our lives when we have such thoughts as, "I can't . . ." and "It's too big, scary, or hard."

Acceptance

Acceptance literally means to "take what is offered." **Acceptance** involves fully embracing one's experience at the moment just as it is, without judging it. Acceptance is central to Buddhism, and there is a Zen story about a man who comes home from work and finds that his house has burned down. He looks at the charred remains of his dwelling and simply says, "Is that so." The man is recognizing *what is* and experiencing it fully without evaluating it. Many people confuse such acceptance with passive resignation and giving up, which is not acceptance. "Is that so" is an acknowledgement of the experience as it is, without judgment. Acceptance involves only moment-to-moment experiencing of what is and does not imply that one cannot do something to change the situation in the future (such as the man's building a new house).

Acceptance of pleasant experiences is easy, while acceptance of painful experiences often is very hard. Not resisting, not fighting off, not defending oneself against psychological pain is counterintuitive and goes against habitual human responses (like pulling your hand away from a hot surface). However, letting go of attempts to struggle with and control one's pain (acceptance) can be the most adaptive response because it gives the person space to maneuver. This process can be likened to the experience of trying to extricate one's fingers from a Chinese finger trap.[7]

A Chinese finger trap (see Figure 14-2) is a tube of woven straw, about 5 inches long and ½ inch in diameter. You may have played with one as a child. You slide one index finger into each end of the tube and push them in snuggly. Then, you try to get your fingers out. To do that, most people will pull their index fingers apart. But when you do, the tube tightens uncomfortably around your index fingers. And, the harder you pull, the more stuck you become. Pulling out of the tube seems like the best (and most natural) solution. Yet, it doesn't work.

The same outcome often occurs when people struggle to get out of their "problematic" thoughts and feelings. Freeing your fingers from the trap requires you to *push your fingers in* rather than pull them out, which gives you more wriggle room. And, similarly, ceasing to struggle with and resist your problems—in a sense, pushing yourself into or staying with your problems—may provide the psychological space to get "unstuck."

FIGURE 14-2

A Chinese finger trap; used as an analogy to the negative consequences of struggling with problems

Mindfulness

Mindfulness involves purposely paying attention without judgment to whatever is happening at the moment.[8] The concept of mindfulness, like acceptance, has been around a long time and is a core precept of Buddhism. The Sanskrit word *buddha* refers to awakening in the sense of being totally present in the moment and just experiencing what is there. Sound easy? Actually, it is very difficult because we live a good portion of our lives in our heads—interpreting, evaluating, and judging ourselves, our thoughts and feelings, the past and future, others, and the world. Rather than being mindful, most of the time we are mind*less*. For example, you've no doubt had the experience while reading of getting to the bottom of a page and realizing that you have no idea of what you have just read. Let's hope you are reading mindfully right now.

As you may have surmised, the concepts of mindfulness and acceptance go hand in hand.[9] Acceptance requires mindfulness, or being fully present without judgment or evaluation, and the gentle observing of mindfulness is acceptance. Together, mindfulness and acceptance can be applied in therapy to undermine clients' struggle and resistance, while freeing up their energy to create the kind of life they wish to live. Mindful-acceptance is a skill that is cultivated in third-generation behavior therapies through a variety of exercises.[10] Participation Exercise 14-2 is

---

PARTICIPATION EXERCISE 14-2

Mindful Breathing

There is no behavior that we engage in more often than breathing, yet we usually are unaware of it, except when we are breathing hard. Becoming mindful of your breathing might seem easy, but it is not, as you will discover when you do this simple exercise. Mindful breathing is a skill that must be cultivated with practice. Here's what you have to do.

You will need a space where you can sit comfortably and undisturbed for 5 minutes (or longer if you like, but 5 minutes is a good starting point). Set a kitchen timer or watch with a countdown timer for 5 minutes.

Sit upright with your hands gently resting on your lap. Close your eyes lightly. Gently guide your attention to the natural rhythm of your breathing and the sensations you experience, wherever they are for you—in your chest, in your belly, in your nose or mouth. Simply notice your breath as you breathe in . . . and out . . . in . . . and out. There's no need to regulate your breathing by making the breath faster or slower, deeper or shallower. Just allow your breathing to occur as it does (which is being mindful).

When your mind wanders to anything other than your breath, notice that you are thinking about something else and gently return to focusing on your breath. You may have to refocus on your breath many times, and that is just fine (it happens to everyone).

Continue to just be aware of your breath until your timer sounds. (This exercise can be relaxing, so you may choose to continue longer.) When you're ready, gradually widen your attention and gently open your eyes with the intention of bringing this focused observing (mindfulness) to your experiences throughout the day (which we'll explore later in Participation Exercise 14-5). Practice this exercise daily for at least a week.

an example of one of them, and a good foundational exercise for your learning to be a more mindful observer in your daily life. You should read the Participation Exercise now, but you'll probably want to complete it later.

Creating a Life Worth Living

The final theme of third-generation behavior therapies is that the overall goal of therapy is to help clients live in ways that are consistent with their values— what is meaningful to them. Consider a woman for whom spending time with family is paramount. If a fear of flying keeps her from visiting her children who live in a distant state, the goal of therapy might be for her to get on a plane and fly to see her children. It would be better if she got on the plane with little or no fear, but it is more important that she gets on the plane so that she can be with her family. The theme of helping clients create *a life worth living* plays out in all third-generation behavior therapies.

With the core themes of third-generation behavior therapies in mind, let's see how they guide the specific therapies. We'll present three prime examples of the third-generation approach: Acceptance and Commitment Therapy, dialectical behavior therapy, and mindfulness-based cognitive therapy.[c]

ACCEPTANCE AND COMMITMENT THERAPY (ACT)

Courtesy of Steven Hayes

Steven Hayes

Acceptance and Commitment Therapy (**ACT**; pronounced *act*) has two major goals: (1) acceptance of unwanted thoughts and feelings whose occurrence or disappearance clients cannot control, and (2) commitment and action in the service of a life consistent with clients' personal values.[11] ACT, which has been spearheaded by Steven Hayes, involves both acceptance and change, which is primarily second-order change where the function, not the form or frequency, of the "problem behavior" is modified.[d]

ACT Change Processes

From the ACT perspective, the primary source of clients' problems is **psychological inflexibility**, a narrowing of options for behaving, which leaves a person feeling "stuck." ACT focuses on fostering **psychological flexibility**— that is, having options for behaving available, which occurs when people mindfully accept their distressing thoughts and feelings and engage in behaviors that are consistent with their values. This is accomplished in ACT using a variety of experiential, metaphorical, and second-order change methods.

Psychological inflexibility is created and maintained by six interrelated core processes: cognitive fusion, attachment to the conceptualized self, experiential

---

[c]There are a number of other behavior therapies that are related to third-generation therapies, including three that were discussed in earlier chapters: behavioral activation (Chapter 6), functional analytic psychotherapy (Chapter 6), and integrative behavioral couple therapy (Chapter 13).

[d]ACT is based on a new behavioral account of human language and cognition known as *Relational Frame Theory* (Blackledge, 2003; Hayes, Barnes-Holmes, & Roche, 2001). The theory focuses on the capacity humans have for relating events in infinite ways (for example, same as, similar to, cause of, part of). Initially, this capacity is learned directly through modeling and shaping, and it can be applied thereafter in novel and arbitrary ways that are not explicitly taught.

TABLE **14-1**

Processes Thought to Be Responsible for Psychological Inflexibility (before ACT) and for Psychological Flexibility (desired outcome of ACT)

Psychological Inflexibility (Before ACT)	Psychological Flexibility (Desired outcome of ACT)
cognitive fusion	cognitive defusion
attachment to the conceptualized self	detachment from the conceptualized self
experiential avoidance	experiential acceptance
disconnection from the present moment	mindful contact with the present moment
unclear values	clear values
inaction with respect to values	value-guided action

Source: © 2008 Michael D. Spiegler

avoidance, disconnection from the present moment, unclear values, and inaction with respect to values. These core processes, which are the targets of ACT, are listed in Table 14-1 in the left-hand column, and the parallel core processes that foster psychological flexibility—the desired outcome of ACT—are listed in the right-hand column. In the following six sections, we will discuss each of the sources of psychological inflexibility and the ACT strategies that are used to increase psychological flexibility. The title of each section names the source of inflexibility and the corresponding outcome that would result in flexibility.

Cognitive Fusion Versus Cognitive Defusion

Cognitive fusion is the tendency for humans to take their thoughts literally and to believe that they are accurately describing how things are rather than seeing them as what they are—that is, *just thoughts*. For instance, if someone said the word *lemon*, it is likely that you could see it in your mind's eye and see its color and shape and perhaps experience some of its tartness. Yet, thinking *lemon* does not make you a lemon, right? You are not that thought.

This point is often lost on people suffering from psychological pain. The thought *inadequate* is not just a thought like *lemon* for someone who is severely depressed. It is an unacceptable thought, linked with the self (that is, "*I* am inadequate").

The antidote for cognitive fusion is **cognitive defusion**, which involves letting go of the idea that one's thoughts are valid descriptions and explanations of one's experiences so that they can be seen as only thoughts.[12] Another way to conceptualize this is in terms of the distinction between *self-as-content* (I am my thoughts) and *self-as-process* (I am processing—or doing something with—my thoughts). Self-as-content is cognitive fusion, whereas self-as-process is cognitive defusion.[13] Table 14-2 has examples of the difference between these two ways of dealing with thoughts.

Another ACT strategy for creating cognitive defusion is illustrated in Case 14-1.

TABLE **14-2**

Examples of the Difference Between Self-as-Content (cognitive fusion)
Versus Self-as-Process (cognitive defusion)

Self-as-Content (cognitive fusion)	Self-as-Process (cognitive defusion)
"I am a stupid."	"I am having the thought that I am stupid."
"I am depressed."	"I am experiencing the feeling of depression."
"Nobody loves me."	"I am believing that nobody loves me."
"My life sucks."	"I am making the judgment that my life sucks."
"Nothing will change."	"I am assuming that nothing will change."

CASE **14-1**

Defusing Painful Thoughts Associated with Depression

Martha, a 47-year-old mother of three young children, complained of being barraged by negative thoughts about herself and her life, lethargy, and depressed mood. She was concerned that her depression was interfering with being a "good mother" and worried that her children would pick up on her gloominess and develop depression, too. Martha acted and felt as if her self-depreciating thoughts were accurate descriptions of her, which exacerbated her feeling depressed and "stuck." To counter this cognitive fusion, the therapist asked Martha to engage in a defusion exercise.

Therapist: You've been describing lots of negative thoughts about yourself and your life, your role as a mother, and more. There is a stickiness in there too, like being caught in a spider web. I'd like to see if we can get you some space from those unpleasant thoughts. Are you willing to do an exercise with me?

Client: Sure. I'm game.

Therapist: Let's pick a thought that is upsetting you or that makes you feel sad or blue and write it on an index card. What might one be?

Client: Well, how about, "I'm a bad mother"?

Therapist: Neat. [The therapist's response may appear odd, but it is purposeful. It is aimed at weakening the typical social responses people receive when they express negative thoughts or emotions, such as, "I'm sorry to hear that" or "You really aren't a bad mother." Such responses invalidate the person's painful experiences and thus do not foster acceptance of them.] I'm going to write that thought on an index card. [The therapist does this and then holds it for the client to look at.] What do you see?

Client: Well, I see "I'm a bad mother."

Therapist: Okay. What is that made up of? I mean, what is there on the card if you were to describe it to someone else?

Client: Well . . . I see a bunch of letters and words.

Therapist: Yes, I see that too. Okay, how about another sticky thought you have?

Client: Hmm . . . . "Why can't I just be normal?"

Therapist: Cool. [The therapist writes that thought on another index card and holds it up for the client to see.] Look at this card, what do you see?

Client: A bunch of words again.

Therapist: Let's do one more thought.

Client: Okay. "Will I ever be happy?"

Therapist: Good. [The therapist writes that thought on a card.] So far, we have three index cards with thoughts you just had. And, I'm pretty sure we could keep going for quite a while. But, I'd like you to see if you can sense something here. What are the thoughts like when you were thinking them? What do the thoughts feel like when they show up in your head?

Client: Awful. I can't stand it.

Therapist: How about when we look at them? [The therapist puts all three cards out so the client can see them.] Again, what do you see on the cards?

Client: A whole lot of words.

Therapist: That's it! You can notice your thoughts as just words. In fact, you can also hold them without getting caught up in them. Go ahead and hold out your hand, palm facing up. [The therapist places one of the cards in the client's open hand.] Now, notice the thought you are holding. What is it like to just hold that thought, just look at it?

Client: It feels odd . . . different. Part of me wants to throw it out or burn it. I've never done this before. This isn't like me.

Therapist: That may be true. Notice what it is like to just hold and observe your thoughts, and see that they are just words. Notice something else—you are not your thoughts. A moment ago they were packed in your head, and now they are out and revealed. You can choose to notice them as you are doing now. Heck, you can hold them as you are doing right now, struggle with them, carry them with you, or let them go. That's up to you.

Client: I can see that. The card feels really light, different from what it feels like most of the time.

Therapist: That lightness is what happens when we learn to observe our thoughts. Between now and our next session, would you be willing to commit to do-ing this exercise with good, bad, and ugly thoughts? I'll give you some cards. When a thought shows up, take out a card and write it down. Then, take a few moments to hold the card gently, as you would a young child, and notice the words on the card and see that *you* are not the thoughts. In fact, you can carry your thought cards with you throughout the day. And, any time you wish, you can choose to pull out the cards and simply notice what's on them. This is something you *can* do.

Client: I'll give it a try.

As is typical in ACT, the therapist in Case 14-1 had the client engage in an experiential exercise to see firsthand the worth of the therapy strategy (cognitive defusion) instead of just explaining it to her.

Attachment to the Conceptualized Self Versus Detachment from the Conceptualized Self

Attachment to the conceptualized self is an extreme form of cognitive fusion because it is fusion with one's entire self-concept. People become invested in how they perceive (conceptualize) themselves, which is manifested in the stories they tell themselves and others about who they are and how they got that way. Thus, the person becomes the conceptualized self. The truth of the stories is irrelevant because the individual considers them to be true. Attachment to the conceptualized self results in rigid behaviors aimed at validating or defending one's stories, which contributes to psychological inflexibility.

Consider Andrea's story. She came to therapy with a long history of generalized anxiety that she viewed as the cause of her leading a restricted and unfulfilling life. She spoke of her anxiety as "a chronic illness" that she attributed to her "neurochemistry running amok." Her storyline was essentially this: "I am broken and defective, and I will never get rid of my illness."

Detachment from the conceptualized self involves cognitive defusion, just as cognitive defusion from specific thoughts is implemented to gain psychological flexibility. Clients are encouraged to separate from and become observers of their conceptualized self and recognize that their conceptualized self is *not who they are*, but just a story. For Andrea, this meant learning to notice that her story was one of several possible stories that could be told about her life, and more important, that her current attachment to the defective/disease story was not serving her well.

Experiential Avoidance Versus Experiential Acceptance

Experiential avoidance involves efforts to escape from or avoid unpleasant private events—thoughts, emotions, and bodily sensations—and the circumstances that might occasion them.[14] It also involves attempts to change the form or frequency of these events to make them less painful (in other words, first-order change).[15] Such attempts often require considerable effort, and they may not work in the long term. To experience this for yourself, do the following. Take a few moments to "try hard *not* to think of a pink elephant." After you've tried this, continue reading.[16]

Were you able to do it? Most people have a hard time because *not thinking* about something is, in fact, a thought of it. You may have tried to distract yourself by thinking about something that is clearly not a pink elephant. The problem with distraction is that in order to know that the distracter is not a pink elephant, you must compare the distracter with a pink elephant, and so you are back to thinking about it. Similar processes are at work when people attempt to avoid aversive thoughts and emotions.

Experiential acceptance is the opposite of experiential avoidance. It involves (a) remaining in contact with painful experiences (b) without attempting to alter their form or frequency and (c) persisting in actions that are consistent with one's personal values. Experiential acceptance fosters new and more flexible ways of relating to painful or uncomfortable psychological experiences. The effectiveness of acceptance strategies has been demonstrated[17] in the treatment of such diverse problems as chronic pain,[18] anxiety disorders,[19] self-injurious behaviors,[20] and smoking.[21]

Case 14-2 provides an example of how the function—but not the form or frequency—of painful experiences can be changed through experiential acceptance.

CASE **14-2**
Treatment of Anger by Experiential Acceptance

Larry, a 35-year-old truck driver, came to therapy because he was afraid that his uncontrollable anger would cause his wife to leave him and his children to no longer want to have anything to do with him. He noted that little things just set him off, especially when he was tired. Asked about the little things, Larry talked about his wife and kids' not doing what they should be doing, dinner being late, and the kids' playing too loudly. When Larry got angry, he screamed at his wife and children, and at times threw objects, punched the wall, and hit his wife. When he felt tension building, he usually drank, which made him even more aggressive. He believed that "things only got done" when he became angry ("The wife gets off my back and stops being a slacker, and the kids stay out of my hair"). However, shortly before coming to therapy he had realized that becoming angry only worked in the short term and that the long-term consequences might include losing his family.

The therapist identified a number of behaviors that were examples of Larry's experiential avoidance—that is, escaping from or evading painful aspects of his life: his unwillingness to acknowledge his anger and hurt, verbal and physically aggressive behaviors to avoid demands and obligations, drinking alcohol to calm down and blunt his unpleasant emotions, and blaming his wife and children for not "doing what they were supposed to do."

The therapist asked Larry to reflect on a recent anger episode. Initially, Larry did not want to bring up painful thoughts and feelings, but eventually he agreed. The therapist instructed Larry to watch the anger episode playing out in his imagination, to really get into the experience as if it were happening. As Larry did this, the therapist told him to notice his thoughts, feelings, and urges. The therapist gently encouraged him to go more deeply into the experience with a sense of curiosity and asked him: "What is there besides the anger?" "What do you notice?" "What is it like to feel what you are feeling and think what you are thinking?"

Larry began to tear up as he described feeling inadequate, vulnerable, lonely, and like a loser in the eyes of so many people. The therapist encouraged Larry to just notice the experience without judging it. This was difficult for Larry, as he clearly did not like how he was feeling. After acknowledging the difficulty of what he was asking Larry to do, the therapist

(continued)

CASE **14-2** *(continued)*

encouraged Larry to stay with the experience and see if he could just be there with it (mindfulness), without having to resolve it or push it away.

Following these instructions was a new experience for Larry. He had never allowed himself to explore and touch the hurt underneath his anger without acting on it in some way (his typical experiential avoidance behaviors). To help Larry understand experiential acceptance, the therapist used an analogy with what you should do when you fall into quicksand: you should remain still and make maximum contact with the surface. If you struggle (as in experiential avoidance), you will sink. In the same way, staying with anger and not acting on it is difficult, but adaptive. The therapist pointed out that this was something Larry could choose to do. The therapist asked Larry to practice, outside of therapy, experiencing his hurt and anger with a sense of curiosity and acceptance rather than acting on his emotional pain with avoidance behaviors, especially becoming angry and acting aggressively.

Disconnection from the Present Moment Versus Mindful Contact with the Present Moment

If clients are fused with their private events, they are "living in their heads" and not in contact with what is going on in their life in the present, moment to moment. Not only is their focus on their inner world, but also it is located in the past or future, remembering and anticipating painful events. The antidote to such *disconnection from the present moment* is *mindful contact with the present moment*. A variety of strategies are used to foster mindfulness, such as mindful breathing (Participation Exercise 14-1), and we will describe other strategies later in the section on mindfulness-based cognitive therapy.

Unclear Values Versus Clear Values

Because clients entering therapy are focused on their psychological pain, they often are not in touch with their values—what is really important to them—and their values become fuzzy. Our values provide direction for our actions. Thus, clients who have *unclear values* have difficulty acting. They feel "stuck," and their behavior becomes habitual and automatic, which is a form of psychological inflexibility. One of the goals of ACT is to help clients focus on their values and clarify them. Only with *clear values* can clients direct their behavior toward actions that foster what matters in their lives.

Inaction with Respect to Values Versus Value-Guided Action

Inaction with respect to values is a clear indication of psychological inflexibility. Inaction comes from different sources, including having unclear values. It also is a by-product of experiential avoidance because clients are so consumed with defending themselves from painful experiences that they cannot act. Or, if they do act, their actions are likely to be ineffective or maladaptive and exacerbate their problem. A major goal of ACT is to get clients to act, but their actions must be in the service of their values—in other words, *value-guided action.*

Additionally, clients must make a *commitment* to act, which is different from clients' saying that they will *try* to do a value-guided behavior. The commitment requires that clients do something fully, not part way. It is either doing something or not doing something, which does not include *trying* to do something. You can see for yourself the merits of this approach by taking just a minute to complete Participation Exercise 14-3 before continuing reading.

PARTICIPATION EXERCISE 14-3

I Try—Therefore I Fail

Place a pen (or other small object) on a table or desk in front of you. Then, *try to pick up the pen.* Try as hard as you can to pick it up.

If you picked up the pen, put it down.

Now, *try* again to pick up the pen.

If you picked it up again, put it down and once more *try* to pick it up.

If you did *not* pick up the pen, you did what you were asked to do—namely, *try* to pick up the pen. You were not asked to *pick up* the pen, only to *try* to pick up the pen.

What would "trying to pick up a pen" look like? You can't describe it, because there's no way to *try* to pick up the pen—or to try to do anything. You can only pick it up or not pick it up. Trying is not an option.

You might want to do (not try) this exercise with one or more of your friends. They are likely to fail, as you may have, but they also will benefit from the trying lesson.

Trying is a form of inaction, which is why, in ACT, clients are encouraged never to try anything. Rather, they are encouraged to commit to doing something and then to do it, even if they fail. In the grander scheme, there is no trying to live your life—you need to live it, and preferably, in terms of your values.

ACT as an Approach

In the previous sections, we described a variety of specific strategies and techniques that are used in ACT to undermine the processes that feed psychological inflexibility (see the first column of Table 14-1, page 391) and create psychological flexibility (see the second column of Table 14-1). However, ACT is more than a set of intervention strategies and techniques. ACT is an *approach* to therapy that stresses accepting painful thoughts and feelings and committing to engaging in behaviors in the service of one's values.[22] ACT incorporates both acceptance and change. Although ACT usually promotes second-order change, such change can indirectly bring about first-order change, as you will see in Case 14-3. The case also provides an example of how a first-generation therapy can be used to foster third-generation goals.

CASE **14-3**

Panic Attacks Treated by Interoceptive Exposure to Foster Acceptance[23]

Mark, a 25-year-old shop clerk, had been struggling with panic attacks for 4 years. He reported that his panic attacks had resulted in his dropping out of college and taking a low paying job. He also said that the attacks had kept him from traveling beyond the confines of his small town in the Midwest. This latter limitation had greatly restricted his life and led him to seek therapy.

As part of Mark's treatment, the therapist suggested using interoceptive exposure[24] (see Chapter 9) to develop acceptance and mindfulness of his dreaded panic attacks so that he could do the things he cared about, such as traveling.

To evoke the symptoms Mark experienced during panic attacks, he was asked to breathe through a straw for 30 seconds at a time while holding his nostrils closed. (This technique induces intense physical sensations similar to naturally-occurring panic, such as shortness of breath, choking, suffocation, pounding or racing heart, and dizziness.[25]) During the exposure, the therapist continually reminded Mark of the reason he was being exposed to his panic symptoms: so that he could practice attending closely to the unpleasant sensations he was having and experience them without judging them as painful (mindfulness). Mark was also reminded that this practice was in the service of his being able to have a life worth living.

Following each session of interoceptive exposure, Mark and his therapist discussed the experience. The therapist pointed out that while Mark could not control his panic symptoms, he did have control over his willingness to experience panic. Mark learned to recognize his beating heart and rapid breathing for what they truly were—physical sensations—rather than the terrible things he had been thinking about them (such as, "I'm going crazy" and "I'm having a heart attack"). Through other mindfulness and acceptance exercises, Mark learned to experientially accept his intense discomfort during panic attacks and just observe what was going on. Mark developed a new way of relating to his bodily sensations and judgmental mind by accepting the moments of terror and dread he had. Interestingly, this acceptance had the unintended effect of lowering the frequency and intensity of Mark's panic attacks.

In a 6-month follow-up, Mark reported that he still experienced panic symptoms at times but that he no longer avoided his discomfort. In his words, "I've reclaimed what was always mine: a full life—not free of worry or anxiety—but one where worry and anxiety are in a safe place that feels okay." Mark returned to college and travels when he wishes to.

Interoceptive exposure is a first-generation behavior therapy that is typically used to reduce anxiety. In Mark's case, it was adapted for a third-generation agenda: acceptance of his panic symptoms so that he could "get on with his life"—that is, pursue what was important to him (returning to college and traveling). As this second-order change occurred, Mark also experienced a reduction in the frequency and intensity of his physical and emotional discomfort, which is first-order change and was not the aim of the ACT intervention. However, it came about because as Mark began to do what is important to him, he felt better in general. Additionally, intended or not, exposure to distressing and maladaptive feelings does extinguish them.

Acceptance and Commitment Therapy in Perspective

ACT has been applied to many forms of human suffering, including generalized anxiety disorder,[26] obsessive-compulsive disorder,[27] comorbid anxiety and depressive disorders,[28] worksite stress,[29] depression,[30] substance-related disorders,[31] chronic pain,[32] diabetes,[33] epilepsy,[34] eating disorders,[35] and schizophrenia.[36] To date, there have been approximately 20 randomized controlled trials evaluating ACT outcomes.[37] Despite relatively small sample sizes, the results have been generally supportive—although ACT does not yet qualify as an empirically supported treatment by accepted standards.[38]

In addition to efficacy and effectiveness studies of ACT, basic research on some of the core ACT treatment processes has been carried out. These studies have examined the benefits of acceptance[39] and defusion[40] and the toxic role of experiential avoidance in potentiating emotional distress and limiting adaptive functioning.[41] Although still preliminary, this basic process research is critical for ACT because it is very much a theory-driven therapy, meaning that its interventions are based on the model of psychological inflexibility/flexibility described earlier.[42]

DIALECTICAL BEHAVIOR THERAPY (DBT)

Courtesy of Marsha Linehan

Marsha Linehan

Dialectical behavior therapy (**DBT**; pronounced using the individual letters) was initially developed by Marsha Linehan as an adaptation of first- and second-generation behavior therapies to treat suicidal behaviors.[43] People contemplating suicide lack the skills to construct a life worth living. Thus, in its initial formulation, DBT involved skills training along with exposure therapy and contingency management. However, people who attempt suicide tend to be hypersensitive to criticism and have difficulty regulating their emotions. In her early work, Linehan found that the emphasis on first-order change often resulted in her clients' becoming overaroused and engaging in a variety of therapy-resistant behaviors, such as getting angry at her, storming out of a therapy session, or shutting down emotionally. When she changed the emphasis to acceptance (rather than change), her clients felt that their problems were being ignored, which resulted in extreme hopelessness or rage. Linehan realized that neither extreme—change nor acceptance—was successful, but a synthesis of the two appeared to work, which led to the development of DBT as it is practiced today.[44]

The key word in DBT's name is *dialectical*, which refers to every argument's having an assertion (the thesis) and an opposing position (the antithesis). Often the best resolution incorporates important features of each position in a meaningful way—in other words, a *synthesis*. In DBT, the primary dialectic, or polarity, involves change on one hand and acceptance on the other. DBT involves integrating, or synthesizing, the need for clients to accept who they are with the need to change the way they are living.

DBT has primarily been used to treat clients with borderline personality disorder (BPD), which is characterized by chronic suicidal behavior; other self-destructive behaviors, such as self-mutilation and reckless driving; poor regulation of emotions, including impulsivity; low self-image; and unstable interpersonal relations. Individuals with BPD typically suffer from multiple psychological disorders and have a pattern of never-ending crises. They make excessive use of psychological services and have repeated treatment failures.[45] Not surprisingly, borderline personality disorder is very difficult to treat, and DBT has made a significant contribution to its treatment.

We will describe DBT as it is used to treat borderline personality disorder in outpatient therapy. When DBT is used in an inpatient setting or to treat other disorders, modifications of these procedures may be necessary.[46] The overarching goal of DBT is to move beyond symptom reduction and help clients create a life worth living.

DBT Biosocial Theory of Borderline Personality Disorder

Linehan believes that the crux of BPD is a pervasive problem of emotion regulation that develops and is maintained by the interaction of biological and environmental factors.[47] In her *biosocial theory*, genetics, prenatal conditions, and early life traumas are all hypothesized to lead to changes in the central nervous system that cause people to be more vulnerable to problems of emotion regulation. People with BPD respond in an exaggerated manner to environmental stressors and take longer to return to baseline levels of functioning.[48] The nervous system component becomes particularly problematic when individuals are exposed to invalidating environments.

In an *invalidating environment*, people's painful experiences and emotional responses are discomfirmed, demeaned, minimized, or punished by primary caregivers or other important individuals in their life.[49] For example, they may be given verbal and nonverbal messages such as, "Things aren't that bad," "You don't really want to kill yourself," "Everyone has problems," and "Just stop complaining." Additionally, invalidating environments stress the importance of self-control and self-reliance, which implies that emotion-regulation difficulties are simply due to a lack of will-power, low motivation, and other "character defects."[50] It is easy to see how people exposed to an invalidating environment would come to view themselves as flawed. Taken together, the pervasive emotion-regulation problems associated with BPD that result from the interaction of biological and environmental factors not only interfere with problem-solving abilities but also create problems with interpersonal relationships and the ability to engage in goal-directed behaviors—all in a vicious, self-perpetuating cycle.

DBT Core Treatment Strategies

Two core treatment strategies are used in DBT: validation/acceptance strategies and problem-solving/change strategies. The success of treatment hinges on a flexible application of both strategies at the point that each is warranted for the particular client.

Validation/Acceptance Strategies

Validation/acceptance strategies communicate empathic understanding of the client's emotions, thoughts, and actions and authenticate them. These interventions are important in any therapeutic context to establish rapport. In DBT, they also are needed to counteract the externally-imposed invalidation and self-invalidating behaviors that are common with individuals with pervasive emotion-regulation problems.[51] In attempting to understand a client's problem behavior, identifying the *function* that the behavior serves is paramount. Consider a woman who frequently cuts her arms in response to emotional stress, a frequent self-injurious behavior of clients suffering from BPD.[52] It is all too easy to label the cutting as maladaptive or problematic and therefore invalid or flawed. However, if the cutting provides relief from the client's unbearable emotions (which it typically does), the cutting is valid in the sense that it functions to regulate her emotions. By accepting and validating the client's emotional turmoil and her reason for cutting, the therapist creates space to use problem-solving strategies to help the client find more skillful ways of regulating her emotions. In essence, the therapist communicates to the client: "Your emotions can be very distressing, and it makes sense that you would want to alleviate that distress, which you do by cutting yourself. Perhaps you can learn other, less destructive ways to achieve the same goal." Here, we see the interplay of both acceptance and change strategies. Unless clients believe that the therapist understands what they are experiencing and why they are behaving as they are, they will not be amenable to the therapist's suggestions of alternative problem-solving/change strategies.[53]

Problem-Solving/Change Strategies

DBT utilizes a range of first- and second-generation therapies, including skills training, exposure therapies, contingency management, and cognitive restructuring to affect behavior change. Which change techniques are appropriate depends on the maintaining conditions of the client's problem behaviors. If a problem is maintained by a skills deficit, skills training is called for. If the client can perform the skills necessary for alternative, adaptive behaviors but is not engaging in them because emotions, cognitions, or contingencies are interfering, then exposure therapy, cognitive restructuring, or contingency management would be appropriate, respectively.

The application of these standard behavior therapy procedures often must be modified due to issues that are specific to clients with BPD. For example, clients who have problems with emotion regulation also have difficulties with information processing, which means that the therapist may have to take a more directive role in guiding the client through the procedures than is typical.[54] Another challenge in working with clients suffering from BPD is that the focus of therapy often must shift from session to session because the clients are continually having crises in their lives that require immediate attention. For instance, if the agenda for a therapy session is continuing the exposure therapy for anxiety begun in the previous session, the agenda may have to shift to dealing with such events as the client's losing a job, having a spouse leave, going back to drinking, or being evicted by a landlord. Thus, the course of DBT is rarely a linear progression, and DBT therapists must be able to deal with the client's "crisis of the week" in order to keep the client in therapy and eventually return to the primary goals and target behaviors established at the outset. At the same time, DBT therapists help their clients gain insight into their patterns of crises and maladaptive behaviors and identify alternative, more adaptive ways of behaving in response to life crises that arise.

DBT Treatment Modalities

DBT is delivered in two primary coordinated treatment modalities: individual outpatient therapy and group skills training.[55] Additionally, therapists may provide telephone consultations with clients between sessions to help them apply the skills they have learned in therapy in their everyday lives and to deal with crises.

Individual Therapy

In DBT, individual therapy consists of four overlapping stages.[56] The stage where a client begins treatment depends on the client's current level of functioning. Although the stages are ordered in terms of decreasing severity of the clients' problems, progress through the stages is not necessarily linear, with clients often revisiting issues and therapy procedures from previous stages.[57]

Before the therapist can determine at which stage a client should begin treatment, a thorough behavioral assessment is conducted to determine the nature of the client's problems and their probable maintaining conditions. Then, the therapist and client agree on the goals, target behaviors, and methods of treatment. Finally, in the spirit of therapy's being a collaborative effort, both the client and the therapist commit to engaging in particular behaviors.[58] For example, the client may commit to a specific number of individual therapy sessions and group skills training sessions while the therapist may commit to receiving regular consultation from another therapist about the client's treatment.[e] Once these pretreatment tasks have been completed, the therapist determines the initial stage of treatment that is most appropriate for the client based on the client's current level of functioning.

Stage 1 of DBT treats clients who are at the lowest level of functioning. In this stage, there is a set hierarchy of behavioral targets that involve keeping the client alive, safe, and connected to treatment.[59] They are, in order of importance:

1. Suicidal and other life-threatening behaviors
2. Behaviors that interfere with therapy

[e]It is customary for psychotherapists to receive periodic supervision from another therapist about their cases, but usually clients are unaware of this arrangement. In contrast, DBT therapists specifically tell their clients that they will be receiving such supervision, which demonstrates one way in which therapists contribute to the therapist—client collaboration.

3. Behaviors that degrade the client's quality of life (for example, anxiety or mood disorders, substance abuse, and everyday problems with relationships, employment, and housing)
4. Skills deficits that impede clients' making adaptive life changes

Because of the high risk of self-destructive behaviors among clients with BPD, assuring that they are safe is the first priority. Keeping clients in therapy is the second priority because BPD is associated with multiple treatment failures and a high dropout rate.[60] The third priority involves treating the host of comorbid disorders that are associated with BPD (such as depression and substance abuse). The last priority involves skills training to equip clients with behaviors necessary to create a life worth living. The overall goal of Stage 1 is to help clients get their lives under some control.

Once this goal is achieved, it is possible to deal with clients' painful emotions (such as those due to past traumas) that are interfering with their ability to live meaningfully, in their relationships, jobs, and daily activities. The goals of Stage 2 are for clients to learn to experience emotions with decreased disturbance and to increase their connection to the environment. Stage 2 is difficult for clients because it is here that exposure therapy is employed to desensitize traumatic or other painful experiences that interfere with their lives. If the exposure is not handled judiciously, the client may revert to previous, self-destructive ways of coping with pain and distress, which would require additional Stage 1 interventions.

In Stage 3, clients consolidate what they have learned in Stages 1 and 2. They work on increasing their self-respect, self-efficacy, competence, connections with their environment, and general quality of life. Finally, Stage 4 goes beyond the boundaries of traditional behavior therapy and helps clients develop a sense of freedom, joy of living, or spiritual fulfillment.[61]

Group Skills Training

The weekly individual DBT sessions focus on clients' behavioral and emotional problems, with special emphasis on life-threatening and therapy-interfering behaviors. In addition, due to the range and severity of problems seen in many individuals with borderline personality disorder, clients in DBT typically receive 2½ hours of group skills training each week.[62]

The group skills training sessions are directed by a skills trainer who is someone other than the client's individual therapist. The training typically runs for an entire year and follows a manual consisting of detailed session-by-session instructions and treatment rationales along with handouts for skills training exercises.[63] The skills are taught using the standard skills training procedures described in Chapter 11. Clients develop four types of skills: core mindfulness, interpersonal effectiveness, emotion regulation, and distress tolerance.

Core Mindfulness Skills Core mindfulness skills are based on Zen Buddhist techniques and include skills to focus attention, assume a nonjudgmental stance, and focus awareness on the present moment. These skills are central

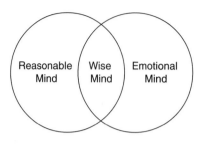

FIGURE 14-3

Wise mind as a synthesis of reasonable mind and emotional mind

to DBT (hence the word *core*) and are covered over the entire year of skills training.

Core mindfulness is based on a model consisting of three states of mind: reasonable mind, emotional mind, and wise mind. *Reasonable mind* involves thinking rationally, with reference to empirical facts—a "cool" approach to problem solving. In contrast, *emotional mind* refers to thinking irrationally without reference to facts and results in exaggerated or distorted thinking that is determined by one's momentary mood—a "hot" approach to problem solving. *Wise mind* is the synthesis of these two polarities (see Figure 14-3), incorporating rationality and emotionality as well as intuition. Mindfulness skills are used to achieve the balance of wise mind.

Interpersonal Effectiveness Skills Assertive behaviors and problem-solving skills help clients obtain what they want, keep them from being taken advantage of, and help them deal with interpersonal conflicts. The goal is for clients to get what they want and solve problems in ways that allow them to maintain relationships (rather than alienating others) and retain their self-respect. Clients are also taught to balance the desires-to-obligations ratio in their lives so that they do not become frustrated with all that they "have to" do and thus not do enough of the things they want to do (the same idea as a balanced lifestyle in relapse prevention described in Chapter 13).

Emotion-Regulation Skills Learning skills to regulate emotions is critical for people with borderline personality disorder. However, this is often difficult for them because their intense and labile emotions have frequently been invalidated by others (for example, "Just calm down and get control of yourself"). Thus, emotion-regulation skills must be taught in a context of emotional self-evaluation.[64]

Emotion regulation requires mindfulness, and emotion-regulation skills consist of observing one's emotions nonjudgmentally and describing, without interpretation, one's current emotional responses. The training involves teaching clients about the nature of emotions and the role emotions play in people's lives as well as debunking common myths about emotions, such as those listed in Table 14-3.

TABLE **14-3**

Common Myths About Emotions Which Are Debunked in DBT Skills Training

There is always a right way to feel in every situation.

Negative feelings are bad and destructive.

If I am emotional, then I am out of control.

All emotions are the result of a bad attitude.

Other people can judge how I am feeling better than I can.

Painful emotions should be avoided.

Source: Adapted from Linehan, 1993b.

Distress Tolerance Skills Given that DBT and other third-generation behavior therapies view discomfort and pain as an unavoidable part of life, learning specific ways to *tolerate* discomfort is important. There are four sets of skills that help clients deal with crises and accepting life as it is in the moment: (1) distracting (to modulate emotional responses), (2) self-soothing, (3) improving the moment (as through cognitive restructuring), and (4) thinking of the pros and cons of tolerating distress.[65]

Dialectical Persuasion

The dialectical perspective or philosophy—finding a synthesis between polar extremes—is the guiding principle in DBT. On a broad level, it is seen in the delicate balancing of acceptance and change throughout treatment. The two case examples of *dialectical persuasion* that follow will give you the flavor of the dialectical interchange that is typical of the therapist—client dialogue in DBT individual therapy sessions.

To modify clients' maladaptive views, DBT may sometimes employ rational disputation as in rational emotive behavior therapy (Chapter 12). However, DBT therapists are more likely to use **dialectical persuasion**, which subtly highlights the inconsistencies in a client's actions, beliefs, and values. The aim is to help the client develop a balanced perspective that is congruent with her or his values (for example, wise mind rather than reasonable or emotional mind).

Consider the case of a woman who habitually burned her arms with a lit cigarette because doing so immediately relieved her intense emotional pain.[66] Not surprisingly, she was reticent to give up this behavior because it served to reduce her emotional pain. In exploring the precipitating events to a recent incident, the woman casually remarked, "The burn really wasn't that bad this time." The therapist followed up on this statement using dialectical persuasion.

Therapist: So what you're saying is that if you saw a person in a lot of emotional pain, say your little niece, and she was feeling as badly as you were the night you burned your arm, that you'd burn her arm with a cigarette to help her feel better.

Client: No, I wouldn't.

Therapist:	Why not?
Client:	I just wouldn't.
Therapist:	I believe you wouldn't, but why not?
Client:	I'd comfort her or do something else to help her feel better.
Therapist:	But what if she was inconsolable, and nothing you did made her feel better? Besides, you wouldn't burn her that badly.
Client:	I just wouldn't do it. It's not right. I'd do something else, but not that.
Therapist:	That's interesting, don't you think?

As this therapist–client dialogue shows, dialectical persuasion subtly highlights the inconsistencies in the client's thought processes in an effort to show the client that there are alternative ways of dealing with her intense emotional distress.

Another example of dialectical persuasion is the *devil's advocate technique*,[67] in which the therapist (1) presents an extreme proposition that could be valid, (2) asks the client if he or she believes the proposition is valid, and then (3) counters the client's attempts to disprove the extreme proposition. The objective is to *dialectically* persuade the client to adopt a point of view that is more moderate than the view the client currently holds. For this technique to be effective, the therapist must be aware of the client's dysfunctional cognitions, engage the client with a seemingly naïve style of speaking, and balance seriousness with a sense of levity.[68] The following therapist–client dialogue illustrates the devil's advocate technique.

Therapist:	Why don't you start by telling me about the argument you had with your boyfriend last night.
Client:	Well, he came home from work really late last night and missed the nice dinner I had made for us, even though we had been planning the date night for over a week now.
Therapist:	That must have really hurt your feelings to plan something nice and have it fall through.
Client:	No, it pissed me off! I mean, he's always doing this—breaking plans with me [said with an upset tone]. It's like he doesn't love me. I think he does this just to hurt me.
Therapist:	I'm sure it's just that he doesn't care about your relationship [said without expressing any emotion].
Client:	What do you mean [confused]?
Therapist:	Well, since he obviously knew about your romantic night and blew it off like it was no big deal, it *must* mean he doesn't care about you.
Client:	I don't know. But still, if he loved me . . . [said in a hesitant tone].
Therapist:	What did he say when he got home?

Client: He made up some excuse about having to finish up a report for his boss or something and said he'd make it up to me next week.

Therapist: So there's no way that he wanted to make it home for dinner and that work interfered.

Client: Well, we've been trying to save money for a vacation, and he has been trying to impress his boss in order to get a promotion.

Therapist: So he missed dinner *and* stayed late to finish a report for his boss, something that might help him get a raise.

Client: I guess so.

Notice how the angry client initially attributed her boyfriend's behavior to his lack of concern and love for her. By playing the devil's advocate, the therapist attempted to "jolt" the client into seeing a different perspective by presenting an extreme version of her dysfunctional beliefs and then continuing to argue along this line of reasoning—but just to the point where the client seemed to soften a bit. The therapist's stance was intended to help the client gain a more balanced perspective (wise mind), allowing her to feel hurt by her boyfriend's missing dinner and, at the same time, appreciating the fact that he missed dinner in the service of doing something nice for her.

Dialectical Behavior Therapy in Perspective

Over the past 15 years, an impressive body of research has demonstrated that DBT is an empirically supported treatment for borderline personality disorder. The evidence includes a number of well-controlled randomized clinical trials, conducted by four independent research teams.[69]

Now that DBT has been established as an empirically supported treatment for borderline personality disorder, the emphasis in DBT research has shifted to identifying its active treatment components and to validating DBT for other problem behaviors.[70] So far, there is modest empirical support for DBT as a treatment for several other psychological problems including depression,[71] eating disorders,[72] intimate partner violence,[73] and BPD with comorbid substance abuse.[74]

In contrast to most behavior therapies, DBT for borderline personality disorder is anything but brief, and typically runs for more than a year. The length of DBT is primarily due to the severity, complexity, and long-standing and pervasive nature of BPD. Thus, it is highly resistant to treatment of any kind. The success of DBT in treating borderline personality disorder arguably makes it the treatment of choice for the disorder.[75]

MINDFULNESS-BASED COGNITIVE THERAPY (MBCT)

Mindfulness-based cognitive therapy (**MBCT**; pronounced using the individual letters), like DBT, was designed to treat a specific problem—in this case, relapse of depression in clients who have recovered from major depressive disorder.[76] A collaborative effort of Zindel Segal, John Teasdale, and

Courtesy of Zindel Segal, John Teasdale, and Mark Williams

Zindel Segal, John Teasdale, and Mark Williams (from left to right)

Mark Williams, MBCT employs mindfulness exercises to teach clients to become more aware of and, at the same time, less engaged with their negative thoughts.

The theory of the recurrence of major depressive episodes that underlies MBCT evolved from Beck's cognitive model,[77] which suggests that vulnerability to recurrent episodes of depression is related to dysfunctional negative cognitions (see Chapter 12). It assumes that people who have had an episode of major depression continue to maintain a high level of negative cognitions even after they have recovered from a previous episode. However, there is evidence to suggest that this is not the case.[78] Rather, it appears that familiar patterns of negative cognitions are *reactivated* by future sad moods.[79] The connection between sad mood and negative cognitions is strengthened with each successive depressive episode, and subsequent episodes are likely to be more intense.

In the treatment of depression, cognitive therapy emphasizes changing the *content* of maladaptive cognitions by using cognitive restructuring to replace unrealistic and unsubstantiated negative thoughts with more realistic positive thoughts. But, cognitive therapy may also implicitly change clients' *awareness of* and *relation to* their negative thoughts.

Specifically, as a result of repeatedly identifying negative thoughts as they arise and standing back from them to evaluate the accuracy or adaptiveness of their content, patients often make a general shift in their *perspective* on negative thoughts and feelings. Instead of viewing thoughts as absolutely true or as descriptive of important self-attributes, patients are able to see negative thoughts and feelings as passing events in the mind that are not necessarily valid reflections of reality or central aspects of [themselves] . . . .[80]

Thus, cognitive therapy may prevent relapse of depression by teaching people to initiate this process when they experience stressors in the future.[81] However, the emphasis in cognitive therapy is to change the content or meaning of negative cognitions. In contrast, mindfulness-based cognitive therapy is a third-generation behavior therapy, and so it focuses on changing clients' attention to their negative cognitions (as well as feelings and bodily sensations) and how they deal with them. MBCT integrates elements of cognitive therapy and the widely used Mindfulness-Based Stress Reduction program developed by Jon Kabat-Zinn and his colleagues.[82]

MBCT Approach and Intervention Strategies

The aim of MBCT is to foster a more decentered perspective of painful negative thoughts and feelings. *Decentering* involves seeing your thoughts as just thoughts and becoming aware that they are not you and not reality.[83] This is what occurred when, earlier in the chapter, you said to yourself, "I am a lemon"; you knew you were not a lemon, even though you had that thought.

In contrast, people who are suffering from depression often do not make the distinction between their negative self-evaluations and themselves. For example, they believe that their thoughts—such as, "I am worthless," "I am incompetent," and "I am a bad person"—are accurate self-descriptions. They need to create psychological space between their thoughts and who they are, which can be achieved through mindfulness practice. With mindfulness practice, a person with depression learns both how to be *less engaged* with negative thoughts and feelings and, at the same time, how to be *more aware* of the negative thoughts and feelings that may signal an impending relapse of depression. Developing increased awareness of negative thoughts and feelings is critical because depression is painful and so the person may avoid or deny early warning signs of a relapse. Such avoidance increases the likelihood that the person will actually experience a relapse because nothing was done to prevent it, which also means that the new depressive episode will likely be more serious.[84]

MBCT Group Training Program

MBCT follows a standard protocol and is delivered over eight weekly, 2-hour sessions in groups of up to 12 clients who are all in a recovery stage of repeated episodes of depression. As with other third-generation behavior therapies, there is explicit attention to balancing acceptance and change. Interestingly, relinquishing attempts to control unwanted thoughts, feelings, and bodily sensations and accepting them is, in itself, a change.

Sessions 1 through 4 focus on learning the fundamental concepts and skills of mindfulness practice, the essence of which is paying attention to present internal and external experiences without evaluating them. Sessions 5 through 8 focus on approaching mood shifts in a more mindful way. Clients learn to notice thoughts and their impact on physical and emotional experiences and accept these thoughts and experiences for what they are (just thoughts and experiences) rather than as valid descriptions of who they are.

Homework exercises are critical for the success of MBCT because the 16 hours of treatment is hardly sufficient for clients to learn and become proficient in mindfulness skills. Additionally, homework exercises foster the transfer of mindfulness into clients' daily activities.

Later elements of MBCT include attention to relapse-prevention strategies, such as involving family members in detecting early warning signs of relapse, engaging in exercises that can help interrupt relapse, and continued practicing of mindfulness skills. The program also includes monthly follow-up meetings for the first 4 months.

Mindfulness, the core of MBCT, is difficult for anyone to learn because most people are not accustomed to being mindful. Consider the fact that we are often multitasking. For example, we drive, talk on our cell phone, and drink coffee at the same time. We go for a run listening to music. In addition, we are constantly thinking about countless things other than what we are doing at the moment. Sound familiar? In each of the examples, we are not being mindful.

The mindfulness skills that clients in MBCT develop foster a new way of relating to everything in their lives as well as to their depressive thoughts and feelings. Participation Exercise 14-4 is an example of one of the many mindfulness exercises used in MBCT. You may want to do it later, but you should read it now as a concrete example of a mindfulness exercise.

PARTICIPATION EXERCISE 14-4

Eating a Raisin Mindfully

For this exercise, you'll need about 5 minutes and one raisin. A raisin is best, but you can substitute a grape, small piece of orange, or gummi bear. There is one essential general instruction: *Whenever you find your mind wandering from the task at hand, just gently return your attention to the raisin and what you are doing with it.* Read over the specific instructions that follow and then begin with the first instruction.

1. Begin by placing the raisin in the palm of your hand. Spend a few moments just looking at it. Really look at it with a sense of curiosity and awe, as if this were the first time you had looked at a raisin. (In fact, it is likely that this is the first time you are truly looking at a raisin.)
2. Gently pick up the raisin with your thumb and index finger and roll it between them. What does the raisin feel like? What are its textures? For this part of the exercise and the remaining parts, it is best to close your eyes because you will no longer be attending to visual sensations.
3. Rub the raisin across your lips, and notice what that feels like.
4. Gently place the raisin on your tongue. Just let it sit on your tongue for a few moments. Don't chew it. Just leave it on your tongue and notice how the raisin feels.

5. When you're ready, begin chewing. Bite the raisin *very slowly* and *gently*, extending the time it takes to bite through it as long as possible. What is that like? What does the raisin feel like between your teeth? What sensations, textures, tastes, and smells do you notice? If you feel the urge to swallow the raisin right away, just notice that urge, and slowly chew the raisin for a minute or so, without swallowing. Finally, go ahead and give in to the urge to swallow it.

Mindfully eating a raisin is used in MBCT to teach clients the general skill of mindfulness. Once clients have experienced what it means to be mindful through this and other exercises, they practice being mindful in their everyday lives. Mindfulness can be applied to any activity one is engaging in, from the mundane, boring tasks we do every day to those that are important or monumental. Being mindful of daily activities allows us to fully experience them and be truly alive in the moment. For clients who are learning mindfulness to help prevent recurrence of major depression, the payoff is particularly high.

The following Participation Exercise, which you'll have to complete later but should read now, provides examples of routine behaviors that you can experience in a new way—mindfully.

PARTICIPATION EXERCISE 14-5

Approaching Daily Tasks Mindfully

Below is a list of some mundane tasks that most people do automatically— that is, *mindlessly*. The next time you find yourself doing one of them, deliberately focus on and pay attention to what you are doing and experiencing at the moment. Approach the task with a sense of curiosity and an openness to whatever you experience. Notice all that is happening outside and inside yourself. And, *whenever you find your mind wandering from the task at hand, just gently return your attention to it.*

1. *Mindful Showering*. This everyday activity is a good one to start with because many people find showering a pleasant, even sensual experience. Next time you shower, notice how the water feels on different parts of your body. Notice the temperature of the water, but don't judge whether it is too hot or too cold or even just right—it is just the temperature that it is. Notice how it feels when the water sprays on to different parts of your body, but don't evaluate whether the spray is too strong or too light. What do you feel as you rub your body with soap and shampoo your hair? Notice what the soap and shampoo smell like. And, as your mind drifts away from showering, gently refocus on showering.

2. *Mindfully Brushing Your Teeth*. Yes, you can even brush your teeth mindfully. Notice what the bristles feel like while you're brushing the front, top, and back of your teeth and how it feels to brush your gums and your tongue. Notice the taste of the toothpaste. Just focus on the simple task of brushing your teeth.

(continued)

3. *Mindful Eating.* Put down the newspaper, book, or magazine—even this textbook. Turn off the computer, TV, and radio. Then, as in Participation Exercise 14-4, in which you mindfully ate a raisin, use all of your senses to fully experience your eating. When the food is in your mouth, close your eyes, eat slowly, and savor the textures, the tastes, and the whole experience.

4. *Mindful Dishwashing.* Start your mindful dishwashing when you have just a few dishes to wash. From the time you turn on the water until you shut it off, focus all of your attention on washing the dishes. Notice how it feels, what it looks like, and what it sounds like to scrape dishes and then to wash them with a sponge or dish rag. As you rinse each dish, watch the water run down the dish and over the side into the sink. Listen to the sound of the water hitting the dish. Although it is easy to do this routine chore while thinking about other things, for once, just wash the dishes and be totally into doing it.

5. *Mindfully Making Your Bed.* Some people make their bed quickly and carelessly, some people do it meticulously, and some people do not make their bed. Few people make their bed mindfully. Pay attention to each component of making the bed, from smoothing the sheets to the last minor adjustments of pillows, blankets, and covers. Watch what you are doing, and notice how the picture of the bed is changing. Be aware of the different textures of the bedding. Feel the kinesthetic sensations of pulling up the covers and tucking in the sheets. Immerse yourself in the whole experience of making your bed.

6. *Mindful Exercising.* Next time you exercise, whatever the activity might be, do so mindfully by focusing totally on the exercising. This means no headphones and music, no watching TV, no talking to other people. Just pay attention to the movements involved, how your muscles feel, and your breathing. Do not evaluate any of these sensations, such as by saying to yourself, "This hurts," "This is hard," or even "This feels good." If you can exercise mindfully, you will have had the full experience of exercising rather than just part of it (as you do when you distract yourself from pain or labored breathing).

These are but a few examples of routine behaviors that you can experience fully by doing them mindfully. Pick one or more from this list or generalize the instructions to any other routine tasks in your life. The more you do things mindfully, the more truly in touch you will be with your life. In fact, tasks you find boring may actually become less boring because you will be experiencing all the nuances that even simple tasks include.

Mindfulness-Based Cognitive Therapy in Perspective

MBCT is the "youngest" of the three third-generation behavior therapies we have discussed, which means that there has been less time to evaluate its effectiveness. Still, empirical support for MBCT's ability to prevent relapse of recurrent major depressive episodes is accumulating.[85] Two randomized clinical trials have been conducted. The first study compared treatment as usual (TAU), such as medication, with MBCT plus TAU to see if the addition of MBCT would reduce the rate of relapse of depressive episodes.[86] The results showed that relapse rates for patients with more extensive histories of recurring depressive episodes were significantly lower with MBCT plus TAU (37%) than with TAU alone (66%). These basic findings also occurred in another randomized controlled trial that showed that MBCT reduced the relapse rate of clients with three or more prior episodes of major depression by more than half compared to clients who received TAU (36% versus 78%).[87]

Although more research needs to be done, these initial findings regarding the efficacy of MBCT in preventing recurrent episodes of major depression are promising.[88] The brevity and group format of MBCT make it an efficient and cost-effective intervention,[89] and clients find it to be an acceptable treatment.[90] There are indications that MBCT may be suitable for depression in old age[91] and depression in children, with some modifications to the standard MBCT protocol.[92] MBCT principles and exercises also may be applicable in a self-help format for people suffering from mild depression. A book has been written for this purpose although its effectiveness has not yet been evaluated.[93] The fact that MBCT is skills-based and administered in a modular format should facilitate its integration with other therapies, and this is being explored with such diverse therapies as DBT[94] and Adlerian therapy.[95] Finally, the feasibility of applying MBCT for disorders and problems other than recurrent major depression is being tested, including bipolar disorder,[96] suicidal behaviors,[97] anxiety disorders,[98] insomnia,[99] and binge eating.[100]

ALL THINGS CONSIDERED: THIRD-GENERATION BEHAVIOR THERAPIES

At the beginning of the chapter, we mentioned that third-generation behavior therapies were somewhat controversial.[101] Now that you have learned about them, you should be aware of an obvious source of controversy—namely, third-generation therapies appear to be very different from first- and second-generation behavior therapies. This can be seen in the themes that run through third-generation therapies: an expanded view of psychological health, a broad view of acceptable therapy outcomes, an emphasis on acceptance and mindfulness strategies, and fostering a life worth living. So, on one hand, they do not seem to fit with the first- and second-generation behavior therapies—with tradition, if you will. On the other hand, the defining themes and characteristics of behavior therapy (discussed in Chapter 1) also characterize third-generation therapies.

A second issue that makes third-generation behavior therapies controversial is the way in which ACT—the most prominent of the third-generation therapies—has been introduced and propagated in the field, which might be summed up as "taking the field by storm." In some cases, proponents implicitly have declared that with the advent of third-generation therapies, the messiah had arrived (or was well on her way). Some critics have described the new generation as a cult.[102] While these descriptions involve hyperbole, they hold some truth. Certainly, third-generation behavior therapies are the current rage in behavior therapy in part because of their fresh and innovative approach and because of their potential to make significant contributions. However, some behavior therapists, even those who are developing third-generation approaches, take a more modest view and consider them to be in their infancy.[103]

The third controversial issue is that, despite some grandiose claims about the success of third-generation therapies, the evidence to date of their efficacy and effectiveness is modest at best.[104] Of the three major third-generation behavior therapies we have looked at, only DBT has met the conventional standards for empirical support (as described in In Theory 4-2), although ACT and MBCT are making strides toward that goal.

To their credit, all three therapies have elaborate theories that are grounded in basic behavioral science to guide the development of their approach and interventions. In the case of ACT, many more studies have been conducted evaluating the underlying theory than the therapy procedures that are derived from the theories.[105] While this research is contributing to our basic understanding of psychological pain and distress, its findings cannot legitimately be used to directly support the therapy procedures that are derived from the theory, as some proponents of ACT have done.

Controversy typically accompanies new ideas in science, and both proponents and opponents of the new ideas tend to get caught up in the controversy and become less objective and open-minded than they would otherwise be. When the dust settles, the merits and contributions of third-generation behavior therapies can be fairly evaluated. Until then, several things seem clear.

The impetus for the development of third-generation behavior therapies was a failure of the first and second generations to adequately address some important clinical challenges. DBT offers new hope for clients with borderline personality disorder, just as MBCT provides an approach for preventing relapse of recurrent episodes of major depression. These are very serious disorders, and previously existing behavior therapies had not made an impact in dealing with the problems they presented. ACT, which targets a wide array of disorders, provides an alternative to traditional first-order change interventions, especially for clients for whom first-order change is not effective. In such cases, second-order change based on acceptance and mindfulness may provide the help clients need to deal with their suffering and live according to their values. As you have seen in Chapters 6–14, there are often a variety of behavior therapy techniques that can treat the same problem. This allows a particular client and his or her specific problem to be matched to the most suitable treatment. So, in addition to being useful when first-order change interventions are not working, ACT and other third-generation behavior therapies may be more applicable to particular clients and problems.

SUMMARY

1. First-generation behavior therapies (Chapters 6–11) and second-generation behavior therapies (Chapters 12–13) focus on changing clients' problem behaviors. Third-generation behavior therapies, which emerged in the 1990s, focus on helping clients accept psychological pain and discomfort (psychological problems)—rather than trying to change them—while they pursue what is important in their lives.

2. Third-generation behavior therapies share the defining themes and characteristics of all behavior therapies and also share five interrelated core themes: (1) an expanded view of psychological health, in which accepting inevitable psychological pain and discomfort is seen as adaptive; (2) a broad view of acceptable therapy outcomes, which includes second-order change that alters the function of problem behaviors rather than first-order change that alters their form or frequency; (3) acceptance (fully embracing one's experience) and (4) mindfulness (purposely and non-judgmentally paying attention to momentary experiences) as general therapeutic strategies; and (5) creating quality of life (a life worth living).

3. Acceptance and Commitment Therapy (ACT) posits that psychological inflexibility—a narrowing of options for behaving—is at the core of psychological suffering and is maintained by six interrelated processes: (1) cognitive fusion (taking thoughts literally rather than seeing them as just thoughts), (2) attachment to the conceptualized self (how we view ourselves), (3) experiential avoidance (escape from or avoidance of unpleasant thoughts and feelings), (4) disconnection from the present moment, (5) unclear personal values, and (6) inaction with respect to values (failure to act in accord with what is personally important). These six sources of psychological inflexibility are treated in ACT to foster psychological flexibility.

4. ACT has been applied to many forms of human suffering and is the most broadly applicable third-generation therapy. Although research has supported its effectiveness, ACT is not yet considered an empirically supported therapy.

5. Dialectical behavior therapy (DBT) was developed specifically to treat borderline personality disorder. DBT involves synthesizing the need for acceptance and change, using both validation/acceptance and problem-solving/change strategies.

6. DBT is administered in two primary modes. Weekly individual DBT sessions focus on clients' behavioral and emotional problems, with special emphasis on life-threatening and therapy-interfering behaviors. Additionally, in weekly group skills training sessions, clients learn core skills in mindfulness, interpersonal effectiveness, emotion regulation, and distress tolerance. The training typically runs for an entire year and follows a manual with detailed session-by-session lessons.

7. The dialectical perspective strives for a synthesis between polar extremes. Using dialectical persuasion, DBT therapists subtly highlight the inconsistencies in clients' actions, beliefs, and values to help them develop a balanced perspective.

8. DBT has been established as an empirically supported treatment for BPD, and its applicability to other disorders is being explored.

9. Mindfulness-based cognitive therapy (MBCT) was designed to treat recurrent episodes of major depression. It integrates elements of cognitive therapy and mindfulness-based stress reduction procedures. Rather than directly changing the content of negative thoughts, as in cognitive therapy, MBCT focuses on changing clients' awareness of and relation to their negative thoughts.

10. MBCT is administered in groups following a set protocol involving eight weekly, 2-hour sessions and homework assignments. Clients are trained to be mindful (intimately aware) of their thoughts, emotions, and bodily sensations through a variety of mindfulness exercises.

11. Initial research evaluating the efficacy of MBCT in preventing recurrent episodes of major depression is promising, and MBCT's brevity and group format make it efficient and cost-effective.

12. Although third-generation behavior therapies are new and controversial, they are making an impact on behavior therapy, especially by providing treatment for difficult clinical problems (borderline personality disorder and relapse of major depression) and offering alternative intervention strategies to first- and second-generation behavior therapies.

REFERENCE NOTES

1. For example, Hayes, 2002, 2004b.
2. Compare with DiGiuseppe, 2008.
3. Anderson, 2008; Arch & Craske, 2008; McCloud, 2006; Hofmann & Asmundson, 2008; Öst, 2008.
4. Hayes, Follette, & Linehan, 2004.
5. Gross, 2002; Gross & Muñoz, 1995; Gutiérrez-Martínez, Luciano-Soriano, Rodríguez-Valverde, & Fink, 2004; Hayes, Luoma, Bond, Masuda, & Lillis, 2006; John & Gross, 2004; Purdon, 1999; Wegner, 1994.
6. Hayes, Follette, & Linehan, 2004.
7. Eifert & Forsyth, 2005; Hayes et al., 1999.
8. Baer, 2003, 2006; Kabat-Zinn, 2003.
9. Roemer & Orsillo, 2008.
10. Baer, 2005.
11. Hayes et al., 1999.
12. Blackledge & Hayes, 2001.
13. Hayes et al., 1999.
14. Hayes et al.,1999; Hayes, Wilson, Gifford, Follette, & Strosahl, 1996.
15. Hayes, 2004a.
16. Compare with Forsyth & Eifert, 2008.
17. Hayes, Luoma, Bond, Masuda, & Lillis, 2006.
18. For example, McCracken, Vowles, & Eccleston, 2005; Vowles & McCracken, 2008.
19. For example, Orsillo & Roemer, 2005; Roemer & Orsillo, 2007.
20. Gratz & Gunderson, 2006.
21. Gifford et al., 2004.
22. Hayes et al., 1999.
23. Adapted from Forsyth & Eifert, 2008.
24. Forsyth, Fusé, & Acheson, in press.
25. Antony, Ledley, Liss, & Swinson, 2006.
26. Dalrymple & Herbert, 2007.
27. Twohig, Hayes, & Masuda, 2006.
28. Forman, Herbert, Moitra, Yeomans, & Geller, 2007.
29. Bond & Bunce, 2000.
30. Dougher & Hackbert, 1994; Zettle, 2007; Zettle & Rains, 1989.
31. Gifford et al., 2004; Hayes et al., 2004; Twohig, Schoenberger, & Hayes, 2007.
32. Dahl, Wilson, & Nilsson, 2004; McCracken, Vowles, & Eccleston, 2005.
33. Gregg, Callaghan, Hayes, & Glenn-Lawson, 2007.
34. Lundgren, Dahl, & Hayes, 2008; Lundgren, Dahl, Melin, & Kies, 2006.
35. Baer, Fischer, & Huss, 2005a; Heffner, Sperry, & Eifert, 2002.

36. Bach & Hayes, 2002; Gaudiano & Herbert, 2006.
37. Hayes, Luoma, Bond, Masuda, & Lillis, 2006.
38. Leahy, 2008; Öst, 2008.
39. Campbell-Sills, Barlow, Brown, & Hofmann, 2006a, 2006b; Eifert & Heffner, 2003; Hayes et al., 1999; Levitt, Brown, Orsillo, & Barlow, 2004.
40. Gutiérrez-Martínez, Luciano-Soriano, Rodríguez-Valverde, & Fink, 2004; Masuda, Hayes, Sackett, & Twohig, 2004.
41. Karekla, Forsyth, & Kelly, 2004; Kashdan, Barrios, Forsyth, & Steger, 2006; Kashdan, Morina, & Priebe, in press; Sloan, 2004.
42. Hayes, Wilson, Gifford, Follette, & Strosahl, 1996; Hayes, Luoma, Bond, Masuda, & Lillis, 2006.
43. Linehan, 1987.
44. Robins, Schmidt, & Linehan, 2004.
45. Linehan, 1993a.
46. Dimeff & Koerner, 2007.
47. Linehan, 1993a.
48. Koerner & Dimeff, 2007.
49. Linehan, 1993a.
50. Koerner & Dimeff, 2007.
51. Linehan, 1993a.
52. Koerner & Dimeff, 2007.
53. Koerner & Dimeff, 2007.
54. Koerner & Dimeff, 2007.
55. Linehan, 1993a.
56. Linehan, 1993a.
57. Koerner & Dimeff, 2007.
58. Koerner & Dimeff, 2007.
59. Koerner & Dimeff, 2007.
60. Linehan, 1993a.
61. Koerner & Dimeff, 2007; Linehan, 1993a.
62. Linehan, 1993a.
63. Linehan, 1993b.
64. Linehan, 1993a.
65. Linehan, 1993a.
66. Koerner & Dimeff, 2007; dialogue p. 11.
67. Goldfried, Linehan, & Smith, 1978.
68. Linehan, 1993a.
69. Lynch, Trost, Salsman, & Linehan, 2007.
70. For example, Lynch, Trost, Salsman, & Linehan, 2007.
71. Lynch, Morse, Mendelson, & Robins, 2003.
72. Safer, Telch, & Agras, 2001; Telch, Agras, & Linehan, 2001.
73. Rathus, Cavuoto, & Passarelli, 2006.
74. Linehan, Schmidt, Dimeff, Craft, Kanter, & Comtois, 1999.
75. For example, Comer, 2008; Lynch, Trost, Salsman, & Linehan, 2007.
76. Segal, Williams, & Teasdale, 2001; Segal, Teasdale, & Williams, 2004.
77. Kovacs & Beck, 1978.
78. Haaga, Dyck, & Ernst, 1991.
79. Segal, Teasdale, &Williams, 2004.
80. Segal, Teasdale, & Williams, 2004, p. 51.
81. Ingram & Hollon, 1986.
82. Kabat-Zinn, 1990.
83. Ingram & Hollon, 1986.
84. Segal, Teasdale, & Williams, 2004.
85. Barnhofer, Duggan, Crane, Hepburn, Fennell, & Williams, 2007; Kenny & Williams, 2007; Kingston, Dooley, Bates, Lawlor, & Malone, 2007; Williams, Russell, & Russell, 2008.
86. Teasdale, Segal, Williams, Ridgeway, Soulsby, & Lau, 2000.
87. Ma & Teasdale, 2004.
88. Williams, Russell, & Russell, 2008.
89. For example, Smith, Graham, & Senthinathan, 2007.
90. Kenny & Williams, 2007.
91. Smith, Graham, & Senthinathan, 2007.
92. Semple, Lee, & Miller, 2006.
93. Williams, Teasdale, Segal, & Kabat-Zinn, 2007.
94. Huss & Baer, 2007.
95. Waller, Carlson, & Englar-Carlson, 2006.
96. Williams et al., 2008.
97. Williams, Duggan, Crane, & Fennell, 2006.
98. Evans, Ferrando, Findler, Stowell, Smart, & Haglin, 2008; Ree & Craigie, 2007.
99. Yook et al., 2008.
100. Baer, Fischer, & Huss, 2005a, 2005b.
101. Anderson, 2008; Arch & Craske, 2008; McCloud, 2006; Hofmann & Asmundson, 2008; Öst, 2008.
102. McCloud, 2006.
103. For example, Segal, Teasdale, & Williams, 2004.
104. Leahy, 2008; Öst, 2008.
105. Hayes, 2008.

PART THREE

Applications to Somatic Problems and Contemporary Behavior Therapy in Perspective

Now that you have digested the appetizers (basic principles) and the main course (behavior therapies), it's time for dessert. Dessert is supposed to be a treat—something different—and we hope that what we have prepared will fit that bill. Whereas Chapters 6–14 were organized by behavior therapies (used to treat various disorders), Chapters 15 and 16 are organized by disorders (treated by various behavior therapies). Chapter 15 covers medical disorders, and Chapter 16 deals with psychological disorders whose primary features are physical problems. You will be familiar with most of the behavior therapy procedures described, but their applications will be new. These applications illustrate the versatility and breadth of behavior therapy principles and procedures and serve as a review of many of the therapies you have read about earlier.

Then, after you've finished dessert, it will be time to sit back and reflect on your elaborate dinner. In place of coffee or tea, in the final chapter we offer the chef's selection of hearty strengths of and tempting challenges to behavior therapy.

15 Applications of Behavior Therapy to Medical Disorders

16 Applications of Behavior Therapy to Psychological Disorders with Primary Physical Characteristics

17 Contemporary Behavior Therapy in Perspective: Strengths and Challenges

15

Applications of Behavior Therapy to Medical Disorders

The application of behavior therapy principles and procedures to physical health and illness burgeoned in the last two decades of the 20th century and is a flourishing endeavor in the new millennium. Much of this work is subsumed under the interdisciplinary field known as *behavioral medicine*.[1] One aspect of the field applies behavioral science, including behavior therapy, to the assessment, treatment, management, rehabilitation, and prevention of physical disease and related behavioral reactions to physical dysfunction.[2]

Behavior therapy serves four functions in dealing with medical disorders: (1) treating medical disorders; (2) increasing adherence to medical treatments, such as taking medication; (3) helping patients cope with treatments and illness; and (4) preventing medical disorders. Table 15-1 describes and gives examples of these four functions. To illustrate each function, we will present representative examples of the medical disorders with which behavior therapy has been used.

TREATMENT OF MEDICAL DISORDERS

Behavior therapy can add to existing medical treatments in three ways. First, behavior therapy can be combined with medical treatments (for example, both relaxation training and medication can be used to control high blood pressure). Second, behavior therapy may be more desirable than medical treatments that are associated with risk (such as surgery) or with undesirable side effects (such as medication). Third, behavior therapy can play an especially important role in cases for which no viable medical treatments exist (as for some types of chronic pain). We will illustrate the use of behavior therapy

TABLE **15-1**

Functions of Behavior Therapy in Dealing with Medical Disorders

Function	Description	Example
TREATMENT	Correct or alleviate a medical condition and the pain and suffering associated with it	Relaxation training to lower blood pressure in patients with essential hypertension
ADHERENCE	Increase patients' following prescribed medical treatments (such as medication, diet, and exercise)	Taking medication at the same time each day so that it will come under stimulus control
COPING	Reduce anxiety, discomfort, and distress associated with medical procedures	Self-instructional training to decrease the anxiety associated with dental work
PREVENTION	Reduce the risk of developing disease, including motivating people to engage in healthful behaviors	Assertion training to promote safer sexual practices (such as refusing to engage in unprotected sex)

to treat medical disorders by describing its application to two medical problems: chronic pain and medically unexplained symptoms.

Chronic Pain

Pain is the most common problem that patients present to physicians as well as the most frequent cause of disability. A distinction usually is made between acute and chronic pain. *Acute pain* is the result of bodily trauma and disappears when the injury heals. Acute pain generally is adaptive in that it signals bodily damage (as when the pain from a pulled muscle alerts you to stop running). *Chronic pain* occurs after an injury has healed or when no trauma exists. Pain is considered chronic if it lasts for at least 6 months.[3] Approximately 30% of the United States population suffer from chronic pain.[4]

Medication is by far the most common treatment for pain, but it has a number of limitations, especially for chronic pain. First, medication may not fully alleviate patients' pain. Second, many drugs lose their effectiveness over time. Third, long-term use of pain medication may lower people's tolerance for mild forms of pain. Fourth, drugs frequently have undesirable side effects (such as drowsiness). Fifth, more potent pain medications may result in physical and psychological dependence.[5] Thus, alternatives to medication are important in the treatment of chronic pain.

Behavioral treatment of chronic pain has two goals: (1) to reduce the patient's subjective discomfort (for example, decreasing the intensity or frequency of headaches) or, when this is not possible, (2) to increase the patient's tolerance for pain through various coping strategies.

Pain as Behavior

How pain is viewed makes a difference. We usually think of pain in terms of the subjective experience of intense physical discomfort. Behavior therapists have found it more useful to view pain as a *behavior* because behaviors can be readily assessed and changed.[6] **Pain behaviors** are overt behaviors that generally indicate a person is experiencing strong physical discomfort—for example, grimacing and saying, "Ouch!" In contrast, **well behaviors** are overt behaviors that typically indicate that a person is not experiencing pain, such as smiling and saying, "I feel good today." Well behaviors compete with pain behaviors. Table 15-2 lists common examples of both pain behaviors and well behaviors.

Pain behaviors, like any other behaviors, are maintained by their antecedents and consequences. A simple example illustrates this conceptualization:

> Vinny is playing a rough game of football with his friends, and his body is becoming badly bruised. However, he does not complain. He continues to play as if nothing hurt. If he did complain, his friends might call him a weakling.
>
> The minute Vinny gets home, the story changes. He slumps into a chair, "unable" to move. He tells his mother that he hurts all over, and she offers to help him upstairs and bring him his dinner in bed.

Clearly, the antecedents and consequences in the two situations are different, and it is easy to see how they influenced Vinny's pain behaviors.

TABLE **15-2**

Examples of Pain Behaviors and Well Behaviors

Pain Behaviors	Well Behaviors
Moaning, screaming	Laughing, singing
Grimacing, wincing	Smiling
Talking about the uncomfortable or unbearable sensations	Talking about feeling good
Moving in a guarded, unnatural manner indicating discomfort (for example, limping)	Moving spontaneously, in an unrestricted manner
Reclining or sitting in order to ease pain	Standing or walking
Restricting activities that might result in pain	Engaging in activities that might result in pain
Requesting and taking pain medication	Refusing pain medication
Requesting help moving	Moving by oneself
Using crutches, cane, walker, or wheelchair	Walking without support

The behavioral conceptualization of pain does not ignore the physical sensation of discomfort caused by the stimulation of pain receptors. The physical sensations of pain are one of the maintaining antecedents of pain behaviors, although they are not antecedents that can be directly changed through behavior therapy. In contrast, situational factors (as in Vinny's case) and a person's ability to cope with discomfort can be changed by behavior therapy.

The consequences of exhibiting pain behaviors often are important maintaining conditions.[7] Significant consequences include (1) social reinforcers, notably attention and sympathy; (2) avoidance of responsibilities (for example, missing work); (3) financial compensation (for instance, disability payments); and (4) receipt of pain medication. Just how closely pain behaviors can be influenced by social attention is illustrated by the case of a 47-year-old man with chronic lower back pain. If you look at Figure 15-1, you can see that the number of pain behaviors the man exhibited clearly varied with the presence or absence of attention from the hospital staff.

Changing the Consequences of Pain Behaviors

One behavioral approach to the treatment of pain is to change the consequences maintaining patients' pain behaviors. The prototype for this approach was developed by Wilbert Fordyce and his colleagues at the University of Washington Pain Clinic.[8] We will describe it in some detail because it is a good illustration of how basic behavior therapy principles are applied to a complex problem.

Wilbert Fordyce

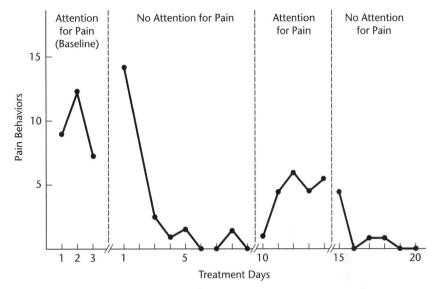

FIGURE 15-1

Effects of professional staff attention on the pain behaviors of a 47-year-old man with chronic lower back pain

Source: Adapted from Fordyce, 1976, p. 89.

The program begins in the hospital and later is extended to the patient's home environment. Assessing the maintaining conditions of the patient's pain behaviors comes first. Often, patients are being reinforced for pain behaviors but not for well behaviors.[9] When this is the case, treatment involves

reversing the contingencies: Reinforcers are administered for well behaviors and withheld for pain behaviors.

The most common reinforcer for pain behaviors is attention from others. Thus, a major focus of the treatment program involves encouraging *everyone* who comes in contact with the patient to ignore or respond matter-of-factly to the patient's pain behaviors in order to extinguish them. At the same time, people are asked to reinforce—as with praise and attention—the patient's well behaviors.

Rest is another reinforcing consequence of pain. Thus, rest is made a consequence of activity (well behaviors) rather than a consequence of pain behaviors. First, the amount of activity the patient can tolerate without experiencing pain, known as the *pain threshold*, is assessed. Then, the initial amount of activity that the patient is required to do is set just below the patient's pain threshold. When the initial amount of activity is reached, the patient is allowed to rest before going on to the next activity. The hospital staff gives the patient attention and praise for completing the activity criterion. As the patient's pain threshold rises, the amount of activity required for rest is gradually increased.

Receiving medication also results in a variety of reinforcing consequences. Positive reinforcers include the pleasant side effects of pain medication (such as feeling "high") and attention from the person administering the medication. Negative reinforcers include relief from physical discomfort and avoiding unpleasant responsibilities (such as household chores).

Pain medication typically is administered on an as-needed basis. In contrast, during the pain treatment program, access to medication is made *time contingent* rather than pain contingent. Patients are given medication at fixed time intervals, whether or not they request it. Over the course of treatment, the medication dosage is gradually reduced (and eventually eliminated in many cases).

After a course of hospital treatment, the patient's therapy continues at home. Systematic procedures are established to ensure that the decrease in pain behaviors transfers from the hospital to the patient's home environment and is maintained over time. The patient's family and close friends are asked to participate in the treatment and are trained in the procedures. For example, they learn to withhold reinforcers for the patient's pain behaviors and to administer reinforcers for the patient's well behaviors.

Although the assistance of family and friends may be reinforced by their observing the patient's progress, that may not be sufficient to maintain their efforts over an extended period. Accordingly, procedures are established to ensure that the help of family and friends are adequately reinforced. For example, patients are instructed to explicitly thank them for their help.

Part of the program also deals with reestablishing previously reinforcing activities in patients' lives. These activities, which often are natural reinforcers, are made contingent on well behaviors. As an example, suppose a woman's walking, bending, and lifting increased in the hospital. If the patient had enjoyed shopping, then she would be allowed to go shopping only if she walked to the store. If having friends visit had been a favorite activity, the patient would be permitted to invite them to her house only if she did some of the preparatory housework.

Treatment Packages for Chronic Pain

Because pain is a multifaceted behavior, treatment packages generally are more effective than single treatments. In one study, for example, clients' using coping skills along with changing simply the consequences of pain resulted in greater pain management than changing consequences alone.[10] The components of treatment packages for pain include changing the maintaining consequences of pain behaviors, cognitive-behavioral coping skills therapy, relaxation training, and biofeedback (as well as nonbehavioral treatments such as medication, physical therapy, and exercise).[11]

Biofeedback provides information (feedback) about a physiological function, such as muscle tension associated with headaches, to help the person modify that function. The individual is "hooked up" to electromechanical equipment, such as a polygraph, that provides the individual with the moment-to-moment status of the physiological function (see Photo 15-1). For example, a tone or visual display indicates the level of muscle tension. Patients are instructed to keep their muscle tension within an acceptable range (although how they achieve this is left up to the patient). Patients learn to

PHOTO 15-1

In biofeedback training, electrodes attached to the client transmit information about a physiological function, such as muscle tension, to electromechanical equipment that provides the client with feedback about a physiological state.

achieve the same outcome without the biofeedback equipment in their home environments by identifying their sensations associated with an optimal physiological level and then using them as cues to modulate the level (employing the same strategies that they used during biofeedback training).

Biofeedback and relaxation training are often used to treat and prevent chronic headaches.[12] For tension headaches, relaxation training and electromyographic (muscle tension) biofeedback appear to be equally effective.[13] For migraine headaches in adults, the combination of relaxation training and thermal (skin temperature) biofeedback results in larger reductions in migraine activity than either treatment alone.[14] Thermal biofeedback may be the treatment of choice for children's migraine headaches.[15] Biofeedback equipment that resembles a computer game has been developed for children and adolescents, and it may increase patients' motivation to undergo and remain in the treatment.[16] A recent meta-analysis clearly demonstrated the efficacy of biofeedback for tension headaches and the effects were maintained over an average of 15 months.[17] Although biofeedback is superior to relaxation, the combination of the two treatments is most effective, especially for children and adolescents.

Adding behavioral parent training to biofeedback for the treatment of migraine headaches has reduced headache frequency in children significantly more than biofeedback alone.[18] When their child is experiencing a headache, the parents are instructed to (1) praise the child for using coping skills, (2) encourage the child to continue normal activities (for example, attending school and performing daily chores), (3) remove attention for pain-related behaviors (for instance, not asking how much the headache hurts), (4) administer pain medication only as prescribed and not on request, (5) treat headaches that require reduction of normal activity as an illness (for example, the child must remain in bed), and (6) recruit others (such as teachers) to follow the same guidelines.

Studies of relaxation training and biofeedback for both migraine and tension headaches have demonstrated an average of 50% reduction in headaches compared with 5% improvement for clients in wait-list control groups and 15% improvement for clients receiving a placebo medication.[19] Biofeedback and relaxation training also can be effective when self-administered with minimal therapist contact.[20]

For reducing both headaches and medication usage, biofeedback-assisted relaxation may be superior to self-relaxation that involves 10 to 15 minutes of relaxing each day while thinking peaceful thoughts.[21] Cognitive therapy and other cognitive-behavioral therapies for migraine headaches do not appear to enhance the effectiveness of biofeedback-assisted relaxation training.[22] As for the mechanisms that are operative with biofeedback-assisted relaxation, it seems to change important physiological functions associated with headaches, such as cerebral blood flow velocity.[23]

In contrast to the poor long-term maintenance typically found with medication for headaches, follow-up studies indicate that behavioral treatments maintain their effectiveness for at least as long as 3 years.[24] Moreover, behavioral treatments for headaches are associated with positive side effects, such as reduction in anxiety and depression, which do not occur with pain medication.[25]

Cognitive-behavioral coping skills treatment packages that include relaxation and cognitive restructuring are effective treatments for managing pain associated with rheumatic diseases.[26] Juvenile rheumatoid arthritis, a chronic and recurrent pain condition, has been treated successfully with relaxation training, breathing exercises, and emotive imagery.[27] Treatment packages incorporating cognitive restructuring, relaxation training, and emotive imagery have been effective in reducing pain from fibromyalgia (a chronic, multi-site pain condition).[28]

Some cognitive-behavioral coping skills treatment packages have been very brief, such as the single-session stress inoculation training program used to help African-American children cope with pain associated with sickle cell anemia, which you read about in Chapter 13 (page 364).[29] In another program involving three 45-minute therapy sessions, African-American adults with sickle cell anemia learned calming self-instructions through modeling and behavior rehearsal to cope with pain.[30] The treatment package also included relaxation training and self-distraction techniques. Sixty-seven patients were assigned either to the cognitive-behavioral coping skills training group or to a control group that received disease education. At a 3-month follow-up, patients who had participated in the coping skills treatment reported significantly less pain and more attempts to cope with pain than patients in the control group. Moreover, on days when they experienced pain, patients receiving the cognitive-behavioral treatment required fewer contacts with health care professionals than patients in the control group.

Learning differential relaxation allows patients to employ muscle relaxation to cope with pain during the course of their daily activities.[31] Often, there are identifiable antecedents to pain that people can use as cues to begin differential relaxation. For example, stress-evoking situations and anxiety often precipitate and exacerbate pain associated with existing medical conditions, such as the uncomfortable itching associated with eczema (skin inflammation) or the physical discomfort associated with menopause, both of which have been successfully treated with relaxation training.[32] To identify situations in which patients are particularly vulnerable to headaches, patients learn to monitor their headaches; they record in a *pain diary* such information as the circumstances in which the pain occurs, what they are doing and thinking at the time, and the consequences of the pain.[33]

In many cases, learning to tolerate chronic pain, rather than reducing it, is the most realistic goal of therapy. Cognitive-behavioral coping skills therapy can help patients achieve this goal. An example is Dennis Turk's stress inoculation training for pain that combines relaxation training, breathing exercises, attention diversion, and emotive imagery.[34] These procedures are similar to the Lamaze method of natural childbirth.[35] In one study of the treatment of chronic pain and whiplash-associated disorders, participants receiving Acceptance and Commitment Therapy showed significant differences in pain disability, life satisfaction, fear of movement, depression, and psychological inflexibility compared with participants in a wait-list control group—although pain intensity did not decrease in either group.[36]

Behavioral Treatment of Chronic Pain in Perspective

Although behavior therapy procedures have been used to treat a variety of pain conditions, most research has focused on lower back pain and headaches. Generally, behavioral treatment of chronic pain has been successful.[37] In the majority of cases, however, patients experience a *reduction* in pain, rather than a complete elimination of pain.[38] The improvement often is substantial enough that patients can resume normal activities despite their still experiencing some physical discomfort. In the case of headaches, treatment gains have been maintained for 1 to 4 years without any specific maintenance procedures.[39] An indirect measure of the effectiveness of behavioral treatments for pain is that most pain clinics employ behavior therapy procedures as part of the treatment packages offered to patients.

Turning to specific treatments, changing maintaining consequences of pain behaviors has been shown to be effective in a number of studies.[40] However, its application has been narrow. It has been applied exclusively to pain associated with physical activity (primarily chronic lower back pain), and it has focused on increasing exercise and activity and decreasing medication usage while ignoring emotional and cognitive aspects of pain.[41] Another potential limitation of the consequential approach concerns transfer to and long-term maintenance in clients' natural environments.[42] The ultimate success of the treatment may depend on instituting specific procedures to foster transfer and maintenance (such as family members' continuing appropriate contingencies), which has not always been done.

Both biofeedback and relaxation training can be effective in treating headaches.[43] Cognitive-behavioral coping skills approaches have been successful in treating a variety of types of pain.[44] Treatment outcomes with patients suffering from chronic pain appear to be enhanced when they are given detailed information about when and how to use coping skills[45] and when coping skills are individualized.[46]

To summarize, four major behavioral interventions have been used to treat chronic pain: changing maintaining consequences, biofeedback, relaxation training, and cognitive-behavioral coping skills therapies. At present, none of the four treatments has been shown to be consistently superior to the others.[47] This state of affairs is not necessarily bad because individual patients differ widely in their responses to the treatments, which means that there is a need for a variety of effective procedures.[48] Moreover, treatment packages consisting of a combination of the four therapies generally are effective.[49]

Medically Unexplained Symptoms

Medically unexplained symptoms refer to physical complaints for which a physical cause cannot be found and that do not fit the criteria for a known psychological disorder (for example, heart palpitations related to panic disorder). The symptoms are chronic and result in decreased activity, social behavior, and work performance.

Medically unexplained symptoms are very common. According to some studies, physical complaints such as fatigue, backache, headache, dizziness, chest pain, and abdominal pain have no demonstrable organic cause in more than 75% of cases.[50] Because the symptoms persist and are unexplained, patients often engage in a continual and costly search for the "correct" diagnosis, which results in multiple diagnostic tests and hospitalizations. Also, such patients often have comorbid psychological disorders, most notably anxiety and depression,[51] and there is a need to treat them as well as the somatic symptoms.[52]

Cognitive-behavioral therapies are used to supplement ongoing medical interventions, replacing medical treatments that involve invasive procedures or negative side effects, and offering alternative treatments where no effective medical interventions exist. The cognitive-behavioral therapies include relaxation training, biofeedback, cognitive restructuring, problem-solving training, assertion training, and collaborative empiricism exercises (derived from cognitive therapy).[53] We will briefly describe the success of cognitive-behavioral therapies in treating three examples of common medically unexplained symptoms: chronic fatigue syndrome, noncardiac chest pain, and fibromyalgia syndrome.

Chronic fatigue syndrome is characterized by disabling fatigue lasting more than 6 months and resulting in a 50% reduction in daily activity. Cognitive-behavioral interventions have resulted in reduced emotional distress, increased activity level, and increased functional abilities (such as daily self-care behaviors),[54] and these interventions appear to be more beneficial than medical treatments alone.[55]

Noncardiac chest pain is persistent chest pain without any identifiable cardiac etiology. The benefits of cognitive-behavioral treatments for this condition include decreased or cessation of chest pain, increased activity, reduced emotional distress, and decreased use of medications.[56] However, studies have yet to demonstrate that the cognitive-behavioral interventions are superior to other treatments and attention-placebo controls.[57]

Fibromyalgia syndrome is a musculoskeletal condition involving diffuse pain of at least 3 months' duration. There is increased pain sensitivity in multiple tender points throughout the body and often stiffness in muscles and connective tissue. Certain forms of fibromyalgia have no identifiable physiological cause. The effects of cognitive-behavioral interventions for fibromyalgia have included reduced pain and emotional distress as well as improved self-efficacy beliefs and quality of life.[58] In some cases, these changes have not exceeded those obtained from less costly, education-only interventions.[59] However, impressive results from a recent study conducted in Spain indicate that not only was stress inoculation training a highly effective treatment for fibromyalgia but that it also was superior to medication.[60]

The treatment of medically unexplained symptoms is an exciting new application of cognitive-behavioral therapies. At present, the research findings appear to support the conclusion that the interventions are promising, but further research is required to demonstrate clear-cut effectiveness.[61]

ADHERENCE TO MEDICAL REGIMENS

Patients' failure to follow medical advice—for example, to take medication or do physical rehabilitation exercises—is a major problem for the medical profession.[62] In fact, nonadherence may occur as frequently as 70% of the time for patients in general[63] and 87% of the time with pediatric patients.[64] Clearly, the most effective treatment is worthless if patients do not avail themselves of it, and, in some cases, adherence can mean the difference between life and death. For instance, nearly perfect adherence to a stringent medication regime is imperative for appropriate HIV disease management.[65]

Early research on increasing adherence to medical regimens attempted to identify patient characteristics associated with nonadherence, such as educational level and personality traits. However, it appears that there is little or no relationship between patient characteristics and nonadherence.[66] It is more useful to view adherence as a *behavior*, rather than a trait,[67] and to develop procedures for accelerating specific adherence behaviors, such as administering frequent, immediate, and meaningful positive reinforcement to enhance parental adherence to their children's health care needs.[68]

With many medical regimens, the immediate consequences of "following doctor's orders" at best are weak because the benefits are usually delayed. At worst, complying with medical regimens may be distinctly aversive, such as taking antibiotics that result in nausea and engaging in exhausting physical rehabilitation exercises.[69] In contrast, patients readily adhere to medical regimens that have immediate benefits, such as taking pain medication.

Adherence can occur only *if the patient first remembers and then is sufficiently motivated* to follow the prescribed treatment. Prompting is used to help patients remember to perform treatment-related behaviors, and reinforcement is employed to provide the motivation.[70]

We will illustrate behavioral interventions for increasing adherence to three important aspects of medical treatment: taking medication, engaging in health-related behaviors (such as following a prescribed diet), and keeping medical appointments.

Taking Medication

High rates of noncompliance with prescribed medication regimens are typical in patient populations.[71] Physicians frequently prescribe regular doses of medication for an extended time, ranging from a week to years (as for essential hypertension, epilepsy, and diabetes). Environmental prompts to remind patients to take medication may be as simple as special labels on medicine bottles, such as a picture of a clock on which the hours the medication needs to be taken are circled,[72] or pill boxes with separate compartments for each day of the week, as shown in Photo 15-2. A more sophisticated prompting device is a portable timer and pill dispenser that sounds a tone when a pill should be taken.[73] The tone continues until a knob is turned that releases a pill into the patient's hand. The advent of handheld computers and cell phones could facilitate elaborate prompting of medical regimens that might include explicit step-by-step directions for carrying out the procedures.[74]

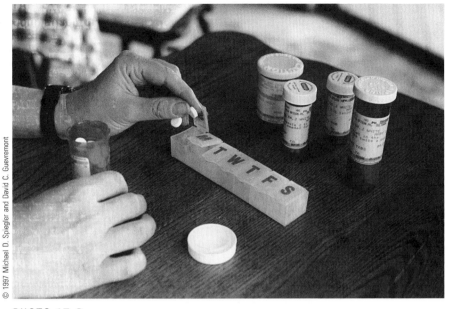

PHOTO 15-2

Patient using a daily pill box, a simple stimulus control device that prompts taking daily medication

Naturalistic stimulus control can be used to tailor a medication schedule to the patient's daily routine so that regularly occurring activities serve as cues for taking medication. This might involve taking medications at the same time each day,[75] with meals, or right before leaving the house in the morning.[76]

Merely remembering to take medication often is not sufficient to ensure adherence. Accordingly, stimulus control procedures generally are supplemented with reinforcement. For example, in one study, the combination of telephone reminders and lottery tickets as reinforcers increased patients' taking anticonvulsive medication an average of 43%.[77] Another example involved a token system for children (ages 8 and 10) to increase using an inhaler for asthma three times a day.[78]

Although prompting and reinforcement can be effective in obtaining adherence to taking medication, when these procedures are discontinued the adherence may not persist.[79] Adherence is more likely to be maintained if self-control skills are added to stimulus control and reinforcement procedures. As an example, one program taught patients with high blood pressure to use stimulus control procedures (for example, to associate pill taking with breakfast) and self-monitoring (of the medication taken and blood pressure).[80] Additionally, every 2 weeks the patients' blood pressure was checked. When their blood pressure was below a set criterion, patients were given a $4 credit toward the purchase of blood pressure recording equipment. Six months after the intervention, patients' medication adherence (assessed by random urine samples) was 80%, compared with 39% for comparable patients who were not in the program.

Punishment procedures have also been used to increase adherence to taking medication. For example, response cost for failure to take doses of Antabuse (a drug used in the treatment of alcohol dependence) has proven effective.[81] In one study, patients who had chronic drinking problems left "security deposits" with their therapist, and forfeited between $5 and $10 for each missed dose during a 3-month treatment contract. The patients missed only 8% of the scheduled clinic visits and were abstinent on 95% of their visits.

Engaging in Health-Related Behaviors

Besides prescribing medication, physicians instruct patients to perform various health-related behaviors, such as maintaining a specific diet, engaging in regular exercise, and monitoring indicators of bodily functions (such as blood glucose level). However, physicians' instructions alone are not likely to change patients' health-related behaviors.[82] Getting children and adolescents to consistently carry out necessary medical procedures is especially difficult, particularly when multiple behaviors are required.[83] For instance, people with diabetes may have to engage in a variety of health care routines, including maintaining dietary restrictions, self-injecting insulin, testing their urine, and taking care of their feet (because of the increased vulnerability to infections from poor circulation in the extremities). Prompting in the form of visual cues generally has a minimal effect on adherence;[84] however, written prompts have been shown to increase self-monitoring of blood glucose levels.[85]

More elaborate prompting involving a 56-step checklist for glucose monitoring was successful with a woman who had serious memory impairment.[86] The patient was verbally prompted to read each instruction, follow it, and check it off before going to the next step. She was praised for correctly performing each step and given corrective feedback for errors. After 90% accuracy was achieved, the prompts and feedback were faded. Whereas before the intervention the patient's accuracy in peforming the behaviors was as low as 40%, after the intervention her accuracy was consistently at or above 90%.

Self-monitoring may be an effective intervention for increasing adherence to simple regimens, such as engaging in a single exercise.[87] However, self-monitoring is likely to be ineffective for complex regimens, such as those required for diabetes.[88]

Reinforcement results in the most consistent adherence to health-related behaviors.[89] Token economy programs have been used to increase compliance with prescribed medical regimens for children with diabetes[90] and children on hemodialysis (a blood purification procedure).[91] The successful use of a token economy with an 82-year-old man to get him to follow a diet, do his exercises, and take his medication after a heart attack was described in Case 8-1 (page 193). Contingency contracts have proved useful with children and adolescents as well as with adults. For example, in a program for children and adolescents with hemophilia (a blood clotting disorder), the use of contingency contracts with token reinforcers resulted in 81% to 90% adherence to exercise and diet over 6 months.[92] Other procedures that enhance adherence to prescribed dietary and exercise regimens are self-monitoring, stimulus control, and relapse prevention procedures.[93]

When low adherence is maintained by a skill deficit in the prescribed medical procedure, modeling can increase adherence.[94] For example, parents of children with hemophilia were taught to administer factor replacement therapy, a complex emergency treatment for bleeding.[95] A nurse practitioner demonstrated the procedure and then gave parents feedback as they rehearsed it. The parents' skill level increased from 15% before the intervention to 92% during the intervention and 97% at follow-up. Modeling also has been helpful in teaching social and coping skills to overcome social barriers to adherence that children and adolescents experience (such as being called "sicky" when abstaining from sports in school).[96] Behavioral parent training is another strategy for enhancing children's adherence to medical regimens, such as prescribed diets for children with cystic fibrosis.[97]

Keeping Medical Appointments

Showing up for scheduled medical appointments is crucial for obtaining medical care and treatment. Telephone calls[98] and mailed reminders[99] are simple, relatively low-cost prompts, but they are not always successful.[100] As with the other targets of adherence, reinforcement generally is the most effective strategy to get people to keep medical appointments. For example, in a treatment program for heroin dependence, clients were given the privilege of taking their methadone (a drug used to treat heroin dependence) at home over the weekend if they made weekly clinic visits. This intervention increased the percentage of appointments kept from 45% to 89%.[101] In a pediatric clinic, the number of appointments that were kept was increased by including parking passes with mailed reminders;[102] the passes allowed parents to park adjacent to the clinic, which saved them time. Similarly, whereas keeping follow-up appointments at a family practice center was unaffected by reminder cards, offering free or reduced-rate appointments significantly increased appointments kept.[103]

COPING WITH MEDICAL/DENTAL PROCEDURES AND ILLNESS

Medical procedures, hospitalization, and even routine visits to the doctor or dentist produce significant stress and anxiety in many individuals. People fear pain, unfamiliar instrumentation and surroundings, separation from loved ones, and receiving a serious diagnosis. Children are particularly vulnerable to these fears.

As you saw in Chapter 11, modeling therapy is used to prepare children and adults for medical treatments. Another strategy is to teach patients coping skills to actively reduce their anxiety and discomfort as they prepare for and undergo treatments. Using coping skills also can facilitate medical procedures (such as lying still during a lumbar puncture) and aid in the recovery process. For surgery, coping skills can (1) improve patients' cooperation before, during, and after surgery; (2) reduce the amount of postoperative analgesic medications required; (3) speed recovery and reduce time spent in the hospital; and (4) reduce the amount of time and support patients require from others during recovery.[104]

To cope with painful medical procedures, children have been taught cognitive-behavioral coping skills, such as progressive relaxation, breathing exercises, emotive/distracting imagery, and the use of positive self-statements.[105] A variant of in vivo desensitization, in which children's preferred activities (such as playing a video game) are paired with stimuli associated with invasive medical procedures, has lowered the distress of children who must repeatedly undergo painful procedures.[106] Treatment packages usually are employed to teach patients to cope with medical procedures and tend to be more effective than single therapies.[107]

Medical procedures need not be painful to cause distress. For example, magnetic resonance imaging (MRI) used for diagnostic purposes may cause claustrophobia (fear of enclosed spaces) because patients are placed in a narrow tube and must remain motionless for extended periods. One approach to reducing such anxiety is to administer a pleasant fragrance during the MRI procedure, which may serve to distract or relax the patient.[108] Another approach used with children is to dispense token reinforcers for lying still during the MRI procedure.[109] Afterwards, the children exchange the tokens for backup reinforcers.

In a related application, a stimulus control procedure called *behavioral momentum compliance training*, along with differential reinforcement and extinction, was used to keep 22-month-old Aaron still while he was undergoing a medical procedure.[110] **Behavioral momentum compliance training** is used to get a client to comply with a low-probability request (one with which the client is not likely to comply) by preceding it with a series of high-probability requests (those with which the client is likely to comply). Aaron's mother first made a series of high-probability requests of Aaron (such as "Touch your head," "Say, 'Mom,'" and "Blow Mom a kiss") and praised him for compliance with each request. Immediately after the series of high-probability requests, Aaron's mother told him, "Hold still," which was a low-probability request. The treatment package resulted in a significant increase in Aaron's remaining still, from 44% to 78% of the time.

Parents' participation in interventions aimed at reducing their children's stress related to medical procedures is beneficial. Pediatric cancer patients undergoing venipuncture (puncturing a vein), for example, cried significantly less when their parents prompted and reinforced (with praise and token reinforcers) their children's engaging in a breathing distraction technique.[111] Parents' participation not only is helpful to their children but also can vicariously reduce parents' anxiety (such as in Case 11-3 [page 271] in which a mother participated in the vicarious extinction of her daughter's fear of dental procedures).[112] Parents whose children are seriously ill and undergoing medical procedures often experience high levels of stress, which may cause or exacerbate their children's anxiety and stress. In contrast, parents who are calm and effectively deal with their own stress are better able to help their children, including serving as coping models for them.

Various programs have been developed to directly treat parents' anxiety about their children's illnesses. For instance, parents whose children underwent painful bone marrow aspirations or lumbar punctures for leukemia were given stress inoculation training to deal with their own anxiety.[113] The training involved three 15-minute training sequences consisting of (1) exposure to a modeling film that provided information and examples of coping behaviors, (2) instruction in using coping self-statements to counter catastrophic self-statements, and (3) relaxation training (including home practice). Other parents received no direct intervention for their own anxiety but participated in their children's cognitive-behavioral treatment. The parents who received stress inoculation training reported lower anxiety and used more positive self-statements than parents who only participated in their children's treatment. As another example, a problem-solving training program has been developed specifically for parents whose children are diagnosed with cancer and who are at increased risk for significant emotional distress.[114]

A variety of treatments have been found to be effective in helping children and adults cope with stress associated with dental visits.[115] For instance, low-income preschool children who had no previous dental treatment benefited from learning to employ relaxation exercises, breathing exercises, and coping words (such as "calm" and "nice").[116] The children also were given descriptive information regarding the dental procedures and the sights, sounds, and physical sensations they would experience. These interventions reduced the children's anxiety and discomfort, physiological arousal, and disruptive behaviors, and they also increased children's cooperation.

Adults with true dental phobia are so anxious about dental procedures that they will not see a dentist even though they may need treatment. Systematic desensitization can be helpful in such cases.[117] In one study, a single-session treatment package consisting of systematic desensitization and stress inoculation training was compared with antianxiety medication (benzodiazepine) and a no-treatment control condition. Both active treatments reduced clients' anxiety during dental procedures significantly more than the control condition. However, at a 2-month follow-up, the clients treated with medication showed a return to pretreatment levels of anxiety, whereas the clients who received the behavioral intervention maintained their treatment gains. Most important, 70% of the clients receiving the behavioral treatment continued to obtain dental care, compared with 20% of those receiving medication—clearly a clinically significant outcome.[118]

When people have a medical crisis, such as learning that they require invasive surgery, they may experience symptoms of anxiety and depression because of unrealistic beliefs, cognitive distortions, and poor coping strategies. Cognitive-behavioral therapies, including stress inoculation training, problem-solving training, and cognitive restructuring, are particularly well suited for treating the distress surrounding medical crises.[119]

People living with HIV often experience anxiety, depression, anger, and stress, and these states are not only psychologically debilitating but they also are associated with more rapid progression of AIDS. A recent meta-analytic study of cognitive-behavioral interventions has demonstrated their efficacy in reducing these emotional states.[120] As an example, group cognitive-behavioral treatment package consisting of relaxation training, cognitive restructuring, assertion training, and anger management was used to assist gay men cope with HIV. Clients receiving the 10-week intervention, in comparison with clients in a wait-list control group, showed significant decreases in depressed mood and anxiety; they also had fewer cases of herpes virus, which is common in people infected with HIV and may contribute to the onset of AIDS.[121]

In addition to helping people cope with the distressing psychological ramifications of illness and medical treatments, behavior therapies have been used to reduce the negative physical side effects of medical treatments. For example, nausea and vomiting often occur with chemotherapy for cancer. These extremely noxious side effects generally begin 1 to 2 hours after the injection of the chemical and can persist as long as 24 hours.[122] Relaxation training has been successful in reducing the frequency and severity of nausea and vomiting.[123] Some patients also experience anticipatory nausea and vomiting,[124] which can be treated by systematic desensitization.[125]

As if the physical side effects of cancer treatment and the pain and fatigue caused by the disease itself were not horrible enough, cancer patients often are demoralized by the hospital social environment, which can result in psychological disorders, including anxiety and depression.[126] Cancer patients may be deprived of social reinforcers,[127] especially patients in isolation (which may be required because chemotherapy compromises the immune system). These patients' social reinforcers are limited to contact with the medical personnel who care for their needs. Accordingly, one of the few ways patients can control their social contacts is to develop symptoms that require close attention.[128] Case 15-1 describes the treatment of physical symptoms that were maintained by nurses' attention.

CASE **15-1**

Physical Symptoms Related to Cancer Treatment Alleviated by Extinction and Differential Reinforcement[129]

Two patients with acute leukemia developed symptoms for which no physical cause could be found. Patient 1, a 24-year-old man, had a deep, raspy cough that did not respond to medication. Patient 2, a 63-year-old woman, regurgitated saliva excessively. Both patients were described as outgoing, friendly, and well adjusted to their illnesses. Their symptoms developed when they were placed in restrictive isolation.

It appeared that the patients' symptoms worsened in the presence of a nurse. This belief was confirmed by a sophisticated systematic naturalistic observation procedure. The symptoms were tape recorded for 16 hours over the course of 2 days in the patients' rooms. Three-minute segments were analyzed for (1) the presence of the symptom (for example, loud, repeated exhalation of air or sounds of spitting), (2) a nurse entering the room (for instance, sounds of the door opening and footsteps), and

(3) talking. The assessment revealed that the patients' symptoms were maintained by a nurse's presence, which served as a setting event. The symptoms were more likely to occur when a nurse was with the patients (the probabilities were .75 and .82 for Patients 1 and 2, respectively) than when the patients were alone (.25 and .18, respectively).

Treatment involved extinction and differential reinforcement of other behaviors. The nurses did not discuss the patients' symptoms with them at any time. If the symptoms continued during standard nursing procedures, the nurse finished the procedures and immediately left the room (extinction). However, if the symptom ceased or did not occur, the nurse remained in the room and talked with the patient for a minimum of 10 minutes after the medical procedures had been completed (differential reinforcement of other behaviors). Within 2 weeks, both patients' symptoms were eliminated.

PREVENTION OF PHYSICAL ILLNESS

Behavior therapy procedures not only have been employed in the treatment of medical disorders, but they also have been applied to preventing physical illness.[130] Behavioral prevention programs have two major aims. One is to *educate* people about the controllable factors that cause and exacerbate illnesses and about specific behaviors that can reduce the risk of developing illnesses. The other aim is to *motivate* people to engage in preventive behaviors. Breast cancer and HIV/AIDS are two areas that have been targets of behavioral prevention.

Breast Cancer Prevention

Breast cancer, a leading cause of death in women, often is curable if detected early.[131] Regular breast self-examination is the simplest and most cost-effective means of early detection. Despite the ease of breast self-examinations, many women do not perform them. One program used biweekly postcards or phone calls to prompt women to do their breast self-examinations.[132] Initially, the women participated in a 1-hour workshop in which they learned how to examine their breasts. The procedure included placing baby oil on their fingers, palpating their breasts, and placing a sheet of tissue on their chests to absorb the oil. The women were instructed to mail the tissue they used, signed and dated, each time they performed the procedure, which provided a measure of the frequency of self-examinations. Compared with women who received no prompts, women who were prompted either by mail or telephone returned more self-examination tissues. However, the frequency of self-examinations decreased over time for both prompted and unprompted women. It is likely that providing reinforcers for breast self-examination would have increased compliance. For example, one study found that women were more likely to perform breast self-examinations when they received a silver dollar each month they had performed their breast self-examination.[133]

HIV/AIDS Prevention

Since it was first identified in 1981, acquired immune deficiency syndrome (AIDS) has become the most serious disease epidemic in the United States,[134] with infection rates rising fastest among heterosexual women.[135] As its name implies, AIDS involves a breakdown in the immune system, rendering the individual vulnerable to a host of diseases. It is caused by the human immunodeficiency virus (HIV), which is transmitted primarily through sexual contact (in semen and vaginal secretions) and direct infusion of contaminated blood (through shared hypodermic needles, blood transfusions, and childbirth).[136] According to the Joint United Nations Programme on HIV/AIDS, as of the end of the year 2000, more than 36 million people were estimated to be living with HIV/AIDS; in the year 2000, AIDS was responsible for the death of an estimated 3 million people. In the United States, more than three-quarters of a million people contracted AIDS between 1980 and 2000, and almost two-thirds of them died from the disease.[137]

Because HIV infection has no known cure, it is a prime candidate for prevention. Fortunately, unlike many other life-threatening diseases with no known cures, the transmission of HIV is linked to specific, identifiable, and potentially changeable patterns of behavior.[138] Preventive efforts have focused on reducing high-risk behaviors (see Table 15-3), especially with gay men, who, in the United States, comprise more than half of the people with AIDS.[139]

Modest and cost-effective programs have attempted to encourage simple safer-sex practices, such as using condoms. For example, to increase gay bar patrons' taking free condoms, signs were posted as prompts.[140] Printed in large blue and red letters on a 1-by-2-foot poster board, the signs read: "In the State

TABLE **15-3**

Behaviors That Place People at High Risk for AIDS and Alternative Low-Risk Behaviors

High-Risk Behaviors	Low-Risk Alternatives
Sexual activities that allow blood-stream exposure to seminal secretions or blood products (such as unprotected anal intercourse and oral sex)	Nonpenetrative sexual acts (such as massage and masturbation) and use of condoms
Sexual contact with multiple partners	Establishment of stable relationships
Frequenting settings where casual or anonymous sexual contacts occur (such as bathhouses and certain pornographic theaters)	Avoidance of high-risk settings and the development of social supports conducive to a nonpromiscuous lifestyle
Excessive use of chemical substances that promote behavioral/sexual disinhibition or impaired judgment	Curtailed use of chemical substances that impair judgment and produce disinhibition

Source: Adapted from Kelly & St. Lawrence, 1987, p. 9.

of Alaska 38 people have died from AIDS. Many more have tested positive. Condoms can reduce the spread of AIDS." Commercially printed signs regarding safer-sex practices to prevent HIV infection also were displayed in rest rooms during the intervention periods and reminded patrons that free condoms were available in the bar. In three different bars, condoms were taken an average of 47% more of the time when prompts were displayed. (Of course, this does not mean that the condoms were used more.)

The primary thrust of behavioral AIDS prevention programs has been to change complex, high-risk sexual behavior patterns by using treatment packages based on the model developed by Jeffrey Kelly and Janet St. Lawrence.[141] Their cognitive-behavioral coping skills model begins with extensive individual assessment, including tests of knowledge of risk behaviors, self-report measures of sexual activity in the recent past, self-monitoring of current risk behaviors, and role-played tests of sexual assertiveness (for instance, refusing a proposition to engage in unsafe sex). The program is conducted in small groups and consists of four basic components:

1. *HIV risk education* involves direct instruction concerning risk factors and ways to reduce them.
2. *Cognitive-behavioral self-management* begins with participants' identifying the maintaining antecedents of their high-risk behaviors (such as setting, mood, and intoxicant use). Then, strategies for changing personal and environmental antecedents to lessen risks are taught. Participants generate and practice self-statements emphasizing that safer practices are possible, will reduce anxiety, and are worthwhile (for example, "I can change my sex practices"; "I'll feel better if I change my sex practices"; and "I did well avoiding that high-risk situation").
3. *Assertion training* teaches participants to refuse high-risk sexual propositions and to insist on engaging in safer sexual activities.
4. *Social skills training* teaches participants how to develop stable relationships involving a mutual commitment to healthful sexual behaviors.

In the final group session, participants identify risk reduction changes that they have made during the program. This session exposes participants to multiple coping models, gives them additional ideas about how they can modify their own behaviors, and strengthens their self-efficacy for reducing high-risk behaviors in their lives.[142]

Cognitive-behavioral coping skills therapies to prevent HIV infection have been used with high-risk adolescents such as those with other sexually transmitted diseases or who have substance abuse problems[143] and those who lack the social behaviors necessary for initiating, maintaining, and terminating social and sexual relationships with persons of the opposite sex.[144] Other targeted groups include teenagers who have run away from home[145] and those living in HIV epicenters;[146] inner-city, low-income men[147] and women;[148] gay and bisexual men;[149] college students;[150] adults with chronic psychiatric disorders such as schizophrenia and depression;[151] and people with mental retardation.[152] Overall, such interventions appear to reduce high-risk sexual behaviors in a variety of age groups and populations, when compared with information-oriented treatments and no treatment.[153] The most common outcome measures used in these studies are (1) number of sexual partners; (2) number of protected and unprotected occasions of oral, anal, and vaginal intercourse; (3) percentage of time condoms are used; and (4) number of sexual encounters with a high-risk partner.[154] Unfortunately, each of these measures is based on self-reports that are easily fabricated. Ideally, these self-report measures should be corroborated by other types of measures, but this is rarely feasible with sexual activity.

The long-term maintenance of reductions in high-risk sexual behaviors brought about through cognitive-behavioral coping skills therapies has not yet been evaluated thoroughly. Initial studies indicate that the effects diminish over time.[155] For example, a 16-month follow-up assessment of 68 gay and bisexual men who had completed a cognitive-behavioral treatment program showed that 40% of the men had returned to unsafe sexual practices. Relapse was more common in men who were younger and who used alcohol or other drugs in conjunction with their high-risk sexual behaviors.[156]

ALL THINGS CONSIDERED: BEHAVIORAL MEDICINE APPLICATIONS

As you have seen, behavior therapy principles and procedures can make important contributions to comprehensive health care. They are especially valuable with regard to helping patients cope with medical treatments and increasing their adherence to medical procedures. Behavior therapy also can play a role in providing alternative treatments for some medical disorders and in preventing disease.

Medicine has traditionally focused on treatment—that is, on getting the patient well. Concern for the psychological well-being of patients in treatment has, all too often, been an afterthought. For example, the practice of waking sleeping patients in the hospital to give them sleeping medication is more than a well-worn joke. Many people may endure inconveniences and discomfort associated with medical treatments because they subscribe to the "no pain, no gain" philosophy. More serious psychological consequences are associated with the intense discomfort and pain brought about by cancer treatment, the dread of undergoing surgery, and the hopelessness and despair caused by chronic illness and its care. Behavior therapy has begun to contribute to alleviating such problems.

Physicians have long recognized that patients' failure to follow prescribed treatment is a major impediment to providing adequate health care. However, neither physicians' skills nor medical technology is suited to changing the prevailing high rate of nonadherence. In contrast, behavior therapists have a large armamentarium of effective procedures for increasing patients' adherence behaviors.

Prevention of physical illness by promoting healthful behaviors and lifestyles also is an area in which behavior therapy procedures can make a difference. For instance, behavior therapy can influence proper diet, regular exercise, and the elimination of harmful drug habits (such as smoking and heavy drinking), all factors that directly enhance physical health. The major obstacle to implementing behavioral prevention programs is one faced by all prevention interventions—namely, the prevailing attitude: "If it ain't broke, don't fix it." The benefits of preventive interventions may not become evident until years after the interventions are implemented. Further, because the goal of prevention is always the *absence* of disease, people may not recognize and appreciate the results of preventive interventions. Consider the fact that, as you read these words, you are unaware that you are breathing normally and that you are seeing the words clearly. In contrast, you would be aware of labored breathing if you had emphysema and of blurred vision if you had cataracts.

A final contribution made by behavior therapy to medicine is in providing alternative forms of treatment. For some medical conditions, such as certain types of chronic pain, existing medical treatments are inadequate. In other cases, existing medical treatments may be associated with potentially serious negative side effects, as with many drugs. Sometimes, the treatments themselves may be potentially life threatening, such as with certain types of medication. In such instances, behavioral treatments may be preferable, especially if they safely provide comparable results. Finally, even putting aside the negative side effects of medication, one advantage that cognitive-behavioral interventions have over medication is that patients learn coping skills. The use of coping skills may be associated with greater long-term maintenance of treatment gains,[157] and the skills may generalize to dealing with other problems people encounter in their lives.

SUMMARY

1. The application of behavior therapy to the assessment, treatment, management, rehabilitation, and prevention of physical disease is part of behavioral medicine.

2. Behavior therapy serves four functions in dealing with medical disorders: treating medical disorders, increasing adherence to medical treatments, helping patients cope with treatments and illness, and preventing medical disorders.

3. Pain behaviors—overt behaviors indicating that the person is experiencing sensations of pain—are accessible to assessment and treatment. Well behaviors are overt behaviors that typically indicate a person is not experiencing pain sensations.

4. One approach to treating pain involves changing the consequences that are maintaining pain behaviors. Social attention, rest, and medication are common reinforcers for pain. Treatment involves extinction of pain behaviors and reinforcement of well behaviors. Attention and rest are made contingent on well behaviors rather than pain behaviors. Pain medication is made time contingent rather than pain contingent.

5. Cognitive-behavioral coping skills treatment packages that include biofeedback and relaxation training also are used to treat pain.

6. Behavioral treatments for pain typically reduce, rather than eliminate, pain. The reduction can be substantial enough for patients to resume their normal activities.

7. Cognitive-behavioral therapies have been used to treat medically unexplained symptoms, such as in chronic fatigue syndrome, noncardiac chest pain, and fibromyalgia syndrome.

8. Following medical advice and engaging in health-related behaviors have been increased by stimulus control, reinforcement, teaching patients self-control skills, and making the consequences of nonadherence unpleasant. Reinforcement generally is the most effective technique for increasing adherence. When low adherence is maintained by skills deficits, modeling is useful.

9. A variety of strategies have been used to help patients and their families deal with the stress, anxiety, discomfort, and pain associated with medical and dental procedures, hospitalization, and illness. They include teaching patients cognitive-behavioral coping skills and employing reinforcement and extinction procedures. Similar procedures also have been used to reduce the negative physical and psychological side effects of medical treatments.

10. Behavioral interventions have been used to help prevent physical illness by educating people about disease and motivating them to engage in healthful, preventive behaviors.

11. Behavior therapies have been applied to breast cancer prevention by using prompting to increase breast self-examination.

12. Treatment programs for decreasing high-risk behaviors for HIV infection have employed education, cognitive-behavioral coping skills therapies, assertion training, and social skills training.

REFERENCE NOTES

1. Nater, Gaab, Rief, & Ehlert, 2006.
2. Pinkerton, Hughes, & Wenrich, 1982.
3. Black, 1975.
4. Bonica & Loeser, 2000.
5. McGrady, 1994; McGrady, Olson, & Kroon, 1995.
6. Compare with Kaplan, 1990.
7. Fordyce, 1976.
8. Fordyce, 1976, 1988.
9. Doleys, Crocker, & Patton, 1982; Flor, Kerns, & Turk, 1987.
10. Kole-Snijderes, Vlaeyen, Rutten-van Molken, Heuts, van Eek, & van Breukelen, 1999.
11. Turk & Meichenbaum, 1989; Turk & Rudy, 1995.
12. Blanchard, 1992; Holroyd & Penzien, 1994.
13. Andrasik & Blanchard, 1987.
14. Holroyd & Penzien, 1994.
15. Andrasik, Larsson, & Grazzi, 2002; Blanchard, 1992.
16. Andrasik, Larsson, & Grazzi, 2002.
17. Nestoriuc, Reif, & Martin, 2008.
18. Allen & Shriver, 1998.
19. Holroyd & Penzien, 1994; McGrady et al., 1999; Penzien & Holroyd, 1994.
20. Larsson & Andrasik, 2002; McGrady et al., 1999.
21. McGrady, Wauquier, McNeil, & Gerard, 1994.
22. Compas, Haaga, Keefe, Leitenberg, & Williams, 1998.
23. Wauquier, McGrady, Aloe, Klausner, & Collins, 1995.
24. Lake & Pingel, 1988.
25. Blanchard, 1992; Nicholson & Blanchard, 1993.
26. Compas, Haaga, Keefe, Leitenberg, & Williams, 1998.

27. Varni, La Greca, & Spirito, 2000.
28. Mason, Goolkasian, & McCain, 1998.
29. Gil et al., 1997.
30. Gil, Carson, Sedway, Porter, Schaeffer, & Orringer, 2000.
31. Linton, 1982; Linton & Melin, 1983.
32. de L. Horne, Taylor, & Varigos, 1999; Wijma, Melin, Nedstrand, & Hammar, 1997.
33. For example, Peterson & Tremblay, 1999.
34. Turk & Meichenbaum, 1989; Turk, Meichenbaum, & Genest, 1983.
35. Lamaze, 1970.
36. Wicksell, Ahlqvist, Bring, Melin, & Olsson, 2008.
37. For example, Blanchard, 1987; Hoffman, Papas, Chatkoff, & Kerns, 2007; Morley, Eccleston, & Williams, 1999; Rokke & al'Absi, 1992.
38. For example, Feuerstein & Gainer, 1982.
39. Blanchard, 1987.
40. For example, Fordyce, 1976; Fordyce & Steger, 1979; Kerns, Turk, Holzman, & Rudy, 1986; Turner, 1982.
41. Schmidt, Gierlings, & Peters, 1989.
42. Cairns & Pasino, 1977; Dolce, Doleys, Raczynski, Lossie, Poole, & Smith, 1986; Doleys, Crocker, & Patton, 1982.
43. For example, Blanchard, 1987; Blanchard et al., 1990.
44. Blanchard, 1987; Turk & Meichenbaum, 1989; Turk, Meichenbaum, & Genest, 1983; Turk & Rudy, 1995.
45. James, Thorn, & Williams, 1993.
46. For example, Osman, Barrios, Osman, Schnekloth, & Troutman, 1994; Rokke & al'Absi, 1992.
47. For example, Blanchard, Theobald, Williamson, Silver, & Brown, 1978; Silver, Blanchard, Williamson, Theobald, & Brown, 1979.
48. For example, Blanchard et al., 1982.
49. For example, Anderson, Lawrence, & Olson, 1981; Turner & Clancy, 1988.
50. For example, Katon & Walker, 1998; Kroenke & Mangelsdorf, 1989.
51. For example, Ginsburg, Riddle, & Davies, 2006.
52. Reigada, Fisher, Cutler, & Warner, 2008.
53. Nezu, Nezu, & Lombardo, 2001.
54. For example, Bertagnolli & Morris, 1997; Deale, Chalder, Marks, & Wessely, 1997.
55. Nezu, Nezu, & Lombardo, 2001.
56. For example, Nezu, Nezu, & Lombardo, 2001; Van Peski-Oosterbaan, Spinhoven, Van der Does, Brushke, & Rooijmans, 1999.

57. Nezu, Nezu, & Lombardo, 2001.
58. For example, Buckelew et al., 1998; Degotardi, Klass, Rosenberg, Fox, Gallelli, & Gottlieb, 2006; Rossy et al., 1999.
59. Nezu, Nezu, & Lombardo, 2001.
60. García, Simón, Durán, Canceller, & Aneiros, 2006.
61. Nezu, Nezu, & Lombardo, 2001.
62. Dunbar & Stunkard, 1979.
63. Pinkston, Carruth, & Goggin, 2008.
64. Varni, LaGreca, & Spirito, 2000.
65. Levine et al., 2006; Pinkston, Carruth, & Goggin, 2008.
66. Marston, 1970; Sackett & Haynes, 1976.
67. For example, Kasl, 1975; Zifferblatt, 1975.
68. Allen & Warzak, 2000.
69. For example, Rounsaville, Rosen, & Carroll, 2008.
70. Haynes, MacDonald, & Garg, 2002.
71. For example, Haynes, MacDonald, Garg, & Montague, 2000; Weiss, 2004.
72. Lima, Nazarian, Charney, & Lahti, 1976.
73. Azrin & Powell, 1969.
74. Newman, Kenardy, Herman, & Taylor, 1996, 1997.
75. Azrin & Teichner, 1998.
76. Compare with Skinner & Vaughan, 1983.
77. Masek, 1982.
78. Da Costa, Rapoff, & Goldstein, 1997.
79. For example, Masek, 1982.
80. Haynes et al., 1976.
81. Bigelow, Strickler, Liebson, & Griffiths, 1976.
82. Orleans, 2000.
83. LaGreca, 1988.
84. For example, Lowe & Lutzker, 1979; compare with Lima, Nazarian, Charney, & Lahti, 1976.
85. Wagner, 1998.
86. Wong, Seroka, & Ogisi, 2000.
87. For example, LaGreca & Ottinger, 1979; Waggoner & LeLieuvre, 1981.
88. Epstein et al., 1981.
89. Epstein et al., 1981.
90. Lowe & Lutzker, 1979.
91. Magrab & Papadopoulou, 1977.
92. Greenan, Powell, & Varni, 1984.
93. For example, Brownell & Cohen, 1995; Dubbert, 1992.
94. For example, Gilbert, Johnson, Spillar, McCallum, Silverstein, & Rosenbloom, 1982.
95. Sergis-Deavenport & Varni, 1982, 1983.
96. Follansbee, LaGreca, & Citrin, 1983; Gross, Johnson, Wildman, & Mullett, 1981.

97. Stark et al., 1993.
98. For example, Turner & Vernon, 1976.
99. For example, Nazarian, Mechaber, Charney, & Coulter, 1974.
100. For example, Barkin & Duncan, 1975; Kidd & Euphrat, 1971.
101. Stitzer, Bigelow, Lawrence, Cohen, D'Lugoff, & Hawthorne, 1977.
102. Friman, Finney, Rapoff, & Christophersen, 1985.
103. Rice & Lutzker, 1984.
104. de L. Horne, Vatmanidis, & Careri, 1994.
105. Dahlquist, Gil, Armstrong, Ginsberg, & Jones, 1985; Jay, Elliott, Katz, & Siegel, 1987; Manne, Redd, Jacobsen, Gorfinkle, Schorr, & Rabkin, 1990; Peterson & Shigetomi, 1981; Rains, 1995.
106. Slifer, Babbitt, & Cataldo, 1995.
107. For example, Peterson & Shigetomi, 1981.
108. Redd, Manne, Peters, Jacobsen, & Schmidt, 1994.
109. Slifer, Cataldo, Cataldo, Llorente, & Gerson, 1993.
110. McComas, Wacker, & Cooper, 1998.
111. Manne, Bakeman, Jacobsen, Gorfinkle, & Redd, 1994.
112. For example, Manne, Redd, Jacobsen, Gorfinkle, Schorr, & Rabkin, 1990; Peterson & Shigetomi, 1981.
113. Jay & Elliott, 1990.
114. Varni, LaGreca, & Spirito, 2000.
115. For example, Nocella & Kaplan, 1982.
116. Siegel & Peterson, 1980.
117. For example, Gatchel, 1980.
118. Thom, Sartory, & Johren, 2000.
119. DiTomasso, Martin, & Kovnat, 2000.
120. Crepaz et al., 2008.
121. Lutgendorf et al., 1997.
122. Redd & Andrykowski, 1982.
123. For example, Compas, Haaga, Keefe, Leitenberg, & Williams, 1998; Lyles, Burish, Krozely, & Oldham, 1982.
124. Morrow & Morrell, 1982.
125. Morrow et al., 1992; Morrow & Morrell, 1982.
126. Cullen, Fox, & Isom, 1976; Holand et al., 1977.
127. Agras, 1976.
128. Redd, 1980.
129. Redd, 1980.
130. Fekete, Antoni, & Schneiderman, 2007.
131. Jansen, 1987.
132. Mayer & Frederiksen, 1986.
133. Solomon et al., 1998.
134. Kelly & St. Lawrence, 1987.
135. Centers for Disease Control and Prevention, 1994.
136. Hall, 1988.
137. National Center for HIV, STD and TB Prevention, 2001.
138. Kelly & St. Lawrence, 1988a.
139. National Center for HIV, STD and TB Prevention, 2001.
140. Honnen & Kleinke, 1990.
141. Kelly, St. Lawrence, Hood, & Brasfield, 1989.
142. McKusick, Wiley, Coates, & Morin, 1986.
143. Metzler, Biglan, Noell, Ary, & Ochs, 2000; St. Lawrence, Brasfield, Jefferson, Alleyne, O'Bannon, & Shirley, 1995; St. Lawrence, Jefferson, Alleyne, & Brasfield, 1995.
144. Nangle & Hansen, 1998.
145. Rotheram-Borus, Koopman, Haignere, & Davies, 1991.
146. Walter & Vaughan, 1993.
147. Kalichman, Cherry, & Browne-Sperling, 1999.
148. For example, Carey et al., 2000; Hobfoll, Jackson, Lavin, Britton, & Shepherd, 1994; Kelly et al., 1994.
149. For example, Kelly, St. Lawrence, Hood, & Brasfield, 1989.
150. For example, Sikkema, Winett, & Lombard, 1995.
151. Kalichman, Sikkema, Kelly, & Bulto, 1995; Weinhardt, Carey, Carey, & Verdecias, 1998.
152. Miltenberger et al., 1999.
153. For example, Carey et al., 2000; Herbst, Kay, Passin, Lyles, Crepaz, & Marin, 2007; Lyles et al., 2007; Metzler, Biglan, Noell, Ary, & Ochs, 2000; St. Lawrence, Jefferson, Alleyne, & Brasfield, 1995; Weinhardt, Carey, Carey, & Verdecias, 1998.
154. For example, Carey et al., 2000; Kalichman, Carey, & Johnson, 1996; Metzler, Biglan, Noell, Ary, & Ochs, 2000.
155. Kalichman, Carey, & Johnson, 1996.
156. Kelly, St. Lawrence, Hood, & Brasfield, 1989.
157. For example, Otto & Gould, 1995; Otto, Gould, & Pollack, 1994.

16

Applications of Behavior Therapy to Psychological Disorders with Primary Physical Characteristics

In addition to its contribution to behavioral medicine described in the previous chapter, behavior therapy plays an important role in the treatment of a variety of psychological disorders whose primary feature is a physical problem. To illustrate this application, we will describe behavior therapy for four such disorders: enuresis, tics and nervous habits, insomnia, and bulimia nervosa.

The distinction between these psychological disorders and the medical problems discussed in Chapter 15 is based on the way they are classified by health professionals.[1] For example, whereas pain and medically unexplained symptoms are considered medical disorders, enuresis and insomnia are viewed as psychological disorders. This distinction is, admittedly, somewhat arbitrary and artificial. Both psychological disorders with primary physical characteristics and medical disorders increasingly are being viewed in terms of an interplay of physical and psychological factors.[2]

ENURESIS

Enuresis is the inability of people beyond the age of 5 to voluntarily control urination, when no known physical cause is involved. Enuresis most frequently occurs during sleep, so treatment efforts have focused on *nocturnal enuresis*, or bedwetting. It is a common problem among children, occurring in approximately 15% to 20% of all 5-year-olds, 5% of 10-year-olds, and 2% of 12- to 14-year-olds.[3] Nocturnal enuresis is more prevalent in boys than in girls.[4]

Urination is the natural response to tension in the bladder as it fills up. Normally, bladder tension wakes us when we are sleeping, and we get out of bed and go to the bathroom. The problem in enuresis is that bladder tension does not wake the person. Traditional verbal psychotherapy generally has been unsuccessful in treating enuresis.[5] In contrast, two behavior therapy procedures—the urine alarm and dry-bed training—have proved to be highly effective.

Urine Alarm

A **urine alarm** is a device that sounds an alarm to wake the child when the child begins to urinate. The original urine alarm was the *bell-and-pad method*; urine that contacts a special pad under the bed sheet completes an electrical circuit that sounds an alarm.[6] Through repeated associations between the alarm and bladder tension, bladder tension alone becomes the stimulus that awakens the child before urination starts. (In classical conditioning terms, the alarm is an UCS that wakes the child [UCR] and bladder tension is a CS that comes to awaken the child [CR].)

Although the bell-and-pad apparatus still is available, a more convenient device generally is used today. It consists of a moisture-sensitive switching system; the sensor end goes inside the client's underpants and is connected to a small alarm that unobtrusively is attached to the client's outer clothing, such as pajamas. This device, which can be purchased over the counter in pharmacies, also is applicable to diurnal (daytime) enuresis, which affects approximately 1% of children over the age of 5.[7]

The urine alarm is very easy to use. It has been employed for more than 70 years,[8] and it continues to be effective 70% to 80% of the time.[9] It has been shown to be superior to medication (imipramine)[10] and traditional psychotherapy.[11] The relapse rate after 6 months has been about 33%, and the predominant reason for relapse has been poor compliance with the procedures.[12] The urine alarm has been used alone and as part of treatment packages.[13] Interestingly, the urine alarm tends to be as effective alone as when it is combined with other behavioral treatments.[14]

Dry-Bed Training

Dry-bed training, developed by Nathan Azrin and his colleagues,[15] is a comprehensive treatment package that employs shaping and overcorrection to teach children the behaviors required to keep their bed dry throughout the night. Table 16-1 outlines the steps involved in dry-bed training. These procedures illustrate the detail and precision inherent in many behavior therapy procedures.

TABLE **16-1**

Protocol for Dry-Bed Training with Parents as Trainers for a 6-Year-Old Boy

I. *Training day*

A. Afternoon

1. Child encouraged to drink favorite beverage to increase urination

2. Child requested to attempt urination every half hour

    a. If child feels urge to urinate, he is asked to wait for increasingly longer periods of time

    b. If child *has* to urinate, he is asked to lie in bed as if asleep, then jump up and go to the bathroom (role-playing what he should do at night); his behavior is then reinforced with a beverage and praise

3. Child motivated to work at dry bed

    a. Parents and child review inconveniences caused by bed-wetting

    b. Parents contract with child for reinforcers to be given after first dry night and after a specified series of dry nights

    c. Child specifies whom he'd like to tell that he is keeping dry

    d. Child is given a chart to mark his progress

B. One hour before bedtime with parents watching

1. Child informed of all phases of procedures

2. Child role-plays cleanliness training (to be used if bed-wetting occurs)

    a. Child required to put on own pajamas

    b. Child required to remove sheets and put them back on

3. Child role-plays positive practice in toileting (to be used if bed-wetting occurs)

    a. Child lies down in bed as if asleep (lights out)

    b. Child counts to 50

    c. Child arises and hurries to bathroom where he tries to urinate

    d. Child returns to bed

    e. Steps a–d repeated 20 times with parents counting

C. At bedtime

1. Child tells parents instructions on accident correction and nighttime awakenings

2. Child continues to drink fluids

(continued)

TABLE **16-1** (*continued*)

3. Parents talk to child about reinforcers and express confidence in child
4. Parents comment on dryness of sheets
5. Child retires for the night

D. Hourly awakenings by parents until 1 A.M.
   1. If child is dry
      a. Minimal prompt (light touching) used to awaken (stronger prompt used if child doesn't wake)
      b. Child asked if he needs to urinate
         i. If he can wait another hour
            (a) Parents praise his urinary control
            (b) Child returns to bed
         ii. If he must urinate
            (a) Child goes to bathroom
            (b) Parents praise him for correct toileting
            (c) Child returns to bed
      c. Child feels sheets and comments on their dryness
      d. Parents praise child for having dry bed
      e. Child given fluids (discontinued after 11 P.M.)
      f. Child returns to sleep
   2. When an accident has occurred
      a. Parent awakens child and reprimands him for wetting
      b. Parent directs child to bathroom to finish urinating
      c. Child given cleanliness training
         i. Child changes pajamas
         ii. Child removes wet sheets and places them in laundry basket
         iii. Child obtains clean sheets and remakes bed
      d. Positive practice in correct toileting (20 times) performed immediately after cleanliness training

      e. Child reminded that positive practice is necessary before going to bed the next evening

E. Parents check child half hour earlier than normal waking the next morning
   1. If bed is wet, steps under IIB (below) implemented

II. *Posttraining (after training day)*

   A. If bed dry in the morning
      1. Parents point out to child half hour before his usual bedtime that he does not have to practice (because bed was dry that morning) and so he can do what he wants in the half hour before going to bed
      2. Parents point out child's chart that shows his progress toward reinforcers
      3. Parents tell visitors to the home how child is keeping his bed dry
      4. Parents remark on child's success at least three times a day

   B. If bed wet in the morning
      1. Parents wake child half hour earlier, prompt him to check his sheets, and ask him to say what he should do
      2. Child required to change bed and pajamas
      3. Child engages in positive practice in correct toileting (20 times)
      4. Child engages in positive practice (20 times) half hour before bed that night
      5. Child marks chart and is told "We will try again tomorrow"
      6. Parents tell visitors to the home that the child is learning to keep his bed dry

Source: Based on Azrin & Thienes, 1978.

Treatment begins with a night of intensive training. The child is awakened every hour to urinate if necessary and to be praised for having a dry bed. When an accident occurs, the child goes through a two-phase overcorrection procedure. First comes *cleanliness training*, a form of restitution in which the client changes the wet nightclothes and sheets. Second, there is repeated *positive practice*, which consists of (1) the child's lying in bed for a count of 50, then (2) hurrying to the bathroom and attempting to urinate, and finally (3) returning to bed. In addition, during the day the child practices retaining urine in the bladder by using **retention control training**.[16] This procedure involves shaping the retention of increasingly greater amounts of urine (created by frequently drinking favorite beverages) for increasingly longer periods.

Dry-bed training usually is implemented by the child's parents after they have been trained in the procedures by the therapist, which takes about an hour and a half.[17] However, the child is made largely responsible for carrying out the dry-bed training procedures. For example, the therapist first teaches the procedures to the child, who then explains them to the parents and requests their help in carrying them out.[18] The emphasis in dry-bed training is on the child's developing self-control skills and being reinforced for accomplishments. When accidents occur, the child assumes responsibility for correcting them by cleaning up and then by practicing the behaviors required to prevent accidents in the future.

Dry-bed training eliminates enuresis more quickly and results in longer-lasting effects than the urine alarm.[19] The results of one study with 44 children between the ages of 3 and 15 (with an average age of 7) illustrate the rapidity and long-lasting effectiveness of dry-bed training.[20] Before dry-bed training, the children were wetting their beds an average of 92% of nights. On the first day after the intensive training, bedwetting was reduced to 18% and it gradually

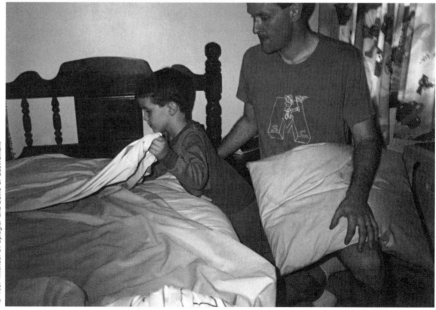

© 1997 Michael D. Spiegler and David C. Guevremont

PHOTO 16-1
As part of dry-bed training, the child is responsible for changing bedding after accidents

decreased from there. At a 5-month follow-up, bedwetting was occurring on only 4% of the nights, a level that was maintained 1 year later.

The major limitation of dry-bed training is that it is labor-intensive and complex and therefore less likely to be used than much simpler therapies, such as the urine alarm.[21] Modified, shortened versions of dry-bed training have been developed[22] and have been shown to be effective and still superior to the urine-alarm alone.[23] Dry-bed training occasionally is used for adults, and one study revealed that eight of nine clients who had had enuresis most of their lives remained continent at a 6-year follow-up.[24]

Dry-Pants Method

The principles of dry-bed training have been extended to normal daytime toilet training with impressive results.[25] Most children learn to use the toilet over a period of several months, and parental attempts to hasten the process generally have little effect.[26] Several methods of intensive reinforcement training have been moderately successful in reducing training time to approximately 1 month.[27] In contrast, using the **dry-pants method** (the daytime version of dry-bed training), children ranging in age from 20 to 36 months have been toilet trained in an average of 4 hours, and the average is 2 hours for children older than 26 months.[28]

A simplified variation of the dry-pants method was used to toilet train John, a 21-year-old man with profound mental retardation who lived in a residential facility.[29] Over the years, many previous attempts to toilet train John had failed. Throughout the day, John was given large amounts of liquid and was taken to the bathroom every 30 minutes. An alarm system was attached to the inside of the toilet bowl and was activated by a small amount of urine. When the alarm sounded, a staff member praised John and reinforced him with food. John also wore a dry-pants alarm that signaled toileting accidents. When an accident occurred, a staff member took John to a private area, mildly reprimanded him (for example, "No, don't wet your pants"), and then withdrew social attention as John's clothing was changed and for an additional 10 minutes thereafter. The intervention resulted in a significant increase in John's urinating appropriately and a reduction in his toileting accidents. At a 3-month follow-up, John was completely continent.

TIC DISORDERS AND NERVOUS HABITS

A *tic* is a recurring, sudden, rapid movement or vocalization. Examples of *motor tics* are repetitive neck jerking, shoulder twitching, facial grimacing, and slapping oneself. Examples of *vocal tics* are repetitive throat clearing, snorting, and grunting. Although tics are largely involuntary, people can suppress them for varying lengths of time. Tics usually begin in childhood, are three times more common in males, and are exacerbated by stress. Children and adolescents who exhibit tics are viewed negatively by their peers,[30] and adults' social and occupational functioning may be impaired because of social ostracism and anxiety about exhibiting tics in the presence of others. In severe cases, tics may directly interfere with a person's daily functioning, as when eye blinking makes reading difficult. *Tourette's disorder* is the most serious tic disorder, involving multiple motor and vocal tics (which sometimes include involuntarily and inappropriately uttering obscenities).[31]

Medication is the most common treatment for tics, but its use is problematic. In the case of Tourette's disorder, for example, the frequency of tics is only reduced by about 50%,[32] and unwanted side effects have been noted in about 80% of clients taking medication.[33] Further, only about 20% to 30% of clients continue taking medication on a long-term basis.[34] Clearly, alternative treatments are needed. Five behavioral treatments have been used to treat tics: massed negative practice, changing maintaining consequences, progressive relaxation, self-monitoring, and habit reversal.

Massed negative practice, the most frequently used behavioral treatment for tics, has the client deliberately perform the tic as rapidly as possible. This is done for a set time (for example, 30 minutes), with short rest periods (for instance, 1 minute of rest for each 4 minutes of performing the tic).[35] Negative practice has been moderately successful in reducing the frequency of tics for some people,[36] with an average reduction of about 60%.[37]

Changing the maintaining consequences of tics is the second most frequently employed behavior therapy. Differential reinforcement[38] as the sole treatment is effective in reducing tics in children,[39] and it also is effective when combined with other therapies.[40] Punishment, including contingent electric shock[41] and time out from positive reinforcement,[42] also can reduce tic frequency. However, the treatment effects with punishment may not transfer from the therapy setting to the client's natural environment and may be only temporary;[43] moreover, punishment procedures are generally less preferable than reinforcement procedures.

Using progressive relaxation is consistently effective in decreasing tics *while* the clients are relaxing.[44] However, the tics tend to return shortly after relaxation sessions have ended.[45]

Self-monitoring can be an effective treatment for tics.[46] Although self-monitoring typically is an assessment procedure (see Chapter 5), it is sometimes specifically used to modify a target behavior. Self-monitoring makes clients more aware of their tics, which is an essential component of effective treatment.

To summarize, massed negative practice, changing maintaining consequences, progressive relaxation, and self-monitoring all are moderately effective treatments for tics. To increase their effectiveness, various combinations of these treatments generally are used. However, by far the most effective treatment package for tics is habit reversal.

Habit Reversal for Tics

Habit reversal is another potent therapy developed by Azrin and his colleagues.[47] It incorporates four components: (1) awareness training, (2) competing response training, (3) relaxation training, and (4) reinforcement. Awareness training and competing response training seem to be the most important components.[48]

Awareness training, which includes self-monitoring, involves extensive self-assessment to ensure that the client is aware of the frequency and severity of the tics, their environmental antecedents, and the individual responses that make up the tics. Clients and family members keep a record of when, how often, where, and with whom tics occur. Because knowing the specific component responses involved is necessary to control tics, clients are asked to observe their tics by looking in a mirror or videotaping themselves. They learn to detect the first signs of tics so that they will be able to stop the tics early in their sequence.

In *competing response training*, clients practice performing a response that (1) competes with the tic, (2) can be sustained for several minutes, (3) is compatible with everyday activities, and (4) is inconspicuous to others.[49] Table 16-2 provides examples of competing responses for various kinds of tics.[50]

Clients are taught progressive relaxation and are instructed to practice it daily. Additionally, they are taught to use differential relaxation in their daily lives whenever they feel anxious or emit a tic. Family members are asked to praise the client when they observe that the client is tic free or shows a significant reduction in tics. Clients compile a list of the negative consequences of emitting tics (such as embarrassment and being restricted in their activities) and the positive consequences of eliminating tics (such as feeling confident and being able to engage in desired activities). They write the list on a card that they carry with them, and they periodically refer to it to remind themselves of the benefits of engaging in habit reversal procedures. Children are given specific reinforcers for completing therapy assignments and reducing tics below a predetermined goal level.

TABLE **16-2**
Examples of Competing Responses for Tics Used in Habit Reversal

Tics	*Competing Responses*
HEAD JERK	Isometric contraction of neck flexor muscles: pull chin down and in, head in, eyes forward
SHOULDER SHRUG	Isometric contraction of shoulder depressor muscles: push elbow toward hip
HEAD SHAKE	Slow isometric contraction of neck muscles with eyes forward until head can be held perfectly still
ARM JERK	Push hand down on thigh or stomach and push elbow in toward hip
LEG JERK	If sitting, place feet on floor and push down; if standing, lock knees
EYE BLINK	Systematic, soft blinking at rate of one blink every 3–5 seconds; frequent downward glance every 5–10 seconds
ORAL VOCAL TICS	Continuous slow, rhythmic breathing through nose with mouth closed
NASAL VOCAL TICS	Continuous slow, rhythmic breathing through mouth

Source: Based on Azrin & Peterson, 1988b.

Habit reversal consistently has been shown to be highly effective in treating tics,[51] reducing them by about 90%, compared with roughly 50% with medication.[52] Besides tics, habit reversal is used to treat various nervous habits.[53]

Habit Reversal for Nervous Habits

Nervous habits treated by habit reversal include thumb sucking,[54] fingernail biting,[55] and bruxism (teeth grinding).[56] We will illustrate the use of habit reversal for nervous habits with trichotillomania[57] and stuttering.[58]

Trichotillomania is an impulse-control disorder in which people repeatedly pluck hair from different parts of their body. As an example of how habit reversal is used to treat chronic trichotillomania, consider the treatment employed with three 12-year-olds (two girls and one boy).[59] During awareness training, the clients learned to detect their hair pulling, first by describing what hair felt like between their fingers and then by actually feeling their hair between their fingers without actually pulling out their hair. In competing response training, each client identified several behaviors that were incompatible with hair pulling (such as crossing one's arms and sitting on one's hands). The therapist instructed the clients to use these competing responses every time they are aware that they are pulling their hair or having an urge to do so. The clients simulated hair pulling and engaged in the competing response for 1 minute, which was repeated 12 to 15 times. The therapist taught the clients' parents first to prompt their child to engage in a competing response when they observed their child pulling out hair and then to praise the child for performing the competing response. Habit reversal resulted in significant reductions in hair pulling with all three clients.

Stuttering affects nearly 1% of adults and 5% to 10% of children,[60] and it is the most prevalent maladaptive habit in individuals with mental retardation, occurring in up to 32% of that population.[61] The most common competing response employed in habit reversal for stuttering is *regulated breathing exercises* that consist of relaxing, slowly inhaling deeply through the nose, and slowly exhaling through the mouth. Habit reversal not only decreases stuttering but also can increase the naturalness of speech, including the rate of speech (which often is slow and labored in people who stutter).[62]

One limitation of habit reversal is that it generally requires considerable time—from the therapist, the client, and family members (when they participate in the treatment). However, this is not always the case. In one study, five boys between the ages of 5 and 11 received a single session of habit reversal training in their homes for stuttering.[63] During awareness training, each child and his parents together practiced identifying the occurrences of stuttering from videotaped speech samples of the child, which were made ahead of time. Both the child and his parents learned and practiced regulated breathing exercises as the competing response. The child was taught to stop speaking when he began to stutter and begin regulated breathing. Parents provided social support and praise when their son applied the habit reversal procedures. Habit reversal resulted in significant reductions in stuttering in four of the five children, and three of the children maintained these gains for up to 9 months. The parents, who were an integral part of the therapy, found habit reversal to be an acceptable treatment.

Although habit reversal often is a sufficient treatment for decreasing clients' maladaptive habits, it sometimes needs to be augmented with additional procedures to achieve the desired outcome. For example, when habit reversal only minimally reduced a 6-year-old girl's trichotillomania and thumb sucking, differential reinforcement and response cost were added, which resulted in near zero levels of both deceleration target behaviors.[64] Similarly, adding response cost to habit reversal resulted in further reductions in a 14-year-old boy's disruptive outbursts during athletic events.[65] Brief booster training sessions also can enhance long-term maintenance of treatment gains following habit reversal.[66]

Although habit reversal is primarily used to treat tics and nervous habits, it also has been applied to a variety of other problems, including overeating,[67] eczema (skin inflammation),[68] and temporomandibular disorders (TMD or TMJ; pain in the jaw and surrounding structures).[69] For example, the effectiveness of habit reversal in treating TMD was compared to a standard dental intervention in which patients wore an appliance (splint) in the mouth for up to 20 hours a day.[70] Patients in the habit reversal group carried electronic pagers and were paged once every 2 hours during the day to prompt the prescribed therapy procedures: first, becoming aware of the position of their teeth and tension in their masticatory (chewing) muscles and then, opening their mouth (thereby unclenching their teeth) and relaxing the masticatory muscles. Both treatments were effective and were maintained at a 1-year follow-up. Although habit reversal was not superior to the standard treatment, it has the advantage of being less intrusive and less costly.

INSOMNIA AND SLEEP PROBLEMS

Insomnia refers to difficulties in falling or staying asleep that result in personal distress and affect one's daytime performance, mood, and general psychological well-being and that are not directly caused by a medical condition or the effects of drugs.[71] It is estimated that 15% to 20% of adults suffer from chronic insomnia and that 30% to 40% experience occasional or transient insomnia.[72] Sedatives or other sleep-inducing medications are the most common treatment for adult insomnia. Sedating drugs—usually antihistamines—also are widely prescribed for infant and childhood sleep difficulties.[73] A number of potential problems are associated with using sleep medications, including deterioration in daytime functioning, rebound insomnia (greater difficulty sleeping after discontinuing sleep medication), psychological and physiological dependence on the drug, and financial expense.[74] Given the high prevalence of sleep problems among both children and adults and the disadvantages of using drug therapy, psychological treatments play an important role in the treatment of chronic sleep problems. Behavior therapies are among the most effective psychological treatments.[75]

Infant and Childhood Sleep Problems

Sleep problems in infants and children up to age 6 usually involve refusal to go to bed, difficulty in settling down and falling asleep, and nighttime awakening and crying. Such sleep disturbances are chronic problems for 15% to 35% of children under the age of 5.[76] Not surprisingly, parents typically respond to their child's sleep problems with some form of attention, which can reinforce the sleep disturbance. When parental attention is the primary maintaining condition of infant and toddler sleep disturbances, extinction is the treatment of choice.[77]

In the standard application of extinction for infant sleep problems, parents refrain from attending to their child after placing the child in bed (as in Case 7-1, page 151). Attention is withheld if the child refuses to get into bed or to go to sleep and if the child wakes up and cries during the night. This simple procedure is highly effective in decreasing children's refusal to go to bed or sleep and the frequency and duration of awakenings during the night; it also improves children's general sleep quality. The improvements have been shown to last at least 2 years after the treatment ends.[78] A major advantage of extinction is that it is simple for parents to learn and implement. In addition, extinction, along with changing setting events (which you'll read about in the next section), has been effective in preventing infant sleep problems.[79]

Despite the demonstrated effectiveness of extinction for infant sleep problems, some parents are unwilling to use it because, understandably, they are upset by their child's crying and sleep problems and they feel compelled to provide comfort. Another factor that makes extinction unacceptable as a treatment to some parents is the occasional occurrence of extinction bursts—the temporary, initial increase in the deceleration target behavior that is common with extinction (such as increased crying when the child is put to bed).[80] Moreover, some critics have argued that extinction is unethical because it damages the parent–child relationship, such as by decreasing the infant's security.[81] In fact, the empirical evidence suggests just the opposite. Studies reveal that infants treated by extinction appear to be more secure and exhibit fewer negative emotional responses (such as crying) than do untreated infants with sleep problems.[82]

To deal with parental objections to using extinction to treat their child's sleep problems, modified extinction procedures to render them more palatable for parents have been developed. The simplest modification allows parents to make a specified number of brief, time-limited checks on their child if the child cries after having been put to bed (for instance, looking in on the child for 15 seconds or less, no more often than once every 20 minutes).[83]

Graduated extinction is a more complex modification that involves either gradually increasing the time the parent ignores the child's bedtime crying[84] or gradually decreasing the time the parent spends attending to the child when the child awakens during the night.[85] The increments are individualized for each family. Parents tend to find modified extinction procedures more acceptable,[86] but they generally are less effective than standard extinction procedures.[87]

When children's sleep disturbances are not being maintained by parental attention, alternative interventions are needed. Such is the case with episodes of *sleep terrors*, in which a child wakes up screaming with diffuse fear and agitation. The child has no recollection of dreaming and does not remember the incident in the morning. It is difficult to comfort a child who has had a sleep terror. It is estimated that between 1% and 6% of children experience sleep terrors,[88] and the exact causes are unknown. Sleep terrors in children are not believed to be triggered or maintained by parental attention, but they possibly are maintained by a disruption in the sleep cycle.

Scheduled awakenings are an effective behavioral intervention for sleep terrors. For a particular child, sleep terrors occur at about the same time each night (usually in the first third of the child's sleep period). Parents are instructed to awaken the child approximately 30 minutes before the anticipated sleep terror episode. The parent lightly touches or moves the child until his or her eyes open, and then the child is allowed to fall back asleep. Scheduled awakenings are carried out until the child achieves a specified number of nights without experiencing a sleep terror episode. Scheduled awakenings have resulted in significant reductions in children's sleep terrors.[89]

Adult Insomnia

Adult insomnia is maintained primarily by three antecedent conditions: inappropriate setting events for sleeping, excessive muscle tension, and excessive worry. Three behavior therapies are used to change these maintaining conditions: changing setting events, progressive relaxation training, and cognitive restructuring, respectively.

Changing Setting Events

Some people have difficulty falling asleep because, for them, being in bed has strong associations with a host of activities other than sleeping, including reading, watching TV, snacking, talking on the phone, and worrying about not being able to fall asleep. Modifying setting events is effective when insomnia is maintained by such non–sleep-related setting events.

Procedures for adjusting setting events to treat insomnia, developed by Richard Bootzin,[90] establish a client's bed as a clear-cut cue for sleeping and *only* for sleeping. Clients are instructed to follow three basic rules.[91]

Courtesy of Richard Bootzin

Richard Bootzin

1. Get into bed *only* when you are sleepy.
2. Use your bed *only* for sleeping. (The one exception is for sexual behavior, but only if you feel relaxed or sleepy afterward. If sex leaves you wide awake, engage in it somewhere other than the bed in which you sleep.)
3. If you cannot fall asleep within 15 minutes, get out of bed and go into another room. Return to your bed only when you are sleepy. If you still cannot fall asleep, repeat this step. (It does not seem to matter what you do when you get out of bed, as long as the activity is not stimulating, which includes watching TV or working on a computer.)

In addition to these rules that establish appropriate setting events, clients also are asked to follow two other rules that promote good sleep habits.

4. Get up at the same time every morning, regardless of what time you go to bed. (This routine allows you to establish a regular sleep rhythm.)
5. Do not take naps. (Napping can disrupt the regular sleep rhythm and makes it harder to fall asleep at night.)

These procedures are highly effective for treating sleep-onset insomnia.[92] They consistently have been shown to be superior to no treatment and placebo control conditions in decreasing sleep-onset latency, the time it takes to fall asleep.

Modifying setting events has been an effective treatment for older adults who often experience sleep-onset problems and frequent nighttime awakenings.[93] In one study with adults aged 47 to 76, changing setting events was combined with *sleep education*, which provides clients with information about behaviors that facilitate sleep (such as daily exercise) and behaviors that interfere with sleep (such as consuming alcohol before retiring).[94] This treatment package was compared with sleep education alone, sleep education plus relaxation training, and a no-treatment control group.

Interestingly, all the clients, including those in the control group, showed improvement immediately after treatment in self-report measures, including the number of nighttime awakenings, feeling depressed, and feeling refreshed upon awakening. Because clients in the control group also reported these improvements, it was not possible to conclude that any of the treatments were responsible for the positive changes. However, at a 2-year follow-up, clients who had been taught to change setting events reported shorter sleep-onset latencies and had the highest ratings of sleep quality. It is noteworthy that these clients were still using the setting events intervention. Two factors may have accounted for the long-lasting effects: changing setting events was easy to implement, and the new, appropriate setting events became a natural part of the clients' lives.

These factors also may explain why, in general, modifying setting events is the single most effective treatment for adult insomnia.[95] When insomnia is secondary to other problems, such as with chronic pain, establishing setting events conducive to sleep is used as part of a treatment package.[96]

Many everyday behaviors besides falling asleep are maintained by setting events, which means that they can be influenced by changing setting events. Studying is a common example, and you might benefit from doing Participation Exercise 16-1 (now or at a later time).

| PARTICIPATION EXERCISE 16-1 | # Modifying Setting Events to Enhance Studying |

Studying is maintained by a host of setting events, including the time of day, the physical setting, and the presence of other students. If your study habits are being maintained by inappropriate setting events, modifying these events may increase the efficiency and effectiveness of your studying.

Using the rules for treating insomnia described earlier in the text as models, make a list of rules to establish setting events that will prompt you to study and will make studying more productive, including increasing

(continued)

concentration and decreasing distractions. Consider the following situational factors and how differences in them affect your studying.

1. *When* you study. This includes the days of the week, the time of day, and the length of study sessions and breaks. What time parameters are optimal for you?
2. *Where* you study. This includes the general location (for instance, in your room or at the library) and the specific physical setup (for example, at a desk or on your bed). What factors facilitate your studying (such as ample lighting and optimal temperature) and inhibit your studying (such as noise and interruptions)?
3. *With whom* you study. Do you study more efficiently by collaborating with one or more other students or by yourself? If you study by yourself, is your studying facilitated by others' studying around you (such as in a study lounge) or by being alone?

After you have compiled your rules, refer to your Student Resource Manual for examples of possible rules. Finally, you might want to follow your rules and see if they affect your studying. If some of your inefficient or ineffective study habits are maintained by setting events, appropriately modifying the events will make a difference.

Relaxation Training

People who have problems sleeping often report being "all keyed up" and "tense" before going to bed. When insomnia is maintained by muscle tension, training in progressive relaxation is the treatment of choice. Once clients have learned progressive relaxation, they use the relaxation skills when they get into bed to go to sleep. Clients using progressive relaxation in systematic desensitization sometimes get so relaxed that they fall asleep while visualizing scenes. Although this interferes with systematic desensitization, it is precisely the desired outcome for clients who have difficulty falling asleep.

For decreasing sleep-onset latency, progressive relaxation consistently has been found to be superior to no treatment[97] but only inconsistently superior to placebo conditions.[98] Clients who receive relaxation training may not routinely show improvements in their daytime functioning (for example, alertness during the day).[99] However, relaxation training may serve as a daytime coping skill for dealing with daily stressors,[100] which is beneficial because many clients with chronic insomnia report high levels of daytime anxiety. Finally, relaxation training can facilitate clients' attempts to stop using sleep medications.[101]

The effectiveness of relaxation training for insomnia can be enhanced by (1) greater individualization of treatment, (2) a larger number of treatment sessions,[102] and (3) increased practice in relaxation exercises between therapy sessions.[103] Standard progressive relaxation training appears to be as effective as electromyographic (muscle tone) biofeedback-assisted relaxation training, particularly for clients with sleep-onset problems. Thus, the additional cost of using biofeedback appears to be unwarranted.[104]

Cognitive Restructuring

Worry is a common maintaining antecedent of sleep problems. The worry can be about anything, including interpersonal problems, work, or health. And, not infrequently, people worry about their sleep difficulties—as the classic quip puts it: Insomnia wouldn't be bad if I didn't lie awake worrying about it. We will focus on this last problem to illustrate the use of cognitive restructuring to deal with worry that interferes with sleep.

When excessive worry about not sleeping and about the possible negative consequences of sleep loss is a maintaining antecedent of sleep problems, cognitive restructuring may be the treatment of choice. Typically, the worry is the result of faulty or distorted beliefs about sleeping, involving one of the following themes: exaggerated ideas about the negative consequences of sleep loss (for instance, "If I don't get a good night's sleep, I'll flunk my exam tomorrow"), unrealistic expectations about what constitutes acceptable sleep requirements (such as, "I can't function on fewer than 9 hours of sleep"), and beliefs about not having control over one's sleeping (for example, "I'm 'wired' when I get into bed, there's nothing I can do to fall asleep"). A client's specific sleep-related cognitions can be assessed initially with a direct self-report inventory. For example, the Personal Beliefs and Attitudes About Sleep inventory contains common thoughts about sleep problems (see Table 16-3) which clients rate on a scale ranging from *strongly agree* to *strongly disagree*.[105]

Cognitive restructuring for insomnia involves three steps: (1) identifying unrealistic, maladaptive sleep-related cognitions; (2) challenging the validity of these cognitions; and (3) replacing unrealistic, maladaptive cognitions with realistic, adaptive ones. For example, "If I don't fall asleep soon, I won't get anything done tomorrow" might be more realistically and adaptively restructured as, "If I don't fall asleep soon, I may be tired tomorrow but I'll still be able to function." Note that the adaptive thoughts realistically acknowledge that sleep loss may have some negative consequences, but not the catastrophic consequences predicted by the maladaptive thoughts. With a more realistic outlook, worry about loss of sleep will diminish, which, in turn, will make it more likely that the person will be able to fall asleep.

Cognitive restructuring for insomnia has been shown to be effective compared with no-treatment control conditions.[106] Although cognitive restructuring

TABLE **16-3**

Examples of Items from the Personal Beliefs and Attitudes About Sleep Inventory That Clients Rate on a Scale Ranging from *Strongly Agree* to *Strongly Disagree*

I am worried that if I go for one or two nights without sleep, I may have a "nervous breakdown."
After a poor night's sleep, I know that it will interfere with my daily activities the next day.
I feel that insomnia is basically the result of aging and there isn't much that can be done about this problem.
My sleep is getting worse all the time, and I don't believe anyone can help.
When I sleep poorly on one night, I know that it will disturb my sleep schedule for the whole week.

Source: Adapted from Sloan, Hauris, Bootzin, Morin, Stevenson, & Shapiro, 1993.

can be used as the sole treatment for insomnia, it generally is part of a treatment package.[107]

Cognitive-Behavioral Treatment Packages for Adult Insomnia

We'll begin our discussion of cognitive-behavioral treatment packages of adult insomnia with an example of a treatment package for adults who had suffered from insomnia for an average of more than 11 years.[108] Therapy was conducted individually and typically required 8 to 10 therapy sessions. The components of the treatment package were cognitive restructuring, changing setting events, sleep education, and sleep restriction. *Sleep restriction* involves limiting the time spent in bed to the actual time a client usually sleeps. For example, if a client typically spends 10 hours in bed but sleeps only 5 hours, the client would be instructed to stay in bed for only 5 hours, no matter how much of that time the client is asleep. Clients also kept a *sleep diary* that included such information as bedtime, arising time, daytime naps, frequency of night awakenings, sleep quality (rated on a 5-point scale), and medication intake (see Figure 16-1 for an excerpt from a sleep diary). Finally,

Day/date:	Monday, 2/14
Naps	11:15 a.m.–12:05 p.m. (50 min.) 3:30–4:00 p.m. (30 min.)
Medication Intake	None
Bedtime	10:30 p.m.
Nighttime Awakenings	12:50 a.m. 3:35 a.m.
Sleep Quality (5-point rating)	2
Arising Time	7:10 a.m.

Day/date:	Tuesday, 2/15
Naps	11:30 a.m.–12:15 p.m. (45 min.)
Medication Intake	Sominex—2 pills at 10:30 p.m.
Bedtime	11:20 p.m.
Nighttime Awakenings	1:20 a.m. 4:10 a.m.
Sleep Quality (5-point rating)	2
Arising Time	7:45 a.m.

FIGURE 16-1

Excerpt from a sleep diary

therapists offered clients who were using sleep medication a withdrawal plan to decrease or eliminate drug use.

The treatment package significantly reduced clients' sleep-onset latency, awakenings during the night, and early morning awakenings. Significant reductions in clients' use of sleep medication also occurred; the number of clients who had habitually used sleep medication decreased by 54% by the end of therapy. Similar results have been obtained using short-term cognitive-behavioral therapy for older adults (with an average age of 67) suffering from insomnia.[109]

Cognitive-behavioral treatment packages also have been administered in small groups (five to seven clients)[110] and in brief telephone consultations.[111] One such group treatment package for clients whose insomnia was related to chronic pain combined sleep education (which included specific information about pain-related sleep problems), changing setting events, relaxation training, and cognitive restructuring.[112] The treatment was administered in seven 2-hour weekly sessions. Compared with a wait-list control condition, the treatment package improved clients' self-reports of sleep-onset latency, the number of awakenings after falling asleep, and sleep quality; it also reduced sleep-interfering movement during sleep (as measured by a monitor, worn on the wrist, which continuously recorded movement).

The frequency and severity of chronic insomnia is pronounced in older adults (with estimates of occurrence being between 20% and 30% of that population).[113] A meta-analysis of cognitive-behavioral treatment packages for later-life insomnia has indicated that they are effective.[114] Moreover, some studies have demonstrated that cognitive-behavioral interventions are more effective than sleep medication.[115]

Although the efficacy of a variety of cognitive-behavioral interventions for treating insomnia have been well documented in controlled studies conducted in research settings,[116] it is important to know if these interventions can be effectively delivered in sleep clinics where most clients receive help. This question was addressed by examining the results of 47 case studies of clients who were treated for insomnia in a sleep clinic.[117] (This investigation is an example of using a series of case studies to provide evidence of the effectiveness of an intervention.) The treatments included sleep restriction, modification of setting events, relaxation training, cognitive therapy, and sleep education. On average, clients undergoing the clinic-based treatment showed a 65% reduction in sleep latency, a 46% decrease in nightly awakenings, a 48% reduction in time awake after sleep onset, and a 13% increase in total sleep time. These data are comparable to results obtained in research settings. Total sleep time was the outcome measure least affected by the treatment, improving only 13%. This is not surprising because sleep restriction and modification of setting events (such as getting out of bed if one does not fall asleep in 15 minutes) may initially decrease sleep time. Fortunately, there is evidence that total sleep time eventually increases.

Treatment packages for insomnia may be more effective than single therapies, especially when a client's sleeping problems result from more than one category of maintaining conditions. For example, changing setting events and relaxation training have been shown to be more effective than changing setting events alone.[118] To decrease dependence on sleep medication, treatment packages that combine medication-tapering schedules and cognitive-behavioral procedures have proved successful.[119] Although treatment packages for insomnia are effective, research has not yet indicated which specific combinations of therapies are optimal and which clients are likely to benefit most from treatment packages rather than single therapies.[120]

BULIMIA NERVOSA

Bulimia nervosa (or *bulimia*, for short) is a serious eating disorder characterized by binge eating and then purging what has been eaten.[121] *Binge eating* involves consuming large quantities of high-caloric food (often junk food) in a brief period. The person then *purges* what has been eaten, most often by self-induced vomiting and also through the abuse of laxatives and diuretics. Clients with bulimia nervosa typically are preoccupied with their body image and weight, and purging prevents the person from gaining weight following binge eating episodes. Bulimia affects 1% to 3% of women (it is rare in men), primarily in industrialized countries, and typically begins in late adolescence or early adulthood. Recurrent purging after binge eating can result in serious medical problems, including loss of bodily fluids and electrolytes as well as damage to the esophagus and teeth caused by stomach acid that is regurgitated.[122]

Treatment of bulimia generally consists of a multifaceted cognitive-behavioral treatment package that can be implemented in as few as 20 sessions, individually or in groups.[123] The treatment is a prime example of the rich integration of behavioral and cognitive components that characterizes much of the practice of contemporary behavior therapy.

After providing the client with information about bulimia, nutrition, and weight regulation,[124] a combination of the following eight procedures is used.

1. *Self-monitoring.* Self-monitoring of binge eating and purging episodes and the circumstances surrounding them is the clients' first task and continues throughout the treatment. Clients also record their daily food and liquid intake and sometimes the type of food and the time and place of eating. The self-monitoring records help identify maintaining conditions of binging and purging episodes and provide a continuous measure of change.

2. *Changing setting events.* The therapist teaches the client to adjust setting events related to eating, such as eating at specified times, eating in a particular location, and buying only foods that the client is unlikely to binge on. The aim of these procedures is for the client to develop habits of eating three regular meals a day plus planned snacks.

3. *Scheduling competing activities.* The client learns to schedule pleasurable between-meal activities that reduce the likelihood of binge eating. Such competing behaviors include engaging in moderate exercise and work that holds the client's attention.

4. *Cognitive restructuring.* Clients are trained to identify and alter their dysfunctional thoughts and attitudes about eating, food, and body image. People suffering from bulimia typically have rigid and perfectionist attitudes

regarding their body shape and weight, eating, and dieting (for example, "I'll never be happy until I'm thin").[125]

5. *Collaborative empiricism.* Clients engage in empirical hypothesis testing designed to challenge their dysfunctional beliefs and thoughts (as is done in cognitive therapy). For example, a client who erroneously believed that she weighed well above normal for her height could check a current table of normal weight ranges.

6. *Problem solving.* Clients learn problem-solving skills to help them cope with stress-evoking events that have been associated with binge eating. Clients are encouraged to anticipate these stressors so that they can solve problems before binge eating is imminent.[126]

7. *Flooding with response prevention.* Binge eating and the threat of gaining weight typically evoke a great deal of anxiety in clients with bulimia. Purging reduces the anxiety, which negatively reinforces purging. Flooding is used to break this vicious cycle.[127] In the presence of a therapist, clients are encouraged to eat the foods on which they typically binge (often sweet and soft-textured foods that can be rapidly swallowed), but not to excess. After this exposure, clients are instructed not to vomit (response prevention). The flooding session is terminated only when the strong urge to purge dissipates. Although flooding can be effective, it does not appear to be a necessary treatment component.[128] In some cases, flooding may make the treatment package less effective[129] because clients are reluctant to participate in the unpleasant flooding procedures.[130]

8. *Relapse prevention.* Bulimia tends to occur in cycles[131] and is characterized by relapses.[132] Thus, preparing clients for the possibility that the bulimic behaviors will return in the future is important.[133] Accordingly, clients identify high-risk situations for binge eating and rehearse coping strategies that can be used if the situations occur, including their recruiting and using social support from family and friends.

The comprehensive cognitive-behavioral treatment package we have just described is generally considered the treatment of choice for bulimia.[134] Well-controlled studies support its efficacy, showing an average reduction in clients' binge eating ranging from 93% to 73% and an average reduction in purging ranging from 94% to 77%.[135] For clients who do not experience significant changes in their binge eating habits after a standard number of sessions, additional therapy sessions can be beneficial.[136]

The cognitive-behavioral treatment package for bulimia consistently is superior to traditional verbal/interpersonal psychotherapies[137] and antidepressant medication (which has been used to treat depression related to bulimia).[138] Compared with medication, the treatment package is more effective in reducing the frequency of binge and purging episodes as well as feelings of depression.[139] The treatment package often results in more rapid changes in clients' binging and purging behaviors than alternative treatments.[140] Additionally, the treatment package consistently improves clients' beliefs and attitudes about their body and weight[141] and most studies show significant improvements in self-esteem and social functioning.[142] Moreover, cognitive-behavioral interventions for bulimia can be administered success-fully through cost-effective self-help formats.[143]

Long-term maintenance of treatment gains from the cognitive-behavioral treatment package have been found in some,[144] but not all,[145] studies. Cognitive interventions that target clients' maladaptive cognitions that maintain binge eating and purging may be especially important in fostering long-term maintenance of treatment gains.[146]

ALL THINGS CONSIDERED: APPLICATIONS OF BEHAVIOR THERAPY TO PSYCHOLOGICAL DISORDERS WITH PRIMARY PHYSICAL CHARACTERISTICS

Behavior therapy for psychological disorders with primary physical character-istics provides alternatives to traditional medical interventions that are more intrusive and have serious negative side effects. The predominant use of seda-tives or other sleep-inducing drugs to treat insomnia is a prime example. Pro-longed use of sleep medication may actually interfere with sleeping, can lead to diminished daytime functioning, and may result in psychological and phys-ical dependence on the drugs.

Although the problems we discussed in this chapter are classified as psy-chological rather than medical, their physical aspects can have serious medi-cal implications. Thus, physical factors that may cause/exacerbate or result from the psychological disorders, must be assessed because they may need to be treated directly. For example, bedwetting can be caused by medication the client is currently taking (such as diuretics) and general medical conditions (such as diabetes); sleep difficulties can result from drug use (for instance, use of amphetamines) and medical conditions (for instance, hyperthyroidism); and bulimia nervosa often results in dental problems, damage to the esopha-gus, and low levels of electrolytes due to repeated regurgitation.

Because clients with enuresis, tic disorders, and bulimia nervosa are likely to experience guilt, embarrassment, and shame, treating clients with these dis-orders requires an especially good therapist–client relationship. For instance, the client must trust the therapist sufficiently to reveal embarrassing behav-iors, and the therapist must trust the client to be honest and straightforward in reporting about these personally sensitive problems.

Many of the behavior therapy interventions used to treat psychological disorders with primary physical characteristics involve self-control techniques. For example, habit reversal for tic disorders teaches clients to "catch" their maladaptive behaviors early in their sequence and counter them with com-peting responses. Gaining self-control over so-called involuntary physical disabilities (such as tics) is likely to increase clients' self-efficacy about their ability to modify them, and enhanced self-efficacy may be one of the factors responsible for the success of habit reversal for tics (see In Theory 11-2, page 275).

The use of treatment packages is another common element in the behav-ior therapy treatment of psychological disorders with primary physical characteristics. Dry-bed training for enuresis, habit reversal for tics, and cognitive-behavioral treatment packages for insomnia and bulimia nervosa all involve multifaceted approaches.

SUMMARY

1. Behavior therapy treats a variety of psychological disorders whose primary feature is a physical problem.

2. The urine alarm is an efficient and effective treatment for nocturnal enuresis. An alarm is activated when urine contacts a special pad under the child's bed sheet or in the child's underpants. Through repeated pairings of the alarm and bladder tension, bladder tension alone comes to awaken the child before urination begins.

3. Dry-bed training is a highly effective treatment package for nocturnal enuresis that uses shaping and overcorrection to teach children the behaviors required to keep their beds dry throughout the night. The dry-pants method is an extension of dry-bed training that is used for normal daytime toilet training.

4. Behavioral treatments for tics include massed negative practice, changing maintaining consequences, progressive relaxation, and self-monitoring. Habit reversal, the most effective treatment, incorporates four components: awareness training, relaxation training, competing response training, and reinforcement. Awareness training and competing response training are the critical components. Habit reversal also is used to treat nervous habits such as compulsive hair pulling and stuttering.

5. When sleep problems in infants and children are maintained by parental attention, extinction, involving withholding attention for nighttime crying, is a simple and effective treatment. Modified forms of extinction may be more acceptable to parents but somewhat less effective. Sleep terrors, which are not maintained by attention, can be treated by scheduled awakenings before the onset of a sleep terror episode.

6. For adult insomnia, changing setting events establishes a client's being in bed as a clear-cut cue only for sleeping. Relaxation training helps clients reduce muscle tension associated with insomnia before going to bed. Cognitive restructuring reduces worry, such as about sleeping, by identifying, challenging, and replacing maladaptive beliefs with adaptive cognitions.

7. Treatment packages involving changing setting events, relaxation training, cognitive restructuring, sleep restriction, and sleep education for insomnia are appropriate when a client's sleeping problems are the result of multiple maintaining conditions.

8. The treatment of choice for bulimia nervosa is a comprehensive cognitive-behavioral treatment package that includes self-monitoring, changing setting events, competing activities, cognitive restructuring, collaborative empiricism, problem solving, flooding with response prevention, and relapse prevention.

REFERENCE NOTES

1. American Psychiatric Association, 1994; World Health Organization, 1992.
2. Friedman, Sobel, Myers, Caudill, & Benson, 1995; Schell, 1996.
3. Lovibond & Coote, 1970; Oppel, Harper, & Rider, 1968; Yates, 1970.
4. American Psychiatric Association, 1994.
5. For example, Deleon & Mandell, 1966; Werry & Cohrssen, 1965; Yates, 1970.
6. Mowrer & Mowrer, 1938.
7. Friman & Vollmer, 1995.
8. Houts, 2003.
9. Houts, Berman, & Abramson, 1994; Rushton, 1989; Walker, Milling, & Bonner, 1988.
10. Wagner, Johnson, Walker, Carter, & Witner, 1982.
11. Novick, 1966; Werry & Cohrssen, 1965.
12. Deleon & Sacks, 1972; Doleys, 1977.
13. Azrin, Sneed, & Foxx, 1973; Houts, Peterson, & Whelan, 1986; Ikeda, Koga, & Minami, 2006.
14. Houts, Berman, & Abramson, 1994.
15. Azrin, Sneed, & Foxx, 1973.
16. Kimmel & Kimmel, 1970; Paschalis, Kimmel, & Kimmel, 1972.
17. Azrin, Thienes-Hontos, & Besalel-Azrin, 1979.
18. Azrin, Thienes-Hontos, & Besalel-Azrin, 1979.
19. Azrin, Sneed, & Foxx, 1974; Nawaz, Griffiths, & Tappin, 2002.
20. Azrin, Thienes-Hontos, & Besalel-Azrin, 1979.
21. Rushton, 1989.
22. Mellon & McGrath, 2000.
23. Nawaz, Griffiths, & Tappin, 2002.
24. Van Son, Van Heesch, Mulder, & Van Londen, 1995.
25. Foxx & Azrin, 1973a, 1973b.
26. For example, Madsen, Hoffman, Thomas, Karopsak, & Madsen, 1969.
27. For example, Madsen, Hoffman, Thomas, Karopsak, & Madsen, 1969; Mahoney, Van Wagenen, & Meyerson, 1971.
28. Foxx & Azrin, 1973a.
29. Wilder, Higbeen, Williams, & Nachtwey, 1997.
30. Boudjouk, Woods, Miltenberger, & Long, 2000; Long, Woods, Miltenberger, Fuqua, & Boudjouk, 1999.
31. American Psychiatric Association, 1994; Bauer & Shea, 1984; Cohen, Leckman, & Shaywitz, 1984.
32. Peterson & Azrin, 1993; Shapiro & Shapiro, 1984; Shapiro et al., 1989.
33. Shapiro & Shapiro, 1984.
34. Cohen, Leckman, & Shaywitz, 1984.
35. Yates, 1958.
36. For example, Browning & Stover, 1971; Storms, 1985.
37. Azrin & Peterson, 1988a; Turpin, 1983.
38. For example, Schulman, 1974; Tophoff, 1973; Varni, Boyd, & Cataldo, 1978; Wagaman, Miltenberger, & Woods, 1995.
39. Wagaman, Miltenberger, & Williams, 1995.
40. Azrin & Peterson, 1988a.
41. For example, Barr, Lovibond, & Katsaros, 1972; Clark, 1966.
42. For example, Canavan & Powell, 1981; Varni, Boyd, & Cataldo, 1978.
43. For example, Barr, Lovibond, & Katsaros, 1972; Canavan & Powell, 1981; Lahey, McNees, & McNees, 1973.
44. For example, Franco, 1981; Friedman, 1980.
45. Peterson & Azrin, 1990.
46. For example, Billings, 1978; Hutzell, Platzek, & Logue, 1974; Thomas, Abrams, & Johnson, 1971.
47. Azrin & Nunn, 1973.
48. Miltenberger, Fuqua, & McKinley, 1985.
49. Carr, 1995.
50. See Carr, 1995.
51. Cook & Blacher, 2007; Himle, Wood, Piacentini, & Walkup, 2006; Peterson, 2007; Peterson & Azrin, 1993.
52. Peterson & Azrin, 1993.
53. Miltenberger, Fuqua, & Woods, 1998; Peterson, Campise, & Azrin, 1994; Woods & Miltenberger, 1995.
54. For example, Long, Miltenberger, & Rapp, 1999; Rapp, Miltenberger, Galensky, Roberts, & Ellingson, 1999; Woods, Murray, Fuqua, Seif, Boyer, & Siah, 1999.
55. Long, Miltenberger, Ellingson, & Ott, 1999.
56. Bebko & Lennox, 1988; Miltenberger, Fuqua, & Woods, 1998.
57. For example, Lerner, Franklin, Meadows, Hembree, & Foa, 1998; Tarnowski, Rosen, McGrath, & Drabman, 1987.
58. For example, Wagaman, Miltenberger, & Arndorfer, 1993; Wagaman, Miltenberger, & Woods, 1995.
59. Rapp, Miltenberger, Long, Elliott, & Lumley, 1998.
60. Elliott, Miltenberger, Rapp, Long, & McDonald, 1998.

61. Long, Miltenberger, & Rapp, 1998.
62. de Kinkelder & Boelens, 1998.
63. Elliott, Miltenberger, Rapp, Long, & McDonald, 1998.
64. Long, Miltenberger, & Rapp, 1999.
65. Allen, 1998.
66. Elliott, Miltenberger, Rapp, Long, & McDonald, 1998; Rapp, Miltenberger, Galensky, Roberts, & Ellingson, 1999.
67. Nunn, Newton, & Faucher, 1992.
68. de L. Horne, White, & Varigos, 1989.
69. Peterson, Dixon, Talcott, & Kelleher, 1993.
70. Glaros, Lausten, & Franklin, 2007.
71. For example, Murtagh & Greenwood, 1995; Sloan & Shapiro, 1993.
72. For example, Murtagh & Greenwood, 1995.
73. For example, France & Hudson, 1993.
74. For example, Murtagh & Greenwood, 1995.
75. Lichstein & Riedel, 1994.
76. For example, Blampied & France, 1993; France & Hudson, 1993.
77. For example, Didden, Curfs, Sikkema, & de Moor, 1998; France & Hudson, 1990, 1993; Williams, 1959.
78. For example, France & Hudson, 1990.
79. For example, Ashbaugh & Peck, 1998; Wolfson, Lacks, & Futterman, 1992.
80. France & Hudson, 1990, 1993.
81. France, 1992.
82. France, 1992.
83. For example, Pritchard & Appleton, 1988.
84. For example, Durand & Mindell, 1990; Rolider & Van Houten, 1984.
85. For example, Lawton, France, & Blampied, 1991.
86. For example, Hall & Nathan, 1992.
87. For example, Lawton, France, & Blampied, 1991.
88. American Psychiatric Association, 2000a.
89. Durand & Mindell, 1999; Johnson & Lerner, 1985.
90. Bootzin, 1972; Bootzin, Epstein, & Wood, 1991.
91. Bootzin & Engle-Friedman, 1987; France & Hudson, 1990.
92. Bootzin & Perlis, 1992; Espie, Lindsay, Brooks, Hood, & Turvey, 1989; Lichstein & Riedel, 1994.
93. Backhaus, Hohagen, Voderholzer, & Riemann, 2001; Bootzin & Epstein, 2000; King, Dudley, Melvin, Pallant, & Morawetz, 2001; Reidel & Lichstein, 2000.
94. Engle-Friedman, Bootzin, Hazlewood, & Tsao, 1992.
95. Lichstein & Riedel, 1994.
96. Degotardi, Klass, Rosenberg, Fox, Gallelli, & Gottlieb, 2006.
97. Nicassio, Boylan, & McCabe, 1982.
98. Lacks, Bertelson, Gans, & Kunkel, 1983; Nicassio, Boylan, & McCabe, 1982.
99. Means, Lichstein, Epperson, & Johnson, 2000.
100. Bootzin & Perlis, 1992.
101. Lichstein, Peterson, Riedel, Means, Epperson, & Aguillard, 1999.
102. Carlson & Hoyle, 1993.
103. Lichstein, 1988; Lichstein & Riedel, 1994.
104. Bootzin & Perlis, 1992; Borkovec, Grayson, & O'Brien, 1979; Hauri, 1981.
105. Sloan, Hauris, Bootzin, Morin, Stevenson, & Shapiro, 1993.
106. Morin, 1993; Morin, Kowatch, Barry, & Walton, 1993.
107. For example, Jacobs, Benson, & Friedman, 1993; Lichstein & Riedel, 1994.
108. Morin, Stone, McDonald, & Jones, 1994.
109. Morin, Kowatch, Barry, & Walton, 1993.
110. Jansson & Linton, 2005; Rosenlicht, 2007; Verbeek, Konings, Aldenkamp, Declerck, & Klip, 2006.
111. Bastien, Morin, Ouellet, Blais, & Bouchard, 2004.
112. Currie, Wilson, Pontefract, & deLaplante, 2000.
113. Irwin, Cole, & Nicassio, 2006.
114. Irwin, Cole, & Nicassio, 2006; McCurry, Logsdon, Teri, & Vitiello, 2007.
115. Cook, Nau, & Lichstein, 2005; Sivertsen et al., 2006.
116. Morin, 2004; Morin, Culvert, & Schwartz, 1994; Murtagh & Greenwood, 1995.
117. Perlis et al., 2000.
118. Jacobs et al., 1993.
119. Morin, Stone, McDonald, & Jones, 1994.
120. Lacks & Morin, 1992; Murtagh & Greenwood, 1995; Smith & Perlis, 2006.
121. American Psychiatric Association, 1994.
122. American Psychiatric Association, 1994.
123. Smith, Marcus, & Eldredge, 1994.
124. Olmsted, Davis, Rockert, Irvine, Eagle, & Garner, 1991.
125. For example, Heatherton & Baumeister, 1991.
126. Smith, Marcus, & Eldredge, 1994.
127. Kennedy, Katz, Neitzert, Ralevski, & Mendlowitz, 1995; Leitenberg, 1993.
128. Wilson, Eldredge, Smith, & Niles, 1991.

129. Agras, Schneider, Arnow, Raeburn, & Telch, 1989.

130. Smith, Marcus, & Eldredge, 1994; Sturmey, 1992.

131. Keller, Herzog, Lavori, Bradburn, & Mahoney, 1992.

132. Mitchell, Pyle, Hatsukami, Goff, Glotter, & Harper, 1989.

133. Wilson et al., 1999.

134. Agras, 1993; American Psychiatric Association, 2000b; Fairburn, Marcus, & Wilson, 1993; Latner & Wilson, 2000.

135. Wilson & Fairburn, 1993, 1998.

136. Eldredge et al., 1997.

137. Agras, Walsh, Fairburn, Wilson, & Kraemer, 2000; DeAngelis, 2002; Kirkley, Schneider, Agras, & Bachman, 1985.

138. Leitenberg, Rosen, Wolf, Vara, Detzer, & Srebnik, 1994; Wilson & Fairburn, 1993.

139. Whital, Agras, & Gould, 1999.

140. Wilson et al., 1999.

141. For example, Garner, Rockert, Davis, Garner, Olmsted, & Eagle, 1993.

142. For example, DeAnglis, 2002; Shiina et al., 2005.

143. Carter & Fairburn, 1998; Fairburn, 1995; Wilson, Vitousek, & Loeb, 2000.

144. For example, Fairburn, Jones, Peveler, Hope, & O'Connor, 1993.

145. For example, Agras, Telch, Arnow, Eldredge, & Marnell, 1997; Agras, Walsh, Fairburn, Wilson, & Kraemer, 2000; Eldredge et al., 1997.

146. Thackwray, Smith, Bodfish, & Meyers, 1993; compare with Wolf & Crowther, 1992.

17

Contemporary Behavior Therapy in Perspective
Strengths and Challenges

Major Strengths of Behavior Therapy
Precision in Specifying Goals, Target
  Behaviors, and Therapy Procedures
Efficacy and Effectiveness
Efficiency
Breadth and Complexity of Applications
Ethical Practices in Behavior Therapy

Challenges
Enhancing Durability of Change
Preventing Psychological Disorders and
  Problems
Treating Culturally Diverse Clients
Providing Behavior Therapy for Elderly
  Clients

Employing Technology in Behavior
  Therapy
Using Precise Terminology
Promoting Widespread Use of Empirically
  Supported Behavior Therapies

**All Things Considered: Behavior
Therapy**
Participation Exercise 17-1: Demythifying
  Myths About Contemporary Behavior
  Therapy

SUMMARY
REFERENCE NOTES

Having come this far in the book, you know what behavior therapy is and have seen the wide range of assessment and therapy procedures it employs; you've also become aware of the broad spectrum of problems it treats. What, then, is left for this last chapter? We have chosen two topics. First, we think it is important to review the major strengths of contemporary behavior therapy. And, so as not to just rest on the laurels of the field, we then will suggest some critical challenges that we believe behavior therapists must deal with. In essence, then, this chapter discusses where behavior therapy is now and where it needs to be going in the future.

MAJOR STRENGTHS OF BEHAVIOR THERAPY

What do you consider the major strengths of behavior therapy? Before reading further, take a moment to answer that question.

We have chosen to highlight five strengths of behavior therapy: (1) precision in specifying goals, target behaviors, and procedures; (2) efficacy and effectiveness; (3) efficiency; (4) breadth and complexity of applications; and (5) ethical practices.

Precision in Specifying Goals, Target Behaviors, and Therapy Procedures

Because goals are very specific and target behaviors are defined in unambiguous, measurable terms in behavior therapy, explicit criteria for evaluating the success of treatment can be established. This allows the client and therapist to objectively determine progress in therapy and when it can be terminated. In contrast, many types of psychotherapy employ goals that are implicit and vaguely defined (for example, "gaining insight" about one's problems or "feeling better"), and selecting specific targets of treatment is not considered a critical part of therapy. In such cases, progress and success are "measured" by the therapist's subjective opinion.

The therapy procedures used in behavior therapy also are precisely specified. (See the procedures for dry-bed training in Table 16-1 [page 449] for a prime example.) This practice has four benefits. First, therapists can use the specific therapy procedures that have been found to be effective. Second, behavior therapists can explain to clients exactly what the therapy will entail, which enables clients to provide truly informed consent. Third, detailed descriptions of therapy procedures are invaluable in training behavior therapists. Finally, independent researchers can test the efficacy and effectiveness of behavioral interventions because the procedures are clearly specified.

Efficacy and Effectiveness

The bottom line for any psychotherapy is its success, which is measured in terms of *change*. The question is: How much has the client changed with respect to the goals of therapy? Because the goals in behavior therapy are specific, clear-cut, and measurable, the success of treatment is easy to determine for an *individual* client.[a] In contrast, making statements about the *general* efficacy and effectiveness of a behavior therapy is complex. It requires asking a series of qualifying questions, including: For what problem or disorder? For which client population? And in what context?

Even when carefully qualified questions are asked, a host of practical, methodological, and ethical problems may hinder research efforts.[1] For one thing, researchers use multiple criteria to assess the effectiveness of therapy: meaningfulness of change, transfer and generalization of change, maintenance of change over time, and acceptability of the therapy. To their credit, behavior therapists are increasingly examining the usefulness of therapies in terms of each of these criteria.[2]

Behavior therapy arguably has the broadest and strongest empirical base among psychotherapies.[3] Two prime examples are exposure therapies for anxiety disorders and cognitive therapy for depression. Today, managed care organizations dictate the treatments that are acceptable for particular disorders and therefore the treatments for which therapists can be reimbursed. Because of their strong empirical support, many behavior therapies are among the most frequently "approved" treatments.[4]

It is noteworthy that behavior therapy fares well in comparison to medication, which is the treatment most frequently employed for psychological disorders.[5] Despite the effectiveness of many drug treatments, behavior therapies are often a more desirable form of treatment because they may work as well as drug treatments for many disorders and may reduce relapse rates better than medication.

The existence of a strong empirical base for the effectiveness of behavior therapy procedures stems from the commitment behavior therapists have to evaluating the treatment procedures scientifically. Moreover, not only have behavior therapists accepted the difficult challenge of conducting psychotherapy outcome studies, but they also have been loud and stringent critics of their own research.[6] And, incidentally, the research ethic in behavior therapy has had an impact beyond behavior therapy in that it has encouraged outcome research on other forms of psychotherapy.[7]

Efficiency

The efficiency of a therapy is another important factor in assessing its value. Efficient therapies are those that (1) achieve the goals of therapy quickly and (2) are cost-effective for both therapists and clients, in terms of time and money.

Behavior therapy often brings about change relatively quickly, especially compared with traditional verbal psychotherapies. This is attributable to two factors. First, many behavior therapy techniques act quickly because they

---

[a]Strictly speaking, the fact that a client's goals have been met does not necessarily mean that the therapy caused the change. It always is possible that some other factors occurring at the same time as the therapy (such as changes in relationships or work) were responsible. Controlled research, such as a single-subject reversal study or a multiple baseline study, is necessary to draw more definitive conclusions about the effectiveness of therapy procedures for an individual client.

directly change the present maintaining conditions of the target behavior. Occasionally, the target behavior is altered almost immediately (as when powerful reinforcers are completely eliminated for a maladaptive behavior and provided exclusively for alternative, adaptive behaviors).

A second factor responsible for change in a relatively short time is that behavior therapy does not only take place during therapy sessions. Clients in behavior therapy often do much of their therapeutic work outside the therapy sessions. For example, for every hour in a therapy session, a client might do 3 hours of homework assignments. If the therapy involved 20 weekly, hour-long sessions, then the total amount of therapy would be 80 hours (not 20).[8] In contrast, a client would spend more than a year and a half in weekly sessions of verbal psychotherapy to receive the equivalent number of hours of treatment. Moreover, the client in behavior therapy would have completed treatment more than a year earlier. Homework assignments not only shorten the duration of therapy, but they also are cost-effective because the therapist is not present. Similarly, therapists' time is saved when nonprofessional change agents—such as parents, teachers, friends, and spouses—are trained to implement therapy procedures in clients' natural environments. Directing behavior therapy procedures by telephone[9] and through portable, palmtop (handheld) and home computers (as we describe later) is another means of making treatment more cost-effective.

In addition to valuing effective therapies, managed health care providers are interested in their clients' receiving brief, cost-effective treatment (for obvious financial reasons).[10] Most behavior therapies are short-term.[11] Nonetheless, the health care industry's demands for briefer treatments—along with the personal, practical, and economic advantages for clients—has increasingly led behavior therapists to develop abbreviated treatments by reducing them to their essential components.[12]

Breadth and Complexity of Applications

Behavior therapy is broadly applied, serving clients of all ages and with various cultural backgrounds who exhibit the gamut of psychological disorders.[13] It is appropriate for meeting the needs of certain groups of clients for whom traditional verbal psychotherapy has been ineffective, including infants, young children, elderly individuals,[14] people with low intelligence, and people who do not speak.[15] Clients who cannot afford expensive, long-term therapy have benefited from relatively efficient and therefore less costly behavior therapy interventions. Behavior therapy has made inroads in the treatment of disorders that are relatively unresponsive to other forms of psychological treatment, such as schizophrenia, attention deficit hyperactivity disorder, borderline personality disorder, and a number of disorders characterized by physical problems, such as pain, enuresis, and tic disorders. Finally, behavior therapy is implemented in settings where traditional psychotherapy is not typically employed, including the home, schools, and industry.

An early criticism of behavior therapy was that it dealt only with simple problems. From your reading about behavior therapy, it should be clear that contemporary behavior therapy is used to treat many complex problems.

Behavioral treatment of posttraumatic stress disorder, depression, eating disorders, and couple relationship problems are but a few examples.

Ethical Practices in Behavior Therapy

Our discussion of ethical issues in the practice of behavior therapy throughout the book has focused on the two concerns critics have most frequently voiced: depriving clients of their rights and harming clients. One strength of behavior therapy is that its practices serve to *protect* clients' rights and provide treatment that is beneficial. Behavior therapists have developed specific, rather stringent guidelines to assure ethical conduct (see Table 1-1, page 13).

The scientific approach that is a hallmark of behavior therapy contributes to ethical practices in a number of ways. The detailed specification of goals and target behaviors make the process of evaluating the success of therapy clear to all parties involved. This standard also minimizes the chances that therapy will continue longer than is necessary. Psychotherapy sometimes is prolonged because clients become overly dependent on their therapists. Although this dependence may be inappropriate, it is not unethical. In contrast, it is unethical for therapists to prolong therapy because of *their* dependence on clients. Therapists are vulnerable to this pitfall because their clients provide them with potent reinforcers, including the satisfaction of helping others and, of course, clients' fees. Continually evaluating clients' progress in behavior therapy provides a partial safeguard against therapists' inappropriately prolonging treatment. Additionally, treatment with behavior therapies is relatively brief compared with many other psychotherapies. Thus, clients' problems are alleviated as quickly as possible, which is clearly an ethical practice.

Behavior therapies are empirically tested to ensure that clients receive effective treatment. Moreover, when therapy procedures could *conceivably* be harmful, such as by temporarily inducing anxiety with prolonged/intense exposure therapy, behavior therapists have empirically verified that such harm does not occur. In the rare instances that physically aversive stimuli, such as shock, are used, a cost-benefit analysis is always made, the client's informed consent to undergo the treatment is obtained, and specific procedures are instituted to assure that the therapy is used ethically (see Chapter 7, page 174).

Collaboration between therapist and client—an essential element of behavior therapy—also serves to protect clients' rights. Clients decide on the treatment goals. The therapist provides clients with detailed information about the specific therapy procedures that are appropriate for their particular problems, and clients participate in choosing the specific therapy procedures that will be employed.[16] Clients are active participants in the therapy process, including being responsible for carrying out aspects of the treatment on their own. Such involvement decreases the chances that clients will become victims of ethical violations.

In Chapter 2, we commented on the heightened scrutiny with regard to ethical issues that behavior therapy received in its formative years. It is worth noting that this "special attention" may have been a blessing in disguise. By alerting behavior therapists to potential ethical violations, the early scrutiny may have contributed to the sensitivity to clients' welfare that has become an essential element in the practice of behavior therapy.

CHALLENGES

The strengths of behavior therapy notwithstanding, behavior therapy currently faces a number of challenges. Again, before you continue reading, you might find it instructive to think of significant challenges that you believe exist.

We will highlight seven important challenges: (1) enhancing durability of change, (2) preventing psychological disorders and problems, (3) treating culturally diverse clients, (4) providing behavior therapy for elderly clients, (5) employing technology in behavior therapy, (6) using precise terminology, and (7) promoting widespread use of empirically supported behavior therapies.

Enhancing Durability of Change

Ideally, changes that occur in a client's problems as a result of behavior therapy will endure after treatment has ended. However, this goal, which behavior therapy shares with all psychotherapies, is not easily attained.[17] A major reason is that treatment focuses on initiating change in clients' behaviors, and the process of *initiating* change and the process of *maintaining* change often are different. In some cases, changes brought about through therapy do endure; however, often it is necessary to introduce specific strategies to promote long-term maintenance of change. This can be done in the course of therapy or after the therapy has ended.

Within-Therapy Interventions to Enhance Durability of Change

Two broad strategies are employed *during* behavior therapy to foster durability of treatment gains: (1) providing clients with self-control coping skills and (2) structuring clients' natural environments where the treatment gains need to be maintained. Teaching clients self-control coping skills is the easier and more frequently used strategy. The goal is for clients to use the coping skills to handle any recurrences of the problem in the future. Problem solving, self-instructions, cognitive restructuring, and muscle relaxation are examples of self-control coping skills that might be appropriate. Central to the success of this approach is that clients understand that behavior therapy is an educational enterprise designed to help them cope more adaptively with their problems rather than to "cure" them of their ills.[18] Recent evidence shows that continuing to use skills learned in therapy increases maintenance of treatment gains after therapy has ended.[19]

The second strategy for promoting durability of treatment gains during therapy is to ensure that the client's natural environments will provide the necessary antecedents and consequences to maintain the new adaptive behaviors developed in therapy. This strategy is more complicated and requires more time than teaching clients coping skills. First, clients may need to institute setting events in their natural environments that will support the changes achieved during therapy. Second, significant people in the clients' lives may need to be trained to continue treatment procedures begun in therapy. For instance, therapists may teach parents to apply the same reinforcement contingencies that were used in therapy so that their child's adaptive behaviors will persist.

Even with such deliberate strategies to promote long-term maintenance, durability of treatment gains is not guaranteed. It is impossible to anticipate all the future life events that may interfere with clients' dealing effectively with problems treated in therapy. Further, the less similar a client's future problems are to the problems that treatment specifically focused on, the less likely it is that the treatment gains will endure. Finally, if old problems recur or new problems arise long after the termination of therapy, it is likely that the client will either have lost proficiency in the coping skills learned in therapy or will not remember to apply them.

Despite these obstacles, behavior therapies seem to promote long-term maintenance as well as or better than most other therapies. (It is not possible to say this definitively because long-term maintenance data are unavailable for many other therapies.) With some disorders, both immediate and long-term effectiveness of behavioral interventions are very impressive. For example, outcome studies of cognitive-behavioral therapy for panic disorder indicate not only that panic attacks are eliminated in more than 80% of clients immediately after treatment (which is as good or better than existing drug therapies) but also that clients remain free of panic attacks for at least 2 years.[20]

Nonetheless, in many cases, long-term maintenance of treatment gains in behavior therapy is far from optimal in an absolute sense.[21] In other words, even if behavior therapy is as successful as or better than other treatments, the extent of long-term maintenance may be less than desirable. For example, only about half the couples treated by traditional cognitive-behavioral couple therapy retain the benefits after 2 years.[22]

Posttherapy Interventions to Enhance Durability of Change

Behavior therapists increasingly are relying on posttherapy interventions to enhance long-term maintenance of treatment gains. *Relapse prevention* is the most comprehensive posttherapy approach for promoting long-term maintenance (see Chapter 13). A second approach is to offer clients *booster sessions* after therapy has ended. In essence, therapists give clients one or a few brief refresher sessions. For example, booster sessions commonly are employed after aversion therapy because the treatment effects tend to deteriorate over time but can be renewed with periodic booster sessions (see Chapter 7).[23] This may be because substance-related disorders and paraphilias, the problems most commonly treated by aversion therapy, are highly resistant to change. Other problems that are difficult to treat, such as obsessive-compulsive disorder, often require booster sessions as well.[24]

A third potential approach for fostering lasting change would provide *maintenance treatment* for extended periods after therapy has terminated—in some cases, for the remainder of a client's life. This is a radical idea for behavior therapists because behavior therapy has a tradition of providing relatively brief treatment and the approach, at first glance, seems to resemble traditional long-term psychotherapy. However, maintenance treatment is different from long-term psychotherapy, in which the therapy *itself*—that is, the process of initiating change—requires years to complete.

Maintenance treatment is less intense and less frequent than the initial treatment. It is made available to clients either on a regular basis (for example, once every 6 months) or on an as-needed basis, often over many years. Maintenance treatment has been suggested for such divergent populations and problems as couples experiencing difficulties in their relationship[25] and adolescents' engaging in delinquent behaviors.[26] The need for maintenance treatment in many cases stems from the sobering fact that

> no matter how potent the technology, after treatment ends other salient life events gradually become more important in influencing . . . [clients'] functioning. . . . The solution cannot simply be more and better therapy technology during the active therapy phase. Rather, maintenance may be facilitated to a greater extent by creating a context for the therapist to remain a continuing presence in . . . [clients'] lives. . . .[27]

Maintenance treatment is an intriguing idea, albeit one that has yet to be tested.

Although behavior therapy is among the most effective forms of intervention for many disorders, treatment effects often deteriorate over time.[28] Thus, promoting the long-term maintenance of therapeutic change has been and remains the most difficult challenge for behavior therapy (as well as other psychotherapies).[29]

Preventing Psychological Disorders and Problems

The primary objective of behavior therapy is to alleviate the human suffering that results from psychological disorders. Clearly, behavior therapy has made major advances toward achieving this goal. Behavioral principles and procedures could make an even greater contribution if they were employed more extensively to *prevent* the occurrence of psychological disorders. Some behavior therapy procedures are immediately applicable to prevention, such as stress inoculation training and problem-solving training. Others must be adapted because there are fundamental differences between treatment and prevention[30] (just as there are differences between initiating and maintaining change[31]).

Prevention might be especially germane to problems for which behavior therapy has been least effective. For instance, substance-related disorders are notoriously resistant to change, largely because of the powerful immediate consequences of many drugs. Although behavior therapy has been among the most effective psychotherapies in treating addictive behaviors,[32] the success rate is far below that achieved with many other problems treated by behavior therapy. In some cases, continued efforts to improve interventions have made little difference.[33] And, given the immense economic cost of treatment for and consequences of addictive behaviors, prevention is likely to be more cost-effective.[34] Thus, it may be a better strategy to *prevent* substance-related disorders from developing in the first place.

Prevention programs for substance-abuse that target school-age children and adolescents do exist. Often, however, they merely provide information, advice, or warnings. The popular "Just Say No" campaign, for instance, is not likely to be very effective because it does not teach youngsters the assertive behaviors they require to successfully refuse drugs. In contrast, there are cognitive-behavioral programs for preventing depression that teach children and adolescents coping skills to deal with stress-evoking events that are likely to trigger depression.[35] These programs usually are offered to groups identified as being at risk for developing depression, such as children from households containing significant parental conflict[36] and adolescents whose parents have depressive disorders.[37] Similar coping-skills interventions might be effective in preventing anxiety disorders[38] and even substance-related disorders in at-risk adolescents.

The idea of behavioral prevention is not new.[39] You have read about behavioral programs developed to prevent couple relationship problems (Chapter 13), depression (Chapter 14), and medical disorders (Chapter 15), for example. Recently, behavior therapists have begun to explore interventions for preventing posttraumatic stress disorder in trauma victims.[40] However, the number of preventive efforts is very small relative to treatment efforts.[41] Also, behavioral preventive interventions for the most part have been narrow in scope, focusing on children and adolescents[42] and on medical disorders and associated psychological disorders (such as post-surgery depression).

The potential for preventing psychological disorders using behavioral interventions is great, and it is an important challenge for the future. There are four major obstacles facing preventive efforts.[43] First, people are generally not strongly motivated to participate in prevention programs because they are not presently experiencing the need for help and so participation rates may be as low as 20% to 30%.[44] Second, long-term maintenance of the benefits of preventive interventions may not occur because the target of prevention is not likely to occur for many years.[45] Third, many prevention programs are begun as research efforts, and often they are not continued after the research is completed.[46] Finally, because prevention efforts target the future development of disorders, they require long-term evaluation of their effects, which conflicts with social and political pressures for instant success. For example, legislators who authorize funding for prevention programs expect to see the benefits quickly, which is not possible.

Treating Culturally Diverse Clients

Over the past 20 years, behavior therapists have become increasingly aware of the need to be responsive to *specific* issues of ethnic and cultural minorities, and you have seen examples of these efforts in preceding chapters. Empirical evidence from a variety of sources points to this need. The United States is becoming increasingly ethnically diverse, with ethnic minorities comprising an estimated 25% of the population.[47] Yet, a content analysis of research articles published in the 1970s through the early 1990s in three leading behavior therapy journals revealed that only 1.3% focused on U.S. ethnic minority groups.[48] The need for more behavior therapists who are members of ethnic minority groups is documented by the finding that although the U.S. population is becoming more diverse, the demographics of students being trained in behavior therapy and of faculty at behavior therapy training institutions has remained stable.[49]

Before addressing some specific challenges regarding cultural diversity that behavior therapists need to address, one important point should be kept in mind. Behavior therapy is inherently suited to assessing and treating clients from diverse ethnic and cultural backgrounds by virtue of its basic principles. The emphasis on the role of the environment, including the client's sociocultural background and unique life circumstances, is a key element in assessing the maintaining conditions of each client's problems. A number of behavioral assessment procedures—especially systematic naturalistic observation, self-monitoring, and physiological measures—are likely to be culturally unbiased.[50] Treatments are designed based on the unique maintaining conditions of the client's target behavior, and standard therapy procedures are tailored for each client.[51] These assets that the behavioral approach brings to the treatment of problems of diverse clients notwithstanding, many specific issues require increased attention.[52]

Cultural identity—as well as race, gender, and sexual orientation—can affect the course and outcome of therapy.[53] For instance, some African-American clients' distrust of European-American therapists may reflect a healthy response to the realities of racism. However, a culturally insensitive therapist may misinterpret this as paranoid behavior. As another example, in the area of child rearing, there are important cultural differences regarding issues such as methods of discipline and family privacy. Unfortunately, there are no data to suggest how to modify and tailor behavioral parent training to ethnic minority families. Research is needed to provide (1) greater understanding of how different ethnic groups perceive, define, and interpret problem behaviors (for example, whether non–European-Americans view noncompliance with parental requests, a major focus of behavioral parent training, as problematic); (2) information about the acceptability of specific behavioral treatment components, such as reinforcement versus punishment-based therapies, in different cultures;[54] and (3) data on the relative effectiveness of traditional behavioral parent training for ethnic minority families.[55]

Assessment methods should be chosen with the client's cultural background in mind. For example, many Native Americans value paying attention to *actions* rather than to verbal accounts, and they believe that asking questions is rude.[56] Accordingly, a Native-American client might have more confidence in systematic naturalistic observation than in an interview as a means of assessment. Culturally sensitive assessment also requires that behavior therapists be aware of cultural differences in the primary symptoms that clients with a particular disorder exhibit. For example, Chinese and Southeast Asian refugees in the United States suffering from depression frequently exhibit somatic complaints, such as headaches and chest pains, more than a sad mood.[57]

Providing behavior therapy interventions and a therapeutic environment that are sensitive to differences among clients of varying cultural backgrounds is challenging.[58] To begin with, clients' cultural identities impact their preferences for type of therapy and therapist style. For instance, many Asian-American clients prefer a therapist who serves as an authority figure.[59] Japanese-American women, who are unaccustomed to directly communicating negative emotions or private topics with strangers, are likely to prefer indirect means of communication, such as through the use of a thought diary rather than through verbal reports.[60] Therapy with Hispanic clients may be more effective when the therapist allows for a period of familiarizing "small talk" before launching into goal-directed activities.

The particular therapy procedures chosen must take into account unique aspects of the client's general cultural identity.[61] For example, because Native Americans value action over words, they are more likely to find the collaborative empiricism of cognitive therapy (that is, gathering evidence for one's beliefs) more acceptable than the rational disputation of rational emotive behavior therapy. Clients from cultures that stigmatize having psychological problems (for example Portuguese, Pakistani, and ultra-Orthodox Jewish) and seeking treatment for them (for example, German and French Canadian)[62] may find problem-solving therapy acceptable because *solving problems* does not have the same negative connotations as *therapy*. And, attempting to increase eye contact as part of social skills training with Navajos might be inappropriate because, in their culture, extended eye contact is viewed as an aggressive act.[63]

Effective therapy with clients from diverse backgrounds requires that the therapist become knowledgeable about as well as sensitive and open to issues such as (1) what people in the client's culture consider normal and abnormal behavior (for instance, seeing and speaking with entities from the spirit world may be regarded as normal), (2) clients' culturally based conceptions of psychological problems, (3) cultural differences in acceptable social behaviors (for example, Japanese women traditionally behave unassertively), and (4) who are considered appropriate and inappropriate behavior change agents (for instance, in some Southeast Asian cultures, a woman is not permitted to be alone with a man other than her husband).[64]

Behavior therapists have begun to attend to the impact of cultural diversity as well as other forms of diversity, such as age,[65] gender,[66] and sexual orientation.[67] Most of the work so far has consisted of proposing guidelines, including recommendations of appropriate therapy techniques for clients with particular cultural and ethnic backgrounds. Regrettably, these guidelines have a number of serious flaws.[68] First, in many cases the recommended practices for different ethnic minority groups are very similar. For example, a problem-centered, present-oriented approach has been suggested as optimal for Latino,[69] Japanese-American,[70] and African-American clients.[71] Second, the recommendations often are already an integral part of the practice of behavior therapy. In the previous example, behavior therapy is a problem-centered and present-oriented approach to treatment. Thus, nothing new has been added to already established practices. Third, many of the guidelines proposed for clients with a specific ethnic background stem from cultural stereotypes,[72] and it may be difficult to distinguish between useful generalizations and misleading stereotypes.[73] Fourth, a number of proposed guidelines are not specific to behavior therapy, but rather could be applied to any professional/business dealings with people. For instance, it has been recommended that behavior therapists address Latino clients respectfully by referring to them as *Señorita*, *Señora*, or *Señor* along with their last names and maintaining a humble attitude while interacting with them.[74] Fifth, and most important, the guidelines that have been proposed thus far rest on speculation gleaned from cultural norms.[75] It will be important in the future to develop empirically based recommendations for optimally serving diverse clients. This will require specifically testing the efficacy and effectiveness of behavior therapies with culturally diverse clients, which, to date, has generally not been done (despite exceptions you have read about in this book).[76]

Providing Behavior Therapy for Elderly Clients

As with cultural minorities, the elderly population is increasing yet remains underserved by behavior therapists. One commentator has mused that

> if an alien were to land on Earth and survey the activities of behavior therapists . . .
> the alien easily could decide that behavior therapy is intended for adults aged 18
> to 40. . . . Although this conclusion could be argued with, in some respects
> the alien's observations accurately reflect the majority of . . . [behavior
> therapists'] research and clinical efforts.[77]

Among the reasons for this state of affairs is that elderly clients do not have access to treatment when they are homebound. One alternative is to provide treatment in clients' homes, as through high-quality self-help manuals and interactive computer programs (as discussed in the next the section).[78]

Both general and specific guidelines are being proposed for customizing behavior therapy for elderly clients. General considerations include (1) slower pacing of treatment, (2) use of multimodal presentations (such as both visual and auditory), (3) increased use of modeling and behavior rehearsal, (4) use of memory aids (such as audiotapes and notebooks), and (5) interdisciplinary coordination of therapy (for example, with medical and social welfare personnel).[79]

Behavior therapists have begun to examine the effectiveness of behavior therapies with older adults for specific disorders, including schizophrenia,[80] depression,[81] sexual dysfunction,[82] and anxiety disorders.[83] These efforts involve identifying useful adaptations of standard therapies for elderly clients. For example, older adults with anxiety disorders appear to respond more favorably to brief/graduated exposure therapies than prolonged/intense exposure therapies. Additionally, for older adults with musculoskeletal conditions (such as arthritis), competing responses other than progressive relaxation (in which muscle tensing may be painful) are more appropriate; examples include listening to relaxing music and emotive imagery.[84]

Research has demonstrated that older adults suffering from depression respond well to brief cognitive-behavioral interventions with little alteration of the basic procedures.[85] However, when introducing the therapy to older clients, it may be necessary to dispel prevalent myths about elderly people, psychological disorders, and psychotherapy. These myths include: "Depression is a normal part of aging," "Therapy is only for 'crazy' people," and "You can't teach an old dog new tricks."[86]

Most nursing homes for the elderly have a small number of staff members who must care for a large number of residents. This poses major problems for dealing with disruptive behaviors that elderly residents with dementia exhibit. The typical solution is to use psychotropic medication as a "chemical restraint," which raises serious ethical issues.[87] Behavior therapy interventions may provide an alternative means of reducing disruptive behaviors. This effect was demonstrated in a nursing home in which psychotropic medication was frequently used to control behavioral problems (rather than treat psychiatric disorders). Thirty one residents (with a mean age of 80) who suffered from dementia had their medication dosage reduced and were treated for behaviors that the staff thought interfered most with the residents' functioning (verbally disruptive behaviors and demanding or combative behaviors).[88] The treatment consisted of modeling appropriate alternative behaviors, covert behavior rehearsal, and reinforcement. This treatment package led to improvement in the residents' overall functioning, and staff reports of disruptive behaviors declined.

Providing care for elderly people who are physically and cognitively challenged can be very stressful, especially when the person is a family member, and helping family caregivers deal with their stress is another arena in which behavior therapy could prove beneficial.[89] For example, in one program, the emotional stress of caregivers was reduced when they were taught cognitive-behavioral coping skills to manage their own distressing thoughts and actions and to deal with the problem behaviors of their care recipients.[90]

Employing Technology in Behavior Therapy

Behavior therapy has always made use of simple technology, such as mechanical devices for recording behaviors (see Chapter 5), a battery-operated apparatus for individually administering response cost to students in a classroom (see Chapter 7), the Self-Injurious Behavior Inhibiting System (see Chapter 7), and the use of video modeling (see Chapter 11). Occasionally, more sophisticated and costly technology has been used, such as biofeedback for pain (see Chapter 15) and virtual reality for exposure therapy (see Chapter 9).

For the most part, however, behavior therapy has not made extensive use of technology. In one way, this is a virtue. Technology often makes procedures complicated and costly, whereas simplicity has distinct advantages in therapy. All other things being equal, the simpler the therapy procedures, the more likely they are to work, especially when clients self-administer them.

Nonetheless, there are ways in which behavior therapy could use existing and future technology, especially technology that is readily accessible and relatively inexpensive.[91] For example, clients could use personal computers or cell phones to transmit information to their therapist by e-mail or on a Website. At the beginning of therapy, clients could send completed assessment forms, such as direct self-report inventories. During therapy, clients could keep the therapist informed of the outcome of ongoing homework assignments, such as their self-monitoring and practicing coping skills. This would allow therapists to provide feedback and modify assignments before the next therapy session, which, in some cases, might reduce the number of therapy sessions required.

Palmtop computers have been employed in the treatment of anxiety.[92] In the case of panic disorder, the palmtop computer, which clients are instructed to carry with them at all times, serves three purposes: (1) prompting clients to self-monitor the frequency and severity of their panic attacks; (2) prompting them to perform homework assignments; and (3) guiding clients through interoceptive exposure, cognitive restructuring, and breathing exercises.[93]

Increasingly, computers are being used to deliver therapy.[94] There is preliminary evidence for the effectiveness of cognitive-behavioral *computer-based therapy* (therapy solely via the computer) and *computer-assisted therapy* (combination of face-to-face and computer therapy) for a number of disorders in adults, including anxiety[95] and depression.[96] However, relatively few computer-based therapy programs for children and adolescents have been adequately tested, although the preliminary tests are promising.[97]

An interactive video program has been developed to teach parenting skills to teenage parents or parents-to-be.[98] The program teaches the skills through modeling, behavior rehearsal, and feedback for both correct and incorrect choices of solutions to problem situations. Participants control the pace of the lessons, and their success with each unit determines the content of the next unit. Another example of an interactive, computer-based program targets the reduction of alcohol consumption of clients who drink heavily.[99] The self-control training package consists of goal setting, self-monitoring, self-reinforcement, stimulus control procedures, coping skills training, and relapse prevention.

An Internet-guided self-help program for the treatment of phobic and panic disorders has shown some success.[100] Clients seeking help at a clinic were randomly assigned to a cognitive-behavior treatment package (including relaxation training and cognitive restructuring) with and without self-exposure exercises over 10 weeks. All clients in the Internet program had six brief telephone support calls. Both treatments led to improvements, but the clients who engaged in self-exposure improved significantly more.

As the preceding examples suggest, the use of computer-assisted therapy may be a promising way to enhance the cost-effectiveness of therapies by reducing therapist contact-time with the client. Moreover, computer-assisted behavior therapy (1) can provide standardized therapy procedures and facilitate dissemination of empirically supported treatments; (2) may be useful for reaching a wide audience of clients with limited English proficiency because the computer programs can be translated into any language; (3) allows clients to control the pace of their treatment; (4) affords clients privacy, which may increase the acceptability of therapy; and (5) increases the accessibility of treatment to clients who are unable to engage in face-to-face behavior therapy (such as clients who live in isolated areas). Disadvantages of computer-assisted behavior therapy include (1) the absence of a face-to-face therapist–client relationship; (2) reduced ability to individualize therapy; (3) potentially greater difficulties in monitoring clients' compliance with prescribed treatment procedures; and (4) the danger of violation of confidentiality with Internet-based treatments.[101]

Using Precise Terminology

Precision is essential to the scientific ethic inherent in behavior therapy, and precision in specifying goals, target behaviors, and treatment procedures is a strength of behavior therapy. Yet, behavior therapists frequently use imprecise terminology in at least three ways.

First, some standard terms in the field are inaccurate and potentially misleading. A prime example is *time out from positive reinforcement*. The correct term for the technique, as it is practiced, is *time out from generalized reinforcers*. This is because what the client is temporarily deprived of (for example, participating in enjoyable activities) has not been identified as a *reinforcer* for the client (in order words, it is not known if it would increase the future occurrence of a behavior). Instead, the typical time-out environment (a bare room or facing a blank wall) removes *potential* reinforcers for the client, things that generally serve as reinforcers for similar clients—that is, generalized reinforcers. Also, the abbreviated term *time out* has the unfortunate negative connotation of isolation similar to solitary confinement. This association is erroneous because the time-out period is brief.

Another example of imprecise terminology is the indiscriminate use of the term *reward* as a synonym for *reinforcer*. A reward specifically refers to a pleasant consequence for engaging in a behavior, but not necessarily one that increases the likelihood that the person will perform the behavior again (which is what defines a reinforcer).

A second problem with imprecision of terms is that behavior therapists frequently label behavior therapy procedures inconsistently in their writing and speech. The result is that it is unclear which therapy procedure is being referred to. This issue was discussed in In Theory 10-2 (page 258) with regard to exposure therapies. It is even more problematic with cognitive-behavioral therapies, where many published reports indicate that clients were treated by "cognitive-behavioral therapy," without specifying which of the many variants of cognitive-behavioral therapy was used. Among the causes of this problem are the faulty assumption that behavior therapists will know what is meant by a particular therapy label and the fact that often there are no agreed-upon definitions. A prototypical example is the use of the generic term *cognitive-behavioral therapy* (which includes many therapies) to refer to *cognitive therapy* (the specific therapy originally developed by Beck).[102] To add to the confusion, some people use the term *cognitive therapy* as a generic label for all therapies that change clients' cognitions or views of the world including interventions that are not behavior therapy, such as fixed-role therapy and other constructivist psychotherapies.

The result of the lack of agreed-upon and adhered-to labels for behavior therapies is that interpreting the results of studies of behavior therapies can be ambiguous and misleading.[103] This is especially problematic when a study reports the use of a treatment package and does not specify its components. Recently, an international group of psychotherapists, led by veteran behavior therapist Isaac Marks in England, have begun to develop a lexicon of common language for all psychotherapies, which, if followed, should mitigate the problem of the absence of standard definitions for therapy procedures.[104] Of course, whether the standard definitions are used remains to be seen.

A third way in which behavior therapists use terminology carelessly concerns the words they use to refer to clients. Behavior therapy deals with behaviors—what people *do*—rather than hypothetical traits or intrapsychic states. This means that behavior therapists should view their clients as human beings who *exhibit* maladaptive behaviors that are a part of their disorder or who *suffer from* psychological disorders. Clients are not their disorders and should not be equated with them (no more than people with diabetes or cancer should be viewed entirely in terms of their physical illness). Thus, labeling clients in terms of their disorder should be verboten for behavior therapists (as was discussed in In Theory 5-1, page 82), but it is common practice. It is easier to refer to a client as *a schizophrenic* or as *an obsessive-compulsive* than to say that the client "*has schizophrenia*" or "*suffers from obsessive-compulsive disorder.*" However, this sloppiness of language all too often results in viewing clients solely in terms of their problems, rather than as *people with problems*. This distinction is meaningful and the failure to make it has serious negative consequences, including the deleterious effects of labeling people and stigmatizing them. Granted, labeling clients is a widespread practice among mental health workers of all theoretical persuasions and professions. However, behavior therapists are particularly guilty when they label people because doing so is counter to their theoretical perspective. As testament to the feasibility of communicating about clients without labeling them, this entire book has been written without once describing clients as their disorders.

The challenge with regard to precision in terminology is straightforward. Behavior therapists must practice what they preach and be in concert with their scientific approach to therapy, which includes being precise.

Promoting Widespread Use of Empirically Supported Behavior Therapies

For a large array of problems and client populations, a majority of the psychotherapies that have been deemed *empirically supported* are behavior therapies.[105] Nonetheless, mental health practitioners in general have not widely adopted these treatment methods.[106]

Consider a few examples of the underutilization of empirically supported behavior therapies. Although interoceptive exposure therapy (see Chapter 9) is the treatment of choice for panic disorder, most clients with panic disorder do not receive this treatment.[107] Similarly, although cognitive-behavioral approaches are among the treatments of choice for bulimia nervosa, they have not been widely implemented.[108] And, despite evidence that 70% of children with enuresis are successfully treated by urine alarm systems, less than 5% of primary care physicians recommend it.[109] The list of poorly utilized empirically validated treatments could be extended, and it is clear that increasing the use of effective behavior therapies is important. After all, the most effective treatments are only effective if they are used.

What accounts for the underuse of effective therapies? To begin with, therapists who are not behaviorally oriented may choose, on theoretical or ideological grounds, not to employ empirically supported behavior therapies. For example, from a psychoanalyst's perspective, it is necessary to explore clients' unconscious memories that hold the key to clients' problems, which, of course, behavior therapies do not do.

A second explanation stems from the fact that, in contrast to behavior therapists, most nonbehavioral clinicians were not trained to value an empirical approach to treating clients[110] and to use empirically supported procedures.[111] The majority of practicing psychotherapists classify themselves as *eclectic*, which means that they use a variety of therapy techniques from a number of different theoretical approaches. Eclectic psychotherapists choose the therapy techniques they employ for each client based on their intuition and clinical experience—what they *believe* will work best for the client. Obviously, the eclectic psychotherapists' approach of selecting appropriate treatments is quite different from the behavior therapists' approach of selecting treatments that have been empirically supported for a particular disorder.

Finally, practicing clinicians may not be aware of or may not have access to empirically supported behavior therapies. Behavior therapists have recently begun to address this problem by considering ways of disseminating effective treatments.[112]

The use of treatment manuals is a major strategy for increasing the dissemination of empirically supported behavior therapies.[113] Treatment manuals contain detailed session-by-session procedures for the treatment of a specific disorder. Manuals used in clinical practice have evolved from research protocols employed in efficacy studies[114] and are adapted to community-based settings. As an example, a program for training school counselors to treat anxiety disorders with inner-city students employed a modified cognitive-behavioral treatment that had been shown to be efficacious in randomized clinical trials.[115]

A major advantage of well-written treatment manuals is that therapists who have not otherwise been trained in a therapy can implement it using the manual.[116] Although treatment manuals make empirically supported treatments available to clinicians, their existence does not necessarily assure that clinicians will use them. For instance, a recent survey of therapists treating eating disorders revealed that only 6% indicated that they used treatment manuals.[117]

The major criticism of using treatment manuals is that adhering to the standard procedures does not allow the treatment to be tailored for clients' unique problems.[118] However, those in favor of treatment manuals note that using them does not preclude therapists' applying their clinical judgment to adjust procedures so that they fit for individual clients.[119] The challenge is to be able to modify the standard procedures while still maintaining the elements that are essential to a treatment's effectiveness.

The availability of treatment manuals makes empirically supported behavior therapies accessible to clinicians, but the major obstacle to dissemination is influencing clinicians to use them.[120] It requires educating and convincing the majority of clinicians who are less scientifically oriented than behavior therapists about the merits of using empirically supported treatments. This clearly is a challenge for the future.

ALL THINGS CONSIDERED: BEHAVIOR THERAPY

Once upon a time—actually about 50 years ago—behavior therapy was like a new family of kids that moved into the psychotherapy neighborhood that was inhabited almost exclusively by one dominant family, psychoanalysis. Accordingly, behavior therapy initially had a hard time gaining acceptance. When verbal taunts (such as behavior therapy treated only the simplest problems or resulted in symptom substitution) did not scare behavior therapists away, the old-timers placed seemingly impossible barriers in their path. Behavior therapists were allowed to treat only the most difficult cases, those for whom established therapies had been ineffective. Believing they were omnipotent, as youngsters often do, the new kids enthusiastically accepted the challenge. The result was some remarkable successes with so-called hopeless clients. So it came to pass that the established family had no choice but to allow the new family, which by this time had expanded in size, to take up legitimate residence in the neighborhood.

At this point, the kids had grown into teenagers, and they began to fight among themselves (which was predictable now that their common external adversaries were leaving them alone). Some of the teenagers began to *think*—a process that most of the other teens did not trust because they could not see it. The result of this infighting was an *informal* division into a behavioral side of the family and a cognitive-behavioral side. The cognitive-behavioral side eventually came to outnumber the behavioral side.[121] Sibling rivalry still arises occasionally,[122] but for the most part, harmony exists because the siblings recognize that they are part of the same family—behavior therapy.[123]

Recently, a new tension has arisen in the family with the advent of a third generation of behavior therapies. While most members of the third generation acknowledge that they are related to previous generations, a few especially vocal members are prone to asserting their independence and an assumption of superiority that is no doubt due to the exuberance and hubris of youth, which may diminish with maturity.

The behavior therapy family has grown considerably over the past 50 years in both number and stature. Today it is the predominant family in the psychotherapy neighborhood. The stature of behavior therapy in the current practice of psychotherapy is largely due to its effectiveness that is substantiated by a strong body of empirical evidence. Although all behavior therapies do not have equally high levels of empirical support, behavior

therapists are committed to subjecting their interventions to empirical validation, which is an expensive endeavor in terms of both time and money.
Behavior therapy's scientific ethic is perhaps its most unifying tenet.

Despite the strengths of behavior therapy, it is not a panacea. The effectiveness of behavior therapy in general varies with different disorders and client populations. Further, not all clients favor the behavioral approach, with
its emphasis on direct, concrete solutions to psychological problems.

Looking ahead, the advent of managed health care has raised many issues regarding the future of the treatment of psychological disorders.
Although it is too early to know all the implications of a predominant managed health care system, three imperatives are clear. First, accountability is
essential. Therapists must specify (1) the problems being treated, (2) clear-
cut goals and criteria for determining whether the goals have been met, and
(3) the specific treatment procedures being employed.[124] Accountability
should be an easy requirement for behavior therapists to meet because precision and measurement are essential elements of their approach. Second, the
treatments used must be empirically supported for the psychological disorder being treated.[125] Fortunately, behavior therapies are treatments of choice
for many disorders.[126] Third, managed health care emphasizes short-term
and cost-effective treatment. Generally, behavior therapies are relatively
brief, involving fewer therapy sessions and less overall professional time
than many other types of therapy.[127] Further, the emphasis on providing clients with self-control coping skills is cost-effective over time. What all this
means is that behavior therapy should fare well in the era of managed
health care.[128]

The commitment to empirical accountability in behavior therapy has
resulted in almost continual change in the field. Behavior therapists have
remained relatively open to new ideas, relying on empirical evidence to determine their merit. For instance, the current acceptance of cognitive factors in
behavior therapy, which initially had focused exclusively on overt behaviors,
came about because research demonstrated the effectiveness of cognitive-
behavioral therapies.

The fact that behavior therapists are self-critical is indicative of their
open-mindedness. They have increasingly recognized and accepted the limitations of behavior therapy as challenges to be addressed.[129] One example is
recognizing that procedures instituted during therapy do not ensure the durability of treatment effects. Thus, posttherapy procedures, including protracted
maintenance treatment, may be necessary with some problems and client
populations. Another example is acknowledging that traditional change strategies used in behavior therapy may not always be optimal. In some cases, acceptance strategies, such as those used in third-generation behavior therapies,
may be more effective in helping clients cope with their problems and make
their lives personally meaningful.

Continual self-assessment and a willingness to change characterize the dy-
namic field of behavior therapy. For us, these practices make being behavior
therapists exciting and challenging. Having come to the end of our book, we
hope you share our enthusiasm.

Demythifying Myths About Contemporary Behavior Therapy

You began your introduction to behavior therapy by judging whether 14 statements about behavior therapy were true or false (in Participation Exercise 1-1). You learned that all the statements are predominantly false; they all are commonly held myths or misconceptions about behavior therapy. At this point, you should know *why* each of the statements is predominantly false. As a final check of your understanding of contemporary behavior therapy, read each of the statements again and write specific reasons why each is false. When you have finished, compare your reasons with those in your Student Resource Manual.

1. Behavior therapy is the application of well-established laws of learning.
2. Behavior therapy directly changes symptoms of a disorder.
3. A trusting relationship between client and therapist is not necessary for behavior therapy to be effective.
4. Behavior therapy does not deal with problems of feelings, such as depression and anger.
5. Generally, little verbal interchange takes place between the therapist and client in behavior therapy.
6. The client's cooperation is not necessary for behavior therapy to be successful.
7. Most clients in behavior therapy are treated in fewer than five sessions.
8. Behavior therapy is not applicable to changing mental processes such as thoughts and beliefs.
9. Positive reinforcement works better with children than with adults.
10. Many behavior therapy procedures use painful or aversive treatments.
11. Behavior therapy primarily deals with relatively simple problems, such as phobias (for example, fear of snakes) or undesirable habits (for instance, smoking).
12. The behavior therapist determines the goals of therapy.
13. The behavior therapist primarily is responsible for the success of therapy.
14. Because behavior therapy treats the symptoms of a disorder and not its underlying cause, once the symptoms are removed, others will develop because the cause of the symptoms has not been treated.

SUMMARY

1. Five major strengths of behavior therapy are its precision in specifying goals, target behaviors, and procedures; its efficacy and effectiveness; its efficiency; its breadth and complexity of applications; and its ethical practices.
2. One major challenge for behavior therapy is designing procedures that increase the durability of change when treatment ends. The two major strategies used to enhance durability during behavior therapy are

teaching clients self-control coping skills and ensuring that clients' natural environments provide the necessary antecedents and consequences to maintain treatment gains. Three posttherapy strategies are used to promote durability of treatment gains: relapse prevention, booster sessions, and maintenance treatment.

3. A second major challenge for behavior therapy is to develop prevention programs using behavioral principles and techniques. Prevention is especially germane to problems for which behavior therapies have been least effective or for which there is no available treatment.

4. Providing assessment and therapy procedures that are sensitive to culturally diverse clients is a third challenge. Behavior therapy practices are, in general, sensitive to diversity because assessment and therapy procedures are tailored to the unique needs of each client. However, behavior therapies need to be empirically validated with minority populations. Many suggestions have been made for providing behavior therapy for clients from specific cultural backgrounds, but so far there is no empirical support for them.

5. Providing behavior therapy that is effective for the growing elderly population represents a fourth challenge.

6. Greater use of technology to enhance the efficiency and effectiveness of behavior therapy procedures is a fifth challenge.

7. Using precise terminology is a sixth challenge. Some standard terms in the field are inaccurate and potentially misleading, there are frequent inconsistencies in the labeling of behavior therapy procedures, and behavior therapists often label their clients in terms of their disorders rather than as clients with disorders.

8. A final challenge for behavior therapy is the promotion of widespread use of empirically supported behavior therapies. Treatment manuals are a major way in which these therapies can be widely disseminated.

9. Because behavior therapy emphasizes accountability, has demonstrated effectiveness, and is relatively brief, the field should fare well in this era of managed health care.

REFERENCE NOTES

1. Bergin & Strupp, 1972; Gottman & Markman, 1978; Strupp, 1978.
2. For example, Risley, 1995.
3. American Psychological Association, 1995; Crits-Christoph, Wilson, & Hollon, 2005; Deacon & Abramowitz, 2004; Kroenke, 2007; Sanderson, 2003; Weisz, Weersing, & Henggeler, 2005.
4. Addis & Carpenter, 1997; Kendall & Chambless, 1998.
5. DeAngelis, 2008.
6. Christensen, Jacobson, & Babcock, 1995; Franks, 1995; Jacobson, 1989, 1991.
7. Goldfried & Castonguay, 1993.
8. Compare with White, 1995.
9. For example, Lovell, Fullalove, Garvey, & Brooker, 2000.
10. For example, Barnett, 1996; Bracero, 1996; Cantor, 1995.
11. For example, Giles, 1991; Giles, Prial, & Neims, 1993.
12. For example, Weersing, Gonzalez, Campo, & Lucas, 2008.
13. For example, Agras & Berkowitz, 1994; Chen, 1995; Cottraux, 1993; Simos & Dimitriou, 1994.
14. For example, Beck, 1997; Dick-Siskin, 2002; Lemsky, 1996.

15. For example, Cottraux, 1993.
16. Compare with Richard, 1995.
17. For example, Barlow, 1994; Milne & Kennedy, 1993.
18. For example, Nelson & Politano, 1993.
19. Powers, Thompson, & Gallagher-Thompson, 2008.
20. Barlow, 1994.
21. For example, Chorpita, 1995; Shea et al., 1992.
22. Christensen, Jacobson & Babcock, 1995.
23. Rachman & Teasdale, 1969; Voegtlin, Lemere, Broz, & O'Hollaren, 1941.
24. Turner, Beidel, Spaulding, & Brown, 1995.
25. Jacobson, 1989.
26. Wolf, Braukmann, & Ramp, 1987.
27. Jacobson, 1989, p. 329.
28. Kendall, 1989.
29. Barlow, 1994; Chorpita, 1995; Shea et al., 1992.
30. Spiegler, 1983.
31. Jacobson, 1989.
32. For example, Foreyt, 1987, 1990.
33. For example, Bennett, 1987.
34. Compare with Foster, Jones, & Group, 2006.
35. Wolfe, Dozois, Fisman, & DePace, 2008.
36. Jaycox, Reivich, Gillham, & Seligman, 1994.
37. Clarke, Hawkins, Murphy, Sheeber, Lewinsohn, & Seeley, 1995.
38. Miller, 2008.
39. Poser, 1970; Spiegler, 1980.
40. Gray & Litz, 2005; Resnick, Acierno, Kilpatrick, & Holmes, 2005.
41. Rapee, 2008; Whittal, 2008.
42. For example, Clarke, Hawkins, Murphy, Sheeber, Lewinsohn, & Seeley, 1995; Jaycox, Reivich, Gillham, & Seligman, 1994; Miller, 2008; Wolfe, Dozois, Fisman, & DePace, 2008.
43. Rapee, 2008.
44. Gillham, Reivich, Jaycox, & Seligman, 1995; Heinrichs, Bertram, Kuschel, & Hahlweg, 2005.
45. Spence, Sheffield, & Donovan, 2005.
46. For example, Headey et al., 2006.
47. Iwamasa, 1997.
48. Iwamasa & Smith, 1996.
49. Neal-Barnett & Smith, 1996; Safren, 2001.
50. Paniagua, 1998.
51. For example, Hanson, Zamboanga, & Sedlar, 2000; Tanaka-Matsumi, Seiden, & Lam, 1996.
52. For example, Hanson, Zamboanga, & Sedlar, 2000; Harper & Iwamasa, 2000; Paniagua, 1998.
53. Hatch, Friedman, & Paradis, 1996; Landrine & Klonoff, 1995; Paradis, Friedman, Hatch, & Ackerman, 1996.
54. For example, Borrego, Ibanez, Spendlove, & Pemberton, 2007.
55. Forehand & Kotchik, 1996.
56. Reyna, 1996.
57. Tanaka-Matsumi & Higginbotham, 1994.
58. Iwamasa, 1996; Martin, 1995.
59. Chen, 1995; Toyokawa & Nedate, 1996.
60. Toyokawa & Nedate, 1996.
61. Fudge, 1996; Simos & Dimitriou, 1994; Tanaka-Matsumi & Higginbotham, 1994.
62. McGoldrick, Giordano, & Garcia-Preto, 2005.
63. Tanaka-Matsumi, Higginbotham, & Chang, 2002.
64. Tanaka-Matsumi, Higginbotham, & Chang, 2002; Tanaka-Matsumi & Seiden, 1994; Tanaka-Matsumi, Seiden, & Lam, 1996.
65. For example, Lemsky, 1996; Malec, 1995; Zeiss & Steffen, 1996.
66. For example, McNair, 1996; Thase, Reynolds, Frank, Simons, McGeary, 1994.
67. Chesney & Folkman, 1994; Hunter & Schaecher, 1994; Mylott, 1994; Purcell, Campos, & Perilla, 1996.
68. Compare with Iwamasa, 1999.
69. Organista & Muñoz, 1996.
70. Toyokawa & Nedate, 1996.
71. McNair, 1996.
72. For example, Abudabbeh & Hays, 2006; McNair, 1996; Organista & Muñoz, 1996; Paradis, Cukor, & Friedman, 2006.
73. Preciado, 1999.
74. Organista & Muñoz, 1996.
75. Huey & Pan, 2006.
76. For example, Horrell, 2008.
77. Beck, 1997, p. 1.
78. Azar, 2002.
79. Beck, 1997; Dick-Siskin, 2002.
80. Bartels, Mueser, & Miles, 1997.
81. Beck, 1997.
82. Fisher, Swingen, & O'Donahue, 1997; Sorocco, Kasl-Godley, & Zeiss, 2002.
83. Beck & Stanley, 1997.
84. Wetherell, 2002.
85. For example, Scogin & McElreath, 1994; Teri, Curtis, Gallagher-Thompson, & Thompson, 1994.
86. Dick-Siskin, 2002.
87. Office of Inspector General, 1996.

88. Mansdorf, Calapai, Caselli, Burstein, & Dimant, 1999.
89. Coon & Thompson, 2002.
90. Gallagher-Thompson et al., 2000.
91. For example, Gale, 1996.
92. Newman, Consoli, & Taylor, 1997, 1999.
93. Newman, Kenardy, Herman, & Taylor, 1997.
94. Marks, Cavanagh, Gega, 2007.
95. For example, Anderson, Jacobs, & Rothbaum, 2004; Klein, Richards, & Austin, 2006; Marks, Kenwright, McDonough, Whittaker, & Mataix-Cols, 2004.
96. For example, Andersson, Bergström, Holländare, Carlbring, Kaldo, & Ekelius, 2005; Christensen, Griffiths, & Jorm, 2004.
97. Khanna & Kendall, 2008; Ritterband, Andersson, Christensen, Carlbring, & Cuijpers, 2006; Spence, Holmes, March, & Lipp, 2006.
98. Lagges & Gordon, 1999.
99. Hester & Delaney, 1997.
100. Schneider, Mataix-Cols, Marks, & Bachofen, 2005.
101. Newman, Consoli, & Taylor, 1997.
102. Beck, 2005.
103. For example, Rao, Beidel, & Murray, 2008.
104. Common Language for Psychotherapy, 2008; Marks, Goldfried, Sungur, Newman, Moore, & Stricker, 2005.
105. Kendall & Chambless, 1998.
106. Becker, Zayfert, & Anderson, 2004; Cook, Schnurr, & Foa, 2004; Persons, 1997.
107. Barlow, 1994.
108. Wilson, 1997b.
109. Rushton, 1989.
110. Date, 1996.
111. Task Force, 1995.
112. Hansen, 2001; Persons, 1995, 1997; Wilson, 1997b.
113. For example, Addis & Carpenter, 1997; Heimberg, 1998.
114. Carroll & Rounsaville, 2008; Nezu & Nezu, 2008.
115. Ginsburg, Becker, Kingery, & Nichols, 2008.
116. McCulloch & McMurran, 2007.
117. Tobin, Banker, Weisberg, & Bowers, 2007.
118. Westin, Novotny, & Thompson-Brenner, 2004.
119. For example, Fairburn, Cooper, Shafran, & Wilson, 2008; Kendall & Beidas, 2007; Levitt, Malta, Martin, Davis, & Cloitre, 2007.
120. DiGiuseppe, 2007; Young, Connolly, & Lohr, 2008.
121. Craighead, 1990.
122. For example, Hawkins, 1997.
123. Compare with Hawkins, 1997.
124. For example, Cavaliere, 1995.
125. For example, Strosahl, 1995, 1996.
126. For example, Kendall & Chambless, 1998
127. For example, Bergan, 1995; Strosahl, 1995.
128. For example, Giles, 1991; Giles, Prial, Neims, 1993; compare with Cone, Alexander, Lichtszajn, & Mason, 1996.
129. Goldfried & Castonguay, 1993.

APPENDIX

Guidelines for Choosing a Behavior Therapist*

After the decision to seek therapy has been made, an individual may feel unsure about how to choose a therapist. Persons seeking therapy often find that they have no standards to use in evaluating potential therapists. There are many competent therapists of varying theoretical persuasions. The purpose of this guide is to provide you with information that might be useful in selecting a behavior therapist. No guideline can provide strict rules for selecting the best therapist for a particular individual. We can, however, suggest questions you might ask and areas of information you might want to cover with a potential behavior therapist before you make a final decision.

WHAT IS BEHAVIOR THERAPY?

There is no single definition of behavior therapy. Although some common points of view are shared by most behavior therapists, there is a wide diversity among those persons who call themselves behavior therapists. The definition that follows is meant to give you a general idea of what behavior therapy is. It is not, however, an absolute definition. The particular behavior therapist you select may agree with some parts of it and disagree with other parts. The following definition is adapted from "Behavior Modification: Perspective on a Current Issue," published by the National Institute of Mental Health:

> Behavior therapy is a particular kind of therapy that involves the application of findings from behavioral science research to help individuals change in ways they would like to change. There is an emphasis in behavior therapy on checking up

*The "Guidelines" were written by Marsha Linehan, Ph.D. (University of Washington, Seattle) during her tenure as membership chairperson of the Association for Advancement of Behavior Therapy, with a committee consisting of Richard Bootzin, Ph.D., Joseph Cautela, Ph.D., Perry London, Ph.D., Morris Perloff, Ph.D., Richard Stuart, D.S.W., and Todd Risley, Ph.D.

on how effective the therapy is by monitoring and evaluating the individual's progress. Most behaviorally oriented therapists believe that the current environment is most important in affecting the person's present behavior. Early life experiences, long-time intrapsychic conflicts, or the individual's personality structure are considered to be of less importance than what is happening in the person's life at the present time. The procedures used in behavior therapy are generally intended to improve the individual's self-control by expanding the person's skills, abilities, and independence.

QUALIFICATIONS AND TRAINING NECESSARY FOR PARTICULAR MENTAL HEALTH PROFESSIONALS

Behavior therapy can be done by a number of different mental health professionals. Competent behavior therapists are trained in many different disciplines, and the distinction between different types of mental health professions can sometimes be confusing. Therefore, we have listed below a brief description of the training received by different types of professionals who may offer behavior therapy.

Psychiatric Social Workers

A psychiatric social worker must have a college degree, plus at least 2 years of graduate training in a program accredited by the Council on Social Work Education. A psychiatric social worker who is certified by the Academy of Certified Social Workers (ACSW) must have a master's or doctoral degree in social work (M.S.W. or D.S.W.) from a program approved by the Council on Social Work Education, 2 years of post-degree experience in the practice of social work, and membership in the National Association of Social Workers. In addition, the certified psychiatric social worker must pass a written exam and submit several professional references. Licensing procedures vary from state to state.

Psychologists

Psychologists usually have doctoral degrees (Ph.D., Ed.D., or Psy.D.) from graduate programs approved by the American Psychological Association. The *National Register of Health Service Providers in Psychology* lists psychologists who have a doctoral degree from a regionally accredited university, have at least 2 years of supervised experience in health services, 1 of which is postdoctoral, and are licensed or certified by the state for the independent practice of psychology. After 5 years of post-doctoral experience, a psychologist may apply for credentials from the American Board of Professional Psychology. This involves a review by the Board of the applicant's experience and an examination that the applicant must pass. Licensing or certification procedures vary from state to state.

Psychiatrists

A psychiatrist must have a medical degree. Although technically an individual can practice psychiatry having had four years of medical school and a 1-year medical internship, most psychiatrists continue their training in a 3-year residency program in psychiatry. Psychiatrists who have Board certification have had 2 years of post-residency experience in practicing psychiatry and must have passed an examination given by the American Board of Psychiatry and Neurology.

PRACTICAL INFORMATION ABOUT THERAPISTS

You have the right to obtain the following information about any potential therapist. This information may be obtained from the referral person, over the phone with the therapist, or at your first visit with the therapist. Although you may not feel that all this information is relevant, you will need a substantial amount of it in order to evaluate whether a particular therapist would be good for you.

Your first session with a therapist should always be a consultation. This session does not commit you to working with the therapist. The goals in the first session should be to find out whether therapy would be useful for you and whether this particular therapist is likely to be helpful to you. During this session you may want to discuss with your therapist any values which are particularly important to you. If your therapist's views are very different from yours, you may want to find a therapist with whom you are more compatible. An important aspect of therapy for you will be the relationship between you and the therapist. This first session is a time for you to determine whether you will feel comfortable and confident working with this particular therapist.

The following are things you need to know about a prospective therapist.

Training and Qualifications

An earlier section of this guide gives a description of the qualifications and amount of training necessary for an individual to obtain a particular mental health-related degree. You should find out whether the individual therapist is licensed or certified by your state. If the person is not licensed or certified by your state, you may want to ask whether the person is being supervised by another mental health professional.

Because behavior therapists vary in types of training, there are no set rules on which professional qualifications would be best for any given person. It is common, though, for clients to want to know about the training, experience, and other professional qualifications of a potential therapist. Good therapists will not mind being asked questions about their qualifications and will freely give you any professional information which you request. If a therapist does not answer your questions, you should consult another therapist.

Fees

Many people feel uncomfortable asking about fees. However, it is important information which a good therapist will be quite willing to give a potential client. The following are financial questions you may want to cover with a therapist. This information may be obtained over the phone or during your first visit. You will want to know:

1. How much does the therapist charge per session?
2. Does the therapist charge according to income (sliding scale)?
3. Does the therapist charge for the initial session? (Since many therapists *do* charge for the initial session, you should get this information before your first visit.)
4. Is there a policy concerning vacations and missed or cancelled sessions? Is there a charge?
5. Will your health insurance cover you if you see this therapist?
6. Will the therapist want you to pay after each session, or will you be billed periodically?

Other Questions

The following are other questions you may want to ask a potential therapist:

1. How many times a week will the therapist want to see you?
2. How long will each session last?
3. How long does the therapist expect treatment to last? (Some therapists only do time-limited therapy, whereas others set no such limits.)
4. What are some of the treatment approaches likely to be used?
5. Does the therapist accept phone calls at the office or at home?
6. When your therapist is out of town or otherwise unavailable, is there someone else you can call if an emergency arises?
7. Are there any limitations on confidentiality?

QUESTIONS TO ASK WHEN DECIDING ON A THERAPIST

A behavior therapist will devote the first few sessions to assessing the extent and causes of the concerns that you have. Generally, your therapist will be asking quite specific questions about the concerns or problems causing you distress and about when and where these occur. As the assessment progresses, you can expect that you and your therapist will arrive at mutually agreeable goals for how you want to change. If you cannot agree on the goals of therapy, you should consider finding another therapist.

Once the initial goals are decided upon, you can expect the therapist to discuss with you one or more approaches for helping you reach your goals. As you continue therapy, you can expect your therapist to continually evaluate with you your progress toward these goals. If you are not progressing, or if progress is too slow, your therapist will most likely suggest modifying or changing the treatment approach. At each of these points you may want to ask yourself the following questions:

1. Do you understand what the therapist has asked you to do?
2. Do the therapist's instructions seem relevant to your objectives?
3. Do you believe that following these instructions is likely to help you make significant progress?

4. Has the therapist given you a choice of alternative therapy approaches?
5. Has the therapist explained possible side effects of the therapy?
6. Do you know what the therapist's own values are, to the extent that they are relevant to your problem?

WHAT TO DO IF YOU ARE DISSATISFIED WITH YOUR THERAPIST

Talk with Your Therapist

People often feel angry or frustrated at times about their therapy. If you do, you should discuss these concerns, dissatisfactions, and questions with the therapist. A good therapist will be open to hearing them and discussing your dissatisfactions with you.

Get a Second Opinion

If you feel that the issues and problems you have raised with your therapist are not being resolved, you may want to consider asking for a consultation with another professional. Usually the therapist you are seeing can suggest someone you can consult. If your therapist objects to your consulting another professional, you should change to another therapist who will not object.

Consider Changing Therapists

Many people feel that it is never acceptable to change therapists once therapy has begun. This is simply not true. Good therapists realize that they might not be appropriate for every person.

The most important thing you need to ask yourself when deciding to continue with a particular therapist is "Am I changing in the direction I want to change?" If you do not feel that you are improving, and if, after discussing this with your therapist, it does not appear likely to you that you will improve with this therapist, you should consult another therapist.

HOW TO GET THE NAMES OF BEHAVIOR THERAPISTS

If you don't already have the name of a therapist, you might try some of the following suggestions:

1. Ask for recommendations from your family physician, friends, and relatives.
2. Look through the Association for Behavioral and Cognitive Therapies Membership Directory. ABCT is not a certifying organization, and not all members listed offer behavior therapy. However, you might call people listed in the directory to ask for a referral. Members are listed by city and state, as well as alphabetically. You can write or call ABCT, 305 Seventh Avenue, 16th Floor, New York, NY 10001, phone (212) 647-1890, or visit www.ABCT.org.
3. Call your state psychological association or district psychiatric association, and ask for a referral. You can locate your state psychological association by writing or calling the American Psychological Association, 750 First Street, N.E., Washington, DC 20002, phone (800) 374-2721 or

(202) 336-5500, or by visiting www.APA.org. Only certified or licensed professionals will be referred by these organizations. District psychiatric associations can be found by calling or writing the American Psychiatric Association, 1000 Wilson Boulevard, Suite 1825, Arlington, VA 22209, phone (703) 907-7300; or by visiting www.psych.org.

4. Call the university psychology, social work, or medical school psychiatry departments in your area and ask for a referral. Ask to speak with someone in clinical or counseling psychology, the chairperson of the social work department, or the chairperson of the department of psychiatry.

5. Call your local community mental health clinic. The clinic may have a behavior therapist on the staff or be able to give you a referral.

6. Look in the directories of the American Psychological Association and the American Psychiatric Association. Copies of these directories should be in your public library. Members in these organizations will often be able to give you a referral.

7. Look in the *National Register of Health Service Providers in Psychology*, published by the Council of National Health Service Providers in Psychology, 1120 "G" Street, N.W., Suite 330, Washington, DC 20005, phone (202) 783-7663; or www.nationalregister.org. People listed might be able to give you a referral.

8. Look in the National Association of Social Workers' *Register of Clinical Social Workers*, published by the National Association of Social Workers, 750 First Street, N.E., Suite 700, Washington, DC 20002, phone (202) 408-8600; or www.socialworkers.org. People listed might be able to give you a referral.

GLOSSARY OF BEHAVIOR THERAPY TERMS

ABA study Single-subject reversal study consisting of three phases: baseline (A), treatment (B), and reversal (to baseline) (A).

ABAB study Single-subject reversal study consisting of four phases: baseline (A), treatment (B), reversal (to baseline) (A), and reinstatement of treatment (B).

ABC model Temporal sequence of antecedents, behavior, and consequences.

acceleration target behavior Adaptive behavior that is increased in therapy.

acceptability Measure of how palatable therapy procedures are to clients, therapists, and change agents.

acceptance Fully embracing one's experience at the moment, just as it is, and without judging it.

Acceptance and Commitment Therapy (ACT) Third-generation behavior therapy that fosters acceptance of unwanted thoughts and feelings and a commitment to acting in accord with one's values.

activity schedule List of the day's activities used in cognitive therapy to provide structure in clients' lives and motivate them to remain active.

adaptation period Initial period in systematic naturalistic observation in which observations are made, but the data are not used; allows the client to become accustomed to the observer's presence in order to reduce reactivity.

antecedents Events that occur or that are present before a behavior is performed.

anxiety hierarchy List of events that elicit anxiety, ranked in order of increasing anxiety.

anxiety-induction therapy Exposure therapy in which the client's level of anxiety is heightened initially in order to reduce it eventually.

assertion training Specific skills training procedures used to teach assertive behaviors.

assertive behaviors Actions that secure and maintain what one is entitled to without infringing on the rights of others.

automatic thoughts Maladaptive thoughts that appear to arise reflexively, without prior deliberation or reasoning.

aversion therapy Treatment that directly decelerates a maladaptive behavior by associating it with an unpleasant stimulus.

backup reinforcer Reinforcer that can be purchased with tokens in a token economy.

baseline Measurement of the natural occurrence of a target behavior prior to the introduction of treatment. It provides a standard for evaluating changes in a target behavior after a treatment has been introduced.

behavior Anything a person does.

behavior rehearsal Therapy procedure in which a client practices performing a target behavior.

behavioral activation Therapy, primarily used for depression, that identifies a client's reinforcing activities and then initiates the client's engaging in them.

behavioral approach (or avoidance) test Simulated observation to assess fear; clients are asked to engage in a series of steps that involve progressively more fear-inducing behaviors.

behavioral deficit Adaptive behavior that a client is not performing often enough, long enough, or intensely enough.

behavioral excess Maladaptive behavior that a client is performing too often, for too long, or too intensely.

behavioral momentum compliance training Technique used to get a client to comply with a low-probability request (one with which the client is not likely to comply) by preceding it with a series of high-probability requests (those with which the client is likely to comply).

behavioral parent training Treatment package taught to parents consisting of acceleration and deceleration behavior therapy procedures to effectively manage their child's behavioral problems.

biofeedback Specific information clients receive about their physiological processes.

booster treatment Additional treatment after therapy has been terminated, which is designed to promote long-term maintenance of therapeutic gains.

brief/graduated exposure therapy Treatment for anxiety in which the client experiences an anxiety-evoking event for a short period and in a gradual manner.

caring-days technique Behavioral couple therapy procedure in which each partner deliberately performs behaviors that the other partner believes indicate caring.

case study Research method that provides a detailed description of what transpires during the treatment of an individual client.

checklist List of potential problem behaviors; someone who knows the client well checks those behaviors that are problematic for the client.

clinical significance Change following therapy that makes a practical difference in the client's life.

cognitive defusion Letting go of the idea that one's thoughts are valid descriptions and explanations of one's experiences and seeing them as just thoughts.

cognitive fusion Tendency for humans to take their thoughts literally and to believe that they accurately describe how things are, rather than seeing them as just thoughts.

cognitive processing therapy Adaptation of cognitive therapy for stress disorders in which clients' written accounts of their precipitating trauma are used.

cognitive restructuring Cognitive-behavioral technique of recognizing maladaptive thoughts and replacing them with adaptive ones.

cognitive restructuring therapy Cognitive-behavioral treatment that teaches clients to substitute adaptive cognitions for the distorted, illogical, and erroneous cognitions that are maintaining their problem behaviors.

cognitive therapy Cognitive restructuring therapy that emphasizes empirically testing hypotheses about the validity of maladaptive beliefs.

cognitive-behavioral coping skills therapy Treatment that teaches clients specific cognitive and overt-behavioral skills to deal effectively with difficult situations.

cognitive-behavioral therapy Treatment that changes cognitions that are the maintaining conditions of psychological disorders.

collaborative empiricism Cognitive therapy procedure in which the therapist and client work together to frame the client's irrational beliefs as hypotheses and design homework "experiments" that the client uses to test these hypotheses.

competing responses Two behaviors that cannot easily be performed simultaneously.

consequences Events that occur as a result of a behavior being performed.

contingency contract Written agreement among the client, the therapist, and other change agents that specifies the relationship between target behaviors and their consequences.

continuous reinforcement schedule Schedule of reinforcement in which the target behavior is reinforced every time it is performed.

control group Clients in a therapy outcome experiment who do not receive the therapy and serve as a comparison with clients who receive the therapy.

coping desensitization Variation of systematic desensitization in which clients use anxiety-related bodily sensations as cues to actively cope with anxiety.

coping model Model who initially experiences difficulty performing a behavior and gradually becomes competent at it.

covert behavior Behavior that cannot be directly observed in other people, such as thinking and feeling.

covert behavior rehearsal Procedure in which clients visualize their practicing performing a target behavior.

covert modeling Procedure in which clients visualize a model's behaviors.

covert sensitization Aversion therapy in which an aversive stimulus and a maladaptive target behavior are associated completely in the client's imagination.

cue exposure Exposure therapy that exposes clients to cues associated with their addictive behaviors but prevents clients from engaging in the behaviors.

dead person rule "Never ask a client to do something a dead person can 'do'" reminds therapists to phrase target behaviors as active rather than passive behaviors.

deceleration target behavior Maladaptive behavior that is decreased in therapy.

dialectical behavior therapy (DBT) Third-generation behavior therapy for treating borderline personality disorder that includes individual therapy to deal with clients' immediate problems and group skills training.

dialectical persuasion Subtly highlighting the inconsistencies in a client's actions, beliefs, and values to help the client develop a balanced perspective that is congruent with her or his values.

differential reinforcement Indirectly decelerating a maladaptive behavior by reinforcing an alternative acceleration target behavior.

differential reinforcement of competing behaviors Indirectly decelerating a maladaptive behavior by reinforcing acceleration target behaviors that interfere with the simultaneous performance of the deceleration target behavior.

differential reinforcement of incompatible behaviors Indirectly decelerating a maladaptive behavior by reinforcing acceleration target behaviors that preclude the simultaneous performance of the deceleration target behavior.

differential reinforcement of low response rates Indirectly decelerating a maladaptive behavior by reinforcing the behavior when it occurs at a less frequent rate.

differential reinforcement of other (or alternative) behaviors Indirectly decelerating a maladaptive behavior by reinforcing any behaviors other than the deceleration target behavior.

differential relaxation Relaxing all muscles not essential to the behavior being performed.

direct self-report inventory
Questionnaire containing brief statements or questions requiring simple, discrete answers; clients' complete it themselves to provide information about their problem behaviors.

dry-bed training Treatment package for enuresis consisting of shaping and overcorrection.

dry-pants method Daytime version of dry-bed training.

effectiveness/effective The success of therapy in actual clinical settings (compare with *efficacy*).

efficacy/efficacious The success of therapy when it is assessed under ideal conditions—in research settings using rigorous controls and standardized procedures (compare with *effectiveness*).

emotive imagery Exposure therapy procedure in which the client uses pleasant thoughts as competing responses for anxiety.

environment All external influences on behaviors.

experiential avoidance Efforts to escape from or avoid unpleasant thoughts, emotions, and bodily sensations and the circumstances that might elicit them.

experiment Research method involving groups of clients; all the clients are dealt with in the same way except that some clients receive the therapy being tested and others do not.

exposure therapy Treatment for anxiety (and other negative emotional responses) that exposes clients, under carefully controlled conditions, to stimuli that create the anxiety.

extinction Process of withdrawing or withholding reinforcers in order to decrease maladaptive behaviors.

eye movement desensitization and reprocessing (EMDR) Exposure-based treatment package for alleviating upsetting memories about traumatic experiences; its basic components are imaginal flooding, cognitive restructuring, and the induction of rapid, rhythmic eye movements.

fading Process of gradually withdrawing prompts as the client performs the acceleration target behavior more frequently.

fear survey schedule Direct self-report inventory for rating the severity of fear or anxiety elicited by various situations and objects.

first-order change Changing the form or frequency of problem behaviors.

flooding Prolonged/intense in vivo or imaginal exposure to highly anxiety-evoking stimuli.

follow-up assessment (or follow-up) Measurement of the client's functioning some time after therapy has been terminated to determine the durability of the treatment effects.

functional analytic psychotherapy Behavior therapy that shapes clients' appropriate and adaptive interpersonal behaviors as they occur in the client–therapist relationship.

functional communication training Variant of differential reinforcement that teaches clients to use acceptable ways of communicating the desire for a reinforcer as an alternative to their typical unacceptable means of communicating the same message.

generalization Process in which changes occurring as a result of therapy influence behaviors other than those that were specifically treated.

generalized imitation The basic ability to learn by imitating others.

generalized reinforcer Event that functions as a reinforcer for many people.

graded task assignment Cognitive therapy shaping technique in which clients are encouraged to perform small sequential steps leading to a goal.

group contingency Procedure in which the behaviors of a group of clients as a whole determine the consequences for each member of the group.

group hierarchy Common anxiety hierarchy used for all the clients in group systematic desensitization.

habit reversal Treatment package for tics and nervous habits incorporating awareness training, relaxation training, competing response training, and reinforcement.

homework assignments Specific therapeutic activities that clients carry out on their own in their everyday environments.

imitation Response in which a person behaves like a model who the person has observed.

implosive therapy Imaginal, prolonged/intense exposure therapy in which the client visualizes exaggerated scenes that include hypothesized stimuli related to the client's anxiety.

in vivo Term used to designate therapy procedures implemented in the client's natural environment (Latin for "in life").

in vivo desensitization Brief/graduated exposure to actual anxiety-evoking events.

in vivo flooding Prolonged/intense exposure to actual anxiety-evoking stimuli.

individual contingency Procedure in which the behaviors of an individual client determine the consequences for that client.

integrative behavioral couple therapy Behavioral couple therapy that employs techniques to create acceptance of one's partner's upsetting behaviors.

intermittent reinforcement schedule Schedule of reinforcement in which only some of the occurrences of a target behavior are reinforced.

interobserver reliability Extent to which two or more observers agree on their observations of a client's behaviors.

interoceptive exposure Therapy procedure that induces physical sensations of panic attacks so that clients can practice using cognitive-behavioral coping skills to deal with panic attacks.

interrater reliability Extent to which two or more raters agree on their ratings of a client's behaviors.

live model Model who is actually present ("in the flesh").

long-term maintenance (or maintenance) Durability over time of changes that occur as a result of therapy.

maintaining antecedents Prerequisites and situational cues, present before a behavior is performed, that set the stage for or elicit the behavior.

maintaining conditions Antecedents and consequences of a behavior that cause the behavior to be performed.

maintaining consequences Events that occur as a result of a behavior being performed and increase the likelihood that the behavior will be repeated.

maintenance *See* long-term maintenance.

massed negative practice Treatment for tics in which the client deliberately performs the tic as rapidly as possible for a set period.

mastery and pleasure rating Cognitive therapy technique in which clients rate the degree of success and enjoyment they experience engaging in an activity.

mastery model Model who, from the outset, performs a target behavior competently.

meta-analysis Research method that integrates and compares empirical findings from multiple studies regarding a specific research question.

mindfulness Paying attention without judgment to whatever is happening at the moment.

mindfulness-based cognitive therapy (MBCT) Third-generation behavior therapy for preventing recurrence of episodes of major depression; mind-fulness exercises are employed to teach clients to become more aware of and less engaged with their negative thoughts.

model Person who demonstrates a behavior for another person.

modes of behavior The four types of behavior that are assessed and treated in behavior therapy: overt actions, cognitions, emotions, and physiological responses.

multimethod assessment Use of two or more methods to gather information about a target behavior and its maintaining conditions.

multimodal assessment Assessment of two or more of the four modes of behavior.

multiple baseline study Evaluates the effects of a therapy for multiple target behaviors, clients, or settings.

natural model Person in a client's natural environment who exhibits behaviors that the client can benefit from observing.

natural reinforcer A reinforcer that is readily available to clients in their natural environments.

negative punishment Removing a pleasant or desirable consequence for a behavior, which decreases the likelihood that the behavior will be repeated.

negative reinforcement Removing an unpleasant or undesirable consequence for a behavior, which increases the likelihood that the behavior will be repeated.

negative reinforcer Stimulus that is removed or avoided as a consequence of a behavior's being performed, which increases the likelihood that the behavior will be repeated.

noncontingent reinforcement Variant of differential reinforcement in which the reinforcer identified as maintaining a problem behavior is administered on a frequent fixed-interval schedule whether or not the client engages in the deceleration target behavior.

observer In modeling therapy, a client who observes a model's demonstrating a behavior.

overcorrection Punishment technique in which a client corrects the harmful effects of a deceleration target behavior (restitution) and then intensively practices an alternative acceleration target behavior (positive practice).

overt behavior Behavior that can be observed directly by other people.

pain behaviors Overt behaviors generally indicating a person is experiencing pain sensations (such as grimacing and saying, "Ouch!").

participant modeling Treatment in which the therapist models the target behavior for the client and then physically prompts the client to perform the target behavior.

perceived self-efficacy A person's belief that he or she can master a situation or be successful at performing a task.

physically aversive consequences Physically painful or noxious consequences used to decelerate a maladaptive target behavior.

positive punishment Presenting an unpleasant or undesirable consequence that decreases the likelihood that a behavior will be repeated.

positive reinforcement Presenting a pleasant or desirable consequence that increases the likelihood that a behavior will be repeated.

positive reinforcer Event presented as a consequence of a behavior's being performed, which increases the likelihood that the behavior will be repeated.

Premack principle Principle stating that a higher-probability behavior will serve as a reinforcer for a lower-probability behavior.

probable maintaining conditions The antecedents and consequences of a behavior that appear to be causing a behavior.

problem-solving therapy Cognitive-behavioral coping skills therapy in which clients use a series of systematic steps for solving a problem for which they specifically have sought treatment.

problem-solving training Cognitive-behavioral coping skills training to prepare people to use a series of systematic steps for dealing with problems that they may encounter in their daily lives.

progressive relaxation Systematically relaxing groups of skeletal muscles.

prolonged/intense exposure therapy Treatment in which the client experiences a highly anxiety-evoking event for a lengthy period (in order to ultimately reduce the anxiety).

prompt Cue that reminds, instructs, or guides a client to perform a behavior.

prompting Reminding, instructing, or guiding a client to perform a behavior.

psychological flexibility Having options for the behaviors one can engage in.

psychological inflexibility Narrowing of options for the behaviors one can engage in.

punisher Consequence of a behavior that decreases the likelihood that it will be repeated.

punishment Process by which the consequence of a behavior decreases the like-lihood that the behavior will be repeated.

rapid smoking Aversion therapy in which clients take one puff of a cigarette every 6 seconds, inhaling normally, and continue until they can no longer tolerate the procedure.

rating scale List of potential problem behaviors; someone who knows the client well rates the frequency or severity of each behavior for the client.

rational emotive behavior therapy (REBT) Cognitive restructuring therapy in which clients' irrational thoughts are directly challenged and replaced with rational thoughts.

rational emotive education Training in which children and adolescents learn to apply the basic principles and procedures of rational emotive behavior therapy in their daily lives.

reactivity Phenomenon in which people's behaviors change because they know they are being observed.

reinforcement Process by which the consequence of a behavior increases the likelihood that the behavior will be repeated.

reinforcer Consequence of a behavior that increases the likelihood that the behavior will be repeated.

reinforcer sampling Procedure for making a generalized reinforcer into a reinforcer for an individual client. The client first receives the generalized reinforcer noncontingently; then, when the client comes to value it, the client receives it contingently.

reinforcing agent A person who administers reinforcers.

relapse prevention Procedure for promoting long-term maintenance that involves identifying situations in which clients are likely to relapse, developing skills to cope with such situations, and creating a lifestyle balance that decreases the chances of relapse.

response cost Punishment technique in which a client's access to a valued item or privilege is removed as a consequence of performing a maladaptive behavior.

response prevention Exposure therapy procedure in which clients remain exposed to the threatening situation without engaging in their typical maladaptive anxiety-reducing responses.

retention control training Procedure used in treating enuresis that involves shaping the retention of increasingly greater amounts of urine for increasingly longer periods.

reversal phase Phase in a reversal study in which the therapy is withdrawn temporarily while the target behavior continues to be measured.

reversal study Single-subject study in which the therapy is applied to the target behavior and then is withdrawn temporarily to determine whether the therapy is causing the change in the target behavior.

role-playing Assessment or therapy technique in which clients act as if they were in actual problem situations to provide the therapist with samples of how they typically behave in the situations (assessment) or to practice adaptive behaviors (therapy).

schemas Broad, pervasive cognitive themes about oneself, others, and the world, which may stem from childhood experiences and are further developed throughout one's lifetime.

second-order change Changing the function of problem behaviors rather than their form or frequency.

self-control approach Training clients to initiate, implement, and evaluate behavior therapy procedures on their own.

self-efficacy *See* perceived self-efficacy.

self-instructional training Cognitive-behavioral coping skills therapy that teaches clients to instruct themselves verbally (usually silently) to cope effectively with difficult situations.

self-modeling Therapy procedure in which clients serve as their own models, by observing themselves on videotape or in their imaginations performing an acceleration target behavior.

self-recording (self-monitoring) Clients' observing and keeping records of their target behaviors.

self-reinforcement Process by which clients administer reinforcers to themselves for performing target behaviors.

self-talk What people "say" to themselves when they are thinking.

setting events Environmental conditions that elicit a behavior.

shaping Reinforcing components of a target behavior that are successively closer approximations of the complete target behavior.

simulated observation Observing a client's behaviors under conditions set up to resemble those in the client's natural environment.

situation-specific Term used to indicate that behaviors are influenced by the specific environmental context in which they are performed.

skills training Treatment package— including modeling, behavior rehearsal, and reinforcement—used to teach clients skills.

social reinforcers Reinforcers consisting of attention and affirmation from other people.

social skills Interpersonal competencies needed to interact successfully with others.

social validity Therapy outcome measure that evaluates whether a client's behaviors are similar to the behaviors of individuals judged to be functioning adaptively.

stimulus control Prompts or setting events that "set the stage" for behaviors to occur.

stimulus control procedures Procedures that change behaviors by modifying prompts or setting events.

stress inoculation training Cognitive-behavioral coping skills therapy in which clients learn coping skills for dealing with stressful situations and then practice the skills while being exposed to stressors.

Subjective Units of Discomfort scale (SUDs) Scale clients use to rate the level of anxiety they experience in anxiety-evoking situations; usually the scale ranges from 0, representing total calm, to 100, representing the highest level of anxiety the client can imagine.

symbolic model Model who is observed indirectly, such as on television, in books, and in one's imagination.

systematic desensitization Brief/graduated exposure therapy in which a client imagines successively more anxiety-evoking situations while engaging in a behavior that competes with anxiety.

systematic naturalistic observation Observation and recording of a predetermined set of overt behaviors as the client performs them in her or his natural environment.

tangible reinforcers Material objects that serve as reinforcers.

target behavior Aspect of a client's problem that is a relatively narrow and discrete behavior that can be clearly defined and easily measured; the focus of treatment in behavior therapy.

theft reversal Overcorrection treatment for stealing that involves exaggerated restitution, wherein a client is required not only to return the stolen items to the victim but also to purchase additional similar items for the victim.

thought stopping Cognitive-behavioral therapy in which clients interrupt disturbing thoughts by saying "Stop!" (usually silently) and then substitute a prepared pleasant thought for the disturbing thought.

time out from positive reinforcement (or time out) Punishment technique in which a client's access to generalized reinforcers is withdrawn for a few minutes after the client engages in a maladaptive behavior, often by placing the client in a time-out room or area.

time-out room Isolated room in which a client spends a time-out period with no access to generalized reinforcers.

token economy System for motivating clients in which they earn token reinforcers for adaptive behaviors and lose tokens for maladaptive behaviors; the tokens are exchanged for backup reinforcers.

token reinforcers Symbolic reinforcers, such as money and points, that can be exchanged for desired tangible reinforcers and reinforcing activities.

tokens In a token economy, symbolic reinforcers, such as money and points, that clients earn for performing adaptive behaviors and lose for performing maladaptive behaviors.

traditional behavioral couple therapy Behavioral couple therapy that focuses on communication and problem-solving skills training and increasing positive behavior exchanges.

transfer Process in which what is learned and practiced in one setting (such as in therapy) carries over to other settings (such as at home).

treatment group Clients in a therapy outcome experiment who receive the therapy.

treatment manual (or protocol) Detailed, session-by-session procedures for a therapist to follow in using a particular therapy.

treatment package Treatment consisting of two or more therapy procedures.

treatment plan The specific, individualized details of how the therapy procedures will be implemented for a particular client.

urine alarm Device to treat nocturnal enuresis that sounds an alarm to wake a child when the child begins to urinate; eventually the child associates bladder tension with awakening.

vicarious consequences Consequences of a model's behaviors that indicate the consequences that observers are likely to receive for imitating the model.

vicarious extinction Process by which a client's fear is reduced by observing a model perform the feared behavior without the model's incurring negative consequences.

vicarious punishment Consequences of a model's acts that decrease the likelihood that an observer will imitate the model.

vicarious reinforcement Consequences of a model's acts that increase the likelihood that an observer will imitate the model.

well behaviors Overt behaviors generally indicating that a person is not experiencing pain sensations.

GLOSSARY OF PSYCHOLOGICAL DISORDERS AND PROBLEMS

addictive behavior Recurrent use of substances (for example, alcohol) or engaging in other activities (for example, compulsive gambling) that involve physiological or psychological dependence and result in maladaptive consequences for the individual and others.

agoraphobia Anxiety disorder characterized by intense fear and avoidance of public places or other situations from which escape might be difficult should the individual experience anticipated incapacitating panic-like symptoms (*see* panic attack).

anorexia nervosa Eating disorder characterized by distorted body image, intense fear of gaining weight, intentional reduction in food intake, and excessive exercise, resulting in dangerously low body weight.

antisocial behavior Action characterized by a blatant disregard for and violation of other people's rights.

Asperger syndrome (disorder) Pervasive developmental disorder marked by impaired social interactions and limited repetitive patterns of behavior but with minimal impairment of cognitive functioning and language.

attention deficit hyperactivity disorder (ADHD) Disorder emerging in early childhood characterized by age-inappropriate inattention and hyperactive and impulsive behaviors.

autistic disorder Developmental disorder beginning in infancy characterized by severely impaired social interaction, delayed language development and communication, and highly restrictive and repetitive patterns of behavior.

binge eating Pattern of maladaptive eating in which a person consumes excessively large quantities of (usually high-caloric) food in a short period.

bipolar disorder Mood disorder characterized by fluctuations between depression and manic states.

body dysmorphic disorder Maladaptive preoccupation with an imagined defect or minor flaw in one's appearance.

borderline personality disorder Chronic and pervasive pattern of instability of interpersonal relationships, distorted self-image, poor regulation of emotions, and extreme impulsive behaviors.

bulimia nervosa Eating disorder involving recurrent episodes of uncontrolled binge eating followed by purging (through self-induced vomiting or abusing laxatives) to avoid weight gain.

chronic fatigue syndrome Pervasive fatigue lasting more than 6 months and resulting in a 50% reduction in daily activities.

chronic pain Pain occurring for a duration of at least 6 months after an injury has healed or when no trauma exists.

chronic psychiatric disorder Psychiatric disorder characterized by longstanding and severe psychological impairment in one's ability to function independently (such as schizophrenia).

compulsions Repetitive actions and ritualistic behaviors intended to suppress obsessions.

conversion disorder Physical impairment, such as paralysis or blindness, occurring in the absence of a known medical condition and associated with psychological factors.

delusions Blatantly false, maladaptive and disturbing beliefs people steadfastly hold despite contrary evidence (most often associated with schizophrenia).

dementia Progressive deterioration of brain functioning characterized by deficits in memory, abstract thinking, problem solving, judgment, and motor control.

depression Mood disorder characterized by intense sadness, feelings of despair and hopelessness, inability to experience pleasure, decreased physical energy, lack of motivation, distorted thinking, and often physical complaints.

developmental disability Handicapping condition in which one or more aspects of a person's development (for instance, intellectual, language, motor) are significantly delayed in comparison with the development of others of the same age.

eating disorder Disturbed pattern of eating associated with individuals' distorted perceptions of their body shape and weight.

enuresis Recurrent involuntary bedwetting or wetting of one's clothes after age 5, which has no organic cause.

essential hypertension Chronic high blood pressure with no apparent directly treatable physical cause.

generalized anxiety disorder Anxiety disorder characterized by excessive diffuse worry, tension, apprehension, and often physical complaints.

hallucinations False sensory perceptions that people experience as real (generally associated with schizophrenia).

hypertension *See* essential hypertension.

impulsive behavior Behavior characterized by a lack of forethought about the consequences of one's actions.

insomnia Difficulties initiating and maintaining sleep.

irritable bowel syndrome Stress-related disorder that results in abdominal pain and discomfort associated with altered bowel function, including constipation and diarrhea.

mental retardation Significantly subaverage intellectual functioning accompanied by difficulties with everyday, adaptive functioning.

nervous habit Repetitive manipulation of objects or movement of body parts, usually occurring when a person is anxious or experiencing stress.

obesity Weighing 20% or more than the maximum appropriate weight for a person (based on age, sex, height, and body build).

obsessions Persistent, unwanted intrusive thoughts.

obsessive-compulsive disorder Anxiety disorder involving unwanted, persistent intrusive thoughts (obsessions) and repetitive, ritualistic behaviors (compulsions) intended to suppress the obsessions.

oppositional behaviors Disruptive behaviors involving acting contrary to what is expected or requested by an authority figure.

panic attack Unexpected sudden occurrence of intense apprehension and terror accompanied by physical symptoms, such as shortness of breath, dizziness, heart palpitations, and chest pain.

panic disorder Anxiety disorder characterized by repeated panic attacks (*see* panic attack).

paraphilia Sexually deviant behavior in which a person is sexually aroused by socially inappropriate objects or individuals.

personality disorder Longstanding, pervasive pattern of maladaptive behaviors that are inflexible and involve distress and impairment.

phobic disorder Anxiety disorder characterized by disproportionate and irrational fear of specific objects, activities, or situations resulting in a compelling desire to avoid the feared stimuli.

posttraumatic stress disorder Anxiety disorder that emerges sometime after experiencing a traumatic event; it is characterized by emotional numbness, heightened vigilance and arousal, and the reliving of the traumatic event through mental flashbacks and nightmares.

ruminative vomiting (rumination disorder) Regurgitating and reswallowing of partially digested food, which interferes with nutritional intake and weight gain.

schizophrenia Severe, chronic psychiatric disorder characterized by hallucinations and delusions, emotional blunting, disorganized thought and speech, social withdrawal, and bizarre actions.

selective mutism Refusal to speak in certain social situations despite being able to speak.

self-injurious behaviors Physically harmful behaviors (such as head banging) people deliberately inflict on themselves.

separation anxiety Anxiety in children that involves excessive fear that harm will come to oneself or one's primary caregivers while apart from them, resulting in extreme distress when separating from primary caregivers.

sexual dysfunction Impaired functioning in sexual relations involving diminished sexual arousal and desire, inability to achieve sexual gratification, or the experience of pain during sexual intercourse.

skills deficit Absence of adaptive skills that impairs a person's functioning.

social anxiety Irrational fear and avoidance of social situations.

social phobia Anxiety disorder characterized by fear of scrutiny by others and being embarrassed in social situations.

social withdrawal Deliberate avoidance of being in the presence of other people.

substance abuse Recurrent substance use resulting in significant personal distress or adverse consequences.

substance dependence Disorder involving recurrent substance use that results in a physiological or psychological need for the substance in addition to personal distress and adverse consequences.

tic disorder Pattern of recurring, sudden, rapid involuntary motor movements or vocalizations.

Tourette's disorder Severe tic disorder involving multiple sudden, involuntary motor movements and vocalizations.

transvestic behavior (transvestism) Paraphilia in which a person is sexually aroused by dressing in clothing of the opposite sex.

Type A behavior Pattern of behavior characterized by competitive, achievement-oriented behaviors; engaging in multiple tasks simultaneously; and a constant monitoring of time.

REFERENCES

ABLON, J. S., & MARCI, C. (2004). Psychotherapy process: The missing link: Comment on Westen, Novotny, & Thompson-Brenner. *Psychological Bulletin, 130,* 664–668.

ABRAHMS, J. L. (1983). Cognitive-behavioral strategies to induce and enhance a collaborative set in distressed couples. In A. Freeman (Ed.), *Cognitive therapy with couples and groups* (pp. 125–155). New York: Plenum.

ABRAMOWITZ, J. S. (1996). Variants of exposure and response prevention in the treatment of obsessive-compulsive disorder: A meta-analysis. *Behavior Therapy, 27,* 583–600.

ABRAMOWITZ, J. S. (2001). Treatment of scrupulous obsessions and compulsions using exposure and response prevention: A case report. *Cognitive and Behavioral Practice, 8,* 79–85.

ABRAMOWITZ, J. S., FOA, E. B., & FRANKLIN, M. E. (2003). Exposure and ritual prevention for obsessive-compulsive disorder: Effects of intensive versus twice-weekly sessions. *Journal of Consulting and Clinical Psychology, 71,* 394–398.

ABRAMS, M., & ELLIS, A. (1994). Rational emotive behaviour therapy in the treatment of stress. *British Journal of Guidance and Counselling, 22,* 39–50.

ABUDABBEH, N., & HAYS, P. A. (2006). Cognitive-behavioral therapy with people of Arab heritage. In P. A. Hays & G. Y. Iwamasa (Eds.), *Culturally responsive cognitive-behavioral therapy: Assessment, practice, and supervision* (pp. 161–175). Washington, DC: American Psychological Association.

ACHENBACH, T. M. (1978). The Child Behavior Profile, I: Boys aged 6–11. *Journal of Consulting and Clinical Psychology, 46,* 478–488.

ADAMS, C. D., & KELLEY, M. L. (1992). Managing sibling aggression: Overcorrection as an alternative to time-out. *Behavior Therapy, 23,* 707–717.

ADDIS, M. E., & CARPENTER, K. M. (1997). Treatment manuals and the future of behavior therapy. *the Behavior Therapist, 20,* 53–55.

ADDIS, M. E., & JACOBSON, N. S. (2000). A closer look at the treatment rationale and homework compliance in cognitive-behavioral therapy for depression. *Cognitive Therapy and Research, 24,* 313–326.

AGRAS, W. S. (1976). Behavior modification in the general hospital psychiatric unit. In H. Leitenberg (Ed.), *Handbook of behavior modification and behavior therapy* (pp. 547–565). Englewood Cliffs, NJ: Prentice Hall.

AGRAS, W. S. (1993). Short-term psychological treatments for binge eating. In C. G. Fairburn & G. T. Wilson (Eds.), *Binge eating: Nature, assessment and treatment* (pp. 270–286). New York: Guilford.

AGRAS, W. S., & BERKOWITZ, R. I. (1994). Behavior therapy. In R. E. Hales, S. C. Yudofsky, & J. A. Talbott (Eds.), *The American Psychiatric Press textbook of psychiatry* (2nd ed., pp. 1061–1081). Washington, DC: American Psychiatric Press.

AGRAS, W. S., KAZDIN, A. E., & WILSON, G. T. (1979). *Behavior therapy: Toward an applied clinical science.* San Francisco: W. H. Freeman.

AGRAS, W. S., SCHNEIDER, J. A., ARNOW, B., RAEBURN, S. D., & TELCH, C. F. (1989). Cognitive-behavioral treatment with and without exposure plus response-prevention of bulimia nervosa: A reply to Leitenberg and Rosen. *Journal of Consulting and Clinical Psychology, 57,* 778–779.

AGRAS, W. S., TELCH, C. F., ARNOW, B., ELDREDGE, K., & MARNELL, M. (1997). One-year follow-up of cognitive-behavioral therapy for obese individuals with binge eating disorder. *Journal of Consulting and Clinical Psychology, 65,* 343–347.

AGRAS, W. S., WALSH, B. T., FAIRBURN, C. G., WILSON, G. T., & KRAEMER, H. C. (2000). A multicenter comparison of cognitive-behavioral therapy and interpersonal psychotherapy for bulimia nervosa. *Archives of General Psychiatry, 57,* 459–466.

AHRENS, J., & REXFORD, L. (2002). Cognitive processing therapy for incarcerated adolescents with PTSD. *Journal of Aggression, Maltreatment & Trauma, 6,* 201–216.

AIKEN, L. R. (1996). *Personality assessment: Methods and practices* (2nd ed.). Seattle: Hogrefe & Huber.

AJIBOLA, O., & CLEMENT, P. W. (1995). Differential effects of methylphenidate and self-reinforcement on attention-deficit hyperactive disorder. *Behavior Modification, 19,* 211–233.

ALBERTI, R., & EMMONS, M. (2001). *Your perfect right: Assertiveness and equality in your life and relationships* (8th ed.). San Luis Obispo, CA: Impact Publishers.

ALEXOPOULOS, G. S., RAUE, P., & AREAN, P. A. (2003). Problem-solving therapy versus supportive therapy in geriatric major depression with executive dysfunction. *American Journal of Geriatric Psychiatry, 11,* 46–52.

ALFORD, B. A. (1986). Behavioral treatment of schizophrenic delusions: A single-case experimental analysis. *Behavior Therapy, 17,* 637–644.

ALFORD, B. A., & BECK, A. T. (1994). Cognitive therapy of delusional beliefs. *Behaviour Research and Therapy, 32,* 369–380.

ALFORD, B. A., & BECK, A. T. (1997). *The integrative power of cognitive therapy.* New York: Guilford.

ALFORD, B. A., & CORREIA, C. J. (1994). Cognitive therapy of schizophrenia: Theory and empirical status. *Behavior Therapy, 25,* 17–33.

ALFORD, B. A., FREEMAN, A., BECK, A. T., & WRIGHT, F. (1990). Brief focused cognitive therapy of panic disorder. *Psychotherapy, 27,* 230–234.

ALLEN, K. D. (1998). The use of an enhanced simplified habit-reversal procedure to reduce disruptive outbursts during athletic performance. *Journal of Applied Behavior Analysis, 31,* 489–492.

ALLEN, K. D., DANFORTH, J. S., & DRABMAN, R. S. (1989). Videotaped modeling and film distraction for fear reduction in adults undergoing hyperbaric oxygen therapy. *Journal of Consulting and Clinical Psychology, 57,* 554–558.

ALLEN, K. D., & SHRIVER, M. D. (1998). Role of parent-mediated pain behavior management strategies in biofeedback treatment of childhood migraines. *Behavior Therapy, 29,* 477–490.

ALLEN, K. D., & WARZAK, W. J. (2000). The problem of parental nonadherence in clinical behavior analysis: Effective treatment is not enough. *Journal of Applied Behavior Analysis, 33,* 373–391.

ALLEN, L. B., McHUGH, R. K., & BARLOW, D. H. (2008). Emotional disorders: A unified protocol. In D. H. Barlow (Ed.), *Clinical handbook of psychological disorders: A step-by-step treatment manual* (4th ed., pp. 216–249). New York: Guilford.

ALLEN, S. N., & BLOOM, S. L. (1994). Group and family treatment of post-traumatic stress disorder. *The Psychiatric Clinics of North America, 8,* 425–438.

ALTMAIER, E. M., LEARY, M. R., HALPERN, S., & SELLERS, J. E. (1985). Effects of stress inoculation and participant modeling on confidence and anxiety: Testing predictions of self-efficacy theory. *Journal of Social and Clinical Psychology, 3,* 500–505.

ALVAREZ, M. F. (1997). Using REBT and supportive psychotherapy with post-stroke patients. *Journal of Rational-Emotive & Cognitive-Behavior Therapy, 15,* 231–245.

AMERICAN PSYCHIATRIC ASSOCIATION. (1987). *Diagnostic and statistical manual of mental disorders* (3rd ed., rev.). Washington, DC: Author.

AMERICAN PSYCHIATRIC ASSOCIATION. (1994). *Diagnostic and statistical manual of mental disorders* (4th ed.). Washington, DC: Author.

AMERICAN PSYCHIATRIC ASSOCIATION. (2000a). *Diagnostic and statistical manual of mental disorders* (4th ed., text rev.). Washington, DC: Author.

AMERICAN PSYCHIATRIC ASSOCIATION. (2000b). *Practice guidelines for the treatment of eating disorders.* Washington, DC: Author.

AMERICAN PSYCHOLOGICAL ASSOCIATION. (1995). Training in and dissemination of empirically-validated psychological treatments: Report and recommendations. *The Clinical Psychologist, 48,* 3–24.

ANANT, S. S. (1968). The use of verbal aversion (negative conditioning) with an alcoholic: A case report. *Behaviour Research and Therapy, 6,* 695–696.

ANDERSON, D. (2008). Introduction. *the Behavior Therapist, 31,* 145–146.

ANDERSON, N. B., LAWRENCE, P. S., & OLSON, T. W. (1981). Within-subject analysis of autogenic training and cognitive coping training in the treatment of tension headache pain. *Journal of Behavior Therapy and Experimental Psychiatry, 12,* 219–223.

ANDERSON, P., JACOBS, C., & ROTHBAUM, B. O. (2004). Computer-supported cognitive behavioral treatment of anxiety disorders. *Journal of Clinical Psychology, 60,* 253–267.

ANDERSON, P., ROTHBAUM, B. O., & HODGES, L. F. (2003). Virtual reality exposure in the treatment of social anxiety: Two case reports. *Cognitive and Behavioral Practice, 10,* 240–247.

ANDERSSON, G., BERGSTRÖM, J., HOLLÄNDARE, F., CARLBRING, P., KALDO, V., & EKELIUS, L. (2005). Internet-based self-help for depression: Randomised controlled trial. *British Journal of Psychiatry, 187,* 456–461.

ANDRASIK, F., & BLANCHARD, E. B. (1987). Task force report on the biofeedback treatment of tension headache. In J. P. Hatch, J. D. Rugh, & J. G. Fisher (Eds.), *Biofeedback studies in clinical efficacy* (pp. 281–321). New York: Plenum.

ANDRASIK, F., LARSSON, B., & GRAZZI L. (2002). Biofeedback treatment of recurrent headaches in children and adolescents. In V. Guidetti, G. Russell, M. Sillanpaa, & P. Winner (Eds.), *Headache and migraine in childhood and adolescence* (pp. 317–332). London: Martin Dunitz.

ANESKO, K. M., & O'LEARY, S. G. (1982). The effectiveness of brief parent training for the management of children's homework problems. *Child & Family Behavior Therapy, 4,* 113–126.

ANTON, W. D. (1976). An evaluation of outcome variables in the systematic desensitization of test anxiety. *Behaviour Research and Therapy, 14,* 217–224.

ANTONI, M. H., KUMAR, M., IRONSON, G., CRUESS, D. G., LUTGEN-DORF, S., KLIMAS, N., et al. (2000). Cognitive-behavioral stress management intervention effects on anxiety, 24-hr urinary norepinephrine output, and T-cytotoxic/suppressor cells over time among symptomatic HIV-infected gay men. *Journal of Consulting and Clinical Psychology, 68,* 31–45.

ANTONI, M. H., LEHMAN, J. M., KILBOURN, K. M., BOYERS, A. E., CULVER, J. L., ALFERI, S. M., et al. (2001). Cognitive-behavioral stress management intervention decreases the prevalence of depression and enhances benefit finding among woman under treatment for early-stage breast cancer. *Health Psychology, 20,* 20–32.

ANTONUCCIO, D. O., DANTON, W. G., & DENELSKY, G. Y. (1995). Psychotherapy versus medication for depression: Challenging the conventional wisdom with data. *Professional Psychology: Research and Practice, 26,* 574–585.

ANTONUCCIO, D. O., THOMAS, M., & DANTON, W. G. (1997). A cost-effectiveness analysis of cognitive behavior therapy and fluoxetine (Prozac) in the treatment of depressions. *Behavior Therapy, 28,* 187–210.

ANTONY, M. M., LEDLEY, D. R., LISS, A., & SWINSON, R. P. (2006). Responses to symptom induction exercises in panic disorder. *Behaviour Research and Therapy, 44,* 85–98.

ANTONY, M. M., McCABE, R. E., LEEUW, I., SANO, N., & SWINSON, R. P. (2001). Effect of distraction and coping styles on in vivo exposure for specific phobia of spiders. *Behaviour Research and Therapy, 39,* 1137–1150.

ARCH, J. J., & CRASKE, M. G. (2008). Acceptance and commitment therapy and cognitive behavioral therapy for anxiety disorders: Different treatments, similar mechanisms? *Clinical Psychology: Science & Practice, 5,* 263–279.

AREAN, P. A., PERRI, M. G., NEZU, A. M., SCHEIN, R. L., CHRISTOPHER, F., & JOSEPH, T. X. (1993). Comparative effectiveness of social problem-solving therapy and reminiscence therapy as treatments for depression in older adults. *Journal of Consulting and Clinical Psychology, 61,* 1003–1010.

ARMSTRONG, K. J., & DRABMAN, R. S. (1998). Treatment of a nine year old girl's masturbatory behavior. *Child & Family Behavior Therapy, 20,* 55–62.

ARNARSON, E. O. (1994). The saga of behavioural cognitive intervention. *Behavioural and Cognitive Psychotherapy, 22,* 105–109.

ARNKOFF, D. B., & GLASS, C. R. (1992). Cognitive therapy and psychotherapy: A century of change. In D. K. Freedheim (Ed.), *History of psychotherapy: A century of change* (pp. 657–694). Washington, DC: American Psychological Association.

ASHBAUGH, R., & PECK, S. M. (1998). Treatment of sleep problems in a toddler: A replication of the faded bedtime with response cost protocol. *Journal of Applied Behavior Analysis, 31,* 127–129.

ASHEM, B., & DONNER, L. (1968). Covert sensitization with alcoholics: A controlled replication. *Behaviour Research and Therapy, 6,* 7–12.

ASSOCIATION FOR BEHAVIORAL AND COGNITIVE THERAPIES. (2008). *About behavioral & cognitive therapy.* Retrieved May 30, 2008, from http://www.aabt.org/about/?fa= aboutBCT

Asylum on the front porch: Community life for the mentally retarded. (1974). *Innovations, 1,* 11–14.

ATTHOWE, J. M., JR., & KRASNER, L. (1968). Preliminary report on the application of contingent reinforcement procedures (token economy) on a "chronic" psychiatric ward. *Journal of Abnormal Psychology, 73,* 37–43.

AUSTIN, J., ALVERO, A. M., & OLSON, R. (1998). Prompting patron safety belt use at a restaurant. *Journal of Applied Behavior Analysis, 31,* 655–657.

AUSTIN, J., HACKETT, S., GRAVINA, N., & LEBBON, A. (2006). The effects of prompting and feedback on drivers' stopping at stop signs. *Journal of Applied Behavior Analysis, 39,* 117–121.

AXELROD, S. (1998). *How to use group contingencies* (2nd ed.). Austin, TX: Pro-Ed.

AXELROD, S., BRANTNER, J. P., & MEDDOCK, T. D. (1978). Overcorrection: A review and critical analysis. *Journal of Special Education, 12,* 367–391.

AXELROD, S., & HALL, S. V. (1999). *Behavior modification: Basic principles* (2nd ed.). Austin, TX: Pro-Ed.

AYDIN, G., & YERIN, O. (1994). The effect of a story-based cognitive behavior modification procedure on reducing children's test anxiety before and after cancellation of an important examination. *International Journal for the Advancement of Counselling, 17,* 149–161.

AYLLON, T. (1963). Intensive treatment of psychotic behavior by stimulus satiation and food reinforcement. *Behaviour Research and Therapy, 1,* 53–61.

AYLLON, T. (1965). Some behavioral problems associated with eating in chronic schizophrenic patients. In L. P. Ullmann & L. Krasner (Eds.), *Case studies in behavior modification* (pp. 73–84). New York: Holt, Rinehart & Winston.

AYLLON, T., & AZRIN, N. H. (1965). The measurement and reinforcement of behavior of psychotics. *Journal of the Experimental Analysis of Behavior, 8,* 357–383.

AYLLON, T., & AZRIN, N. H. (1968). *The token economy: A motivational system for therapy and rehabilitation.* New York: Appleton-Century-Crofts.

AYLLON, T., & MICHAEL, J. (1959). The psychiatric nurse as a behavioral engineer. *Journal of the Experimental Analysis of Behavior, 2,* 323–334.

AZAR, B. (2002, March). Helping older adults get on the technological bandwagon. *Monitor on Psychology, 33,* 28–29.

AZRIN, N. H., & BESALEL[-AZRIN], V. A. (1999). *How to use positive practice, self-correction, and overcorrection* (2nd ed.). Austin, TX: Pro-Ed.

AZRIN, N., EHLE, C., & BEAUMONT, A. (2006). Physical exercise as a reinforcer to promote calmness of an ADHD child. *Journal of Behavior Modification, 30,* 564–570.

AZRIN, N. H., GOTTLIEB, L., HUGHART, L., WESOLOWSKI, M. D., & RAHN, T. (1975). Eliminating self-injurious behavior by educative procedures. *Behaviour Research and Therapy, 13,* 101–111.

AZRIN, N. H., & HOLZ, W. C. (1966). Punishment. In W. K. Honig (Ed.), *Operant behavior: Areas of research and application* (pp. 380–447). New York: Appleton-Century-Crofts.

AZRIN, N. H., McMAHON, P. T., DONAHUE, B., BESALEL, V. A., LAPINSKI, K. J., KOGAN, E. S. , et al. (1994). Behavior therapy for drug abuse: A controlled treatment outcome study. *Behaviour Research and Therapy, 32,* 857–866.

AZRIN, N. H., & NUNN, R. G. (1973). Habit reversal: A method of eliminating nervous habits and tics. *Behaviour Research and Therapy, 11,* 619–628.

AZRIN, N. H., & PETERSON, A. L. (1988a). Behavior therapy for Tourette's syndrome and tic disorders. In D. J. Cohen, R. D. Bruun, & J. F. Leckman (Eds.), *Tourette's syndrome and tic disorders: Clinical understanding and treatment* (pp. 238–255). New York: Wiley.

AZRIN, N. H., & PETERSON, A. L. (1988b). Habit reversal for the treatment of Tourette syndrome. *Behaviour Research and Therapy, 26,* 347–351.

AZRIN, N. H., & POWELL, J. (1968). Behavioral engineering: The reduction of smoking behavior by a conditioning apparatus and procedure. *Journal of Applied Behavior Analysis, 1,* 193–200.

AZRIN, N. H., & POWELL, J. (1969). Behavioral engineering: The use of response priming to improve prescribed self-medication. *Journal of Applied Behavior Analysis, 2,* 39–42.

AZRIN, N. H., & POWERS, M. A. (1975). Eliminating classroom disturbances of emotionally disturbed children by positive practice procedures. *Behavior Therapy, 6,* 525–534.

AZRIN, N. H., SNEED, T. J., & FOXX, R. M. (1973). Dry bed: A rapid method of eliminating bedwetting (enuresis) of the retarded. *Behaviour Research and Therapy, 11,* 427–434.

AZRIN, N. H., SNEED, T. J., & FOXX, R. M. (1974). Dry-bed training: Rapid elimination of childhood enuresis. *Behaviour Research and Therapy, 12,* 147–156.

AZRIN, N., & TEICHNER, G. (1998). Evaluation of an instructional program for improving medication compliance for chronically mentally ill outpatients. *Behaviour Research and Therapy, 36,* 849–861.

AZRIN, N. H., & THIENES, P. (1978). Rapid elimination of enuresis by intensive learning without a conditioning apparatus. *Behavior Therapy, 9,* 342–354.

AZRIN, N. H., THIENES-HONTOS, P., & BESALEL-AZRIN, V. (1979). Elimination of enuresis without a conditioning apparatus: An extension by office instruction of the child and parents. *Behavior Therapy, 10,* 14–19.

AZRIN, N. H., VINAS, V., & EHLE, C. T. (2007). Physical activity as reinforcement for classroom calmness of ADHD children: A preliminary study. *Child & Family Behavior Therapy, 29,* 1–7.

AZRIN, N. H., & WESOLOWSKI, M. D. (1974). Theft reversal: An overcorrection procedure for eliminating stealing by retarded persons. *Journal of Applied Behavior Analysis, 7,* 577–581.

AZRIN, N. H., & WESOLOWSKI, M. D. (1975). Eliminating habitual vomiting in a retarded adult by positive practice and self-correction. *Journal of Behavior Therapy and Experimental Psychiatry, 6,* 145–148.

BABCOCK, R. A., SULZER-AZAROFF, B., SANDERSON, M., & SCIBAK, J. (1992). Increasing nurses' use of feedback to promote infection-control practices in a head-injury treatment center. *Journal of Applied Behavior Analysis, 25,* 621–627.

BACH, P., & HAYES, S. C. (2002). The use of Acceptance and Commitment Therapy to prevent the rehospitalization of psychotic patients: A randomized controlled trial. *Journal of Consulting and Clinical Psychology, 70,* 1129–1139.

BACKHAUS, J., HOHAGEN, F., VODERHOLZER, U., & RIEMANN, D. (2001). Long-term effectiveness of a short-term cognitive-behavioral group treatment for primary insomnia. *European Archives of Psychiatry and Clinical Neuroscience, 25,* 35–41.

BAER, D. M. (1999). *How to plan for generalization* (2nd ed.). Austin, TX: Pro-Ed.

BAER, D. M., & GUESS, D. (1971). Receptive training of adjectival inflections in mental retardates. *Journal of Applied Behavior Analysis, 4,* 129–139.

BAER, D. M., & GUESS, D. (1973). Teaching productive noun suffixes to severely retarded children. *American Journal of Mental Deficiency, 77,* 498–505.

BAER, L., HURLEY, J. D., MINICHIELLO, W. E., OTT, B. D., PENZEL, F., & RICCIARDI, J. (1992). EMDR workshop: Disturbing issues? *the Behavior Therapist, 15,* 110–111.

BAER, R. A. (2003). Mindfulness training as a clinical intervention: A conceptual and empirical review. *Clinical Psychology: Science and Practice, 10,* 125–143.

BAER, R. A. (Ed.). (2005). Mindfulness-based treatment approaches: Clinician's guide to evidence base and applications. New York: Academic Press.

BAER, R. A. (Ed.). (2006). *Mindfulness-based treatment approaches: Clinician's guide to evidence base and applications.* San Diego: Elsevier Academic Press.

BAER, R. A., FISCHER, S., & HUSS, D. B. (2005a). Mindfulness and acceptance in the treatment of disordered eating. *Journal of Rational-Emotive & Cognitive Behavior Therapy, 23,* 281–300.

BAER, R. A., FISCHER, S., & HUSS, D. B. (2005b). Mindfulness-based cognitive therapy applied to binge eating: A case study. *Cognitive and Behavioral Practice, 123,* 351–358.

BAILEY, J. S., TIMBERS, G. D., PHILLIPS, E. L., & WOLF, M. M. (1971). Modification of articulation errors of predelinquents by their peers. *Journal of Applied Behavior Analysis, 4,* 265–281.

BAILEY, J. S., WOLF, M. M., & PHILLIPS, E. L. (1970). Home-based reinforcement and the modification of predelinquents' classroom behavior. *Journal of Applied Behavior Analysis, 3,* 223–233.

BAKKEN, J., MILTENBERGER, R. G., & SCHAUSS, S. (1993). Teaching parents with mental retardation: Knowledge versus skills. *American Journal of Mental Retardation, 97,* 405–417.

BALLARD, K. D., & CROOKS, T. J. (1984). Videotape modeling for preschool children with low levels of social interaction and low peer involvement in play. *Journal of Abnormal Child Psychology, 12,* 95–110.

BALTER, R., & UNGER, P. (1997). REBT stress management with patients with chronic fatigue syndrome. *Journal of Rational-Emotive & Cognitive-Behavior Therapy, 15,* 223–230.

BANARJEE, S. P. (1999). Behavioral psychotherapy in Singapore. *the Behavior Therapist, 22,* 80, 91–91.

BANDURA, A. (1969). *Principles of behavior modification.* New York: Holt, Rinehart & Winston.

BANDURA, A. (Ed.). (1971). *Psychological modeling: Conflicting theories.* Chicago: Aldine-Atherton.

BANDURA, A. (1976). Effecting change through participant modeling. In J. D. Krumboltz & C. E. Thoresen (Eds.), *Counseling methods* (pp. 248–265). New York: Holt, Rinehart & Winston.

BANDURA, A. (1977a). Self-efficacy: Toward a unifying theory of behavioral change. *Psychological Review, 84,* 191–215.

BANDURA, A. (1977b). *Social learning theory.* Englewood Cliffs, NJ: Prentice Hall.

BANDURA, A. (1978). Reflections on self-efficacy. In S. Rachman (Ed.), *Advances in behaviour research and therapy* (Vol. 1, pp. 237–269). Oxford, UK: Pergamon.

BANDURA, A. (1984). Recycling misconceptions of perceived self-efficacy. *Cognitive Therapy and Research, 8,* 231–255.

BANDURA, A. (1986a). From thought to action: Mechanisms of personal agency. *New Zealand Journal of Psychology, 15,* 1–17.

BANDURA, A. (1986b). *Social foundations of thought and action: A social cognitive theory.* Englewood Cliffs, NJ: Prentice Hall.

BANDURA, A. (1997). *Self-efficacy: The exercise of control.* San Francisco: W. H. Freeman.

BANDURA, A. (2001, June). *On shaping one's future: The primacy of human agency.* Keynote address presented at the meeting of the American Psychological Society, Toronto.

BANDURA, A. (2008). Reconstrual of "free will" from the agentic perspective of social cognitive theory. In J. Baer, J. C. Kaufman, & R. F. Baumeister (Eds.), *Are we free? Psychology and free will* (pp. 86–127). New York: Oxford University Press.

BANDURA, A., JEFFERY, R. W., & GAJDOS, E. (1975). Generalizing change through participant modeling with self-directed mastery. *Behaviour Research and Therapy, 13,* 141–152.

BANDURA, A., & WALTERS, R. H. (1963). *Social learning and personality development.* New York: Holt, Rinehart & Winston.

BARCLAY, D. R., & HOUTS, A. C. (1995). Parenting skills: A review and developmental analysis of training content. In W. O'Donohue & L. Krasner (Eds.), *Handbook of psychological skills training: Clinical techniques and applications* (pp. 195–228). Boston: Allyn & Bacon.

BARKER, J. B., & JONES, M. V. (2006). Using hypnosis, technique refinement, and self-modeling to enhance self-efficacy: A case study in cricket. *The Sport Psychologist, 20,* 94–110.

BARKIN, R. M., & DUNCAN, R. (1975). Broken appointments: Questions, not answers. *Pediatrics, 55,* 747–748.

BARKLEY, R. A. (1987). *Defiant children: A clinician's manual for parent training.* New York: Guilford.

BARKLEY, R. A. (1989). *Defiant children.* New York: Guilford.

BARKLEY, R. A., GUEVREMONT, D. C., ANASTOPOULOS, A. D., & FLETCHER, K. (1992). A comparison of three family therapy programs for treating family conflicts in adolescents with attention deficit hyperactivity

disorder. *Journal of Consulting and Clinical Psychology, 60,* 450–462.

BARLOW, D. H. (1988). *Anxiety and its disorders: The nature and treatment of anxiety and panic.* New York: Guilford.

BARLOW, D. H. (1993). Covert sensitization for paraphilia. In J. R. Cautela & A. J. Kearney (Eds.), *Covert conditioning casebook* (pp. 185–198). Pacific Grove, CA: Brooks/Cole.

BARLOW, D. H. (1994). Psychological interventions in the era of managed competition. *Clinical Psychology: Science and Practice, 1,* 109–122.

BARLOW, D. H. (2000). Evidence-based practice: A world view. *Clinical Psychology: Science and Practice, 7,* 241–242.

BARLOW, D. H., & CERNEY, J. A. (1988). *Psychological treatment of panic.* New York: Guilford.

BARLOW, D. H., GORMAN, J. M., SHEAR, M. K., & WOODS, S. W. (2000). Cognitive-behavioral therapy, imipramine, or their combination for panic disorder. *Journal of the American Medical Association, 283,* 2529–2536.

BARLOW, D. H., & HERSEN, M. (1984). *Single case experimental designs: Strategies for studying behavior change* (2nd ed.). New York: Pergamon Press.

BARLOW, D. H., O'BRIEN, G. T., & LAST, C. A. (1984). Couples treatment of agoraphobia. *Behavior Therapy, 15,* 41–58.

BARNETT, J. E. (1996). Managed care: Time to fight or flee? *Psychotherapy Bulletin, 31,* 54–58.

BARNHOFER, T., DUGGAN, D., CRANE, C., HEPBURN, S., FENNELL, M., & WILLIAMS, J. M. G. (2007). Effects of meditation on frontal alpha asymmetry in previously suicidal patients. *NeuroReport, 18,* 707–712.

BARR, R. F., LOVIBOND, S. H., & KATSAROS, E. (1972). Giles de la Tourette's syndrome in a brain-damaged child. *Medical Journal of Australia, 2,* 372–374.

BARRIOS, B. A. (1988). On the changing nature of behavioral assessment. In A. S. Bellack & M. Hersen (Eds.), *Behavioral assessment: A practical handbook* (3rd ed., pp. 3–41). Elmsford, NY: Pergamon.

BARRY, J. V. (1958). *Alexander Maconochie of Norfolk Island: A study of a pioneer in penal reform.* London: Oxford University Press.

BARRY, N. J., & OVERMANN, P. B. (1977). Comparison of the effectiveness of adult and peer models with EMR children. *American Journal of Mental Deficiency, 82,* 33–36.

BARTELS, S. J., MUESER, K. T., & MILES, K. M. (1997). Functional impairments in elderly patients with schizophrenia and major affective illness in the community: Social skills, living skills, and behavior problems. *Behavior Therapy, 28,* 43–63.

BARTON, E. J., & ASCIONE, F. R. (1984). Direct observation. In T. H. Ollendick & M. Hersen (Eds.), *Child behavioral assessment* (pp. 166–194). Elmsford, NY: Pergamon.

BARTON, E. S., GUESS, D., GARCIA, E., & BAER, D. M. (1970). Improvement of retardates' mealtime behaviors by timeout procedures using multiple base-line techniques. *Journal of Applied Behavior Analysis, 3,* 77–84.

BARZOUKA, K., BERGELES, N., & HATZIHARISTOS, D. (2007). Effect of simultaneous model observation and self-modeling of volleyball skill acquisition. *Perceptual and Motor Skills, 104,* 32–42.

BAŞOĞLU, M., LIVANOU, M., ŞALCIOĞLU, E., & KALENDER, D. (2003). A brief behavioural treatment of chronic post-traumatic stress disorder in earthquake survivors: Results from an open clinical trial. *Psychological Medicine, 33,* 647–654.

BASTIEN, C. H., MORIN, C. M., OUELLET, M.-C., BLAIS, F. C., & BOUCHARD, S. (2004). Cognitive-behavioral therapy for insomnia: Comparison of individual therapy, group therapy, and telephone consultations. *Journal of Consulting and Clinical Psychology, 72,* 653–659.

BATEMAN, K., HANSEN, L., TURKINGTON, D., & KINGDON, D. (2007). Cognitive behavioral therapy reduces suicidal ideation in schizophrenia: Results from a randomized controlled trial. *Suicide and Life-Threatening Behavior, 37,* 284–290.

BATTERSBY, M., OAKES, J., TOLCHARD, B., FORBES, A., & POLS, R. (2008). Cognitive behavioral therapy for problem gamblers. In M. Zangeneh, A. Blaszczynski, & N. Turner (Eds.), *In the pursuit of winning* (pp. 179–197). New York: Springer.

BAUCOM, B., CHRISTENSEN, A., & YI, J. C. (2005). Integrative behavioral couple therapy. In J. L. Lebow (Ed.), *Handbook of clinical family therapy* (pp. 329–352). Hoboken, NJ: Wiley.

BAUCOM, D. H., & EPSTEIN, N. (1990). *Cognitive-behavioral marital therapy.* New York: Brunner/Mazel.

BAUCOM, D. H., GORDON, K. C., SNYDER, D. K., ATKINS, D. C., & CHRISTENSEN, A. (2006). Treating affair couples: Clinical considerations and initial findings. *Journal of Cognitive Psychotherapy, 20,* 375–392.

BAUCOM, D. H., HAHLWEG, K., & KUSCHEL, A. (2003). Are waiting-list control groups needed in future marital therapy outcome research? *Behavior Therapy, 34,* 179–188.

BAUCOM, D. H., & HOFFMAN, J. A. (1986). The effectiveness of marital therapy: Current status and applications to the clinical setting. In N. S. Jacobson & A. S. Gurman (Eds.), *Clinical handbook of marital therapy* (pp. 597–620). New York: Guilford.

BAUCOM, D. H., SHOHAM, V., MUESER, K. T., DAIUTO, A. D., & STICKLE, T. R. (1998). Empirically supported couple and family interventions for marital distress and adult mental health problems. *Journal of Consulting and Clinical Psychology, 66,* 53–88.

BAUER, A. M., & SHEA, T. M. (1984). Tourette syndrome: A review and educational implications. *Journal of Autism and Developmental Disorders, 14,* 69–80.

BAXTER, L. R., SCHWARTZ, J. M., BERGMAN, K. S., SZUBA, M. P., GUZE, B. H., MAZZIOTTA, J. C., et al. (1992). Caudate glucose metabolic rate changes with both drug and behavior therapy for obsessive-compulsive disorder. *Archives of General Psychiatry, 49,* 681–689.

BEACH, S. R. H., & O'LEARY, K. D. (1992). Treating depression in the context of marital discord: Outcome predictors of response of marital therapy versus cognitive therapy. *Behavior Therapy, 23,* 507–528.

BEACH, S. R. H., WHISMAN, M. A., & O'LEARY, K. D. (1994). Marital therapy for depression: Theoretical foundation, current status, and future directions. *Behavior Therapy, 25,* 345–371.

BEAUCHAMP, T. L., & WALTERS, L. (Eds.). (1978). *Contemporary issues in bioethics.* Encino, CA: Dickenson.

BEBKO, J. M., & LENNOX, C. (1988). Teaching the control of diurnal bruxism to two children with autism using a simple cueing procedure. *Behavior Therapy, 19,* 249–255.

BECK, A. T. (1963). Thinking and depression. *Archives of General Psychiatry, 9,* 324–333.

BECK, A. T. (1967). *Depression: Clinical, experimental, and theoretical aspects.* New York: Hoeber.

BECK, A. T. (1972). *Depression: Causes and treatment.* Philadelphia: University of Pennsylvania Press.

BECK, A. T. (1976). *Cognitive therapy and the emotional disorders.* New York: International Universities Press.

BECK, A. T. (1988). Cognitive approaches to panic disorder: Theory and therapy. In S. Rachman & J. D. Maser (Eds.), *Panic: Psychological perspectives* (pp. 91–109). Hillsdale, NJ: Erlbaum.

BECK, A. T. (1989). *Love is never enough.* New York: Harper & Row (Perennial Library).

BECK, A. T. (2005). The current state of cognitive therapy: A 40-year retrospective. *Archives of General Psychiatry, 62,* 953–959.

BECK, A. T., & EMERY, G. (1985). *Anxiety disorders and phobias: A cognitive perspective.* New York: Basic Books.

BECK, A. T., & FREEMAN, A. (1989). *Cognitive therapy of personality disorders.* New York: Guilford.

BECK, A. T., RUSH, A. J., SHAW, B. F., & EMERY, G. (1979). *Cognitive therapy of depression.* New York: Guilford.

BECK, A. T., & STEER, R. A. (1993). *Beck Depression Inventory* (rev. ed.). San Antonio, TX: Psychological Corporation.

BECK, A. T., & WEISHAAR, M. [E.] (1989). Cognitive therapy. In A. Freeman, K. M. Simon, L. E. Beutler, & H. Arkowitz (Eds.), *Comprehensive handbook of cognitive therapy* (pp. 21–36). New York: Plenum.

BECK, A. T., WRIGHT, F. D., NEWMAN, C. F., & LIESE, B. S. (1993). *Cognitive therapy of substance abuse.* New York: Guilford.

BECK, J. G. (1997). Mental health in the elderly—Challenges for behavior therapy: Introduction to the special series. *Behavior Therapy, 28,* 1–2.

BECK, J. G., & STANLEY, M. A. (1997). Anxiety disorders in the elderly: The emerging role of behavior therapy. *Behavior Therapy, 28,* 83–100.

BECKER, C. B., ZAYFERT, C., & ANDERSON, E. (2004). A survey of psychologists' attitudes towards and utilization of exposure therapy for PTSD. *Behaviour Research and Therapy, 42,* 277–292.

BECKER, R. E., & HEIMBERG, R. G. (1988). Assessment of social skills. In A. S. Bellack & M. Hersen (Eds.), *Behavioral assessment: A practical handbook* (3rd ed., pp. 365–395). Elmsford, NY: Pergamon.

BECKER, W. (1971). *Parents are teachers: A child management program.* Champaign, IL: Research Press.

BEIDEL, D. C., & TURNER, S. M. (1986). A critique of the theoretical bases of cognitive-behavioral theories and therapy. *Clinical Psychology Review, 6,* 177–197.

BEIDEL, D. C., & TURNER, S. M. (1998). *Shy children, phobic adults: The nature and treatment of social phobia.* Washington, DC: American Psychological Association.

BEIDEL, D. C., TURNER, S. M., & MORRIS, T. L. (1995). A new inventory to assess childhood social anxiety and phobia: The social phobia and anxiety inventory for children. *Psychological Assessment, 7,* 73–79.

BEIDEL, D. C., TURNER, S. M., & MORRIS, T. L. (2000). Behavioral treatment of childhood social phobia. *Journal of Consulting and Clinical Psychology, 68,* 1072–1080.

BELCHIC, J. K., & HARRIS, S. L. (1994). The use of multiple peer exemplars to enhance the generalization of play skills to the siblings of children with autism. *Child & Family Behavior Therapy, 16,* 1–24.

BELLACK, A. S., HERSEN, M., & TURNER, S. M. (1979). Relationship of role playing and knowledge of appropriate behavior to assertion in the natural environment. *Journal of Consulting and Clinical Psychology, 47,* 670–678.

BELLACK, A. S., MORRISON, R. L., WIXTED, J. T., & MUESER, K. T. (1990). An analysis of social competence in schizophrenia. *British Journal of Psychiatry, 156,* 809–818.

BELLACK, A. S., & MUESER, K. T. (1994). Schizophrenia. In L. W. Craighead, W. E. Craighead, A. E. Kazdin, & M. J. Mahoney (Eds.), *Cognitive and behavioral interventions: An empirical approach to mental health problems.* Needham Heights, MA: Allyn & Bacon.

BELL-DOLAN, D. J. (1995). Social cue interpretation of anxious children. *Journal of Clinical Child Psychology, 24,* 1–10.

BELLINI, S., & AKULLIAN, J. (2007a). Increasing social engagement in young children with autism spectrum disorders using video self-modeling. *School Psychology Review, 36*, 80–90.

BELLINI, S., & AKULLIAN, J. (2007b). A meta-analysis of video modeling and video self-modeling interventions for children and adolescents with autism spectrum disorders. *Exceptional Children, 73*, 264–287.

BENNETT, W. (1987). Dietary treatments of obesity. In R. J. Wurtman & J. J. Wurtman (Eds.), *Human obesity* (pp. 250–263). New York: New York Academy of Sciences.

BENTALL, R. P., HADDOCK, G., & SLADE, P. D. (1994). Cognitive behavior therapy for persistent auditory hallucinations: From theory to therapy. *Behavior Therapy, 25*, 51–66.

BENTALL, R. P., HIGSON, P., & LOWE, C. (1987). Teaching self-instructions to chronic schizophrenic patients: Efficacy and generalization. *Behavioural Psychotherapy, 15*, 58–76.

BENTON, M. K., & SCHROEDER, H. E. (1990). Social skills training with schizophrenics: A meta-analytic evaluation. *Journal of Consulting and Clinical Psychology, 58*, 741–747.

BERGAN, J. (1995). Behavioral training and the new mental health: Are we learning what we need to know? *the Behavior Therapist, 18*, 161–164, 166.

BERGIN, A. E., & STRUPP, H. H. (Eds.). (1972). *Changing frontiers in the science of psychotherapy.* Chicago: Aldine-Atherton.

BERMAN, S. L., WEEMS, C. F., SILVERMAN, W. K., & KURTINES, W. M. (2000). Predictors of outcome of exposure-base cognitive and behavioral treatments for phobic and anxiety disorders in children. *Behavior Therapy, 31*, 713–731.

BERNAD-RIPOLL, S. (2007). Using a self-as-model video combined with Social Stories™ to help a child with Asperger syndrome understand emotions. *Focus on Autism and Other Developmental Disabilities, 22*, 100–106.

BERNARD, M. E. (1990). Rational-emotive therapy with children and adolescents: Treatment strategies. *School Psychology Review, 19*, 294–303.

BERNARD, M. E., & DIGIUSEPPE, [A.] (1989). Rational-emotive therapy today. In M. E. Bernard & R. [A.] DiGiuseppe (Eds.), *Inside rational-emotive therapy: A critical appraisal of the theory and therapy of Albert Ellis* (pp. 1–7). San Diego: Academic Press.

BERNARD, M. E., & JOYCE, M. R. (1984). *Rational-emotive therapy with children and adolescents: Theory, treatment strategies, preventative methods.* New York: Wiley.

BERNSTEIN, D. A., BORKOVEC, T. D., & HAZLETT-STEVENS, H. (2000). *New directions in progressive relaxation training: A guidebook for helping professionals.* Westport, CT: Praeger.

BERTAGNOLLI, A., & MORRIS, S. (1997). Cognitive-behavioral interventions with chronic fatigue syndrome: A single case study. *Journal of Cognitive Psychotherapy: An International Quarterly, 11*, 127–139.

BEUTLER, L. E., & GUEST, P. D. (1989). The role of cognitive change in psychotherapy. In A. Freeman, K. M. Simon, L. E. Beutler, & H. Arkowitz (Eds.), *Comprehensive handbook of cognitive therapy* (pp. 123–142). New York: Plenum.

BIGELOW, G., LIEBSON, I., & GRIFFITHS, R. (1974). Alcoholic drinking: Suppression by a brief time-out procedure. *Behaviour Research and Therapy, 12*, 107–115.

BIGELOW, G., STRICKLER, D., LIEBSON, L., & GRIFFITHS, R. (1976). Maintaining disulfiram ingestion among outpatient alcoholics: A security-deposit contingency contracting procedure. *Behaviour Research and Therapy, 14*, 378–381.

BIGELOW, K. M., HUYNEN, K. B., & LUTZKER, J. R. (1993). Using a changing criterion design to teach fire escape to a child with developmental disabilities. *Journal of Developmental and Physical Disabilities, 5*, 121–128.

BIGELOW, K. M., & LUTZKER, J. R. (1998). Using video to teach planned activities to parents reported for child abuse. *Child & Family Behavior Therapy, 20*, 1–14.

BIGGAM, F. H., & POWER, K. G. (1999). Social problem-solving skills and psychological distress among incarcerated young offenders: The issue of bullying and victimization. *Cognitive Therapy and Research, 23*, 307–326.

BILLINGS, A. (1978). Self-monitoring in the treatment of tics: A single subject analysis. *Journal of Behavior Therapy and Experimental Psychiatry, 9*, 339–342.

BLACK, D. (1987). A minimal intervention program and a problem-solving program for weight control. *Cognitive Therapy and Research, 11*, 107–120.

BLACK, R. G. (1975). The chronic pain syndrome. *Surgical Clinics of North America, 55*, 4–4.

BLACKLEDGE, J. T. (2003). An introduction to relational frame theory: Basics and applications. *The Behavior Analyst Today, 3*, 421–433.

BLACKLEDGE, J. T., & HAYES, S. C. (2001). Emotion regulation in Acceptance and Commitment Therapy. *JCLP/In Session: Psychotherapy in Practice, 57*(2), 243–255.

BLAMPIED, N. M. (1999). Cognitive-behavior therapy in Aptearoa, New Zealand. *the Behavior Therapist, 22*, 173–178.

BLAMPIED, N. M., & FRANCE, K. G. (1993). A behavioral model of infant sleep disturbance. *Journal of Applied Behavior Analysis, 26*, 477–492.

BLAMPIED, N. M., & KAHAN, E. (1992). Acceptability of alternative punishments: A community survey. *Behavior Modification, 16*, 400–413.

BLANCHARD, E. B. (1987). Long-term effects of behavioral treatment of chronic headache. *Behavior Therapy, 18*, 375–385.

BLANCHARD, E. B. (1992). Psychological treatment of benign headache disorders. *Journal of Consulting and Clinical Psychology, 60*, 537–551.

BLANCHARD, E. B., ANDRASIK, F., NEFF, D. F., ARENA, J. G., AHLES, T. A., JURISH, S. E., et al. (1982). Biofeedback and relaxation training with three kinds of headaches: Treatment effects and their prediction. *Journal of Consulting and Clinical Psychology, 50*, 562–575.

BLANCHARD, E. B., APPLEBAUM, K. A., RADNITZ, C. L., MORRILL, B., MICHULTKA, D., KIRSCH, C., et al. (1990). A controlled evaluation of thermal biofeedback and thermal biofeedback combined with cognitive therapy in the treatment of vascular headache. *Journal of Consulting and Clinical Psychology, 58*, 216–224.

BLANCHARD, E. B., THEOBALD, D. E., WILLIAMSON, D. A., SILVER, B. V., & BROWN, D. A. (1978). Temperature biofeedback in the treatment of migraine headaches. *Archives of General Psychiatry, 35*, 581–588.

BLANKSTEIN, K. R., & SEGAL, Z. V. (2001). Cognitive assessment: Issues and methods. In K. S. Dobson (Ed.), *Handbook of cognitive-behavioral therapies* (2nd ed., pp. 40–85). New York: Guilford.

BLOXHAM, G., LONG, C. G., ALDERMAN, N., & HOLLIN, C. R. (1993). The behavioral treatment of self-starvation and severe self-injury in a patient with borderline personality disorder. *Journal of Behavior Therapy and Experimental Psychiatry, 24,* 261–267.

BLUMBERG, E. J., HOVELL, M. F., WERNER, C. A., KELLEY, N. J., SIPAN, C. L., BURKHAM, S. M., et al. (1997). Evaluating AIDS-related social skills in Anglo and Latino adolescents. *Behavior Modification, 21,* 281–307.

BLY, R. (1990). *Iron John: A book about men.* Reading, MA: Addison-Wesley.

BOCKTING, C. L. H., SCHENE, A. H., SPINHOVEN, P., KOETER, M. W. J., WOUTERS, L. F., HUYSER, J., et al. (2005). Preventing relapse/recurrence in recurrent depression with cognitive therapy: A randomized controlled trial. *Journal of Consulting and Clinical Psychology, 73,* 647–657.

BOELEN, P. A., DE KEIJSER, J., VAN DEN HOUT, M. A., & VAN DEN BOUT, J. (2007). Treatment of complicated grief: A comparison between cognitive-behavioral therapy and supportive counseling. *Journal of Consulting and Clinical Psychology, 75,* 277–284.

BOND, F. W., & BUNCE, D. (2000). Mediators of change in emotion-focused and problem-focused worksite stress management interventions. *Journal of Occupational Health Psychology, 5,* 156–163.

BONICA, J. J., & LOESER, J. D. (2000). History of pain concepts and therapies. In J. D. Loeser, S. H. Butler, C. R. Chapman, & D. C. Turk (Eds.), *Bonic's management of pain* (3rd ed., pp. 3–16). Philadelphia: Lippincott Williams & Wilkins.

BOOTZIN, R. R. (1972). Stimulus control treatment for insomnia. *Proceedings of the 80th annual convention of the American Psychological Association, 7,* 395–396.

BOOTZIN, R. R., & ENGLE-FRIEDMAN, M. (1987). Sleep disturbances. In B. Edelstein & L. Carstensen (Eds.), *Handbook of clinical gerontology* (pp. 238–251). Elmsford, NY: Pergamon.

BOOTZIN, R. R., & EPSTEIN, D. R. (2000). Stimulus control. In K. L. Lichstein & C. M. Morin (Eds.), *Treatment of late-life insomnia* (pp. 167–184). Thousand Oaks, CA: Sage.

BOOTZIN, R. R., EPSTEIN, D., & WOOD, J. M. (1991). Stimulus control instructions. In P. Hauri (Ed.), *Case studies in insomnia* (pp. 19–28). New York: Plenum.

BOOTZIN, R. R., & PERLIS, M. L. (1992). Nonpharmacologic treatments of insomnia. *Journal of Clinical Psychiatry, 53,* 37–41.

BORCKARDT, J. J., NASH, M. R., MURPHY, M. D., MOORE, M., SHAW, D., & O'NEIL, P. (2008). Clinical practice as natural laboratory for psychotherapy research: A guide to case-based time-series analysis. *American Psychologist, 63,* 77–95.

BORDNICK, P. S., ELKINS, R. L., ORR, T. W., WALTERS, P., & THYER, B. A. (2004). Evaluating the relative effectiveness of three aversion therapies designed to reduce craving among cocaine abusers. *Behavioral Interventions, 19,* 1–24.

BORKOVEC, T. D. (1970). *The comparative effectiveness of systematic desensitization and implosive therapy and the effect of expectancy manipulation on the elimination of fear.* Unpublished doctoral dissertation, University of Illinois, Champaign.

BORKOVEC, T. D. (1972). Effects of expectancy on the outcome of systematic desensitization and implosive treatments for analogue anxiety. *Behavior Therapy, 3,* 29–40.

BORKOVEC, T. D., & COSTELLO, E. (1993). Efficacy of applied relaxation and cognitive-behavioral therapy in the treatment of generalized anxiety disorder. *Journal of Consulting and Clinical Psychology, 61,* 611–619.

BORKOVEC, T. D., GRAYSON, J. B., & O'BRIEN, G. T. (1979). Relaxation treatment of pseudoinsomnia and idiopathic insomnia: An electroencephalographic evaluation. *Journal of Applied Behavior Analysis, 12,* 37–54.

BORKOVEC, T. D., & MATHEWS, A. M. (1988). Treatment of nonphobic anxiety disorders: A comparison of nondirective, cognitive, and coping desensitization therapy. *Journal of Consulting and Clinical Psychology, 56,* 877–884.

BORKOVEC, T. D., & WHISMAN, M. A. (1996). Psychosocial treatment for generalized anxiety disorder. In M. R. Mavissakalian & R. F. Prien (Eds.), *Long term treatments of anxiety disorders* (pp. 171–199). Washington, DC: American Psychiatric Press.

BORNAS, X., FULLANA, M. A., TORTELLA-FELIU, M., LLABRÉS, J., & DE LA BANDA, G. G. (2001). Computer-assisted therapy in the treatment of flight phobia: A case report. *Cognitive and Behavioral Practice, 8,* 234–240.

BORNSTEIN, P. H., HAMILTON, S. B., & BORNSTEIN, M. T. (1986). Self-monitoring procedures. In A. Ciminero, K. Calhoun, & H. Adams (Eds.), *Handbook of behavioral assessment* (2nd ed., pp. 176–225). New York: Wiley.

BORREGO, J., IBANEZ, E. S., SPENDLOVE, S. J., & PEMBERTON, J. R. (2007). Treatment acceptability among Mexican American parents. *Behavior Therapy, 38,* 218–227.

BORREGO, J., & URQUIZA, A. J. (1998). Importance of therapist use of social reinforcement with parents as a model of parent-child relationships: An example with parent-child interaction therapy. *Child & Family Behavior Therapy, 20,* 27–54.

BOTELLA, C., BAÑOS, R. M., PERPIÑA, C., VILLA, H., ALCAÑIZ, M., & REY, A. (1998). Virtual reality treatment of claustrophobia: A case report. *Behaviour Research and Therapy, 36,* 239–246.

BOUDIN, H. M. (1972). Contingency contracting as a therapeutic tool in deceleration of amphetamine use. *Behavior Therapy, 3,* 602–608.

BOUDJOUK, P. J., WOODS, D., MILTENBERGER, R. G., & LONG, E. S. (2000). Negative peer evaluation in adolescents: Effects of tic disorders and trichotillomania. *Child & Family Behavior Therapy, 22,* 17–28.

BOUHENIE, G., & MOORE, T. E. (2000). EMDR and the scientific perspective. *the Behavior Therapist, 23,* 154–158.

BOULOUGOURIS, J. C., MARKS, I. M., & MARSET, P. (1971). Superiority of flooding (implosion) to desensitization for reducing pathological fear. *Behaviour Research and Therapy, 9,* 7–16.

BOUTELLE, K. N. (1998). The use of exposure with response prevention in a male anorexic. *Journal of Behavior Therapy and Experimental Psychiatry, 29,* 79–84.

BOWERS, W. A. (1989). Cognitive therapy with inpatients. In A. Freeman, K. M. Simon, L. E. Beutler, & H. Arkowitz (Eds.), *Comprehensive handbook of cognitive therapy* (pp. 583–596). New York: Plenum.

BRACERO, W. (1996). The story hour: Narrative and multicultural perspectives on managed care and time-limited psychotherapy. *Psychotherapy Bulletin, 31,* 59–65.

BRADLEY, R., GREENE, J., RUSS, E., DUTRA, L., & WESTEN, D. (2005). A multidimensional meta-analysis of psychotherapy for PTSD. *American Journal of Psychiatry, 162,* 214–227.

BRAET, C., & WINCKEL, M. V. (2000). Long-term follow-up of a cognitive behavioral treatment program for obese children. *Behavior Therapy, 31,* 55–74.

BRASWELL, L., & KENDALL, P. C. (2001). Cognitive-behavioral therapy with youth. In K. S. Dobson (Ed.), *Handbook of cognitive-behavioral therapies* (2nd ed., pp. 246–294). New York: Guilford.

BRAUKMANN, C. J., & WOLF, M. M. (1987). Behaviorally based group homes for juvenile offenders. In E. K. Morris & C. J. Braukmann (Eds.), *Behavioral approaches to crime and delinquency: A handbook of applications, research, and concepts* (pp. 135–159). New York: Plenum.

BRAUKMANN, C. J., WOLF, M. M., & KIRIGIN RAMP, K. A. (1985). *Follow-up of group home youths into young adulthood* (Progress Report, Grant MH20030). Lawrence: Achievement Place Research Project, University of Kansas.

BRAY, M. A., & KEHLE, T. J. (1998). Self-modeling as an intervention for stuttering. *School Psychology Review, 27,* 587–598.

BRAY, M. A., & KEHLE, T. J. (2001). Long-term follow-up of self-modeling as an intervention for stuttering. *School Psychology Review, 30,* 135–141.

BRAZELTON, T. B. (1987, June). Are we frightening our children? *Family Circle,* pp. 98, 100, 124.

BREINER, J. L., & FOREHAND, R. [L.] (1981). An assessment of the effects of parent training on clinic-referred children's school behavior. *Behavioral Assessment, 3,* 31–42.

BRESTAN, E. V., EYBERG, S. M., BOGGS, S. R., & ALGINA, J. (1997). Parent-child interaction therapy: Parent's perceptions of untreated siblings.

Child & Family Behavior Therapy, 19, 13–28.

BRIGHAM, F. J., BAKKEN, J. P., SCRUGGS, T. E., & MASTROPIERE, M. A. (1992). Cooperative behavior management: Strategies for promoting a positive classroom environment. *Education and Training in Mental Retardation, 27,* 3–12.

BRINKMEYER, M. Y., & EYBERG, S. M. (2003). Parent-child interaction therapy for oppositional children. In A. E. Kazdin (Ed.), *Evidence-based psychotherapies for children and adolescents* (pp. 204–223). New York: Guilford.

BRISTOL, M. M., & SLOANE, H. N. (1974). Effects of contingency contracting on study rate and test performance. *Journal of Applied Behavior Analysis, 7,* 271–285.

BRODER, M. S. (2000). Making optimal use of homework to enhance your therapeutic effectiveness. *Journal of Rational-Emotive & Cognitive-Behavior Therapy, 18,* 3–18.

BROWN, E. J., HEIMBERG, R. G., & JUSTER, H. R. (1995). Social phobia subtype and avoidant personality disorder: Effect on severity of social phobia, impairment, and outcome of cognitive-behavioral treatment. *Behavior Therapy, 26,* 467–486.

BROWN, G. K., TEN HAVE, T., HENRIQUES, G. R., XIE, S. X., HOLLANDER, J. E., & BECK, A. T. (2005). Cognitive therapy for the prevention of suicide attempts: A randomized controlled trial. *Journal of the American Medical Association, 294,* 563–570.

BROWN, K. A., WACKER, D. P., DERBY, K. M., PECK, S. M., RICHMAN, D. M., SASSO, G. M., et al. (2000). Evaluating the effects of functional communication training in the presence and absence of establishing operations. *Journal of Applied Behavior Analysis, 33,* 53–71.

BROWNELL, K. D., & COHEN, L. R. (1995). Adherence to dietary regimens 1: An overview of research. *Behavioral Medicine, 20,* 149–154.

BROWNING, R. M., & STOVER, D. O. (1971). *Behavior modification in child treatment: An experimental and clinical approach.* Chicago: Aldine-Atherton.

BRYANT, L. E., & BUDD, K. S. (1982). Self-instructional training to increase independent work performance in preschoolers. *Journal of Applied Behavior Analysis, 15,* 259–271.

BRYSON, B. (1999). *A walk in the woods.* New York: Broadway Books.

BUCELL, M. (1979). *An empirically derived self-report inventory for the assessment of assertive behavior.* Unpublished doctoral dissertation, Kent State University, Kent, OH.

BUCHANAN, J. A., & HOULIHAN, D. (2008). The use of in vivo desensitization for the treatment of a specific phobia of earthworms. *Clinical Case Studies, 7,* 12–24.

BUCHER, B., & LOVAAS, O. I. (1968). Use of aversive stimulation in behavior modification. In M. R. Jones (Ed.), *Miami Symposium on the Prediction of Behavior 1967: Aversive stimulation* (pp. 77–145). Coral Gables, FL: University of Miami Press.

BUCKELEW, S. P., CONWAY, R., PARKER, J., DEUSER, W. E., READ, J., WITTY, T. E., et al. (1998). Biofeedback/relaxation training and exercise interventions for fibromyalgia: A prospective study. *Arthritis Care and Research, 11,* 169–209.

BUCKLEY, S. D., & NEWCHOK, D. K. (2006). Analysis and treatment of problem behavior evoked. *Journal of Applied Behavior Analysis, 39,* 141–144.

BUDD, K. S., WORKMAN, D. E., LEMSKY, C. M., & QUICK, D. M. (1994). The Children's Headache Assessment Scale (CHAS): Factor structure and psychometric properties. *Journal of Behavioral Medicine, 17,* 159–179.

BUDNEY, A. J., HIGGINS, S. T., RADONOVICH, K. J., & NOVY, P. L. (2000). Adding voucher-based incentives to coping skills and motivational enhancement improves outcomes during treatment for marijuana dependence. *Journal of Consulting and Clinical Psychology, 68,* 1051–1061.

BUGGEY, T. (2005). Video self-modeling applications with students with autism spectrum disorder in a small private school setting. *Focus on Autism and Other Developmental Disabilities, 20,* 52–63.

BUJOLD, A., LADOUCEUR, R., SYLVAIN, C., & BOISVERT, J. (1994). Treatment of pathological gamblers: An experimental study. *Journal of Behavior Therapy and Experimental Psychiatry, 25,* 275–282.

BURGIO, L. D., WHITMAN, T. L., & JOHNSON, M. R. (1980). A self-instructional package for increasing attending behavior in educable mentally retarded children. *Journal of Applied Behavior Analysis, 13,* 443–459.

Burham, J. J., & Gullone, E. (1997). The Fear Survey Schedule for Children-II: A psychometric investigation with American data. *Behaviour Research and Therapy, 35,* 165–173.

Burman, B., Margolin, G., & John, R. S. (1993). America's angriest home videos: Behavioral contingencies observed in home reenactments of marital conflict. *Journal of Consulting and Clinical Psychology, 61,* 28–39.

Burns, D. [D.] (1980). *Feeling good.* New York: Morrow.

Burns, D. D., & Nolen-Hoeksema, S. (1992). Therapeutic empathy and recovery from depression in cognitive-behavioral therapy: A structural equation model. *Journal of Consulting and Clinical Psychology, 60,* 441–449.

Burns, D. D., & Sprangler, D. L. (2000). Does psychotherapy homework lead to improvements in depression in cognitive-behavioral therapy or does improvement lead to increased homework compliance? *Journal of Consulting and Clinical Psychology, 69,* 46–56.

Bushell, D., Jr. (1978). An engineering approach to the elementary classroom: The Behavior Analysis Follow Through Project. In C. A. Catania & T. A. Brigham (Eds.), *Handbook of applied behavior analysis: Social and instructional processes* (pp. 525–563). New York: Irvington.

Bushman, B. B. (2008). Does teaching problem-solving skills matter? An evaluation of problem-solving skills training for the treatment of social behavioral problems in children. *Dissertation Abstracts International: Section B: The Sciences and Engineering, 68(9-B),* 6292.

Butler, G. (1985). Exposure as a treatment for social phobia: Some instructive difficulties. *Behaviour Research and Therapy, 23,* 651–657.

Butler, L. R., & Luiselli, J. K. (2007). Escape-maintained problem behavior in a child with autism: Antecedent functional analysis and intervention evaluation of noncontingent escape and instructional fading. *Journal of Positive Behavior Interventions, 9,* 195–202.

Cahill, S. P., Rauch, S. A., Hembree, E. A., & Foa, E. B. (2004). Effect of cognitive-behavioral treatments for PTSD on anger. In S. Taylor (Ed.), *Advances in the treatment of posttraumatic stress disorder:*

Cognitive-behavioral perspectives (pp. 175–196). New York: Springer.

Cahoon, D. D. (1968). Symptom substitution and the behavior therapies: A reappraisal. *Psychological Bulletin, 69,* 149–156.

Cairns, D., & Pasino, J. A. (1977). Comparison of verbal reinforcement and feedback in operant treatment of disability due to low back pain. *Behavior Therapy, 8,* 621–630.

Calamari, J. E., Faber, S. D., Hitsman, B. L., & Poppe, C. J. (1994). Treatment of obsessive compulsive disorder in the elderly: A review and case example. *Journal of Behavior Therapy and Experimental Psychiatry, 25,* 95–104.

Callahan, E. J., & Leitenberg, H. (1973). Aversion therapy for sexual deviation: Contingent electric shock and covert sensitization. *Journal of Abnormal Psychology, 81,* 60–73.

Camp, B. W., & Bash, M. A. S. (1981). *Think aloud: Increasing social and cognitive skills—A problem-solving program for children (primary level).* Champaign, IL: Research Press.

Camp, B. W., Blom, G. E., Herbert, F., & Van Doorwick, W. J. (1977). "Think aloud": A program for developing self-control in young aggressive boys. *Journal of Abnormal Child Psychology, 5,* 157–169.

Campbell, J. (1988). *The power of myth.* New York: Doubleday.

Campbell, R. V., & Lutzker, J. R. (1993). Using functional equivalence training to reduce severe challenging behavior: A case study. *Journal of Developmental and Physical Disabilities, 5,* 203–215.

Campbell-Sills, L., Barlow, D. H., Brown, T. A., & Hofmann, S. G. (2006a). Acceptability and suppression of negative emotion in anxiety and mood disorders. *Emotion, 6,* 587–595.

Campbell-Sills, L., Barlow, D. H., Brown, T. A., & Hofmann, S. G. (2006b). Effects of suppression and acceptance on emotional responses on individuals with anxiety and mood disorders. *Behavior Research and Therapy, 44,* 1251–1263.

Canavan, A. G. M., & Powell, G. E. (1981). The efficacy of several treatments of Gilles de la Tourette's syndrome as assessed in a single case. *Behaviour Research and Therapy, 19,* 549–556.

Cano, A., & Leonard, M. (2006). Integrative behavioral couple therapy

for chronic pain: Promoting behavior change and emotional acceptance. *Journal of Clinical Psychology, 62,* 1409–1418.

Cantor, D. W. (1995). Maintaining our professional integrity in the era of managed care. *Psychotherapy Bulletin, 30,* 27–28.

Carey, M. P., Braaten, L. S., Maisto, S. A., Gleason, J. R., Forsyth, A. D., Durant, L. E., et al. (2000). Using information, motivation enhancement, and skills training to reduce the risk of HIV infection for low-income urban woman: A second randomized clinical trial. *Health Psychology, 19,* 3–11.

Carey, R. G., & Bucher, B. B. (1981). Identifying the educative and suppressive effects of positive practice and restitutional overcorrection. *Journal of Applied Behavior Analysis, 14,* 71–80.

Carey, R. G., & Bucher, B. B. (1986). Positive practice over-correction: Effects of reinforcing correct performance. *Behavior Modification, 10,* 73–92.

Carlin, A. S., Hoffman, H. G., & Weghorst, S. (1997). Virtual reality and tactile augmentation in the treatment of spider phobia: A case report. *Behaviour Research and Therapy, 35,* 153–158.

Carlson, C. L., Mann, M., & Alexander, D. K. (2000). Effects of reward and response cost on the performance and motivation of children with ADHD. *Cognitive Therapy and Research, 24,* 87–98.

Carlson, C. L., & Tamm, L. (2000). Responsiveness of children with attention deficit-hyperactivity disorder to reward and response cost: Differential impact on performance and motivation. *Journal of Consulting and Clinical Psychology, 68,* 73–83.

Carlson, C. R., & Bernstein, D. A. (1995). Relaxation skills training: Abbreviated progressive relaxation. In W. O'Donohue & L. Krasner (Eds.), *Handbook of psychological skills training: Clinical techniques and applications* (pp. 20–35). Boston: Allyn & Bacon.

Carlson, C. R., & Hoyle, R. H. (1993). Efficacy of abbreviated progressive muscle relaxation training: A quantitative review of behavioral medicine research. *Journal of Consulting and Clinical Psychology, 61,* 1059–1067.

CARMODY, T. P. (1992). Preventing relapse in the treatment of nicotine addiction: Current issues and future directions. *Journal of Psychoactive Drugs, 24,* 131–158.

CARR, E. G., & DURAND, V. M. (1985). Reducing behavior problems through functional communication training. *Journal of Applied Behavior Analysis, 18,* 111–126.

CARR, E. G., LEVIN, L., McCONNACHIE, G., CARLSON, J. I., KEMP, D. C., & SMITCH, C. E. (1994). *Communication-based intervention for problem behavior: A user's guide for producing positive change.* Baltimore: Brookes.

CARR, J. E. (1995). Competing responses for the treatment of Tourette syndrome and tic disorders. *Behaviour Research and Therapy, 33,* 455–456.

CARRINGTON, P., LEHRER, P. M., & WITTENSTROM, K. (1997). A children's self-management system for reducing homework-related problems: Parent efficacy ratings. *Child & Family Behavior Therapy, 19,* 1–22.

CARROLL, K. M. (1996). Relapse prevention as a psychosocial treatment: A review of controlled clinical trials. *Experimental and Clinical Psychopharmacology, 4,* 46–54.

CARROLL, K. M., & ROUNSAVILLE, B. J. (2008). Efficacy and effectiveness in developing treatment manuals. In A. M. Nezu & C. M. Nezu (Eds.). *Evidence-based outcome research: A practical guide to conducting randomized controlled trials for psychosocial interventions* (pp. 219, 243). New York: Oxford University Press.

CARROLL, K. M., ROUNSAVILLE, B. J., & GAWIN, F. H. (1991). A comparative trial of psychotherapies for ambulatory cocaine abusers: Relapse prevention and interpersonal psychotherapy. *American Journal of Drug and Alcohol Abuse, 17,* 229–247.

CARSTENSEN, L. L., & FISHER, J. E. (1991). Problems of the institutionalized elderly. In P. A. Wisocki (Ed.), *Handbook of clinical behavior therapy for the elderly client* (pp. 337–362). New York: Plenum.

CARTER, J. C., & FAIRBURN, C. G. (1998). Cognitive-behavioral self-help for binge eating disorder: A controlled effectiveness study. *Journal of Consulting and Clinical Psychology, 66,* 616–623.

CARTWRIGHT, D. E. (1955). Effectiveness of psychotherapy: A critique of the spontaneous remission argument. *Journal of Counseling Psychology, 2,* 290–296.

CASEY, S. D., & MERICAL, C. L. (2006). The use of functional communication training without additional treatment procedures in an inclusive school setting. *Behavioral Disorders, 32,* 46–54.

CASH, T. F., & LAVALLEE, D. M. (1997). Cognitive-behavioral body-image therapy: Extended evidence of the efficacy of a self-directed program. *Journal of Rational-Emotive & Cognitive-Behavior Therapy, 15,* 281–294.

CASTANEDA, C. A. (1972). *A separate reality: Further conversations with Don Juan.* New York: Pocket Books.

CAUCE, A. M. (1995, May). *Consequences of introducing culture/diversity into the research context.* Paper presented at the Conference on Marital and Family Therapy Outcome and Process Research: State of the Science, Philadelphia.

CAUTELA, J. R. (1966). Treatment of compulsive behavior by covert sensitization. *Psychological Record, 16,* 33–41.

CAUTELA, J. R. (1967). Covert sensitization. *Psychological Reports, 20,* 459–468.

CAUTELA, J. R. (1970). The use of covert sensitization in the treatment of alcoholism. *Psychotherapy: Theory, Research and Practice, 7,* 86–90.

CAUTELA, J. R. (1972). Rationale and procedures for covert conditioning. In R. D. Rubin, H. Fensterheim, J. D. Henderson, & L. P. Ullmann (Eds.), *Advances in behavior therapy* (pp. 85–96). New York: Academic Press.

CAUTELA, J. R. (1982). Covert conditioning with children. *Journal of Behavior Therapy and Experimental Psychiatry, 13,* 209–214.

CAUTELA, J. R. (1993). Insight in behavior therapy. *Journal of Behavior Therapy and Experimental Psychiatry, 24,* 155–159.

CAUTELA, J. R., & KASTENBAUM, R. (1967). A reinforcement survey schedule for use in therapy, training, and research. *Psychological Reports, 20,* 1115–1130.

CAUTELA, J. R., & KEARNEY, A. J. (1993). *Covert conditioning casebook.* Pacific Grove, CA: Brooks/Cole.

CAVALIER, A. R., FERRETTI, R. P., & HODGES, A. E. (1997). Self-management within a classroom token economy with learning disabilities. *Research on Developmental Disabilities, 18,* 167–178.

CAVALIERE, F. (1995, October). Payers demand increased provider documentation. *APA Monitor, 26,* p. 41.

CAYNER, J. J., & KILAND, J. R. (1974). Use of brief time out with three schizophrenic patients. *Journal of Behavior Therapy and Experimental Psychiatry, 5,* 141–145.

CENTERS FOR DISEASE CONTROL AND PREVENTION. (1994). *HIV/AIDS surveillance report.* Atlanta: Author.

CERVONE, D., & PEAKE, P. K. (1986). Anchoring, efficacy, and action: The influence of judgmental heuristics on self-efficacy judgments and behavior. *Journal of Personality and Social Psychology, 50,* 492–501.

CERVONE, D., & SCOTT, W. D. (1995). Self-efficacy theory of behavioral change: Foundations, conceptual issues, and therapeutic implications. In W. O'Donohue & L. Krasner (Eds.), *Theories of behavior therapy* (pp. 349–383). Washington, DC: American Psychological Association.

CHADWICK, P. D. J., & LOWE, C. F. (1990). Measurement and modification of delusional beliefs. *Journal of Consulting and Clinical Psychology, 58,* 225–232.

CHAMBERLIN, J. (2008, September). Cool tools for school. *GradPSYCH, 6*(3), 24–26.

CHAMBLESS, D. L. (1985). Agoraphobia. In M. Hersen & A. S. Bellack (Eds.), *Handbook of clinical behavior therapy with adults* (pp. 49–87). New York: Plenum.

CHAMBLESS, D. L., FOA, E. B., GROVES, G. A., & GOLDSTEIN, A. J. (1982). Exposure and communications training in the treatment of agoraphobia. *Behaviour Research and Therapy, 20,* 219–231.

CHAMBLESS, D. L., & HOLLON, S. D. (1998). Defining empirically supported therapies. *Journal of Consulting and Clinical Psychology, 66,* 7–18.

CHAMBLESS, D. L., & WILLIAMS, K. E. (1995). A preliminary study of African Americans with agoraphobia: Symptoms severity and outcome of treatment with in vivo exposure. *Behavior Therapy, 26,* 501–515.

CHANDLER, G. M., BURCK, H. D., & SAMPSON, J. P. (1986). A generic computer program for systematic desensitization: Description, construction and case study. *Journal of Behavior Therapy and Experimental Psychiatry, 17,* 171–174.

CHANG, E. C., D'ZURILLA, T. J., & SANNA, L. J. (Eds.). (2004). *Social problem solving: Theory, research, and training*. Washington, DC: American Psychological Association.

CHANG, G., CARROLL, K. M., BEHR, H. M., & KOSTEN, T. R. (1992). Improving treatment outcome in pregnant opiate-dependent women. *Journal of Substance Abuse Treatment*, 9, 327–330.

CHAPMAN, S., FISHER, W., PIAZZA, C. C., & KURTZ, P. F. (1993). Functional assessment and treatment of life-threatening drug ingestion in a dually diagnosed youth. *Journal of Applied Behavior Analysis*, 26, 255–256.

CHARD, K. M. (2005). An evaluation of cognitive processing therapy for the treatment of posttraumatic stress disorder related to childhood sexual abuse. *Journal of Consulting and Clinical Psychology*, 73, 965–971.

CHARLOP, M. H., & MILSTEIN, J. P. (1989). Teaching autistic children conversational speech using video modeling. *Journal of Applied Behavior Analysis*, 22, 275–285.

CHARLOP, M. H., SCHREIBMAN, L., & TRYON, A. S. (1983). Learning through observation: The effects of peer modeling on acquisition and generalization in autistic children. *Journal of Abnormal Child Psychology*, 11, 355–366.

CHEMTOB, C. M., NOVACO, R. W., HAMADA, R. S., & GROSS, D. M. (1997). Cognitive-behavioral treatment for severe anger in posttraumatic stress disorder. *Journal of Consulting and Clinical Psychology*, 65, 184–189.

CHEN, C. P. (1995). Counseling applications of RET in a Chinese cultural context. *Journal of Rational-Emotive & Cognitive-Behavior Therapy*, 13, 117–129.

CHESNEY, M. A., & FOLKMAN, S. (1994). Psychological impact of HIV disease and implications for intervention. *Psychiatric Clinics of North America*, 17, 163–182.

CHORPITA, B. F. (1995). Eventual responders: What do we do when treatments do not work? *the Behavior Therapist*, 18, 140–141.

CHRISTENSEN, A., ATKINS, D. C., BERNS, S., WHEELER, J., BAUCOM, D. H., & SIMPSON, L. E. (2004). Traditional versus integrative behavioral couple therapy for significantly and chronically distressed married couples.

Journal of Consulting and Clinical Psychology, 72, 176–191.

CHRISTENSEN, A., ATKINS, D. C., YI, J., BAUCOM, D. H., & GEORGE, W. H. (2006). Couple and individual adjustment for 2 years following a randomized clinical trial comparing traditional versus integrative behavioral couple therapy. *Journal of Consulting and Clinical Psychology*, 74, 1180–1191.

CHRISTENSEN, A., JACOBSON, N. S., & BABCOCK, J. C. (1995). Integrative behavioral couple therapy. In N. S. Jacobson & A. S. Gurman (Eds.), *Clinical handbook of marital therapy* (2nd ed., pp. 31–64). New York: Guilford.

CHRISTENSEN, H., GRIFFITHS, K. M., & JORM, A. F. (2004). Delivering interventions for depression by using the internet: Randomised controlled trial. *British Medical Journal*, 31, 265.

CHRISTIAN, L., & POLING, A. (1997). Using self-management procedures to improve the productivity of adults with developmental disabilities in a competitive employment setting. *Journal of Applied Behavior Analysis*, 30, 169–172.

CHRISTOPHERSEN, E. R. (1977). *Little people: Guidelines for common sense child rearing*. Lawrence, KS: H & H Enterprises.

CIGRANG, J. A., PETERSON, A. L., & SCHOBITZ, R. P. (2005). Three American troops in Iraq: Evaluation of a brief exposure therapy treatment for the secondary prevention of combat-related PTSD. *Pragmatic Case Studies in Psychotherapy*, 1, 1–25.

CIHAK, D., ALBERTO, P. A., & FREDRICK, L. D. (2007). Use of brief functional analysis and intervention evaluation in public settings. *Journal of Positive Behavior Interventions*, 9, 80–93.

CLARE, S. K., JENSON, W. R., KEHLE, T. J., & BRAY, M. A. (2000). Self-modeling as a treatment for increasing on-task behavior. *Psychology in the Schools*, 37, 517–522.

CLARK, D. F. (1966). Behaviour therapy of Gilles de la Tourette's syndrome. *British Journal of Psychiatry*, 112, 771–778.

CLARK, G. R., BUSSONE, A., & KIVITZ, M. S. (1974). Elwyn Institute's community living program. *The Challenge*, 17, 14–15.

CLARK, G. R., KIVITZ, M. S., & ROSEN, M. (1972). From research to

community living. *Human Needs*, 1, 25–28.

CLARKE, G. N., HAWKINS, W., MURPHY, M., SHEEBER, L. B., LEWINSOHN, P. M., & SEELEY, J. R. (1995). Targeted prevention of unipolar depressive disorder in an at-risk sample of high school adolescents: A randomized trial of a group cognitive intervention. *Journal of the American Academy of Child and Adolescent Psychiatry*, 34, 312–321.

CLARKE, M. A., BRAY, M. A., KEHLE, T. J., & TRUSCOTT, S. D. (2001). A school-based intervention designed to reduce the frequency of tics in children with Tourette's syndrome. *School Psychology Review*, 30, 11–22.

CLARKE, S., & DUNLAP, G.A. (2008). A descriptive analysis of intervention research published in the Journal of Positive Behavior Interventions: 1999 through 2005. *Journal of Positive Behavior Interventions*, 10, 67–71.

CLEES, T. J. (1994–95). Self-recording of students' daily schedules of teachers' expectancies: Perspectives on reactivity, stimulus control, and generalization. *Exceptionality*, 5, 113–129.

CLOITRE, M. (1995). An interview with Edna Foa. *the Behavior Therapist*, 18, 177–181.

CLOSE, J. M. (2000). Planned activities with and without a timeout component for families reported for child maltreatment. *Dissertation Abstracts International*, 60, 6350–6350.

CLUM, G. A., CLUM, G. A., & SURLS, R. (1993). A meta-analysis of treatment for panic disorder. *Journal of Consulting and Clinical Psychology*, 61, 317–326.

CLUM, G. A., & FEBBRARO, G. A. R. (2004). Social problem solving and suicide risk. In E. C. Chang, T. J. D'Zurilla, & L. J. Sanna (Eds.), *Social problem solving: Theory, research, and training* (pp. 67–82). Washington, DC: American Psychological Association.

COCCO, N., & SHARPE, L. (1993). An auditory variant of eye movement desensitization in a case of childhood post-traumatic stress disorder. *Journal of Behavior Therapy and Experimental Psychiatry*, 24, 373–377.

COE, D. A., BABBIT, R. L., WILLIAMS, K. E., HAJIMIHALIS, C., SNYDER, A. M., BALLARD, C., et al. (1997). Use of extinction and reinforcement to increase food consumption and reduce expulsion. *Journal of Applied Behavior Analysis*, 30, 581–583.

COFER, C. N., & APPLEY, M. H. (1964). *Motivation: Theory and research.* New York: Wiley.

COFFEY, S. F., SCHUMACHER, J. A., BRIMO, M. L., & BRADY, K. T. (2005). Exposure therapy for substance abusers with PTSD: Translating research to practice. *Behavior Modification, 29,* 10–38.

COFFMAN, S. J., MARTELL, C. R., DIMIDJIAN, S., GALLOP, R., & HOLLON, S. D. (2007). Extreme nonresponse in cognitive therapy: Can behavioral activation succeed where cognitive therapy fails? *Journal of Consulting and Clinical Psychology, 75,* 531–541.

COHEN, D. J., LECKMAN, J. F., & SHAYWITZ, B. (1984). *A physician's guide to diagnosis and treatment of Tourette syndrome: A neurological multiple tic disorder.* New York: Tourette Syndrome Association.

COHEN, J. (1988). *Statistical power analysis for the behavioral sciences* (2nd ed.). New York: Academic Press.

COLDWELL, S. E., GETZ, T., MILGROM, P., PRALL, C. W., SPADAFORA, A., & RAMSAY, D. S. (1998). CARL: A LabVIEW 3 computer program for conducting exposure therapy for the treatment of dental injection fear. *Behaviour Research and Therapy, 36,* 429–441.

COLE, G. A., MONTGOMERY, R. W., WILSON, K. M., & MILAN, M. A. (2000). Parametric analysis of overcorrection duration effects: Is longer really better than shorter? *Behavior Modification, 24,* 359–377.

COLES, M. E., HART, T. A., & HEIMBERG, R. G. (2001). Cognitive-behavioral group treatment for social phobia. In R. Crozier & L. E. Alden (Eds.), *International handbook or social anxiety* (pp. 449–469). New York: Wiley.

COLLIER, W. C., & MARLATT, G. A. (1995). Relapse prevention. In A. J. Goreczny (Ed.), *Handbook of health and rehabilitation psychology* (pp. 307–321). New York: Plenum.

COMBS, M. L., & LAHEY, B. B. (1981). A cognitive social skills training program: Evaluation with young children. *Behavior Modification, 5,* 39–60.

COMER, R. J. (2008). *Fundamentals of abnormal psychology* (5th ed.). New York: Worth.

COMMON LANGUAGE FOR PSYCHOTHERAPY. (2008, June 10). Retrieved June 10, 2008, from http://www.commonlanguagepsychotherapy.org/

COMPAS, B. E., HAAGA, D. A. [F.], KEEFE, F. J., LEITENBERG, H., & WILLIAMS, D. A. (1998). Sampling of empirically supported psychological treatments from health psychology: Smoking, chronic pain, cancer, and bulimia nervosa. *Journal of Consulting and Clinical Psychology, 66,* 89–112.

CONE, J. D. (1993). The current state of behavioral assessment. *European Journal of Psychological Assessment, 9,* 175–181.

CONE, J. D. (1998). Psychometric considerations: Concepts, contents, and methods. In M. Hersen & A. S. Bellack (Eds.), *Behavioral assessment: A practical handbook* (4th ed., pp. 22–46). Boston: Allyn & Bacon.

CONE, J. D., ALEXANDER, K., LICHTSZAJN, J. L., & MASON, R. L. (1996). Re-engineering clinical training curricula to meet challenges beyond the year 2000. *the Behavior Therapist, 19,* 65–70.

CONSTANTINO, G., MALGADY, R. G., & ROGLER, L. G. (1986). Cuento therapy: A culturally sensitive modality for Puerto Rican children. *Journal of Consulting and Clinical Psychology, 54,* 639–645.

COOK, C. R., & BLACHER, J. (2007). Evidence-based psychosocial treatments for tic disorders. *Clinical Psychology: Science and Practice, 14,* 252–267.

COOK, J. M., SCHNURR, P. P., & FOA, E. B. (2004). Bridging the gap between posttraumatic stress disorder research and clinical practice: The example of exposure therapy. *Psychotherapy: Theory, Research, Practice, Training, 41,* 374–387.

COOK, K. G., NAU, S. D., & LICHSTEIN, K. L. (2005). Behavioral treatment of late-life insomnia. In L. VandeCreek (Ed.), *Innovations in clinical practice: Focus on adults* (pp. 65–81). Sarasota, FL: Professional Resource Press/Professional Resource Exchange.

COOK, S., PETERSON, L., & DILILLO, D. (1999). Fear and exhilaration in response to risk: An extension of a model of injury risk in a real-world context. *Behavior Therapy, 30,* 5–15.

COON, D. W., & THOMPSON, L. W. (2002). Family caregivers for older adults: Ongoing and emergent themes for the behavior therapist. *the Behavior Therapist, 25,* 17–20.

COOPER, J. O., HERON, T. E., & HEWARD, W. L. (1987). *Applied behavior analysis.* Columbus, OH: Merrill.

COOPER, L. J., WACKER, D. P., BROWN, K., MCCOMAS, J. J., PECK, S. M., DREW, J., et al. (1999). Use of a concurrent operants paradigm to evaluate positive reinforcers during treatment of food refusal. *Behavior Modification, 23,* 3–40.

CORRIGAN, S. A., THOMPSON, K. E., & MALOW, R. M. (1992). A psychoeducational approach to prevent HIV transmission among injection drug users. *Psychology of Addictive Behaviors, 6,* 114–119.

COSTENBADER, V., & READING-BROWN, M. (1995). Isolation timeout used with students with emotional disturbance. *Exceptional Children, 61,* 353–363.

COTHARIN, R. L., & MIKULAS, W. L. (1975). Systematic desensitization of racial emotional responses. *Journal of Behavior Therapy and Experimental Psychiatry, 6,* 347–348.

COTTER, L. H. (1967). Operant conditioning in a Vietnamese mental hospital. *American Journal of Psychiatry, 124,* 23–28.

COTTRAUX, J. (1990). "Cogito ergo sum": Cognitive-behavior therapy in France. *the Behavior Therapist, 13,* 189–190.

COTTRAUX, J. (1993). Behavioral psychotherapy applications in the medically ill. *Psychotherapy and Psychosomatics, 60,* 116–128.

COUSINS, N. (1979). *Anatomy of an illness.* New York: Norton.

COUSINS, N. (1989). *Head first: The biology of hope.* New York: Dutton.

COWLEY, G. (1994, June 20). Waving away the pain. *Newsweek, 123,* 70–71.

COX, B. J., FERGUS, K. D., & SWINSON, R. P. (1994). Patient satisfaction with behavioral treatments for panic disorder with agoraphobia. *Journal of Anxiety Disorders, 8,* 193–206.

COX, B. S., COX, A. B., & COX, D. J. (2000). Motivating signage prompts safety belt use among drivers exiting senior communities. *Journal of Applied Behavior Analysis, 33,* 635–638.

COYNE, L. W., FAUL, L. A., & GROSS, A. M. (2000). Harnessing environmental contingencies to enhance social skills: The case of Mike J. *Cognitive and Behavioral Practice, 7,* 231–235.

CRADOCK, C., COTLER, S., & JASON, L. A. (1978). Primary prevention: Immunization of children for speech anxiety. *Cognitive Therapy and Research, 2,* 389–396.

CRAIG, K. D. (1986). Social modeling influences: Pain in context. In R. A. Sternbach (Ed.), *The psychology of pain* (2nd ed., pp. 67–95). New York: Raven Press.

CRAIGHEAD, W. E. (1990). There's a place for us: All of us. *Behavior Therapy, 21,* 3–23.

CRAIGHEAD, W. E., KAZDIN, A. E., & MAHONEY, M. J. (1976). *Behavior modification: Principles, issues, and applications.* Boston: Houghton Mifflin.

CRAIGHEAD, W. E., KIMBALL, W. H., & REHAK, P. J. (1979). Mood changes, physiological responses, and self-statements during social rejection imagery. *Journal of Consulting and Clinical Psychology, 47,* 385–396.

CRASKE, M. G., & BARLOW, D. H. (2008). Panic disorder and agoraphobia. In D. H. Barlow (Ed.), *Handbook of psychological disorders: A step-by-step treatment manual* (4th ed., pp. 1–64). New York: Guilford.

CREER, T. L., & MIKLICH, D. R. (1970). The application of a self-modeling procedure to modify inappropriate behavior: A preliminary report. *Behaviour Research and Therapy, 8,* 91–92.

CREPAZ, N., PASSIN, W. F., HERBST, J. H., RAMA, S. M., MALOW, R. M., PURCELL, D. W., et al. (2008). Meta-analysis of cognitive-behavioral interventions on HIV-positive persons' mental health and immune functioning. *Health Psychology, 27,* 4–14.

CRITCHFIELD, T. S., & VARGAS, E. A. (1991). Self-recording, instructions, and public self-graphing. *Behavior Modification, 15,* 95–112.

CRITS-CHRISTOPH, P., WILSON, T. G., & HOLLON, S. D. (2005). Empirically supported psychotherapies: Comment on Westen, Novotny, and Thompson-Brenner (2004). *Psychological Bulletin, 131,* 412–417.

CSIKSZENTMIHALYI, M. (1990). *Flow: The psychology of optimal experience.* New York: Harper & Row.

CSIKSZENTMIHALYI, M., & CSIKSZENTMIHALYI, I. S. (Eds.). (1988). *Optimal experience: Psychological studies of flow in consciousness.* New York: Cambridge University Press.

CULLEN, J. W., FOX, B. H., & ISOM, R. N. (1976). *Cancer: The behavioral dimension.* New York: Raven Press.

CUNLIFFE, T. (1992). Arresting youth crime: A review of social skills training with young offenders. *Adolescence, 27,* 891–899.

CURRIE, S. R., WILSON, K. G., PONTEFRACT, A. J., & DELAPLANTE, L. (2000). Cognitive-behavioral treatment of insomnia secondary to chronic pain. *Journal of Consulting and Clinical Psychology, 68,* 407–416.

DA COSTA, I. G., RAPOFF, M. A., & GOLDSTEIN, G. L. (1997). Improving adherence to medication regimens for children with asthma and its effect on clinical outcome. *Journal of Applied Behavior Analysis, 30,* 687–691.

DAHL, J., WILSON, K. G., & NILSSON, A. (2004). Acceptance and Commitment Therapy and the treatment of persons at risk for long-term disability resulting from stress and pain symptoms: A preliminary randomized trial. *Behavior Therapy, 35,* 785–802.

DAHLQUIST, L. M., GIL, K. M., ARMSTRONG, F. D., GINSBERG, A., & JONES, B. (1985). Behavioral management of children's distress during chemotherapy. *Journal of Behavior Therapy and Experimental Psychiatry, 16,* 325–329.

DALEY, M. F. (1969). The "Reinforcement Menu": Finding effective reinforcers. In J. D. Krumboltz & C. E. Thoresen (Eds.), *Behavioral counseling: Cases and techniques* (pp. 42–45). New York: Holt, Rinehart & Winston.

DALRYMPLE, K. L., & HERBERT, J. D. (2007). Acceptance and Commitment Therapy for generalized social anxiety disorder: A pilot study. *Behavior Modification, 31,* 543–568.

DANAHER, B. G. (1974). Theoretical foundations and clinical applications of the Premack principle: Review and critique. *Behavior Therapy, 5,* 307–324.

DANFORTH, J. S. (1998). The outcome of parent training using the behavior management flow chart with mothers and their children with oppositional defiant disorder and attention-deficit hyperactivity disorder. *Behavior Modification, 22,* 443–473.

DAPCICH-MIURA, E., & HOVELL, M. F. (1979). Contingency management of adherence to a complex medical regimen in an elderly heart patient. *Behavior Therapy, 10,* 193–201.

DATE, A. (1996). On maintaining an empirical orientation in an "alternative ways of knowing" world. *the Behavior Therapist, 19,* 86.

DATTILIO, F. M. (1999). Cognitive behavior therapy in Cuba. *the Behavior Therapist, 22,* 78, 91.

DATTILIO, F. M., & PADESKY, C. A. (1990). *Cognitive therapy with couples.* Sarasota, FL: Professional Resource Exchange.

DAUNIC, A. P., SMITH, S. W., BRANK, E. M., & PENFIELD, R. D. (2006). Classroom-based cognitive-behavioral intervention to prevent aggression: Efficacy and social validity. *Journal of School Psychology, 44,* 123–139.

DAVIDSON, P. R., & PARKER, K. C. H. (2001). Eye movement desensitization and reprocessing (EMDR): A meta-analysis. *Journal of Consulting and Clinical Psychology, 69,* 305–316.

DAVIS, C. A., & FOX, J. (1999). Evaluating environmental arrangements as setting events: Review and implications of measurement. *Journal of Behavioral Education, 9,* 77–96.

DAVIS, M. (2006). Neural systems involved in fear and anxiety measured with fear-potentiated startle. *American Psychologist, 61,* 741–756.

DAVIS, M., MYERS, K. M., CHHATWAL, J., & RESSLER, K. J. (2006). Pharmacological treatments that facilitate extinction of fear: Relevance to psychotherapy. *NeuroRx, 3,* 82–96.

DAVIS, P. K., & CHITTUM, R. (1994). A group-oriented contingency to increase leisure activities of adults with traumatic brain injury. *Journal of Applied Behavior Analysis, 27,* 553–554.

DAVIS, R. A. (1979). The impact of self-modeling on problem behaviors in school-age children. *School Psychology Digest, 8,* 128–132.

DAVIS, T. E., III, KURTZ, P. F., GARDNER, A. W., & CARMAN, N. B. (2007). Cognitive-behavioral treatment for specific phobias with a child demonstrating severe problem behavior and developmental delays. *Research in Developmental Disabilities, 28,* 546–558.

DAVISON, G. C. (1976). Homosexuality: The ethical challenge. *Journal of Consulting and Clinical Psychology, 44,* 157–162.

DAVISON, G. C., D'ZURILLA, T. J., GOLDFRIED, M. R., PAUL, G. L., & VALINS, S. (1968, August). In M. R. Goldfried (Chair), *Cognitive processes in behavior modification.* Symposium presented at the meeting of the American Psychological Association, San Francisco.

DAVISON, G. C., & LAZARUS, A. A. (1995). The dialectics of science and practice. In S. C. Hayes, V. M. Follette, R. M. Dawes, & K. E. Grady (Eds.), *Scientific standards of psychological practice: Issues and recommendations* (pp. 95–120). Reno, NV: Context Press.

DAVISON, G. C., NAVARRE, S. G., & VOGEL, R. S. (1995). The articulated thoughts in simulated situations paradigm: A think-aloud approach to cognitive assessment. *Current Directions in Psychological Science, 4,* 29–33.

DAVISON, G. C., & STUART, R. B. (1975). Behavior therapy and civil liberties. *American Psychologist, 30,* 755–763.

DAVISON, G. C., VOGEL, R. S., & COFFMAN, S. G. (1997). Think-aloud approaches to cognitive assessment and the Articulated Thoughts in Simulated Situations paradigm. *Journal of Consulting and Clinical Psychology, 65,* 950–958.

DAWE, G. F., & HART, D. S. (1986, June). *Covert modeling and rehearsal in the treatment of social anxiety.* Paper presented at the meeting of the Canadian Psychological Association, Toronto.

DAWSON, B., DE ARMAS, A., MCGRATH, M. L., & KELLY, J. A. (1986). Cognitive problem-solving training to improve child-care judgment of child neglectful parents. *Journal of Family Violence, 1,* 209–221.

DAY, L., & REZNIKOFF, M. (1980). Preparation of children and parents for treatment at a children's psychiatric clinic through videotaped modeling. *Journal of Consulting and Clinical Psychology, 48,* 303–304.

DEACON, B. J., & ABRAMOWITZ, J. S. (2004). Cognitive and behavioral treatments for anxiety disorders: A review of meta-analytic findings. *Journal of Clinical Psychology, 60,* 429–441.

DEALE, A., CHALDER, T., MARKS, I. [M.], & WESSELY, S. (1997). Cognitive behavior therapy for chronic fatigue syndrome: A randomized control trial. *American Journal of Psychiatry, 154,* 408–414.

DEANGELIS, T. (2002). Promising treatments for anorexia and bulimia. *Monitor on Psychology, 33,* 38–41.

DEANGELIS, T. (2008, February). When do meds make the difference? *Monitor on Psychology, 39,* 48–51.

DEFFENBACHER, J. L., DAHLEN, E. R., LYNCH, R. S., MORRIS, C. D., &
GOWENSMITH, W. N. (2000). An application of Beck's cognitive therapy to general anger reduction. *Cognitive Therapy and Research, 24,* 689–697.

DEFFENBACHER, J. [L.], FILETTI, L., LYNCH, R., & DAHLEN, E. (2000, August). *Interventions for the reduction of driving anger.* Paper presented at the 108th Annual Convention of the American Psychological Association, Washington, DC.

DEFFENBACHER, J. [L.], HUFF, M., LYNCH, R., OETTING, E., & SALVATORE, N. (2000). Characteristics and treatment of high-anger drivers. *Journal of Counseling Psychology, 47,* 5–17.

DEGOTARDI, P. J., KLASS, E. S., ROSENBERG, B. S., FOX, D. G., GALLELLI, K. A., & GOTTLIEB, B. S. (2006). Development and evaluation of a cognitive-behavioral intervention for juvenile fibromyalgia. *Journal of Pediatric Psychology, 31,* 714–723.

DEITZ, S. M. (1977). An analysis of programming DRL schedules in educational settings. *Behaviour Research and Therapy, 15,* 103–111.

DEITZ, S. M., & REPP, A. C. (1973). Decreasing classroom misbehavior through the use of DRL schedules of reinforcement. *Journal of Applied Behavior Analysis, 6,* 457–463.

DEITZ, S. M., REPP, A. C., & DEITZ, D. E. D. (1976). Reducing inappropriate classroom behavior of retarded students through three procedures of differential reinforcement. *Journal of Mental Deficiency Research, 20,* 155–170.

DE JONG, P. J., VORAGE, I., & VAN DEN HOUT, M. A. (2000). Counterconditioning in the treatment of spider phobia: Effects on disgust, fear, and valence. *Behaviour Research and Therapy, 38,* 1055–1069.

DE KINKELDER, M., & BOELENS, H. (1998). Habit-reversal treatment for children's stuttering: Assessment in three settings. *Journal of Behavior Therapy and Experimental Psychiatry, 29,* 261–265.

DELANO, M. E. (2007). Improving written language performance of adolescents with Asperger syndrome. *Journal of Applied Behavior Analysis, 40,* 345–351.

DELEON, G., & MANDELL, W. (1966). A comparison of conditioning and psychotherapy in the treatment of functional enuresis. *Journal of Clinical Psychology, 22,* 326–330.
DELEON, G., & SACKS, S. (1972). Conditioning functional enuresis: A four-year follow-up. *Journal of Consulting and Clinical Psychology, 39,* 299–300.

DE L. HORNE, D. J., TAYLOR, M., & VARIGOS, G. (1999). The effects of relaxation with and without imagery in reducing anxiety and itchy skin in patients with eczema. *Behavioural and Cognitive Psychotherapy, 27,* 143–151.

DE L. HORNE, D. J., VATMANIDIS, P., & CARERI, A. (1994). Preparing patients for invasive medical and surgical procedures 1: Adding behavioral and cognitive interventions. *Behavioral Medicine, 20,* 5–13.

DE L. HORNE, D. J., WHITE, A. E., & VARIGOS, G. A. (1989). A preliminary study of psychological therapy in the management of atopic eczema. *British Journal of Medical Psychology, 62,* 241–248.

DEMBER, W. N. (1974). Motivation and the cognitive revolution. *American Psychologist, 29,* 161–168.

DE MOOR, J., DIDDEN, R., & TOLBOOM, J. (2005). Severe feeding problems secondary to anatomical disorders: Effectiveness of behavioural treatment in three school-aged children. *Educational Psychology, 25,* 325–340.

DEPP, C., & LEBOWITZ, B. D. (2007). Clinical trials: Bridging the gap between efficacy and effectiveness. *International Review of Psychiatry, 19,* 531–539.

DE QUIRÓS ARAGÓN, M. B., LABRADOR, F. J., & DE ARCE, F. (2005). Evaluation of a group cue exposure treatment for opiate addicts. *The Spanish Journal of Psychology, 8,* 229–237.

DERBY, K. M., WACKER, D. P., BERG, W., DERAAD, A., ULRICH, S., ASMUS, J., et al. (1997). The long-term effects of functional communication training in home settings. *Journal of Applied Behavior Analysis, 30,* 587–531.

DERBY, K. M., WACKER, D. P., SASSO, G., STEEGE, M., NORTHUP, J., CIGLAND, K., et al. (1992). Brief functional assessment techniques to evaluate aberrant behavior in an outpatient setting: A summary of 79 cases. *Journal of Applied Behavior Analysis, 25,* 713–721.

DERUBEIS, R. J., TANG, T. Z., & BECK, A. T. (2001). Cognitive therapy. In K. S. Dobson (Ed.), *Handbook of cognitive-behavioral therapies*

(2nd ed., pp. 349–392). New York: Guilford.

DEVILLY, G. J., & SPENCE, S. H. (1999). The relative efficacy and treatment distress of EMDR and a cognitive behavioral trauma treatment protocol in the amelioration of post-traumatic stress disorder. *Journal of Anxiety Disorders, 13*, 131–157.

DEWHURST, D. T. (1993). Using the self-control triad to treat tension headache in a child. In J. R. Cautela & A. J. Kearney (Eds.), *Covert conditioning casebook* (pp. 75–81). Pacific Grove, CA: Brooks/Cole.

DICK-SISKIN, L. P. (2002). Cognitive-behavioral therapy with older adults. *the Behavior Therapist, 25*, 3–4, 6.

DIDDEN, R., CURFS, L. M. G., SIKKEMA, S. P. E., & DE MOOR, J. (1998). Functional assessment and treatment of sleeping problems with developmentally disabled children: Six case studies. *Journal of Behavior Therapy and Experimental Psychiatry, 29*, 85–97.

DIEFENBACH, G. J., ABRAMOWITZ, J. S., & NORBERG, M. M. (2007). Changes in quality of life following cognitive-behavioral therapy for obsessive-compulsive disorder. *Behaviour Research and Therapy, 45*, 3060–3068.

DIFEDE, J., CUKOR, J., JAYASINGHE, N., PATT, I., JEDEL, S., SPIELMAN, L., et al. (2007). Virtual reality exposure therapy for the treatment of post-traumatic stress disorder following September 11, 2001. *Journal of Clinical Psychiatry, 68*, 1639–1647.

DIFEDE, J., CUKOR, J., PATT, I., GOISAN, C., & HOFFMAN, H. (2006). The application of virtual reality to the treatment of PTSD following the WTC attack. *Annals of the New York Academy of Sciences, 1071*, 500–501.

DIFEDE, J., & ESKRA, D. (2002). Cognitive processing therapy for PTSD in a survivor of the World Trade Center bombing: A case study. In S. N. Gold & J. Faust (Eds.), *Trauma practice in the wake of September 11*, 2001 (pp. 155–165). New York: Haworth Press.

DIFEDE, J., & HOFFMAN, H. G. (2002). Virtual reality exposure therapy for World Trade Center post-traumatic stress disorder: A case report. *Cyberpsychology & Behavior, 5*, 529–535.

DIGENNARO, F. D., MARTENS, B. K., & MCINTYRE, L. L. (2005). Increasing treatment integrity through negative reinforcement: Effects on teacher and student behavior. *School Psychology Review, 34*, 220–231.

DIGIUSEPPE, R. A. (1981). Cognitive therapy with children. In G. Emery, S. D. Hollon, & R. C. Bedrosian (Eds.), *New directions in cognitive therapy: A casebook* (pp. 50–67). New York: Guilford.

DIGIUSEPPE, R. [A.] (1989). Cognitive therapy with children. In A. Freeman, K. M. Simon, L. E. Beutler, & H. Arkowitz (Eds.), *Comprehensive handbook of cognitive therapy* (pp. 515–533). New York: Plenum.

DIGIUSEPPE, R. [A.] (2007). Dissemination of CBT research results: Preaching to the uninterested or engaging in scientific debate. *the Behavior Therapist, 30*, 117–120.

DIGIUSEPPE, R. [A.] (2008). Surfing the waves of behavior therapy. *the Behavior Therapist, 31*, 154–155.

DIMEFF, L. A., & KOERNER, K. (Eds.). (2007). *Dialectical behavior therapy in clinical practice: Applications across disorders and settings.* New York: Guilford.

DIMIDJIAN, S., HOLLON, S. D., DOBSON, K. S., SCHMALING, K. B., KOHLENBERG, R. J., ADDIS, M. E., et al. (2006). Randomized trial of behavioral activation, cognitive therapy, and antidepressant medication in the acute treatment of adults with major depression. *Journal of Consulting and Clinical Psychology, 74*, 658–670.

DITOMASSO, R. A., MARTIN, D. M., & KOVNAT, K. D. (2000). In F. M. Dattilio & A. Freeman (Eds.), *Cognitive-behavioral strategies for crisis intervention* (2nd ed., pp. 409–428). New York: Guilford.

DOBSON, K. S., HOLLON, S. D., DIMIDJIAN, S., SCHMALING, K. B., KOHLENBERG, R. J., GALLOP, R. J., et al. (2008). Randomized trial of behavioral activation, cognitive therapy, and antidepressant medication in the prevention of relapse and recurrence in major depression. *Journal of Consulting and Clinical Psychology, 76*, 468–477.

DOIRON, J. P., & NICKI, R. M. (2007). Prevention of pathological gambling: A randomized controlled trial. *Cognitive Behaviour Therapy, 36*, 74–84.

DOLCE, J. J., DOLEYS, D. M., RACZYNSKI, J. M., LOSSIE, J., POOLE, L., & SMITH, M. (1986). The role of self-efficacy expectancies in the prediction of pain tolerance. *Pain, 27*, 261–272.

DOLEYS, D. M. (1977). Behavioral treatment of nocturnal enuresis in children: A review of the recent literature. *Psychological Bulletin, 84*, 30–54.

DOLEYS, D. M., CROCKER, M., & PATTON, D. (1982). Response of patients with chronic pain to exercise quotas. *Physical Therapy, 62*, 1111–1114.

DOLEZAL, D. N., WEBER, K. P., EVAVOLD, J. J., WYLIE, J., & MCLAUGHLIN, T. F. (2007). The effects of a reinforcement package for on-task and reading behavior with at-risk and middle school students with disabilities. *Child & Family Behavior Therapy, 29*, 9–25.

DONAHUE, B., THEVENIN, D. M., & RUNYON, M. K. (1997). Behavioral treatment of conversion disorder in adolescence: A case example of Globus Hystericus. *Behavior Modification, 21*, 231–251.

DONOHUE, B. C., VAN HASSELT, V. B., & HERSEN, M. (1994). Behavioral assessment and treatment of social phobia: An evaluative review. *Behavior Modification, 18*, 262–288.

DOOLEY, R. T., & HALFORD, W. K. (1992). A comparison of relapse prevention with nicotine gum or nicotine fading in modification of smoking. *Australian Psychologist, 27*, 186–191.

DOSS, B. D., THUM, Y. M., SEVIER, M., ATKINS, D. C., & CHRISTENSEN, A. (2005). Improving relationships: Mechanisms of change in couple therapy. *Journal of Consulting and Clinical Psychology, 73*, 624–633.

DOUGHER, M. J. (1993). Covert sensitization in the treatment of deviant sexual arousal. In J. R. Cautela & A. J. Kearney (Eds.), *Covert conditioning casebook* (pp. 199–207). Pacific Grove, CA: Brooks/Cole.

DOUGHER, M. J., & HACKBERT, L. (1994). A behavior-analytic account of depression and a case report using acceptance-based procedures. *The Behavior Analyst, 17*, 321–334.

DOUGHTY, S. S., & ANDERSON, C. M. (2006). Effects of noncontingent reinforcement and functional communication training on problem behavior and mands. *Education & Treatment of Children, 29*, 23–50.

DOWNS, A. F. D., ROSENTHAL, T. L., & LICHSTEIN, K. L. (1988). Modeling therapies reduce avoidance of bath-time by the institutionalized elderly. *Behavior Therapy, 19*, 359–368.

DOWRICK, P. W. (1978). Suggestions for the use of edited video replay in training behavioral skills. *Journal of Practical Approaches to Developmental Handicap, 2,* 21–24.

DOWRICK, P. W. (1991). *Practical guide to using video in the behavioral sciences.* New York: Wiley.

DOWRICK, P. W. (1994). Video psychology. In R. J. Corsini (Ed.), *Encyclopedia of psychology* (2nd ed., pp. 566–567). New York: Wiley.

DOWRICK, P. W. (1999). A review of self modeling and related interventions. *Applied & Preventive Psychology, 8,* 23–39.

DOWRICK, P. W. (2007). Community-driven learning activities, creating futures: 30,000 people can't be wrong—Can they? *American Journal of Community Psychology, 39,* 13–19.

DOWRICK, P. W., KIM-RUPNOW, W. S., & POWER, T. J. (2006). Video feedforward for reading. *The Journal of Special Education, 39,* 194–207.

DOWRICK, P. W., & RAEBURN, J. M. (1995). Self-modeling: Rapid skill training for children with physical disabilities. *Journal of Developmental and Physical Disabilities, 7,* 25–37.

DOWRICK, P. W., TALLMAN, B. I., & CONNER, M. E. (2005). Constructing better future via video. *Journal of Prevention & Intervention in the Community, 29,* 131–144.

DOWRICK, P. W., & WARD, K. M. (1997). Video feedforward in the support of a man with intellectual disability and inappropriate sexual behaviour. *Journal of Intellectual and Developmental Disability, 22,* 147–160.

DRYDEN, W., & ELLIS, A. (2001). Rational emotive behavior therapy. In K. S. Dobson (Ed.), *Handbook of cognitive-behavioral therapies* (2nd. ed., pp. 295–348). New York: Guilford.

DRYDEN, W., & HILL, L. K. (Eds.). (1993). *Innovations in rational-emotive therapy.* Newbury Park, CA: Sage.

DUBBERT, P. M. (1992). Exercise in behavioral medicine. *Journal of Consulting and Clinical Psychology, 60,* 613–618.

DUCHARME, D. E., & HOLBORN, S. W. (1997). Programming generalization of social skills in preschool children with hearing impairments. *Journal of Applied Behavior Analysis, 30,* 639–651.

DUCHARME, J. M., & VAN HOUTEN, R. (1994). Operant extinction in the treatment of severe maladaptive behavior: Adapting research to practice. *Behavior Modification, 18,* 139–170.

DUDLEY, R., DIXON, J., & TURKINGTON, D. (2005). CBT for a person with schizophrenia: Systematic desensitization for phobias led to a positive symptom improvement. *Behavioural and Cognitive Psychotherapy, 33,* 249–254.

DULEY, S. M., CANCELLI, A. A., KRATOCHWILL, T. R., BERGAN, J. R., & MEREDITH, K. E. (1983). Training and generalization of motivational analysis interview assessment skills. *Behavioral Assessment, 5,* 281–293.

DUNBAR, J. M., & STUNKARD, A. J. (1979). Adherence to diet and drug regimens. In R. Levy, B. Rifkin, B. Dennis, & N. Ernst (Eds.), *Nutrition, lipids, and coronary heart disease* (pp. 391–423). New York: Raven Press.

DUNKEL, L. D., & GLAROS, A. G. (1978). Comparison of self-instructional and stimulus control treatments for obesity. *Cognitive Therapy and Research, 2,* 75–78.

DUNLAP, G., ESTER, T., LANGHANS, S., & FOX, L. (2006). Functional communication training with toddlers in home environments. *Journal of Early Intervention, 28,* 81–86.

DUPAUL, G. J., GUEVREMONT, D. C., & BARKLEY, R. A. (1992). Behavioral treatment of attention-deficit hyperactivity disorder in the classroom: The use of the attention training system. *Behavior Modification, 16,* 204–225.

DUPAUL, G. J., & WEYANDT, L. L. (2006). School-based intervention for children with attention deficit hyperactivity disorder: Effects on academic, social, and behavioural functioning. *International Journal of Disability, Development and Education, 53,* 161–176.

DURAND, V. M. (1999). Functional communication training using assistive devices: Recruiting natural communities of reinforcement. *Journal of Applied Behavior Analysis, 32,* 247–267.

DURAND, V. M., & MINDELL, J. A. (1990). Behavioral treatment of multiple childhood sleep disorders. *Behavior Modification, 14,* 37–49.

DURAND, V. M., & MINDELL, J. A. (1999). Behavioral interventions for childhood sleep terrors. *Behavior Therapy, 30,* 705–715.

DYER, W. (1977). *Your erroneous zones.* New York: Funk & Wagnalls.

D'ZURILLA, T. J., & CHANG, E. C. (1995). The relations between social problem solving and coping. *Cognitive Therapy and Research 19,* 547–562.

D'ZURILLA, T. J., CHANG, E. C., NOTTINGHAM, E. J., & FACCINI, L. (1998). Social problem-solving deficits and hopelessness, depression, and suicide risk in college students and psychiatric inpatients. *Journal of Clinical Psychology, 54,* 1–17.

D'ZURILLA, T. J., & GOLDFRIED, M. R. (1971). Problem solving and behavior modification. *Journal of Abnormal Psychology, 78,* 107–126.

D'ZURILLA, T. J., & MASCHKA, G. (1988, November). *Outcome of problem-solving approach to stress management: I. Comparison with social support.* Paper presented at the annual meeting of the Association for Advancement of Behavior Therapy, New York.

D'ZURILLA, T., & NEZU, A. (1982). Social problem solving in adults. In P. Kendall (Ed.), *Advances in cognitive-behavioral research and therapy* (Vol. 1, pp. 285–315). New York: Academic Press.

D'ZURILLA, T. J., & NEZU, A. M. (1999). *Problem-solving therapy: A social competence approach to clinical intervention* (2nd ed.). New York: Springer.

D'ZURILLA, T. J., & NEZU, A. M. (2001). Problem-solving therapies. In K. S. Dobson (Ed.), *Handbook of cognitive-behavioral therapies* (2nd ed., pp. 211–245). New York: Guilford.

D'ZURILLA, T. J., & NEZU, A. M. (2007). *Problem-solving therapy: A positive approach to clinical intervention.* New York: Springer.

D'ZURILLA, T. J., NEZU, A. M., & MAYDEU-OLIVARES, A. (2002). *Social problem-solving inventory-revised (SPSI-R): Manual.* North Tonawanda, NY: Multi-Health Systems.

ECTON, R. B., & FEINDLER, E. L. (1990). Anger control training for temper control disorders. In E. L. Feindler & G. R. Kalfus (Eds.), *Adolescent behavior therapy handbook* (pp. 351–371). New York: Springer.

EDELMAN, R. E., & CHAMBLESS, D. L. (1993). Compliance during sessions and homework in exposure-based treatment of agoraphobia. *Behaviour Research and Therapy, 31,* 767–773.

EDGETTE, J. S., & PROUT, M. F. (1989). Cognitive and behavioral approaches to the treatment of anorexia nervosa. In A. Freeman,

K. M. Simon, L. E. Beutler, & H. Arkowitz (Eds.), *Comprehensive handbook of cognitive therapy* (pp. 367–384). New York: Plenum.

EIFERT, G. H., & FORSYTH, J. P. (2005). *Acceptance and Commitment Therapy for anxiety disorders: A Practitioner's treatment guide to using mindfulness, acceptance, and values-based behavior change strategies.* Oakland, CA: New Harbinger.

EIFERT, G. H., & HEFFNER, M. (2003). The effects of acceptance versus control contexts on avoidance of panic-related symptoms. *Journal of Behavior Therapy and Experimental Psychiatry, 34,* 293–312.

EIFERT, G. H., & WILSON, P. H. (1991). The triple response approach to assessment: A conceptual and methodological reappraisal. *Behaviour Research and Therapy, 29,* 283–292.

EISLER, R. M., HERSEN, M., & MILLER, P. M. (1973). Effects of modeling on components of assertive behavior. *Journal of Behavior Therapy and Experimental Psychiatry, 4,* 1–6.

EISLER, R. M., HERSEN, M., MILLER, P. M., & BLANCHARD, E. B. (1975). Situational determinants of assertive behaviors. *Journal of Consulting and Clinical Psychology, 43,* 330–340.

EITZEN, D. S. (1975). The effects of behavior modification on the attitudes of delinquents. *Behaviour Research and Therapy, 13,* 295–299.

ELDREDGE, K. L., AGRAS, W. S., ARNOW, B., TELCH, C. F., BELL, S., CASTONGUAY, L., et al. (1997). The effects of extending cognitive-behavioral therapy for binge eating disorder among initial treatment nonresponders. *International Journal of Eating Disorders, 21,* 347–352.

ELLIOTT, A. J., MILTENBERGER, R. G., RAPP, J. T., LONG, E. S., & McDONALD, R. (1998). Brief application of simplified habit reversal to treat stuttering in children. *Journal of Behavior Therapy and Experimental Psychiatry, 29,* 289–302.

ELLIS, A. (1959). *Psychotherapy session with an eight year old female bedwetter.* [Cassette recording]. New York: Institute for Rational-Emotive Therapy.

ELLIS, A. (1962). *Reason and emotion in psychotherapy.* New York: Lyle Stuart.

ELLIS, A. (1970). *The essence of rational psychotherapy: A comprehensive approach in treatment.* New York: Institute for Rational Living.

ELLIS, A. (1989a). Comments on my critics. In M. E. Bernard & R. [A.] DiGiuseppe (Eds.), *Inside rational-emotive therapy: A critical appraisal of the theory and therapy of Albert Ellis* (pp. 199–233). San Diego: Academic Press.

ELLIS, A. (1989b). The history of cognition in psychotherapy. In A. Freeman, K. M. Simon, L. E. Beutler, & H. Arkowitz (Eds.), *Comprehensive handbook of cognitive therapy* (pp. 5–20). New York: Plenum.

ELLIS, A. (1993). Changing rational-emotive therapy (RET) to rational emotive behavior therapy (REBT). *the Behavior Therapist, 16,* 257–258.

ELLIS, A. (1994a). A corrective note on O'Donohue and Szymanski's study of logical analysis and REBT's use of empirical hypothesis testing as well as logical analysis. *Journal of Rational-Emotive & Cognitive-Behavior Therapy, 12,* 73–76.

ELLIS, A. (1994b). Ellis, Albert. *Current Biography, 65,* 6–10.

ELLIS, A. (1994c). General semantics and rational emotive behavior therapy. In P. D. Johnston, D. D. Bourland, & J. Klein (Eds.), *More E-prime: To be or not II* (pp. 213–240). Concord, CA: International Society for General Semantics.

ELLIS, A. (1994d). Post-traumatic stress disorder (PTSD): A rational emotive behavioral theory. *Journal of Rational-Emotive & Cognitive-Behavior Therapy, 12,* 3–25.

ELLIS, A. (1994e). Radical behavioral treatment of private events: A response to Michael Dougher. *the Behavior Therapist, 17,* 219–221.

ELLIS, A. (1995). Changing rational-emotive therapy (RET) to rational-emotive behavior therapy (REBT). *Journal of Rational-Emotive & Cognitive-Behavior Therapy, 13,* 85–89.

ELLIS, A. (1999). Rational emotive behavior therapy and cognitive behavior therapy for elderly people. *Journal of Rational-Emotive & Cognitive-Behavior Therapy, 17,* 5–18.

ELLIS, A., & ABRAMS, M. (2009). *Personality theories: Critical perspectives.* Los Angeles: Sage.

ELLIS, A., & BERNARD, M. E. (Eds.). (1983). *Rational-emotive approaches to the problems of childhood.* New York: Plenum.

ELLIS, A., & BERNARD, M. E. (1985). What is rational-emotive therapy (RET)? In A. Ellis & R. M. Grieger (Eds.), *Handbook of rational-emotive therapy* (pp. 1–30). New York: Springer.

ELLIS, A., & DRYDEN, W. (1987). *The practice of rational-emotive therapy.* New York: Springer.

ELLIS, A., & DRYDEN, W. (1993). A therapy by any other name? An interview. *The Rational Emotive Therapist, 1,* 34–37.

ELLIS, C. R., SINGH, N. N., CREWS, W. D., BONAVENTURA, S. H., GEHIN, J. M., & RICKETTS, R. W. (1997). Pica. In N. N. Singh (Ed.), *Prevention and treatment of severe behavior problems: Models and methods in developmental disabilities* (pp. 253–269). Pacific Grove, CA: Brooks/Cole.

ELSESSER, K., VAN BERKEL, M., SARTORY, G., BIERMANN-GÖCKE, W., & ÖHL, S. (1994). The effects of anxiety management training on psychological variables and immune parameters in cancer patients: A pilot study. *Behavioural and Cognitive Psychotherapy, 22,* 13–23.

EMERSON, E. (1993). Challenging behaviours and severe learning disabilities: Recent developments in behavioural analysis and intervention. *Behavioural and Cognitive Psychotherapy, 21,* 171–198.

EMMELKAMP, P. M. G. (1994). Behavior therapy with adults. In A. E. Bergin & S. L. Garfield (Eds.), *Handbook of psychotherapy and behavior change* (4th ed., pp. 379–427). New York: Wiley.

EMMELKAMP, P. M., KRIJN, M., HULSBOSCH, A. M., DE VRIES, S., SCHUEMIE, M. J., & VAN DER MAST, C. A. (2002). Virtual reality treatment versus exposure in vivo: A comparative evaluation in acrophobia. *Behaviour Research and Therapy, 40,* 509–516.

EMMELKAMP, P. M. G., DE HAAN, E., & HOOGDUIN, C. A. L. (1990). Marital adjustment and obsessive-compulsive disorder. *British Journal of Psychiatry, 156,* 55–60.

EMMELKAMP, P. M. G., & WESSELS, H. (1975). Flooding in imagination versus flooding in vivo: A comparison with agoraphobics. *Behaviour Research and Therapy, 13,* 7–15.

ENG, R. V. (2008). Improving treatment acceptability among teachers by increasing knowledge of ADHD. *Dissertation Abstracts International Section A: Humanities and Social Sciences, 68*(7-A), 2807.

ENGLE-FRIEDMAN, M., BOOTZIN, R. R., HAZLEWOOD, L., & TSAO, C. (1992). An evaluation of behavioral treatments for insomnia in the older adult. *Journal of Clinical Psychology, 48*, 77–90.

EPSTEIN, E. E., & MCCRADY, B. S. (1998). Behavioral couples treatment of alcohol and drug use disorders: Current status and innovations. *Clinical Psychology Review, 18*, 689–711.

EPSTEIN, L. H., BECK, S., FIGUEROA, J., FARKAS, G., KAZDIN, A. E., DANEMAN, D., et al. (1981). The effects of targeting improvements in urine glucose on metabolic control in children with insulin dependent diabetes. *Journal of Applied Behavior Analysis, 14*, 365–375.

EPSTEIN, L. H., & MASEK, B. J. (1978). Behavioral control of medicine compliance. *Journal of Applied Behavior Analysis, 11*, 1–9.

EPSTEIN, N., & BAUCOM, D. H. (1989). Cognitive-behavioral marital therapy. In A. Freeman, K. M. Simon, L. E. Beutler, & H. Arkowitz (Eds.), *Comprehensive handbook of cognitive therapy* (pp. 491–513). New York: Plenum.

ESPIE, C. A., LINDSAY, W. R., BROOKS, D. N., HOOD, E. H., & TURVEY, T. (1989). A controlled comparative investigation of psychological treatments for chronic sleep-onset insomnia. *Behaviour Research and Therapy, 27*, 79–88.

ESVELDT-DAWSON, K., & KAZDIN, A. E. (1998). *How to maintain behavior* (2nd ed.). Austin, TX: Pro-Ed.

Ethical issues for human services. (1977). *Behavior Therapy, 8*, v–vi.

EVANS, J. H., FERRE, L., FORD, L. A., & GREEN, J. L. (1995). Decreasing attention deficit hyperactivity disorder symptoms utilizing an automated classroom reinforcement device. *Psychology in the Schools, 32*, 210–219.

EVANS, P. D., & KELLAM, A. M. P. (1973). Semi-automated desensitization: A controlled clinical trial. *Behaviour Research and Therapy, 11*, 641–646.

EVANS, S., FERRANDO, S., FINDLER, M., STOWELL, C., SMART, C., & HAGLIN, D. (2008). Mindfulness-based cognitive therapy for generalized anxiety disorder. *Journal of Anxiety Disorders, 22*, 716–721.

EVERETT, G. E., OLMI, D. J., EDWARDS, R. P., TINGSTROM, D. H., STERLING-TURNER, H. E., & CHRIST, T. J. (2007). An empirical investigation of time-out with and without escape extinction to treat escape-maintained noncompliance. *Behavior Modification, 31*, 412–434.

EYSENCK, H. J. (1952). The effects of psychotherapy: An evaluation. *Journal of Consulting Psychology, 16*, 319–324.

FABIANO, G. A. (2007). Father participation in behavioral parent training for ADHD: Review and recommendations for increasing inclusion and engagement. *Journal of Family Psychology, 21*, 683–693.

FABIANO, G. A., & PELHAM, W. E. (2003). Improving the effectiveness of behavioral classroom interventions for ADHD: A case study. *Journal of Emotional and Behavioral Disorders, 11*, 122–128.

FAIRBURN, C. G. (1995). *Overcoming binge eating.* New York: Guilford.

FAIRBURN, C. G. (Ed.). (2008). *Cognitive-behavioral therapy and eating disorders.* New York: Guilford.

FAIRBURN, C. G., COOPER, Z., SHAFRAN, R., & WILSON, G. T. (2008). Eating disorders: A transdiagnostic protocol. In D. H. Barlow (Ed.), *Clinical handbook of psychological disorders: A step-by-step treatment manual* (4th ed., pp. 578–614). New York: Guilford.

FAIRBURN, C. G., JONES, R., PEVELER, R. C., HOPE, R. A., & O'CONNOR, M. E. (1993). Psychotherapy and bulimia nervosa: The long-term effects of interpersonal psychotherapy, behavior therapy, and cognitive behavior therapy for bulimia nervosa. *Archives of General Psychiatry, 50*, 419–428.

FAIRBURN, C. G., MARCUS, M. D., & WILSON, G. T. (1993). Cognitive-behavioral therapy for binge eating and bulimia nervosa: A comprehensive treatment manual. In C. G. Fairburn & G. T. Wilson (Eds.), *Binge eating: Nature, assessment and treatment* (pp. 361–404). New York: Guilford.

FALLOON, I. R. H., & COVERDALE, J. H. (1994). Cognitive-behavioural family interventions for major mental disorders. Special issue: Behaviour therapy and schizophrenia: I. *Behaviour Change, 11*, 213–222.

FALS-STEWART, W., MARKS, A. P., & SCHAFER, J. (1993). A comparison of behavioral group therapy and individual behavior therapy in treating obsessive-compulsive disorder. *Journal of Mental and Nervous Disease, 181*, 189–193.

FARMER, R. F., & CHAPMAN, A. L. (2008). Changing behavior by building skills. In R. F. Farmer & A. L. Chapman (Eds.), *Behavioral interventions in cognitive behavior therapy: Practical guidance for putting theory into action* (pp. 177–201). Washington, DC: American Psychological Association.

FARRELL, L. V., COX, M. G., & GELLER, E. S. (2007). Prompting safety-belt use in the context of a belt-use law: The flash-for-life revisited. *Journal of Safety Research, 38*, 407–411.

FARRELL, S. P., HAINS, A. A., & DAVIES, W. H. (1998). Cognitive behavioral interventions for sexually abused children exhibiting PTSD symptomology. *Behavior Therapy, 29*, 241–255.

FECTEAU, G., & NICKI, R. (1999). Cognitive behavioural treatment of post traumatic stress disorder after motor vehicle accident. *Behavioural and Cognitive Psychotherapy, 27*, 201–214.

FEENY, N. C., HEMBREE, E. A., & ZOELLNER, L. A. (2003). Myths regarding exposure therapy for PTSD. *Cognitive and Behavioral Practice, 10I*, 85–90.

FEINDLER, E. L., ECTON, R. B., KINGSLEY, D., & DUBEY, D. R. (1986). Group anger-control training for institutionalized psychiatric male adolescents. *Behavior Therapy, 17*, 109–123.

FEINDLER, E. L., MARRIOTT, S. A., & IWATA, M. (1984). Group anger-control training for junior high school delinquents. *Cognitive Therapy and Research, 8*, 299–311.

FEINDLER, E. L., RATHUS, J. H., & SILVER, L. B. (Eds.). (2003). *Assessment of family violence: A handbook for researchers and practitioners.* Washington, DC: American Psychological Association.

FEKETE, E. M., ANTONI, M. H., & SCHNEIDERMAN, N. (2007). Psychosocial and behavioral interventions for chronic medical conditions. *Current Opinion in Psychiatry, 20*, 152–157.

FELL, C. (Trans. and Ed.). (1975). *Egils saga.* London: Dent.

FERRITOR, D. E., BUCKHOLDT, D., HAMBLIN, R. L., & SMITH, L. (1972). The noneffects of contingent reinforcement for attending behavior on work accomplished. *Journal of Applied Behavior Analysis, 5*, 7–17.

FERSTER, C. B. (1973). A functional analysis of depression. *American Psychologist, 28,* 857–870.

FESTINGER, L. (1957). *A theory of cognitive dissonance.* Stanford, CA: Stanford University Press.

FEUERSTEIN, M., & GAINER, J. (1982). Chronic headache: Etiology and management. In D. M. Doleys, R. L. Meredith, & A. R. Ciminero (Eds.), *Behavioral medicine: Assessment and treatment strategies* (pp. 199–249). New York: Plenum.

FINK, C. M., TURNER, S. M., & BEIDEL, D. C. (1996). Culturally relevant factors in the behavioral treatment of social phobia: A case study. *Journal of Anxiety Disorders, 10,* 201–209.

FINNEY, J. W., MILLER, K. M., & ADLER, S. P. (1993). Changing protective and risky behaviors to prevent child-to-parent transmission of cytomegalovirus. *Journal of Applied Behavior Analysis, 26,* 471–472.

FISHER, E., & THOMPSON, J. K. (1994). A comparative evaluation of cognitive-behavioral therapy (CBT) versus exercise therapy (ET) for the treatment of body image disturbance: Preliminary findings. *Behavior Modification, 18,* 171–185.

FISHER, J. E., SWINGEN, D. N., & O'DONAHUE, W. (1997). Behavioral interventions for sexual dysfunction in the elderly. *Behavior Therapy, 28,* 65–82.

FITZPATRICK, K. K., WITTE, T. K., & SCHMIDT, N. B. (2005). Randomized controlled trial of a brief problem-oriented intervention for suicidal ideation. *Behavior Therapy, 36,* 323–333.

FIXSEN, D. L., PHILLIPS, E. L., PHILLIPS, E. A., & WOLF, M. M. (1976). The teaching-family model of group home treatment. In W. E. Craighead, A. E. Kazdin, & M. J. Mahoney, *Behavior modification: Principles, issues, and applications.* (pp. 310–320). Boston: Houghton Mifflin.

FLANAGAN, R., POVALL, L., DELLINO, M., & BYRNE, L. (1998). A comparison of problem-solving with and without rational emotive behavior therapy to improve children's social skills. *Journal of Rational-Emotive & Cognitive-Behavior Therapy, 16,* 125–134.

FLEECE, L. (1995). [Review of the book The therapeutic relationship in behavioural psychotherapy]. *the Behavior Therapist, 18,* 142.

FLOR, H., KERNS, R. D., & TURK, D. C. (1987). The role of spouse reinforcement, perceived pain, and activity levels of chronic pain patients. *Journal of Psychosomatic Research, 31,* 251–259.

FOA, E. B. (2000). Psychosocial treatment of posttraumatic stress disorder. *Journal of Clinical Psychiatry, 61* (Suppl. 5), 43.

FOA, E. B., DANCU, C. V., HEMBREE, E. A., JAYCOX, L. H., MEADOWS, E. A., & STREET, G. P. (1999). A comparison of exposure therapy, stress inoculation training, and their combination for reducing posttraumatic stress disorder in female assault victims. *Journal of Consulting and Clinical Psychology, 67,* 194–200.

FOA, E. B., DAVIDSON, J. R. T., & FRANCES, A. (1999). The Expert Consensus Guidelines Series: Treatment of posttraumatic stress disorder. *Journal of Clinical Psychiatry, 60,* 4–76.

FOA, E. B., HEMBREE, E. A., CAHILL, S. P., RAUCH, S. A. M., RIGGS, D. S., FEENY, N. C., et al. (2005). Randomized trial of prolonged exposure for posttraumatic stress disorder with and without cognitive restructuring: Outcome at academic and community clinics. *Journal of Consulting and Clinical Psychology, 73,* 953–964.

FOA, E. B., HUPPERT, J. D., & CAHILL, S. P. (2006). Emotional processing theory: An update. In B. O. Rothbaum (Ed.), *Pathological anxiety: Emotional processing in etiology and treatment* (pp. 3–24). New York: Guilford.

FOA, E. B., & ROTHBAUM, B. O. (1989). Behavioural psychotherapy for post-traumatic stress disorder. *International Review of Psychiatry, 1,* 219–226.

FOA, E. B., & ROTHBAUM, B. O. (1998). *Treating the trauma of rape: Cognitive-behavioral therapy for PTSD.* New York: Guilford.

FOA, E. B., ROTHBAUM, B. O., & KOZAK, M. J. (1989). Behavioral treatments for anxiety and depression. In P. C. Kendall & D. Watson (Eds.), *Anxiety and depression: Distinctive and overlapping features* (pp. 413–454). New York: Academic Press.

FOA, E. B., ROTHBAUM, B. O., RIGGS, D. S., & MURDOCK, T. B. (1991). Treatment of posttraumatic stress disorder in rape victims: A comparison between cognitive-behavioral

procedures and counseling. *Journal of Consulting and Clinical Psychology, 59,* 715–723.

FOA, E. B., STEKETEE, G. S., TURNER, R. M., & FISCHER, S. C. (1980). Effectiveness of imaginal exposure to feared disasters in obsessive-compulsive checkers. *Behaviour Research and Therapy, 18,* 449–455.

FOLLANSBEE, D. J., LA GRECA, A. M., & CITRIN, W. S. (1983). Coping skills training for adolescents with diabetes. (Abstract) *Diabetes, 32*(Suppl. 1), 147.

FORBES, D., CREAMER, M., & RYCROFT, P. (1994). Eye movement desensitization and reprocessing in posttraumatic stress disorder: A pilot study using assessment measures. *Journal of Behavior Therapy and Experimental Psychiatry, 25,* 113–120.

FORDYCE, W. [E.] (1976). *Behavioral methods for chronic pain and illness.* St. Louis: Mosby.

FORDYCE, W. E. (1988). Pain and suffering: A reappraisal. *American Psychologist, 43,* 276–283.

FORDYCE, W. E., & STEGER, J. C. (1979). Chronic pain. In O. F. Pomerleau & J. P. Brady (Eds.), *Behavioral medicine: Theory and practice* (pp. 125–153). Baltimore: Williams & Wilkins.

FOREHAND, R. [L.], & KING, H. E. (1977). Noncompliant children: Effects of parent training on behavior and attitude. *Behavior Modification, 1,* 93–108.

FOREHAND, R. [L.], & KOTCHIK, B. A. (1996). Cultural diversity: A wake-up call for parent training. *Behavior Therapy, 27,* 187–206.

FOREHAND, R. [L.], & LONG, N. (1988). Outpatient treatment of the acting-out child: Procedures, long-term follow-up data, and clinical problems. *Archives in Behaviour Research and Therapy, 10,* 129–177.

FOREHAND, R. L., & MCMAHON, R. J. (1981). *Helping the non-compliant child: A clinician's guide to parent training.* New York: Guilford.

FOREMAN, S. A. (1980). A comparison of cognitive training and response cost procedures in modifying aggressive behavior of elementary school children. *Behavior Therapy, 11,* 594–600.

FOREYT, J. P. (1987). The addictive disorders. In G. T. Wilson, C. M. Franks, P. C. Kendall, & J. P. Foreyt (Eds.), *Review of behavior therapy: Theory and practice* (Vol. 11, pp. 187–233). New York: Guilford.

Foreyt, J. P. (1990). The addictive disorders. In C. M. Franks, G. T. Wilson, P. C. Kendall, & J. P. Foreyt (Eds.), *Review of behavior therapy: Theory and practice* (Vol. 12, pp. 178–224). New York: Guilford.

Forman, E. M., Herbert, J. D., Moitra, E., Yeomans, P. D., & Geller, P. A. (2007). A randomized controlled effectiveness trial of acceptance and commitment therapy and cognitive therapy for anxiety and depression. *Behavior Modification, 31*, 772–799.

Forsyth, J. P., & Eifert, G. H. (2008). The mindfulness and acceptance workbook for anxiety: A guide to breaking free from anxiety, phobias, and worry using Acceptance and Commitment Therapy. Oakland, CA: New Harbinger.

Forsyth, J. P., Fusé, T. M., & Acheson, D. A. (in press). Interoceptive exposure for panic disorder.In W. O'Donohue, J. Fisher, & S. C. Hayes (Eds.), *Cognitive behavior therapy: Applying empirically supported techniques in your practice* (2nd ed.). New York: Wiley.

Foster, E., Jones, D., & Group, C. P. P. R. (2006). Can a costly intervention be cost-effective? *Archives of General Psychiatry, 63*, 1284–1291.

Foster, S. L., Bell-Dolan, D. J., & Burge, D. A. (1988). Behavioral observation. In A. S. Bellack & M. Hersen (Eds.), *Behavioral assessment: A practical handbook* (3rd ed., pp. 119–160). Elmsford, NY: Pergamon.

Foster, S. L., & Cone, J. D. (1980). Current issues in direct observation. *Behavioral Assessment, 2*, 313–338.

Foster, S. L., & Cone, J. D. (1986). Design and use of direct observation. In A. R. Ciminero, K. S. Calhoun, & H. A. Adams (Eds.), *Handbook of behavioral assessment* (2nd ed., pp. 253–324). New York: Wiley.

Fox, D. K., Hopkins, B. L., & Anger, W. K. (1987). The long-term effects of a token economy on safety performance in open-pit mining. *Journal of Applied Behavior Analysis, 20*, 215–224.

Fox, R. A., & Deshaw, J. M. (1993a). Milestone reinforcer survey. *Education and Training in Mental Retardation, 28*, 257–261.

Fox, R. A., & Deshaw, J. M. (1993b). *Milestone reinforcer survey manual.* Rockford, IL: Milestone Inc.

Foxx, R. M., & Azrin, N. H. (1972). Restitution: A method of eliminating aggressive-disruptive behavior of retarded and brain damaged patients. *Behaviour Research and Therapy, 10*, 15–27.

Foxx, R. M., & Azrin, N. H. (1973a). Dry pants: A rapid method of toilet training children. *Behaviour Research and Therapy, 11*, 435–442.

Foxx, R. M., & Azrin, N. H. (1973b). *Toilet training the retarded: A rapid program for day and night time independent toileting.* Champaign, IL: Research Press.

Foxx, R. M., & Faw, G. D. (1990). Long-term follow-up of echolalia and question answering. *Journal of Applied Behavior Analysis, 23*, 387–396.

Foxx, R. M., Faw, G. D., & Weber, G. (1991). Producing generalization of inpatient adolescents' social skills with significant adults in a natural environment. *Behavior Therapy, 22*, 85–99.

Foxx, R. M., & Garito, J. (2007). The long term successful treatment of the very severe behaviors of a preadolescent with autism. *Behavioral Interventions, 22*, 69–82.

Foxx, R. M., Martella, R. C., & Marchand-Martella, N. E. (1989). The acquisition, maintenance, and generalization of problem-solving skills by closed head-injured adults. *Behavior Therapy, 20*, 61–76.

Foxx, R. M., & Meindl, J. (2007). The long term successful treatment of the aggressive-destructive behaviors of a preadolescent with autism. *Behavioral Interventions, 22*, 83–97.

Frame, C. L., & Matson, J. L. (1987). *Handbook of assessment in childhood psychopathology: Applied issues in differential diagnosis and treatment evaluation.* New York: Plenum.

France, K. G. (1992). Behavioral characteristics and security in sleep disturbed infants treated with extinction. *Journal of Pediatric Psychology, 17*, 467–475.

France, K. G., & Hudson, S. M. (1990). Behavior management of infant sleep disturbance. *Journal of Applied Behavior Analysis, 23*, 91–98.

France, K. G., & Hudson, S. M. (1993). Management of infant sleep disturbance: A review. *Clinical Psychology Review, 13*, 635–647.

Franco, D. D. (1981). Habit reversal and isometric tensing with motor tics. *Dissertation Abstracts International, 42*, 3418B.

Franco, D. P., Christoff, K. A., Crimmins, D. B., & Kelly, J. A. (1983). Social skills training for an extremely shy young adolescent: An empirical case study. *Behavior Therapy, 14*, 568–575.

Franco, H., Galanter, M., Casteeda, R., & Paterson, J. (1995). Combining behavioral and self-help approaches in the inpatient management of dually diagnosed patients. *Journal of Substance Abuse, 12*, 227–232.

Franklin, M. E., Abramowitz, J. S., Kozak, M. J., Levitt, J. T., & Foa, E. B. (2000). Effectiveness of exposure and ritual prevention for obsessive-compulsive disorder randomized compared with non-randomized samples. *Journal of Consulting and Clinical Psychology, 68*, 594–602.

Franklin, M. E., & Foa, E. B. (2008). Obsessive-compulsive disorder. In D. H. Barlow (Ed.), *Clinical handbook of psychological disorders: A step-by-step treatment manual* (4th ed., pp. 164–215). New York: Guilford.

Franks, C. M. (1963). Behavior therapy, the principles of conditioning and the treatment of the alcoholic. *Quarterly Journal of Studies on Alcohol, 24*, 511–529.

Franks, C. M. (1969). Introduction: Behavior therapy and its Pavlovian origins: Review and perspectives. In C. M. Franks (Ed.), *Behavior therapy: Appraisal and status* (pp. 1–26). New York: McGraw-Hill.

Franks, C. M. (1995). RET, REBT and Albert Ellis. *Journal of Rational-Emotive & Cognitive-Behavior Therapy, 13*, 91–95.

Franks, C. M., & Wilson, G. T. (Eds.). (1973). *Annual review of behavior therapy: Theory and practice* (Vol. 1). New York: Brunner/Mazel.

Franks, C. M., & Wilson, G. T. (Eds.). (1976). *Annual review of behavior therapy: Theory and practice* (Vol. 4). New York: Brunner/Mazel.

Franks, C. M., & Wilson, G. T. (Eds.). (1978). *Annual review of behavior therapy: Theory and practice* (Vol. 6). New York: Brunner/Mazel.

Franks, C. M., & Wolfe, J. L. (2008). Albert Ellis (1913–2007): Appreciation and perspective by two who knew him well. *the Behavior Therapist, 31*, 3–7.

FREEMAN, A., & SIMON, K. M. (1989). Cognitive therapy of anxiety. In A. Freeman, K. M. Simon, L. E. Beutler, & H. Arkowitz (Eds.), *Comprehensive handbook of cognitive therapy* (pp. 347–365). New York: Plenum.

FREEMAN, A., & WHITE, D. M. (1989). The treatment of suicidal behavior. In A. Freeman, K. M. Simon, L. E. Beutler, & H. Arkowitz (Eds.), *Comprehensive handbook of cognitive therapy* (pp. 321–346). New York: Plenum.

FREESTON, M. H., LEGER, E., & LADOUCEUR, R. (2001). Cognitive therapy for obsessive thoughts. *Cognitive and Behavioral Practice, 8,* 61–78.

FREUD, S. (1955). Analysis of a phobia in a five-year-old boy. In J. Strachey (Ed. and Trans.), *The standard edition of the complete psychological works of Sigmund Freud* (Vol. 10). London: Hogarth. (Originally published 1909)

FRIEDBERG, R. D., CROSBY, L. E., FRIEDBERG, B. A., RUTTER, J. G., & KNIGHT, K. R. (2000). Making cognitive behavioral therapy user-friendly to children. *Cognitive and Behavioral Practice, 6,* 189–200.

FRIEDBERG, R. D., VIGLIONE, D. J., STINSON, B. L., BEAL, K. G., FIDALEO, R. A., & CELESTE, B. (1999). Perceptions of treatment helpfulness and depressive symptomatology in psychiatric inpatients on a cognitive therapy unit. *Journal of Rational-Emotive & Cognitive-Behavior Therapy, 17,* 33–50.

FRIEDMAN, R., SOBEL, D., MYERS, P., CAUDILL, M., & BENSON, H. (1995). Behavioral medicine, clinical health psychology, and cost offset. *Health Psychology, 14,* 509–518.

FRIEDMAN, S. (1980). Self-control in the treatment of Gilles de la Tourette's syndrome: Case study with 18-month follow-up. *Journal of Consulting and Clinical Psychology, 48,* 400–402.

FRIEDMAN, S., SMITH, L. C., HALPERN, B., LEVINE, C., PARADIS, C., VISWANATHAN, R., et al. (2003). Obsessive-compulsive disorder in a multi-ethnic urban outpatient clinic: Initial presentation and treatment outcome with exposure and ritual prevention. *Behavior Therapy, 34,* 397–410.

FRIMAN, P. C., FINNEY, J. W., RAPOFF, M. A., & CHRISTOPHERSEN, E. R. (1985). Improving pediatric appointment keeping with reminders and reduced response requirements. *Journal of Applied Behavior Analysis, 18,* 315–321.

FRIMAN, P. C., & VOLLMER, D. (1995). The successful use of the nocturnal urine alarm for diurnal enuresis. *Journal of Applied Behavior Analysis, 28,* 89–90.

FRISBY, C. (1990). A teacher inservice model for problem solving in classroom discipline: Suggestions for the school psychologist. *School Psychology Quarterly, 5,* 211–232.

FRISCH, M. B., & FROBERG, W. (1987). Social validation of assertion strategies for handling aggressive criticism: Evidence for consistency across situations. *Behavior Therapy, 18,* 181–191.

FRUEH, B. C. (1995). Self-administered exposure therapy by a Vietnam veteran with PTSD. *American Journal of Psychiatry, 152,* 1831–1832.

FRUEH, B. C., TURNER, S. M., & BEIDEL, D. C. (1995). Exposure therapy for combat-related PTSD: A critical review. *Clinical Psychology Review, 15,* 799–817.

FRYE, A. A., & GOODMAN, S. H. (2000). Which social problem-solving components buffer depression in adolescent girls? *Cognitive Therapy and Research, 24,* 637–650.

FUDGE, R. C. (1996). The use of behavior therapy in the development of ethnic consciousness: A treatment model. *Cognitive and Behavioral Practice, 3,* 317–335.

GALASSI, F., QUERCIOLI, S., CHARISMAS, D., NICCOLAI, V., & BARCIULLI, E. (2007). Cognitive-behavioral group treatment for panic disorder with agoraphobia. *Journal of Clinical Psychology, 63,* 409–416.

GALE, B. M. (1996). Is this the year you become friends with technology? *the Behavior Therapist, 19,* 82–83.

GALLAGHER-THOMPSON, D., LOVETT, S., ROSE, J., MCKIBBIN, C., COON, D. W., FUTTERMAN, A., et al. (2000). Impact of psychoeducational interventions on distressed family care-givers. *Journal of Clinical Geropsychology, 6,* 91–110.

GAMBRILL, E. [D.] (1985). Social skill training with the elderly. In L. L'Abate & M. A. Milan (Eds.), *Handbook of social skills training and research* (pp. 326–327). New York: Wiley.

GAMBRILL, E. [D.] (1995a). Assertion skills training. In W. O'Donohue & L. Krasner (Eds.), *Handbook of psychological skills training: Clinical techniques and applications* (pp. 81–118). Boston: Allyn & Bacon.

GAMBRILL, E. [D.] (1995b). Helping shy, socially anxious, and lonely adults: A skill-based contextual approach. In W. O'Donohue & L. Krasner (Eds.), *Handbook of psychological skills training: Clinical techniques and applications* (pp. 247–286). Boston: Allyn & Bacon.

GAMBRILL, E. D., & RICHEY, C. A. (1975). An assertion inventory for use in assessment and research. *Behavior Therapy, 6,* 550–561.

GAMITO, P., OLIVEIRA, J., MORAIS, D., SARAIVA, T., ROSA, P., LEAL, A., et al. (2007). War PTSD: A VR pre-trial case study. *Annual Review of Cybertherapy and Telemedicine, 5,* 191–198.

GANNON, P., HARMON, M., & WILLIAMS, B. F. (1997). An in-home token system for a student with attention deficit hyperactivity disorder. *Journal of Special Education, 21,* 33–40.

GARCÍA, J., SIMÓN, M. A., DURÁN, M., CANCELLER, J., & ANEIROS, F. J. (2006). Differential efficacy of a cognitive-behavioral intervention versus pharmacological treatment in the management of fibromyalgic syndrome. *Psychology, Health & Medicine, 11,* 498–506.

GARCIA-PALACIOS, A., HOFFMAN, H., CARLIN, A., FURNESS, T. A., III, & BOTELLA, C. (2002). Virtual reality in the treatment of spider phobia: A controlled study. *Behaviour Research and Therapy, 40,* 983–993.

GARLAND, J. (1985). Adaptation skills in the elderly, their supporters and careers. Special issue: Sharing psychological skills: Training non-psychologists in the use of psychological techniques. *British Journal of Medical Psychology, 58,* 267–274.

GARNER, D. M., ROCKERT, W., DAVIS, R., GARNER, M. V., OLMSTED, M. P., & EAGLE, M. (1993). Comparison of cognitive-behavioral and supportive-expressive therapy for bulimia nervosa. *American Journal of Psychiatry, 150,* 37–46.

GARRATT, G., INGRAM, R. E., & RAND, K. L. (2007). Cognitive processes in cognitive therapy: Evaluation of the mechanisms of change in the treatment of depression. *Clinical Psychology: Science and Practice, 14,* 224–239.

GASTON, L., GOLDFRIED, M. R., GREENBERG, L. S., HORVATH, A. O., RAUE, P. J., & WATSON, J. (1995). The therapeutic alliance in psychodynamic, cognitive-behavioral, and experimental therapies. *Journal of Psychotherapy Integration, 5*, 1–26.

GATCHEL, R. J. (1980). Effectiveness of two procedures for reducing dental fear: Group-administered desensitization and group education and discussion. *Journal of the American Dental Association, 101*, 634–637.

GAUDIANO, B. A., & HERBERT, J. D. (2006). Acute treatment of inpatients with psychotic symptoms using Acceptance and Commitment Therapy: Pilot results. *Behaviour Research & Therapy, 44*, 415–437.

GEER, J. H. (1965). The development of a scale to measure fear. *Behaviour Research and Therapy, 3*, 45–53.

GEISS, S. K., & O'LEARY, K. D. (1981). Therapist ratings of frequency and severity of marital problems: Implications for research. *Journal of Marital and Family Therapy, 7*, 515–520.

GENEST, M., & TURK, D. C. (1981). Think-aloud approaches to cognitive assessment. In T. V. Merluzzi, C. R. Glass, & M. Genest (Eds.), *Cognitive assessment* (pp. 233–269). New York: Guilford.

GERARDI, M., ROTHBAUM, B. O., & RESSLER, K. (2008). Virtual reality exposure therapy using a virtual Iraq: Case report. *Journal of Traumatic Stress, 21*, 209–213.

GERARDI, M., ROTHBAUM, B. O., RESSLER, K., HEEKIN, M., & RIZZO, A. A. (2008). Virtual reality exposure therapy using a virtual Iraq: Case report. *Journal of Traumatic Stress, 21*, 1–5.

GETKA, E. J., & GLASS, C. R. (1992). Behavioral and cognitive-behavioral approaches to the reduction of dental anxiety. *Behavior Therapy, 23*, 433–448.

GIFFORD, E. V., KOHLENBERG, B. S., HAYES, S. C., ANTONUCCIO, D. O., PIASECKI, M. M., RASMUSSEN-HALL, M. L., et al. (2004). Applying a functional acceptance based model to smoking cessation: An initial trial of Acceptance and Commitment Therapy. *Behavior Therapy, 35*, 689–705.

GIL, K. M., CARSON, J. W., SEDWAY, J. A., PORTER, L. S., SCHAEFFER, J. J. W., & ORRINGER, E. (2000). Follow-up coping skills training in adults with sickle cell disease: Analysis of daily pain and coping practice diaries. *Journal of Consulting and Clinical Psychology, 68*, 85–90.

GIL, K. M., WILSON, J. J., EDENS, J. L., WORKMAN, E., READY, J., SEDWAY, J., et al. (1997). Cognitive coping skills training with sickle cell disease pain. *International Journal of Behavioral Medicine, 4*, 364–377.

GILBERT, B. O., JOHNSON, S. B., SPILLAR, R., MCCALLUM, M., SILVERSTEIN, J. H., & ROSENBLOOM, A. (1982). The effects of a peer-modeling film on children learning to self-inject insulin. *Behavior Therapy, 13*, 186–193.

GILES, T. R. (1991). Managed mental health care and effective psychotherapy: A step in the right direction? *Journal of Behaviour Therapy and Experimental Psychiatry, 22*, 83–86.

GILES, T. R., PRIAL, E. M., & NEIMS, D. M. (1993). Evaluating psychotherapies: A comparison of effectiveness. *International Journal of Mental Health, 22*, 43–65.

GILLHAM, J. E., REIVICH, K. J., JAYCOX, L. H., & SELIGMAN, M. E. P. (1995). Prevention of depressive symptoms in school children: Two-year follow-up. *Psychological Science, 6*, 343–351.

GILLIES, L. A., HASHMALL, J. M., HILTON, N. Z., & WEBSTER, C. D. (1992). Relapse prevention in pedophiles: Clinical issues and program development. Special issue: Violence and its aftermath. *Canadian Psychology, 33*, 199–210.

GINSBURG, G. S., BECKER, K. D., KINGERY, J. N., & NICHOLS, T. (2008). Transporting CBT for childhood anxiety disorders into inner-city school-based mental health clinics. *Cognitive and Behavioral Practice, 15*, 148–158.

GINSBURG, G. S., RIDDLE, M., & DAVIES, M. (2006). Somatic symptoms in children and adolescents with anxiety disorders. *Journal of the American Academy of Child and Adolescent Psychiatry, 45*, 1179–1187.

GLAESER, B. C., PIERSON, M. R., & FRITSCHMAN, N. (2003). Comic strip conversations: A positive behavioral support strategy. *Teaching Exceptional Children, 36*, 14–19.

GLANTZ, K., RIZZO, A. A., & GRAAP, K. (2003). Virtual reality for psychotherapy: Current reality and future possibilities. *Psychotherapy: Theory, Research, Practice, Training, 40*, 55–67.

GLANZ, M. D. (1989). Cognitive therapy with the elderly. In A. Freeman, K. M. Simon, L. E. Beutler, & H. Arkowitz (Eds.), *Comprehensive handbook of cognitive therapy* (pp. 467–489). New York: Plenum.

GLAROS, A. G., LAUSTEN, L., & FRANKLIN, K. L. (2007). Comparison of habit reversal and a behaviorally-modified dental treatment for temporomandibular disorders: A pilot investigation. *Applied Psychophysiology and Biofeedback, 32*, 149–154.

GLASER, B. A., KRONSNOBLE, K. M., & FORKNER, C. B. W. (1997). Parents and teachers as raters of children's problem behavior. *Child & Family Behavior Therapy, 19*, 1–13.

GLASGOW, R. E. (1975). In vivo prolonged exposure in treatment of urinary retention. *Behavior Therapy, 6*, 701–702.

GLASS, C. R., & ARNKOFF, D. B. (1989). Behavioral assessment of social anxiety and social phobia. *Clinical Psychology Review, 9*, 75–90.

GLASS, C. R., & ARNKOFF, D. B. (1992). Behavior therapy. In D. K. Freedheim (Ed.), *History of psychotherapy: A century of change* (pp. 587–628). Washington, DC: American Psychological Association.

GLASS, C. R., & ARNKOFF, D. B. (1994). Validity issues in self-statement measures of social phobia and social anxiety. *Behaviour Research and Therapy, 32*, 255–267.

GLASS, C. R., & ARNKOFF, D. B. (1997). Questionnaire methods of cognitive self-statement assessment. *Journal of Consulting and Clinical Psychology, 65*, 911–927.

GLASS, C. R., GOTTMAN, J. M., & SHMURAK, S. H. (1976). Response acquisition and cognitive self-statement modification approaches to dating skills training. *Journal of Counseling Psychology, 23*, 520–526.

GLASS, C. R., MERLUZZI, T. V., BIEVER, J. L., & LARSEN, K. H. (1982). Cognitive assessment of social anxiety: Development and validation of a self-statement questionnaire. *Cognitive Therapy and Research, 6*, 37–55.

GLYNN, S. M. (1990). Token economy approaches for psychiatric patients. *Behavior Modification, 14*, 383–407.

GLYNN, S. M., ETH, S., RANDOLPH, E. T., FOY, D. W., URBAITIS, M., BOXER, L., et al. (1999). A test of behavioral family therapy to augment exposure for combat-related posttraumatic stress disorder. *Journal of Consulting and Clinical Psychology, 67,* 243–251.

GOETZ, E. M., HOLMBERG, M. C., & LEBLANC, J. M. (1975). Differential reinforcement of other behavior and non-contingent reinforcement as control procedures during the modification of a preschooler's compliance. *Journal of Applied Behavior Analysis, 8,* 77–82.

GOLD, S. R., LETOURNEAU, E. J., & O'DONOHUE, W. (1995). Sexual interaction skills. In W. O'Donohue & L. Krasner (Eds.), *Handbook of psychological skills training: Clinical techniques and applications* (pp. 229–246). Boston: Allyn & Bacon.

GOLDFRIED, M. R. (1971). Systematic desensitization as training in self-control. *Journal of Consulting and Clinical Psychology, 37,* 228–234.

GOLDFRIED, M. R. (1988). Application of rational restructuring to anxiety disorders. *The Counseling Psychologist, 16,* 50–68.

GOLDFRIED, M. R., & CASTONGUAY, L. G. (1993). Behavior therapy: Redefining strengths and limitations. *Behavior Therapy, 24,* 505–526.

GOLDFRIED, M. R., & DAVISON, G. C. (1994). *Clinical behavior therapy* (expanded ed.). New York: Wiley.

GOLDFRIED, M. R., GREENBERG, L. S., & MARMAR, C. (1990). Individual psychotherapy: Process and outcome. *Annual Review of Psychology, 41,* 659–688.

GOLDFRIED, M. R., LINEHAN, M. M., & SMITH, J. L. (1978). The reduction of test anxiety through cognitive restructuring. *Journal of Consulting and Clinical Psychology, 46,* 32–39.

GOLDFRIED, M. R., & SPRAFKIN, J. N. (1974). *Behavioral personality assessment.* Morristown, NJ: General Learning Press.

GOLDIAMOND, I. (1974). Toward a constitutional approach to social problems: Ethical and constitutional issues raised by applied behavior analysis. *Behaviorism, 2,* 1–79.

GOLDSTEIN, H., & MOUSETIS, L. (1989). Generalized language learning by children with severe mental retardation: Effects of peers' expressive modeling. *Journal of Applied Behavior Analysis, 22,* 245–259.

GOSSETTE, R. L., & O'BRIEN, R. M. (1993). Efficacy of rational emotive therapy (RET) with children: A critical reappraisal. *Journal of*

Behavior Therapy and Experimental Psychiatry, 24, 15–25.

GOTTMAN, J. M., & MARKMAN, H. J. (1978). Experimental designs in psychotherapy research. In S. L. Garfield & A. E. Gergin (Eds.), *Handbook of psychotherapy and behavior change: An empirical analysis* (2nd ed., pp. 23–62). New York: Wiley.

GOTTMAN, J. [M.], & RUSHE, R. (1995). Communication skills and social skills approaches to treating ailing marriages: A recommendation for a new marital therapy called "Minimal Marital Therapy." In W. O'Donohue & L. Krasner (Eds.), *Handbook of psychological skills training: Clinical techniques and applications* (pp. 287–305). Boston: Allyn & Bacon.

GOUBOTH, D., WILDER, D. A., & BOOHER, J. (2007). The effects of signaling stimulus presentation during non-contingent reinforcement. *Journal of Applied Behavior Analysis, 40,* 725–730.

GOULD, M. S., & SHAFFER, D. (1986). The impact of suicide in television movies: Evidence of imitation. *New UK Journal of Medicine, 31,* 690–694.

GOULD, R. A., & OTTO, M. W. (1995). Cognitive-behavioral treatment of social phobia and generalized anxiety disorder. In M. H. Pollack, M. W. Otto, & J. F. Rosenbaum (Eds.), *Challenges in psychiatric treatment: Pharmacological and psychosocial strategies* (pp. 171–200). New York: Guilford.

GOULD, R. A., OTTO, M. W., & POLLACK, M. H. (1995). A meta-analysis of treatment outcome for panic disorder. *Clinical Psychology Review, 15,* 819–844.

GRAF, A. (2003). A psychometric test of a German version of the SPSI-R. *Zeitschrift für Differentielle und Diagnostische Psychologie, 24,* 277–291.

GRANDY, S. E., & PECK, S. M. (1997). The use of functional assessment and self-management with a first grader. *Child & Family Behavior Therapy, 19,* 29–43.

GRATZ, K. L., & GUNDERSON, J. G. (2006). Preliminary data on an acceptance-based emotion regulation group intervention for deliberate self-harm among women with borderline personality disorder. *Behavior Therapy, 37,* 25–35.

GRAUBARD, P. S., ROSENBERG, H., & MILLER, M. B. (1974). Student

applications of behavior modification to teachers and environments or ecological approaches to social deviancy. In R. Ulrich, T. Stachnik, & J. Mabry (Eds.), *Control of human behavior* (Vol. 3, pp. 421–436). Glenview, IL: Scott Foresman.

GRAVE, D. G. (1999). Cognitive behavior therapy in obesity: Standard techniques and new trends. *Psicoterapia and Cognitiva e Comportamentale, 5,* 31–44.

GRAVES, R., OPENSHAW, D., & ADAMS, G. R. (1992). Adolescent sex offenders and social skills training. *International Journal of Offender Therapy and Comparative Criminology, 36,* 139–153.

GRAY, M. J., & LITZ, B. T. (2005). Behavioral interventions for recent trauma: Empirically informed practice guidelines. *Behavior Modification, 29,* 189–215.

GRAZIANO, A. M., DEGIOVANNI, I. S., & GARCIA, K. A. (1979). Behavioral treatment of children's fears: A review. *Psychological Bulletin, 86,* 804–830.

GRAZIANO, A. M., & RAULIN, M. L. (2007). *Research methods: A process of inquiry* (6th ed.). Boston: Allyn & Bacon.

GREAVES, D. (1997). The effects on rational-emotive parent education on the stress of mothers with young children with Down syndrome. *Journal of Rational-Emotive & Cognitive-Behavior Therapy, 15,* 249–267.

GREEN, L. (1978). Temporal and stimulus factors in self-monitoring of obese persons. *Behavior Therapy, 8,* 328–341.

GREENAN, E., POWELL, C., & VARNI, J. W. (1984). *Adherence to therapeutic exercise by children with hemophilia.* Unpublished manuscript. Cited in LaGreca, A. M. (1988). Adherence to prescribed medical regimens. In D. K. Routh (Ed.), *Handbook of pediatric psychology* (pp. 299–320). New York: Guilford.

GREENE, L., KAMPS, D., WYBLE, J., & ELLIS, C. (1999). Home-based consultation for parents of young children with behavioral problems. *Child & Family Behavior Therapy, 21,* 19–45.

GREENE, R. W. (2001). *The explosive child* (2nd ed.). New York: HarperCollins.

GREGG, J. A., CALLAGHAN, G. M., HAYES, S. C., & GLENN-LAWSON, J. L. (2007). Improving diabetes self-management through acceptance, mindfulness, and values: A randomized controlled trial. *Journal of Consulting and Clinical Psychology, 75,* 336–343.

GRIFFITHS, D., FELDMAN, M. A., & TOUGH, S. (1997). Programming generalization of social skills in adults with developmental disabilities: Effects on generalization and social validity. *Journal of Applied Behavior Analysis, 28,* 253–269.

GRIFFITHS, R., BIGELOW, G., & LIEBSON, I. (1974). Suppression of ethanol self-administration in alcoholics by contingent time-out from social interactions. *Behaviour Research and Therapy, 12,* 327–334.

GRODEN, J. (1993). The use of covert procedures to reduce severe aggression in a person with retardation and behavioral disorders. In J. R. Cautela & A. J. Kearney (Eds.), *Covert conditioning casebook* (pp. 144–152). Pacific Grove, CA: Brooks/Cole.

GROSS, A. M., JOHNSON, W. G., WILDMAN, H. E., & MULLETT, M. (1981). Coping skills training with insulin dependent preadolescent diabetics. *Child Behavior Therapy, 3,* 141–153.

GROSS, A. M., & WIXTED, J. T. (1988). Assessment of child behavior problems. In A. S. Bellack & M. Hersen (Eds.), *Behavioral assessment: A practical handbook* (3rd ed., pp. 578–608). Elmsford, NY: Pergamon.

GROSS, J. J. (2002). Emotion regulation: Affective, cognitive, and social consequences. *Psychophysiology, 39,* 281–291.

GROSS, J. J., & MUÑOZ, R. F. (1995). Emotion regulation and mental health. *Clinical Psychology: Science and Practice, 2,* 151–164.

GROTH, A. N. (1980). *Men who rape: The psychology of the offender.* New York: Plenum.

GROTHBERG, E. H., FEINDLER, E. L., WHITE, C. B., & STUTMAN, S. S. (1991). Using anger management for prevention of child abuse. In P. Keller & S. Heyman (Eds.), *Innovations in clinical practice: A source book* (Vol. 10, pp. 5–21). Sarasota, FL: Professional Resource Press/ Professional Resource Exchange.

GRUDER, C. L., MERMELSTEIN, R. J., KIRKENDOL, S., HEDEKER, D., WONG, S. C., SCHRECKENGOST, J., et al. (1993). Effects of social support and relapse prevention training as

adjuncts to a televised smoking-cessation intervention. *Journal of Consulting and Clinical Psychology, 61,* 113–120.

GUESS, D., & BAER, D. M. (1973). An analysis of individual differences in generalization between receptive and productive language in retarded children. *Journal of Applied Behavior Analysis, 6,* 311–329.

GUEVREMONT, D. C. (1987). *A contingency contract to reduce fighting among siblings.* Unpublished manuscript, West Virginia University.

GUEVREMONT, D. C. (1990). Social skills and peer relationship training. In R. A. Barkley (Ed.), *Attention deficit hyperactivity disorder* (pp. 540–572). New York: Guilford.

GUEVREMONT, D. C., & DUMAS, M. C. (1996). *Impact of multiple setting events on social interactions of children with ADHD.* Unpublished manuscript, Blackstone Valley Psychological Institute, North Smithfield, RI.

GUEVREMONT, D. C., & DUMAS, M. C. (2002). *Impact of setting events on the social interactions of boys with attention deficit hyperactivity disorder.* Unpublished manuscript.

GUEVREMONT, D. C., DuPAUL, G. J., & BARKLEY, R. A. (1990). Diagnosis and assessment of attention deficit hyperactivity disorder in children. *Journal of School Psychology, 28,* 51–78.

GUEVREMONT, D. C., & FOSTER, S. L. (1992). Impact of social problem solving on the behavior of aggressive boys: Generalization, maintenance, and social validation. *Journal of Abnormal Child Psychology, 26,* 112–121.

GUEVREMONT, D. C., OSNES, P. G., & STOKES, T. F. (1986a). Preparation for effective self-management: The development of generalized verbal control. *Journal of Applied Behavior Analysis, 19,* 99–104.

GUEVREMONT, D. C., OSNES, P. G., & STOKES, T. F. (1986b). Programming maintenance following correspondence training with children. *Journal of Applied Behavior Analysis, 19,* 215–219.

GUEVREMONT, D. C., OSNES, P. G., & STOKES, T. F. (1988). The functional role of verbalizations in the generalization of self-instructional training with children. *Journal of Applied Behavior Analysis, 21,* 45–55.

GUEVREMONT, D. C., & SPIEGLER, M. D. (1990, November). *What do*

behavior therapists really do? A survey of the clinical practice of AABT members. Paper presented at the meeting of the Association for Advancement of Behavior Therapy, San Francisco.

GUEVREMONT, D. C., TISHELMAN, A. C., & HULL, D. B. (1985). Teaching generalized self-control to attention-deficit boys with mothers as adjunct therapists. *Child & Family Behavior Therapy, 7,* 23–36.

GUMPEL, T. P., & FRANK, R. (1999). An expansion of the peer-tutoring paradigm: Cross-age peer tutoring of social skills among social rejected boys. *Journal of Applied Behavior Analysis, 32,* 115–118.

GUTENTAG, S., & HAMMER, D. (2000). Shaping oral feeding in a gastronomy tube-dependent child in natural settings. *Behavior Modification, 24,* 395–410.

GUTIÉRREZ-MARTÍNEZ, O., LUCIANO-SORIANO, C., RODRÍGUEZ-VALVERDE, M., & FINK, B. C. (2004). Comparison between an acceptance-based and a cognitive-control-based protocol for coping with pain. *Behavior Therapy, 35,* 767–783.

HAAGA, D. A. F. (1990). Issues in relating self-efficacy to smoking relapse: Importance of an "Achilles' heel" situation and of prior quitting experience. *Journal of Substance Abuse, 2,* 191–200.

HAAGA, D. A. F., & DAVISON, G. C. (1989a). Outcome studies of rational-emotive therapy. In M. E. Bernard & R. [A.] DiGiuseppe (Eds.), *Inside rational-emotive therapy: A critical appraisal of the theory and therapy of Albert Ellis* (pp. 155–197). San Diego: Academic Press.

HAAGA, D. A. F., & DAVISON, G. C. (1989b). Slow progress in rational-emotive therapy outcome research: Etiology and treatment. *Cognitive Therapy and Research, 13,* 493–508.

HAAGA, D. A. [F.], & DAVISON, G. C. (1993). An appraisal of rational-emotive therapy. *Journal of Consulting and Clinical Psychology, 61,* 215–220.

HAAGA, D. A. F., DYCK, M. J., & ERNST, D. (1991). Empirical status of cognitive theory of depression. *Psychological Bulletin, 110,* 215–236.

HACKMANN, A., & McCLEAN, C. (1975). A comparison of flooding and thought stopping in the treatment of obsessional neurosis. *Behaviour Research and Therapy, 13,* 263–269.

HAGOPIAN, L. P., CROCKETT, J. L., VAN STONE, M., DELEON, I. G., & BOWMAN, L. G. (2000). Effects of noncontingent reinforcement on problem behavior and stimulus engagement: The role of satiation, extinctions, and alternative reinforcement. *Journal of Applied Behavior Analysis, 33*, 433–449.

HAGOPIAN, L. P., & SLIFER, K. J. (1993). Treatment of separation anxiety disorder with graduated exposure and reinforcement targeting school attendance: A controlled case study. *Journal of Anxiety Disorders, 7*, 271–280.

HAHLWEG, K., & MARKMAN, H. J. (1988). Effectiveness of behavioral marital therapy: Empirical status of behavioral techniques in preventing and alleviating marital distress. *Journal of Consulting and Clinical Psychology, 56*, 440–447.

HALL, A. C., & NATHAN, P. R. (1992, July). *The management of night wakening and settling problems in young children: Efficacy of a behavioral group parent training programme.* Paper presented at the Fourth World Congress of Behavior Therapy, Queensland, Australia.

HALL, N. R. S. (1988). The virology of AIDS. *American Psychologist, 43*, 907–913.

HALL, R. V., & HALL, M. C. (1982). *How to negotiate a behavioral contract.* Austin, TX: Pro-Ed.

HALL, R. V., & HALL, M. L. (1998a). *How to select reinforcers* (2nd ed.). Austin, TX: Pro-Ed.

HALL, R. V., & HALL, M. L. (1998b). *How to use systematic attention and approval* (2nd ed.). Austin, TX: Pro-Ed.

HANNIE, T. J., JR., & ADAMS, H. E. (1974). Modification of agitated depression by flooding: A preliminary study. *Journal of Behavior Therapy and Experimental Psychiatry, 5*, 161–166.

HANSELL, J., & DAMOUR, L. (2008). *Abnormal psychology* (2nd ed.). New York: Wiley.

HANSEN, D. J. (2001). Public education and media dissemination: An interview with Albert Ellis. *the Behavior Therapist, 24*, 117–121.

HANSEN, D. J., ST.LAWRENCE, J. S., & CHRISTOFF, K. A. (1985). Effects of interpersonal problem-solving training with chronic aftercare patients on problem-solving component skills and effectiveness of solutions. *Journal of Consulting and Clinical Psychology, 53*, 167–174.

HANSEN, D. J., ZAMBOANGA, B. L., & SEDLAR, G. (2000). Cognitive-behavior therapy for ethnic minority adolescents: Broadening our perspectives. *Cognitive and Behavioral Practice, 7*, 54–60.

HARDING, J., WACKER, D. P., BERG, W. K., BARRETTO, A., & RINGDAHL, J. (2005). Evaluation of relations between specific antecedent stimuli and self-injury during functional analysis conditions. *American Journal of Mental Retardation, 110*, 205–215.

HARING, T. G., BREEN, C. G., WEINER, J., KENNEDY, C. H., & BEDNERAH, F. (1995). Using videotape modeling to facilitate generalized purchasing skills. *Journal of Behavioral Education, 5*, 29–53.

HARPER, G. W., & IWAMASA, G. Y. (2000). Cognitive-behavioral therapy with ethnic minority adolescents: Therapist perspectives. *Cognitive and Behavioral Practice, 7*, 37–53.

HARRIS, S., DAVIES, M. F., & DRYDEN, W. (2006). An experimental test of a core REBT hypothesis: Evidence that irrational beliefs lead to physiological as well as psychological arousal. *Journal of Rational-Emotive & Cognitive-Behavior Therapy, 24*, 1–9.

HARRIS, S. L., & ROMANCZYK, R. G. (1976). Treating self-injurious behavior of a retarded child by overcorrection. *Behavior Therapy, 7*, 235–239.

HARRIS, V. W., & SHERMAN, J. A. (1974). Homework assignments, consequences, and classroom performance in social studies and mathematics. *Journal of Applied Behavior Analysis, 7*, 505–519.

HARTL, T. L., & FROST, R. O. (1999). Cognitive-behavioral treatment of compulsive hoarding: A multiple baseline experimental case study. *Behaviour Research and Therapy, 37*, 451–461.

HARTMANN, D. P. (1982). Assessing the dependability of observational data. In D. P. Hartmann (Ed.), *New directions for methodology of social and behavioral science: Using observers to study behavior* (pp. 51–65). San Francisco: Jossey-Bass.

HARTMANN, D. P., & WOOD, D. D. (1982). Observational methods. In A. S. Bellack, M. Hersen, & A. E. Kazdin (Eds.), *International handbook of behavior modification and therapy* (pp. 109–138). New York: Plenum.

HARVEY, A., WATKINS, E., MANSELL, W., & SHAFRAN, R. (2004). *Cognitive behavioral processes across psychological disorders: A transdiagnostic approach to research and treatment.* Oxford, UK: Oxford University Press.

HATCH, M. L., FRIEDMAN, S., & PARADIS, C. M. (1996). Behavioral treatment of obsessive-compulsive disorder in African Americans. *Cognitive and Behavioral Practice, 3*, 303–315.

HAUGHTON, E., & AYLLON, T. (1965). Production and elimination of symptomatic behavior. In L. P. Ullmann & L. Krasner (Eds.), *Case studies in behavior modification* (pp. 94–98). New York: Holt, Rinehart & Winston.

HAURI, P. (1981). Treating psychophysiological insomnia with biofeedback: A replication study. *Biofeedback and Self-Regulation, 7*, 752–758.

HAWKEN, L. S., & HESS, R. S. (2006). Special section: Changing practice, changing schools. *School Psychology Quarterly, 21*, 91–111.

HAWKINS, R. P. (1997). Can behavior therapy be saved from triviality? Commentary on "Thirty years of behavior therapy." *Behavior Therapy, 28*, 637–645.

HAWKINS, R. P., & FORSYTH, J. P. (1997). The behavior analytic perspective: Its nature, prospects, and limitations for behavior therapy. *Journal of Behavior Therapy and Experimental Psychiatry, 28*, 7–16.

HAY, W. M., HAY, L. R., & NELSON, R. O. (1977). The adaptation of covert modeling procedures in the treatment of chronic alcoholism and obsessive-compulsive behavior: Two case reports. *Behavior Therapy, 8*, 70–76.

HAYES, S. C. (2002). Acceptance, mindfulness and science. *Clinical Psychology: Science and Practice, 9*, 101–106.

HAYES, S. C. (2004a). Acceptance and Commitment Therapy and the new behavior therapies: Mindfulness, acceptance, and relationship. In S. C. Hayes, V. M. Follette, & M. Linehan (Eds.), *Mindfulness and acceptance: Expanding the cognitive-behavioral tradition* (pp. 1–29). New York: Guilford.

HAYES, S. C. (2004b). Acceptance and Commitment Therapy, Relational Frame Theory, and the third wave of behavioral and cognitive therapies. *Behavior Therapy, 35,* 639–666.

HAYES, S. C. (2008). Climbing our hills: A beginning conversation on the comparison of acceptance and commitment therapy and traditional cognitive behavioral therapy. *Clinical Psychology: Science & Practice, 5,* 286–295.

HAYES, S. C., BARNES-HOLMES, D., & ROCHE, B. (2001). *Relational frame theory: A post-Skinnerian account of human language and cognition.* New York: Kluwer.

HAYES, S. C., BISSETT, R., KORN, Z., ZETTLE, R. D., ROSENFARB, I., COOPER, L., et al. (1999). The impact of acceptance versus control rationales on pain tolerance. *The Psychological Record, 49,* 33–47.

HAYES, S. C., FOLLETTE, V. M., & LINEHAN, M. (Eds.). (2004). Mindfulness and acceptance: Expanding the cognitive-behavioral tradition. New York: Guilford.

HAYES, S. C., LUOMA, J. B., BOND, F. W., MASUDA, A., & LILLIS, J. (2006). Acceptance and commitment therapy: Model, processes, and outcomes. *Behaviour Research and Therapy, 44,* 1–25.

HAYES, S. C., WILSON, K. G., GIFFORD, E. V., BISSETT, R., PIASECKI, M., BATTEN, S. V., et al. (2004). A preliminary trial of Twelve-Step Facilitation and Acceptance and Commitment Therapy with polysubstance-abusing methadone-maintained opiate addicts. *Behavior Therapy, 35,* 667–688.

HAYES, S. C., WILSON, K. G., GIFFORD, E. V., FOLLETTE, V. M., & STROSAHL, K. (1996). Experiential avoidance and behavioral disorders: A functional dimensional approach to diagnosis and treatment. *Journal of Consulting and Clinical Psychology, 64,* 1152–1168.

HAYNES, R. B., McDONALD, H. P., & GARG, A. X. (2002). Helping patients followed prescribed treatment: Clinical applications. *Journal of the American Medical Association, 288,* 2880–2883.

HAYNES, R. B., McDONALD, H. P., GARG, A. X., & MONTAGUE, P. (2000). Interventions for helping patients to follow prescription medications. *Cochrane Database Systematic Review, 2,* CD000011.

HAYNES, R. B., SACKETT, D. L., GIBSON, E. S., TAYLOR, D. W., HACKETT, B. C., ROBERTS, R. S., et al. (1976). Improvement of medication compliance in uncontrolled hypertension. *Lancet, 1,* 1265–1268.

HAYNES, S. N. (1978). *Principles of behavioral assessment.* New York: Gardner.

HEADEY, A., PIRKIS, J., MERNER, B., VANDENHEUVEL, A., MITCHELL, P., ROBINSON, J., et al. (2006). A review of 156 local projects funded under Australia's National Suicide Prevention Strategy: Overview and lessons learned. *Australian e-Journal for the Advancement of Mental Health, 5*(3), 1–15.

HEARD, K., & WATSON, T. S. (1999). Reducing wandering by persons with dementia using differential reinforcement. *Journal of Applied Behavior Analysis, 32,* 381–384.

HEATHERTON, T. F., & BAUMEISTER, R. F. (1991). Binge eating as escape from self-awareness. *Psychological Bulletin, 110,* 86–108.

HEATON, R. C., & SAFER, D. J. (1982). Secondary school outcome following a junior high school behavioral program. *Behavior Therapy, 13,* 226–231.

HEDBERG, A. G., & CAMPBELL, L. (1974). A comparison of four behavioral treatments of alcoholism. *Journal of Behavior Therapy and Experimental Psychiatry, 5,* 251–256.

HEFFNER, M., SPERRY, J., & EIFERT, G. H. (2002). Acceptance and commitment therapy in the treatment of an adolescent female with anorexia nervosa: A case example. *Cognitive and Behavioral Practice, 9,* 232–236.

HEGEL, M. T., & FERGUSON, R. J. (2000). Differential reinforcement of other behavior (DRO) to reduce aggressive behavior following traumatic brain injury. *Behavior Modification, 24,* 94–101.

HEIMBERG, R. G. (1998). Manual-based treatment: An essential ingredient of clinical practice in the 21st century. *Clinical Psychology: Science and Practice, 5,* 387–390.

HEIMBERG, R. G., SALZMAN, D. G., HOLT, C. S., & BLENDELL, K. A. (1993). Cognitive-behavioral group treatment for social phobia: Effectiveness at five-year followup. *Cognitive Therapy and Research, 17,* 325–339.

HEINRICHS, N., BERTRAM, H., KUSCHEL, A., & HAHLWEG, K. (2005). Parent recruitment and retention in a universal prevention program for child behavior and emotional problems: Barriers to research and program participation. *Prevention Science: The Official Journal of The Society for Prevention Research, 6,* 275–286.

HEMBREE, E. A., & FOA, E. B. (2003). Interventions for trauma-related emotional disturbances in adult victims of crime. *Journal of Traumatic Stress, 16,* 187–199.

HEMBREE, E. A., FOA, E. B., DORFAN, N. M., STREET, G. P., KOWALSKI, J., & TU, X. (2003). Do patients drop out prematurely from exposure therapy for PTSD? *Journal of Traumatic Stress, 16,* 555–562.

HERBERT, J. D., GAUDIANO, B. A., RHEINGOLD, A. A., MYERS, V. H., DALRYMPLE, K, & NOLAN, E. M. (2005). Social skills training augments the effectiveness of cognitive behavioral group therapy for social anxiety disorder. *Behavior Therapy, 36,* 125–138.

HERBST, J. H., KAY, L. S., PASSIN, W. F., LYLES, C. M., CREPAZ, N., & MARIN, B. V. (2007). A systematic review and meta-analysis of behavioral interventions to reduce HIV risk behaviors of Hispanics in the United States and Puerto Rico. *AIDS and Behavior, 11,* 25–47.

HERMANN, J. A., DE MONTES, A. I., DOMINGUEZ, B., MONTES, F., & HOPKINS, B. L. (1973). Effects of bonuses for punctuality on the tardiness of industrial workers. *Journal of Applied Behavior Analysis, 6,* 563–570.

HERRING, M., & NORTHUP, J. (1998). The generalization of social skills for a child with behavior disorders in the school setting. *Child & Family Behavior Therapy, 20,* 51–65.

HERSEN, M., EISLER, R. M., MILLER, P. M., JOHNSON, M. B., & PINKSTON, S. G. (1973). Effects of practice, instructions, and modeling on components of assertive behavior. *Behaviour Research and Therapy, 11,* 443–451.

HESTER, R. K., & DELANEY, H. D. (1997). Behavioral self-control program for Windows: Results of a controlled clinical trial. *Journal of Consulting and Clinical Psychology, 65,* 686–693.

HEWARD, W. L., DARDIG, J. C., & ROSSETT, A. (1979). *Working with parents of handicapped children.* Columbus, OH: Merrill.

HIGGINS, S. T., & SILVERMAN, K. (2008). Introduction. In S. T. Higgins, K. Silverman, & S. H. Heil (Eds.), *Contingency management in substance abuse treatment* (pp. 1–15). New York: Guilford.

HIGGINS, S. T., SILVERMAN, K., & HEIL, S. H. (Eds.). (2008). *Contingency management in substance abuse treatment.* New York: Guilford.

HIGGINS, S. T., WONG, C. J., BADGER, G. J., OGDEN, D. H., & DANTONA, R. (2000). Contingent reinforcement increases cocaine abstinence during outpatient treatment and 1 year of follow-up. *Journal of Consulting and Clinical Psychology, 68,* 64–72.

HILL, P. (1989). Behavioural psychotherapy with children. *International Review of Psychiatry, 1,* 257–266.

HILLIARD, R. B. (1993). Single-case methodology in psychotherapy process and outcome research. *Journal of Consulting and Clinical Psychology, 61,* 373–380.

HIMADI, B., OSTEEN, F., & CRAWFORD, E. (1993). Delusional verbalizations and beliefs. *Behavioral Residential Treatment, 8,* 229–242.

HIMLE, M. B., WOODS, D. W., PIACENTINI, J. C., & WALKUP, J. T. (2006). Brief review of habit reversal training for Tourette syndrome. *Journal of Clinical Neurology, 21,* 719–725.

HIRSCHSTEIN, M., & FREY, K. S. (2006). Promoting behavior and beliefs that reduce bullying: The steps to respect program. In S. R. Jimerson & M. Furling (Eds.), *Handbook of school violence and school safety: From research to practice* (pp. 309–323). Mahwah, NJ: Lawrence Erlbaum.

HITCHCOCK, C. H., DOWRICK, P. W., & PRATER, M. A. (2003). Video self-modeling intervention in school-based settings: A review. *Remedial and Special Education, 24,* 36–46.

HITCHCOCK, C. H., PRATER, M. A., & DOWRICK, P. W. (2004). Reading comprehension and fluency: Examining the effects of tutoring and video self-modeling on first-grade students with reading difficulties. *Learning Disability Quarterly, 27,* 89–103.

HOBFOLL, S. E., JACKSON, A. P., LAVIN, J., BRITTON, P. J., & SHEPHERD, J. B. (1994). Reducing inner-city women's AIDS risk activities: A study of single, pregnant women. *Health Psychology, 13,* 397–403.

HODGES, L. F., ROTHBAUM, B. O., KOOPER, R., OPDYKE, D., MEYER, T., DE GRAFF, J. J., et al. (1994). *Presence as the defining factor in a VR application: Virtual reality graded exposure in the treatment of acrophobia.* (Tech. Rep. #GITGVU-94-6). Atlanta: Georgia Institute of Technology.

HODGINS, D. C., WYNNE, H., & MAKARCHUCK, K. (1999). Pathways to recovery from gambling problems: Follow-up from a general population survey. *Journal of Gambling Studies, 15,* 93–104.

HODGSON, R. J., & RACHMAN, S. (1970). An experimental investigation of the implosive technique. *Behaviour Research and Therapy, 8,* 21–27.

HOFFMAN, B. M., PAPAS, R. K., CHATKOFF, D. K., & KERNS, R. D. (2007). Meta-analysis of psychological interventions for chronic lower back pain. *Health Psychology, 26,* 1–9.

HOFMANN, S. G. (2004). Cognitive mediation of treatment change in social phobia. *Journal of Consulting and Clinical Psychology, 72,* 393–399.

HOFMANN, S. G., & ASMUNDSON, G. J. (2008). Acceptance and mindfulness-based therapy: New wave or old hat? *Clinical Psychology Review, 28,* 1–16.

HOGAN, R. A. (1968). The implosive technique. *Behaviour Research and Therapy, 6,* 423–432.

HOGAN, R. A. (1969). Implosively oriented behavior modification: Therapy considerations. *Behaviour Research and Therapy, 7,* 177–184.

HOGAN, R. A., & KIRCHNER, J. H. (1967). A preliminary report of the extinction of learned fears via a short term implosive therapy. *Journal of Abnormal Psychology, 72,* 106–111.

HOLAND, J., PLUMB, M., YATES, J., HARRIS, S., TUTTOLOMONDO, A., HOLMES, J., et al. (1977). Psychological response of patients with acute leukemia to germ-free environments. *Cancer, 36,* 871–879.

HOLLON, S. D., & BECK, A. T. (1986). Research on cognitive therapies. In S. L. Garfield & A. E. Bergin (Eds.), *Handbook of psychotherapy and behavior change* (3rd ed., pp. 443–482). New York: Wiley.

HOLLON, S. D., & BECK, A. T. (1994). Cognitive and cognitive behavioral therapies. In A. E. Bergin & S. L. Garfield (Eds.), *Handbook of psychotherapy and behavior change* (4th ed., pp. 428–466). New York: Wiley.

HOLLON, S. D., SHELTON, R. C., & DAVIS, D. D. (1993). Cognitive therapy for depression: Conceptual issues and clinical efficacy. *Journal of Consulting and Clinical Psychology, 61,* 270–275.

HOLLON, S. D., STEWART, M. O., & STRUNK, D. (2006). Enduring effects of cognitive behavior therapy in the treatment of depression and anxiety. *Annual Review of Psychology, 57,* 285–315.

HOLROYD, K. A. (1976). Cognition and desensitization in the group treatment of test anxiety. *Journal of Consulting and Clinical Psychology, 44,* 991–1001.

HOLROYD, K. A., & PENZIEN, D. B. (1994). Psychosocial interventions in the management of recurrent headache disorders 1: Overview and effectiveness. *Behavioral Medicine, 20,* 53–63.

HOMME, L. E. (1971). *How to use contingency contracting in the classroom.* Champaign, IL: Research Press.

HOMME, L. E., C'DE BACA, P., DEVINE, J. V., STEINHORST, R., & RICKERT, E. J. (1963). Use of the Premack principle in controlling the behavior of nursery school children. *Journal of the Experimental Analysis of Behavior, 6,* 544.

HONNEN, T. J., & KLEINKE, C. L. (1990). Prompting bar patrons with signs to take free condoms. *Journal of Applied Behavior Analysis, 23,* 215–217.

HOOD, K., & EYBERG, S. M. (2003). Outcomes of parent child interaction therapy: Mothers' reports on maintenance three to six years after treatment. *Journal of Clinical Child and Adolescent Psychology, 32,* 419–429.

HOPKO, D. R., BELL, J. L., ARMENTO, M. E. A., HUNT, M. K., & LEJUEZ, C. W. (2005). Behavior therapy for depressed cancer patients in primary care. *Psychotherapy: Theory, Research, Practice, Training, 42,* 236–243.

HOPKO, D. R., HOPKO, S. D., & LEJUEZ, C. W. (2004). Behavioral activation as an intervention for co-existent depressive and anxiety symptoms. *Clinical Case Studies, 3,* 37–48.

HOPKO, D. R., LEJUEZ, C. W., LEPAGE, J., HOPKO, S. D., & MCNEIL, D. W. (2003). A brief behavioral activation treatment for depression: A randomized trial within an inpatient psychiatric hospital. *Behavior Modification, 27,* 458–469.

HOPKO, D. R., LEJUEZ, C. W., RUGGIERO, K. J., & EIFERT, G. H. (2003). Contemporary behavioral activation treatments for depression: Procedures, principles, and progress. *Clinical Psychology Review, 23,* 699–717.

HOPKO, D. R., SANCHEZ, L., HOPKO, S. D., DVIR, S., & LEJUEZ, C. W. (2003). Behavioral activation and the prevention of suicide in patients with borderline personality disorder. *Journal of Personality Disorders, 17,* 460–478.

HORAN, J. J., HACKETT, G., BUCHANAN, J. D., STONE, C. I., & STONE, D. D. (1977). Coping with pain: A component analysis of stress inoculation. *Cognitive Therapy and Research, 1,* 211–221.

HORAN, J. J., HACKETT, G., NICHOLAS, W. C., LINBERG, S. E., STONE, C. I., & LUKASKI, H. C. (1977). Rapid smoking: A cautionary note. *Journal of Consulting and Clinical Psychology, 45,* 341–343.

HORAN, J. J., & JOHNSON, R. G. (1971). Coverant conditioning through a self-management application of the Premack principle: Its effect on weight reduction. *Journal of Behavior Therapy and Experimental Psychiatry, 2,* 243–249.

HORNE, A. M., & MATSON, J. L. (1977). A comparison of modeling, desensitization, flooding, study skills, and control groups for reducing test anxiety. *Behavior Therapy, 8,* 1–8.

HORNER, R. D., & KEILITZ, I. (1975). Training mentally retarded adolescents to brush their teeth. *Journal of Applied Behavior Analysis, 8,* 301–309.

HORRELL, S. C. V. (2008). Effectiveness of cognitive-behavioral therapy with adult ethnic minority clients: A review. *Professional Psychology: Research and Practice, 39,* 160–168.

HOSFORD, R., & BROWN, S. (1975). Innovations in behavioral approaches to counseling. *Focus on Guidance, 8,* 1–11.

HOUSE, A. S. (2006). Increasing the usability of cognitive processing therapy for survivors of child sexual abuse. *Journal of Child Sexual Abuse, 15,* 87–103.

HOUTS, A.C. (2003). Behavioral treatment for enuresis. In A.E. Kazdin & J.R. Weisz (Eds.), *Evidence-based psychotherapies for children and adolescents* (pp. 389–406). New York: Guilford.

HOUTS, A. C., BERMAN, J. S., & ABRAMSON, H. (1994). Effectiveness of psychological and pharmacological treatments for nocturnal enuresis. *Journal of Consulting and Clinical Psychology, 62,* 737–745.

HOUTS, A. C., PETERSON, J. K., & WHELAN, J. P. (1986). Prevention of relapse in Full-Spectrum Home Training for primary enuresis: A components analysis. *Behavior Therapy, 17,* 462–469.

HRYDOWY, E. R., STOKES, T. F., & MARTIN, G. (1984). Training elementary students to prompt teacher praise. *Education and Treatment of Children, 7,* 99–108.

HUANG, W., & CUVO, A. J. (1997). Social skills training for adults with mental retardation in job-related settings. *Behavior Modification, 21,* 3–44.

HUEY, S., JR., & PAN, D. (2006). Culture-responsive one-session treatment for phobic Asian Americans: A pilot study. *Psychotherapy: Theory, Research, Practice, Training, 43,* 549–554.

HUGHES, C., & RUSCH, F. R. (1989). Teaching supported employees with severe mental retardation to solve problems. *Journal of Applied Behavior Analysis, 22,* 365–372.

HUMMEL, R. M., & GROSS, A. M. (2001). Socially anxious children: An observational study of parent-child interaction. *Child & Family Behavior Therapy, 23,* 19–42.

HUMPHREYS, L., FOREHAND, R. [L.], MCMAHON, R. J., & ROBERTS, M. (1978). Parent behavioral training to modify child noncompliance: Effects on untreated siblings. *Journal of Behavior Therapy and Experimental Psychiatry, 9,* 235–238.

HUNT, J. G., FITZHUGH, L. C., & FITZHUGH, K. B. (1968). Teaching "exit-ward" patients appropriate personal appearance by using reinforcement techniques. *American Journal of Mental Deficiency, 73,* 41–45.

HUNT, J. G., & ZIMMERMAN, J. (1969). Stimulating productivity in a simulated sheltered workshop setting. *American Journal of Mental Deficiency, 74,* 43–49.

HUNTER, J., & SCHAECHER, R. (1994). AIDS prevention for lesbian, gay, and bisexual adolescents. (Special Issue: HIV/AIDS). *Families in Society, 75,* 346–354.

HUNTER, R. H. (1995). Benefits of competency-based treatment programs. *American Psychologist, 50,* 509–513.

HUSS, D. B., & BAER, R. A. (2007). Acceptance and change: The integration of mindfulness-based cognitive therapy into ongoing dialectical behavior therapy in a case of borderline personality disorder with depression. *Clinical Case Studies, 61,* 17–33.

HUTZELL, R., PLATZEK, D., & LOGUE, P. (1974). Control of Gilles de la Tourette's syndrome by self-monitoring. *Journal of Behavior Therapy and Experimental Psychiatry, 5,* 71–76.

IGUCHI, M. Y., BELDING, M. A., MORRAL, A. R., LAMB, R. J., & HUSBAND, S. D. (1997). Reinforcing operants other than abstinence in drug abuse treatment: An effective alternative for reducing drug use. *Journal of Consulting and Clinical Psychology, 65,* 421–428.

IKEDA, K., KOGA, A., & MINAMI, S. (2006). Evaluation of a cure process during alarm treatment for nocturnal enuresis. *Journal of Clinical Psychology, 62,* 1245–1257.

INGRAM, R. E., & HOLLON, S. D. (1986). Cognitive therapy for depression from an information processing perspective. In R. E. Ingram (Ed.), *Information processing approaches to clinical psychology* (pp. 261–280). Orlando, FL: Academic Press.

INTERIAN, A., ALLEN, L. A., GARA, M. A., & ESOBAR, J. I. (2008). A pilot study of culturally adapted cognitive behavior therapy for Hispanics with major depression. *Cognitive and Behavioral Practice, 15,* 67–75.

IRVIN, J. E., BOWERS, C. A., DUNN, M. E., & WANG, M. C. (1999). Efficacy of relapse prevention: A meta-analytic review. *Journal of Consulting and Clinical Psychology, 67,* 563–570.

IRWIN, M. R., COLE, J. C., & NICASSIO, P. M. (2006). Comparative meta-analysis of behavioral interventions for insomnia and their efficacy in middle-aged adults and in older adults 55+ years of age. *Health Psychology, 25,* 3–14.

ISAACS, W., THOMAS, I., & GOLDIAMOND, I. (1960). Application of operant conditioning to reinstate verbal behavior in psychotics. *Journal of Speech and Hearing Disorders, 25,* 8–12.

ISRAEL, A. C., GUILE, C. A., BAKER, J. E., & SILVERMAN, W. K. (1994). An evaluation of enhanced self-regulation training in the treatment of childhood obesity. *Journal of Pediatric Psychology, 19,* 737–749.

ITARD, J. M. G. (1962). *The wild boy of Aveyron.* New York: Appleton-Century-Crofts.

IWAMASA, G. Y. (1996). Introduction to the special series: Ethnic and cultural diversity in cognitive and behavioral practice. *Cognitive and Behavioral Practice, 3,* 209–213.

IWAMASA, G. Y. (1997). Behavior therapy and a culturally diverse society: Forging an alliance. *Behavior Therapy, 28,* 347–358.

IWAMASA, G. Y. (1999). Behavior therapy and cultural diversity: Is there a commitment? *the Behavior Therapist, 22,* 193.

IWAMASA, G. Y., & SMITH, S. K. (1996). Ethnic diversity in behavioral psychology. *Behavior Modification, 20,* 45–59.

IWATA, B. A. (1987). Negative reinforcement in applied behavior analysis: An emerging technology. *Journal of Applied Behavior Analysis, 20,* 361–378.

IWATA, B. A. (1994). Functional analysis methodology: Some closing comments. *Journal of Applied Behavior Analysis, 27,* 413–418.

IWATA, B. A., VOLLMER, T. R., & ZARCONE, J. R. (1990). The experimental (functional) analysis of behavior disorders: Methodology, applications, and limitations. In A. C. Repp & N. N. Singh (Eds.), *Perspectives on the use of nonaversive and aversive interventions for persons with developmental disabilities* (pp. 301–330). Sycamore, IL: Sycamore Publishing.

IYER, E. S., & KASHYAP, R. K. (2007). *Journal of Consumer Behaviour, 6,* 32–47.

JABERGHADERI, N., GREENWALD, R., RUBIN, A., DOLATABADIM S., & ZAND, S. O. (2004). A comparison of CBT and EMDR for sexually abused Iranian girls. *Clinical Psychology and Psychotherapy, 11,* 358–368.

JACKSON, H. J., & FRANCEY, S. M. (1985). The use of hypnotically induced covert modelling in the desensitization of an escalator phobia. *Australian Journal of Clinical and Experimental Hypnosis, 13,* 55–58.

JACOBS, G. D., BENSON, H., & FRIEDMAN, R. (1993). Home-based central nervous system assessment of a multifactor behavioral intervention for chronic sleep-onset insomnia. *Behavior Therapy, 24,* 159–174.

JACOBS, G. D., ROSENBERG, P. A., FRIEDMAN, R., MATHESON, J., PEAVY,

G. M., DOMAR, A. D., et al. (1993). Multifactor behavioral treatment of chronic sleep-onset insomnia using stimulus control and the relaxation response: A preliminary study. *Behavior Modification, 17,* 498–509.

JACOBS, M. K., & COCHRAN, S. D. (1982). The effects of cognitive restructuring on assertive behavior. *Cognitive Therapy and Research, 6,* 63–76.

JACOBSON, E. (1929). *Progressive relaxation.* Chicago: University of Chicago Press.

JACOBSON, E. (1934). *You must relax.* Chicago: University of Chicago Press.

JACOBSON, N. S. (1985). The role of observational measures in behavior therapy outcome research. *Behavioral Assessment, 7,* 297–308.

JACOBSON, N. S. (1988). Defining clinically significant change: An introduction. *Behavior Therapy, 10,* 131–132.

JACOBSON, N. S. (1989). The maintenance of treatment gains following social learning-based marital therapy. *Behavior Therapy, 20,* 325–336.

JACOBSON, N. S. (1991, September). Marital therapy: Theory and treatment considerations. Workshop sponsored by the Rhode Island Psychological Association, Warwick, RI.

JACOBSON, N. S. (1992). Behavioral couple therapy: A new beginning. *Behavior Therapy, 23,* 493–506.

JACOBSON, N. S. (1993). Introduction to special section on couples and couple therapy. *Journal of Consulting and Clinical Psychology, 61,* 5.

JACOBSON, N. S., & ADDIS, M. E. (1993). Research on couples and couple therapy: What do we know, where are we going? *Journal of Consulting and Clinical Psychology, 61,* 85–93.

JACOBSON, N. S., & CHRISTENSEN, A. (1996). *Acceptance and change in couple therapy: A therapist's guide to transforming relationships.* New York: Norton.

JACOBSON, N. S., CHRISTENSEN, A., PRINCE, S. E., CORDOVA, J., & ELDRIDGE, K. (2000). Integrative behavioral couple therapy: An acceptance-based, promising new treatment for couple discord. *Journal of Consulting and Clinical Psychology, 68,* 351–355.

JACOBSON, N. S., & MARGOLIN, G. (1979). *Marital therapy: Strategies based on social learning and behavior exchange principles.* New York: Brunner/Mazel.

JAMES, J. E. (1985). Desensitization treatment of agoraphobia. *British Journal of Clinical Psychology, 24,* 133–134.

JAMES, J. E. (1986). Review of the relative efficacy of imaginal and in vivo flooding in the treatment of clinical fear. *Behavioural Psychotherapy, 14,* 183–191.

JAMES, L. D., THORN, B. E., & WILLIAMS, D. A. (1993). Goal specification in cognitive-behavioral therapy for chronic headache pain. *Behavior Therapy, 24,* 305–320.

JAMES, S. D., & EGEL, A. L. (1986). A direct prompting strategy for increasing reciprocal interactions between handicapped and non-handicapped siblings. *Journal of Applied Behavior Analysis, 19,* 173–186.

JANDA, L. H., & RIMM, D. C. (1972). Covert sensitization in the treatment of obesity. *Journal of Abnormal Psychology, 80,* 37–42.

JANNOUN, L., MUNBY, M., CATALAN, J., & GELDER, M. (1980). A home-based treatment program for agoraphobia: Replication and controlled evaluation. *Behavior Therapy, 11,* 294–305.

JANSEN, M. (1987). Women's health issues: An emerging priority for health psychology. In G. C. Stone, S. M. Weiss, J. D. Matarazzo, N. E. Miller, J. Rodin, C. D. Belar, et al. (Eds.), *Health psychology: A discipline and a profession* (pp. 249–264). Chicago: University of Chicago Press.

JANSSON, M., & LINTON, S. J. (2005). Cognitive-behavioral group therapy as an early intervention for insomnia: A randomized controlled study. *Journal of Occupational Rehabilitation, 15,* 177–190.

JASON, L. A. (1985). Using a token-actuated timer to reduce television viewing. *Journal of Applied Behavior Analysis, 18,* 269–272.

JAY, S. M., & ELLIOTT, C. H. (1990). A stress inoculation program for parents whose children are undergoing painful medical procedures. *Journal of Consulting and Clinical Psychology, 58,* 799–804.

JAY, S. M., ELLIOTT, C. H., KATZ, E., & SIEGEL, E. (1987). Cognitive-behavioral and pharmacologic interventions for children's distress during painful medical procedures. *Journal of Consulting and Clinical Psychology, 55,* 860–865.

JAY, S. M., ELLIOTT, C. H., OZOLINS, M., OLSON, R. A., & PRUITT, S. D. (1985). Behavioral management of children's distress during painful medical procedures. *Behaviour Research and Therapy, 23,* 513–520.

JAYCOX, L. H., REIVICH, K. J., GILLHAM, J., & SELIGMAN, M. E. P. (1994). Prevention of depressive symptoms in school children. *Behaviour Research and Therapy, 32,* 801–816.

JENSEN, B. J., & HAYNES, S. N. (1986). Self-report questionnaires and inventories. In A. R. Ciminero, K. S. Calhoun, & H. A. Adams (Eds.), *Handbook of behavioral assessment* (2nd ed., pp. 150–179). New York: Wiley.

JOHN, O. P., & GROSS, J. J. (2004). Healthy and unhealthy emotion regulation: Personality processes, individual differences, and life span development. *Journal of Personality, 72,* 1301–1333.

JOHNSON, B. M., MILTENBERGER, R. G., EGEMO-HELM, K., JOSTAD, C. M., FLESSNER, C., & GATHERIDGE, B. (2005). Evaluation of behavioral skills training for teaching abduction-prevention skills to young children. *Journal of Applied Behavior Analysis, 38,* 67–78.

JOHNSON, B. M., MILTENBERGER, R. G., KNUDSON, P., EGEMO-HELM, K., KELSO, P., JOSTAD, C., et al. (2006). A preliminary evaluation of two behavioral skills training procedures for teaching abduction-prevention skills to schoolchildren. *Journal of Applied Behavior Analysis, 39,* 25–34.

JOHNSON, C. M., & LERNER, M. (1985). Amelioration of infant sleep disturbance: II. Effects of scheduled awakenings by compliant parents. *Infant Mental Health Journal, 6,* 21–30.

JOHNSON, S. M., & BOLSTAD, O. D. (1973). Methodological issues in naturalistic observation: Some problems and solutions for field research. In L. A. Hamerlynck, L. C. Handy, & E. J. Mash (Eds.), *Behavior change: Methodology, concepts, and practice.* Champaign, IL: Research Press.

JOHNSON, W. G., CORRIGAN, S. A., & MAYO, L. L. (1987). Innovative treatment approaches to bulimia nervosa. Special issue: Recent advances in behavioral medicine. *Behavior Modification, 11,* 373–388.

JOHNSTON, C., HOMMERSEN, P., & SEIPP, C. (2008). Acceptability of behavioral and pharmacological treatments for attention-deficit/hyperactivity disorder: Relations to child and parent characteristics. *Behavior Therapy, 39,* 22–32.

JONES, K. M., & FRIMAN, P. C. (1999). A case study of behavioral assessment and treatment of insect phobia. *Journal of Applied Behavior Analysis, 32,* 95–98.

JONES, M. C. (1924). A laboratory study of fear: The case of Peter. *Pedagogical Seminar, 31,* 308–315.

JONES, M. L., EYBERG, S. M., ADAMS, C. D., & BOGGS, S. R. (1998). Treatment acceptability of behavioral interventions for children: An assessment by mothers of children with disruptive behavior disorders. *Child & Family Behavior Therapy, 20,* 15–26.

JONES, R. J., & TIMBERS, G. D. (1983). *Professional parenting for juvenile offenders.* (Final Report, Grant MH15776). Morgantown, NC: BIABH Study Center.

JORGENSEN, R. S., & CAREY, M. P. (1994). Supplementing relaxation training with "aromatherapy": An in-depth comparison of two clients. *Anxiety Disorders Practice Journal, 1,* 59–76.

JOSMAN, N., SOMER, E., REISBERG, A., WEISS, P. L., GARCIA-PALACIOS, A., & HOFFMAN, H. (2006). Designing a virtual environment for PTSD in Israel: A protocol. *Cyberpsychology and Behavior, 9,* 241–244.

JOYCE, M. R. (1995). Emotional relief for parents: Is rational-emotive parent education effective? *Journal of Rational-Emotive & Cognitive-Behavior Therapy, 13,* 55–75.

JURGELA, A. R. (1993). The use of covert conditioning to treat self-injurious behavior. In J. R. Cautela & A. J. Kearney (Eds.), *Covert conditioning casebook* (pp. 172–184). Pacific Grove, CA: Brooks/Cole.

KABAT-ZINN, J. (1990). *Full catastrophe living: The program of the stress reduction clinic at the University of Massachusetts Medical Center.* New York: Delta.

KABAT-ZINN, J. (2003). Mindfulness-based interventions in context: Past, present, and future. *Clinical Psychology: Science and Practice, 10,* 144–156.

KAESTLE, C. F. (Ed.). (1973). *Joseph Lancaster and the monitorial school movement: A documentary history.* New York: Teachers College Press.

KAHLE, A. L., & KELLEY, M. L. (1994). Children's homework problems: A comparison of goal setting and parent training. *Behavior Therapy, 25,* 275–290.

KAHN, J. S., KEHLE, T. J., JENSON, W. R., & CLARK, E. (1990). Comparison of cognitive-behavioral, relaxation, and self-modeling interventions for depression among middle-school students. *School Psychology Review, 19,* 196–211.

KAHNG, S. W., HENDRICKSON, D. J., & VU, C. P. (2000). Comparison of single and multiple functional communication training responses for the treatment of problem behavior. *Journal of Applied Behavior Analysis, 33,* 321–324.

KALAWSKY, R. S. (1993). *The science of virtual reality and virtual environments.* Reading, MA: Addison-Wesley.

KALICHMAN, S. C., CAREY, M. P., & JOHNSON, B. T. (1996). Prevention of sexually transmitted HIV infection: A meta-analytic review of the behavioral outcome literature. *Annals of Behavioral Medicine, 18,* 6–15.

KALICHMAN, S. C., CHERRY, C., & BROWNE-SPERLING, F. (1999). Effectiveness of a video-based motivational skills-building HIV-reduction intervention for inner-city African American men. *Journal of Consulting and Clinical Psychology, 67,* 959–966.

KALICHMAN, S. C., SIKKEMA, K., KELLY, J. A., & BULTO, M. (1995). Use of a brief behavioral skills intervention to prevent HIV infection among chronic mentally ill adults. *Psychiatric Services, 46,* 275–280.

KALLMAN, W. M., HERSEN, M., & O'TOOLE, D. H. (1975). The use of social reinforcement in a case of conversion reaction. *Behavior Therapy, 6,* 411–413.

KALMUSS, D. (1984). The intergenerational transmission of marital aggression. *Journal of Marriage and the Family, 46,* 11–19.

KAMINER, Y., & SHAHAR, A. (1987). The stress inoculation training management of self-mutilating behavior: A case study. *Journal of Behavior Therapy and Experimental Psychiatry, 18,* 289–292.

KAPLAN, D. A. (1982). Behavioral, cognitive, and behavioral-cognitive approaches to group assertion training therapy. *Cognitive Therapy and Research, 6,* 301–314.

KAPLAN, H. S. (1974). *The new sex therapy: Active treatment of sexual dysfunctions.* New York: Brunner/Mazel.

KAPLAN, H. S. (1975). *The illustrated manual of sex therapy.* New York: Quadrangle.

KAPLAN, R. M. (1990). Behavior as the central outcome in health care. *American Psychologist, 45,* 1211–1220.

KAREKLA, M., FORSYTH, J. P., & KELLY, M. M. (2004). Emotional avoidance and panicogenic responding to a biological challenge procedure. *Behavior Therapy, 35,* 725–746.

KASHDAN, T. B., BARRIOS, V., FORSYTH, J. P., & STEGER, M. F. (2006). Experiential avoidance as a generalized psychological vulnerability: Comparisons with coping and emotion regulation strategies. *Behaviour Research and Therapy, 9,* 1301–1320.

KASHDAN, T. B., MORINA, N., & PRIEBE, S. (in press). Post-traumatic stress disorder, social anxiety disorder, and depression in survivors of the Kosovo War: Experiential avoidance as a contributor to distress and quality of life. *Journal of Anxiety Disorders.*

KASL, S. V. (1975). Issues in patient adherence to health care regimens. *Journal of Human Stress, 1,* 5–17.

KATON, W. J., & WALKER, E. A. (1998). Medically unexplained symptoms in primary care. *Journal of Clinical Psychiatry, 59,* 15–21.

KAYSEN, D., LOSTUTTER, T. W., & GOINES, M. A. (2005). Cognitive processing therapy for acute stress disorder resulting from an anti-gay assault. *Cognitive and Behavioral Practice, 12,* 278–289.

KAZANTIS, N., DEANE, F. P., RONAN, K. R., & L'ABATE, L. (Eds.). (2005). *Using homework assignments in cognitive behavior therapy.* New York: Routledge Press.

KAZDIN, A. E. (1972). Response cost: The removal of conditioned reinforcers for therapeutic change. *Behavior Therapy, 3,* 533–546.

KAZDIN, A. E. (1974a). Comparative effects of some variations of covert modeling. *Journal of Behavior Therapy and Experimental Psychiatry, 5,* 225–231.

KAZDIN, A. E. (1974b). Covert modeling, model similarity, and reduction of avoidance behavior. *Behavior Therapy, 5,* 325–340.

KAZDIN, A. E. (1974c). The effect of model identity and fear-relevant similarity on covert modeling. *Behavior Therapy, 5,* 624–635.

KAZDIN, A. E. (1974d). Effects of covert modeling and model reinforcement on assertive behavior. *Journal of Abnormal Psychology, 83,* 240–252.

KAZDIN, A. E. (1974e). Reactive self-monitoring: The effects of response desirability, goal setting, and feedback. *Journal of Counsulting and Clinical Psychology, 5,* 704–716.

KAZDIN, A. E. (1976). Effects of covert modeling, multiple models, and model reinforcement on assertive behavior. *Behavior Therapy, 7,* 211–222.

KAZDIN, A. E. (1977a). Assessing the clinical or applied importance of behavior change through social validation. *Behavior Modification, 1,* 427–452.

KAZDIN, A. E. (1977b). Extensions of reinforcement techniques to socially and environmentally relevant behaviors. In M. Hersen, R. M. Eisler, & P. M. Miller (Eds.), *Progress in behavior modification* (Vol. 4, pp. 39–67). New York: Academic Press.

KAZDIN, A. E. (1977c). *The token economy: A review and evaluation.* New York: Plenum.

KAZDIN, A. E. (1978). *History of behavior modification: Experimental foundations of contemporary research.* Baltimore: University Park Press.

KAZDIN, A. E. (1979). Vicarious reinforcement and punishment in operant programs for children. *Child Behavior Therapy, 1,* 13–36.

KAZDIN, A. E. (1980). Acceptability of alternative treatments for deviant child behavior. *Journal of Applied Behavior Analysis, 13,* 259–273.

KAZDIN, A. E. (1987). *Conduct disorders in childhood and adolescence.* Newbury Park, CA: Sage.

KAZDIN, A. E. (1989). *Behavior modification in applied settings* (4th ed.). Pacific Grove, CA: Brooks/Cole.

KAZDIN, A. E. (1992). *Research design in clinical psychology* (2nd ed.). Boston: Allyn & Bacon.

KAZDIN, A. E. (1994). *Behavior modification in applied settings* (5th ed.). Pacific Grove, CA: Brooks/Cole.

KAZDIN, A. E. (2003). Problem-solving skills training and parent management training for conduct disorders. In A. E. Kazdin & J. R. Weisz (Eds.), *Evidence-based psychotherapies for children and adolescents* (pp. 241–262). New York: Guilford.

KAZDIN, A. E. (2005). *Parent management training: Treatment for oppositional, aggressive, and antisocial behavior in children and adolescents.* New York: Oxford University Press.

KAZDIN, A. E. (2008). Evidence-based treatment and practice: New opportunities to bridge clinical research and practice, enhance the knowledge base, and improve patient care. *American Psychologist, 63,* 146–159.

KAZDIN, A. E. (in press). Psychosocial treatments for conduct disorders in children and adolescents. In A. E. Kazdin & J. M. Gorman (Eds.), *A guide to treatments that work* (3rd ed.). New York: Oxford University Press.

KAZDIN, A. E., ESVELDT-DAWSON, K., FRENCH, N. H., & UNIS, A. S. (1987). Problem-solving skills training and relationship therapy in the treatment of antisocial child behavior. *Journal of Consulting and Clinical Psychology, 55,* 76–85.

KAZDIN, A. E., & GEESEY, S. (1977). Simultaneous-treatment design comparisons of the effects of reinforcers for one's peers versus for oneself. *Behavior Therapy, 8,* 682–693.

KAZDIN, A. E., & MASCITELLI, S. (1982). Behavioral rehearsal, self-instructions, and homework practice in developing assertiveness. *Behavior Therapy, 13,* 346–360.

KAZDIN, A. E., & WILCOXON, L. A. (1976). Systematic desensitization and nonspecific treatment effects: A methodological evaluation. *Psychological Bulletin, 83,* 729–758.

KAZDIN, A. E., & WILSON, G. T. (1978). *Evaluation of behavior therapy: Issues, evidence, and research strategies.* Cambridge, MA: Ballinger.

KEANE, T. M., FAIRBANK, J. A., CADDELL, J. M., & ZIMERING, R. T. (1989). Implosive (flooding) therapy reduces symptoms of PTSD in Vietnam combat veterans. *Behavior Therapy, 20,* 245–260.

KEARNEY, A. B. (1993). The use of covert conditioning in the treatment of obsessive compulsive disorder. In J. R. Cautela & A. J. Kearney (Eds.), *Covert conditioning casebook* (pp. 22–37). Pacific Grove, CA: Brooks/Cole.

KEARNEY, A. J. (1993). The use of covert conditioning in a hypnotic context to treat anticipatory anxiety and postoperative pain. In J. R. Cautela & A. J. Kearney (Eds.), *Covert conditioning casebook* (pp. 99–107). Pacific Grove, CA: Brooks/Cole.

KEARNS, H., FORBES, A., & GARDINER, M. (2007). A cognitive behavioural coaching intervention for the treatment of perfectionism and self-handicapping in a nonclinical population. *Behaviour Change, 24,* 157–172.

KEENEY, K. M., FISHER, W. W., ADELINIS, J. D., & WILDER, D. A. (2000). The effects of response cost in the treatment of aberrant behavior maintained by negative reinforcement. *Journal of Applied Behavior Analysis, 33,* 225–258.

KEHLE, T. J., CLARK, E., JENSON, W. R., & WAMPOLD, B. E. (1986). Effectiveness of self-observation with behavior disordered elementary school children. *School Psychology Review, 15,* 289–295.

KEHLE, T. J., MADAUS, R., BARATTA, V. S., & BRAY, M. A. (1998). Augmented self-modeling as a treatment for children with selective mutism. *Journal of School Psychology, 36,* 247–260.

KEHLE, T. J., OWEN, S. V., & CRESSY, E. T. (1990). The use of self-modeling as an intervention in school psychology: A case study of an elective mute. *School Psychology Review, 19,* 115–121.

KEIJSERS, G. P. J., SCHAAP, C. P. D. R., & HOOGDUIN, C. A. L. (2000). The impact of interpersonal patient and therapist behavior on outcome in cognitive-behavior therapy. *Behavior Modification, 24,* 264–297.

KELLER, F. S. (1968). "Good-bye, teacher..." *Journal of Applied Behavior Analysis, 1,* 79–89.

KELLER, M. B., HERZOG, D. B., LAVORI, P. W., BRADBURN, I. S., & MAHONEY, E. M. (1992). The naturalistic history of bulimia nervosa: Extraordinary high rates of chronicity, relapse, recurrence, and psychosocial morbidity. *International Journal of Eating Disorders, 12,* 1–9.

KELLEY, M. L. (1990). *School-home notes: Promoting children's classroom success.* New York: Guilford.

KELLY, G. A. (1955). *The psychology of personal constructs.* New York: Norton.

KELLY, J. A., MURPHY, D. [A.], WASHINGTON, C., WILSON, T., KOOB, J., DAVIS, D., et al. (1994). Effects of HIV/AIDS prevention groups for high-risk women in urban primary health care clinics. *American Journal of Public Health, 84,* 1918–1922.

KELLY, J. A., & ST. LAWRENCE, J. [S.] (1987). The prevention of AIDS:

Roles for behavioral intervention. *Scandinavian Journal of Behaviour Therapy, 16,* 5–19.

KELLY, J. A., & ST. LAWRENCE, J. S. (1988a). *The AIDS health crisis: Psychological and social intervention.* New York: Plenum.

KELLY, J. A., & ST. LAWRENCE, J. S. (1988b). AIDS prevention and treatment: Psychology's role in the health crisis. *Clinical Psychology Review, 8,* 255–284.

KELLY, J. A., ST. LAWRENCE, J. S., HOOD, H. V., & BRASFIELD, T. L. (1989). Behavioral intervention to reduce AIDS risk activities. *Journal of Consulting and Clinical Psychology, 57,* 60–67.

KENDALL, P. C. (1987). Cognitive processes and procedures in behavior therapy. In G. T. Wilson, C. M. Franks, P. C. Kendall, & J. P. Foreyt (Eds.), *Review of behavior therapy: Theory and practice* (Vol. 11, pp. 114–153). New York: Guilford.

KENDALL, P. C. (1989). The generalization and maintenance of behavior change: Comments, considerations, and the "no-cure" criticism. *Behavior Therapy, 20,* 357–364.

KENDALL, P. C. (1993). Cognitive-behavioral therapies with youth: Guiding theory, current status, and emerging developments. *Journal of Consulting and Clinical Psychology, 61,* 235–247.

KENDALL, P. C. (1994). Treating anxiety disorders in children: Results of a randomized clinical trial. *Journal of Consulting and Clinical Psychology, 62,* 100–110.

KENDALL, P. C. (1998). Empirically supported psychological therapies. *Journal of Consulting and Clinical Psychology, 66,* 3–6.

KENDALL, P. C. (1999). Clinical significance. *Journal of Consulting and Clinical Psychology, 67,* 283–284.

KENDALL, P. C. (2000). *Child & adolescent therapy: Cognitive-behavioral procedures* (2nd ed.). New York: Guilford.

KENDALL, P. C., & BEIDAS, R. S. (2007). Smoothing the trail for dissemination of evidence-based practices for youth: Flexibility within fidelity. *Professional Psychology: Research and Practice, 38,* 13–20.

KENDALL, P. C., & BRASWELL, L. (1985). *Cognitive-behavioral therapy for impulsive children.* New York: Guilford.

KENDALL, P. C., & CHAMBLESS, D. L. (Eds.). (1998). Empirically

supported psychological therapies. (Special Section). *Journal of Consulting and Clinical Psychology, 66,* 3–161.

KENDALL, P. C., CHU, B., PIMENTEL, S., & CHOUDHURY, M. (2000). Treating anxiety disorders in youth. In P. C. Kendall (Ed.), *Child and adolescent therapy: Cognitive-behavioral procedures* (2nd ed., pp. 235–287). New York: Guilford.

KENDALL, P. C., & FINCH, A. J. (1978). A cognitive-behavioral treatment for impulsivity: A group comparison study. *Journal of Consulting and Clinical Psychology, 46,* 110–118.

KENDALL, P. C., & GEROW, M. A. (1995). *Long-term follow-up of a cognitive-behavioral therapy for anxiety-disordered youth.* Unpublished manuscript.

KENDALL, P. C., HAAGA, D. A. F., ELLIS, A., BERNARD, M., DIGIUSEPPE, R. [A.], & KASSINOVE, H. (1995). Rational-emotive therapy in the 1990s and beyond: Current status, recent revisions, and research questions. *Clinical Psychology Review, 15,* 169–185.

KENDALL, P. C., HOLMBECK, G., & VERDUIN, T. (2004). Methodology, design, and evaluation in psychotherapy research. In M. Lambert (Ed.), *Bergin and Garfield's Handbook of psychotherapy and behavior change* (5th ed., pp. 16–43). New York: Wiley.

KENDALL, P. C., NAY, W. R., & JEFFERS, J. (1975). Timeout duration and contrast effects: A systematic evaluation of a successive treatments design. *Behavior Therapy, 6,* 609–615.

KENDALL, P. C., & SHELDRICK, R. C. (2000). Normative data for normative comparisons. *Journal of Consulting and Clinical Psychology, 68,* 767–773.

KENDALL, P. C., & WILCOX, L. E. (1980). Cognitive-behavioral treatment for impulsivity: Concrete versus conceptual training in non-self-controlled problem children. *Journal of Consulting and Clinical Psychology, 48,* 80–91.

KENNEDY, S. H., KATZ, R., NEITZERT, C. S., RALEVSKI, E., & MENDLOWITZ, S. (1995). Exposure with response prevention treatment of anorexia nervosa-bulimic subtype and bulimia nervosa. *Behaviour Research and Therapy, 33,* 685–689.

KENNY, F. T., MOWBRAY, R. M., & LALANI, S. (1978). Faradic disruption of obsessive ideation in the treatment of obsessive neurosis. *Behavior Therapy, 9,* 209–221.

KENNY, M., & WILLIAMS, J. M. G. (2007). Treatment-resistant depressed patients show a good response to mindfulness-based cognitive therapy. *Behaviour Research and Therapy, 45,* 617–625.

KENT, R. N., & FOSTER, S. (1977). Direct observational procedures: Methodological issues in naturalistic settings. In A. R. Ciminero, K. S. Calhoun, & H. E. Adams (Eds.), *Handbook of behavioral assessment* (pp. 279–328). New York: Wiley.

KEOGH, D. A., FAW, G. D., WHITMAN, T. L., & REID, D. H. (1984). Enhancing leisure skills in severely retarded adolescents through a self-instructional treatment package. *Analysis and Intervention in Developmental Disabilities, 4,* 333–351.

KERN, J. M. (1982). Predicting the impact of assertive, empathic-assertive, and nonassertive behavior: The assertiveness of the assertee. *Behavior Therapy, 13,* 486–498.

KERN, J. M., CAVELL, T. A., & BECK, B. (1985). Predicting differential reactions to males' versus females' assertions, empathic-assertions, and nonassertions. *Behavior Therapy, 16,* 63–75.

KERN, L., & DUNLAP, G. (1998). Curricular modifications to promote desirable classroom behavior. In J. K. Luiselli & M. J. Cameron (Eds.), *Antecedent control* (pp. 289–307). Baltimore: Brookes.

KERNS, R. D., TURK, D. C., HOLZMAN, A. D., & RUDY, T. E. (1986). Comparison of cognitive-behavioral and behavioral approaches to outpatient treatment of chronic pain. *Clinical Journal of Pain, 1,* 195–203.

KETTLEWELL, P. W., MIZES, J. S., & WASYLYSHYN, N. A. (1992). A cognitive-behavioral group treatment of bulimia. *Behavior Therapy, 23,* 657–670.

KHANNA, M. S., & KENDALL, P. C. (2008). Computer-assisted CBT for child anxiety: The coping can CD-ROM. *Cognitive and Behavioral Practice, 15,* 159–165.

KIDD, A. H., & EUPHRAT, J. L. (1971). Why prospective outpatients fail to make or keep appointments. *Journal of Clinical Psychology, 27,* 94–95.

KILPATRICK, D. G., & BEST, C. L. (1984). Some cautionary remarks on treating sexual assault victims with implosion. *Behavior Therapy, 15,* 421–423.

KIMMEL, H. D., & KIMMEL, E. (1970). An instrumental conditioning method for treatment of enuresis. *Journal of Behavior Therapy and Experimental Psychiatry, 1,* 121–124.

KING, N. J., DUDLEY, A., MELVIN, G., PALLANT, J., & MORAWETZ, D. (2001). Empirically supported treatments for insomnia. (Special Issue). *Scandinavian Journal of Behaviour Therapy, 30,* 23–32.

KING, N. J., MURIS, P., & OLLENDICK, T. H. (2005). Childhood fears and phobias: Assessment and treatment. *Child and Adolescent Mental Health, 10,* 50–56.

KING, N. J., OLLENDICK, T. H., MURPHY, G. C., & TIBGE, B. (1997). Behavioural assessment of childhood phobias: A multi-method approach. *Scandinavian Journal of Behaviour Therapy, 26,* 3–10.

KING, N. J., TONGE, B. J., HEYNE, D., PRITCHARD, M., ROLLINGS, S., YOUNG, D., et al. (1998). Cognitive-behavioral treatment of school-refusing children: A controlled evaluation. *Journal of the Academy of Child and Adolescent Psychiatry, 37,* 395–403.

KINGDON, D. [G.], RATHOD, S., HANSEN, L., NAEEM, F., & WRIGHT, J. H. (2007). Combining cognitive therapy and pharmacotherapy for schizophrenia. *Journal of Cognitive Psychotherapy, 21,* 28–36.

KINGDON, D. G., & TURKINGTON, D. (2005). *Cognitive therapy of schizophrenia.* New York: Guilford.

KINGSTON, T., DOOLEY, B., BATES, A., LAWLOR, E., & MALONE, K. (2007). Mindfulness-based cognitive therapy for residual depressive symptoms. *Psychology & Psychotherapy, 80,* 193–203.

KIRBY, K. C., FOWLER, S. A., & BEAR, D. M. (1991). Reactivity in self-recording: Obtrusiveness of recording procedure and peer comments. *Journal of Applied Behavior Analysis, 24,* 487–498.

KIRBY, K. C., MARLOWE, D. B., CARRIGAN, D. R., & PLATT, J. J. (1998). Counselor prompts to increase condom taking during treatment for cocaine dependence. *Behavior Modification, 22,* 29–44.

KIRIGIN, K. A., BRAUKMANN, C. J., ATWATER, J., & WOLF, M. M. (1982). An evaluation of Achievement Place (Teaching-Family) group homes for juvenile offenders. *Journal of Applied Behavior Analysis, 15,* 1–16.

KIRKLEY, B. G., SCHNEIDER, J. A., AGRAS, W. S., & BACHMAN, J. A. (1985). Comparison of two group treatments for bulimia. *Journal of Consulting and Clinical Psychology, 53,* 43–48.

KITFIELD, E. B., & MASALSKY, C. J. (2000). Negative reinforcement-based treatment to increase food intake. *Behavior Modification, 24,* 600–608.

KLEIN, B., RICHARDS, J. C., & AUSTIN, D. W. (2006). Efficacy of internet therapy for panic disorder. *Journal of Behavior Therapy and Experimental Psychiatry, 37,* 213–238.

KLEINER, L., MARSHALL, W. L., & SPEVACK, M. (1987). Training in problem solving and exposure treatment for agoraphobic with panic attacks. *Journal of Anxiety Disorders, 1,* 219–238.

KLEINKNECHT, R. A. (1993). Rapid treatment of blood and injection phobias with eye movement desensitization. *Journal of Behavior Therapy and Experimental Psychiatry, 24,* 211–217.

KLEINKNECHT, R. A., & BERNSTEIN, D. A. (1979). Short term treatment of dental avoidance. *Journal of Behavior Therapy and Experimental Psychiatry, 10,* 311–315.

KLESGES, R. C., MALOTT, J. M., & UGLAND, M. (1984). The effects of graded exposure and parental modeling on the dental phobias of a four-year-old girl and her mother. *Journal of Behavior Therapy and Experimental Psychiatry, 15,* 161–164.

KLINGMAN, A., MELAMED, B. G., CUTHBERT, M. I., & HERMECZ, D. A. (1984). Effects of participant modeling on information acquisition and skill utilization. *Journal of Consulting and Clinical Psychology, 52,* 414–422.

KLORMAN, R., HILPERT, P. L., MICHAEL, R., LAGANA, C., & SVEEN, O. B. (1980). Effects of coping and mastery modeling on experienced and inexperienced pedodontic patients' disruptiveness. *Behavior Therapy, 11,* 156–168.

KNAUS, W. J. (1985). Student burnout: A rational-emotive education treatment approach. In A. Ellis & M. Bernard (Eds.), *Clinical applications of rational-emotive therapy* (pp. 257–276). New York: Plenum.

KNAUS, W. J., & HABERSTROH, N. (1993). A rational-emotive education program to help disruptive mentally retarded clients develop self-control. In W. Dryden & L. K. Hill (Eds.),

Innovations in rational-emotive therapy (pp. 201–217). Newbury Park, CA: Sage.

KNEEBONE, I. I., & AL-DAFTARY, S. (2006). Flooding treatment of phobia to having her feet touched by physiotherapists, in a young woman with Down's syndrome and a traumatic brain injury. *Neuropsychological Rehabilitation, 16,* 230–236.

KNIGHT, M. F., & MCKENZIE, H. S. (1974). Elimination of bedtime thumbsucking in home settings through contingent reading. *Journal of Applied Behavior Analysis, 7,* 33–38.

KOEGEL, L. K., STIEBEL, D., & KOEGEL, R. L. (1998). Reducing aggression in children with autism toward infant or toddler siblings. *Journal of the Association for Persons with Severe Handicaps, 23,* 111–118.

KOERNER, K., & DIMEFF, L. A. (2007). Overview of dialectical behavior therapy. In L. A. Dimeff & K. Koerner, K. (Eds.), *Dialectical behavior therapy in clinical practice: Applications across disorders and settings* (pp. 1–18). New York: Guilford.

KOHLENBERG, R. J., KANTER, J. W., BOLLING, M., WEXNER, R., PARKER, C., & TSAI, M. (2004). Functional analytic psychotherapy, cognitive therapy, and acceptance. In S. C. Hayes, V. M. Follette, & M. Linehan (Eds.), *Mindfulness and acceptance: Expanding the cognitive-behavioral tradition* (pp. 96–119). New York: Guilford.

KOHLENBERG, R. J., & TSAI, M. (1991). *Functional Analytic Psychotherapy (FAP): Creating intense and curative therapeutic relationships.* New York: Plenum.

KOHLENBERG, R. J., & TSAI, M. (1995). Functional analytic psychotherapy: A behavioral approach to intensive treatment. In W. T. O'Donohue & L. Krasner (Eds.), *Theories of behavior therapy: Exploring behavior change* (pp. 637–658). Washington, DC: American Psychological Association.

KOKOSZKA, A., POPIEL, A., & SITARZ, M. (2000). Cognitive-behavioral therapy in Poland. *the Behavior Therapist, 23,* 209–216.

KOLE-SNIJDERES, A. M. K., VLAEYEN, J. W. S., RUTTEN-VAN MOLKEN, M. P. M. H.,HEUTS, P. H. T. G., VAN EEK, H., & VAN BREUKELEN, G. (1999). Chronic low-back pain: What does cognitive coping skills training add to operant behavioral treatment? Results of a randomized clinical trial. *Journal of Consulting and Clinical Psychology, 67,* 931–944.

KONSTANTOPOULOS, S., & HEDGES, L. V. (2006). Meta-analysis. In D. Kaplan (Ed.), *The Sage Handbook of quantitative methodology for the social sciences* (pp. 281–283). Thousand Oaks, CA: Sage Publications.

KOPEC, A. M., BEAL, D., & DIGIUSEPPE, R. [A.] (1994). Training in RET: Disputational strategies. *Journal of Rational-Emotive & Cognitive-Behavior Therapy, 12,* 47–60.

KORNFELD, A. D. (1989). Mary Cover Jones and the Peter case: Social learning versus conditioning. *Journal of Anxiety Disorders, 3,* 187–195.

KORNHABER, R. C., & SCHROEDER, H. E. (1975). Importance of model similarity on extinction of avoidance behavior in children. *Journal of Consulting and Clinical Psychology, 43,* 601–607.

KOVACS, M. B., & BECK, A. T. (1978). Maladaptive cognitive structures in depression. *American Journal of Psychiatry, 135,* 525–533.

KOZAK, M. J., FOA, E. B., & STEKETEE, G. (1988). Process and outcome of exposure treatment with obsessive-compulsives: Psychophysiological indicators of emotional processing. *Behavior Therapy, 19,* 157–169.

KRAKAUER, J. (1995, October). Loving them to death. *Outside, 20,* pp. 72–80, 82, 142–143.

KRAMER, F. M., & STALKER, L. A. (1989). Treatment of obesity. In A. Freeman, K. M. Simon, L. E. Beutler, & H. Arkowitz (Eds.), *Comprehensive handbook of cognitive therapy* (pp. 385–401). New York: Plenum.

KRAPFL, J. E. (1967). *Differential ordering of stimulus presentation and semi-automated versus live treatment in the systematic desensitization of snake phobia.* Unpublished doctoral dissertation, University of Missouri.

KROENKE, K. (2007). Efficacy of treatment for somatoform disorders: A review of randomized controlled trials. *Psychosomatic Medicine, 69,* 881–888.

KROENKE, K., & MANGELSDORF, A. D. (1989). Common symptoms in ambulatory care: Incidence, evaluation, therapy, and outcome. *American Journal of Medicine, 86,* 262–266.

KROP, H., & BURGESS, D. (1993a). Use of covert conditioning to treat excessive masturbation. In J. R. Cautela & A. J. Kearney (Eds.), *Covert conditioning casebook* (pp. 208–216). Pacific Grove, CA: Brooks/Cole.

KROP, H., & BURGESS, D. (1993b). The use of covert modeling in the treatment of a sexual abuse victim. In J. R. Cautela & A. J. Kearney (Eds.), *Covert conditioning casebook* (pp. 153–158). Pacific Grove, CA: Brooks/Cole.

KUEHLWEIN, K. T. (1992). Working with gay men. In A. Freeman & F. M. Dattilio (Eds.), *Comprehensive casebook of cognitive therapy* (pp. 249–255). New York: Plenum.

KURTZ, P. F., CHIN, M. D., HUETE, J. M., TARBOX, R. S. F., O'CONNOR, J. T., PACLAWSKYJ, T. R., et al. (2003). Functional analysis and treatment of self-injurious behavior in young children: A summary of 30 cases. *Journal of Applied Behavior Analysis, 36,* 205–219.

KUTCHINS, H., & KIRK, S. A. (1995). Should DSM be the basis for teaching social work practice in mental health? No! *Journal of Social Work Education, 31,* 159–168.

LABERGE, B., GAUTHIER, J. G., COTE, G., PLAMONDON, J., & CORMIER, H. J. (1993). Cognitive-behavioral therapy of panic disorder with secondary major depression: A preliminary investigation. *Journal of Consulting and Clinical Psychology, 61,* 1028–1037.

LABOUVIE-VIEF, G., & GONDA, J. (1976). Cognitive strategy training and intellectual performance in the elderly. *Journal of Gerontology, 31,* 327–332.

LACKS, P., BERTELSON, A. D., GANS, L., & KUNKEL, J. (1983). The effectiveness of three behavioral treatments for different degrees of sleep-onset insomnia. *Behavior Therapy, 14,* 593–605.

LACKS, P., & MORIN, C. M. (1992). Recent advances in the assessment and treatment of insomnia. *Journal of Consulting and Clinical Psychology, 60,* 586–594.

LAGGES, A. M., & GORDON, D. A. (1999). Use of an interactive laser-disc parent training program with teenage parents. *Child & Family Behavior Therapy, 21,* 19–35.

LA GRECA, A. M. (1988). Adherence to prescribed medical regimens. In D. K. Routh (Ed.), *Handbook of pediatric psychology* (pp. 299–320). New York: Guilford.

La Greca, A. M., & Ottinger, D. R. (1979). Self-monitoring and relaxation training in the treatment of medically ordered exercise in a 12-year-old female. *Journal of Pediatric Psychology, 4,* 49–54.

Lahey, B. B., McNees, M. P., & McNees, M. C. (1973). Control of an obscene "verbal tic" through time out in an elementary classroom. *Journal of Applied Behavior Analysis, 6,* 101–104.

Lake, A. E., & Pingel, J. D. (1988). Brief versus extended relaxation: Relationship to improvement at follow-up in mixed headache patients. *Medical Psychotherapy, 1,* 119–129.

Lam, D. H., Bright, J., Jones, S., Hayward, P., Schuck, N., Chisholm, D., et al. (2000). Cognitive therapy for bipolar illness—A pilot study of relapse prevention. *Cognitive Therapy and Research, 24,* 503–520.

Lamaze, F. (1970). *Painless childbirth.* Chicago: Henry Regery.

Lamb, R. J., Morral, A. R., Kirby, K. C., Javors, M. A., Galbicka, G., & Iguchi, M. (2007). Contingencies for change in complacent smokers. *Experimental and Clinical Psychopharmacology, 15,* 245–255.

Lamontagne, Y., & Marks, I. M. (1973). Psychogenic urinary retention: Treatment of prolonged exposure. *Behavior Therapy, 4,* 581–585.

Lancaster, J. (1805). *Improvements in education, as it respects the industrious classes of the community* (3rd ed.). London: Darton and Harvey.

Lando, H. A. (1975). A comparison of excessive and rapid smoking in the modification of chronic smoking behavior. *Journal of Consulting and Clinical Psychology, 43,* 350–355.

Landrine, H., & Klonoff, E. (1995). Cultural diversity and the silence of behavior therapy. *the Behavior Therapist, 18,* 187–189.

Lang, P. J. (1969). The mechanics of desensitization and the laboratory study of fear. In C. M. Franks (Ed.), *Behavior therapy: Appraisal and status* (pp. 160–191). New York: McGraw-Hill.

Lang, P. J., Melamed, B. G., & Hart, J. A. (1970). A psychophysiological analysis of fear modification using an automated desensitization procedure. *Journal of Abnormal Psychology, 76,* 220–234.

Larson, K., & Ayllon, T. (1990). The effects of contingent music and differential reinforcement on infantile colic. *Behaviour Research and Therapy, 28,* 119–125.

Larsson, B., & Andrasik, F. (2002). Relaxation treatment of recurrent headaches in children and adolescents. In V. Guidetti, G. Russell, M. Sillanpaa, & P. Winner (Eds.), *Headache and migraine in childhood and adolescence* (pp. 307–316). London: Martin Dunitz.

Lascelles, M., Cunningham, S., McGrath, P., & Sullivan, M. (1989). Teaching coping skills to adolescents with migraine. *Journal of Pain and Symptom Management, 4,* 135–145.

Latner, J. D., & Wilson, G. T. (2000). Cognitive-behavioral therapy and nutritional counseling in the treatment of bulimia nervosa and binge eating. *Eating Behaviors, 1,* 3–21.

Lauterbach, W. (1999). Cognitive behavior therapy in the Russian society. *the Behavior Therapist, 22,* 16.

Lavigna, G. W., & Donnellan, A. M. (1986). *Alternatives to punishment: Solving behavior problems with nonaversive strategies.* New York: Irvington.

Lavin, N. I., Thorpe, J. G., Barker, J. C., Blakemore, C. B., & Conway, C. G. (1961). Behaviour therapy in a case of transvestism. *Journal of Nervous and Mental Disease, 133,* 346–353.

Lawson, D. M., & May, R. B. (1970). Three procedures for the extinction of smoking behavior. *Psychological Record, 20,* 151–157.

Lawton, C., France, K. G., & Blampied, N. M. (1991). Treatment of infant sleep disturbance by graduated extinction. *Child & Family Behavior Therapy, 13,* 39–56.

Lazarus, A. A. (1959). The elimination of children's phobias by deconditioning. *Medical Proceedings, 5,* 261–265.

Lazarus, A. A. (1961). Group therapy of phobic disorders by systematic desensitization. *Journal of Abnormal and Social Psychology, 63,* 505–510.

Lazarus, A. A. (1966). Broad-spectrum behaviour therapy and the treatment of agoraphobia. *Behaviour Research and Therapy, 4,* 95–97.

Lazarus, A. A. (1967). In support of technical eclecticism. *Psychological Reports, 21,* 415–416.

Lazarus, A. A. (1971). *Behavior therapy and beyond.* New York: McGraw-Hill.

Lazarus, A. A. (1973). On assertive behavior: A brief note. *Behavior Therapy, 4,* 697–699.

Lazarus, A. A. (1976). *Multimodal behavior therapy.* New York: Springer.

Lazarus, A. A. (1989a). *The practice of multimodal therapy.* Baltimore: Johns Hopkins University Press.

Lazarus, A. A. (1989b). The practice of rational-emotive therapy. In M. E. Bernard & R. [A.] DiGiuseppe (Eds.), *Inside rational-emotive therapy: A critical appraisal of the theory and therapy of Albert Ellis* (pp. 95–112). San Diego: Academic Press.

Lazarus, A. A., & Abramovitz, A. (1962). The use of "emotive imagery" in the treatment of children's phobias. *Journal of Mental Science, 108,* 191–195.

Lazarus, A. A., Davison, G. C., & Polefka, D. A. (1965). Classical and operant factors in the treatment of a school phobia. *Journal of Abnormal Psychology, 70,* 225–229.

Lazarus, R. S., & Folkman, S. (1984). *Stress, appraisal, and coping.* New York: Springer.

Leahy, R. L. (2007). Emotional schemas and resistance to change in anxiety disorders. *Cognitive and Behavioral Practice, 14,* 36–45.

Leahy, R. L. (2008). A closer look at ACT. *the Behavior Therapist, 31,* 148–150.

Leahy, R. L., Beck, A. T., & Beck, J. S. (2005). Cognitive therapy of personality disorders. In S. Strack (Ed.), *Personology: Essays in honor of Theodore Millon.* New York: Wiley.

Ledwidge, B. (1978). Cognitive behavior modification: A step in the wrong direction? *Psychological Bulletin, 85,* 353–375.

Ledwidge, B. (1979). Cognitive behavior modification: A rejoinder. *Cognitive Therapy and Research, 3,* 133–140.

Lee, C., Gavriel, H., Drummond, P., Richards, J., & Greenwald, R. (2002). Treatment of posttraumatic stress disorder: A comparison of stress inoculation training with prolonged exposure and eye movement desensitization and reprocessing. *Journal of Clinical Psychology, 58,* 1071–1089.

Lee, E. S. (1951). Negro intelligence and selective migration: A Philadelphia test of the Klineberg hypothesis. *American Review, 16,* 227–232.

Lee, J. H., Ku, J., Kim, K., Kim, B., Kim, I. Y., Yang, B.-H., et al. (2003). Experimental application of virtual reality for nicotine craving through cue exposure. *CyberPsychology & Behavior, 6,* 275–280.

Lee, J.-H., Kwon, H., Choi, J., & Yang, B.-H. (2007). Cue-exposure therapy to decrease alcohol craving in virtual environment. *CyberPsychology & Behavior, 10,* 617–623.

Lee, N. K., & Oei, T. P. S. (1993). Exposure and response prevention in anxiety disorders: Implications for treatment and relapse prevention in problem drinkers. *Clinical Psychology Review, 13,* 619–632.

Leitenberg, H. (1976). Behavioral approaches to treatment of neuroses. In H. Leitenberg (Ed.), *Handbook of behavior modification and behavior therapy* (pp. 124–167). Englewood Cliffs, NJ: Prentice Hall.

Leitenberg, H. (1993). Treatment of bulimia nervosa. In T. R. Giles (Ed.), *Handbook of effective psychotherapy* (pp. 279–302). New York: Plenum.

Leitenberg, H., Burchard, D., Burchard, N., Fuller, E. J., & Lysaght, T. V. (1977). Using positive reinforcement to suppress behavior: Some experimental comparisons with sibling conflict. *Behavior Therapy, 8,* 168–182.

Leitenberg, H., Gross, J., Peterson, J., & Rosen, J. C. (1984). Analysis of an anxiety model in the process of change during exposure plus response prevention treatment of bulimia nervosa. *Behavior Therapy, 15,* 3–20.

Leitenberg, H., & Rosen, J. C. (1988). Cognitive-behavioral treatment of bulimia nervosa. In M. Hersen, R. M. Eisler, & P. M. Miller (Eds.), *Progress in behavior modification* (Vol. 23, pp. 11–32). Newbury Park, CA: Sage.

Leitenberg, H., Rosen, J. C., Wolf, J., Vara, L. S., Detzer, M. J., & Srebnik, D. (1994). Comparison of cognitive-behavior therapy and desipramine in the treatment of bulimia nervosa. *Behaviour Research and Therapy, 32,* 37–45.

Lejuez, C. W., Hopko, D. R., LePage, J., Hopko, S. D., & McNeil, D. W. (2001). A brief behavioral activation treatment for depression. *Cognitive and Behavioral Practice, 8,* 164–175.

Lemsky, C. M. (1996). Adapting behavioral interventions for brain injured older adults. *the Behavior Therapist, 19,* 9–12.

Lennox, D. B., Miltenberger, R. G., & Donnelly, D. R. (1987). Response interruption and DRL for the reduction of rapid eating. *Journal of Applied Behavior Analysis, 20,* 279–284.

Lerman, D. C., & Iwata, B. A. (1995). Prevalence of the extinction burst and its attenuation during treatment. *Journal of Applied Behavior Analysis, 28,* 93–94.

Lerman, D. C., & Iwata, B. A. (1996). Developing a technology for the use of operant extinction in clinical settings: An examination of basic and applied research. *Journal of Applied Behavior Analysis, 29,* 345–382.

Lerman, D. C., Iwata, B. A., & Wallace, M. D. (1999). Side effects of extinction: Prevalence of bursting and aggression during the treatment of self-injurious behavior. *Journal of Applied Behavior Analysis, 32,* 1–8.

Lerner, J., Franklin, M. E., Meadows, E. A., Hembree, E., & Foa, E. B. (1998). Effectiveness of a cognitive-behavioral treatment program for trichotillomania: An uncontrolled evaluation. *Behavior Therapy, 29,* 157–171.

Lester, D. (1987). Indirect evidence for effects of suggestion in suicide: A critical mass hypothesis. *Psychological Reports, 61,* 576.

Leung, N., Waller, G., & Thomas, G. (2000). Outcome of group cognitive-behavioral therapy for bulimia nervosa: The role of core beliefs. *Behaviour Research and Therapy, 38,* 145–156.

Levin, R. B., & Gross, A. M. (1984). Reactions to assertive versus nonassertive behavior. *Behavior Modification, 8,* 581–592.

Levine, A. J., Hinkin, C. H., Marion, S., Keuning, A., Castellon, S. A., Lam, M. N., et al. (2006). Adherence to antiretroviral medications in HIV: Differences in data collected via self-report and electronic monitoring. *Health Psychology, 25,* 329–335.

Levis, D. J. (1980). Implementing the technique of implosive therapy. In A. Goldstein & E. B. Foa (Eds.), *Handbook of behavioral interventions: A clinical guide* (pp. 92–151). New York: Wiley.

Levis, D. J. (1988). Observations and experience from clinical practice: A critical ingredient for advancing behavioral theory and therapy. *the Behavior Therapist, 11,* 95–99.

Levis, D. J. (1993). The power of extrapolating basic laboratory principles: The behavioural-cognitive approach of implosive therapy. *Behaviour Change, 10,* 154–161.

Levis, D. J., & Carrera, R. N. (1967). Effects of 10 hours of implosive therapy in the treatment of outpatients: A preliminary report. *Journal of Abnormal Psychology, 72,* 504–508.

Levis, D. J., & Malloy, P. F. (1982). Research in infrahuman and human conditioning. In G. T. Wilson & C. M. Franks (Eds.), *Contemporary behavior therapy: Conceptual and empirical foundations* (pp. 65–118). New York: Guilford.

Levitt, E. E. (1957). The results of psychotherapy with children: An evaluation. *Journal of Consulting Psychology, 21,* 189–196.

Levitt, E. E. (1963). Psychotherapy with children: A further evaluation. *Behaviour Research and Therapy, 1,* 45–51.

Levitt, J. T., Brown, T. A., Orsillo, S. M., & Barlow, D. H. (2004). The effects of acceptance versus suppression of emotion on subjective and psychophysiological response to carbon dioxide challenge in patients with panic disorder. *Behavior Therapy, 35,* 747–766.

Levitt, J. T., Malta, L. S., Martin, A., Davis, L., & Cloitre, M. (2007). The flexible application of a manualized treatment for PTSD symptoms and functional impairment related to the 9/11 World Trade Center attack. *Behaviour Research and Therapy, 45,* 1419–1433.

Lewinsohn, P. M. (1974). A behavioral approach to depression. In R. M. Friedman & M. M. Katz (Eds.), *The psychology of depression: Contemporary theory and research* (pp. 157–185). New York: Wiley.

Lewinsohn, P. M., Clarke, G. N., & Rohde, P. (1994). Psychological approaches to the treatment of depression in adolescents. In W. M. Reynolds & H. F. Johnston (Eds.), *Handbook of depression in children and adolescents* (pp. 309–344). New York: Plenum.

Lewinsohn, P. M., & Rohde, P. (1993). The cognitive-behavioral treatment of depression in adolescents: Research and suggestions. *The Clinical Psychologist, 46,* 177–183.

Lewis, D. (1875). *Chastity or our secret sins.* Philadelphia: Maclean.

Libb, J. W., & Clements, C. B. (1969). Token reinforcement in an exercise program for hospitalized geriatric patients. *Perceptual and Motor Skills, 28,* 957–958.

Liberman, R. P., Eckman, T. A., & Marder, S. R. (2001). Training in social problem solving among persons with schizophrenia. *Psychiatric Services, 52,* 31–33.

Liberman, R. P., Wallace, C. J., Blackwell, G. [A.], Eckman, T. A., Vaccaro, J. V., & Kuehnel, T. G. (1993). Innovations in skills training for the seriously mentally ill: The UCLA social and independent living skills modules. *Innovations and Research, 2,* 43–60.

Liberman, R. P., Vaccaro, J. V., & Corrigan, P. W. (1995). Psychiatric rehabilitation. In H. I. Kaplan & B. J. Sadock (Eds.), *Comprehensive textbook of psychiatry* (6th ed., pp. 2696–2717). Baltimore: Williams & Wilkins.

Liberman, R. P., Wallace, C. J., Blackwell, G. A., & Vaccaro, J. V. (1993, November). *Integrating skills training with assertive case management in the rehabilitation of persons with schizophrenia.* Paper presented at a meeting of Psychiatric Research in the Department of Veterans Affairs, Washington, DC.

Lichstein, K. L. (1988). *Clinical relaxation strategies.* New York: Wiley.

Lichstein, K. L., Peterson, B. A., Riedel, B. W., Means, M. K., Epperson, M. T., & Aguillard, R. N. (1999). Relaxation to assist sleep medication withdrawal. *Behavior Modification, 23,* 379–402.

Lichstein, K. L., & Riedel, B. W. (1994). Behavioral assessment and treatment of insomnia: A review with an emphasis on clinical application. *Behavior Therapy, 25,* 659–688.

Lichtenstein, E., & Glasgow, R. E. (1977). Rapid smoking: Side effects and safeguards. *Journal of Consulting and Clinical Psychology, 45,* 815–821.

Lichtenstein, E., Harris, D. E., Birchler, G. R., Wahl, J. M., & Schmahl, D. P. (1973). Comparison of rapid smoking, warm, smoky air and attention-placebo in the modification of smoking behavior. *Journal of Consulting and Clinical Psychology, 40,* 92–98.

Lichtenstein, E., & Rodrigues, M. R. P. (1977). Long-term effects of rapid smoking treatment for dependent cigarette smokers. *Addictive Behaviors, 2,* 109–112.

Lick, J. R. (1975). Expectancy, false galvanic skin response feedback and systematic desensitization in the modification of a phobic behavior. *Journal of Consulting and Clinical Psychology, 43,* 557–567.

Liddell, A., Di Fazio, L., Blackwood, J., & Ackerman, C. (1994). Long-term follow-up of treated dental phobics. *Behaviour Research and Therapy, 32,* 605–610.

Liebert, R. M., & Spiegler, M. D. (1994). *Personality: Strategies and issues* (7th ed.). Pacific Grove, CA: Brooks/Cole.

Liese, B. S. (1994). Brief therapy, crisis intervention and the cognitive therapy of substance abuse. *Crisis Intervention, 1,* 11–29.

Lima, J., Nazarian, L., Charney, E., & Lahti, C. (1976). Compliance with short-term antimicrobial therapy: Some techniques that help. *Pediatrics, 57,* 383–386.

Lindberg, J. S., Iwata, B. A., Roscoe, E. M., Worsdell, A. S., & Hanley, G. P. (2003). Treatment efficacy of noncontingent reinforcement during brief and extended application. *Journal of Applied Behavior Analysis, 36,* 1–19.

Lindsley, O. R. (1956). Operant conditioning methods applied to research in chronic schizophrenia. *Psychiatric Research Reports, 5,* 118–139.

Lindsley, O. R. (1960). Characteristics of the behavior of chronic psychotics as revealed by free-operant conditioning methods. *Diseases of the Nervous System (Monograph Supplement), 21,* 66–78.

Lindsley, O. R. (1963). Free-operant conditioning and psychotherapy. *Current Psychiatric Therapies, 3,* 47–56.

Lindsley, O. R. (1966). An experiment with parents handling behavior at home. *Johnstone Bulletin (Johnstone Training Center, Bordentown, NJ), 9,* 27–36.

Lindsley, O. R. (1968). A reliable wrist counter for recording behavior rates. *Journal of Applied Behavior Analysis, 1,* 77–78.

Linehan, M. M. (1987). Dialectical behavioral therapy: A cognitive behavioral approach to parasuicide. *Journal of Personality Disorders, 1,* 328–333.

Linehan, M. M. (1993a). *Cognitive-behavioral treatment of borderline personality disorder.* New York: Guilford.

Linehan, M. M. (1993b). *Skills training manual for treating borderline personality disorder.* New York: Guilford.

Linehan, M. M., & Dexter-Mazza, E. T. (2008). Dialectical behavior therapy for borderline personality disorder. In D. H. Barlow (Ed.), *Clinical handbook of psychological disorders: A step-by-step treatment manual* (4th ed., pp. 365–420). New York: Guilford.

Linehan, M. M., Schmidt, H., Dimeff, L. A., Craft, J. C., Kanter, J., & Comtois, K. A. (1999). Dialectical behavior therapy for patients with borderline personality disorder and drug dependence. *American Journal of Addictions, 8,* 279–292.

Linscheid, T. R., Hartel, F., & Cooley, N. (1993). Are aversive procedures durable? A five year follow-up of three individuals treated with contingent electric shock. *Child and Adolescent Mental Health Care, 3,* 67–76.

Linscheid, T. R., Iwata, B. A., Ricketts, R. W., Williams, D. E., & Griffin, J. C. (1990). Clinical evaluation of the self-injurious behavior inhibiting system (SIBIS). *Journal of Applied Behavior Analysis, 23,* 53–78.

Linton, S. J. (1982). Applied relaxation as a method of coping with chronic pain: A therapist's guide. *Scandinavian Journal of Behaviour Therapy, 11,* 161–174.

Linton, S. J., & Melin, L. (1983). Applied relaxation in the management of chronic pain. *Behavioural Psychotherapy, 11,* 337–350.

Lochman, J. E. (1985). Effects of different treatment lengths in cognitive behavioral interventions with aggressive boys. *Child Psychiatry and Human Development, 16,* 45–56.

Lochman, J. E. (2003). Preventive intervention with precursors to substance abuse. In W. J. Bukowski & Z. Slaboda (Eds.), *Handbook of drug abuse theory, science, and practice* (pp. 307–326). New York: Plenum.

Lochman, J. E., & Curry, J. F. (1986). Effects of social problem-solving training and self-instruction training with aggressive boys. *Journal of Clinical Child Psychology, 15,* 159–164.

Lochman, J. E., Nelson, W. M., III, & Sims, J. P. (1981). A cognitive-behavioral program for use with aggressive children. *Journal of Clinical Child Psychology, 13,* 527–538.

LOCHMAN, J. E., WHIDBY, J. M., & FITZGERALD, D. P. (2000). Cognitive-behavioral assessment and treatment with aggressive children. In P. C. Kendall (Ed.), *Child and adolescent therapy: Cognitive-behavioral procedures* (2nd ed., pp. 31–87). New York: Guilford.

LOCKE, E. A. (1979). Behavior modification is not cognitive and other myths: A reply to Ledwidge. *Cognitive Therapy and Research, 3,* 119–126.

LODGE, J., TRIPP, G., & HARTE, D. K. (2000). Think-aloud, thought-listing, and video-mediated recall procedures in the assessment of children's self-talk. *Cognitive Therapy and Research, 24,* 399–418.

LOEBER, S., CROISSANT, B., HEINZ, A., MANN, K., & FLOR, H. (2006). Cue exposure in the treatment of alcohol dependence: Effects on drinking outcome, craving and self-efficacy. *British Journal of Clinical Psychology, 45,* 515–529.

LOFTUS, E. (1979). *Eyewitness testimony.* Cambridge, MA: Harvard University Press.

LOMBARDO, T. W., & GRAY, M. T. (2005). Beyond exposure for post-traumatic stress disorder (PTSD) symptoms: Broad-spectrum PTSD treatment strategies. *Behavior Modification, 29,* 3–9.

LONG, E. S., MILTENBERGER, R. G., ELLINGSON, S. A., & OTT, S. M. (1999). Augmenting simplified habit reversal in the treatment of oral-digital habits exhibited by individuals with mental retardation. *Journal of Applied Behavior Analysis, 32,* 353–365.

LONG, E. S., MILTENBERGER, R. G., & RAPP, J. T. (1998). A survey of habit behaviors exhibited by individuals with mental retardation. *Behavioral Interventions, 13,* 79–89.

LONG, E. S., MILTENBERGER, R. G., & RAPP, J. T. (1999). Simplified habit reversal plus adjunct contingencies in the treatment of thumb sucking and hair pulling in a young child. *Child & Family Behavior Therapy, 21,* 45–58.

LONG, E. S., WOODS, D. W., MILTENBERGER, R. [G.], FUQUA, R. W., & BOUDJOUK, P. J. (1999). Examining the social effects of habit behaviors exhibited by individuals with mental retardation. *Journal of Mental and Physical Disabilities, 11,* 295–312.

LONG, P., FOREHAND, R. [L.], WIERSON, M., & MORGAN, A. (1993). Does parent training with young non-compliant children have long-term effects? *Behaviour Research and Therapy, 32,* 101–107.

LOVAAS, O. I. (1977). *The autistic child: Language development through behavior modification.* New York: Irvington.

LOVAAS, O. I. (1987). Behavioral treatment and normal educational and intellectual functioning in young autistic children. *Journal of Consulting and Clinical Psychology, 55,* 3–9.

LOVAAS, O. I., & SIMMONS, J. Q. (1969). Manipulation of self-destruction in three retarded children. *Journal of Applied Behavior Analysis, 2,* 143–157.

LOVELL, K., FULLALOVE, L., GARVERY, R., & BROOKER, C. (2000). Telephone treatment of obsessive-compulsive disorder. *Behavioural and Cognitive Psychotherapy, 28,* 87–91.

LOVIBOND, S. H., & COOTE, M. A. (1970). Enuresis. In C. G. Costello (Ed.), *Symptoms of psychopathology: A handbook* (pp. 373–396). New York: Wiley.

LOWE, K., & LUTZKER, J. R. (1979). Increasing compliance to a medical regimen with a juvenile diabetic. *Behavior Therapy, 10,* 57–64.

LUBORSKY, L. (1954). A note on Eysenck's article "The effects of psychotherapy: An evaluation." *British Journal of Psychology, 45,* 129–131.

LUCIC, K. S., STEFFEN, J. J., HARRIGAN, J. A., & STUEBING, R. C. (1991). Progressive relaxation training: Muscle contraction before relaxation? *Behavior Therapy, 22,* 249–256.

LUISELLI, J. K. (1993). Training self-feeding skills in children who are deaf and blind. *Behavior Modification, 17,* 457–473.

LUKINS, R., DAVAN, I. G. P., & DRUMMOND, P. D. (1997). A cognitive behavioural approach to preventing anxiety during magnetic resonance imaging. *Journal of Behavior Therapy and Experimental Psychiatry, 28,* 97–104.

LUMAN, M., OOSTERIAAN, J., HYDE, C., VAN MEEL, C. S., & SERGEANT, J. A. (2007). Heart rate and reinforcement sensitivity in ADHD. *Journal of Child Psychology and Psychiatry, 48,* 890–898.

LUMLEY, V. A., MILTENBERGER, R. G., LONG, E. S., RAPP, J. T., & ROBERTS, J. A. (1998). Evaluation of a sexual abuse prevention program for adults with mental retardation. *Journal of Applied Behavior Analysis, 31,* 91–101.

LUNDGREN, T., DAHL, J., & HAYES, S. C. (2008). Evaluation of mediators of change in the treatment of epilepsy with acceptance and commitment therapy. *Journal of Behavior Medicine, 31,* 225–235.

LUNDGREN, T., DAHL, J., MELIN, L., & KIES, B. (2006). Evaluation of acceptance and commitment therapy for drug refractory epilepsy: A randomized controlled trial in South Africa—A pilot study. *Epilepsia, 47,* 2173–2179.

LUNDQUIST, L. M., & HANSEN, D. J. (1998). Enhancing treatment adherence, social validity, and generalization of parent-training interventions with physically abusive and neglectful families. In J. Lutzker (Ed.), *Handbook of child abuse research and treatment* (pp. 449–471). New York: Plenum.

LUSSIER, J. P., HEIL, S. H., MONGEON, J. A., BADGER, G. J., & HIGGINS, S. T. (2006). A meta-analysis of voucher-based reinforcement therapy for substance use disorders. *Addition, 101,* 192–203.

LUTGENDORF, S. K., STARR, K., MCCABE, P., ANTONI, M. H., IRONSON, G., KLIMAS, N., et al. (1997). Cognitive-behavioral stress management decreases dysphoric mood and herpes simplex virus-type 2 antibody titers in symptomatic HIV-seropositive gay men. *Journal of Consulting and Clinical Psychology, 65,* 31–43.

LUTZKER, J. R., HUYNEN, K. B., & BIGELOW, K. M. (1998). Parent training. In V. B. Van Hasselt & M. Michel (Eds.), *Handbook of psychological treatment protocols for children and adolescents* (pp. 467–500). Mahwah, NJ: Erlbaum.

LUTZKER, J. R., & STEED, S. E. (1998). Parent training for families of children with developmental disabilities. In J. M. Briesmeister & C. E Schaefer (Eds.), *Handbook of parent training: Parents as cotherapists for children's behavior problems* (2nd ed., pp. 281–307). New York: Wiley.

LYLES, C. M., KAY, L. S., CREPAZ, N., HERBST, J. H., PASSIN, W. F., KIM, A. S., et al. (2007). Best-evidence interventions: Findings from a systematic review of HIV behavioral interventions for US populations at high risk, 2000–2004. *American Journal of Public Health, 97,* 133–143.

LYLES, J. M., BURISH, T. G., KROZELY, M. G., & OLDHAM, R. K. (1982). Efficacy of relaxation training and guided imagery in reducing the aversiveness of cancer chemotherapy. *Journal of Consulting and Clinical Psychology, 50,* 509–524.

LYNCH, T. R, MORSE, J. Q., MENDELSON, T., & ROBINS, C. J. (2003). Dialectical behavior therapy for depressed older adults: A randomized pilot study. *American Journal of Geriatrics, 11,* 33–45.

LYNCH, T. R., TROST, W.T., SALSMAN, N., & LINEHAN, M. M. (2007). Dialectical behavior therapy for borderline personality disorder. *Annual Review of Clinical Psychology, 3,* 181–205.

LYONS, L. C., & WOODS, P. J. (1991). The efficacy of rational-emotive therapy: A quantitative view of the outcome research. *Clinical Psychology Review, 11,* 357–369.

MA, S. H., & TEASDALE, J. D. (2004). Mindfulness-based cognitive therapy for depression: Replication and exploration of differential relapse prevention effects. *Journal of Consulting and Clinical Psychology, 72,* 31–40.

MAAG, J. W., & KOTLASH, J. (1994). Review of stress inoculation training with children and adolescents: Issues and recommendations. *Behavior Modification, 18,* 443–469.

MACCOBY, N., FARQUHAR, J. W., WOOD, P. D., & ALEXANDER, J. (1977). Reducing the risk of cardiovascular disease: Effects of a community-based campaign on knowledge and behavior. *Journal of Community Health, 3,* 100–114.

MACCURBREY, J. (1971). Verbal operant conditioning with young institutionalized Down's syndrome children. *American Journal of Mental Deficiency, 75,* 676–701.

MACCULLOCH, M. (2006). Effects of EMDR on previously abused child molesters: Theoretical reviews and preliminary findings from Ricci, Clayton, and Shapiro. *The Journal of Forensic Psychiatry & Psychology, 17,* 531–537.

MACKENZIE, E. P., FITE, P. J., & BATES, J. E. (2004). Predicting outcome in behavioral parent training: Expected and unexpected results. *Child & Family Behavior Therapy, 26,* 37–53.

MACKENZIE-KEATING, S. E., & MCDONALD, L. (1990). Overcorrection: Reviewed, revisited, and revised. *The Behavior Analyst, 13,* 39–48.

MACMILLAN, V., GUEVREMONT, D. C., & HANSEN, D. J. (1989). Problem-solving training with a multidistressed abusive mother. *Journal of Family Violence, 3,* 69–81.

MACONOCHIE, A. (1848). *The mark system.* London: John Ollivier.

MACPHILLAMY, D., & LEWINSOHN, P. M. (1971). *The Pleasant Events Schedule.* (Mimeo). Eugene: University of Oregon.

MADSEN, C. H., HOFFMAN, M., THOMAS, D. R., KOROPSAK, E., & MADSEN, C. K. (1969). Comparison of toilet training techniques. In D. M. Gelfand (Ed.), *Social learning in childhood* (pp. 104–112). Pacific Grove, CA: Brooks/Cole.

MADSEN, C. K., GREER, R. D., & MADSEN, C. H. (1975). *Research in music behavior: Modifying music behavior in the classroom.* New York: Teachers College Press.

MAEDA, M. (1985). The effects of combinations of vicarious reinforcement on the formation of assertive behaviors in covert modeling. *Japanese Journal of Behavior Therapy, 10,* 34–44. (English abstract)

MAGEE, S. K., & ELLIS, J. (2000). Extinction effects during the assessment of multiple problem behaviors. *Journal of Applied Behavior Analysis, 33,* 313–316.

MAGILL-EVANS, J., HARRISON, M. J., BENZIES, K., GIERL, M., & KIMAK, C. (2007). Effects of parenting education on first-time fathers' skills in interactions with their infants. *Fathering, 5,* 42–57.

MAGRAB, P. R., & PAPADOPOULOU, Z. L. (1977). The effects of a token economy on dietary compliance for children on hemodialysis. *Journal of Applied Behavior Analysis, 10,* 573–578.

MAHONEY, K., VAN WAGENEN, R. K., & MEYERSON, L. (1971). Toilet training of normal and retarded children. *Journal of Applied Behavior Analysis, 4,* 173–181.

MAHONEY, M. J., LYDDON, W. J., & ALFORD, D. J. (1989). An evaluation of the rational-emotive theory of psychotherapy. In M. E. Bernard & R. [A.] DiGiuseppe (Eds.), *Inside rational-emotive therapy: A critical appraisal of the theory and therapy of Albert Ellis* (pp. 69–94). San Diego: Academic Press.

MALEC, J. F. (1995). Behavior therapy and cognitive decline in the elderly. *the Behavior Therapist, 18,* 161–169.

MALETZKY, B. M. (1974). "Assisted" covert sensitization in the treatment of exhibitionism. *Journal of Consulting and Clinical Psychology, 42,* 34–40.

MALETZKY, B. M. (1993). Assisted covert sensitization: Application to a bisexual pedophile. In J. R. Cautela & A. J. Kearney (Eds.), *Covert conditioning casebook* (pp. 217–234). Pacific Grove, CA: Brooks/Cole.

MALLESON, N. (1959). Panic and phobia. *Lancet, 1,* 225–227.

MALONEY, D. M., FIXSEN, D. L., & PHILLIPS, E. L. (1981). The Teaching-Family model: Research and dissemination in a service program. *Children and Youth Services Review, 3,* 343–355.

MALONEY, K. B., & HOPKINS, B. L. (1973). The modification of sentence structure and its relationship to subjective judgments of creativity in writing. *Journal of Applied Behavior Analysis, 6,* 425–433.

MANCIL, G. R., CONROY, M. A., NAKAO, T., & ALTER, P. J. (2006). Functional communication training in the natural environment: A pilot investigation with a young child with autism spectrum disorder. *Education & Treatment of Children, 29,* 615–633.

MANN, R. A. (1972). The behavior-therapeutic use of contingency contracting to control an adult behavior problem: Weight control. *Journal of Applied Behavior Analysis, 5,* 99–109.

MANN, R. A. (1976). The use of contingency contracting to facilitate durability of behavior change: Weight loss maintenance. *Addictive Behaviors, 1,* 245–249.

MANNE, S. L., BAKEMAN, R., JACOBSEN, P. B., GORFINKLE, K., & REDD, W. H. (1994). An analysis of a behavioral intervention for children undergoing venipuncture. *Health Psychology, 13,* 556–566.

MANNE, S. L., REDD, W. H., JACOBSEN, P. B., GORFINKLE, K., SCHORR, O., & RABKIN, B. (1990). Behavioral interventions to reduce child and parent distress during venipuncture. *Journal of Consulting and Clinical Psychology, 58,* 565–572.

MANSDORF, I. J., CALAPAI, P., CASELLI, L., BURSTEIN, Y., & DIMANT, J. (1999). Reducing psychotropic medication usage in nursing home residents: The effects of behaviorally oriented psychotherapy. *the Behavior Therapist, 22,* 21–23, 29.

MARGOLIN, G., MICHELLI, J., & JACOBSON, N. (1988). Assessment of marital dysfunction. In A. S. Bellack & M. Hersen (Eds.), *Behavioral assessment: A practical handbook* (3rd ed., pp. 441–489). Elmsford, NY: Pergamon.

MARISSEN, M. A. E., FRANKEN, I. H. A., BLANKEN, P., VAN DEN BRINK, W., & HENDRICKS, V. M. (2005). Cue exposure therapy for opiate dependent clients. *Journal of Substance Use, 10,* 97–105.

MARISSEN, M. A. E., FRANKEN, I. H. A., BLANKEN, P., VAN DEN BRINK, W., & HENDRICKS, V. M. (2007). Cue exposure therapy for the treatment of opiate addiction: Results of a randomized controlled clinical trial. *Psychotherapy and Psychosomatics, 76,* 97–105.

MARKMAN, H. J., FLOYD, F. J., STANLEY, S. M., & LEWIS, H. (1986). Prevention. In N. S. Jacobson & A. S. Gurman (Eds.), *Clinical handbook of marital therapy* (pp. 173–195). New York: Guilford.

MARKMAN, H. J., FLOYD, F. J., STANLEY, S. M., & STORAASLI, R. D. (1988). Prevention of marital distress: A longitudinal investigation. *Journal of Consulting and Clinical Psychology, 56,* 210–217.

MARKMAN, H. J., LEBER, B., CORDOVA, A. D., & ST. PETERS, M. (1995). Behavioral observation and family psychology: Strange bedfellows or happy marriage? *Journal of Family Psychology, 9,* 371–379.

MARKMAN, H. J., RENICK, M. J., FLOYD, F. J., STANLEY, S. M., & CLEMENTS, M. (1993). Preventing marital distress through communication and conflict management training: A 4-and 5-year follow-up. *Journal of Consulting and Clinical Psychology, 61,* 70–77.

MARKMAN, H. J., STANLEY, S. M., JENKINS, N. H., PETRELLA, J. N., & WADSWORTH, M. E. (2006). Preventive education: Distinctives and directions. *Journal of Cognitive Psychotherapy, 20,* 411–433.

MARKMAN, H. J., WILLIAMS, T., EINHORN, L., & STANLEY, S. M. (2008). The new frontier in relationship education: Innovations and challenges in dissemination. *the Behavior Therapist, 31,* 14–17.

MARKS, I. [M.] (1978). Behavioral psychotherapy of adult neurosis. In S. L. Garfield & A. E. Bergin (Eds.), *Handbook of psychotherapy and behavior change: An empirical analysis* (2nd ed., pp. 493–547). New York: Wiley.

MARKS, I. M., CAVANAGH, K., & GEGA, L. (2007). *Hands-on help: Computer-aided psychotherapy.* New York: Routledge.

MARKS, I. M., GOLDFRIED, M. R. (Moderators), SUNGUR, M., NEWMAN, M. G., MOORE, K., & STRICKER, G. (Panelists). (2005). *Towards a common language in psychotherapy.* Panel discussion presented at the annual meeting of the Association for Behavioral and Cognitive Therapies, Washington, DC.

MARKS, I. M., KENWRIGHT, M., MCDONOUGH, M., WHITTAKER, M., & MATAIX-COLS, D. (2004). Saving clinicians' time by delegating routine aspects of therapy to a computer: A randomized controlled trial in phobia/panic disorder. *Psychological Medicine, 34,* 9–17.

MARLATT, G. A., & BARRETT, K. (1994). Relapse prevention. In M. Galanter & H. D. Kleber (Eds.), *The textbook of substance abuse treatment* (pp. 285–299). Washington, DC: American Psychiatric Press.

MARLATT, G. A., & DONOVAN, D. M. (Eds.). (2005). *Relapse prevention: Maintenance strategies in the treatment of addictive behaviors* (2nd ed.). New York: Guilford.

MARLATT, G. A., & GORDON, J. R. (Eds.). (1985). *Relapse prevention: Maintenance strategies in the treatment of addictive behaviors.* New York: Guilford.

MARLATT, G. A., & TAPERT, S. F. (1993). Harm reduction: Reducing the risks of addictive behaviors. In J. S. Baer, G. A. Marlatt, & R. J. McMahon (Eds.), *Addictive behaviors across the lifespan* (pp. 243–273). Newbury Park, CA: Sage.

MARLOW, A. G., TINGSTROM, D. H., OLMI, D. J., & EDWARDS, R. P. (1997). The effects of classroom-based time-in/time-out on compliance rates in children with speech/language disabilities. *Child & Family Behavior Therapy, 19,* 1–14.

MARSHALL, W. L., GAUTHIER, J., & GORDON, A. (1979). The current status of flooding therapy. In M. Hersen, R. M. Eisler, & P. M. Miller (Eds.), *Progress in behavior modification* (Vol. 7, pp. 205–275). New York: Academic Press.

MARSTON, M. V. (1970). Compliance with medical regimens: A review of the literature. *Nursing Research, 19,* 312–323.

MARTELL, C. R., ADDIS, M. E., & JACOBSON, N. S. (2001). *Depression in context: Strategies for guided action.* New York: Norton.

MARTELL, C. R., & PRINCE, S. E. (2005). Treating infidelity in same-sex couples. *Journal of Clinical Psychology, 61,* 1429–1438.

MARTIN, G., & PEAR, J. (2007). *Behavior modification: What it is and how to do it* (8th ed.). Upper Saddle River, NJ: Pearson.

MARTIN, S. (1995, October). Ethnic issues deeply entwined in family therapy. *APA Monitor, 26,* 38.

MARTINEZ-MALLÉN, E., CASTRO-FORNIELES, J., LÁZARO, L., MORENO, E., MORER, A., FONT, E., et al. (2007). Cue exposure in the treatment of resistant adolescent bulimia nervosa. *International Journal of Eating Disorders, 40,* 596–601.

MARTINEZ-TABOAS, A., & NAVAS-ROBLETO, J. J. (2000). Cognitive behavior therapy in Puerto Rico. *the Behavior Therapist, 23,* 184–187.

MASEK, B. J. (1982). Compliance and medicine. In D. M. Doleys, R. L. Meredith, & A. R. Ciminero (Eds.), *Behavioral medicine: Assessment and treatment strategies* (pp. 527–545). New York: Plenum.

MASON, L. W., GOOLKASIAN, P., & MCCAIN, G. A. (1998). Evaluation of a multimodal treatment program for fibromyalgia. *Journal of Behavioral Medicine, 21,* 163–178.

MASTERS, J. C., BURISH, T. G., HOLLON, S. D., & RIMM, D. C. (1987). *Behavior therapy: Techniques and empirical findings* (3rd ed.). San Diego: Harcourt Brace Jovanovich.

MASTERS, W. H., & JOHNSON, V. E. (1970). *Human sexual inadequacy.* Boston: Little, Brown.

MASUDA, A., HAYES, S. C., SACKETT, C. F., & TWOHIG, M. P. (2004). Cognitive defusion and self-relevant negative thoughts: Examining the impact of a ninety year old technique. *Behaviour Research and Therapy, 42,* 477–485.

MATHEWS, A. M., GELDER, M. G., & JOHNSTON, D. W. (1981). *Agoraphobia: Nature and treatment.* New York: Guilford.

MATHEWS, A. M., JOHNSTON, D. W., LANCASHIRE, M., MUNBY, M., SHAW, P. M., & GELDER, M. G. (1976). Imaginal flooding and exposure to real phobic situations: Treatment outcome with agoraphobic patients. *British Journal of Psychology, 129*, 362–371.

MATHEWS, A. M., TEASDALE, J., MUNBY, M., JOHNSTON, D. W., & SHAW, P. M. (1977). A home-based treatment for agoraphobia. *Behavior Therapy, 8*, 915–924.

MATSON, J. L., BAMBURG, J., SMALLS, Y., & SMIROLDO, B. B. (1997). Evaluating behavioral techniques in training individuals with severe and profound mental retardation to use functional independent living skills. *Behavior Modification, 21*, 533–534.

MATSON, J. L., SEVIN, J. A., & BOX, M. L. (1995). Social skills in children. In W. O'Donohue & L. Krasner (Eds.). *Handbook of psychological skills training: Clinical techniques and applications* (pp. 36–53). Boston: Allyn & Bacon.

MATSON, J. L., SMALLS, Y., HAMPFF, A., SMIROLDO, B. B., & ANDERSON, S. J. (1998). A comparison of behavioral techniques to teach functional independent-living skills to individuals with severe and profound mental retardation. *Behavior Modification, 22*, 298–306.

MATTICK, R. P., & PETERS, L. (1988). Treatment of severe social phobia: Effects of guided exposure with and without cognitive restructuring. *Journal of Consulting and Clinical Psychology, 56*, 251–260.

MAUDE-GRIFFEN, P. M., HOHENSTEIN, J. M., HUMFLEET, G. L., REILLY, P. M., TUSEL, D. J., & HALL, S. M. (1998). Superior efficacy of cognitive-behavioral therapy for urban crack cocaine abusers: Main and matching effects. *Journal of Consulting and Clinical Psychology, 66*, 832–837.

MAUGHAN, D. R., CHRISTIANSEN, E., JENSON, W. R., OLYMPIA, D., & CLARK, E. (2005). Behavioral parent training as a treatment for externalizing behaviors and disruptive behavior disorders: A meta-analysis. *School Psychology Review, 34*, 267–286.

MAYDEU-OLIVARES, A., & D'ZURILLA, T. J. (1997). The factor structure of the Problem Solving Inventory. *European Journal of Psychological Assessment, 13*, 206–215.

MAYDEU-OLIVARES, A., RODRIGUEZ-FORNELLS, A., GOMEZ-BENITO, J., & D'ZURILLA, T. J. (2000). Psychometric properties of the Spanish adaptation of the Social Problem-Solving Inventory-Revised (SPSI-R). *Personality and Individual Differences, 29*, 699–708.

MAYER, J. A., & FREDERIKSEN, L. W. (1986). Encouraging long-term compliance with breast self-examination: The evaluation of prompting strategies. *Journal of Behavioral Medicine, 9*, 179–189.

MAYHEW, G. L., & HARRIS, F. C. (1978). Some negative side effects of a punishment procedure for stereotyped behavior. *Journal of Behavior Therapy and Experimental Psychiatry, 9*, 245–251.

MAZALESKI, J. L., IWATA, B. A., VOLLMER, T. R., ZARCONE, J. R., & SMITH, R. G. (1993). Analysis of the reinforcement and extinction components in contingencies with self-injury. *Journal of Applied Behavior Analysis, 26*, 143–156.

MAZUR, T., & MICHAEL, P. M. (1992). Outpatient treatment for adolescents with sexually inappropriate behavior. *Journal of Offender Rehabilitation, 18*, 191–203.

MCADAM, D. B., & CUVO, A. J. (1994). Textual prompts as an antecedent cue self-management strategy for persons with mild disabilities. *Behavior Modification, 18*, 47–65.

MCCABE, R. E., BLANKSTEIN, K. R., & MILLS, J. S. (1999). Interpersonal sensitivity and social problem-solving: Relation with academic and social self-esteem, depressive symptoms, and academic performance. *Cognitive Therapy and Research, 23*, 587–604.

MCCAIN, A. P., & KELLEY, M. L. (1993). Managing the classroom behavior of an ADHD preschooler: The efficacy of a school-home note intervention. *Child & Family Behavior Therapy, 15*, 33–44.

MCCAIN, A. P., & KELLEY, M. L. (1994). Improving classroom performance in underachieving adolescents: The additive effects of response cost to a school-home note system. *Child & Family Behavior Therapy, 16*, 27–41.

MCCALLIE, M. S., BLUM, C. M., & HOOD, C. J. (2006). Progressive muscle relaxation. *Journal of Human Behavior in the Social Environment, 13*, 51–66.

MCCART, M. R., PRIESTER, P. E., DAVIES, W. H., & AZEN, R. (2006).

Differential effectiveness of behavioral parent-training and cognitive-behavioral therapy for antisocial youth: A meta-analysis. *Journal of Abnormal Child Psychology, 34*, 527–543.

MCCARTHY, B. [W.] (1989). A cognitive-behavioral approach to sex therapy. In A. Freeman, K. M. Simon, L. E. Beutler, & H. Arkowitz (Eds.), *Comprehensive handbook of cognitive therapy* (pp. 435–447). New York: Plenum.

MCCARTHY, B. W. (2001). Relapse prevention strategies and techniques with erectile dysfunction. *Journal of Sex & Marital Therapy, 27*, 1–8.

MCCARTHY, G. W., & CRAIG, K. D. (1995). Flying therapy for flying phobia. *Aviation, Space, and Environmental Medicine, 66*, 1179–1184.

MCCATHIE, H., & SPENCE, S. H. (1991). What is the Revised Fear Survey Schedule for Children measuring? *Behaviour Research and Therapy, 29*, 495–502.

MCCLAUGHLIN, T. F. (1982). An analysis of token reinforcement: A control group comparison with special education youth employing measures of clinical significance. *Child & Family Behavior Therapy, 3*, 43–50.

MCCLOUD, J. (2006, February 13). Happiness isn't normal. *Time Magazine, 167*(7), 58–60, 63–64, 67.

MCCOMAS, J. J., WACKER, D. P., & COOPER, L. J. (1998). Increasing compliance with medical procedures: Application of the high-probability request procedure for a toddler. *Journal of Applied Behavior Analysis, 31*, 287–290.

MCCONAGHY, N. (1988). Assessment of sexual dysfunction and deviation. In A. S. Bellack & M. Hersen (Eds.), *Behavioral assessment: A practical handbook* (3rd ed., pp. 490–541). Elmsford, NY: Pergamon.

MCCONNACHIE, G., & CARR, E. G. (1997). The effects of child behavior problems on the maintenance of intervention fidelity. *Behavior Modification, 21*, 123–158.

MCCONNELL, J. V. (1990). Negative reinforcement and positive punishment. *Teaching of Psychology, 17*, 247–249.

MCCORDICK, S. M., KAPLAN, R. M., FINN, M. E., & SMITH, S. H. (1979). Cognitive behavior modification and modeling for test anxiety. *Journal of Consulting and Clinical Psychology, 47*, 419–420.

McCracken, J. (2000). Tic disorders. In H. Kaplan & B. Sadock (Eds.), *Comprehensive textbook of psychiatry* (7th ed., pp. 2711–2719). Philadelphia: Lippincott Williams & Wilkins.

McCracken, L. M., Vowles, K. E., & Eccleston, C. (2005). Acceptance-based treatment for persons with complex, long standing chronic pain: A preliminary analysis of treatment outcome in comparison to a waiting phase. *Behaviour Research and Therapy, 43,* 1335–1346.

McCulloch, A., & McMurran, M. (2007). The features of a good offender treatment programme manual: A delphi survey of experts. *Psychology, Crime & Law, 13,* 265–274.

McCurry, S. M., Logsdon, R. G., Teri, L., & Vitiello, M. V. (2007). Evidence-based psychological treatment for insomnia in older adults. *Psychology and Aging, 22,* 18–27.

McEvoy, P. M. (2007). Effectiveness of cognitive behavioural group therapy for social phobia in a community clinic: A benchmarking study. *Behaviour Research and Therapy, 45,* 3030–3040.

McFall, R. M., & Lillesand, D. B. (1971). Behavior rehearsal with modeling and coaching in assertion training. *Journal of Abnormal Psychology, 77,* 313–323.

McGill, P., Teer, K., Rye, L., & Hughes, D. (2005). Staff reports of setting events associated with challenging behavior. *Behavior Modification, 29,* 599–615.

McGinn, L. K., & Young, J. E. (1996). Schema-focused therapy. In P. M. Salkovskis (Ed.), *Frontiers of cognitive therapy* (pp. 182–207). New York: Guilford.

McGinn, L. K., Young, J. E., & Sanderson, W. C. (1995). When and how to do longer term therapy without feeling guilty. *Cognitive and Behavioral Practice, 2,* 187–212.

McGinnis, J. C., Friman, P. C., & Carlyon, W. D. (1999). The effect of token awards on "intrinsic" motivation for doing math. *Journal of Applied Behavior Analysis, 32,* 375–379.

McGlynn, F. D., Moore, P. M., Rose, M. P., & Lazarte, A. (1995). Effects of relaxation training on fear and arousal during in vivo exposure to a caged snake among DSM-III-R simple (snake) phobics. *Journal of Behavior Therapy and Experimental Psychiatry, 26,* 1–8.

McGlynn, F. D., Smitherman, T. A., & Gothard, K. D. (2004). Comment on the status of systematic desensitization. *Behavior Modification, 28,* 194–205.

McGoey, K. E., & DuPaul, G. J. (2000). Token reinforcement and response cost procedures: Reducing the disruptive behavior of preschool children with attention-deficit/hyperactivity disorder. *School Psychology Quarterly, 15,* 330–343.

McGoldrick, M., Giordano, J., & Garcia-Preto, N. (Eds.). (2005). *Ethnicity and family therapy* (3rd ed.). New York: Guilford.

McGrady, A. (1994). Effects of group relaxation training and thermal biofeedback on blood pressure and related physiological and psychological variables in essential hypertension. *Biofeedback and Self-Regulation, 19,* 51–66.

McGrady, A., Olson, R. P., & Kroon, J. S. (1995). Biobehavioral treatment of essential hypertension. In M. S. Schwartz (Ed.), *Biofeedback: A practitioner's guide* (pp. 445–467). New York: Guilford.

McGrady, A., Wauquier, A., McNeil, A., & Gerard, G. (1994). Effects of biofeedback-assisted relaxation on migraine headache and changes in cerebral blood flow velocity in the middle cerebral artery. *Headache, 34,* 424–428.

McGrady, A. V., Andrasik, F., Davies, T., Striefel, S., Wickra-Masekera, I., Baskin, S. M., et al. (1999). Psychophysiologic therapy for chronic headache in primary care. *Primary Care Companion Journal of Clinical Psychiatry, 1,* 96–102.

McGraw-Hunter, M., Faw, G. D., & Davis, P. K. (2006). The use of video self-modeling and feedback to teach cooking skills to individuals with traumatic brain injury: A pilot study. *Brain Injury, 20,* 1061–1068.

McKay, D. (1997). A maintenance program for obsessive-compulsive disorder using exposure with response prevention: 2 year follow-up. *Behaviour Research and Therapy, 35,* 367–369.

McKay, D. (1999). Two-year follow-up of behavioral treatment and maintenance for body dysmorphic disorder. *Behavior Modification, 23,* 620–629.

McKay, D., Todaro, J., Neziroglu, F., Campisi, T., Moritz, E. K., & Yaryura-Tobias, J. A. (1997). Body dysmorphic disorder: A preliminary evaluation of treatment and maintenance using exposure with response prevention. *Behaviour Research and Therapy, 35,* 67–70.

McKusick, L., Wiley, J., Coates, T. J., & Morin, S. F. (1986, November). *Predictors of AIDS behavioral risk reduction: The AIDS behavioral research project.* Paper presented at the New Zealand AIDS Foundation Prevention Education Planning Workshop, Auckland.

McManus, F., Clark, D. M., & Hackmann, A. (2000). Specificity of cognitive biases in social phobia and their role in recovery. *Behavioural and Cognitive Psychotherapy, 28,* 201–209.

McNair, L. D. (1996). African American women and behavior therapy: Integrating theory, culture, and clinical practice. *Cognitive and Behavioral Practice, 3,* 337–349.

McNees, M. P., Egli, D. S., Marshall, D. S., Schnelle, R. S., Schnelle, J. F., & Risley, T. R. (1976). Shoplifting prevention: Providing information through signs. *Journal of Applied Behavior Analysis, 9,* 399–405.

McNeil, C. B., Clemens-Mowrer, L., Gurwitch, R. H., & Funderburk, B. W. (1994). Assessment of a new procedure to prevent timeout escape in preschoolers. *Child & Family Behavior Therapy, 16,* 27–35.

Meadowcroft, P., Hawkins, R. P., Trout, B. A., Grealish, E. M., & Stark, L. J. (1982, September). *Making foster-family-based treatment accountable: The issue of quality control.* Paper presented at the meeting of the American Psychological Association, Washington, DC.

Meadows, E. A., & Foa, E. B. (1998). Intrusion, arousal, and avoidance. In V. M. Follette, J. I. Ruzek, & F. R. Abueg (Eds.), *Cognitive-behavioral therapies for trauma* (pp. 100–123). New York: Guilford.

Mealiea, W. L., & Nawas, M. M. (1971). The comparative effectiveness of systematic desensitization and implosive therapy in the treatment of snake phobia. *Journal of Behavior Therapy and Experimental Psychiatry, 2,* 85–94.

MEANS, M. K., LICHSTEIN, K. L., EPPERSON, M. T., & JOHNSON, C. T. (2000). Relaxation therapy for insomnia: Nighttime and day time effects. *Behaviour Research and Therapy, 38,* 665–678.

MEHARG, S. S., & WOLTERSDORF, M. A. (1990). Therapeutic uses of videotape self-modeling: A review. *Advances in Behaviour Research and Therapy, 12,* 85–99.

MEHTA, M. (1990). A comparative study of family-based and patient-based behavioral management in obsessive-compulsive disorder. *British Journal of Psychiatry, 157,* 133–135.

MEICHENBAUM, D. [H.] (1971). Examination of model characteristics in reducing avoidance behavior. *Journal of Personality and Social Psychology, 17,* 298–307.

MEICHENBAUM, D. [H.] (1974). Self-instructional training: A cognitive prosthesis for the aged. *Human Development, 17,* 273–280.

MEICHENBAUM, D. [H.] (1975). Enhancing creativity by modifying what subjects say to themselves. *American Educational Research Journal, 12,* 129–145.

MEICHENBAUM, D. [H.] (1977). *Cognitive-behavior modification: An integrative approach.* New York: Plenum.

MEICHENBAUM, D. H. (1985). *Stress inoculation training.* Elmsford, NY: Pergamon.

MEICHENBAUM, D. [H.] (1991, February–March). *Cognitive behavioral therapy.* Workshop sponsored by the Institute for the Advancement of Human Behavior (Portola Valley, CA), Chicago.

MEICHENBAUM, D. [H.] (1994). *A clinical handbook/practical therapist manual for assessing and treating adults with post-traumatic stress disorder (PTSD).* Waterloo, Ontario: Institute Press.

MEICHENBAUM, D. [H.] (2007). Stress inoculation training: A preventative and treatment approach. In P. M. Lehrer, R. L. Woolfolk, & W. E. Sime (Eds.), *Principles and practice of stress management* (3rd ed., pp. 497–516). New York: Guilford.

MEICHENBAUM, D. [H.], & CAMERON, R. (1972). *Stress inoculation: A skills training approach to anxiety management.* Unpublished manuscript, University of Waterloo, Ontario.

MEICHENBAUM, D. [H.], & CAMERON, R. (1973). Training schizophrenics to talk to themselves: A means of developing attentional controls. *Behavior Therapy, 4,* 515–534.

MEICHENBAUM, D. H., & DEFFENBACHER, J. L. (1988). Stress inoculation training. *The Counseling Psychologist, 16,* 69–90.

MEICHENBAUM, D. [H.], GILMORE, B., & FEDORAVICIUS, A. (1971). Group insight vs. group desensitization in treating speech anxiety. *Journal of Consulting and Clinical Psychology, 36,* 410–421.

MEICHENBAUM, D. [H.], & GOODMAN, J. (1971). Training impulsive children to talk to themselves: A means of developing self-control. *Journal of Abnormal Psychology, 77,* 115–126.

MELAMED, B. G. (1979). Behavioral approaches to fear in dental settings. In M. Hersen, R. M. Eisler, & P. M. Miller (Eds.), *Progress in behavior modification* (Vol. 7, pp. 172–205). New York: Academic Press.

MELAMED, B. G., HAWES, R. R., HELBY, E., & GLICK, J. (1975). Use of filmed modeling to reduce uncooperative behavior of children during dental treatment. *Journal of Dental Research, 54,* 797–801.

MELAMED, B. G., & SIEGEL, L. J. (1975). Reduction of anxiety in children facing hospitalization and surgery by use of filmed modeling. *Journal of Consulting and Clinical Psychology, 43,* 511–521.

MELLON, M. W., & MCGRATH, M. L. (2000). Empirically supported treatments in pediatric psychology: Nocturnal enuresis. *Journal of Pediatric Psychology, 25,* 193–214.

MENZIES, R. G., & CLARKE, J. C. (1993). A comparison of in vivo and vicarious exposure in the treatment of childhood water phobia. *Behaviour Research and Therapy, 31,* 9–15.

MESSMAN-MOORE, T. L., & RESICK, P. A. (2002). Brief treatment of complicated PTSD and peritraumatic responses in a client with repeated sexual victimization. *Cognitive and Behavioral Practice, 9,* 89–99.

METZ, J. R. (1965). Conditioning generalized imitation in autistic children. *Journal of Experimental Child Psychology, 2,* 389–399.

METZLER, C. W., BIGLAN, A., NOELL, J., ARY, D. V., & OCHS, L. (2000). A randomized controlled trial of a behavioral intervention to reduce high-risk sexual behavior among adolescents in STD clinics. *Behavior Therapy, 31,* 27–54.

MEYER, R. G. (1975). A behavioral treatment of sleepwalking associated with test anxiety. *Journal of Behavior Therapy and Experimental Psychiatry, 6,* 167–168.

MEYER, V., ROBERTSON, J., & TATLOW, A. (1975). Home treatment of an obsessive-compulsive disorder by response prevention. *Journal of Behavior Therapy and Experimental Psychiatry, 6,* 37–38.

MEYERS, A., MERCATORIS, M., & SIROTA, A. (1976). Use of covert self-instruction for the elimination of psychotic speech. *Journal of Consulting and Clinical Psychology, 44,* 480–483.

MICHAEL, J. (2000). Implications and refinements of the establishing operations concept. *Journal of Applied Behavior Analysis, 33,* 401–410.

MIDDLETON, M. B., & CARTLEDGE, G. (1995). The effects of social skills instruction and parental involvement on the aggressive behaviors of African American males. *Behavioral Medicine, 19,* 192–210.

MIKLOWITZ, D. J. (2008). Biopolar disorder. In D. H. Barlow (Ed.), *Handbook of psychological disorders: A step-by-step treatment manual* (4th ed., pp. 421–462). New York: Guilford.

MIKULAS, W. L., & COFFMAN, M. F. (1989). Home-based treatment of children's fear of the dark. In C. E. Schaefer & J. M. Briesmeister (Eds.), *Handbook of parent training: Parents as co-therapists for children's behavior problems* (pp. 179–202). New York: Wiley.

MIKULAS, W. L., COFFMAN, M. F., DAYTON, D., FRAYNE, C., & MAIER, P. L. (1985). Behavioral bibliotherapy and games for treating fear of the dark. *Child & Family Behavior Therapy, 7,* 1–7.

MILAN, M. A. (1987). Token economy programs in closed institutions. In E. K. Morris & C. J. Braukmann (Eds.), *Behavioral approaches to crime and delinquency: A handbook of applications, research, and concepts* (pp. 195–222). New York: Plenum.

MILES, H., PETERS, E., & KUIPERS, E. (2007). Service-user satisfaction with CBT for psychosis. *Behavioural and Cognitive Psychotherapy, 35,* 109–116.

MILGROM, P., MANCL, L., KING, B., & WEINSTEIN, P. (1995). Origins of childhood dental fear. *Behaviour Research and Therapy, 33,* 313–319.

MILLER, D. L., & KELLEY, M. L. (1992). Treatment acceptability: The effects, marital adjustment, and child behavior. *Child & Family Behavior Therapy*, 14, 11–23.

MILLER, D. L., MANNE, S., & PALEVSKY, W. (1998). Acceptance of behavioral interventions for children with cancer: Perceptions of parents, nurses, and community controls. *Journal of Pediatric Psychology*, 23, 267–271.

MILLER, D. N., & COLE, C. L. (1998). Effects of social skills training on an adolescent with comorbid conduct disorder and depression. *Child & Family Behavior Therapy*, 20, 35–53.

MILLER, H. R., & NAWAS, M. M. (1970). Control of aversive stimulus termination in systematic desensitization. *Behaviour Research and Therapy*, 8, 57–61.

MILLER, L. D. (2008). Facing fears: The feasibility of anxiety universal prevention efforts with children and adolescents. *Cognitive and Behavioral Practice*, 15, 2835–2835.

MILLER, P. M. (1972). The use of behavioral contracting in the treatment of alcoholism: A case report. *Behavior Therapy*, 3, 593–596.

MILNE, D., & KENNEDY, S. (1993). The utility of consumer satisfaction data: A case study in organizational behaviour management. *Behavioural and Cognitive Psychotherapy*, 21, 281–291.

MILTENBERGER, R. G. (2000). Behavioral skills training to remediate deviant social behavior of an adolescent in residential treatment. *Cognitive and Behavioral Practice*, 7, 236–238.

MILTENBERGER, R. G., FUQUA, R. W., & MCKINLEY, T. (1985). Habit reversal with muscle tics: Replication and component analysis. *Behavior Therapy*, 16, 39–50.

MILTENBERGER, R. G., FUQUA, R. W., & WOODS, D. W. (1998). Applying behavior analysis to clinical problems: Review and analysis of habit reversal. *Journal of Applied Behavior Analysis*, 31, 447–469.

MILTENBERGER, R. G., ROBERTS, J. A., ELLINGSON, S., GALENSKY, T., RAPP, J. T., LONG, E. S., et al. (1999). Training and generalization of sexual abuse prevention skills for woman with mental retardation. *Journal of Applied Behavior Analysis*, 32, 385–388.

MILTENBERGER, R. G., & THIESSE-DUFFY, E. (1988). Evaluation of home-based programs for teaching personal safety skills to children. *Journal of Applied Behavior Analysis*, 21, 81–87.

MINKIN, N., BRAUKMANN, C. J., MINKIN, B. L., TIMBERS, G. D., TIMBERS, B. J., FIXSEN, D. L., et al. (1976). The social validation and training of conversational skills. *Journal of Applied Behavior Analysis*, 9, 127–139.

MINNEKER-HUGEL, E., UNLAND, H., & BUCHKREMER, G. (1992). Behavioral relapse prevention strategies in smoking cessation. *The International Journal of the Addictions*, 27, 627–634.

MINOR, S. W., LEONE, C., & BALDWIN, R. T. (1984). A comparison of in vivo and imaginal participant modeling. *Journal of Clinical Psychology*, 40, 717–720.

MISCHEL, W. (1968). *Personality and assessment*. New York: Wiley.

MISCHEL, W. (1973). On the empirical dilemmas of psychodynamic approaches: Issues and alternatives. *Journal of Abnormal Psychology*, 82, 335–344.

MITCHELL, J. E., PYLE, R. L., HATSUKAMI, D., GOFF, G., GLOTTER, D., & HARPER, J. (1989). A 2–5 year follow-up study of patients treated for bulimia nervosa. *International Journal of Eating Disorders*, 8, 157–165.

MOHR, D. C., HART, S., & VELLA, L. (2007). Reduction in disability in a randomized controlled trial of telephone-administered cognitive-behavioral therapy. *Health Psychology*, 26, 554–563.

MOHR, D. C., LIKOSKY, W., BERTAGNOLLI, A., GOODKIN, D. E., VAN DER WENDE, J., DWYER, P., et al. (2000). Telephone-administered cognitive-behavioral therapy for the treatment of depressive symptoms in multiple sclerosis. *Journal of Consulting and Clinical Psychology*, 68, 356–361.

MONSON, C. M., SCHNURR, P. P., RESICK, P. A., FRIEDMAN, M. J., YOUNG-XU, Y., & STEVENS, S. P. (2006). Cognitive processing therapy for veterans with military-related posttraumatic stress disorder. *Journal of Consulting and Clinical Psychology*, 74, 898–907.

MONTI, P. M., ABRAMS, D. B., KADDEN, R. M., & COONEY, N. L. (1989). *Treating alcohol dependence*. New York: Guilford.

MONTI, P. M., ROHSENOW, D. J., RUBONIS, A. V., NIAURA, R. S., SIROTA, A. D., COLBY, S. M., et al. (1993). Cue exposure with coping skills treatment for male alcoholics: A preliminary investigation. *Journal of Consulting and Clinical Psychology*, 61, 1011–1019.

MOORE, N. (1965). Behavior therapy in bronchial asthma: A controlled study. *Journal of Psychosomatic Research*, 9, 257–276.

MOORE, V., & CALLIAS, M. (1987). A systematic approach to teaching reading and spelling to a nine-year-old boy with severely impaired literacy skills. *Educational Psychology*, 7, 103–115.

MORGAN, D. L., & MORGAN, R. K. (2001). Single-subject research design: Bringing science to managed care. *American Psychologist*, 56, 119–127.

MORGAN, W. G. (1974). The shaping game: A teaching technique. *Behavior Therapy*, 5, 271–272.

MORGANSTERN, K. P. (1973). Implosive therapy and flooding procedures: A critical review. *Psychological Bulletin*, 79, 318–334.

MORGANSTERN, K. P. (1976). Behavioral interviewing: The initial stages of assessment. In M. Hersen & A. S. Bellack (Eds.), *Behavioral assessment: A practical approach* (pp. 51–76). Oxford, UK: Pergamon.

MORIN, C. M., CULVERT, J. P., & SCHWARTZ, S. M. (1994). Nonpharmacological interventions for insomnia: A meta-analysis of treatment efficacy. *American Journal of Psychiatry*, 151, 1172–1180.

MORIN, C. M. (1993). *Insomnia: Psychological assessment and management*. New York: Guilford.

MORIN, C. M. (2004). Cognitive-behavioral approaches to the treatment of insomnia. *Journal of Clinical Psychiatry*, 65, 33–40.

MORIN, C. M., KOWATCH, R. A., BARRY, T., & WALTON, E. (1993). Cognitive-behavior therapy for late-life insomnia. *Journal of Consulting and Clinical Psychology*, 61, 137–146.

MORIN, C. M., STONE, J., MCDONALD, K., & JONES, S. (1994). Psychological management of insomnia: A clinical replication series with 100 patients. *Behavior Therapy*, 25, 291–309.

MORLEY, S., ECCLESTON, C., & WILLIAMS, A. (1999). Systematic review and meta-analysis of randomized controlled trials of cognitive behavior therapy and behavior therapy for chronic pain in adults, excluding headache. *Pain*, 80, 1–13.

MORRIS, C. W., & COHEN, R. (1982). Cognitive considerations in cognitive behavior modification. *School Psychological Review, 11,* 14–20.

MORRIS, R. J., & KRATOCHWILL, T. R. (1983). *Treating children's fears and phobias.* Elmsford, NY: Pergamon.

MORRISON, A. P. (1998). A cognitive analysis of auditory hallucinations: Are voices to schizophrenia what bodily sensations are to panic? *Behavioural and Cognitive Psychotherapy, 26,* 289–302.

MORRISON, A. P., & RENTON, J. C. (2001). Cognitive therapy for auditory hallucinations: A theory-based approach. *Cognitive and Behavioral Practice, 8,* 147–160.

MORRISON, A. P., RENTON, J., FRENCH, P., & BENTALL, R. P. (2008). *Think you're crazy? Think again: A resource book for cognitive therapy for psychosis.* London: Routledge.

MORRISON, A. P., RENTON, J., WILLIAMS, S., & DUNN, H. (1999). *An effectiveness study of cognitive therapy for psychosis: Preliminary findings.* Paper presented at the 3rd International Conference on Psychological Treatment of Schizophrenia, Oxford, UK.

MORRISON, R. L. (1988). Structured interviews and rating scales. In A. S. Bellack & M. Hersen (Eds.), *Behavioral assessment: A practical handbook* (3rd ed., pp. 252–277). Elmsford, NY: Pergamon.

MORROW, G. R. (1986). Effect of the cognitive hierarchy in the systematic desensitization treatment of anticipatory nausea in cancer patients: A component comparison with relaxation only, counseling, and no treatment. *Cognitive Therapy and Research, 10,* 421–446.

MORROW, G. R., ASBURY, R., HAMMON, S., DOBKIN, P., CARUSO, L., PANDYA, K., et al. (1992). Comparing the effectiveness of behavioral treatment for chemotherapy-induced nausea and vomiting when administered by oncologists, oncology nurses, and clinical psychologists. *Health Psychology, 11,* 250–256.

MORROW, G. R., & MORRELL, C. (1982). Behavioral treatment for the anticipatory nausea and vomiting induced by cancer chemotherapy. *New UK Journal of Medicine, 307,* 1476–1480.

MOSES, A. N., & HOLLANDSWORTH, J. G. (1985). Relative effectiveness of education alone versus stress inoculation training in treatment of

dental phobia. *Behavior Therapy, 16,* 531–537.

MOSS, J., OLIVER, C., HALL, S., ARRON, K., SLONEEM, J., & PETTY, J. (2005). The association between environmental and self-injurious behaviour in Cornelia de Lange syndrome. *Journal of Intellectual Disability Research, 49,* 269–277.

MOWRER, O. H. (1960). *Learning theory and the symbolic processes.* New York: Wiley.

MOWRER, O. H., & MOWRER, W. M. (1938). Enuresis: A method for its study and treatment. *American Journal of Orthopsychiatry, 8,* 436–447.

MUDFORD, O. C. (1995). An intrusive and restrictive alternative to contingent shock. *Behavioral Interventions, 10,* 87–99.

MULICK, P. S., & NAUGLE, A. E. (2004). Behavioral activation for comorbid PTSD and major depression: A case study. *Cognitive and Behavioral Practice, 11,* 378–386.

MUNBY, M., & JOHNSTON, D. W. (1980). Agoraphobia: The long-term follow-up of behavioural treatment. *British Journal of Psychiatry, 137,* 418–427.

MURAN, E., & DIGIUSEPPE, R. [A.] (2000). Rape trauma. In F. M. Dattilio & A. Freeman (Eds.), *Cognitive-behavioral strategies for crisis intervention* (2nd ed., pp. 84–125). New York: Guilford.

MURTAGH, D. R. R., & GREENWOOD, K. M. (1995). Identifying effective psychological treatments for insomnia: A meta-analysis. *Journal of Consulting and Clinical Psychology, 63,* 79–89.

My tonsillectory coloring book. (1969). Bob Knight and Associates.

MYERS, K. M., & DAVIS, M. (2007). Mechanisms of fear extinction. *Molecular Psychiatry, 12,* 120–150.

MYLOTT, K. (1994). Twelve irrational ideas that drive gay men and women crazy. *Journal of Rational-Emotive & Cognitive-Behavior Therapy, 12,* 61–71.

NANGLE, D. W., CARR-NANGLE, R. E., & HANSEN, D. J. (1994). Enhancing generalization of a contingency-management intervention through the use of family problem-solving training: Evaluation with a severely conduct-disordered adolescent. *Child & Family Behavior Therapy, 15,* 65–76.

NANGLE, D. W., & HANSEN, D. J. (1998). Adolescent heterosocial competence

revisited: Implications for an expanded conceptualization for the prevention of high-risk sexual interactions. *Education and Treatment of Children, 21,* 431–446.

NATER, U. M., GAAB, J., RIEF, W., & EHLERT, U. (2006). Recent trends in behavioral medicine. *Current Opinion in Psychiatry, 19,* 180–183.

NATHAN, P. E. (1976). Alcoholism. In H. Leitenberg (Ed.), *Handbook of behavior modification and behavior therapy* (pp. 3–44). Englewood Cliffs, NJ: Prentice Hall.

NATHAN, P. E. (2005). Bring home the psychological immediacy of the Iraqi battlefield. *Pragmatic Case Studies in Psychotherapy, 1,* 1–3.

NATIONAL CENTER FOR HIV, STD AND TB PREVENTION. (2001). *HIV/AIDS Surveillance Report.* Retrieved February 17, 2002, from http://www.cdc.gov/hiv stats/hasr1202.htm

NAWAS, M. M., WELSCH, W. V., & FISHMAN, S. T. (1970). The comparative effectiveness of pairing aversive imagery with relaxation, neutral tasks and muscular tension in reducing snake phobia. *Behaviour Research and Therapy, 6,* 63–68.

NAWAZ, S., GRIFFITHS, P., & TAPPIN, D. (2002). Parent-administered modified dry-bed training for childhood nocturnal enuresis: Evidence for superiority over urine-alarm conditioning when delivery factors are controlled. *Behavioral Interventions, 17,* 247–260.

NAZARIAN, L. F., MECHABER, J., CHARNEY, E., & COULTER, M. P. (1974). Effects of a mailed appointment reminder on appointment keeping. *Pediatrics, 5,* 49–52.

NEAL-BARNETT, A. M., & SMITH, J. M., SR. (1996). African American children and behavior therapy: Considering the Afrocentric approach. *Cognitive and Behavioral Practice, 3,* 351–369.

NEILL, J. (2008). *Meta-analysis research methodology.* Retrieved August 5, 2008. from http://wilderdom.com/research/meta-analysis.html#PrimaryStudies

NEIMEYER, R. A. (2000). Constructivist psychotherapies. In *Encyclopedia of psychology.* Washington, DC: American Psychological Association.

NEIMEYER, R. A., & RASKIN, J. D. (Eds.). (2000). *Constructions of disorder: Meaning-making frameworks for psychotherapy.* Washington, DC: American Psychological Association.

NEIMEYER, R. A., & RASKIN, J. D. (2001). Varieties of constructivism in psychotherapy. In K. S. Dobson (Ed.), *Handbook of cognitive-behavioral therapies* (2nd ed., pp. 393–430). New York: Guilford.

NEISWORTH, J. T., & MOORE, F. (1972). Operant treatment of asthmatic responding with the parent as therapist. *Behavior Therapy, 3,* 95–99.

NELSON, W. M., III, & FINCH, A. J., JR. (2000). Managing anger in youth. In P. C. Kendall (Ed.), *Child and adolescent therapy: Cognitive-behavioral procedures* (2nd ed., pp. 129–170). New York: Guilford.

NELSON, W. M., III, & POLITANO, P. M. (1993). The goal is to say "goodbye" and have the treatment effects generalize and maintain: A cognitive-behavioral view of termination. *Journal of Cognitive Psychotherapy, 7,* 251–263.

NEMETZ, G. H., CRAIG, K. D., & REITH, G. (1978). Treatment of female sexual dysfunction through symbolic modeling. *Journal of Consulting and Clinical Psychology, 46,* 62–73.

NESBITT, E. B. (1973). An escalator phobia overcome in one session of flooding in vivo. *Journal of Behavior Therapy and Experimental Psychiatry, 4,* 405–406.

NESTORIUC, Y., RIEF, W., & MARTIN, A. (2008). Meta-analysis of biofeedback for tension-type headache: Efficacy, specificity, and treatment moderators. *Journal of Consulting and Clinical Psychology, 76,* 379–396.

NEVO, O., & SHAPIRA, J. (1988). The use of humor by pediatric dentists. *Journal of Children in Contemporary Society, 20,* 171–178.

New tool: "Reinforcement" for good work. (1971, December 18). *Business Week,* 76–77.

NEWMAN, C., & ADAMS, K. (2004). Dog gone good: Managing dog phobia in a teenage boy with a learning disability. *British Journal of Learning Disabilities, 32,* 35–38.

NEWMAN, C. F., & HAAGA, D. A. F. (1995). Cognitive skills training. In W. O'Donohue & L. Krasner (Eds.), *Handbook of psychological skills training: Clinical techniques and applications* (pp. 119–143). Boston: Allyn & Bacon.

NEWMAN, M. G., CONSOLI, A., & TAYLOR, C. (1997). Computers in assessment and cognitive behavior treatment of clinical disorders: Anxiety as a case in point. *Behavior Therapy, 28,* 211–235.

NEWMAN, M. G., CONSOLI, A., & TAYLOR, C. (1999). A palm-top computer program for the treatment of generalized anxiety disorder. *Behavior Modification, 23,* 597–619.

NEWMAN, M. G., HOFMANN, S. G., TRABERT, W., ROTH, W. T., & TAYLOR, C. B. (1994). Does behavioral treatment of social phobia lead to cognitive changes? *Behavior Therapy, 25,* 503–517.

NEWMAN, M. G., KENARDY, J., HERMAN, S., & TAYLOR, C. B. (1996). The use of hand-held computers as an adjunct to cognitive-behavior therapy. *Computers in Human Behavior, 12,* 135–143.

NEWMAN, M. G., KENARDY, J., HERMAN, S., & TAYLOR, C. B. (1997). Comparison of palmtop computer-assisted-brief cognitive behavioral treatment for panic disorder. *Journal of Consulting and Clinical Psychology, 65,* 178–183.

NEWSTROM, J., MCCLAUGHLIN, T. F., & SWEENEY, W. J. (1999). The effects of contingency contracting to improve the mechanics of written language with a middle school student with behavior disorders. *Child & Family Behavior Therapy, 21,* 39–48.

NEZIROGLU, F. A., & YARYURA-TOBIAS, J. A. (1993). Exposure, response prevention, and cognitive therapy in the treatment of body dysmorphic disorder. *Behavior Therapy, 24,* 431–438.

NEZU, A. [M.] (1996). The main thing. *the Behavior Therapist, 19,* 36–39.

NEZU, A. M. (2004). Problem solving and behavior therapy revisited. *Behavior Therapy, 35,* 1–33.

NEZU, A. M., & NEZU, C. M. (2008). Ensuring treatment integrity. In A. M. Nezu & C. M. Nezu (Eds.), *Evidence-based outcome research: A practical guide to conducting randomized controlled trials for psychosocial interventions* (pp. 263–281). New York: Oxford University Press.

NEZU, A. M., NEZU, C. M., & D'ZURILLA, T. J. (2007). *Solving life's problems: A 5-step guide to enhanced well-being.* New York: Springer.

NEZU, A. M., NEZU, C. M., D'ZURILLA, T. J., & ROTHENBERG, J. L. (1996). Problem-solving therapy. In J. S. Kantor (Ed.), *Clinical depression during addiction recovery: Processes,* diagnosis, and treatment (pp. 187–219). New York: Marcel Dekker.

NEZU, A. M., NEZU, C. M., & LOMBARDO, E. R. (2001). Cognitive-behavioral therapy for medically unexplained symptoms: A critical review of the treatment literature. *Behavior Therapy, 32,* 537–583.

NEZU, C. M., NEZU, A. M., & HOUTS, P. S. (1993). Multiple applications of problem-solving principles in clinical practice. In K. T. Kuehlwein & H. Rosen (Eds.), *Cognitive therapies in action: Evolving innovative practice* (pp. 353–378). San Francisco: Jossey-Bass.

NICASSIO, P. M., BOYLAN, M. B., & MCCABE, T. G. (1982). Progressive relaxation, EMG biofeedback and biofeedback placebo in the treatment of sleep-onset insomnia. *British Journal of Medical Psychology, 55,* 159–166.

NICHOLSON, N. L., & BLANCHARD, E. B. (1993). A controlled evaluation of behavioral treatment of chronic headache in the elderly. *Behavior Therapy, 24,* 395–408.

NIELSEN, S. L. (2001). Accommodating religion and integrating religious material during rational emotive behavior therapy. *Cognitive and Behavior Practice, 8,* 34–39.

NIETZEL, M. T., BERNSTEIN, D. A., & RUSSELL, R. L. (1988). Assessment of anxiety and fear. In A. S. Bellack & M. Hersen (Eds.), *Behavioral assessment: A practical handbook* (3rd ed., pp. 280–312). Elmsford, NY: Pergamon.

NINNESS, H. A. C., ELLIS, J., & NINNESS, S. K. (1999). Self-assessment as a learned reinforcer during computer interactive math performance: An experimental analysis. *Behavior Modification, 23,* 403–418.

NISHITH, P., NIXON, R. D. V., & RESICK, P. A. (2005). Resolution of trauma-related guilt following treatment of PTSD in female rape victims: A result of cognitive processing therapy targeting comorbid depression? *Journal of Affective Disorders, 86,* 259–265.

NOCELLA, J., & KAPLAN, R. (1982). Training children to cope with dental treatment. *Journal of Pediatric Psychology, 7,* 175–178.

NOMELLINI, S., & KATZ, R. C. (1983). Effects of anger control training on abusive parents. *Cognitive Therapy and Research, 7,* 57–68.

NOVACO, R. W. (1975). *Anger control: The development and evaluation of an experimental treatment*. Lexington, MA: Lexington Books.

NOVACO, R. [W.] (1977a). A stress-inoculation approach to anger management in the training of law enforcement officers. *American Journal of Community Psychology, 5*, 327–346.

NOVACO, R. [W.] (1977b). Stress inoculation: A cognitive therapy for anger and its application to a case of depression. *Journal of Consulting and Clinical Psychology, 45*, 600–608.

NOVICK, J. (1966). Symptomatic treatment of acquired and persistent enuresis. *Journal of Abnormal Psychology, 71*, 363–368.

NUNES, D. L., MURPHY, R. J., & RUPRECHT, M. L. (1977). Reducing self-injurious behavior of severely retarded individuals through withdrawal-of-reinforcement procedures. *Behavior Modification, 1*, 499–516.

NUNN, R. G., NEWTON, K. S., & FAUCHER, P. (1992). 2.5 year follow-up of weight and body mass index values in the Weight Control for Life Program: A descriptive analysis. *Addictive Behaviors, 17*, 579–585.

O'BANION, D. R., & WHALEY, D. L. (1981). *Behavior contracting: Arranging contingencies of reinforcement*. New York: Springer.

O'CALLAGHAN, M. E., & COUVADELLI, B. (1998). Use of self-instructional strategies with three neurologically impaired adults. *Cognitive Therapy and Research, 22*, 91–107.

O'CALLAGHAN, P. M., REITMAN, D., NORTHRUP, J., HUPP, S. D. A., & MURPHY, M. A. (2003). Promoting social skills generalization with ADHD-diagnosed children in a sports setting. *Behavior Therapy, 34*, 313–330.

OCKENE, J. K., EMMONS, K. M., MERMELSTEIN, R. J., PERKINS, K. A., BONOLLO, D. S., VOORHEES, C. C., et al. (2000). Relapse and maintenance issues for smoking cessation. *Health Psychology, 19*, 17–31.

O'CONNOR, R. D. (1969). Modification of social withdrawal through symbolic modeling. *Journal of Applied Behavior Analysis, 2*, 15–22.

O'DONOHUE, W., & NOLL, J. (1995). Problem-solving skills. In W. O'Donohue & L. Krasner (Eds.), *Handbook of psychological skills training: Clinical techniques and applications* (pp. 144–160). Boston: Allyn & Bacon.

OEI, T. P. S., & SHUTTLEWOOD, G. J. (1997). Comparison of specific and nonspecific factors in group cognitive therapy for depression. *Journal of Behavior Therapy and Experimental Psychiatry, 28*, 221–231.

O'FARRELL, T. J. (1994). Marital therapy and spouse-involved treatment with alcoholic patients. *Behavior Therapy, 25*, 391–406.

O'FARRELL, T. J., & FALS-STEWART, W. (2000). Behavioral couples therapy for alcoholism and drug abuse. *the Behavior Therapist, 23*, 49–54, 70.

OFFICE OF INSPECTOR GENERAL. (1996, May). *Mental health services in nursing facilities*. (Publication OEI-02-91-00860). Washington, DC: U.S. Department of Health and Human Services.

OLDENBURG, D. (1994, April 12). In the eye of the beholder. *The Washington Post*, p. E5.

O'LEARY, K. D. (1972). The assessment of psychopathology in children. In H. C. Quay & J. S. Werry (Eds.), *Psychopathological disorders of childhood* (pp. 234–272). New York: Wiley.

O'LEARY, K. D., & RATHUS, J. H. (1993). Clients' perceptions of therapeutic helpfulness in cognitive and marital therapy for depression. *Cognitive Therapy and Research, 17*, 225–233.

O'LEARY, K. D., & WILSON, G. T. (1975). *Behavior therapy: Application and outcome*. Englewood Cliffs, NJ: Prentice Hall.

OLLENDICK, T. [H.], KING, N., & CHORPITA, B. (2006). Empirically supported treatments for children and adolescents. In P. C. Kendall (Ed.), *Child and adolescent therapy: Cognitive-behavioral procedures* (3rd ed., pp. 492–520). New York: Guilford.

OLLENDICK, T. H. (1979). Fear reduction techniques with children. In M. Hersen, R. M. Eisler, & P. M. Miller (Eds.), *Progress in behavior modification* (Vol. 8, pp. 127–168). New York: Academic Press.

OLLENDICK, T. H. (1983). Reliability and validity of the Revised Fear Survey Schedule for Children (FSSC-R). *Behaviour Research and Therapy, 21*, 685–692.

OLLENDICK, T. H., & CERNY, J. A. (1981). *Clinical behavior therapy with children*. New York: Plenum.

OLLENDICK, T. H., & GREENE, R. W. (1998). Principles and practices of behavioral assessment with children. In C. R. Reynolds (Ed.), *Comprehensive clinical psychology: Assessment* (Vol. 4, pp. 131–155). Oxford: Elsevier Science.

OLLENDICK, T. H., HAGOPIAN, L. P., & KING, N. J. (1997). Specific phobias in children. In G. C. L. Davey (Ed.), *Phobia: A handbook of theory, research, and treatment* (pp. 201–224). New York: Wiley.

OLLENDICK, T. H., & MATSON, J. L. (1978). Overcorrection: An overview. *Behavior Therapy, 9*, 830–842.

OLMSTED, M. P., DAVIS, R., ROCKERT, W., IRVINE, M. J., EAGLE, M., & GARNER, D. M. (1991). Efficacy of a brief group psychoeducational intervention for bulimia nervosa. *Behaviour Research and Therapy, 29*, 71–83.

OLSON, R. L., & ROBERTS, M. W. (1987). Alternative treatments for sibling aggression. *Behavior Therapy, 18*, 243–250.

OMIZO, M. M., LO, F. G., & WILLIAMS, E. (1986). Rational-emotive education, self-concept, and locus of control among learning disabled students. *Journal of Humanistic Education and Development, 25*, 58–69.

O'NEILL, R. E., HORNER, R. H., ALBIN, R. W., STOREY, K., & SPRAGUE, J. R. (1990). *Functional analysis of problem behavior: A practical assessment guide*. Pacific Grove, CA: Brooks/Cole.

OPDYKE, J. (2008, July 6). Bad behavior? What does the contract say? *The Providence Sunday Journal*, p. F6.

OPPEL, W. C., HARPER, P. A., & RIDER, R. V. (1968). Social, psychological and neurological factors associated with nocturnal enuresis. *Pediatrics, 42*, 627–641.

O'REILLY, D., & DILLENBURGER, K. (1997). Compliance training as an intervention for antisocial behaviour: A pilot study. In K. Dillenburger, M. F. O'Reilly, & M. Keenan (Eds.), *Advances in behaviour analysis* (pp. 134–156). Dublin, Ireland: University College Dublin Press.

ORGANISTA, K. C. (2006). Cognitive-behavioral therapy with Latinos and Latinas. In P. A. Hays & G. Y. Iwamasa (Eds.), *Culturally responsive cognitive-behavioral therapy: Assessment, practice, and supervision* (pp. 73–96). Washington, DC: American Psychological Association.

ORGANISTA, K. C., & MUÑOZ, R. F. (1996). Cognitive behavioral therapy with Latinos. *Cognitive and Behavioral Practice, 3*, 255–270.

ORLEANS, C. T. (2000). Promoting the maintenance of health behavior change: Recommendations for the next generation of research and practice. *Health Psychology, 19,* 76–83.

ORSILLO, S. M., & ROEMER, L. (Eds.) (2005). *Acceptance and mindfulness-based approaches to anxiety: Conceptualization and treatment.* New York: Springer.

OSMAN, A., BARRIOS, F. X., OSMAN, J. R., SCHNEKLOTH, R., & TROUTMAN, J. A. (1994). The pain anxiety symptoms scale: Psychometric properties in a community sample. *Journal of Behavioral Medicine, 17,* 511–522.

ÖST, L. G. (1989). One-session treatment for specific phobias. *Behaviour Research and Therapy, 27,* 1–7.

ÖST, L. G. (2001). *One-session treatment of a patient with specific phobia* [Videotape]. (Available from http://aabt.org/publication/videotapes/arch_worldround.html)

ÖST, L. [G.], (2008). Efficacy of the third wave of behavioral therapies: A systematic review and meta-analysis. *Behaviour Research and Therapy, 46,* 296–321.

ÖST, L. [G.], BRANDENBERG, M., & ALM, T. (1997). One versus five sessions of exposure in the treatment of flying phobia. *Behaviour Research and Therapy, 35,* 987–996.

ÖST, L. [G.], & BREITHOLZ, E. (2000). Applied relaxation vs. cognitive therapy in the treatment of generalized anxiety disorder. *Behaviour Research and Therapy, 38,* 777–790.

ÖST, L. [G.], FEREBEE, I., & FURMARK, T. (1997). One-session group therapy of spider phobia: Direct versus indirect treatments. *Behaviour Research and Therapy, 35,* 721–732.

ÖST, L. [G.], THULIN, U., & RAMNERÖ, J. (2004). Cognitive behavior therapy vs exposure in vivo in the treatment of panic disorder with agrophobia. *Behaviour Research and Therapy, 42,* 1105–1127.

OSTROFF, R. B., & BOYD, J. H. (1987). Television and suicide: Comment. *New UK Journal of Medicine, 316,* 876–877.

OTTO, M. W. (2006). Disseminating CBT: By the 10,000 or by the 1. *the Behavior Therapist, 29,* 197–198.

OTTO, M. W., & GOULD, R. A. (1995). Maximizing treatment-outcome for panic disorder: Cognitive-behavioral strategies. In M. H. Pollack, M. W. Otto, & J. F. Rosenbaum (Eds.), *Challenges in psychiatric treatment: Pharmacological and psychosocial strategies* (pp. 113–140). New York: Guilford.

OTTO, M. W., GOULD, R. A., & POLLACK, M. H. (1994). Cognitive-behavioral treatment of panic disorder: Considerations for the treatment of patients over the long term. *Psychiatric Annals, 24,* 307–315.

OTTO, M. W., & HINTON, D. E. (2006). Modifying exposure-based CBT for Cambodian refugees with posttraumatic stress disorder. *Cognitive and Behavioral Practice, 13,* 261–270.

OTTO, M. W., PENAVA, S. J., POLLACK, R. A., & SMOLLER, J. W. (1995). Cognitive-behavioral and pharmacologic perspectives on the treatment of post-traumatic stress disorder. In M. H. Pollack, M. W. Otto, & J. F. Rosenbaum (Eds.), *Challenges in psychiatric treatment: Pharmacological and psychosocial strategies* (pp. 219–260). New York: Guilford.

OTTO, M. W., & POLLACK, M. H. (1994). Treatment strategies for panic disorder: A debate. *Harvard Review of Psychiatry, 2,* 166–170.

OTTO, M. W., POLLACK, M. H., GOULD, R. A., WORTHINGTON, J. J., MCARDLE, E. T., & ROSENBAUM, J. F. (2000). A comparison of the efficacy of clonazepam and cognitive-behavioral group therapy for the treatment of social phobia. *Journal of Anxiety Disorders, 14,* 345–358.

OTTO, M. W., POLLACK, M. H., SACHS, G. S., REITER, S. R., MELTZER-BRODY, S., & ROSENBAUM, J. F. (1993). Discontinuation of benzodiazepine treatment: Efficacy of cognitive-behavioral therapy for patients with panic disorder. *American Journal of Psychiatry, 150,* 1485–1490.

OUIMETTE, P. C., FINNEY, J. W., & MOOS, R. H. (1997). Twelve-step and cognitive-behavioral treatment for substance abuse: A comparison of treatment effectiveness. *Journal of Consulting and Clinical Psychology, 65,* 230–240.

OVERHOSER, J. C., & FINE, M. A. (1994). Cognitive-behavioral treatment of excessive interpersonal dependency: A four-stage psychotherapy model. *Journal of Cognitive Psychotherapy: An International Quarterly, 8,* 55–70.

OWUSU-BEMPAH, J. P., & HOWITT, D. (1985). The effects of self-modeling on cigarette smoking behavior. *Current Psychological Research and Reviews, 4,* 133–142.

OZER, E. M., & BANDURA, A. (1990). Mechanisms governing empowerment effects: A self-efficacy analysis. *Journal of Personality and Social Psychology, 58,* 472–486.

PACE, G. M., IVANCIC, M. T., EDWARDS, J. L., IWATA, B. A., & PAGE, T. J. (1985). Assessment of stimulus preference and reinforcer value with profoundly retarded individuals. *Journal of Applied Behavior Analysis, 18,* 249–255.

PADESKY, C. A., & BECK, A. T. (2003). Science and philosophy: Comparison of cognitive therapy and rational emotive behavior therapy. *Journal of Cognitive Psychotherapy, 17,* 211–224.

PANIAGUA, F. A. (1998). *Assessing and treating culturally diverse clients: A practical guide* (2nd ed.). Thousand Oaks, CA: Sage.

PAQUETTE, V., LÉVESQUE, J., MENSOUR, B., LEROUX, J-M., BEUDOIN, G., BOURGOUIN, P., et al. (2003). "Change the mind and you change the brain": Effects of cognitive-behavioral therapy on the neural correlates of spider phobia. *Neuroimage, 18,* 401–409.

PARADIS, C. M., CUKOR, D., & FRIEDMAN, S. (2006). Cognitive-behavioral therapy with Orthodox Jews. In P. A. Hays & G. Y. Iwamasa (Eds.), *Culturally responsive cognitive-behavioral therapy: Assessment, practice, and supervision* (pp. 161–175). Washington, DC: American Psychological Association.

PARADIS, C. M., FRIEDMAN, S., HATCH, M. L., & ACKERMAN, R. (1996). Cognitive behavioral treatment of anxiety disorders in Orthodox Jews. *Cognitive and Behavioral Practice, 3,* 271–288.

PARK, W. D., & WILLIAMS, G. T. (1986). Encouraging elementary school children to refer themselves for counseling. *Elementary School Guidance and Counseling, 21,* 8–14.

PARSONS, T. D., & RIZZO, A. A. (2008). Affective outcomes of virtual reality exposure therapy for anxiety and specific phobias: A meta-analysis. *Journal of Behavior Therapy and Experimental Psychiatry, 39,* 250–261.

PASCHALIS, A. P., KIMMEL, H. D., & KIMMEL, E. (1972). Further study of diurnal instrumental conditioning in the treatment of enuresis nocturna. *Journal of Behavior Therapy and Experimental Psychiatry, 3,* 253–256.

PATTERSON, G. R. (1974). Interventions for boys with conduct problems: Multiple settings, treatments, and criteria. *Journal of Consulting and Clinical Psychology, 42,* 471–481.

PATTERSON, G. R. (1982). *Coercive family processes.* Eugene, OR: Castalia Press.

PATTERSON, G. R., CHAMBERLAIN, P., & REID, J. B. (1982). A comparative evaluation of a parent-training program. *Behavior Therapy, 13,* 638–650.

PATTERSON, G. R., & FORGATCH, M. S. (1985). Therapist behavior as a determinant for client noncompliance: A paradox for the behavior modifier. *Journal of Consulting and Clinical Psychology, 53,* 846–851.

PATTERSON, G. R., & GULLION, M. E. (1976). *Living with children: New methods for parents and teachers.* Champaign, IL: Research Press.

PATTERSON, G. R., RAY, R. S., SHAW, D. A., & COBB, T. A. (1969). *A manual for coding of family interactions.* New York: Microfiche Publications.

PATTERSON, G. R., & REID, J. B. (1970). Reciprocity and coercion: Two facets of social systems. In C. Neuringer & J. L. Michael (Eds.), *Behavior modification in clinical psychology* (pp. 133–177). New York: Appleton-Century-Crofts.

PATTERSON, G. R., REID, J. B., & DISHION, T. J. (1992). *Antisocial boys.* Eugene, OR: Castalia Press.

PAUL, G. L. (1966). *Insight vs. desensitization in psychotherapy.* Stanford, CA: Stanford University Press.

PAUL, G. L. (1969). Outcome of systematic desensitization: II. Controlled investigations of individual treatment, technique variations, and current status. In C. M. Franks (Ed.), *Behavior therapy: Appraisal and status* (pp. 105–159). New York: McGraw-Hill.

PAUL, G. L., & LENTZ, R. J. (1977). *Psychosocial treatment of chronic mental patients: Milieu vs. social learning programs.* Cambridge, MA: Harvard University Press.

PAUL, G. L., & SHANNON, D. T. (1966). Treatment of anxiety through systematic desensitization in therapy groups. *Journal of Abnormal Psychology, 71,* 124–135.

PAVLOV, I. P. (1927). *Conditioned reflexes.* New York: Live-right.

PAVULURI, M. (2008). *What works for bipolar kids.* New York: Guilford.

PEDALINO, E., & GAMBOA, V. U. (1974). Behavior modification and absenteeism: Intervention in one industrial setting. *Journal of Applied Psychology, 59,* 694–698.

PEDEN, A. R., RAYENS, M. K., HALL, L. A., & GRANT, E. (2005). Testing an intervention to reduce negative thinking, depressive symptoms, and chronic stressors in low-income single mothers. *Journal of Nursing Scholarship, 37,* 268–274.

PEED, S., ROBERTS, M., & FOREHAND, R. [L.] (1977). Evaluation of the effectiveness of a standardized parent training program in altering the interaction of mothers and their noncompliant children. *Behavior Modification, 1,* 323–350.

PEMBERTON, J. R., & BORREGO, J., JR. (2007). Increasing acceptance of behavioral child management techniques: What do parents say? *Child & Family Behavior Therapy, 29,* 27–45

PENAVA, S. J., OTTO, M. W., MAKI, K. M., & POLLACK, M. H. (1998). Rate of improvement during cognitive-behavioral group treatment for panic disorder. *Behaviour Research and Therapy, 36,* 665–673.

PENISTON, E. (1975). Reducing problem behaviors in the severely and profoundly retarded. *Journal of Behavior Therapy and Experimental Psychiatry, 6,* 295–299.

PENZIEN, D. B., & HOLROYD, K. A. (1994). Psychosocial interventions in the management of recurrent headache disorders 2: Description of treatment techniques. *Behavioral Medicine, 20,* 64–73.

PERLIS, M., ALOIA, M., MILLIKAN, A., BOEHMLER, J., SMITH, M., GREENBLATT, D., et al. (2000). Behavioral treatment of insomnia: A clinical case series study. *Journal of Behavioral Medicine, 23,* 149–161.

PERSONS, J. B. (1989). *Cognitive therapy in practice: A case formulation approach.* New York: Norton.

PERSONS, J. [B.] (1994). Is behavior therapy boring? *the Behavior Therapist, 17,* 190.

PERSONS, J. B. (1995). Why practicing psychologists are slow to adopt empirically-validated treatments. In S. C. Hayes, V. M. Follette, R. M. Dawes, & K. E. Grady (Eds.), *Scientific standards of psychological practice: Issues and recommendations* (pp. 141–157). Reno, NV: Context Press.

PERSONS, J. B. (1997). Dissemination of effective methods: Behavior therapy's next challenge. *Behavior Therapy, 28,* 465–471.

PERSONS, J. B., BOSTROM, A., & BERTAGNOLLI, A. (1999). Results of randomized controlled trials of cognitive therapy for depression generalize to private practice. *Cognitive Therapy and Research, 23,* 535–548.

PETERS, L. (2000). Discriminant validity of the Social Phobia and Anxiety Inventory (SPAI), the Social Phobias Scale (SPS) and the Social Interaction Anxiety Scale (SIAS). *Behaviour Research and Therapy, 38,* 943–950.

PETERSON, A. L. (2007). Psychosocial management of tics and intentional repetitive behaviors associated with Tourette syndrome. In D. W. Woods, J. C. Piacentini, & J. T. Walkup (Eds.), *Treating Tourette syndrome and tic disorders: A guide for practitioners* (pp. 154–184). New York: Guilford.

PETERSON, A. L., & AZRIN, N. H. (1990, November). *A comparison of behavioral procedures for the treatment of Tourette syndrome.* Paper presented at the meeting of the Association for Advancement of Behavior Therapy, San Francisco.

PETERSON, A. L., & AZRIN, N. H. (1993). Behavioral and pharmacological treatments for Tourette syndrome: A review. *Applied and Preventive Psychology, 2,* 231–242.

PETERSON, A. L., CAMPISE, R. L., & AZRIN, N. H. (1994). Behavioral and pharmacological treatments for tic and habit disorders: A review. *Developmental and Behavioral Pediatrics, 15,* 430–441.

PETERSON, A. L., DIXON, D. C., TALCOTT, W., & KELLEHER, W. J. (1993). Habit reversal treatment of temporomandibular disorders: A pilot investigation. *Journal of Behavior Therapy and Experimental Psychiatry, 24,* 49–55.

PETERSON, L., & BELL-DOLAN, D. (1995). Treatment outcome research in child psychology: Realistic coping with the "Ten Commandments of Methodology." *Journal of Clinical Child Psychology, 24,* 149–162.

PETERSON, L., CROWSON, J., SALDANA, L., & HOLDRIDGE, S. (1999). Of needles and skinned knees: Children's coping with medical procedures and minor injuries for self and others. *Health Psychology, 18,* 197–200.

PETERSON, L., & RIDLEY-JOHNSON, R. (1980). Pediatric hospital response to survey on prehospital preparation for children. *Journal of Pediatric Psychology, 5,* 1–7.

PETERSON, L., SCHULTHEIS, K., RIDLEY-JOHNSON, R., MILLER, D. J., & TRACY, K. (1984). Comparison of three modeling procedures on the presurgical and postsurgical reactions of children. *Behavior Therapy, 15,* 197–203.

PETERSON, L., & SHIGETOMI, C. (1981). The use of coping techniques to minimize anxiety in hospitalized children. *Behavior Therapy, 12,* 1–14.

PETERSON, L., & TREMBLAY, G. (1999). Self-monitoring in behavioral medicine: Children. *Psychological Assessment, 11,* 458–465.

PETERSON, P. L., & LOWE, J. B. (1992). Preventing fetal alcohol exposure: A cognitive behavioral approach. *The International Journal of the Addictions, 27,* 613–626.

PETRONKO, M. R., HARRIS, S. L., & KORMANN, R. J. (1994). Community-based behavioral training approaches for people with mental retardation and mental illness. *Journal of Consulting and Clinical Psychology, 62,* 49–54.

PHILLIPS, D., FISCHER, S. C., & SINGH, R. (1977). A children's reinforcement survey schedule. *Journal of Behavior Therapy and Experimental Psychiatry, 8,* 131–134.

PHILLIPS, E. L. (1968). Achievement Place: Token reinforcement procedures in a home-style rehabilitation setting for "pre-delinquent" boys. *Journal of Applied Behavior Analysis, 1,* 213–223.

PHILLIPS, E. L., PHILLIPS, E. A., FIXSEN, D. L., & WOLF, M. M. (1971). Achievement Place: Modification of the behaviors of pre-delinquent boys within a token economy. *Journal of Applied Behavior Analysis, 4,* 45–59.

PHILLIPS, E. L., PHILLIPS, E. A., WOLF, M. M., & FIXSEN, D. L. (1973). Achievement Place: Development of the elected manager system. *Journal of Applied Behavior Analysis, 6,* 541–561.

PIERCE, K. L., & SCHREIBMAN, L. (1994). Teaching daily living skills to children with autism in unsupervised settings through pictorial self-management. *Journal of Applied Behavior Analysis, 27,* 471–481.

PIERCE, T. W. (1995). Skills training in stress management. In W. O'Donohue & L. Krasner (Eds.), *Handbook of psychological skills training: Clinical techniques and applications* (pp. 306–319). Boston: Allyn & Bacon.

PIERSON, M. R., & GLAESER, B. C. (2005). Extension of research on social skills training using comic strip conversations to students without autism. *Education and Training in Developmental Disabilities, 40,* 279–284.

PIGOTT, H. E., & GONZALES, F. P. (1987). The efficacy of videotape self-modeling to treat an electively mute child. *Journal of Clinical Child Psychology, 16,* 106–110.

PIGOTT, H. E., & HEGGIE, D. L. (1986). Interpreting the conflicting results of individual versus group contingencies on classrooms: The targeted behavior as a mediating variable. *Child & Family Behavior Therapy, 7,* 1–15.

PINA, A. A., SILVERMAN, W. K., FUENTES, R. M., KURTINES, W. M., & WEEMS, C. F. (2003). Exposure-based cognitive-behavioral treatment for phobic and anxiety disorders: Treatment effects and maintenance for Hispanic/Latino relative to European-American youths. *Journal of the American Academy of Child & Adolescent Psychiatry, 42,* 1179–1187.

PINCUS, D. B., SANTUCCI, L. C., EHRENREICH, J. T., & EYBERG, S. M. (2008). The implementation of modified parent-child interaction therapy for youth with separation anxiety disorder. *Cognitive and Behavioral Practice, 15,* 118–125.

PINKERTON, S. S., HUGHES, H., & WENRICH, W. W. (1982). *Behavioral medicine: Clinical applications.* New York: Wiley.

PINKSTON, E. M., LINSK, N. L., & YOUNG, R. N. (1988). Home-based behavioral family therapy of the impaired elderly. *Behavior Therapy, 19,* 331–344.

PINKSTON, M. M., CARRUTH, T. C., & GOGGIN, K. J. (2008). Empathic jelly beans: One behavioral intervention begets another. *the Behavior Therapist, 31,* 53–57.

PITMAN, R. K., ALTMAN, B., GREENWALD, R., LONGPRE, R. E., MACKLIN, M. L., POIRE, R. E., et al. (1991). Psychiatric complications during flooding therapy for post-traumatic stress disorder. *Journal of Clinical Psychiatry, 52,* 17–20.

PITTS, C. E. (1976). Behavior modification—1787. *Journal of Applied Behavior Analysis, 9,* 146–146.

POCHE, C., BROUWER, R., & SWEARINGEN, M. (1981). Teaching self-protection to young children. *Journal of Applied Behavior Analysis, 14,* 169–176.

POCHE, C., YODER, P., & MILTENBERGER, R. [G.] (1988). Teaching self-protection to children using television techniques. *Journal of Applied Behavior Analysis, 21,* 253–261.

POLAHA, J. A., & ALLEN, K. D. (2000). Using technology to automate off-task behavior: Classroom management made simple. *Proven Practice, 2,* 52–56.

POLING, A., & RYAN, C. (1982). Differential-reinforcement-of-other-behavior schedules. *Behavior Modification, 6,* 3–21.

POLLACK, M. H., OTTO, M. W., KASPI, S. P., HAMMERNESS, P. G., & ROSENBAUM, J. F. (1994). Cognitive behavior therapy for treatment-refractory panic disorder. *Journal of Clinical Psychiatry, 55,* 200–205.

POLLACK, M. J., FLEMING, R. K., & SULZER-AZAROFF, B. (1994). Enhancing professional performance through organizational change. *Behavioral Interventions, 9,* 27–42.

POLLARD, N. L. (1998). Development of social interaction skills in preschool children with autism: A review of the literature. *Child & Family Behavior Therapy, 20,* 1–16.

POOLE, A. D., SANSON-FISHER, R. W., GERMAN, G. A., & HARKER, J. (1980). The rapid-smoking technique: Some physiological effects. *Behaviour Research and Therapy, 18,* 581–586.

POSAVAC, H. D., SHERIDAN, S. M., & POSAVAC, S. S. (1999). A cueing procedure to control impulsivity in children with attention deficit hyperactivity disorder. *Behavior Modification, 23,* 234–253.

POSER, E. G. (1970). Toward a theory of behavioral prophylaxis. *Journal of Behavior Therapy and Experimental Psychiatry, 1,* 39–43.

POSER, E. [G.], & KING, M. (1975). Strategies for the prevention of maladaptive fear responses. *Canadian Journal of Behavioural Science, 7,* 279–294.

POSSEL, P., BALDUS, C., HORN, A. B., GROEN, G., & HAUTZINGER, M.

(2005). Influence of general self-efficacy on the effects of a school-based universal primary prevention program of depressive symptoms in adolescents: A randomized and controlled follow-up study. *Journal of Child Psychology and Psychiatry, 46,* 982–994.

POSSELL, L. E., KEHLE, T., MCLOUGHLIN, C. S., & BRAY, M. A. (1999). Self-modeling as an intervention to reduce disruptive classroom behavior. *Cognitive and Behavioral Practice, 6,* 99–105.

POWELL, E. (1996). *Sex on your terms.* Boston: Allyn & Bacon.

POWELL, R. A., SYMBALUK, D. G., & HONEY, P. L. (2008). *Introduction to learning and behavior* (3rd ed.). Belmont, CA: Wadsworth.

POWERS, D. V., THOMPSON, L. W., & GALLAGHER-THOMPSON, D. (2008). The benefits of using psychotherapy skills following treatment for depression: An examination of "Afterwork" and a test of the skills hypothesis in older adults. *Cognitive and Behavioral Practice, 15,* 194–202.

POWERS, M. B., & EMMELKAMP, P. M. G. (2008). Virtual reality exposure therapy for anxiety disorders: A meta-analysis. *Journal of Anxiety Disorders, 22,* 561–569.

POWERS, M. B., SMITS, J. A. J., & TELCH, M. J. (2004). Disentangling the effects of safety-behavior utilization and safety-behavior availability during exposure-based treatment: A placebo-controlled trial. *Journal of Consulting and Clinical Psychology, 72,* 448–454.

PRECIADO, J. (1999). Behavior therapy's commitment to cultural diversity: The case of Hispanics. *the Behavior Therapist, 22,* 199–200, 207.

PREMACK, D. (1965). Reinforcement theory. In D. Levine (Ed.), *Nebraska symposium on motivation* (pp. 123–180). Lincoln: University of Nebraska Press.

PRINCE, D., & DOWRICK, P. W. (1984, November). *Self-modeling in the treatment of depression: Implications for video in behavior therapy.* Paper presented at the meeting of the Association for Advancement of Behavior Therapy, Philadelphia.

PRITCHARD, A., & APPLETON, P. (1988). Management of sleep problems in preschool children. *Early Child Development and Care, 34,* 227–240.

PROCHASKA, J., SMITH, N., MARZILLI, R., COLBY, J., & DONOVAN, W. (1974).

Remote-control aversive stimulation in the treatment of head-banging in a retarded child. *Journal of Behavior Therapy and Experimental Psychiatry, 5,* 285–289.

PROPST, L. R., OSTROM, R., WATKINS, P., DEAN, T., & MASHBURN, D. (1992). Comparative efficacy of religious and non-religious cognitive-behavioral therapy for the treatment of clinical depression in religious individuals. *Journal of Consulting and Clinical Psychology, 60,* 94–103.

PURCELL, D. W., CAMPOS, P. E., & PERILLA, J. L. (1996). Therapy with lesbians and gay men: A cognitive behavioral perspective. *Cognitive and Behavioral Practice, 3,* 391–415.

PURDON, C. (1999). Thought suppression and psychopathology. *Behaviour Research and Therapy, 37,* 1029–1054.

RACHMAN, S. (1959). The treatment of anxiety and phobic reactions by systematic desensitization psychotherapy. *Journal of Abnormal and Social Psychology, 58,* 259–263.

RACHMAN, S. (1967). Systematic desensitization. *Psychological Bulletin, 67,* 93–103.

RACHMAN, S. (1972). Clinical application of observational learning, imitation and modeling. *Behavior Therapy, 3,* 379–397.

RACHMAN, S. (1990). *Fear and courage* (2nd ed.). New York: W. H. Freeman.

RACHMAN, S., & HODGSON, R. (1980). *Obsessions and compulsions.* Englewood Cliffs, NJ: Prentice Hall.

RACHMAN, S., & TEASDALE, J. (1969). *Aversion therapy and behaviour disorders: An analysis.* Coral Gables: University of Miami Press.

RACHMAN, S. J., & WILSON, G. T. (1980). *The effects of psychological therapy* (2nd, enlarged ed.). Oxford, UK: Pergamon.

RAINS, J. C. (1995). Treatment of obstructive sleep apnea in pediatric patients: Behavioral intervention for compliance with nasal continuous positive airway pressure. *Clinical Pediatrics, 34,* 535–541.

RAM, N., & MCCULLAGH, P. (2003). Self-modeling: Influence on psychological responses and physical performance. *The Sport Psychologist, 17,* 220–241.

RAMIREZ, S. Z., & KRATOCHWILL, T. R. (1990). Development of the Fear Survey Schedule for Children With and Without Mental Retardation. *Behavioral Assessment, 12,* 457–470.

RANKIN, W. H. (1960). *The man who rode the thunder.* Englewood Cliffs, NJ: Prentice Hall.

RAO, N., MOELY, B. E., & LOCKMAN, J. J. (1987). Increasing social participation in preschool social isolates. *Journal of Clinical Child Psychology, 16,* 178–183.

RAO, P. A., BEIDEL, D. C., & MURRAY, M. J. (2008). Social skills interventions for children with Asperger's syndrome or high-functioning autism: A review and recommendations. *Journal of Autism and Developmental Disorders, 38,* 353–361.

RAPEE, R. M. (2008). Prevention of mental disorders: Promises, limitations, and barriers. *Cognitive and Behavioral Practice, 15,* 47–52.

RAPP, J. T., MILTENBERGER, R. G., GALENSKY, T. L., ROBERTS, J., & ELLINGSON, S. A. (1999). Brief functional analysis and simplified habit reversal treatment of thumb sucking in fraternal twin brothers. *Child & Family Behavior Therapy, 21,* 1–17.

RAPP, J. T., MILTENBERGER, R. G., LONG, E. S., ELLIOTT, A. J., & LUMLEY, V. A. (1998). Simplified habit reversal treatment for chronic hair pulling in three adolescents: A clinical replication with direct observation. *Journal of Applied Behavior Analysis, 31,* 299–302.

RASING, E. J., CONINX, F., DUKER, P. C., & VAN DEN HURK, A. J. (1994). Acquisition and generalization of social behavior in language-disabled deaf adolescents. *Behavior Modification, 18,* 411–442.

RASMUSSEN, K., & O'NEILL, R. E. (2006). The effects of fixed-time reinforcement schedules on problem behavior of children with emotional and behavioral disorders in a day-treatment classroom setting. *Journal of Applied Behavioral Analysis, 39,* 453–457.

RATHOD, S., KINGDON, D., WEIDEN, P., & TURKINGTON, D. (2008). Cognitive-behavioral therapy for medication-resistant schizophrenia: A review. *Journal of Psychiatric Practice, 14,* 22–33.

RATHUS, J. H., CAVUOTO, N. & PASSARELLI, V. (2006). Dialectical behavior therapy (DBT): A mindfulness-based treatment for intimate partner violence. In R. A. Baer (Ed.), *Mindfulness-based treatment approaches: Clinician's guide to evidence base and applications* (pp. 333–358). San Diego: Elsevier Academic Press.

RATHUS, S. A. (1973). A 30-item schedule for assessing assertive behavior. *Behavior Therapy, 4,* 398–406.

RAUE, P. J., CASTONGUAY, L. G., & GOLDFRIED, M. R. (1993). The working alliance: A comparison of two therapies. *Psychotherapy Research, 3,* 197–207.

RAUE, P. J., & GOLDFRIED, M. R. (1994). The therapeutic alliance in cognitive-behavior therapy. In A. O. Horvath & L. S. Greenberg (Eds.), *The working alliance: Theory, research, and practice* (pp. 131–152). New York: Wiley.

RAW, M., & RUSSELL, M. A. H. (1980). Rapid smoking, cue exposure and support in the modification of smoking. *Behaviour Research and Therapy, 18,* 363–372.

REDD, W. [H.] (1980). Stimulus control and extinction of psychosomatic symptoms in cancer patients in protective isolation. *Journal of Consulting and Clinical Psychology, 48,* 448–455.

REDD, W. H., & ANDRYKOWSKI, M. A. (1982). Behavioral intervention in cancer treatment: Controlling aversion reactions to chemotherapy. *Journal of Consulting and Clinical Psychology, 50,* 1018–1029.

REDD, W. H., MANNE, S. L., PETERS, B., JACOBSEN, P. B., & SCHMIDT, H. (1994). Fragrance administration to reduce anxiety during MR imaging. *Journal of Magnetic Resonance, 4,* 623–626.

REE, M. J., & CRAIGIE, M. A. (2007). Outcomes following mindfulness-based cognitive therapy in a heterogenous sample of adult outpatients. *Behaviour Change, 24,* 70–86.

REHM, L. P. (1988). Assessment of depression. In A. S. Bellack & M. Hersen (Eds.), *Behavioral assessment: A practical handbook* (3rd ed., pp. 313–364). Elmsford, NY: Pergamon.

REHM, L. P., & ROKKE, P. D. (1988). Self-management therapies. In K. S. Dobson (Ed.), *Handbook of cognitive-behavioral therapies* (pp. 136–166). New York: Guilford.

REID, J. B., EDDY, M., BANK, L., & FETROW, R. (1994, November). *Some preliminary findings from a universal prevention program for conduct disorder.* Paper presented at the Fourth Annual National Prevention Conference, Washington, DC.

REID, J. B., PATTERSON, G. R., & SNYDER, J. (Eds.). (2002). *Antisocial behavior in children and adolescents: A developmental analysis and model for intervention.* Washington, DC: American Psychological Association.

REID, R. (1996). Research in self-monitoring with students with learning disabilities: The present, the prospects, the pitfalls. *Journal of Learning Disabilities, 29,* 317–331.

REID, R. (1999). Attention deficit hyperactivity disorder: Effective methods for the classroom. *Focus on Exceptional Children, 32,* 1–20.

REIDEL, B. W., & LICHSTEIN, K. L. (2000). Insomnia in older adults. In W. K. Whitbourne (Ed.), *Psychopathology in later adulthood* (pp. 299–322). New York: Wiley.

REIGADA, L. C., FISHER, P. H., CUTLER, C., & WARNER, C. M. (2008). An innovative treatment approach for children with anxiety disorders and medically unexplained somatic complaints. *Cognitive and Behavioral Practice, 15,* 140–147.

REIMRINGER, M. J., MORGAN, S. W., & BRAMWELL, P. F. (1970). Succinylcholine as a modifier of acting-out behavior. *Clinical Medicine, 77,* 28–29.

REINECKE, M. A. (2000). Suicide and depression. In F. M. Dattilio & A. Freeman (Eds.), *Cognitive-behavioral strategies for crisis intervention* (2nd ed., pp. 84–125). New York: Guilford.

REITMAN, D., HUMMEL, R., FRANZ, D. Z., & GROSS, A. M. (1998). A review of methods and instruments for assessing externalizing disorders: Theoretical and practical considerations in rendering a diagnosis. *Clinical Psychology Review, 18,* 555–584.

RENFREY, G. S. (1992). Cognitive-behavior therapy and the Native American client. *Behavior Therapy, 23,* 321–340.

RENTZ, T. O., POWERS, M. B., SMITS, J. A. J., COUGLE, J. R., & TELCH, M. J. (2003). Active-imaginal exposure: Examination of a new behavioral treatment for cynophobia (dog phobia). *Behaviour Research and Therapy, 41,* 1337–1353.

RESICK, P. A., MONSON, C. M., & RIZVI, S. L. (2008). Posttraumatic stress disorder. In D. H. Barlow (Ed.), *Clinical handbook of psychological disorders: A step-by-step treatment manual* (4th ed., pp. 65–122). New York: Guilford.

RESICK, P. A., NISHITH, P., WEAVER, T. L., ASTIN, M. C., & FEUER, C. A. (2002). A comparison of cognitive-processing therapy with prolonged exposure and a waiting condition for the treatment of chronic post-traumatic stress disorder in female rape victims. *Journal of Consulting and Clinical Psychology, 70,* 867–879.

RESICK, P. A., & SCHNICKE, M. K. (1992). Cognitive processing therapy for sexual assault victims. *Journal of Consulting and Clinical Psychology, 60,* 748–756.

RESICK, P. A., & SCHNICKE, M. K. (1993). *Cognitive processing therapy for rape victims: A treatment manual.* Thousand Oaks, CA: Sage.

RESNICK, H., ACIERNO, R., KILPATRICK, D. G., & HOLMES, M. (2005). Description of an early intervention to prevent substance abuse and psychopathology in recent rape victims. *Behavior Modification, 29,* 156–188.

REYNA, T. (1996). Personal communication.

REYNOLDS, L. K., & KELLEY, M. L. (1997). The efficacy of a response cost-based treatment package for managing aggressive behavior in preschoolers. *Behavior Modification, 21,* 216–230.

RICE, J. M., & LUTZKER, J. R. (1984). Reducing noncompliance to follow-up appointment keeping at a family practice center. *Journal of Applied Behavior Analysis, 17,* 303–311.

RICHARD, J. (1995). Behavioral treatment of an atypical case of obsessive compulsive disorder. *the Behavior Therapist, 18,* 134–135.

RICHARDS, D. A., LOVELL, K., & MARKS, I. M. (1994). Post-traumatic stress disorder: Evaluation of a behavioral treatment program. *Journal of Traumatic Stress, 7,* 669–680.

RICHARDSON, F. C., & SUINN, R. M. (1973). A comparison of traditional systematic desensitization, accelerated massed desensitization, and anxiety management training in the treatment of mathematics anxiety. *the Behavior Therapist, 4,* 212–218.

RICKARDS-SCHLICHTING, K. A., KEHLE, T. J., & BRAY, M. A. (2004). A self-modeling intervention for high school students with public speaking anxiety. *Journal of Applied School Psychology, 20(2),* 47–60.

RICKETTS, R. W., GOZA, A. B., & MATESE, M..(1993). A 4-year follow-up of treatment of self-injury. *Journal of Behavior Therapy and Experimental Psychiatry, 24,* 57–62.

RIECKERT, J., & MOLLER, A. T. (2000). Rational-emotive behavior therapy in the treatment of adult victims of childhood sexual abuse. *Journal of Rational-Emotive & Cognitive-Behavior Therapy, 18,* 87–101.

RIETVELD, C. M. (1983). The training of choice behaviours in Down's syndrome and nonretarded preschool children. *Australia and New Zealand Journal of Developmental Disabilities, 9,* 75–83.

RIMM, D. C., DEGROOT, J. C., BOORD, P., HEIMAN, J., & DILLOW, P.V. (1971). Systematic desensitization of an anger response. *Behaviour Research and Therapy, 9,* 273–280.

RIMM, D. C., & MASTERS, J. C. (1979). *Behavior therapy: Techniques and empirical findings* (2nd ed.). New York: Academic Press.

RIMM, D. C., SAUNDERS, W. D., & WESTEL, W. (1975). Thought stopping and covert assertion in the treatment of snake phobias. *Journal of Consulting and Clinical Psychology, 43,* 92–93.

RISLEY, T. R. (1968). The effects and side effects of punishing the autistic behaviors of a deviant child. *Journal of Applied Behavior Analysis, 1,* 21–34.

RISLEY, T. R. (1995). Get a life! Positive behavioral intervention for challenging behavior through Life Arrangement and Life Coaching. In L. K. Koegel, R. L. Koegel, & G. Dunlap (Eds.), *Community, school, family, and social inclusion through positive behavioral support.* Baltimore: Brookes.

RISO, L. P., DU TOIT, P. L., STEIN, D. J., & YOUNG, J. E. (Eds.). (2007). *Cognitive schemas and core beliefs in psychological problems: A scientist-practitioner guide.* Washington, DC: American Psychological Association.

RITTER, B. (1968a). Effect of contact desensitization on avoidance behavior, fear ratings, and self-evaluative statements. *Proceedings of the American Psychological Association* (pp. 527–528). Washington, DC: American Psychological Association.

RITTER, B. (1968b). The group desensitization of children's snake phobias using vicarious and contact desensitization procedures. *Behaviour Research and Therapy, 6,* 1–6.

RITTER, B. (1969a). Eliminating excessive fears of the environment through contact desensitization. In J. D. Krumboltz & C. E. Thoresen (Eds.), *Behavioral counseling: Cases and techniques* (pp. 168–178). New York: Holt, Rinehart & Winston.

RITTER, B. (1969b). Treatment of acrophobia with contact desensitization. *Behaviour Research and Therapy, 7,* 41–45.

RITTER, B. (1969c). The use of contact desensitization, demonstration-plus-relaxation and demonstration alone in the treatment of acrophobia. *Behaviour Research and Therapy, 7,* 157–164.

RITTERBAND, L. M., ANDERSSON, G., CHRISTENSEN, H. M., CARLBRING, P. & CUIJPERS, P. (2006). Directions for the International Society for Research on Internet Interventions (ISRII). *Journal of Medical Internet Research, 8,* e23.

RIVERA, D., & SMITH, D. D. (1988). Using a demonstration strategy to teach midschool students with learning disabilities how to compute long division. *Journal of Learning Disabilities, 21,* 77–81.

RIZZO, A. A., GRAAP, K., PERLMAN, K., MCLAY, R. N., ROTHBAUM, B. O., REGER, G., et al. (2008). Virtual Iraq: Initial results from a VR exposure therapy application for OIF/OEF combat-related posttraumatic stress disorder. In J. D. Westwood et al. (Eds.), *Studies in health technology and informatics* (pp. 420–425). Amsterdam, NL: IOS Press.

RIZZO, A. A., REGER, G., GAHM, G., DIFEDE, J., & ROTHBAUM, B. O. (2008). Virtual reality exposure therapy for combat related PTSD. In P. Shiromani, T. Keane, & J. LeDoux (Eds.), *Post-traumatic stress disorder: Basic science and clinical practice.* Totowa, NJ: Humana Press.

ROBB, H. B. (2001). Facilitating rational emotive behavior therapy by including religious beliefs. *Cognitive and Behavioral Practice, 8,* 29–34.

ROBERTS, M., WHITE, R., & MCLAUGHLIN, T. F. (1997). Useful classroom accommodations for teaching children with ADD and ADHD. *Journal of Special Education, 21,* 71–84.

ROBIN, A. L., & FOSTER, S. L. (1989). *Negotiating parent adolescent conflict: A behavioral-family-systems approach.* New York: Guilford.

ROBINS, C. J., & HAYES, A. M. (1993). An appraisal of cognitive therapy. *Journal of Consulting and Clinical Psychology, 61,* 205–214.

ROBINS, C. J., SCHMIDT, H., III, & LINEHAN, M. M. (2004). Dialectical behavior therapy: Synthesizing radical acceptance with skillful means. In S. C. Hayes, V. M. Follette, & M. Linehan (Eds.), *Mindfulness and acceptance: Expanding the cognitive-behavioral tradition* (pp. 30–44). New York: Guilford.

ROEMER, L., & ORSILLO, S. M. (2007). An open trial of an acceptance-based behavior therapy for generalized anxiety disorder. *Behavior Therapy, 38,* 72–85.

ROEMER, L., & ORSILLO, S. M. (2008). *Mindfulness- and acceptance-based behavioral therapies in practice.* New York: Guilford.

ROHSENOW, D. J., MONTI, P. M., MARTIN, R. A., MICHALEC, E., & ABRAMS, D. B. (2000). Brief coping skills treatment for cocaine abuse: 12-month substance use outcomes. *Journal of Consulting and Clinical Psychology, 68,* 515–520.

ROJAHN, J., HAMMER, D., & KROEGER, T. L. (1997). Stereotypy. In N. N. Singh (Ed.), *Prevention and treatment of severe behavior problems: Models and methods in developmental disabilities* (pp. 199–216). Pacific Grove, CA: Brooks/Cole.

ROKKE, P. D., & AL'ABSI, M. (1992). Matching pain coping strategies to the individual: A prospective validation of the cognitive coping strategy inventory. *Journal of Behavioral Medicine, 15,* 611–625.

ROKKE, P. D., TOMHAVE, J. A., & JOCIC, Z. (1999). The role of client choice and target selection in self-management therapy for depression in older adults. *Psychology and Aging, 14,* 155–169.

ROKKE, P. D., TOMHAVE, J. A., & JOCIC, Z. (2000). Self-management therapy and educational group therapy for depressed elders. *Cognitive Therapy and Research, 24,* 99–119.

ROLIDER, A., & VAN HOUTEN, R. (1984). Training parents to use extinction to eliminate nighttime crying by gradually increasing the criteria for ignoring crying. *Education and Treatment of Children, 7,* 119–124.

ROLLINGS, J. P., BAUMEISTER, A. A., & BAUMEISTER, A. A. (1977). The use of overcorrection procedures to eliminate the stereotyped behaviors of retarded individuals: An analysis of collateral behaviors and generalization of suppressive effects. *Behavior Modification, 1,* 29–46.

RONAN, K., KENDALL, P. C., & ROWE, M. (1994). Negative affectivity in children: Development and validation of a self-statement questionnaire. *Cognitive Therapy and Research 18*, 509–528.

RORTVEDT, A. K., & MILTENBERGER, R. G. (1994). Analysis of a high-probability instructional sequence and time-out in the treatment of child noncompliance. *Journal of Applied Behavior Analysis, 27*, 327–330.

ROSALES-RUIZ, J., & BAER, D. M. (1997). Behavioral cusps: A developmental and pragmatic concept for behavior analysis. *Journal of Applied Behavior Analysis, 30*, 533–544.

ROSEN, G. M. (1995). On the origin of eye movement desensitization. *Journal of Behavior Therapy and Experimental Psychiatry, 26*, 121–122.

ROSEN, G. M., GLASGOW, R. E., & BARRERA, M. (1976). A controlled study to assess the clinical efficacy of totally self-administered systematic desensitization. *Journal of Consulting and Clinical Psychology, 44*, 208–217.

ROSEN, G. M., & ORENSTEIN, H. (1976). A historical note on thought stopping. *Journal of Consulting and Clinical Psychology, 44*, 1016–1017.

ROSEN, H. S., & ROSEN, L. A. (1983). Eliminating stealing: Use of stimulus control with an elementary student. *Behavior Modification, 7*, 56–63.

ROSEN, R., GOLDSTEIN, I., & HUANG, X-Y. (2007). The treatment satisfaction scale (TSS) is a sensitive measure of treatment effectiveness for both patients and partners: Results of a randomized controlled trial with vardenafil. *Journal of Sexual Medicine, 4*, 1009–1021.

ROSENHAN, D. L. (1973). On being sane in insane places. *Science, 179*, 250–258.

ROSENLICHT, N. (2007). Cognitive-behavioral group therapy for insomnia. *International Journal of Group Psychotherapy, 57*, 117–121.

ROSENTHAL, R. (1969). Interpersonal expectations: Effects of the experimenter's hypothesis. In R. Rosenthal & R. L. Rosnow (Eds.), *Artifact in behavioral research* (pp. 181–277). New York: Academic Press.

ROSENTHAL, T. L., & STEFFEK, B. D. (1991). Modeling applications. In F. H. Kanfer & A. P. Goldstein (Eds.), *Helping people change* (4th ed., pp. 70–122). New York: Pergamon.

ROSS, L. (1977). The intuitive psychologist and his shortcomings. In L. Berkowitz (Ed.), *Advances in experimental social psychology* (Vol. 10, pp. 173–220). New York: Academic Press.

ROSSELLO, J., & BERNAL, G. (1999). The efficacy of cognitive-behavioral and interpersonal treatments for depression in Puerto Rican adolescents. *Journal of Consulting and Clinical Psychology, 67*, 734–745.

ROSSY, L. A., BUCKELEW, S. P., DORR, N., HAFFLUND, K. J., THAYER, J. F., MCINTOSH, M. J., et al. (1999). A meta-analysis of fibromyalgia treatment interventions. *Annals of Behavioral Medicine, 21*, 180–191.

ROTH, A., & FONAGY, P. (1997). *What works for whom? A critical review of psychotherapy research*. London: Guilford.

ROTHBAUM, B. O. (1992). The behavioral treatment of trichotillomania. *Behavioural Psychotherapy, 20*, 85–90.

ROTHBAUM, B. O., ANDERSON, P., ZIMAND, E., HODGES, L., LANG, D., & WILSON, J. (2006). Virtual reality exposure therapy and standard (in vivo) exposure therapy in the treatment of fear of flying. *Behavior Therapy, 37*, 80–90.

ROTHBAUM, B. O., ASTIN, M. C., & MARSTELLER, F. (2005). Prolonged exposure versus eye movement desensitization (EMDR) for PTSD rape victims. *Journal of Traumatic Stress, 18*, 607–616.

ROTHBAUM, B. O., & HODGES, L. F. (1999). The use of virtual reality exposure in the treatment of anxiety disorders. *Behavior Modification, 23*, 507–525.

ROTHBAUM, B. O., HODGES, L. F., KOOPER, R., OPDYKE, D., WILLIFORD, J. S., & NORTH, M. (1995a). Effectiveness of computer-generated (virtual reality) graded exposure in the treatment of acrophobia. *The American Journal of Psychiatry, 152*, 626–628.

ROTHBAUM, B. O., HODGES, L. F., KOOPER, R., OPDYKE, D., WILLIFORD, J. S., & NORTH, M. (1995b). Virtual reality graded exposure in the treatment of acrophobia: A case report. *Behavior Therapy, 26*, 547–554.

ROTHBAUM, B., HODGES, L., READY, D., GRAAP, K., & ALARCON, R. (2001). Virtual reality exposure therapy for Vietnam veterans with posttraumatic stress disorder. *Journal of Clinical Psychiatry, 62*, 617–622.

ROTHBAUM, B. O., HODGES, L. [F.], SMITH, S., LEE, J. H., & PRICE, L. (2000). A controlled study of virtual reality exposure therapy for the fear of flying. *Journal of Consulting and Clinical Psychology, 68*, 1020–1026.

ROTHBAUM, B. O., MEADOWS, E. A., RESICK, P., & FOY, D. W. (2000). Cognitive-behavioral therapy. In E. B. Foa, T. M. Keane, & M. J. Friedman (Eds.), *Effective treatments for PTSD* (pp. 60–83). New York: Guilford.

ROTHBAUM, B. O., & NINAN, P. T. (1999). Manual for the cognitive-behavioral treatment of trichotillomania. In D. J. Stein & G. A. Christenson (Eds.), *Trichotillomania* (pp. 263–284). Washington, DC: American Psychiatric Press.

ROTHERAM-BORUS, M. J., KOOPMAN, C., HAIGNERE, C., & DAVIES, M. (1991). Reducing HIV sexual risk behaviors among runaway adolescents. *Journal of the American Medical Association, 266*, 1237–1241.

ROUNSAVILLE, B. J., ROSEN, M., & CARROLL, K. M. (2008). Medication. In S. T. Higgins, K. Silverman, & S. H. Heil (Eds.), *Contingency management in substance abuse treatment* (pp. 140–158). New York: Guilford.

ROWA, K., ANTONY, M. M., & SWINSON, R. P. (2000). Behavioural treatment of obsessive compulsive disorder. *Behavioural and Cognitive Psychotherapy, 28*, 353–360.

RUDD, M. D., JOINER, T., & RAJAB, M. H. (2001). *Treating suicidal behavior: An effective, time-limited approach*. New York: Guilford.

RUSCH, F. R., HUGHES, C., & WILSON, P. G. (1995). Utilizing cognitive strategies in the acquisition of employment skills. In W. O'Donohue & L. Krasner (Eds.), *Handbook of psychological skills training: Clinical techniques and applications* (pp. 363–382). Boston: Allyn & Bacon.

RUSCH, F. R., MARTIN, J. E., LAGOMARCINO, T. R., & WHITE, D. M. (1987). Teaching task sequencing via verbal mediation. *Education and Training in Mental Retardation, 22*, 229–235.

RUSCH, F. R., MORGAN, T. K., MARTIN, J. E., RIVA, M., & AGRAN, M. (1985). Competitive employment: Teaching mentally retarded employees self-instructional strategies. *Applied Research in Mental Retardation, 6*, 389–407.

RUSCH, M. D., GRUNERT, B. K., MENDELSOHN, R. A., & SMUCKER, M. R. (2000). Imagery rescripting for recurrent, distressing images. *Cognitive and Behavioral Practice, 7,* 173–182.

RUSHALL, B. S., & SIEDENTOP, D. (1972). *The development and control of behavior in sport and physical education.* Philadelphia: Lea & Febiger.

RUSHTON, H. G. (1989). Nocturnal enuresis: Epidemiology, evaluation, and currently available treatment options. *The Journal of Pediatrics, 114,* 691–696.

RYCHTARIK, R. G., SILVERMAN, W. K., LANDINGHAM, W. P. V., & PRUE, D. M. (1984). Treatment of an incest victim with implosive therapy: A case study. *Behavior Therapy, 15,* 410–420.

SACHS, D. A. (1975). Behavioral techniques in a residential nursing home facility. *Journal of Behavior Therapy and Experimental Psychiatry, 26,* 123–127.

SACKETT, D. L., & HAYNES, R. B. (Eds.). (1976). *Compliance with therapeutic regimens.* Baltimore: Johns Hopkins University Press.

SAFER, D. L., TELCH, C. F., & AGRAS, W. (2001). Dialectical behavior therapy for bulimia nervosa. *American Journal of Psychiatry, 158,* 632–634.

SAFREN, S. A. (2001). The continuing need for diversity in cognitive-behavioral therapy training and research. *the Behavior Therapist, 24,* 209.

SAFREN, S. A., HOLLANDER, G., HART, T. A., & HEIMBERG, R. G. (2001). Cognitive-behavioral therapy with lesbian, gay, and bisexual youth. *Cognitive and Behavioral Practice, 8,* 215–223.

SAHAKIAN, B., & CHARLESWORTH, G. (1994). Masked bereavement presenting as agoraphobia. *Behavioural and Cognitive Psychotherapy, 22,* 177–180.

SAIGH, P. A. (1986). In vitro flooding in the treatment of a 6-yr-old boy's posttraumatic stress disorder. *Behaviour Research and Therapy, 24,* 685–688.

SAIGH, P. A. (1987). In vitro flooding of an adolescent's post-traumatic stress disorder. *Journal of Clinical Child Psychology, 16,* 147–150.

SAKUTA, T. (1999). Recent progress in behavioral psychotherapy in Japan. *the Behavior Therapist, 22,* 76–77, 91

SALVY, S.-J., MULICK, J. A., BUTTER, E., BARTLETT, R. K., & LINSCHEID, T. R. (2004). Contingent electric shock (SIBIS) and a conditioned punisher eliminate severe head banging in a preschool child. *Behavioral Interventions, 19,* 59–72.

SANAVIO, E. (1999). Behavioral and cognitive therapy in Italy. *the Behavior Therapist, 22,* 69–75.

SANDERS, M. R., MARKIE-DADDS, C., TULLY, L. A., & BOR, W. (2000). The Triple P-Positive Parenting Program: A comparison of enhanced, standard, and self-directed behavioral family intervention for parents and children with early onset conduct problems. *Journal of Consulting and Clinical Psychology, 68,* 624–640.

SANDERSON, A., & CARPENTER, R. (1992). Eye movement desensitization versus image confrontation: A single-session crossover study of 58 phobic subjects. *Journal of Behavior Therapy and Experimental Psychiatry, 23,* 269–275.

SANDERSON, W. C. (2003). Why empirically supported psychological treatments are important. *Behavior Modification, 27,* 290–299.

SANDERSON, W. C., BECK, A. T., & McGINN, L. K. (1994). Cognitive therapy for generalized anxiety disorder: Significance of comorbid personality disorders. *Journal of Cognitive Psychotherapy, 8,* 13–18.

SANTIAGO-RIVERA, A., KANTER, J., BENSON, G., DEROSE, T., ILLES, R., & REYES, W. (2008). Behavioral activation as an alternative treatment approach for Latinos with depression. *Psychotherapy: Theory, Research, Practice, Training, 45,* 173–185.

SAPER, Z., BLANK, M. K., & CHAPMAN, L. (1995). Implosive therapy as an adjunct treatment in a psychotic disorder: A case report. *Journal of Behavior Therapy and Experimental Psychiatry, 26,* 157–160.

SARASON, I. G. (1975). Test anxiety and the self-disclosing coping model. *Journal of Consulting and Clinical Psychology, 43,* 148–153.

SASSO, G. M., MUNDSCHENK, N. A., MELLOY, K. J., & CASEY, S. D. (1998). A comparison of the effects of organismic and setting variables on the social interaction behavior of children with developmental disabilities and autism. *Focus on Autism and Other Developmental Disabilities, 13,* 2–16.

SAUNDERS, D. G. (1976). A case of motion sickness treated by systematic desensitization and in vivo relaxation.

Journal of Behavior Therapy and Experimental Psychiatry, 7, 381–382.

SCHEERES, K., WENSING, M., KNOOP, H., & BLEIJENBERG, G. (2008). Implementing cognitive behavioral therapy for chronic fatigue syndrome in a mental health center: A benchmarking evaluation. *Journal of Consulting and Clinical Psychology, 76,* 163–171.

SCHELL, B. J. (1996). Chronic disease and psychotherapy: Part I. *Psychotherapy Bulletin, 31,* 21–25.

SCHLESER, R., MEYERS, A., & COHEN, R. (1981). Generalization of self-instructions: Effects of general versus specific content, active rehearsal, and cognitive level. *Child Development, 52,* 335–340.

SCHMIDT, A. J. M., GIERLINGS, R. E. H., & PETERS, M. L. (1989). Environment and interoceptive influences on chronic low back pain behavior. *Pain, 38,* 137–143.

SCHMIDT, N. B., JOINER, T. E., YOUNG, J. E., & TELCH, M. J. (1995). The Schema Questionnaire: Investigation of psychometric properties and the hierarchical structure of a measure of maladaptive schemas. *Cognitive Therapy and Research, 19,* 295–321.

SCHMIDT, N. B., & WOOLAWAY-BICKEL, K. (2000). The effects of treatment compliance on outcome in cognitive-behavioral therapy for panic disorder: Quality versus quantity. *Journal of Consulting and Clinical Psychology, 68,* 13–18.

SCHMIDT, U. (1989). Behavioural psychotherapy for eating disorders. *International Review of Psychiatry, 1,* 245–256.

SCHMITZ, J. M., RHOADES, H., & GRABOWSKI, J. (1994). A menu of potential reinforcers in a methadone maintenance program. *Journal of Substance Abuse Treatment, 11,* 425–431.

SCHNEIDER, A. J., MATAIX-COLS, D., MARKS, I. M., & BACHOFEN, M. (2005). Internet-guided self-help with or without exposure therapy for phobic and panic disorders. *Psychotherapy and Psychosomatics, 74,* 154–164.

SCHNELLE, J. F., KIRCHNER, R. E., MACRAE, J. W., McNEES, M. P., ECK, R. H., SNODGRASS, S., et al. (1978). Police evaluation research: An experimental and cost-benefit analysis of a helicopter patrol in a high crime area. *Journal of Applied Behavior Analysis, 11,* 11–21.

SCHNURR, P. P., FRIEDMAN, M. J., ENGEL, C. C., FOA, E. B., SHEA, M. T., CHOW, B. K., et al. (2007). Cognitive behavioral therapy for posttraumatic stress disorder in women: A randomized controlled trial. *Journal of the American Medical Association*, 297, 820–830.

SCHOLING, A., & EMMELKAMP, P. M. G. (1993a). Cognitive and behavioural treatments of fear of blushing, sweating or trembling. *Behaviour Research and Therapy*, 31, 155–170.

SCHOLING, A., & EMMELKAMP, P. M. G. (1993b). Exposure with and without cognitive therapy for generalized social phobia: Effects of individual and group treatment. *Behaviour Research and Therapy*, 31, 667–681.

SCHROEDER, H. E., & BLACK, M. J. (1985). Unassertiveness. In M. Hersen & A. S. Bellack (Eds.), *Handbook of clinical behavior therapy with adults* (pp. 509–530). New York: Plenum.

SCHULMAN, M. (1974). Control of tics by maternal reinforcement. *Journal of Behavior Therapy and Experimental Psychiatry*, 5, 95–96.

SCHULZ, P. M., HUBER, L. C., & RESICK, P. A. (2006). Practical adaptations of cognitive processing therapy with Bosnian refugees: Implications for adapting practice to a multicultural clientele. *Cognitive and Behavioral Practice*, 13, 310–321.

SCHULZ, P. M., RESICK, P. A., HUBER, L. C., & GRIFFIN, M. G. (2006). The effectiveness of cognitive processing therapy for PTSD with refugees in a community setting. *Cognitive and Behavioral Practice*, 13, 322–331.

SCHWARTZ, C., HOULIHAN, D., KRUEGER, K. F., & SIMON, D. A. (1997). The behavioral treatment of a young adult with post traumatic stress disorder for fear of children. *Child & Family Behavior Therapy*, 19, 37–49.

SCHWARTZ, J. M., STOESSEL, P. W., BAXTER, L. R., MARTIN, K. M., & PHELPS, M. E. (1996). Systematic changes in cerebral glucose metabolic rate after successful behavior modification treatment of obsessive-compulsive disorder. *Archives of General Psychiatry*, 53, 109–113.

SCHWITZGEBEL, L., & SCHWITZGEBEL, K. (1973). *Psychotechnology: Electronic control of mind and behavior.* New York: Holt, Rinehart & Winston.

SCOGIN, F., & MCELREATH, L. (1994). Efficacy of psychosocial treatments for geriatric depression: A quantitative review. *Journal of Consulting and Clinical Psychology*, 62, 69–74.

SEDLAR, G., & HANSEN, D. J. (2001). Anger, child behavior, and family distress: Further evaluation of the Parental Anger Inventory. *Journal of Family Violence*, 16, 361–373.

SEGAL, Z. V., TEASDALE, J. D., & WILLIAMS, J. M. G. (2004). Mindfulness-based cognitive therapy: Theoretical rationale and empirical status. In S. C. Hayes, V. M., Follette, & M. M. Linehan (Eds.), *Mindfulness and acceptance: Expanding the cognitive-behavioral tradition* (pp. 45–65). New York: Guilford.

SEGAL, Z. V., WILLIAMS, J. M. G., & TEASDALE, J. D. (2001). *Mindfulness-based cognitive therapy for depression: A new approach to preventing relapse.* New York: Guilford.

SEIDLER, G. H., & WAGNER, F. E. (2006). Comparing the efficacy of EMDR and trauma-focused cognitive-behavioral therapy in the treatment of PTSD: A meta-analytic study. *Psychological Medicine*, 36, 1515–1522.

SELF-BROWN, S. R., & MATHEWS, S., II. (2003). Effects of classroom structure on student achievement goal orientation. *Journal of Educational Research*, 97, 106–111.

SELIGSON, M. R., & PETERSON, K. E. (Eds.). (1992). *AIDS prevention and treatment: Hope, humor, & healing.* New York: Hemisphere.

SEMPLE, R. J., LEE, J., & MILLER, L. F. (2006). Mindfulness-based cognitive therapy for children. In R. A. Baer (Ed.), *Mindfulness-based treatment approaches: Clinician's guide to evidence base and applications* (pp. 143–166). San Diego: Elsevier Academic Press.

SERGIS-DEAVENPORT, E., & VARNI, J. W. (1982). Behavioral techniques in teaching hemophilia factor replacement procedures to families. *Pediatric Nursing*, 8, 416–419.

SERGIS-DEAVENPORT, E., & VARNI, J. W. (1983). Behavioral assessment and management of adherence to factor replacement therapy in hemophilia. *Journal of Pediatric Psychology*, 8, 367–377.

SHAFFER, H., BECK, J., & BOOTHROYD, P. (1983). The primary prevention of smoking onset: An inoculation approach. *Journal of Psychoactive Drugs*, 15, 177–184.

SHAFTO, F., & SULZBACHER, S. (1977). Comparing treatment tactics with a hyperactive preschool child: Stimulant medication and programmed teacher intervention. *Journal of Applied Behavior Analysis*, 10, 13–20.

SHAH, M., COYLE, Y., KAVANAUGH, A., ADAMS-HUET, B., & LIPSKEY, P. E. (2000). Development and initial evaluation of a culturally sensitive cholesterol-lowering diet program for Mexican and African American patients with systemic lupus erythematosus. *Arthritis Care and Research: Special Issue*, 13, 205–212.

SHANDISH, W. R., & BALDWIN, S. A. (2005). Effects of behavioral marital therapy: A meta-analysis of randomized controlled studies. *Journal of Consulting and Clinical Psychology*, 73, 6–14.

SHANNON, H. D., & ALLEN, T. W. (1998). The effectiveness of a REBT training program in increasing the performance of high school students mathematics. *Journal of Rational-Emotive & Cognitive-Behavior Therapy*, 16, 197–209.

SHAPIRO, A. K., & SHAPIRO, E. (1984). Controlled study of pimozide vs. placebo in Tourette's syndrome. *Journal of the American Academy of Child Psychiatry*, 23, 161–173.

SHAPIRO, D. A., REES, A., BARKHAM, M., HARDY, G., REYNOLDS, S., & STARTUP, M. (1995). Effects of treatment duration and severity of depression on the maintenance of gains after cognitive-behavioral and psychodynamic-interpersonal psychotherapy. *Journal of Consulting and Clinical Psychology*, 63, 378–387.

SHAPIRO, E., SHAPIRO, A. K., FULOP, G., HUBBARD, M., MANDELI, J., NORDLIE, J., et al. (1989). Controlled study of haloperidol, pimozide, and placebo for the treatment of Gilles de la Tourette's syndrome. *Archives of General Psychiatry*, 46, 722–730.

SHAPIRO, E. S., ALBRIGHT, T. S., & AGER, C. L. (1986). Group versus individual contingencies in modifying two disruptive adolescents' behavior. *Professional School Psychology*, 1, 105–116.

SHAPIRO, F. (1989a). Efficacy of the eye movement desensitization procedure in the treatment of traumatic memories. *Journal of Traumatic Stress Studies*, 2, 199–223.

SHAPIRO, F. (1989b). Eye movement desensitization: A new treatment for post-traumatic stress disorder. *Journal of Behavior Therapy and Experimental Psychiatry*, 20, 211–217.

SHAPIRO, F. (1995). *Eye movement desensitization and reprocessing: Basic principles, protocols, and procedures.* New York: Guilford.

SHAPIRO, M. B. (1957). Experimental method in the psychological description of the individual psychiatric patient. *International Journal of Social Psychiatry, 3,* 89–102.

SHAPIRO, M. B. (1966). The single case of clinical-psychological research. *Journal of General Psychology, 74,* 3–23.

SHARIATNIA, K., & D'SOUZA, L. (2007). Effectiveness of cognitive behaviour group therapy on shyness among adolescents in Iran. *Psychological Studies, 52,* 372–376.

SHARP, K. (1981). Impact of interpersonal problem-solving training on preschoolers' social competency. *Journal of Applied Developmental Psychology, 2,* 129–143.

SHEA, M. T., ELKIN, I., IMBER, S. D., SOTSKY, S. M., WATKINS, J. T., COLLINS, J. F., et al. (1992). Course of depressive symptoms over follow-up: Findings from the National Institute of Mental Health Treatment of Depression Collaborative Research Program. *Archives of General Psychiatry, 49,* 782–787.

SHEARD, M., & GOLBY, J. (2006). Effect of a psychological skills training program on swimming performance and positive psychological development. *International Journal of Sport and Exercise Psychology, 4,* 149–169.

SHEEHY, R., & HORAN, J. J. (2005). Effects of stress inoculation training for 1st-year law students. *International Journal of Stress Management, 11,* 41–55.

SHERER, M., PIERCE, K. L., PAREDES, S., KISACKY, K. L., INGERSOLL, B., & SCHREIBMAN, L. (2001). Enhancing conversation skills in children with autism via video technology: Which is better, 'Self' or 'Other' as a model? *Behavior Modification, 25,* 140–158.

SHIINA, A., NAKAZATO, M., MITSUMORI, M., KOIZUMI, H., SHIMIZU, E., FUJISAKI, M., et al. (2005). An open trial of outpatient group therapy for bulimic disorders: Combination program of cognitive behavioral therapy with assertive training and self-esteem enhancement. *Psychiatry and Clinical Neurosciences, 59,* 690–696.

SHIPLEY, R. H., & BOUDEWYNS, P. A. (1980). Flooding and implosive therapy: Are they harmful? *Behavior Therapy, 11,* 503–508.

SHIPLEY, R. H., BUTT, J. H., HORWITZ, B., & FARBRY, J. E. (1978). Preparation for a stressful medical procedure: Effect of stimulus pre-exposure and coping style. *Journal of Consulting and Clinical Psychology, 46,* 499–507.

SHIPLEY, R. H., BUTT, J. H., & HORWITZ, E. A. (1979). Preparation to re-experience a stressful medical examination: Effect of repetitious videotape exposure and coping style. *Journal of Consulting and Clinical Psychology, 47,* 485–492.

SHORKEY, C., & HIMLE, D. P. (1974). Systematic desensitization treatment of a recurring nightmare and related insomnia. *Journal of Behavior Therapy and Experimental Psychiatry, 5,* 97–98.

SHURE, M. B., & SPIVACK, G. (1980). Interpersonal problem-solving as a mediator of behavioral adjustment in preschool and kindergarten children. *Journal of Applied Developmental Psychology, 1,* 29–44.

SIEGEL, L. J., & PETERSON, L. (1980). Stress reduction in young dental patients through coping skills and sensory information. *Journal of Consulting and Clinical Psychology, 48,* 785–787.

SIKKEMA, K., WINETT, R. A., & LOMBARD, D. N. (1995). Development and evaluation of an HIV risk reduction program for female college students. *AIDS Education and Prevention, 7,* 145–159.

SILVER, B. V., BLANCHARD, E. B., WILLIAMSON, D. A., THEOBALD, D. E., & BROWN, D. A. (1979). Temperature biofeedback and relaxation training in the treatment of migraine headache: One year follow-up. *Biofeedback and Self-Regulation, 4,* 359–366.

SILVERMAN, W. H. (1986). Client-therapist cooperation in the treatment of compulsive hand washing. *Journal of Behavior Therapy and Experimental Psychiatry, 17,* 39–42.

SILVERMAN, W. K., GINSBURG, G. S., & KURTINES, W. M. (1995). Clinical issues in treating children with anxiety and phobic disorders. *Cognitive and Behavioral Practice, 2,* 93–117.

SILVERMAN, W. K., KURTINES, W. M., GINSBURG, G. S., WEEMS, C. F., LUMPKIN, P. W., & CARMICHAEL, D. H. (1999). Treating anxiety disorders in children with group cognitive-behavioral therapy: A randomized clinical trial. *Journal of Consulting and Clinical Psychology, 67,* 995–1003.

SILVERMAN, W. K., KURTINES, W. M., GINSBURG, G. S., WEEMS, C. F., RABIAN, B., & SERAFINI, L. T. (1999). Contingency management, self-control, and education support in the treatment of childhood phobic disorders: A randomized clinical trial. *Journal of Consulting and Clinical Psychology, 67,* 675–687.

SILVERMAN, W. K., & RABIAN, B. (1994). Specific phobias. In T. H. Ollendick, N. J. King, & W. Yule (Eds.), *International handbook of phobic and anxiety disorders in children and adolescents* (pp. 87–109). New York: Plenum.

SIMMONS, T. (1993). *A season in the air.* New York: Fawcett Columbine.

SIMON, K. M. (1994). A rapid stabilization cognitive group therapy program for psychiatric inpatients. *Clinical Psychology and Psychotherapy, 1,* 286–297.

SIMOS, G., & DIMITRIOU, E. (1994). Cognitive-behavioural treatment of culturally bound obsessional ruminations: A case report. *Behavioural and Cognitive Psychotherapy, 2,* 325–330.

SINGH, N. N., & BAKKER, L. W. (1984). Suppression of pica by overcorrection and physical restraint: A comparative analysis. *Journal of Autism and Developmental Disorders, 44,* 331–341.

SIPICH, J. F., RUSSELL, R. K., & TOBIAS, L. L. (1974). A comparison of covert sensitization and "nonspecific" treatment in the modification of smoking behavior. *Journal of Behavior Therapy and Experimental Psychiatry, 5,* 201–203.

SISSON, L. A., VAN HASSELT, V. B., & HERSEN, M. (1993). Behavioral interventions to reduce maladaptive responding in youth with dual sensory impairment: An analysis of direct and concurrent effects. *Behavior Modification, 17,* 164–188.

SIU, A. M. H., & SHEK, D. T. L. (2005). The Chinese version of the Social Problem Solving Inventory: Some initial results on reliability and validity. *Journal of Clinical Psychology, 61,* 347–360.

SIVERTSEN, B., OMVIK, S., PALLESEN, S., BJORVATIN, B., HAVIK, O. E., KVALE, G., et al. (2006). Cognitive-behavioral therapy vs Zopiclone for treatment of chronic primary insomnia in older adults: A randomized controlled trial. *JAMA: Journal of the American Medical Association, 295*, 2851–2858.

SKEELS, H. M. (1966). Adult status of children with contrasting early life experiences. *Monographs of the Society for Research in Child Development,* 31 (Whole No. 3).

SKINNER, B. F. (1953). *Science and human behavior.* New York: Macmillan.

SKINNER, B. F. (1954). A new method for the experimental analysis of the behavior of psychotic patients. *Journal of Nervous and Mental Disease, 120,* 403–406.

SKINNER, B. F., SOLOMON, H. C., & LINDSLEY, O. R. (1953, November 30). *Studies in behavior therapy: Status Report I.* Waltham, MA: Metropolitan State Hospital.

SKINNER, B. F., SOLOMON, H. C., LINDSLEY, O. R., & RICHARDS, M. E. (1954, May 31). *Studies in behavior therapy: Status Report II.* Waltham, MA: Metropolitan State Hospital.

SKINNER, B. F., & VAUGHAN, M. E. (1983). *Enjoy old age.* New York: Norton.

SLIFER, K. J., BABBITT, R. L., & CATALDO, M. D. (1995). Simulation and counterconditioning as adjuncts to pharmacotherapy for invasive pediatric procedures. *Journal of Developmental and Behavioral Pediatrics, 16,* 133–141.

SLIFER, K. J., CATALDO, M. F., CATALDO, M. D., LLORENTE, A. M., & GERSON, A. C. (1993). Behavior analysis of motion control for pediatric neuroimaging. *Journal of Applied Behavior Analysis, 26,* 469–470.

SLOAN, D. M. (2004). Emotion regulation in action: Emotional reactivity in experiential avoidance. *Behaviour Research and Therapy, 42,* 1257–1270.

SLOAN, E. P., HAURIS, P., BOOTZIN, R., MORIN, C., STEVENSON, M., & SHAPIRO, C. M. (1993). The nuts and bolts of behavioral therapy for insomnia. *Journal of Psychosomatic Research, 37*(Suppl. 1), 19–37.

SLOAN, E. P., & SHAPIRO, C. M. (1993). [Editorial] *Journal of Psychosomatic Research, 37,* 1–2.

SLOANE, R. B., STAPLES, F. R., CRISTOL, A. H., YORKSTON, N. H., & WHIPPLE, K. (1975). *Psychotherapy versus behavior therapy.* Cambridge, MA: Harvard University Press.

SLOUGH, N. M., MCMAHON, R. J., & CONDUCT PROBLEMS PREVENTION RESEARCH GROUP. (2008). Preventing serious conduct problems in school-age youth: The Fast Track Program. *Cognitive and Behavioral Practice, 15,* 3–17.

SMAGNER, J. P., & SULLIVAN, M. H. (2005). Investigating the effectiveness of behavioral parent training with involuntary clients in child welfare settings. *Research on Social Work Practice, 15,* 431–439.

SMITH, A., GRAHAM, L., & SENTHINATHAN, S. (2007). Mindfulness-based cognitive therapy for recurring depression in older people: A qualitative study. *Aging & Mental Health, 11,* 346–357.

SMITH, B. H., PELHAM, W. E., GNAGY, E., MOLINA, B., & EVANS, S. (2000). The reliability, validity, and unique contribution of self report by adolescents receiving treatment for attention-deficit/hyperactivity disorder. *Journal of Consulting and Clinical Psychology, 68,* 489–499.

SMITH, D. D., & LOVITT, T. C. (1975). The use of modeling techniques to influence acquisition of computational arithmetic skills in learning disabled children. In E. Ramp & G. Semb (Eds.), *Behavior analysis: Areas of research and application* (pp. 283–308). Englewood Cliffs, NJ: Prentice Hall.

SMITH, D. E., MARCUS, M. D., & ELDREDGE, K. L. (1994). Binge eating syndromes: A review of assessment and treatment with an emphasis on clinical application. *Behavior Therapy, 25,* 635–658.

SMITH, M. L., & GLASS, G. V. (1977). Meta-analysis of psychotherapy outcome studies. *American Psychologist, 32,* 752–760.

SMITH, M. T., & PERLIS, M. L. (2006). Who is a candidate for cognitive-behavioral therapy for insomnia? *Health Psychology, 25,* 15–19.

SMITH, R. E. (1973). The use of humor in the counterconditioning of anger responses: A case study. *Behavior Therapy, 4,* 576–580.

SMITH, R. E., & GREGORY, P. B. (1976). Covert sensitization by induced anxiety in the treatment of an alcoholic. *Journal of Behavior Therapy and Experimental Psychiatry, 7,* 31–33.

SMITH, R. E., SMOLL, F. L., & CUMMING, S. P. (2007). Effects of a motivational climate intervention for

coaches on young athletes' sport performance anxiety. *Journal of Sport and Exercise Psychology, 29,* 39–59.

SMITH, R. G., IWATA, B. A., VOLLMER, T. R., & ZARCONE, J. R. (1993). Experimental analysis and treatment of multiply controlled self-injury. *Journal of Applied Behavior Analysis, 26,* 183–196.

SMUCKER, M. R., DANCU, C., FOA, E. B., & NIEDEREE, J. L. (1995). Imagery rescripting: A new treatment for survivors of childhood sexual abuse suffering from posttraumatic stress. *Journal of Cognitive Psychotherapy: An International Quarterly, 9,* 3–17.

SNYDER, D. K. (1997). *Marital Satisfaction Inventory—Revised (MSI-R) Manual.* Los Angeles: Western Psychological Services.

SOBELL, L. C. (1994). AABT coming of middle age. *the Behavior Therapist, 17,* 179–180.

SOBELL, M. B., & SOBELL, L. C. (2000). Stepped care as a heuristic approach to the treatment of alcohol problems. *Journal of Consulting and Clinical Psychology, 68,* 573–579.

SOBELL, M. B., SOBELL, L. C., & LEO, G. I. (2000). Does enhanced social support improve outcomes for problem drinkers in guided self-change treatment? *Journal of Behavior Therapy and Experimental Psychiatry, 31,* 41–54.

SOFRONOFF, K., & WHITTINGHAM, K. (2007). Parent management training to improve competence in parents of children with Asperger syndrome. In J. M. Briesmeister & C. E. Schaefer (Eds.), *Handbook of parent training: Helping parents prevent and solve problem behaviors* (3rd ed., pp. 107–128). Hoboken, NJ: Wiley.

SOKOLOV, A. N. (1972). *Inner speech and thought.* New York: Plenum.

SOLOMON, A., & HAAGA, D. A. F. (1995). Rational-emotive behavior therapy research: What we know and what we need to know. *Journal of Rational-Emotive & Cognitive-Behavior Therapy, 13,* 179–191.

SOLOMON, L. J., FLYNN, B. S., WORDEN, J. K., MICKEY, R. M., SKELLY, J. M., GELLER, B. M., et al. (1998). Assessment of self-reward strategies for maintenance of breast self-examinations. *Journal of Behavioral Medicine, 21,* 83–102.

SOLOMON, R. L. (1964). Punishment. *American Psychologist, 19,* 239–253.

SOLOMON, R. W., & WAHLER, R. G. (1973). Peer reinforcement control of classroom problem behavior. *Journal of Applied Behavior Analysis, 6*, 49–56.

SOLTER, A. (2007). A case of traumatic stress disorder in a 5-month-old infant following surgery. *Infant Mental Health Journal, 28*, 76–96.

SOMERS, J. M., & MARLATT, G. A. (1992). Alcohol problems. In P. H. Wilson (Ed.), *Principles and practice of relapse prevention* (pp. 23–42). New York: Guilford.

SOROCCO, K. H., KASL-GODLEY, J., & ZEISS, A. M. (2002). Fostering sexual intimacy in older adults: The role of the behavior therapist. *the Behavior Therapist, 25*, 21–22.

SOROUDI, N., PEREZ, G. K., GONZALEZ, J. S., GREER, J. A., POLLACK, M. H., OTTO, M. W., et al. (2008). CBT for medication adherence and depression (CBT-AD) in HIV-infected patients receiving methadone maintenance therapy. *Cognitive and Behavioral Practice, 15*, 93–106.

SOWERS, J., RUSCH, F. R., CONNIS, R. T., & CUMMINGS, L. E. (1980). Teaching mentally retarded adults to time manage in a vocational setting. *Journal of Applied Behavior Analysis, 13*, 119–128.

SPENCE, S. H., HOLMES, J., MARCH, S., & LIPP, O. (2006). The BRAVE internet program for children aged 7-12 years from The University of Queensland: The feasibility and outcome of clinic plus internet delivery of cognitive-behavioural therapy for childhood anxiety. *Journal of Consulting and Clinical Psychology, 74*, 614–621.

SPENCE, S. H., SHEFFIELD, J. K., & DONOVAN, C. L. (2005). Long-term outcome of a school-based, universal approach to prevention of depression in adolescents. *Journal of Consulting and Clinical Psychology, 73*, 160–167.

SPIEGEL, S. A., & FOULK, D. (2006). Reducing overweight through a multidisciplinary school-based intervention. *Obesity Research, 14*, 88–96.

SPIEGLER, M. D. (1970, January). A modeling approach. In J. Schwartz (Chair), *Alternatives within behavior modification*. Symposium presented at the meeting of the California State Psychological Association, Monterey.

SPIEGLER, M. D. (1980, November). Behavioral primary prevention:

Introduction and overview. In M. D. Spiegler (Chair), *Behavioral primary prevention: A challenge for the 1980s*. Symposium presented at the meeting of the Association for Advancement of Behavior Therapy, New York.

SPIEGLER, M. D. (1983). *Contemporary behavioral therapy*. Palo Alto, CA: Mayfield.

SPIEGLER, M. D. (1989, March). *Teaching behavior modification experientially through individual behavior change projects: A five-year study*. Paper presented at Teaching of Psychology: Ideas and Innovations, Philadelphia.

SPIEGLER, M. D. (2000, November). *An analogue model to teach behavior therapy experientially*. Paper to be presented at the meeting of the Association for Advancement of Behavior Therapy, New Orleans.

SPIEGLER, M. D. (2005, November). Why this panel? In M. D. Spiegler (Moderator), J. Forsyth, M. R. Goldfried, R. Kohlenberg, M. Linehan, & M. D. Spiegler (Panelists), *The changing face of behavior therapy: Is behavior therapy having an identity crisis?* Washington, DC: Panel discussion presented at the annual meeting of the Association for Behavioral and Cognitive Therapies.

SPIEGLER, M. D. (2008). Behavior therapy I: Traditional behavior therapy. In J. Frew & M. D. Spiegler (Eds.), *Contemporary psychotherapies for a diverse world* (pp. 275–319). Boston: Lahaska/Houghton Mifflin.

SPIEGLER, M. D., & AGIGIAN, H. (1977). *The Community Training Center: An educational-behavioral-social systems model for rehabilitating psychiatric patients*. New York: Brunner/Mazel.

SPIEGLER, M. D., COOLEY, E. J., MARSHALL, G. J., PRINCE, H. T., II, PUCKETT, S. P., & SKENAZY, J. A. (1976). A self-control versus a counterconditioning paradigm for systematic desensitization: An experimental comparison. *Journal of Counseling Psychology, 23*, 83–86.

SPIEGLER, M. D., & GUEVREMONT, D. C. (1994, November). *The relationship between behavior therapy practice and research*. Paper to be presented at the meeting of the Association for Advancement of Behavior Therapy, San Diego.

SPIEGLER, M. D., & GUEVREMONT, D. C. (1998). *Contemporary behavior therapy* (3rd ed.). Pacific Grove, CA: Brooks/Cole.

SPIEGLER, M. D., & GUEVREMONT, D. C. (2002). *Current use of behavior therapies in clinical practice*. Unpublished manuscript, Providence College.

SPIEGLER, M. D., & GUEVREMONT, D. C. (2003). *Contemporary behavior therapy* (4th ed.). Belmont, CA: Wadsworth.

SPIEGLER, M. D., & LIEBERT, R. M. (1970). Some correlates of self-reported fear. *Psychological Reports, 26*, 691–695.

SPIEGLER, M. D., LIEBERT, R. M., MCMAINS, M. J., & FERNANDEZ, L. E. (1969). Experimental development of a modeling treatment to extinguish persistent avoidance behavior (pp. 45–51). In R. D. Rubin & C. M. Franks (Eds.), *Advances in behavior therapy, 1968*. New York: Academic Press.

SPIVACK, G., & SHURE, M. B. (1974). *Social adjustment of young children*. San Francisco: Jossey-Bass.

SPRING, F. L., SIPICH, J. F., TRIMBLE, R. W., & GOECKNER, D. J. (1978). Effects of contingency and noncontingency contracts in the context of a self-control-oriented smoking modification program. *Behavior Therapy, 9*, 967–968.

ST. LAWRENCE, J. S. (1987). Assessment of assertion. In M. Hersen, R. M. Eisler, & P. M. Miller (Eds.). *Progress in behavior modification* (Vol. 12, pp. 152–190). Newbury Park, CA: Sage.

ST. LAWRENCE, J. S., BRASFIELD, T. L., JEFFERSON, K. W., ALLEYNE, E., O'BANNON, R. E., & SHIRLEY, A. (1995). Cognitive behavioral intervention to reduce African American adolescents' risk for HIV infection. *Journal of Consulting and Clinical Psychology, 58*, 432–436.

ST. LAWRENCE, J. S., COOLEY, E. J., HANSEN, D. J., CUTTS, T. F., TISDELLE, D. A., & IRISH, J. D. (1985). Situational context: Effects on perceptions of assertive and unassertive behavior. *Behavior Therapy, 16*, 51–62.

ST. LAWRENCE, J. S., JEFFERSON, K. W., ALLEYNE, E., & BRASFIELD, T. L. (1995). Comparison of education versus behavioral skills training interventions in lowering sexual HIV-risk behavior of substance-dependent adolescents. *Journal of Consulting and Clinical Psychology, 63*, 154–157.

STAMBAUGH, E. E., II. (1977). Audiotaped flooding in outpatient treatment of somatic complaints. *Journal of Behavior Therapy and Experimental Psychiatry, 8*, 173–176.

STAMPFL, T. G. (1961, May). *Implosive therapy: A learning theory derived psychodynamic therapeutic technique.* Colloquium presented at the University of Illinois, Champaign.

STAMPFL, T. G. (1966). Implosive therapy, Part I: The theory. In S. G. Armitage (Ed.), *Behavioral modification techniques in the treatment of emotional disorder* (pp. 12–21). Battle Creek, MI: V. A. Hospital Publications.

STAMPFL, T. G. (1970). Implosive therapy: An emphasis on covert stimulation. In D. J. Levis (Ed.), *Learning approaches to therapeutic behavior change.* Chicago: Aldine.

STAMPFL, T. G., & LEVIS, D. J. (1967). Essentials of implosive therapy: A learning-theory-based psychodynamic behavioral therapy. *Journal of Abnormal Psychology, 72,* 496–503.

STAMPFL, T. G., & LEVIS, D. J. (1973). *Implosive therapy: Theory and technique.* Morristown, NJ: General Learning Press.

STANLEY, M. A., & TURNER, S. M. (1995). Current status of pharmacological and behavioral treatment of obsessive-compulsive disorder. *Behavior Therapy, 26,* 163–186.

STANLEY, S. M., MARKMAN, H. J., ST. PETERS, M., & LEBER, D. (1995). Strengthening marriages and preventing divorce: New directions in prevention research. *Family Relations, 44,* 392–401.

STAR, T. Z. (1986). Group social skills training: A comparison of two coaching programs. *Techniques, 2,* 24–38.

STARK, L. J., COLLINS, F. L., OSNES, P. G., & STOKES, T. F. (1986). Using reinforcement and cueing to increase healthy snack food choices in preschoolers. *Journal of Applied Behavior Analysis, 19,* 367–379.

STARK, L. J., KNAPP, L. G., BOWEN, A. M., POWERS, S. W., JELALIAN, E., EVANS, S., et al. (1993). Increasing calorie consumption in children with cystic fibrosis: Replication with 2-year follow-up. *Journal of Applied Behavior Analysis, 26,* 435–450.

STARK, L. J., POWERS, S. W., JELALIAN, E., RAPE, R. N., & MILLER, D. L. (1994). Modifying problematic mealtime interactions of children with cystic fibrosis and their parents via behavioral parent training. *Journal of Pediatric Psychology, 19,* 751–768.

STEED, S. E., BIGELOW, K. M., HUYNEN, K. B., & LUTZKER, J. R. (1995). The effects of planned activities training, low-demand schedule, and reinforcement sampling on adults with developmental disabilities who exhibit challenging behaviors. *Journal of Developmental and Physical Disabilities, 7,* 303–316.

STEINMARK, S. W., & BORKOVEC, T. D. (1974). Active and placebo treatment effects on moderate insomnia under counterdemand and positive demand instructions. *Journal of Abnormal Psychology, 83,* 157–163.

STEKETEE, G. (1994). Behavioral assessment and treatment planning with obsessive compulsive disorder: A review emphasizing clinical application. *Behavior Therapy, 25,* 613–633.

STEKETEE, G., & LAM, J. (1993). Obsessive-compulsive disorder. In T. R. Giles (Ed.), *Handbook of effective psychotherapy* (pp. 253–278). New York: Plenum.

STEPHENS, R. S., ROFFMAN, R. A., & SIMPSON, E. E. (1994). Treating adult marijuana dependence: A test of the relapse prevention model. *Journal of Consulting and Clinical Psychology, 62,* 92–99.

STERN, R. S., LIPSEDGE, M. S., & MARKS, I. M. (1973). Obsessive ruminations: A controlled trial of thought-stopping technique. *Behaviour Research and Therapy, 11,* 659–662.

STEWART, M. A. (1961). Psychotherapy by reciprocal inhibition. *American Journal of Psychiatry, 118,* 175–177.

STITZER, M., BIGELOW, G., LAWRENCE, C., COHEN, J., D'LUGOFF, B., & HAWTHORNE, J. (1977). Medication take-home as a reinforcer in a methadone maintenance program. *Addictive Behaviors, 2,* 9–14.

STOLZ, S. B. (1977). Why no guidelines for behavior modification? *Journal of Applied Behavior Analysis, 10,* 349–367.

STOLZ, S. B., & ASSOCIATES. (1978). *Ethical issues in behavior modification: Report of the American Psychological Association Commission.* San Francisco: Jossey-Bass.

STONE, G. W. (1994, May 9). Magic fingers. *New York, 27,* pp. 32–37.

STOREY, K., DANKO, C. D., ASHWORTH, R., & STRAIN, P. S. (1994). Generalization of social skills intervention for preschoolers with social delays. *Education and Treatment of Children, 17,* 29–51.

STOREY, K., LAWRY, J. R., ASHWORTH, R., DANKO, C. D., & STRAIN, P. S. (1994). Functional analysis and intervention for disruptive behaviors of a kindergarten student. *Journal of Educational Research, 87,* 361–370.

STORMS, L. (1985). Massed negative practice as a behavioral treatment of Gilles de la Tourette's syndrome. *American Journal of Psychotherapy, 39,* 277–281.

STRAIN, P. S. (Ed.). (1981). *The utilization of classroom peers as behavior change agents.* New York: Plenum.

STRAIN, P. S., SHORES, R. E., & KERR, M. M. (1976). An experimental analysis of "spillover" effects on the social interaction of behaviorally handicapped preschool children. *Journal of Applied Behavior Analysis, 9,* 31–40.

STRAUSS, C. A. (1986). An operant approach to increasing performance of household chores: A case study using behavioral consultation. *Psychological Reports, 58,* 738.

STROSAHL, K. (1995). Behavior therapy 2000: A perilous journey. *the Behavior Therapist, 18,* 130–133.

STROSAHL, K. (1996). Behavior therapy 2000: Three "gold mine-land mine" themes in Generation 2 of health care reform. *the Behavior Therapist, 19,* 52–54.

STRUPP, H. H. (1978). Psychotherapy research and practice: An overview. In S. L. Garfield & A. E. Bergin (Eds.), *Handbook of psychotherapy and behavior change: An empirical analysis* (2nd ed., pp. 3–22). New York: Wiley.

STRUPP, H. H. (1995). The psychotherapist's skills revisited. *Clinical Psychology: Science and Practice, 2,* 70–74.

STUART, G. L., TREAT, T. A., & WADE, W. A. (2000). Effectiveness of an empirically based treatment for panic disorder delivered in a service clinic setting: One year follow-up. *Journal of Consulting and Clinical Psychology, 68,* 506–512.

STUART, R. B. (1967). Behavioral control of overeating. *Behaviour Research and Therapy, 5,* 357–365.

STUART, R. B. (1969). Operant-interpersonal treatment for marital discord. *Journal of Consulting and Clinical Psychology, 33,* 675–682.

STUART, R. B. (1971). Behavioral contracting with the families of delinquents. *Journal of Behavior Therapy and Experimental Psychiatry, 2,* 1–11.

STUART, R. B. (1980). *Helping couples change: A social learning approach to marital therapy.* New York: Guilford.

STUART, R. B., & LOTT, L. A., JR. (1972). Behavioral contracting with delinquents: A cautionary note. *Journal of Behavior Therapy and Experimental Psychiatry, 3,* 161–169.

STURGIS, E. T., & GRAMLING, S. (1988). Psychophysiological assessment. In A. S. Bellack & M. Hersen (Eds.), *Behavioral assessment: A practical handbook* (3rd ed., pp. 213–251). Elmsford, NY: Pergamon.

STURMEY, P. (1992). Treatment acceptability for anorexia nervosa: Effect of treatment type, problem severity, and treatment outcome. *Behavioural Psychotherapy, 20,* 91–93.

SUAREZ, Y., McCUTCHEON, B. A., & ADAMS, H. E. (1976). Flooding and systematic desensitization: Efficacy in subclinical phobias as a function of arousal. *Journal of Consulting and Clinical Psychology, 44,* 872.

SUINN, R. M. (2001). The terrible twos—Anger and anxiety: Hazardous to your health. *American Psychologist, 56,* 27–36.

SUINN, R. [M.], & DEFFENBACHER, J. L. (2002). Anxiety management training. In M. Hersen & W. Sledge (Eds.), *Encyclopedia of psychotherapy* (Vol. 1, pp. 61–69). New York: Elsevier Science.

SUINN, R. M., & RICHARDSON, F. (1971). Anxiety Management Training: A nonspecific behavior therapy program for anxiety control. *Behavior Therapy, 2,* 498–510.

SUKHODOLSKY, D. G., GOLUB, A., STONE, E. C., & ORBAN, L. (2005). Dismantling anger control training for children: A randomized pilot study of social problem-solving versus social skills training components. *Behavior Therapy, 36,* 15–23.

SULLIVAN, K. T., & BRADBURY, T. N. (1996). Preventing marital dysfunction: The primacy of secondary strategies. *the Behavior Therapist, 19,* 33–36.

SULLIVAN, M. A., & O'LEARY, S. G. (1990). Maintenance following reward and cost token programs. *Behavior Therapy, 21,* 139–149.

SUZMAN, K. B., MORRIS, R. D., MORRIS, M. K., & MILAN, M. A. (1997). Cognitive-behavioral remediation of problem solving deficits in children with acquired brain injury. *Journal of Behavior Therapy and Experimental Psychiatry, 28,* 202–212.

SWAN, G. E., & MacDONALD, M. L. (1978). Behavior therapy in practice: A national survey of behavior therapists. *Behavior Therapy, 9,* 799–807.

SWINSON, R. P., FERGUS, K. D., COX, B. J., & WICKWIRE, K. (1995). Efficacy of telephone-administered behavioral therapy for panic disorder with agoraphobia. *Behaviour Research and Therapy, 33,* 465–469.

SWINSON, R. P., & KUCH, K. (1989). Behavioural psychotherapy for agoraphobia. *International Review of Psychiatry, 1,* 195–205.

SZYMANSKI, J., & O'DONOHUE, W. (1995). Self-appraisal skills. In W. O' Donohue & L. Krasner (Eds.). *Handbook of psychological skills training: Clinical techniques and applications* (pp. 161–179). Boston: Allyn & Bacon.

TAN, S. (2007). Use of prayer and scripture in cognitive-behavioral therapy. *Journal of Psychology and Christianity, 26,* 101–111.

TANAKA-MATSUMI, J., & HIGGINBOTHAM, H. N. (1994). Clinical application of behavior therapy across ethnic and cultural boundaries. *the Behavior Therapist, 17,* 123–126.

TANAKA-MATSUMI, J., HIGGINBOTHAM, H. N., & CHANG, R. (2002). Cognitive-behavioral approaches to counseling across cultures: A functional analytic approach for clinical applications. In P. B. Pedersen, J. G. Draguns, W. J. Lonner, & J. E. Trimble (Eds.), *Counseling across cultures* (5th ed., pp. 337–354). Thousand Oaks, CA: Sage.

TANAKA-MATSUMI, J., SEIDEN, D., & LAM, K. N. (1996). The Culturally Informed Functional Assessment (CIFA) Interview: A strategy for cross-cultural behavioral practice. *Cognitive and Behavioral Practice, 3,* 215–233.

TANAKA-MATSUMI, J., & SEIDEN, D. Y. (1994, November). *Functional analytic approaches to cross-cultural therapy.* Paper presented at the meeting of the Association for Advancement of Behavior Therapy, San Diego.

TARBOX, R. S. F., GHEZZI, P. M., & WILSON, G. (2006). The effects of token reinforcement on attending in a young child with autism. *Behavioral Interventions, 21,* 155–164.

TARNOWSKI, K. J., ROSEN, L. A., McGRATH, M. L., & DRABMAN, R. S. (1987). A modified habit reversal procedure in a recalcitrant case of trichotillomania. *Journal of Behavior Therapy and Experimental Psychiatry, 18,* 157–163.

TARRIER, N. (1992). Management and modification of residual positive psychotic symptoms. In M. Birchwood & N. Tarrier (Eds.), *Innovations in the psychological management of schizophrenia* (pp. 147–169). Chichester, UK: Wiley.

TARRIER, N. (2008). Schizophrenia and other psychotic disorders. In D. H. Barlow (Ed.), *Clinical handbook of psychological disorders: A step-by-step treatment manual* (4th ed., pp. 463–491). New York: Guilford.

TARRIER, N., KINNEY, C., McCARTHY, E., HUMPHREYS, L., WITTKOWSKI, A., & MORRIS, J. (2000). Two-year follow-up on cognitive-behavioral therapy and supportive counseling in the treatment of persistent symptoms in chronic schizophrenia. *Journal of Consulting and Clinical Psychology, 68,* 917–922.

TARRIER, N., PILGRIM, H., SOMMERFIELD, C., FARAGHER, B., REYNOLDS, M., GRAHAM, E., et al. (1999). A randomized trial of cognitive therapy and imaginal exposure in the treatment of chronic posttraumatic stress disorder. *Journal of Consulting and Clinical Psychology, 67,* 13–18.

TARRIER, N., SOMMERFIELD, C., PILGRIM, H., & FARAGHER, B. (2000). Factors associated with outcome of cognitive-behavioural treatment of chronic post-traumatic stress disorder. *Behaviour Research and Therapy, 38,* 191–202.

TASK FORCE ON PROMOTION AND DISSEMINATION OF PSYCHOLOGICAL PROCEDURES. (1995). Training in and dissemination of empirically-validated psychological treatments: Report and recommendations. *The Clinical Psychologist, 48,* 3–23.

TATE, B. G., & BAROFF, G. S. (1966). Aversive control of self-injurious behavior in a psychotic boy. *Behaviour Research and Therapy, 4,* 281–287.

TAYLOR, D. W. A. (1971). A comparison of group desensitization with two control procedures in the treatment of test anxiety. *Behaviour Research and Therapy, 9,* 281–284.

TAYLOR, S., THORDARSON, D. S., MAXFIELD, L., FEDOROFF, I. C., LOVELL, K., & ORGODNICZUK, J. (2003). Comparative efficacy, speed, and adverse effects of three PTSD treatments: Exposure therapy, EMDR, and relaxation training. *Journal of Consulting and Clinical Psychology, 71,* 330–338.

TAYLOR, T. K., SCHMIDT, F., PEPLER, D., & HODGINS, C. (1998). A comparison of eclectic treatment with Webster-Stratton's parents and children series in a children's mental health center: A randomized controlled trial. *Behavior Therapy, 29,* 221–240.

TEASDALE, J. D., SEGAL, Z., & WILLIAMS, J. M. G. (1995). How does cognitive therapy prevent depressive relapse and why should attention control (mindfulness) training help? *Behaviour Research and Therapy, 33,* 25–39.

TEASDALE, J. D., SEGAL, Z. V., WILLIAMS, J. M. G., RIDGEWAY, V. A., SOULSBY, J. M., & LAU, M. (2000). Prevention of relapse/recurrence in major depression by mindfulness-based cognitive therapy. *Journal of Consulting and Clinical Psychology, 68,* 615–623.

TELCH, C.F, AGRAS, W., & LINEHAN, M. M. (2001). Dialectical behavior therapy for binge eating disorder. *Journal of Consulting and Clinical Psychology, 69,* 1061–1065.

TERI, L., CURTIS, J., GALLAGHER-THOMPSON, D., & THOMPSON, L. (1994). Cognitive-behavioral therapy with depressed older adults. In L. S. Schneider, C. F. Reynolds, D. B. Lebowitz, & A. J. Friedhoff (Eds.), *Diagnosis and treatment of depression in late life: Results of the NIH consensus development conference* (pp. 279–291). Washington, DC: American Psychiatric Press.

TERJESEN, M. D., DIGIUSEPPE, R., & GRUNER, P. (2000). A review of REBT research in alcohol abuse treatment. *Journal of Rational-Emotive & Cognitive Behavior Therapy, 18,* 165–179.

TESTAL, R., FRANCISCO, J., ORTIZ, C., ANGEL, M., SANTOS, R., & DOLORES, M. (1998). Application of a multimodal programme on a set of disruptive behaviours in a case of mental retardation. *Apuntes de Psicologia, 16,* 5–19.

THACKWRAY, D. E., SMITH, M. C., BODFISH, J. W., & MEYERS, A. W. (1993). A comparison of behavioral and cognitive-behavioral interventions for bulimia nervosa. *Journal of Consulting and Clinical Psychology, 61,* 639–645.

THASE, M. E. (1994). After the fall: Perspectives on cognitive behavioral treatment of depression in the "post-collaborative" era. *the Behavior Therapist, 17,* 48–52.

THASE, M. E., BOWLER, K., & HARDEN, T. (1991). Cognitive behavior therapy of endogenous depression: Part 2: Preliminary findings in 16 unmedicated inpatients. *Behavior Therapy, 22,* 469–477.

THASE, M. E., REYNOLDS, C. F., FRANK, E., SIMONS, A. D., GARAMONI, G. D., MCGEARY, J., et al. (1994). Response to cognitive-behavioral therapy in chronic depression. *The Journal of Psychotherapy Practice and Research, 3,* 204–214.

THASE, M. E., REYNOLDS, C. F., FRANK, E., SIMONS, A. D., MCGEARY, J., FASICZKA, A. L., et al. (1994). Do depressed men and women respond similarly to cognitive behavior therapy? *The American Journal of Psychiatry, 151,* 500–505.

THASE, M. E., SIMONS, A. D., CAHALANE, J. F., & MCGEARY, J. (1991). Cognitive behavior therapy of endogenous depression: Part 1: An outpatient clinical replication series. *Behavior Therapy, 22,* 457–467.

THASE, M. E., & WRIGHT, J. H. (1991). Cognitive behavior therapy manual for depressed inpatients: A treatment protocol outline. *Behavior Therapy, 22,* 579–595.

THOM, A., SARTORY, G., & JOHREN, P. (2000). Comparison between one-session psychological treatment and benzodiazepine in dental phobia. *Journal of Consulting and Clinical Psychology, 68,* 378–387.

THOMAS, E. J., ABRAMS, K. S., & JOHNSON, J. (1971). Self-monitoring and reciprocal inhibition in the modification of multiple tics of Gilles de la Tourette's syndrome. *Journal of Behavior Therapy and Experimental Psychiatry, 2,* 159–171.

THOMPSON, J. K. (1992). Body image: Extent of disturbance, associated features, theoretical models, assessment methodologies, intervention strategies, and a proposal for a new DSM-IV diagnostic category—Body image disorder. In M. Hersen, R. M. Eisler, & P. M. Miller (Eds.), *Progress in behavior modification* (Vol. 28, pp. 3–54). Sycamore, IL: Sycamore Publishing.

THOMPSON, M. M., & MCCREARY, D. R. (2006). Enhancing mental readiness in military personnel. In A. B. Adler,

C. A. Castro, & T. W. Britt (Eds.), *Military life: The psychology of serving in peace and combat: Vol. 2. Operational stress.* (pp. 54–79). Westport, CT: Praeger Security International.

THOMPSON, R. H., IWATA, B. A., CONNERS, J., & ROSCOE, E. M. (1999). Effects of reinforcement for alternative behavior during punishment of self-injury. *Journal of Applied Behavior Analysis, 32,* 317–328.

THORESEN, C. E., & MAHONEY, M. J. (1974). *Behavioral self-control.* New York: Holt, Rinehart & Winston.

THORNDIKE, E. L. (1911). *Animal intelligence: Experimental studies.* New York: Macmillan.

THORNDIKE, E. L. (1931). *Human learning.* New York: Century.

THORNDIKE, E. L. (1933). *An experimental study of rewards.* New York: Teachers College Press.

THYER, B. A. (1985). Audio-taped exposure therapy in a case of obsessional neurosis. *Journal of Behavior Therapy and Experimental Psychiatry, 16,* 271–273.

TIMBERLAKE, E. M. (1981). Child abuse and externalized aggression: Preventing a delinquent lifestyle. In R. J. Hunner & Y. E. Walker (Eds.), *Exploring the relationship between child abuse and delinquency* (pp. 43–51). Montclair, NJ: Allanheld, Osmun.

TIMBERLAKE, W., & FARMER-DOUGAN, V. A. (1991). Reinforcement in applied settings: Figuring out ahead of time what will work. *Psychological Bulletin, 110,* 379–391.

TIMBERS, G. D., TIMBERS, B. J., FIXSEN, D. L., PHILLIPS, E. L., & WOLF, M. M. (1973, August). *Achievement Place for pre-delinquent girls: Modification of inappropriate emotional behaviors with token reinforcement and instructional procedures.* Paper presented at the meeting of the American Psychological Association, Montreal.

TINCH, C. S., & FRIEDBERG, R. D. (1998). The Schema Identification Worksheet. In L. Vanderreek & T. J. Jackson (Eds.), *Innovations in clinical practice* (pp. 247–258). Sarasota, FL: Professional Resource Press.

TOBIN, D. L., BANKER, J. D., WEISBERG, L., & BOWERS, W. (2007). I know what you did last summer (and it was not CBT): A factor analytic model of international psychotherapeutic practice in the eating disorders.

International Journal of Eating Disorders, 40, 754–757.

TOLCHARD, B., THOMAS, L., & BATTERSBY, M. (2006). Single-session exposure therapy for problem gambling: A single-case experimental design. *Behaviour Change, 23*, 148–155.

TOLIN, D. F., & FOA, E. B. (1999). Treatment of a police officer with PTSD using prolonged exposure. *Behavior Therapy, 30*, 527–538.

TONER, B. B., SEGAL, Z. V., EMMOTT, S. D., & MYRAN, D. (2000). *Cognitive-behavioral treatment of irritable bowel syndrome: The brain-gut connection.* New York: Guilford.

TOPHOFF, M. (1973). Massed practice, relaxation, and assertion training in the treatment of Gilles de la Tourette's syndrome. *Journal of Behavior Therapy and Experimental Psychiatry, 4*, 71–73.

TORO, J., CERVERA, M., FELIU, M. H., GARRIGA, N., JOU, M., MARTINEZ, E., et al. (2003). Cue exposure in the treatment of resistant bulimia nervosa. *International Journal of Eating Disorders, 34*, 227–234.

TORRES-MARTINEZ, E., & SPINETTA, M. (1997). Behavior therapy in Argentina. *the Behavior Therapist, 20*, 171–174.

TOWNEND, M. (2002). Individual exposure therapy for delusional disorder in the elderly: A case study of a 71-year-old man. *Behavioural and Cognitive Psychotherapy, 30*, 103–109.

TOYOKAWA, T., & NEDATE, K. (1996). Application of cognitive behavior therapy to interpersonal problems: A case study of a Japanese female client. *Cognitive and Behavioral Practice, 3*, 289–302.

TREMBLAY, G. C., & DRABMAN, R. S. (1997). An intervention for childhood stealing. *Child & Family Behavior Therapy, 19*, 33–40.

TRIP, S., VERNON, A., & McMAHON, J. (2007). Effectiveness of rational-emotive education: A quantitative meta-analytical study. *Journal of Cognitive and Behavioral Psychotherapies, 7*, 81–93.

TROWER, P. (1995). Adult social skills: State of the art and future directions. In W. O'Donohue & L. Krasner (Eds.), *Handbook of psychological skills training: Clinical techniques and applications* (pp. 54–80). Boston: Allyn & Bacon.

TRULL, T. J., NIETZEL, M. T., & MAIN, A. (1988). The use of meta-analysis to assess the clinical significance of

behavior therapy for agoraphobia. *Behavior Therapy, 19*, 527–538.

TRYON, G. S. (1979). A review and critique of thought stopping research. *Journal of Behavior Therapy and Experimental Psychiatry, 10*, 189–192.

TRYON, W. W. (1999). Behavioral diagnosis versus the Diagnostic and Statistical Manual. *the Behavior Therapist, 22*, 3–4, 19.

TRYON, W. W., & PINTO, L. P. (1994). Comparing activity measurements and ratings. *Behavior Modification, 18*, 251–261.

TRZEPACZ, A. M., & LUISELLI, J. K. (2004). Efficacy of stress inoculation training in a case of posttraumatic stress disorder (PTSD) secondary to emergency gynecological surgery. *Clinical Case Studies, 3*, 83–92.

TUCKER, M., SIGAFOOS, J., & BUSHELL, H. (1998). Use of non-contingent reinforcement in the treatment of challenging behavior. *Behavior Modification, 22*, 529–547.

TULL, M. T., SCHULZINGER, D., SCHMIDT, N. B., ZVOLENSKY, M. J., & LEJUEZ, C. W. (2007). Development and initial examination of a brief intervention for heightened anxiety sensitivity among heroin users. *Behavior Modification, 31*, 220–242.

TUNDO, A., SALVATI, L., & BUSTO, G. (2007). Addition of cognitive-behavioral therapy for nonresponders to medication for obsessive-compulsive disorder: A naturalistic study. *Journal of Clinical Psychiatry, 68*, 1552–1556.

TURK, D. [C.] (1975). *Cognitive control of pain: A skill training approach.* Unpublished manuscript, University of Waterloo, Ontario.

TURK, D. [C.] (1976). *An expanded skills training approach for the treatment of experimentally induced pain.* Unpublished doctoral dissertation, University of Waterloo, Ontario.

TURK, D. C., & MEICHENBAUM, D. [H.] (1989). A cognitive-behavioural approach to pain management. In P. D. Wall & R. Melzack (Eds.), *Textbook of pain* (2nd ed.). London: Churchill Livingstone.

TURK, D. C., MEICHENBAUM, D. [H.], & GENEST, M. (1983). *Pain and behavioral medicine.* New York: Guilford.

TURK, D. C., & RUDY, T. E. (1995). Strategies and tactics in the treatment of persistent pain patients. In W. O'Donohue & L. Krasner (Eds.), *Handbook of psychological*

skills training: Clinical techniques and applications (pp. 339–362). Boston: Allyn & Bacon.

TURKAT, I. D., & FEUERSTEIN, M. (1978). Behavior modification and the public misconception. *American Psychologist, 33*, 194.

TURKINGTON, D., SENSKY, T., SCOTT, J., BARNES, T. R. E., NUR, U., SIDDLE, R., et al. (2008). A randomized controlled trial of cognitive-behavior therapy for persistent symptoms in schizophrenia: A five-year follow-up. *Schizophrenia Research, 98*, 1–7.

TURNER, A. J., & VERNON, J. C. (1976). Prompts to increase attendance in a community mental health center. *Journal of Applied Behavior Analysis, 9*, 141–145.

TURNER, J. A. (1982). Comparison of group progressive-relaxation training and cognitive-behavioral group therapy. *Journal of Consulting and Clinical Psychology, 50*, 757–765.

TURNER, J. A., & CLANCY, S. (1988). Comparison of operant behavioral and cognitive-behavioral group treatment for chronic low back pain. *Journal of Consulting and Clinical Psychology, 56*, 261–266.

TURNER, S. M., BEIDEL, D. C., & FRUEH, B. C. (2005). Multicomponent behavioral treatment for chronic combat-related posttraumatic stress disorder: Trauma Management Therapy. *Behavior Modification, 29*, 39–69.

TURNER, S. M., BEIDEL, D. C., & JACOB, R. G. (1994). Social phobia: A comparison of behavior therapy and atenolol. *Journal of Consulting and Clinical Psychology, 62*, 350–358.

TURNER, S. M., BEIDEL, D. C., SPAULDING, S. A., & BROWN, J. M. (1995). The practice of behavior therapy: A national survey of cost and methods. *the Behavior Therapist, 18*, 1–4.

TURPIN, G. (1983). The behavioral management of tic disorders: A critical review. *Advances in Behaviour Research and Therapy, 5*, 203–245.

TUSTIN, R. D., PENNINGTON, B., & BYRNE, M. (1994). Intrusiveness of interventions: Ratings by psychologists. *Behaviour Change, 11*, 68–100.

TWOHIG, M. P., HAYES, S. C., & MASUDA, A. (2006). Increasing willingness to experience obsessions: Acceptance and Commitment Therapy as a treatment for obsessive-compulsive disorder. *Behavior Therapy, 37*, 3–13.

TWOHIG, M. P., SHOENBERGER, D., & HAYES, S. C. (2007). A preliminary investigation of acceptance and commitment therapy as a treatment for marijuana dependence in adults. *Journal of Applied Behavior Analysis, 40,* 619–632.

TWYMAN, J. S., JOHNSON, H., BUIE, J. D., & NELSON, C. M. (1994). The use of a warning procedure to signal a more intrusive timeout contingency. *Behavioral Disorders, 19,* 243–253.

ULLMANN, L. P., & KRASNER, L. (Eds.). (1965). *Case studies in behavior modification.* New York: Holt, Rinehart & Winston.

ULMAN, J. D., & KLEM, J. L. (1975). (Communication). *Journal of Applied Behavior Analysis, 8,* 210.

UPPER, D. (1993). The use of covert reinforcement and thought stopping in treating a young woman's sexual anxiety. In J. R. Cautela & A. J. Kearney (Eds.), *Covert conditioning casebook* (pp. 235–244). Pacific Grove, CA: Brooks/Cole.

VAAL, J. J. (1973). Applying contingency contracting to a school phobic: A case study. *Journal of Behavior Therapy and Experimental Psychiatry, 4,* 371–373.

VALINS, S., & RAY, A. (1967). Effects of cognitive desensitization on avoidance behavior. *Journal of Personality and Social Psychology, 7,* 345–350.

VALLIS, T. M. (1984). A complete component analysis of stress inoculation for pain tolerance. *Cognitive Therapy and Research, 8,* 313–329.

VALLIS, T. M., HOWES, J. L., & STANDAGE, K. (2000). Is cognitive therapy suitable for treating individuals with personality dysfunction? *Cognitive Therapy and Research, 24,* 595–606.

VAN BALKOM, A. J. L. M., VAN OPPEN, P., VERMEULEN, A. W. A., VAN DYCK, R., NAUTA, M. C. E., & VORST, H. C. M. (1994). A meta-analysis on the treatment of obsessive compulsive disorder: A comparison of antidepressants, behavior, and cognitive therapy. *Clinical Psychology Review, 14,* 359–381.

VAN DEN HOOFDAKKER, B. J., VAN DER VEEN-MULDERS, L., & SYTEMA, S. (2007). Effectiveness of behavioral parent training for children with ADHD in routine clinical practice: A randomized controlled study. *Journal of the American Academy of Child & Adolescent Psychiatry, 46,* 1263–1271.

VAN HOUTEN, R. (1998). *How to use prompts to initiate behavior* (2nd ed.). Austin, TX: Pro-Ed.

VAN OPPEN, P., & ARNTZ, A. (1994). Cognitive therapy for obsessive-compulsive disorder. *Behaviour Research and Therapy, 32,* 79–87.

VAN OPPEN, P., DE HANN, E., VAN BALKOM, A. J. L. M., SPINHOVEN, P., HOOGDUIN, K., & VAN DYCK, R. (1995). Cognitive therapy and exposure *in vivo* in the treatment of obsessive-compulsive disorder. *Behaviour Research and Therapy, 33,* 379–390.

VAN PESKI-OOSTERBAAN, A. S., SPINHOVEN, P., VAN DER DOES, A. J., BRUSHKE, A. V. G., & ROOIJMANS, H. G. M. (1999). Cognitive change following cognitive behavioural therapy for non-cardiac chest pain. *Psychotherapy and Psychosomatics, 68,* 214–220.

VAN SON, M., VAN HEESCH, N., MULDER, G., & VAN LONDEN, A. (1995). The effectiveness of dry bed training for nocturnal enuresis in adults: A 3, 5, and 6 years follow-up. *Behaviour Research and Therapy, 33,* 557–559.

VARGAS, J. S., & SHANLEY, D. (1995). Academic skills. In W. O'Donohue & L. Krasner (Eds.), *Handbook of psychological skills training: Clinical techniques and applications* (pp. 180–194). Boston: Allyn & Bacon.

VARNI, J. W., BOYD, E. F., & CATALDO, M. F. (1978). Self-monitoring, external reinforcement, and timeout procedures in the control of high rate tic behaviors in a hyperactive child. *Journal of Behavior Therapy and Experimental Psychiatry, 9,* 353–358.

VARNI, J. W., KATZ, E. R., COLEGROVE, R., JR., & DOLGIN, M. (1993). The impact of social skills training on the adjustment of children with newly diagnosed cancer. *Journal of Pediatric Psychology, 18,* 751–767.

VARNI, J. W., LA GRECA, A. M., & SPIRITO, A. (2000). Cognitive-behavioral interventions for children with chronic health conditions. In K. S. Dobson (Ed.), *Handbook of cognitive-behavioral therapies* (2nd ed., pp. 291–333). New York: Guilford.

VENTIS, W. L. (1973). Case history: The use of laughter as an alternative response in systematic desensitization. *Behavior Therapy, 4,* 120–122.

VERBEEK, I. H., KONINGS, G. M., ALDENKAMP, A. P., DECLERCK, A. C., & KLIP, E. C. (2006). Cognitive-behavioral treatment in clinically referred chronic insomniacs: Group versus individual treatment. *Behavioral Sleep Medicine, 4*(3), 135–151.

VERNON, D. T. A. (1974). Modeling and birth order in responses to painful stimuli. *Journal of Personality and Social Psychology, 29,* 794–799.

VERONEN, L. J., & KILPATRICK, D. G. (1983). Stress management for rape victims. In D. [H.] Meichenbaum & M. E. Jaremko (Eds.), *Stress reduction and prevention* (pp. 341–374). New York: Plenum.

VITTENGL, J. R., CLARK, L. A., DUNN, T. W., & JARRETT, R. B. (2007). Reducing relapse and recurrence in unipolar depression: A comparative meta-analysis of cognitive-behavioral therapy's effects. *Journal of Consulting and Clinical Psychology, 75,* 475–488.

VOEGTLIN, W. L., LEMERE, F., BROZ, W. R., & O'HOLLAREN, P. (1941). Conditioned reflex therapy of chronic alcoholism. *Quarterly Journal of Studies on Alcohol, 2,* 505–511.

VOELTZ, L. M., & EVANS, I. M. (1982). The assessment of behavioral interrelationships in child behavior therapy. *Behavioral Assessment, 4,* 131–165.

VOLLMER, A., & BLANCHARD, E. B. (1998). Controlled comparison of individual versus group cognitive therapy for irritable bowel syndrome. *Behavior Therapy, 29,* 19–33.

VOLLMER, T. R., ROANE, H. S., RINGDAHL, J. E., & MARCUS, B. A. (1999). Evaluating treatment challenges with differential reinforcement of alternative behavior. *Journal of Applied Behavior Analysis, 32,* 9–23.

VOWLES, K. E., & MCCRACKEN, L. M. (2008). Acceptance and values-based action in chronic pain: A study of treatment effectiveness and process. *Journal of Consulting and Clinical Psychology, 76,* 397–407.

WADE, T. C., BAKER, T. B., & HARTMANN, D. P. (1979). Behavior therapists' self-reported views and practices. *the Behavior Therapist, 2,* 3–6.

WAGAMAN, J. R., MILTENBERGER, R. G., & ARNDORFER, R. E. (1993). Analysis of a simplified treatment for stuttering in children. *Journal of Applied Behavior Analysis, 26,* 53–61.

WAGAMAN, J. R., MILTENBERGER, R. G., & WILLIAMS, D. E. (1995). Treatment of a vocal tic by differential reinforcement. *Journal of Behavior*

Therapy and Experimental Psychiatry, 26, 35–39.

WAGAMAN, J. R., MILTENBERGER, R. G., & WOODS, D. (1995). Long-term follow-up of a behavioral treatment for stuttering in children. *Journal of Applied Behavior Analysis, 28*, 233–234.

WAGGONER, C. D., & LELIEUVRE, R. B. (1981). A method to increase compliance to exercise regimens in rheumatoid arthritis patients. *Journal of Behavioral Medicine, 4*, 191–201.

WAGNER, A. M., ZATZICK, D. F., GHESQUIERE, A., & JURKOVICH, G. J. (2007). Behavioral activation as an early intervention for posttraumatic stress disorder and depression among physically injured trauma survivors. *Cognitive and Behavioral Practice, 14*, 341–349.

WAGNER, J. (1998). Improving adherence to diabetes blood glucose monitoring regimens with prompts and unit dose packaging. *the Behavior Therapist, 21*, 157–159.

WAGNER, M. K., & BRAGG, R. A. (1970). Comparing behavior modification approaches to habit decrement—Smoking. *Journal of Consulting and Clinical Psychology, 34*, 258–263.

WAGNER, W., JOHNSON, S. B., WALKER, D., CARTER, R., & WITNER, J. (1982). A controlled comparison of two treatments of nocturnal enuresis. *Journal of Pediatrics, 101*, 302–307.

WAHLER, R. G. (1969). Oppositional children: A quest for parental reinforcement control. *Journal of Applied Behavior Analysis, 2*, 159–170.

WAHLER, R. G., & GRAVES, M. G. (1983). Setting events in social networks: Ally or enemy in child behavior therapy? *Behavior Therapy, 14*, 19–36.

WALD, J., & TAYLOR, S. (2005). Interoceptive exposure therapy combined with trauma-related exposure therapy for post-traumatic stress disorder: A case report. *Cognitive Behaviour Therapy, 34*, 34–40.

WALD, J., & TAYLOR, S. (2007). Efficacy of interoceptive exposure therapy combined with trauma-related exposure therapy for posttraumatic stress disorder: A pilot study. *Journal of Anxiety Disorders, 21*, 1050–1060.

WALKER, C. E., HEDBERG, A., CLEMENT, P. W., & WRIGHT, L. (1981). *Clinical procedures for behavior therapy.* Englewood Cliffs, NJ: Prentice Hall.

WALKER, C. E., MILLING, L. S., & BONNER, B. L. (1988). Incontinence disorders: Enuresis and encopresis. In D. K. Routh (Ed.), *Handbook of pediatric psychology* (pp. 363–397). New York: Guilford.

WALLER, B., CARLSON, J., & ENGLAR-CARLSON, M. (2006). Treatment and relapse prevention of depression using mindfulness-based cognitive therapy and Adlerian concepts. *Journal of Individual Psychology, 62*, 443–454.

WALLER, M. A., & SPIEGLER, M. D. (1997). A cross-cultural perspective on couple differences. *Journal of Couples Therapy, 7*, 83–98.

WALTER, H., & VAUGHAN, R. (1993). AIDS risk reduction among a multiethnic sample of urban high school students. *Journal of the American Medical Association, 270*, 725–730.

WALTON, D., & MATHER, M. D. (1963). The relevance of generalization techniques to the treatment of stammering and phobic symptoms. *Behaviour Research and Therapy, 1*, 121–125.

WASCHBUSCH, D. A., PELHAM, W. E., & MASSETTI, G. (2005). The behavior education support and treatment (BEST) school intervention program: Pilot project data examining school-wide, targeted-school, and targeted-home approaches. *Journal of Attention Disorder, 9*, 313–322.

WASIK, B. H. (1970). The application of Premack's generalization on reinforcement to the management of classroom behavior. *Journal of Experimental Child Psychology, 10*, 33–43.

WASSERMAN, I. M. (1984). Imitation and suicide: A reexamination of the Werther effect. *American Sociological Review, 49*, 427–43.

WATSON, D. L., & THARP, R. G. (1972). *Self-directed behavior: Self-modification for personal adjustment.* Pacific Grove, CA: Brooks/Cole.

WATSON, J. B. (1914). *Behavior: An introduction to comparative psychology.* New York: Holt.

WATSON, J. P., MULLETT, G. E., & PILLAY, H. (1973). The effects of prolonged exposure to phobic situations upon agoraphobic patients treated in groups. *Behaviour Research and Therapy, 11*, 531–545.

WATSON, T. S., & KRAMER, J. J. (1995). Teaching problem solving skills to teachers-in-training: An analogue experimental analysis of three

methods. *Journal of Behavioral Education, 5*, 295–317.

WATT, M., STEWART, S., BIRCH, C., & BERNIER, D. (2006). Brief CBT for high anxiety sensitivity decreases drinking problems, relief alcohol outcome expectancies, and conformity drinking motives: Evidence from a randomized controlled trial. *Journal of Mental Health, 15*, 683–695.

WAUQUIER, A., MCGRADY, A., ALOE, L., KLAUSNER, T., & COLLINS, B. (1995). Changes in cerebral blood flow velocity, associated with biofeedback-assisted relaxation treatment of migraine headaches, are specific for the middle cerebral artery. *Headache, 35*, 358–362.

WEBSTER-STRATTON, C. (1981a). Modification of mothers' behaviors and attitudes through videotape modeling group discussion. *Behavior Therapy, 12*, 634–642.

WEBSTER-STRATTON, C. (1981b). Videotape modeling: A method of parent education. *Journal of Clinical Child Psychology, 10*, 93–97.

WEBSTER-STRATTON, C. (1982a). Long-term effects of a videotape modeling parent education program: Comparison of immediate and 1-year follow-up results. *Behavior Therapy, 13*, 702–714.

WEBSTER-STRATTON, C. (1982b). Teaching mothers through videotape modeling to change their children's behaviors. *Journal of Pediatric Psychology, 7*, 279–294.

WEERSING, V., & WEISZ, J. (2002). Mechanisms of action in youth psychotherapy. *Journal of Child Psychology and Psychiatry, 43*, 3–29.

WEERSING, V. R., GONZALEZ, A., CAMPO, J. V., & LUCAS, A. N. (2008). Brief behavioral therapy for pediatric anxiety and depression: Piloting an integrated treatment approach. *Cognitive and Behavioral Practice, 15*, 126–139.

WEERTMAN, A., & ARNTZ, A. (2007). Effectiveness of treatment of childhood memories in cognitive therapy for personality disorders: A controlled study contrasting methods focusing. *Behaviour Research and Therapy, 45*, 2133–2143.

WEGNER, D. M. (1994). Ironic processes of mental control. *Psychological Review, 101*, 34–52.

WEIDNER, F. (1970). In vivo desensitization of a paranoid schizophrenic. *Journal of Behavior Therapy and Experimental Psychiatry, 1*, 79–81.

WEINHARDT, L. S., CAREY, M. P., CAREY, K. B., & VERDECIAS, R. N. (1998). Increasing assertiveness skills to reduce HIV risk among woman living with a severe and persistent mental illness. *Journal of Consulting and Clinical Psychology, 66,* 680–684.

WEINRACH, S. G. (1995). Rational emotive behavior therapy: A tough-minded therapy for a tender-minded profession. *Journal of Counseling and Development, 73,* 296–300.

WEINSTEIN, M. (1988). Preparation of children for psychotherapy through videotaped modeling. *Journal of Clinical Child Psychology, 17,* 131–136.

WEISHAAR, M. E. (1996). Developments in cognitive therapy: 1960–1996. In W. Dryden (Ed.), *Developments in psychotherapy: Historical perspectives* (pp. 188–212). London: Sage.

WEISS, R. D. (2004). Adherence to pharmacotherapy in patients with alcohol and opiod dependence. *Addiction, 99,* 1382–1392.

WEISZ, J. R., WEERSING, V. R., & HENGGELER, S. W. (2005). Jousting with straw men: Comment on Westen, Novotny, and Thompson-Brenner (2004). *Psychological Bulletin, 131,* 418–426.

WELCH, M. W., & GIST, J. W. (1974). *The open token economy system: A handbook for a behavioral approach to rehabilitation.* Springfield, IL: Charles C Thomas.

WELLS, E. A., PETERSON, P. L., GAINEY, R. R., HAWKINS, J. D., & CATALANO, R. F. (1994). Outpatient treatment for cocaine abuse: A controlled comparison of relapse prevention and twelve-step approaches. *American Journal of Drug and Alcohol Abuse, 20,* 1–17.

WELLS, J. K., HOWARD, G. S., NOWLIN, W. F., & VARGAS, M. J. (1986). Presurgical anxiety and postsurgical pain and adjustment: Effects of a stress inoculation procedure. *Journal of Consulting and Clinical Psychology, 54,* 831–835.

WELLS, K. C. (1994). Parent and family management training. In L. W. Craighead, W. E. Craighead, A. E. Kazdin, & M. J. Mahoney (Eds.), *Cognitive and behavioral interventions: An empirical approach to mental health problems* (pp. 251–266). Boston: Allyn & Bacon.

WELLS, K. C., & EGAN, J. (1988). Social learning and systems family therapy for childhood oppositional disorder: Comparative treatment outcome.

Comprehensive Psychiatry, 29, 138–146.

WELLS, K. C., GRIEST, D. C., & FOREHAND, R. [L.] (1980). The use of a self-control package to enhance temporal generality of a parent training program. *Behaviour Research and Therapy, 18,* 347–353.

WERRY, J. S., & COHRSSEN, J. (1965). Enuresis: An etiologic and therapeutic study. *Journal of Pediatrics, 67,* 423–431.

WERT, B. Y., & NEISWORTH, J. T. (2003). Effects of video self-modeling on spontaneous requesting in children with autism. *Journal of Positive Behavior Interventions, 5,* 30–34.

WESTIN, D., NOVOTNY, C. M., & THOMPSON-BRENNER, H. (2004). The empirical status of empirically supported psychotherapies: Assumptions, findings, and reporting in controlled trials. *Psychological Bulletin, 130,* 631–663.

WETHERELL, J. L. (2002). Behavior therapy for anxious older adults. *the Behavior Therapist, 25,* 16–17.

WHISMAN, M. A. (Ed.). (2008). *Adapting cognitive therapy for depression: Managing complexity and comorbity.* New York: Guilford.

WHITAL, M. L., AGRAS, W. S., & GOULD, R. A. (1999). Bulimia nervosa: A meta-analysis of psychosocial and pharmacological treatments. *Behavior Therapy, 30,* 117–135.

WHITE, G. D., NIELSON, G., & JOHNSON, S. M. (1972). Timeout duration and the suppression of deviant behavior in children. *Journal of Applied Behavior Analysis, 5,* 111–120.

WHITE, J. A., DAVISON, G. C., HAAGA, D. A. F., & WHITE, K. L. (1992). Cognitive bias in the articulated thoughts of depressed and nondepressed psychiatric patients. *Journal of Nervous and Mental Disease, 180,* 77–81.

WHITE, M. (1989). *Selected papers.* Adelaide, South Australia: Dulwich Centre Publications.

WHITE, M. (1995, March). *Re-authoring lives.* Workshop presented in Mansfield, MA.

WHITE-BLACKBURN, G., SEMB, S., & SEMB, G. (1977). The effects of a good-behavior contract on the classroom behaviors of sixth-grade students. *Journal of Applied Behavior Analysis, 10,* 312.

WHITTAL, M. L. (2008). Prevention of mental disorders. *Cognitive and Behavioral Practice, 15,* 1–2.

WHITTAL, M. L., THORDARSON, D. S., & MCLEAN, P. D. (2005). Treatment of obsessive-compulsive disorder: Cognitive behavior therapy vs. exposure and response prevention. *Behaviour Research and Therapy, 43,* 1559–1576.

WICKSELL, R. K., AHLQVIST, J., BRING, A., MELIN, L., & OLSSON, G. L. (2008). Can exposure and acceptance strategies improve functioning and life satisfaction in people with chronic pain and whiplash-associated disorders (WAD)? A randomized controlled trial. *Cognitive Behaviour Therapy, 37,* 169–182.

WIEDERHOLD, B. K., & WIEDERHOLD, M. D. (2005). *Virtual reality therapy for anxiety disorders: Advances in evaluation and treatment.* Washington, DC.: American Psychological Association.

WIJMA, K., MELIN, A., NEDSTRAND, E., & HAMMAR, M. (1997). Treatment of menopausal symptoms with applied relaxation: A pilot study. *Journal of Behavior Therapy and Experimental Psychiatry, 28,* 251–261.

WILDER, D. A., HIGBEEN, T. S., WILLIAMS, W. L., & NACHTWEY, A. (1997). A simplified method of toilet training adults in residential settings. *Journal of Behavior Therapy and Experimental Psychiatry, 28,* 241–246.

WILDER, D. A., NORMAND, M., & ATWELL, J. (2005). Noncontingent reinforcement as treatment for food refusal and associated self-injury. *Journal of Applied Behavior Analysis, 38,* 549–553.

WILFLEY, D. E., SCHWARTZ, M. B., SPURRELL, E. B., & FAIRBURN, C. G. (1997). Assessing the specific psychopathology of binge eating disorder patients: Interview or self-report? *Behaviour Research and Therapy, 35,* 1151–1159.

WILLERMAN, L. (1979). *The psychology of individual and group differences.* San Francisco: W. H. Freeman.

WILLIAMS, C. D. (1959). The elimination of tantrum behavior by extinction procedures: Case report. *Journal of Abnormal and Social Psychology, 59,* 269.

WILLIAMS, D. E., KIRKPATRICK-SANCHEZ, S., & CROCKER, W. T. (1994). A long-term follow-up of treatment for severe self-injury. *Research in Developmental Disabilities, 15,* 487–501.

WILLIAMS, J. M. G., ALATIQ, Y., CRANE, C., BARNHOFER, T., FENNELL, M. J. V.,

DUGGAN, D. S., et al. (2008). Mindfulness-based cognitive therapy (MBCT) in bipolar disorder: Preliminary evaluation of immediate effects on between-episode functioning. *Journal of Affective Disorders, 107*, 275–279.

WILLIAMS, J. M. G., DUGGAN, D. S., CRANE, C., & FENNELL, M. J. V. (2006). Mindfulness-based cognitive therapy for prevention of recurrence of suicidal behavior. *Journal of Clinical Psychology, 62*, 201–210.

WILLIAMS, J. M. G., RUSSELL, I., & RUSSELL, D. (2008). Mindfulness-based cognitive therapy: Further issues in current evidence and future research. *Journal of Consulting and Clinical Psychology, 76*, 524–529.

WILLIAMS, J. M. G., TEASDALE, J. D., SEGAL, Z. V., & KABAT-ZINN, J. (2007). *The mindful way through depression: Freeing yourself from chronic unhappiness.* New York: Guilford.

WILLIAMS, K. E., & CHAMBLESS, D. L. (1994). The results of exposure-based treatment in agoraphobia. In S. Friedman (Ed.), *Anxiety disorders in African Americans* (pp. 149–165). New York: Springer.

WILLIAMS, K. E., CHAMBLESS, D. L., & STEKETEE, G. (1998). Behavioral treatment of obsessive compulsive disorder in African Americans: Clinical issues. *Journal of Behavior Therapy and Experimental Psychiatry, 29*, 163–170.

WILLIAMS, S. L., DOOSEMAN, G., & KLEIFIELD, E. (1984). Comparative effectiveness of guided mastery and exposure treatments for intractable phobias. *Journal of Consulting and Clinical Psychology, 52*, 505–518.

WILLIAMS, S. L., TURNER, S. M., & PEER, D. F. (1985). Guided mastery and performance desensitization treatments for severe acrophobia. *Journal of Consulting and Clinical Psychology, 53*, 237–247.

WILLIAMS, S. L., & ZANE, G. (1989). Guided mastery and stimulus exposure treatments for severe performance anxiety in agoraphobics. *Behaviour Research and Therapy, 27*, 237–245.

WILLIAMSON, D. A., DAVIS, C. J., & PRATHER, R. C. (1988). Assessment of health-related disorders. In A. S. Bellack & M. Hersen (Eds.), *Behavioral assessment: A practical handbook* (3rd ed., pp. 396–440). Elmsford, NY: Pergamon.

WILLIS, R. W., & EDWARDS, J. A. (1969). A study of the comparative effectiveness of systematic desensitization and implosive therapy. *Behaviour Research and Therapy, 7*, 387–395.

WILSON, D. D., ROBERTSON, S. J., HERLONG, L. H., & HAYNES, S. N. (1979). Vicarious effects of time out in the modification of aggression in the classroom. *Behavior Modification, 3*, 97–111.

WILSON, G. T. (1978). On the much discussed nature of the term "behavior therapy." *Behavior Therapy, 9*, 89–98.

WILSON, G. T. (1997a). Behavior therapy at century close. *Behavior Therapy, 28*, 18–23.

WILSON, G. T. (1997b). Treatment manuals in clinical practice. *Behaviour Research and Therapy, 35*, 305–310.

WILSON, G. T., ELDREDGE, K. L., SMITH, D. E., & NILES, B. (1991). Cognitive-behavioral treatment with and without response prevention for bulimia. *Behaviour Research and Therapy, 29*, 575–583.

WILSON, G. T., & FAIRBURN, C. G. (1993). Cognitive treatment for eating disorders. *Journal of Consulting and Clinical Psychology, 61*, 261–269.

WILSON, G. T., & FAIRBURN, C. G. (1998). Treatments for eating disorders. In P. E. Nathan & J. M. Gorman (Eds.), *A guide to treatments that work* (pp. 501–530). New York: Oxford University Press.

WILSON, G. T., LOEB, K. L., WALSH, B. T., LABOUVIE, E., PETKOVA, E., LIU, X., et al. (1999). Psychological versus pharmacological treatments of bulimia nervosa: Predictors and processes of change. *Journal of Consulting and Clinical Psychology, 67*, 451–459.

WILSON, G. T., & TRACEY, D. A. (1976). An experimental analysis of aversive imagery versus electrical aversive conditioning in the treatment of chronic alcoholics. *Behaviour Research and Therapy, 14*, 41–51.

WILSON, G. T., VITOUSEK, K. M., & LOEB, K. L. (2000). Stepped care treatment for eating disorders. *Journal of Consulting and Clinical Psychology, 68*, 564–572.

WILSON, J. Q., & HERRNSTEIN, R. J. (1985). *Crime and human nature.* New York: Simon & Schuster.

WILSON, K., & GALLOIS, C. (1993). *Assertion and its social context.* New York: Pergamon.

Win prizes online at work! (2007, October 29). *Newsweek,* p. E2.

WINCZE, J. P., BACH, A. K., & BARLOW, D. H. (2008). Sexual dysfunction. In D. H. Barlow (Ed.), *Handbook of psychological disorders: A step-by-step treatment manual* (4th ed., pp. 616–661). New York: Guilford.

WINCZE, J. P., & CAIRD, W. K. (1976). The effects of systematic desensitization and video desensitization in the treatment of sexual dysfunction in women. *Behavior Therapy, 7*, 335–342.

WINETT, R. A., & WINKLER, R. C. (1972). Current behavior modification in the classroom: Be still, be quiet, be docile. *Journal of Applied Behavior Analysis, 5*, 499–504.

WITKIEWITZ, K. A., & MARLATT, G. A. (Eds.). (2007). *Therapist's guide to evidence-based relapse prevention.* San Diego: Elsevier Academic Press.

WOLF, E. M., & CROWTHER, J. H. (1992). An evaluation of behavior and cognitive-behavioral group interventions for the treatment of bulimia nervosa in women. *International Journal of Eating Disorder, 22*, 503–517.

WOLF, M. M. (1978). Social validity: The case for subjective measurement or how applied behavior analysis is finding its heart. *Journal of Applied Behavior Analysis, 11*, 203–214.

WOLF, M. M., BRAUKMANN, C. J., & RAMP, K. A. (1987). Serious delinquent behavior as part of a significantly handicapping condition: Cures and supportive environments. *Journal of Applied Behavior Analysis, 20*, 347–359.

WOLFE, D. A., & SANDLER, J. (1981). Training abusive parents in effective child management. *Behavior Modification, 5*, 320–335.

WOLFE, D. A., & WEKERLE, C. (1993). Treatment strategies for child physical abuse and neglect: A critical progress report. *Clinical Psychology Review, 13*, 473–500.

WOLFE, V. V., DOZOIS, D. J. A., FISMAN, S., & DEPACE, J. (2008). Preventing depression among adolescent girls: Pathways toward effective and sustainable programs. *Cognitive and Behavioral Practice, 15*, 36–46.

WOLFSON, A., LACKS, P., & FUTTERMAN, A. (1992). Effects of parent training on infant sleeping patterns, parents' stress, and perceived parental competence. *Journal of Consulting and Clinical Psychology, 60*, 41–48.

WOLPE, J. (1958). *Psychotherapy by reciprocal inhibition.* Stanford, CA: Stanford University Press.

WOLPE, J. (1990). *The practice of behavior therapy* (4th ed.). Elmsford, NY: Pergamon.

WOLPE, J., & LANG, P. J. (1964). A fear survey schedule for use in behavior therapy. *Behaviour Research and Therapy, 2,* 27–30.

WOLPE, J., & LAZARUS, A. A. (1966). *Behavior therapy techniques: A guide to the treatment of neurosis.* New York: Pergamon.

WONG, S. E., MARTINEZ-DIAZ, J. A., MASSEL, H. K., EDELSTEIN, B. A., WIEGAND, W., BOWEN, L., et al. (1993). Conversation skills training with schizophrenic inpatients: A study of generalization across settings and conversants. *Behavior Therapy, 24,* 285–304.

WONG, S. E., SEROKA, P. L., & OGISI, J. (2000). Effects of a checklist on self-assessment of blood glucose level by a memory-impaired woman with diabetes mellitus. *Journal of Applied Behavior Analysis, 33,* 251–254.

WOOD, D. P., MURPHY, J., CENTER, K., REEVES, D., PYNE, J., SHILLING, R., et al. (2007). Combat-related posttraumatic stress disorder: A case report using virtual reality exposure therapy with physiological monitoring. *CyberPsychology & Behavior, 10,* 309–315.

WOODS, D. W., & MILTENBERGER, R. G. (1995). Habit reversal: A review of applications and variations. *Journal of Behavior Therapy and Experimental Psychiatry, 26,* 123–131.

WOODS, D. W., MURRAY, L. K., FUQUA, W., SEIF, T. A., BOYER, L. J., & SIAH, A. (1999). Comparing the effectiveness of similar and dissimilar competing responses in evaluating the habit reversal treatment of oral-digital habits in children. *Journal of Behavior Therapy and Experimental Psychiatry, 30,* 289–300.

WOOLFOLK, A. E., WOOLFOLK, R. L., & WILSON, G. T. (1977). A rose by another name . . . : Labeling bias and attitudes toward behavior modification. *Journal of Consulting and Clinical Psychology, 45,* 184–191.

WORLD HEALTH ORGANIZATION. (1992). *International classification of diseases and related health problems* (10th rev.). Geneva: Author.

WURTELE, S. K. (1990). Teaching personal safety skills to four-year-old

children: A behavioral approach. *Behavior Therapy, 21,* 25–32.

WURTELE, S. K., CURRIER, L. L., GILLISPIE, E. I., & FRANKLIN, C. F. (1991). The efficacy of a parent-implemented program for teaching preschoolers personal safety skills. *Behavior Therapy, 22,* 69–83.

WURTELE, S. K., MARRS, S. R., & MILLER-PERRIN, C. J. (1987). Practice makes perfect? The role of participant modeling in sexual abuse prevention programs. *Journal of Consulting and Clinical Psychology, 55,* 599–602.

WYKES, T., STEELE, C., EVERITT, B., & TARRIER, N. (2008). Cognitive behavioural therapy for schizophrenia: Effect sizes, clinical models and methodological vigor. *Schizophrenia Bulletin, 34,* 523–537.

WYSOCKI, T., HALL, G., IWATA, B., & RIORDAN, M. (1979). Behavioral management of exercise: Contracting for aerobic points. *Journal of Applied Behavior Analysis, 12,* 55–64.

YATES, A. J. (1958). The application of learning theory to the treatment of tics. *Journal of Abnormal and Social Psychology, 56,* 175–182.

YATES, A. J. (1970). *Behavior therapy.* New York: Wiley.

YOOK, K., LEE, S.-H., RYU, M., KIM, K.-H., CHOI, T. K., SUH, S. Y., et al. (2008). Usefulness of mindfulness-based cognitive therapy for treating insomnia in patients with anxiety disorders: A pilot study. *Journal of Nervous and Mental Disease, 196,* 501–503.

YOUNG, J. E. (1994). *Cognitive therapy for personality disorders: A schema-focused approach* (rev. ed.). Sarasota, FL: Professional Resource Press.

YOUNG, J. E., BECK, A. T., & WEINBERGER, A. (1993). Depression. In D. H. Barlow (Ed.), *Clinical handbook of psychological disorders* (2nd ed., pp. 240–277). New York: Guilford.

YOUNG, J., & BEHARY, W. T. (1998). Schema-focused therapy for personality disorders. In N. Tarrier, A. Wells, & G. Haddock (Eds.), *Treating complex cases: The cognitive behavioural therapy approach* (pp. 340–376). New York: Wiley.

YOUNG, J., CONNOLLY, K., & LOHR, J. M. (2008). Fighting the good fight by hunting the dodo bird to extinction: ABCT's dissemination effort. *the Behavior Therapist, 31,* 97–100.

YOUNG, J. E., RYGH, J. L., WEINBERGER, A. D., & BECK, A. T. (2008).

Cognitive therapy for depression. In D. H. Barlow (Ed.), *Handbook of psychological disorders: A step-by-step treatment manual* (4th ed., pp. 250–305). New York: Guilford.

YU, P., HARRIS, G. E., SOLOVITZ, B. L., & FRANKLIN, L. (1986). A social problem-solving intervention for children at high risk for later psychopathology. *Journal of Clinical Child Psychology, 13,* 30–40.

ZANOLLI, K., & DAGGETT, J. (1998). The effects of reinforcement rate on the spontaneous social initiations of socially withdrawn preschoolers. *Journal of Applied Behavior Analysis, 31,* 117–125.

ZEISS, A. M., & STEFFEN, A. (1996). Treatment issues with elderly clients. *Cognitive and Behavioral Practice, 3,* 371–389.

ZEITLIN, S. B., NETTEN, K. A., & HODDER, S. L. (1995). Thought suppression: An experimental investigation of spider phobics. *Behaviour Research and Therapy, 33,* 407–413.

ZETTLE, R. D. (2007). *ACT for depression: A clinician's guide to using Acceptance and Commitment Therapy in treating depression.* Oakland, CA: New Harbinger.

ZETTLE, R. D., & HAYES, S. C. (1982). Rule-governed behavior: A potential theoretical framework for cognitive-behavioral therapy. In P. C. Kendall (Ed.), *Advances in cognitive-behavioral research and therapy* (Vol. 1, pp. 73–118). New York: Academic Press.

ZETTLE, R. D., & RAINS, J. C. (1989). Group cognitive and contextual therapies in treatment of depression. *Journal of Clinical Psychology, 45,* 438–445.

ZIFFERBLATT, S. M. (1975). Increasing patient compliance through the applied analysis of behavior. *Preventive Medicine, 4,* 173–182.

ZIMMERMAN, J., STUCKEY, T. E., GARLICK, B. J., & MILLER, M. (1969). Effects of token reinforcement on productivity in multiple handicapped clients in a sheltered workshop. *Rehabilitation Literature, 30,* 34–41.

ZVOLENSKY, M. J., LEJUEZ, C. W., KAHLER, C. W., & BROWN, R. A. (2003). Integrating an interoceptive exposure-based smoking cessation program into the cognitive-behavioral treatment of panic disorder: Theoretical relevance and case demonstration. *Cognitive and Behavioral Practice, 10,* 347–357.

NAME INDEX

SUBJECT INDEX

Both noncotinjent reinforcement
and Functional communication -
training are used when people behave
inappropriately, in order to abtain reinforcers.

All behaviors are being reinforced